22nd International Metrology Congress (CIM2025)

EPJ Web of Conferences Volume 323 (2025)

Lyon, France
11-14 March 2025

Editor:

J. Lopez

ISBN: 979-8-3313-1773-7

Printed from e-media with permission by:

Curran Associates, Inc.
57 Morehouse Lane
Red Hook, NY 12571

Some format issues inherent in the e-media version may also appear in this print version.

For additional information, please contact EDP Sciences – Web of Conferences
at the address below.

EDP Sciences – Web of Conferences
17, Avenue du Hoggar
Parc d'Activité de Courtabœuf
BP 112
F-91944 Les Ulis Cedex A
France

Phone: +33 (0) 1 69 18 75 75
Fax: +33 (0) 1 69 28 84 91

contact-edps@webofconferences.org

Additional copies of this publication are available from:

Curran Associates, Inc.
57 Morehouse Lane
Red Hook, NY 12571 USA
Phone: 845-758-0400
Fax: 845-758-2633
Email: curran@proceedings.com
Web: www.proceedings.com

TABLE OF CONTENTS

ROBOTIZATION, AUTOMATIZATION & DYNAMIC MEASUREMENT

THERMOMETRY, HYGROMETRY

FLOW

POLLUTANT ANALYSIS

MATERIALS

RADIONUCLIDE, DOSIMETRY & SPECTROSCOPY

ELECTROMAGNETISM

Statement of Peer review

In submitting conference proceedings to *Web of Conferences*, the editors of the proceedings certify to the Publisher that

1. They adhere to its **Policy on Publishing Integrity** in order to safeguard good scientific practice in publishing.
2. All articles have been subjected to peer review administered by the proceedings editors.
3. Reviews have been conducted by expert referees, who have been requested to provide unbiased and constructive comments aimed, whenever possible, at improving the work.
4. Proceedings editors have taken all reasonable steps to ensure the quality of the materials they publish and their decision to accept or reject a paper for publication has been based only on the merits of the work and the relevance to the journal.

Title, date and place of the conference

CIM - Conférence Internationale de Métrologie, march 11th-14th 2025, LYON

Proceedings editor(s):

Collège Français de Métrologie

Date and editor's signature

March 19th 2025, Jérôme LOPEZ, Director of Collège Français de Métrologie

EPJ Web of Conferences **323**, 01001 (2025) https://doi.org/10.1051/epjconf/202532301001
22nd International Metrology Congress

Digital Calibration Certificates (DCC): Benefits and Challenges to overcome for implementation

Martin Koval [1*], *Jiří* Tesař[1], *Shanna* Schönhals[2], *Anjali* Sharma[3], *David* Balslev-Harder[4], *Carlos* Galvan-Hernandez[5], Henri Baumann[6], *David* Mahovský[7]

[1]CMI Czech Metrology Institute, Okružní 31, 63800 Brno, Czech Republic
[2]PTB Physikalisch-Technische Bundesanstalt, Bundesallee 100, 38116, Germany
[3]CSIR National Physical Laboratory, Dr K S Krishnan Marg, New Delhi,110012, India
[4]DFM Danish Fundamental Metrology, Kogle Allé 5, 2970 Hørsholm, Denmark
[5]CENAM Centro Nacional de Metrologia, km 4.6 Carretara a los Cues, CP 76246, Queretaro, México
[6]Federal Institute of Metrology METAS, Lindenweg 50, CH-3003 Bern-Wabern, Switzerland
[7]Slovak University of Technology in Bratislava, Vazovova 5, 81243 Slovak Republic

Abstract. The term Digital Calibration Certificate (DCC) has been increasingly prevalent in the metrology field, with national and international conferences where stakeholders discuss DCC. This article delves into the implications of integrating "D - digitalization" into "CC - calibration certificate," exploring the significant impact this concept brings to well-established practices. DCC represents a logical progression in the digitalization of metrology. Despite the existence of initial DCC implementations, it is essential to highlight the challenges that must be addressed before full-scale deployment. The discussion in the article focuses on raising questions about what DCC represents and the critical areas of focus before full deployment. The transition from paper-based calibration certificates to digital ones involves significant changes in the mindset of society to increase trustworthy in digital technologies. DCCs promise numerous benefits, including enhanced efficiency, traceability, and reliability in calibration processes, aligning with the broader trend of digital transformation in various industries. However, achieving these benefits requires a thorough understanding of the associated challenges. This article examines the aspects of DCCs, aiming to provide an overview of their benefits and the hurdles to be overcome for widespread acceptance.

1 Introduction

What exactly does the "D" in the abbreviation DCC stand for? While it is clear that it means "digital," it brings a revolution in how the CC (Calibration Certificate) is perceived. By adding "D," not only is the physical (paper) form removed, but it also introduces the integration of digital technologies with all their aspects. Digitalization in this context does not merely mean converting a document into a digital format but also encompasses comprehensive changes in the creation, handling, and sharing of calibration data. This step paves the way for better automation, traceability, and reliability in metrological processes. DCC can be considered a significant step in the digitalization of metrology, as it unambiguously demonstrates the benefits that digitalization can bring when applied to one of the fundamental pillars of metrology. If digitalization is effectively and positively implemented in the field of calibration, then its adoption in more advanced metrological processes will become more acceptable, even for a more conservative society. The current state of digitalization is characterized by aggressive development, advancing dynamically. In fields where calibrations are utilized, speed and efficiency are essential, leading to the development of various data standards, language models, big data processing, and an increasing integration of AI into processes. Therefore, it is crucial for DCC to evolve in a way that aligns with the needs of digitalization in metrology while preserving the mission of metrology, ensuring that digitalization technologies are not unintentionally overloaded at the expense of metrology itself. It is more important than ever to keep the essence of metrology as a priority.

2 Benefits of DCC in metrology

Summarizing the benefits of DCC in metrology is a simple task, as they can be observed in all processes that have been successfully automated and digitalized. However, it is certainly worth highlighting some of the significant benefits listed in Table 1.

Table 1. Typical significant benefits of DCC.

Benefit	Justification
Enhanced data access	It enables easy and fast access to information, accelerating various processes related to calibration.

* Corresponding author: martin.koval@cmi.gov.cz

Machine-readable data	Enables optimization for automated processing, eliminating manual data entry and minimizing errors.
Elimination of paper	Transitioning to digital solutions reduces printing and distribution costs, contributing to environmental goals.
Integration support	DCC can be implemented into existing internal IT systems and support interoperability between different platforms.
Automation of metrological processes	Enables more efficient management of calibrations and management of the lifecycle of devices and instruments, improving planning and maintenance.
Support for digital twins	DCC can support digital twin attributes, improving process efficiency and safety across industries.
Improvement of traceability	Replacing paper-based processes with digital solutions enables quick retrieval and monitoring of calibration history.

It is also important to realize that DCC is not the only one pillar of digitalization in metrology so it must fit into the bigger concept of metrology digital for transformation. This means that the DCC concept must be designed to ensure interoperability, compatibility, modularity, and scalability while also establishing clear boundaries to ensure that metrology is always expressed clearly and comprehensibly. For this reason, several working groups focus on the development, implementation, and harmonization of DCC (see Chapter 5).

3 Trustworthiness in DCC

With the upcoming of digitalization and DCC, not only do benefits arise, but also associated challenges that require attention. It is essential to recognize all aspects related to the use of data in digital form, such as hardware and software requirements, cybersecurity, format, data handling, data integrity, data sharing, data copying, etc.

All of this leads to the questions: How can we trust data in the digital world? If we trust information on paper, what must be ensured to establish trust in digital data? If trustworthiness can be achieved in sectors such as banking and healthcare, then there must also be a way to achieve it in metrology. It is possible to identify three user groups (Fig. 1) that have an influence on the progress of DCC:

1. The first group consists of users who need and actively benefit from the "D" in DCC, as outlined in Table 1.
2. The second group includes users who are interested in the content of the CC and actively work with the data but often lack the resources (personnel and/or financial). They tend to wait for partial, ideally global, harmonization before adapting to the trend.
3. The third group consists of users who require CC for compliance reasons, such as audits, but do not practically use the data from CC.

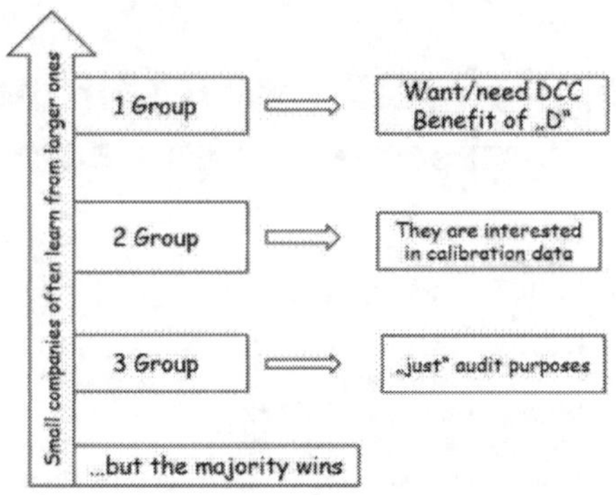

Fig. 1. Interpretation of user distribution influencing the progress of DCC deployment.

This classification reflects reality, and each country has a different distribution of these user groups. In general, small companies learn from large ones, but the principle of "the majority wins" often applies. One of the most common concerns of the second and third groups is the cost of implementing IT infrastructure, whether in terms of financial investment or resource capacity.

4 Challenges in DCC

The biggest challenge in DCC is achieving global harmonization. It is necessary to identify key factors, including:

- Each continent/country may have different expectations regarding DCC.
- The country's level of development/current state of digital/IT infrastructure.
- The society's stance on trustworthiness and acceptance of digital technologies.
- The time required for society to adapt to changes compared to established practices.
- Generation differences.

The aim of each country is to move society forward while avoiding unnecessary pressure for rapid changes. Some societies can adapt to changes more quickly, while others take more time. Therefore, building a digital infrastructure will likely be a long-term process, in some cases taking up to a decade. For this reason, adopting DCC in its advanced form right from the start will be challenging. However, a key driving factor is also generation change, as younger people tend to be more connected to digital technologies and have trust in them.

The available information [1] shows, that one of common concepts of DCC currently used is an embedded digital file within PDFA/3a [2].

Germany is undoubtedly the most progressive country in the field of DCC and its integration with digital infrastructure [3]. They are gradually progressing towards transforming their calibration processes to be based on digital documents and providing the necessary digital quality infrastructure to enable this [4]. Based on the content and attendance numbers of DCC conferences (1-4) [1], it is evident that almost everyone closely involved in this topic follows developments in Germany, including stakeholders that are already implementing DCC in the real field. However, there are still countries that lack the necessary IT/digital infrastructure to fully trust purely digital files. This gap can be attributed to varying levels of societal and technological maturity.

If we look at the technical aspects, the challenges include:

- Unified interpretation,
- Format,
- Compatibility,
- Development,
- Trustworthiness,
- Resources.

Regarding unified interpretation, one of the key advantages of the digital world is the ability to use a standardized, machine-interpretable language. The first step toward this is the creation of a unified digital vocabulary. One of the key working groups addressing this challenge is FMD-TG-MS (FORUM-MD ad hoc Task Group on Metrological Semantics) [15]. For a unified interpretation, it is crucial to maintain consistent semantics and properly structured ontology, which will eliminate barriers related to the use of different data formats such as XML, JSON, JSON-LD, and YAML. Additionally, digitalization constantly evolves, meaning that new formats may develop over time. This brings us to another major challenge - compatibility. While format compatibility is essential, it is also necessary to consider backward compatibility. Since DCCs already exist, future requirements must be designed to ensure that digital files created today can still be used 10-15 years from now. At present, we cannot fully predict what the state of the art will look like in the future, making long-term digital sustainability a critical consideration.

Some recalibration intervals are required every 1-2 years, which, from the perspective of the benefit of historical data traceability, represents only a minor data volume. As mentioned in the introduction, metrology must take precedence over technology. Currently, we can observe how certain IT solutions have become unsustainable within just a few years, while Calibration Certificates (CCs) remain valid. The expiration of calibration is not always strictly defined [5], making it crucial to ensure that DCC validity does not outlast the stability of IT solutions.

A special challenge is trustworthiness. One of the most frequently asked questions is: "How can I trust a digital file?" It is important to emphasize that in the field of software and IT security, it is extremely difficult to claim that something is 100% secure (Secure/Safety) [6]. However, it is possible to implement measures that support trustworthiness. Despite this, various software tools exist to ensure data integrity, such as encryption techniques, digital signatures, and other security mechanisms is generally known that the ingenuity in bypassing such security measures is constantly evolving and, in some cases, is even one step ahead.

Trustworthiness must be realized with precision—it is not enough to rely solely on high-quality software tools. A comprehensive quality management system must also be implemented including personnel training, processes for data and software verification, regular audits, etc. In summarizing these selected aspects, it is pertinent to note the use of resources.

It is natural to recognize that DCC may not be currently suitable for everyone. Implementing DCC brings additional demands on personnel, IT infrastructure, technology, and, of course, financial resources, which are often the decisive factor. However, we can observe a significant shift in the adoption of digital technologies. In relatively a short period, nearly every company has integrated IT into its operations, cloud services have become widely used [7], and the adoption of AI tools has grown rapidly in recent years [8]. From the perspective of the increasing use of digital services, the DCC concept is a logical step forward for metrology. Therefore, it is necessary to establish clear steps to facilitate the adoption of DCC. These steps have already been incorporated into the objectives and tasks of various working groups.

5 Harmonization and working groups focused on DCC

Currently, there are several working groups and projects dedicated to supporting the implementation of DCC. Their objectives include raising awareness about DCC within their fields, monitoring technological advancements, understanding user needs, and collaborating with other working groups to achieve a sufficient level of DCC harmonization that meets the requirements of all users.

Among the most significant international working groups are:

- FMD TG H-DCC/DRMC [9],
- EURAMET TC-IM 1448 [10],
- APMP TG H-DCC [11],
- SIM M4DT TF on DCC [12],
- Project CABUREK MDT-IC [13],

Each working group or project has its specific contribution, whether in technical development, implementation, or harmonization. Each group focuses on specific areas, and their outputs envisioned eventually can converge into an outcome (Fig. 2), which could be directed to FMD TG H-DCC/DRMC: Forum on Metrology and Digitalization ad hoc Task Group on Harmonizing Digital Calibration Certificate and Digital Reference Material Certificate with a global impact.

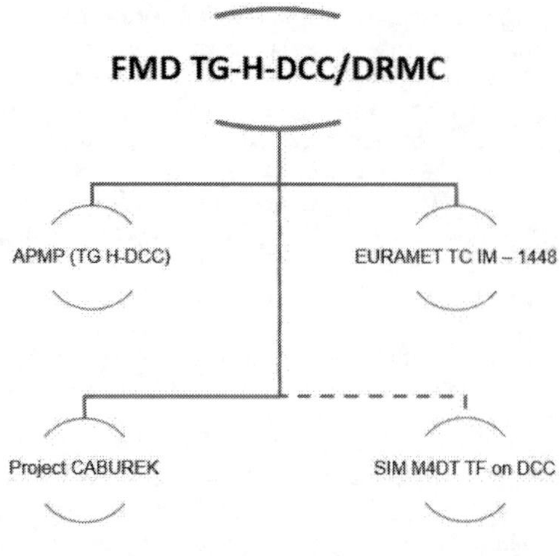

Fig. 2. Schematic representation of growing communication channels between significant working groups and projects focused on DCC.

This Task Group (TG) was established in March 2024 and is part of FMD (Forum on Metrology and Digitalization) [14], whose primary mission is to advise the CIPM (International Committee for Weights and Measures) on the SI Digital Framework and the wider implications of the global digital transformation for metrology and for the international Quality Infrastructure. From the perspective of interactions between TGs and WGs within FMD, in relation to the significance of DCC and DRMC, the following schematic representation can be observed in Fig. 3.

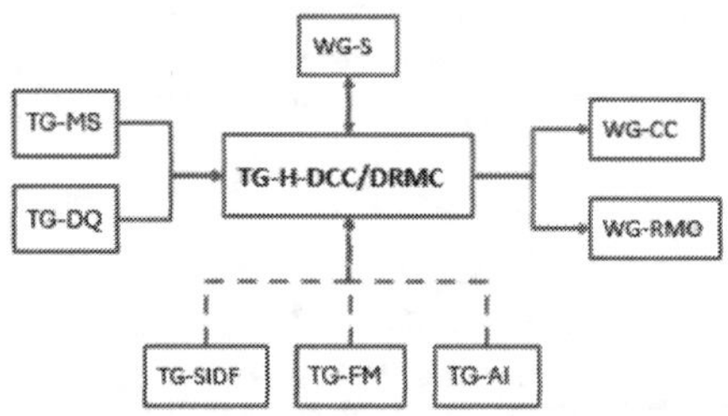

Fig. 3. WGs and TGs interaction in FMD from the perspective of TG-H-DCC/DRMC. (TG-MS: Task Group on Metrological Semantics, TG-DQ: Task Group on Data Quality in Metrology, TG-FM: Task Group on FAIR for Metrology, TG-SIDF: Task Group on SI-digital Framework, TG-AI: Task Group on Secure and Trustworthy AI, FMD-WG-CC: Working Group on coordination between Consultative Committees, WG-RMO: Working Group on coordination between Regional Metrology Organizations, WG-S: Working Group on Strategy.)

From the schematic representation, it is clear that TG-H-DCC/DRMC is not independent and it relies on inputs from other TGs and provides outputs to WGs. Therefore, in addition to the harmonization of DCC/DRMC, this TG also plays a role in the digitalization of metrology as a whole. The establishment of this TG is a significant step toward the implementation of DCC, as it represents a global collaboration across continents. The strategy of this TG is defined through goals and tasks (Fig. 4) to achieve global harmonization for DCC and DRMC.

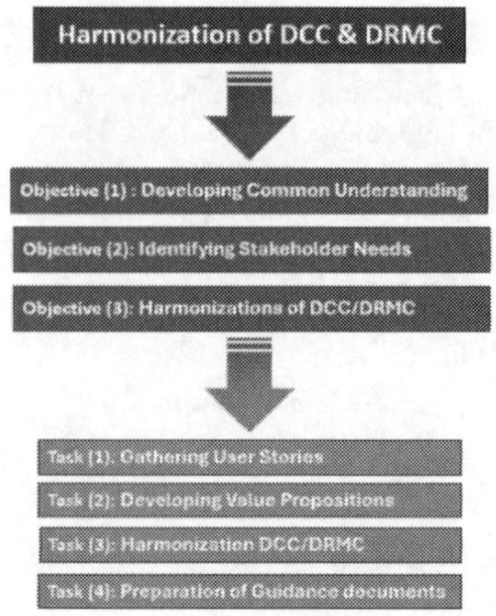

Fig. 4. List of FMD TG-H-DCC/DRMC objectives and tasks.

If we take a closer look at the goals and tasks, the purpose is not to start from scratch. It is essential to summarize what already exists, what is actively used, and continuously update this list. This approach allows for a better identification of the (already extensive) benefits and, more importantly, the needs of stakeholders. This can be achieved through workshops and various conferences. Subsequently, it is possible to consider what will need to be harmonized and what the level of harmonization or its boundaries will be. There are already enough identified assets that can serve as a foundation for further development.

6 The Future of DCC in Metrology

DCC is the future of metrology because we live in a digital age. Metrology is an integral part of this era—just consider the number of sensors surrounding us daily, how many of them are critical, how they influence the quality of our lives, and the key role that calibration plays in ensuring their reliability. The imagination that a single person or a small team is responsible for managing the calibrations of 5,000 devices may seem archaic in today's digital world, but it remains often a reality. The implementation of DCC will likely become as indispensable as the use of smartphones or PCs. Furthermore, new global challenges are emerging where DCC will be essential, including improved product traceability [16 - DPP], utilization in Sensor Networks [17, 18], or training of AI models [8]. Harmonization of DCC is, therefore, more than just desirable, it represents a crucial milestone for the successful digital transformation of metrology.

7 Conclusion

The article points out that DCC brings many benefits as well as challenges that need to be faced. Even though the technical term and the general concept of the DCC has been around for almost a decade, we are still at the beginning. However, with the advancement and development of new technologies, it is only a matter of time before DCC is widely deployed. Before that happens, there is certain "homework" that must be completed to ensure that DCC deployment will be effective and with a vision for the future. DCC is a key factor in the future of digital metrology, but given the enormous number of digital technologies surrounding us, its role is crucial not only for industry but also for society as a whole. As already mentioned in the article, when implementing DCC, it is essential to ensure that new digital technologies do not weaken the role of metrology itself. Most innovations depend on metrology, and if metrology were to be compromised in favor of new technologies, it is highly probable that these very technologies would ultimately be doomed to failure.

The Acknowledgements
This work was partly funded by resources granted to the Czech Metrology Institute by the Ministry of Industry and Trade within the frame of internal research task IF2403601101 and UTR25E601102. Danish Agency for Science and Higher Education with grants to DFM.

References

1. C. Denz, et al., 4th International DCC-Conference 2024-02-27 to 2024-02-29 Proceedings (2024). DOI: 10.7795/810.20240612.
2. G.Boschung, et. al., PDF/A-3 solution for digital calibration certificates, Measurement: Sensors (2021), 100282. https://doi.org/10.1016/j.measen.2021.100282.
3. T. Sołtysiński, J. Niederhausen, S. Eichstädt, Digital Calibration Certificate in a trusted quality infrastructure federated data space: A proof of concept,Measurement: Sensors,(2024),101484, DOI:https://doi.org/10.1016/j.measen.2024.101484.
4. S. Schönhals, et al., Harmonisation processes and practical implementation of machine-interpretable digital calibration certificates, Measurement: Sensors, (2024), 101470. https://doi.org/10.1016/j.measen.2024.101470
5. ISO/IEC 17025:2017, General requirements for the competence of testing and calibration laboratories
6. R. A. Khan, S. U. Khan, H. U. Khan and M. Ilyas, "Systematic Literature Review on Security Risks and its Practices in Secure Software Development," in *IEEE Access*, vol. 10, pp. 5456-5481, 2022, DOI:10.1109/ACCESS.2022.3140181
7. M. M. Lawan, Ch. Oduoza, K. Buckley. (2021). A Systematic Review of Cloud Computing Adoption by Organisations. International Journal of Industrial and Manufacturing Systems Engineering, 6(3), 39-48. https://doi.org/10.11648/j.ijimse.20210603.11
8. C. Alippi, A. Ferrero and V. Piuri, "Artificial intelligence for instruments and measurement applications," in *IEEE Instrumentation & Measurement Magazine*, vol. 1, no. 2, pp. 9-17, June 1998, doi: 10.1109/5289.685492
9. FORUM-MD ad hoc Task Group on Harmonizing DCC and DRMC (FORUM-MD-TG-H-DCC/DRMC).https://www.bipm.org/en/committees/fo/forum-md/wg/forum-md-tg-h-dcc/drmc
10. EURAMET TC-IM 1448: Development of digital calibration certificates. https://www.euramet.org/technical-committees/tc-projects/details/project/development-of-digital-calibration-certificates
11. APMP TG H-DCC, https://www.apmpweb.org/portal/list/index/id/52.html
12. SIM M4DT TF on DCC, https://sim-metrologia.org/about-us/structure/technical-committee/metrology-for-digital-transformation-m4dt/
13. Project CABUREK M4DT-IC Metrology for Digital Transformation in International Cooperation, https://www.m4dt.ptb.de/
14. Forum on Metrology and Digitalization (FORUM-MD).https://www.bipm.org/en/committees/fo/forum-md
15. FORUM-MD ad hoc Task Group on Metrological Semantics (FORUM-MD-TG-MS). https://www.bipm.org/en/committees/fo/forum-md/wg/forum-md-tg-ms
16. DPP – EU's Digital Product Passport: Advancing transparency and sustainability, https://data.europa.eu/en/news-events/news/eus-digital-product-passport-advancing-transparency-and-sustainability
17. M. Koval, J. Tesař, M .Havlíček, General requirements for the competence of testing and calibration laboratories, Acta IMEKO, Vol.12 No. 1(2023).DOI:https://doi.org/10.21014/actaimeko.v12i1.1409
18. S. Tabandeh, Sensor network metrology: Current state and future directions, Measurement: Sensors, (2025),101798.DOI: https://doi.org/10.1016/j.measen.2024.101798

EPJ Web of Conferences **323**, 0100(2(0(5) https://doi.org/10.1051/epjconf/(0(53(30100(
22nd nIt enr Iai nr dMt Iei ai gylCi nget ss

Digitalization in the metrology quality infrastructure – perspectives from Novo Nordisk

Heidi Foldal [1*]
[1]Novo Nordisk A/S, Novo Alle 1, 2880 Bagsvaerd, Denmark
* Corresponding author: hefo@novonordisk.com

Abstract. This paper presents our experiences and challenges with implementing the (DCR) Digital Calibration Request and (DCC) Digital Calibration Certificates initiative in our metrology process at Novo Nordisk, a Danish pharmaceutical company producing medication for chronic diseases. We have a strategic goal to remove all manual transfer of data from our calibration activities, as well as to gain insight by trending on calibration results. Currently, we specify calibration tasks to our suppliers manually, using our IT system, and receive calibration certificates from them mostly as digitally signed PDF-files. We then must manually enter the calibration records into our IT system, which is time-consuming and prone to errors. The DCR/DCC initiative offers a great opportunity to automate both processes companywide, by using standardized and machine-readable formats for exchanging calibration information. Novo Nordisk is actively involved in this initiative, by running pilot projects with several metrology institutes to test the generation and reception of both DCRs and DCCs. However, we have also encountered some data integrity challenges, due to the flexibility of the DCR and DCC schemas. We have realized that, to ensure a robust and reliable transfer process between DCRs, DCCs and our IT system, all these elements must adhere to the ALCOA++ principles, which are a set of criteria for ensuring data quality and traceability in a highly regulated industry.

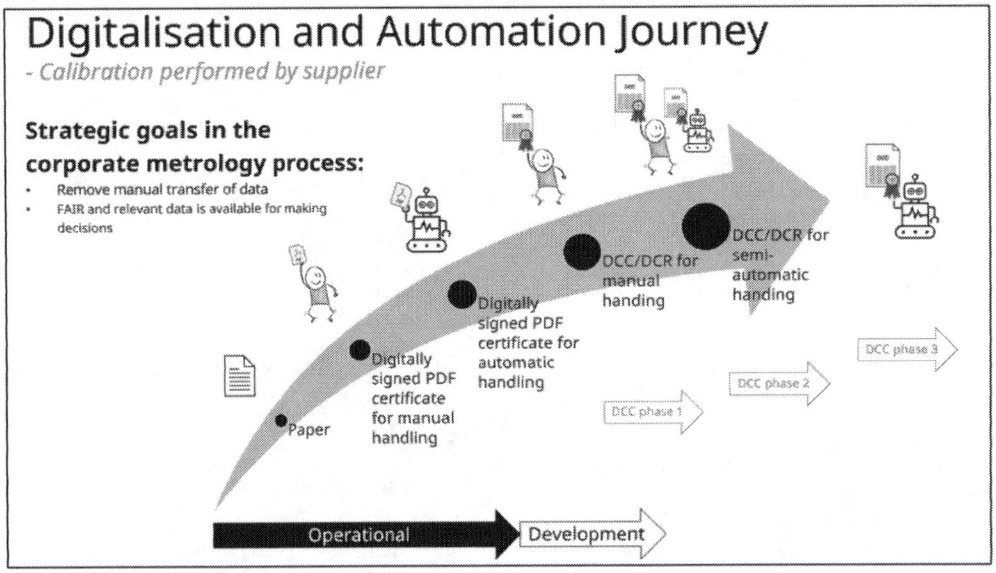

Fig. 1. Digitalisation and automation journey.

1. Introduction

Novo Nordisk, founded in 1923 and based in Denmark, is a global healthcare company focused on providing medication for chronic diseases. Operations are managed through process management across the organizational structure, with the corporate metrology process ensuring reliable and traceable measurements for critical processes. This paper outlines two strategic goals within the corporate metrology process: eliminating manual data transfer and ensuring that data is Findable, Accessible, Interoperable, and Reusable (FAIR) as well as relevant, to support informed decision-making. Pilots are being conducted to implement Digital Calibration Certificates (DCC) and Digital Calibration Requests (DCR).

1.1 Calibration program

The calibration program begins by defining measurement parameters and identifying requirements for these parameters. Calibration requirements for measuring equipment are derived from measurand requirements.

Calibration intervals are determined based on a risk assessment, which considers:
- The impact on Novo Nordisk if measuring equipment does not meet calibration requirements.
- The likelihood of measuring equipment failing to meet calibration requirements.
- Mitigations such as intermediate checks, adjustment limits, and the length of the calibration interval.

A corporate IT system evaluates whether calibration results pass or fail, with the final decision made by a qualified Novo Nordisk employee. If measuring equipment fails to comply with calibration requirements, an investigation is conducted to assess the potential impact on product quality and patient safety since the last successful calibration.

While Novo Nordisk can outsource the execution of calibrations, ultimate responsibility is retained; thus, conformity statements in calibration certificates are not required. All calibration certificates must be delivered to Novo Nordisk.

2. Digitalisation and automation journey

A project has been undertaken to digitize calibration certificates from suppliers in the corporate metrology process. Annually, approximately 20,000 external calibrations are managed, performed by various suppliers across different countries. The digitization process began with the creation of a system for receiving digitally signed PDF certificates for manual handling. Later, the receipt and archiving of these digitally signed PDF certificates were automated. This process is depicted in Figure 1.

2.1 Testing the three-step process

We are testing a three-step process for DCCs and DCRs:
- Manual handling
- Semi-automatic handling
- Fully automated handling

Achieving full automation in our regulated industry is challenging.

2.1.1 Digitally Signed PDF Certificates for Manual Handling

Our metrology process involves receiving digitally signed PDF certificates, verifying data integrity, and archiving. Our records management process specifies the requirements for exchanging these documents with external partners. We have contracts with thirteen suppliers for these certificates. A qualified Novo Nordisk employee verifies the signatures against a root certificate using the Adobe Approved Trust List (AATL) and ensure no changes were made after signing.

2.1.2 Digitally Signed PDF Certificates for Automatic Handling

Ensuring data integrity verification presents challenges for some employees. While it is straightforward to train those who manage digitally signed PDF certificates daily, maintaining competence is more difficult for individuals who handle them infrequently.

In collaboration with the corporate automation department, the corporate metrology process has developed a Robotic Process Automation (RPA) solution for receiving and archiving digitally signed PDF certificates.

The process flow is as follows:
- The supplier sends an email to the software application (BOT).
- The BOT opens the email and reads the email body text, which must adhere to specific syntax requirements.
- The BOT conducts data integrity verification before archiving the certificate(s) in Novo Nordisk's document database.
- Once the certificate(s) are uploaded, the BOT sends a notification to the relevant Novo Nordisk employee with a hyperlink to the certificate in the document database.
- The employee can then review and evaluate the calibration certificate(s) and decide to release or reject the measuring equipment for use.

The syntax requirements in step 2 are necessary due to the lack of machine readability of PDF certificates. Therefore, machine-readable metadata must be included in the email body to facilitate the processing of the PDF certificates.

2.1.3 Manual Handling of DCCs/DCRs

Handling DCCs/DCRs involves logging into Novo Nordisk's IT system, opening the calibration work order, and using middleware to create the DCR. After calibration by a supplier, the employee logs in again, extracts data with middleware, and transfers it back to the IT system. The employee verifies the transfer and signs off the work order. A second person confirms the accuracy and signs for review.

2.1.4 Semi-automatic Handling of DCCs/DCRs

An employee logs into the Novo Nordisk IT system to initiate a calibration work order, generating and sending a DCR to the supplier. After calibration and receipt of the DCC, the data is transferred to the IT system. The employee then verifies and signs off on the data transfer.

2.1.5 Fully Automated Handling of DCCs/DCRs

Fully automated handling functions in a manner like semi-automatic handling as described in section above; however, it does include automation of the work order review process.

3. Development – phase 1: manual handling of dcc/dcr

In the first phase of the DCC pilot (see figure 1), we will apply insights gained from the digitally signed PDF calibration certificate. The DCC in XML format will be embedded into the PDF while maintaining the human-readable PDF for inspections and audits. The PDF will also act as a manual backup if automation fails. This pilot is being conducted with Danish suppliers, including DFM, TI, and FORCE.

3.1 Mapping of Data Flow from Novo Nordisk IT System to DCR

To generate a DCR, it is crucial that data in the Novo Nordisk IT system is FAIR, ensuring retrievability. Analysing all aspects of the calibration request process, including unwritten practices between customer and supplier, identifies three groups of information for the DCR:

Data transferred from the Novo Nordisk IT System:
- Equipment ID number
- Calibration work order
- Requirements for calibration method, environmental conditions, sensor connection, calibration point direction, units for DUT, standard, and expanded uncertainty, and adjustment if limits are exceeded

Standard text describing fundamental requirements:
- Calibration must be performed according to ISO 17025 or a Metrology Quality Agreement between Novo Nordisk and the supplier
- Only one measuring equipment per certificate
- As found and as left calibrations must be in separate certificates
- Consistent units for DUT, standard, and uncertainty
- No conformity statements in the certificate

Manually collected information:
- Contact person (name, initials, email, phone)
- Return address for equipment and certificate

Figure 2 shows an example of mapping data flow from the Novo Nordisk IT System.

3.2 Mapping of Data Flow from DCC to Novo Nordisk IT System

When handling automatic data transfer, it is important to ensure unique data identification in both systems. In the Novo Nordisk IT system, each calibration point has a unique ID, as shown in figure 3. Here, a Device Under Test is referred to as a Unit Under Test (UUT). The first calibration point is labelled 01UUT, the second 02UUT, and so forth. Calibration standards used by suppliers are labelled in a similar manner; for example, 01PRT01 indicates the first point reading, and 02PRT01 the second. Calibration result uncertainties are marked as 01U, 02U, etc.

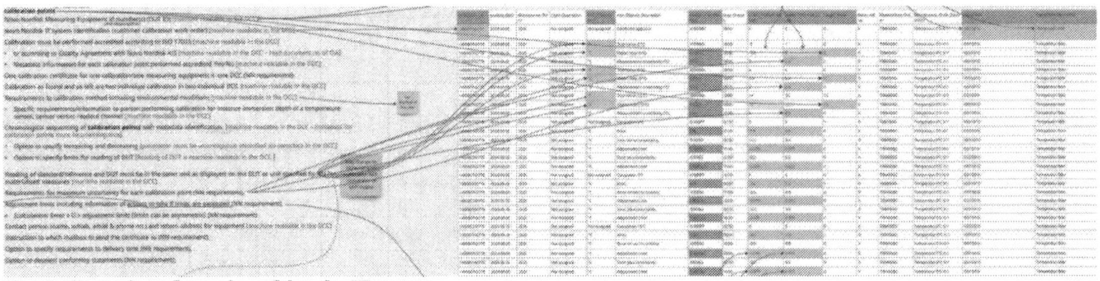

Fig. 2. Illustration of mapping of data for IT system

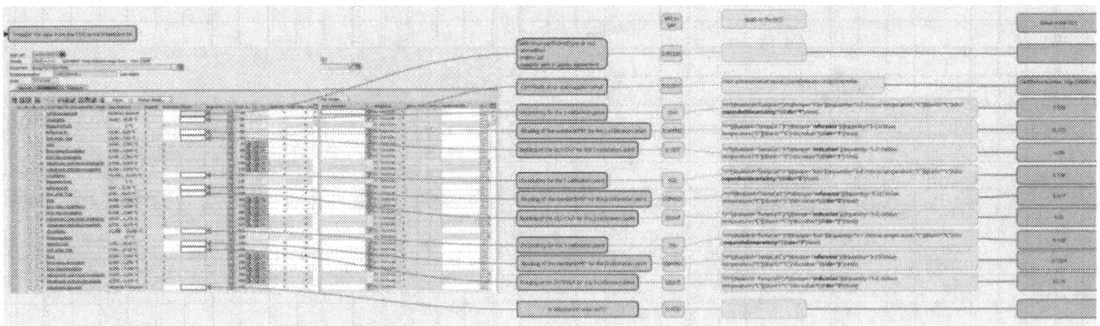

Fig. 3. Illustration of unique data identification.

https://doi.org/10.1051/epjconf/(0(53(30100(

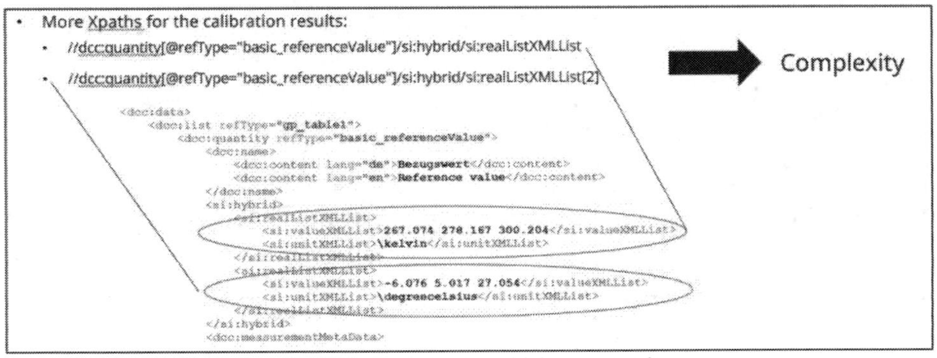

Fig. 4. Illustration of an XPath resulting in multiple query results.

3.3 Ensuring accurate data transfer

To ensure accurate data transfer and reduce transcription errors, calibration results within the DCC must be uniquely identifiable, as specified in section 9.4 of [1].

XPath is used to query XML files. Queries in DCCs should follow consistent, well-defined, and objective XPaths as specified in section 5.5.3 of [1]. XPaths producing multiple results, as seen in figure 4, increase middleware complexity and risk of failure.

While humans can easily distinguish between temperatures in kelvin and Celsius, developing middleware to handle this complicates IT risk assessments, which must validate all potential data transfer issues. Robust XPaths enhance DCC reliability, so the design should simplify creating robust XPaths.

3.3.1 Regulatory Requirements to a Record (ALCOA+)

In the healthcare industry, documentation including calibration certificates are required to meet various regulatory requirements. At Novo Nordisk, the corporate record management process ensures compliance with these standards. Both electronic and paper calibration certificates adhere to the same rules. The ALCOA+ (Attributable, Legible, Contemporaneous, Original, Accurate) principles help ensure that regulatory expectations are met.

Attributable in [1] is ensured by having a clear identification of the individual performing a calibration task and the date or date range for when the calibration was performed. We expect the calibration certificate to be locked for editing with a trusted signature and in a way so it can be verified that the document has not been altered after the last signature was applied.

Legible in [1] covers the record being readable and unambiguous for it to be understandable and usable. This is where the unambiguous identification of calibration data described in section 3.1 becomes important.

Contemporaneous in [1] is covered by section 7.8.1.2 in [2] and is a requirement that specifies that recording of calibration data must be documented when the calibration takes place. By requesting an accredited calibration, the accreditation ensures that the result of the calibration is accurate, clear, unambiguous, and objective.

Original in [1] is also covered by section 7.8.1.2 in [2] and is a requirement to ensure the first capture of calibration results.

Accurate in [1] is a requirement to ensure that the calibration results are a truthful representation of fact which is the intent of [2].

Complete in [1] is a requirement to ensure that all critical information to understand the calibration is captured to ensure that all relevant metadata is available in the DCC and that the information is not deleted or lost.

Consistent in [1] is requirement to help control or standardise the DCC. We need an international standard for the DCC.

Enduring in [1] is a requirement to ensure that the calibration certificate is readable and reliable in the retention period. In Novo Nordisk the retention period for a calibration certificate is ten years. From our experience with digitally signed PDF calibration certificates, we know that the root certificate has an expiry date after typically three years. By uploading the certificates to the Novo Nordisk database upon receival and at the same time ensuring the data integrity we protect the certificates in the entire retention period.

Available in [1] is a requirement to ensure that the calibration certificate is available for Novo Nordisk employees.

3.3.2 Further risk reduction

Section 5.5.3 in [1] gives good practice guidance in reducing risk by having a simple process which is consistent, well defined, and objective. Complex or inconsistent processes with open ends and subjective outcomes lead to increased risk. At Novo Nordisk we prefer simplicity.

4. Why digitalize

At Novo Nordisk, most measuring equipment is calibrated in situ and documented within a corporate IT system. Calibration requirements are accessible to employees via calibration work orders. The readings of the Unit Under Test (UUT) and the standard are directly recorded in the IT system, which then calculates and evaluates whether the calibration has passed or failed to assist the employee in making the final determination. This calibration process is paperless and environmentally friendly, with the capability to trend calibration data as outlined in [3].

Calibrations outsourced to suppliers are also managed within the same IT system, although the digital maturity level is lower. Calibration requirements are available in the IT system for the employee requesting the calibration; however, data covering the calibration requirements, such as calibration points and accuracy requirements, is manually transferred to a letter that is sent to the supplier along with the equipment. After calibration, some departments transfer the calibration result data into the IT system, where it is verified by a second person. Other departments do not transfer this data. The IT system only evaluates calibration data once it has been transferred, and trending on the data is possible only if data transfer occurs. Presently, approximately 25% of all calibration certificates received by Novo Nordisk are digitally signed PDF certificates, indicating progress towards a fully paperless process.

On average, it takes 20 minutes to transfer data from a certificate to the IT system and for a second person to verify the data transfer accuracy. It typically takes 25 minutes to transfer calibration requirements from the IT system to a letter. Additionally, 5% of all revised calibration certificates are due to errors in Novo Nordisk's calibration requests.

The successful transfer of data is just one aspect; true success is achieved when calibration data is used to trend the performance of measuring equipment, build leading indicators, and gain valuable insights for proactive action, as described in [3].

5. Conclusions

The establishment of an international standard for Digital Calibration Certificates (DCC) and Digital Calibration Requests (DCR) is pivotal for successful global implementation. Such a standard ensures that all aspects of DCC and DCR comply with a unified framework, promoting smoother operations across various countries and suppliers. Maintaining data integrity is essential to guarantee trustworthy and reliable information, which is the cornerstone of effective implementation.

A phased implementation approach simplifies change management by breaking down the process into manageable stages. This method allows for thorough planning, monitoring, and adjustment at each phase, thereby reducing the risk of errors and ensuring a seamless transition. Furthermore, being a pioneer comes with challenges and the potential for rework. It is thus crucial to select the right collaboration partner who shares your vision and can offer the expertise and support required for successful implementation.

In conclusion, adhering to international standards, ensuring data integrity, adopting a phased implementation strategy, and partnering with the appropriate collaborators are critical factors for achieving a successful global implementation.

References

[1] Secretariat of the Pharmaceutical Inspection Convention, PIC/S GOOD PRACTICES FOR DATA MANAGEMENT AND INTEGRITY IN REGULATED GMP/GDP ENVIRONMENTS (PI 041-1), 2021, Geneva, Switzerland, https://picscheme.org/docview/4234

[2] International Organization for Standardization, ISO 17025:2017 General requirements for the competence of testing and calibration laboratories, 2017, https://www.iso.org/standard/66912.html

[3] Schroll-Fleischer J., Paustian F. A., Calibration Data Mining – Perspectives from Novo Nordisk, 2024, Novo Nordisk, XXIV IMEKO World Congress, Hamburg, Germany - *Pending Publication.*

 t pp s/dll o.gprj dl0gl0) 1dè: 3conf505) (5(0100(

From a digital calibration certificate to a digital quality infrastructure

Thomas Engel [1*]

[1]Siemens AG, FT RPD CED DPR-DE, Friedrich-Ludwig-Bauer-Straße 3, D-85748 Garching, Germany

Abstract. Digitalizing the quality infrastructure is a very substantial objective for public and industrial stakeholders. A huge variety of quality related documents exist and need to be considered and transformed thoroughly into an appropriate digital representation. Early initiatives were started to digitalize the calibration certificate and the international system of units. GEMIMEG-II was a German lighthouse project with industry partners to verify and enhance the concept of digital calibration certificates for different industrial use-cases. Fundamental requirements of a digital quality document concern the standardisation of content regarding semantics, ontologies and the ability to proof originality and authenticity for all digital quality related documents. A versatile digital quality infrastructure benefits from a common structural concept supporting the variety of quality related documents and bears synergies for commonalities in content. The DX document schema and its underlying norms and standards can serve as a common conceptual framework to generate harmonized quality related digital documents and to exploit the data contained efficiently and unambiguously. International applicability and industrial processes require an efficient, productive and process integrable digital quality infrastructure. Functional requirements and opportunities of a harmonized approach for digital quality related documents will be discussed in depth.

1 Introduction

Product conformity and calibrations are central elements to prove proper design and functionality of a product. Thus, they are core elements needed in a digital quality infrastructure (QI). The German lighthouse project GEMIMEG-II [1], [2] focussed on the application of Digital Calibration Certificates (DCC) in industrial use-cases. The application scenarios were representative for four branches of industry: manufacturing industry, process industry, calibration service providers and autonomous driving. Furthermore, a legal simulation study challenged and approved the evidential value of a digitally signed DCC in comparison to a paper- or pdf-based calibration certificate. The study simulated a court case about a hypothetical damaging event.

QI-Digital is another German lighthouse project to develop concepts and first implementations for a digital quality infrastructure [3]. This project focusses on digitalization of further quality documents like Certificate of Conformity (DCoC), Digital Test Certificate (DTC) and Digital Reference Material Certificates (DRMC). These additional documents were developed based on the actual status of the DCC. GEMIMEG-II and QI-Digital were aligned and complement each other in scope and content.

Digitalization in industry follows the concepts of federated dataspaces for data exchange along process chains and the asset administration shell (AAS) with its respective and dedicated sub-models to supply and receive well-structured datasets [4]. This will eliminate todays' tedious effort to handle and register documents printed on paper or in pdf-data formats [5] and to extract information and data manually.

Legislation in Europe and other parts of the world enforces a fully digital product documentation containing all information in a digital product passport (DPP) [6]. The DPP contains data on resource consumption and data from manufacturing, for customer information and documentation, service and spare parts and finally end of life information for re-use, disassembly and recycling. Product passports come into force for the battery in 02.2027 and for a large variety of industrial products until 2030. To comply with these regulations, data required in the passports can be retrieved from the asset administrations shell and its respective sub-models.

Quality documents like DCoC, DCC, DTC and DRMC are typically passed through to a product customer to prove product quality. As such, they will be part of the AAS and DPP and contained in the AAS sub-model for digital quality documents.

This paper will give more detail on recent and upcoming developments on digital quality documents to enable an efficient digital quality infrastructure.

2 Digitalization of quality documents

To digitalize quality documents effectively, some basic but important preconditions have to be considered. Fig. **1** summarizes major needs. The upper part shows

* Corresponding author: engelthomas@siemens.com

t pp s/dI o.gorj d10gl0) 1de: 3confd505) (5(0100(

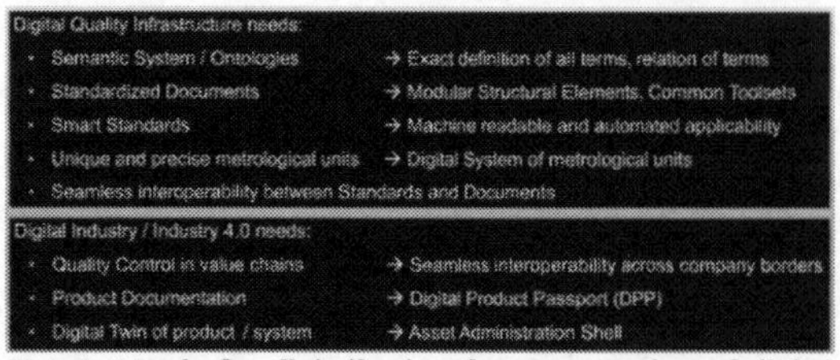

Fig. 1. Needs for digitalization from perspective of digital quality infrastructure and from industry [7]©Creative Commons Attribution 4.0 license

needs from a general QI perspective while the lower part reflects complementing requirements from an industry perspective.

The economic value proposition of digital QI is based on seamless and efficient interoperability of all quality documents including immediate access to data and information contained. Essential prerequisites are exact semantic definitions of all terms used in quality documents. International adherence requires publicly available standards. When available, they will guide, support and harmonize the plurality of current digitalization initiatives. Furthermore, the relation of these terms defines their underlying ontology. Since some terms may exist with a different meaning in different contexts or technical fields, it might be favourable to define separate namespace for distinct technical fields. This will increase efficiency in digitalization and reduce tedious and time-consuming alignment, if possible at all.

Normative work can serve as reference point for available semantics and semantic references including ontologies. These references can be explicit definitions or implicit by specifying semantic terms via their relation to other terminology contained, e.g. in kind of knowledge graphs. The latter would be more adaptive and favourable when computer systems and language models should use them, too. An open but maintained normative framework is desirable to represent the perpetually growing sematic content – e.g. in form of maintained and commented repositories with regular release cycles to keep up pace with the fast evolution of digitalization in different technical fields.

A common structural approach for QI documents enables to transform and represent the semantically defined content of the documents in a modular way, even for different document types. Commonly used modules allow to leverage synergy potential across different QI documents for re-used elements. The modular structure also allows for dedicated toolsets to create, handle or use these documents and all data contained.

QI is based on international standards. Smart standards allow for full interoperability between a given standard and a digital quality document related to it. In future, the content and even formulas could be directly referenced from the standard or even used when preparing the content of a quality document like a DCC or a digital test certificate or measurement protocol.

The originality and authenticity of digital documents is of ultimate importance. Previous paper or pdf-based document have a letter head representing the issuer. For digital document it is necessary to replace the letter head of official documents issued by public authorities and accredited test and calibration bodies by a digital mean. A qualified digital signature with a company's credentials or an official digital seal or accreditation symbol could serve as a versatile solution. Automated tests on the validity of the signature or the document can be performed. In contrast to actual regulations, a digital signature should be made compulsory for QI documents.

The QI documentation also needs to be referenced precisely to the system it is linked to. Unique references are needed. In the framework of the digital nameplate [8], a unique product identifier (UID) is introduced. This could be the one unique reference to a system. Legacy system and common practice have different identifiers in place today. The tool owner my issue his identifier for the system and/or the place where it is used in the process and/or a logic name, where the data is supplied to and/or a unique network identification linked to the hardware. Even qualification service providers tend to issue their own UID to support traceability of their service. A digital QI document must be capable to incorporate those different identifiers with an appropriate reference to the issuer or purpose of this reference. To minimise errors and confusion, the number of such references should be kept as small as possible in QI documents. As an example, a temperature sensor could consist of multiple and modular components, the sensor element, the data transmitter including A/D conversion and a display unit as process indicator. When the entire system is calibrated, all three UIDs must be referenced in the DCC, to specify the system unambiguously.

Many quality documents state measurements and test results and thus need a digital representation of metrological units. The Système International d'Unités, the SI-System, is the international system of metrological units as defined in 1875 [9], 150 years ago, as shown in Fig. *2*. Today, it is based on the seven metrological defining constants. The seven base units are derived from theses constants as defined per 2019-05-19. The actual SI system is tracing back via the evolving definitions to its origin of the meter convention in 1875. Since 2024, it is completely transferred into the digital world with the SI reference point of the BIPM [10]. This reference point provides all the information of units in digital form with full history of the definition of units of the metre convention.

Digital documents need definite metrological units in an explicit digital representation to define measures

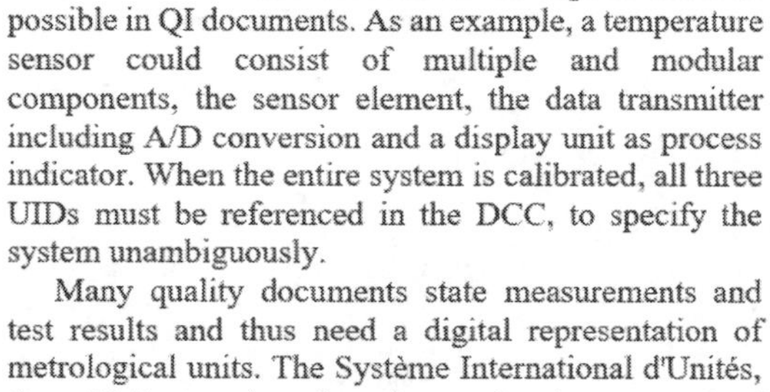

Fig. 2. The first two pages of the meter convention listing the undersigning representatives of the member states, physical artifacts for kilogram and meter. [7, BIPM]

for requirements, specify product features and document measurement results properly. The D-SI system is a very systematic schema to define and represent SI units [11], [12], [13]. It is implemented in XML. It contains the 7 base units and all 22 derived units as defined in the SI-brochure [14] of the Bureau International des Poids et Mesures (BIPM).

Furthermore, the D-SI systematic allows to specify additional units, including imperial units. They can simply be defined as a derivate unit with a unit name, eventually short name of the unit and unit symbol. Those derived units are specified by a combination of the base units in the respective power together with a potential scaling factor. Thus, the D-SI is designed to represent all metrical units used. Meanwhile, complementary implementations of digital representation of the SI are developed, e.g. from a BIPM working group. In the end, it is important to have a versatile and unambiguous system to represent all metrological units in use as a digital unit. This system needs to follow strict rules how units get defined and how new units can be added, in case they are needed. This digital system of units should be represented in international norms to harmonize the digital representation of the SI worldwide.

Today, there is the ISO 80000 framework with many units of measurement represented, but not as digital representation. In parallel, there is the IEC 62720 standard for the common data dictionary (CDD) with a section about the units of measurement (UoM). It lists 1822 units of measurement, some of them at least with some digital expression as a formula. Both standards need to revised to incorporate at least one versatile systematic schema for a digital representation of measurement units. The systematic behind the units defined as a derivative of the base units allows for automated conversion of measurement values to other decimal multiples of the same base unit or alternative derived or imperial units. This is a very powerful feature when aggregating data from different sources. Furthermore, the implementation of digital units in a programming language can be decoupled from the sematic and systematic structural definition of units. To implement this systematic representation of a digital SI in computer readable and executable from, appropriate notations like XML or JSON [15], [16] can be used. In addition, it would be favourable, if all seven base units and the 22 derived units of these standards would be linked to the BIPM refence point to provide full metrological definition complementing today's semantic definitions and descriptions in the standards.

All the aspects mentioned above about standardized and homogenized semantics and ontologies for digital quality documents, standardized digital representation of SI units and smart standards aim at a seamless interoperability between standards and documents in QI. They serve as a common basis for ongoing and future digitalization initiatives in QI and industry. These standards will secure the huge investments to be done for an efficient digital transformation of QI and industry.

Industry is digitalizing its processes as the fourth industrial revolution. Thus, the process of quality control will be digitalized to leverage the value

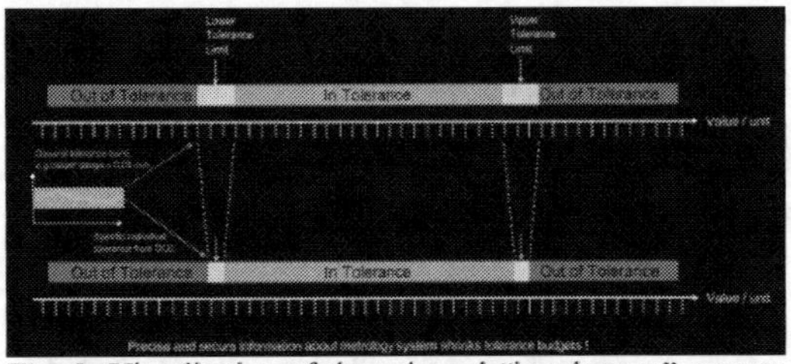

Fig. 3. Visualisation of the enlarged "in tolerance" process window with decreasing tolerances of the measuring system. [2, Fig. 2] ©Creative Commons Attribution 4.0 license

associated with the availability of more detailed knowledge in and about a process. Quality information has to be reported in standardized fashion to enable seamless utilization and interoperability of the respective data. The Asset Administration Shell (AAS) is the concept for seamless data provisioning and interchange as structured datasets allowing for machine interoperability and executability.

The benefit of the availability of precise data in a process is sketched in **Fig. 3**. It shows the significant effect, how the operative process window of a conformity control process can be enlarged. The in-tolerance portion is enlarged, when values from standard tolerance classes of the testing system are replaced by the exact values from a calibration. More precise sensor information increases repeatability and reproducibility of related processes. When calibrations are required and performed to qualify accuracy and precision of the testing system, the exact data is reported in the DCC. The whole calibration data can be extracted automatically in full detail from the DCC. The accuracy of sensor data can be improved by software-based adjustments of data measured at no additional cost.

By 2030, a digital product passport (DPP) is mandatory to deliver industrial products in the European Union and even other regions of the world. These legal requirements enforce to make product documentation, resource consumption and lifecycle data available to customers. Quality documents will be part of the DPP. At the end of life, this compiled and detailed information can be used to minimize the environmental impact of a product and to enable a circular economy by reuse or recycling. This full digital documentation of product related data is a contribution to a real world based digital twin of the respective product. The DPP contains design information and lifecycle information, which can be for example a DCC for calibration and other QI documents.

3 The DX Document Schema

The concept of a common digital document schema called DX-Schema is introduced in multiple publications [1], [2], [17] in detail. Fig. *4* shows the concept idea of the DX-schema. The aim is to derive multiple QI documents from a common, modular semantic basis DX to leverage synergies, reduce implementation efforts while increasing speed of implementation and the maturity of the solution created. Furthermore, all tools needed to create these digital documents or to extract data and/or information from

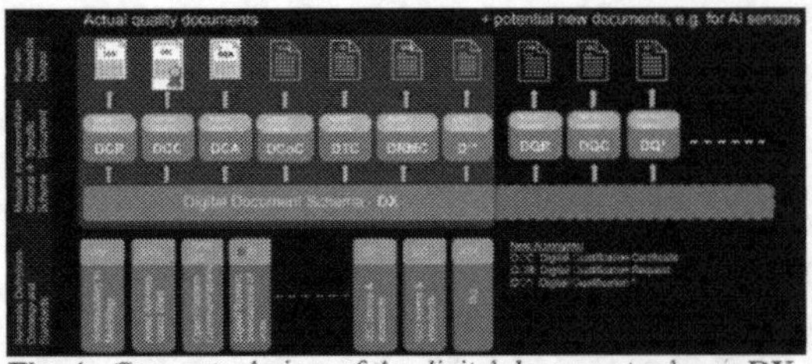

Fig. 4 : Conceptual view of the digital document schema DX, advanced version of *[7]*, p.10 ©Creative Commons Attribution 4.0 license

these documents can be used for multiple documents and thus further synergies can be unlocked.

A more detailed view on some selected and exemplary norms and standards supporting the DX-schema is shown in Fig. *5*. Very general and broadly applicable norms and standards are shown in the left column and more specific standards in the right one. The middle part lists some standards closely related to QI and central documents and certificates to be supported.

The concept for implementing DX based quality documents is shown in Fig. *6*. The DX-schema is a modular structure which contains all sematic definitions and ontologies for the technical terms used for a respective section of a quality document in a separate module. The structure as sketched in Fig. *5* represents the underlying modular concept. To apply this semantic structure to create real documents, an implementation in a computer language is needed. When developing the DCC and the d-SI, XML was chosen as language and an XSD schema was created [12], [18] to define basic rules and logic contained in the schema. The value of this schema definition is, that the content of real documents can be checked automatically for completeness of mandatory entries and some logical relationship between selected data fields. This important feature will help to reduce the number of incomplete or false entries. On larger scale, the data quality in a digital QI will be improved significantly. This results in more robust and resilient digital processes as one lever to increase productivity along value chains.

The DX-schema based digital quality documents can be incorporated into the Digital Quality Document (DQD) sub-model for the AAS, as shown on the right side of Fig. *6*. The common DX schema implies significant synergies to the process, since it reduces or eliminates the need for customized solutions for different quality documents. It reduces implementation and maintenance efforts and related sources of errors.

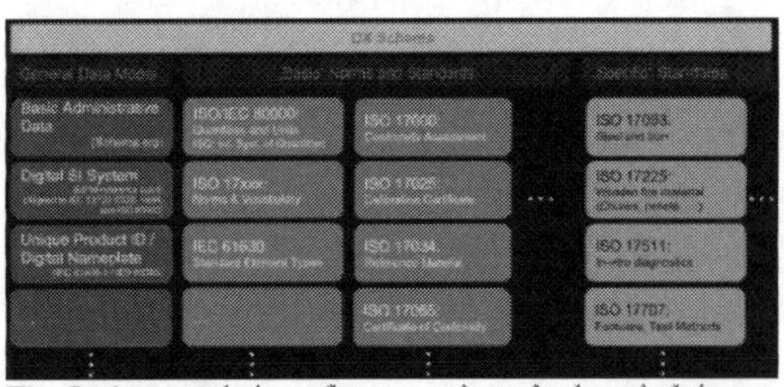

Fig. 5 : Structural view of norms and standards underlying the DX-schema, advanced version of [2], Fig. 7 ©Creative Commons Attribution 4.0 license

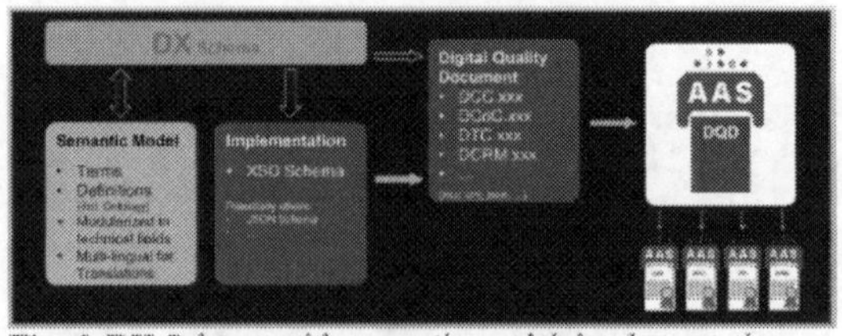

Fig. 6. DX-Schema with semantic model, implementation and digital quality document (DQD), advanced version of [2], fig. 6 ©Creative Commons Attribution 4.0 license

4 Value Stream and Quality Information

A digital QI is based on a variety of different quality documents, which are generated along the product value chain during product generation and its lifecycle. It starts in the early design phase of a product with customer requirements and concepts. They get detailed in the design phase to finalize the product. During design verification, production and quality testing, additional proofs and qualifications are done to qualify a product model and/or a specific serialized product. Qualification results get documented systematically as shown in Fig. *7*. It shows schematically various contributions of quality documents from documentation (D), tests (T), qualifications (Q) and calibrations (C) along a generic product generation process. Certificates of Conformity for a product or a product family can also be provided from third party verification and validation of the product design. All these documents are stored in the manufacturer's ERP system or the asset administration shell (AAS) of the respective product. Only documents relevant to the customer get compiled into the digital product passport which is supplied to the customer together with the finished product. Typically, it will be available to the customer via the serialized link of the unique product identifier (UPI) contained on the digital nameplate (DNP) of the respective product. The access to this information is restricted to control the flow of information and protect business secrets.

When the product is in use, recurring qualifications can be mandatory or required by internal provisions or process guideline to secure product quality. **Fig. *8*** shows a use-case typical for recurring calibrations of a sensor to control product or process properties in a production environment. The diagram shows the complexity that a given sensor type can (1) be purchased from alternative suppliers and (2) recalibrated by one service provider at a time, selected from a group of qualified candidates. All documents related to the sensor need to be stored for

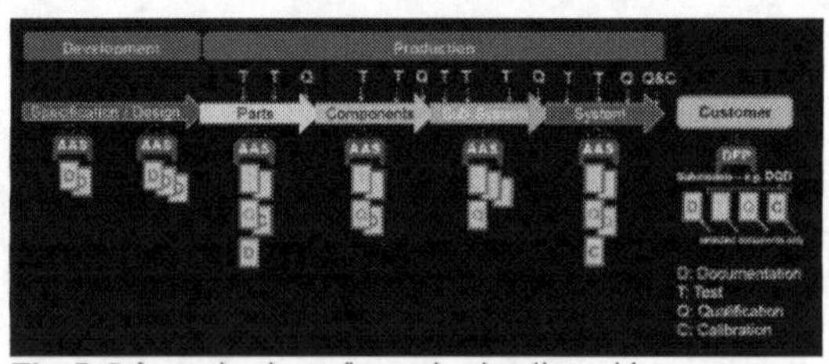

Fig. 7. Schematic view of a production line with a sequence of qualification steps and documentation [7], p. 15 ©Creative Commons Attribution 4.0 license

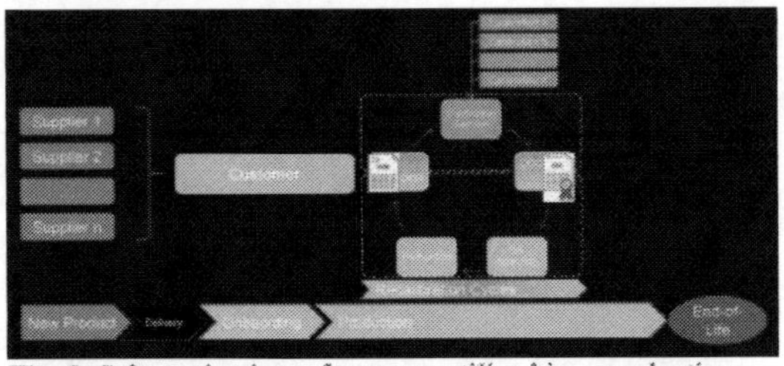

Fig. 8. Schematic view of a sensor utilized in a production line with regular calibrations *[7]* ©Creative Commons Attribution 4.0 license

reference and documentation. The AAS and the DPP are based on a common concept to supply and store the data in a systematic way. The AAS sub-model for Digital Quality Documents (DQD) is the conceptual and practical element to properly supply QI documents into the AAS.

Due to the observation that a variety of quality documents can be derived from a common DX-schema as document semantic system and implementation, it was named Digital Quality Document". This new DQD sub-model is listed in the framework of the Industrial Digital Twin Association (IDTA) [4] and close to its first release. Fig. *9* shows the example of a DCC as it is represented in the AAS-sub-model.

Every quality document like a DCC is integrated into and attributed to the AAS structure of the respective sensor asset. DQDs can also be part of the DPP of that sensor, where the information is listed as a digital quality document sub-model element. Over the lifetime of a specific sensor, a significant number of such quality documents can accumulate in the respective AAS and DPP from recurring qualifications and calibration performed.

Typically, industrial operations are organized in clearly structures processes representing the underlying value stream. The ambition is, to get the same output of processes irrespective of the individual service provider contributing to this process. This aspiration holds true also for QI processes with different service providers involved. For QI documentation, the expectation is to get the respective quality document with the same content and structure, irrespective of the service provider involved. This can only be achieved if there is a qualified and binding regulation about the content and requirements to be analysed and approved by the requested service. A functional requirement specification is needed as input for the service provider. The client has to provide it as a technical sprecification.

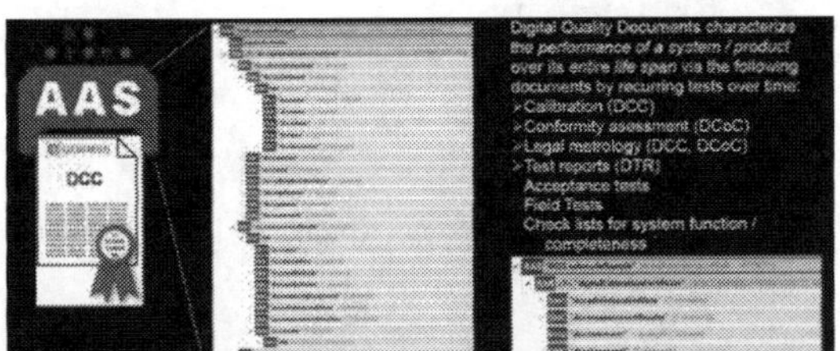

Fig. 9. Digital Quality Document (DQD) sub-model with DCCs as part of the Asset Administration Shell AAS [2], Fig. 10 ©Creative Commons Attribution 4.0 license

To receive a calibration certificate with the expected results on e.g. precision of calibration and setpoints used, a calibration request (DCR) needs to be transferred to the service provider. Fig. *4* shows, that such a request documents (e.g. DCR and DQR) can also be derived from the DX-schema. Fig. *8* gives the example of a DCR on the left side of the feedback loop. Even those request documents can be carried over to the service provider in a DQD dataset of the AAS. Again, benefit is taken from a common structure behind all these documents. The service provider can use the respective request to derive the basic structure of the certificate requested.

To close the feedback loop from a process perspective, the client can use the request specification he issued previously to the service provider. He can double check the final certificate for completeness and correctness of the data contained and thus completion of the qualification task. Full automation at this stage would mean that the invoice from the service provider gets only paid, when this automated check was completed successfully.

5 QI in Dataspaces

Dataspaces are the new concept of digital industry to exchange process relevant information in a structured, controlled and traceable manner. The operator of a dataspace has to provide basic services for general operation, user or partner registration, role management to control access rights to information and documents and so forth. Additionally, the operator has to provide a strong digital trust chain as a basis for all transactions to be executed in the dataspace by all participants. Besides classical customer – supplier transactions, there will be roles of market surveillance, quality service providers from accredited bodies, test- and calibration services, legal metrology and auditors. This list is not exhaustive but shows the complexity of the roles, responsibilities and related access rights and permissions involved. Fig. *10* depicts the functional elements in a dataspace setting. A typical quality process with request and certificate is shown in the horizontal blue box in the middle, the manufacturer – customer – qualification service provider relation is shown in the green box underneath. The outer blue frame represents the administrative and

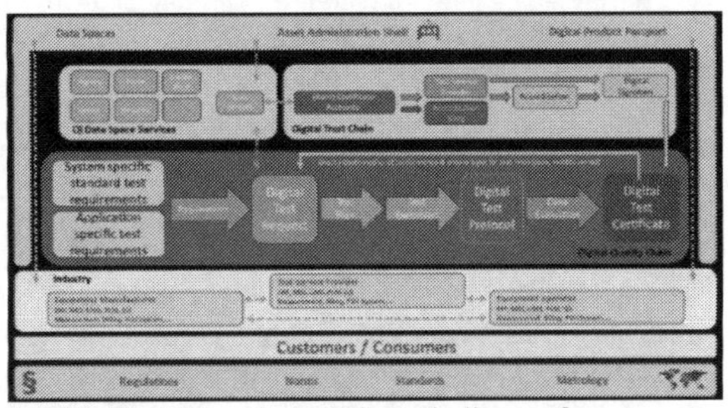

Fig. 10. Workflow oriented schematic diagram for calibrations / tests for a digital QI in a digital environment of dataspaces and AAS, including dataspace services and digital trust chain elements. [2]©Creative Commons Attribution 4.0 license

legislative framework. Dataspace administration and digital trust chain elements are shown in the upper bright boxes.

One strength and benefit of the dataspace concept is, that every participant of a dataspace has only to connect once to this dataspace. This reduces the ever-increasing complexity and maintenance effort to support numerous proprietary interfaces between customers and suppliers or service providers. After registration for the role(s) desired, the dataspace operator will check correctness of data and entitlement for the role(s) requested. Then he will grant the respective access rights and permissions. To interact with all other participants of this dataspace, no further registration nor individual or customized interface needs to be set up and maintained. In that respect, a dataspace simplifies the digital data exchange between its participants significantly.

Another benefit of dataspaces is the feature, that market surveillance or notified bodies can have direct access to the data and documents they need to fulfil their role. Since they might have access to business-critical information, a strict and trusted role and access management is mandatory.

6 Conclusion and Outlook

A seamlessly digitalized quality infrastructure is imperative for an innovative and competitive industry. The growing demand for product specific reporting on product information, resources integrated and consumed during production and lifecycle information on product performance and operational resources is obvious as a global and regional trend. To counteract climate change by informed utilisation of natural resources, enabling circular economy, reducing paperwork for documenting quality are just some demanding challenges for our economy and society. A digital QI bears a huge potential to improve productivity and process yield in industry by making existing information available and machine executable. A fundamental reduction of paper based documentation and related administrative and storage efforts reduces process cost significantly. Improving accessibility and availability of data bears a variety of chances for further process optimization and future business models.

This paper explored the requirements and chances of a digital QI from an industry perspective at some level of detail. The work was based on the outcome of the GEMIMEG-II project which was reflected with respect to the broader requirements of a digital QI and Industry 4.0 demands. Since the whole field of digitalizing industry is developing rapidly, there will be an ongoing process of adopting and enhancing the concepts and implementations discussed here. Nevertheless, it is worthwhile to share such an elaborate project status as it can serve as a common basis for future enhancements.

The author hopes and encourages, that this generic but practical and broad approach of DX based digital documents for a versatile QI will be supported by international organisations in metrology, conformity assessment and standardisation like e.g. the BIPM); the International Electrotechnical Commission (IEC); the International Organization for Standardization (ISO) and the International Organization of Legal Metrology (OIML).

The author is deeply grateful to all members of the GEMIMEG-II project team for numerous valuable and active discussions and the great spirit of collaboration. It was a great honour to work with all of you and to coordinate this ambitious light house project.

The GEMIMEG-II project was funded by the German ministry for economic affairs and climate action based on a decision by the German Bundestag under grant number 01MT20001A.

References

[1] T. Engel, "GEMIMEG-II — How metrology can go digital...," *Meas. Sci. Technol.*, vol. 34, no. 10, p. 104002, Jul. 2023, doi: 10.1088/1361-6501/ace468.

[2] T. Engel and A. Popescu, "GEMIMEG – DIGITALIZATION OF CALIBRATION PROCESSES IN METROLOGY," in Measurement: Sensors. Elsevier, Jan. 2025. doi: https://doi.org/10.1016/j.measen.2024.101474.

[3] "QI-Digital Homepage." [Online]. Available: https://www.qi-digital.de/

[4] "Industrial Digital Twin Association (IDTA): Asset Administration Shell (AAS)." [Online]. Available: https://industrialdigitaltwin.org/en/

[5] "ISO 32000." [Online]. Available: https://www.iso.org/standard/75839.html

[6] "Digital Product Passport." Industrial Digital Twin Association e.V. (IDTA). [Online]. Available: https://dpp40.eu/

[7] T. Engel, "GEMIMEG – DIGITALIZATION OF CALIBRATION PROCESSES IN METROLOGY," XXIV IMEKO World Congress "Think Metrology" August 26 – 29, 2024, Hamburg, Germany, Aug. 2024.

[8] "Digital Nameplate IEC 63365." [Online]. Available: https://webstore.iec.ch/publication/67436

[9] "Meter Convention (authorized text document)." 1875. [Online]. Available: https://www.bipm.org/en/metre-convention

[10] *SI Refernce Point*. [Online]. Available: https://si-digital-framework.org/SI?lang=en

[11] *D-SI Units*. XML. Physikalisch Technische Bundesanstalt. [Online]. Available: https://gitlab1.ptb.de/digitaldynamicmeasurement/dsiUnits

[12] "D-SI XML schema." [Online]. Available: https://doi.org/10.5281/zenodo.4709001

[13] "D-SI GIT repository." [Online]. Available: https://gitlab1.ptb.de/d-ptb/d-si/xsd-d-si

[14] "SI Brochure: The International System of Units (SI)." BIPM - Bureau Internationl des Poids et Mesures. [Online]. Available: https://www.bipm.org/en/publications/si-brochure

[15] *ECMA-404 The JSON Data Interchange Standard*. [Online]. Available: https://www.json.org/json-en.html

[16] *ECMA-404 The JSON data interchange syntax*. [Online]. Available: https://ecma-international.org/publications-and-standards/standards/ecma-404/

[17] S. Hackel, "DX Document Schema," pp. 216–230. [Online]. Available: https://oar.ptb.de/resources/show/10.7795/820.20220411

[18] "Digital Calibration Certificate DCC." [Online]. Available: https://www.ptb.de/dcc/

A digital measurement approach for structural condition assessment of sewers

Luís Lages Martins [1*], *Álvaro* Silva Ribeiro[1], *Maria do Céu* Almeida[2], and *Rita* Salgado Brito[2]

[1]LNEC – National Laboratory for Civil Engineering, Scientific Instrumentation and Information Technologies Centre, Avenida do Brasil 101 1700-066 Lisbon, Portugal
[2] LNEC – National Laboratory for Civil Engineering, Hydraulics and Environment Department, Avenida do Brasil 101 1700-066 Lisbon, Portugal

Abstract. This paper describes the application of photogrammetric digital reconstruction within the context of structural condition assessment of sewers. The acquisition of multiple images of the observation scenario and application of the bundle adjustment technique, supported by computational algorithms dedicated to image parallel computation and clustering, is the base for the approach adopted. An orthographic camera model with uniform scaling was adopted, supported by scale coefficients determined by the relation between digital and actual (SI traceable) dimensions of reference objects visible in the generated model. The paper details experimental and computational methodologies and presents several examples of digital sewer models. Finally, an evaluation of measurement data retrieved from the models is also shown, including identifying uncertainty components related to the input quantities and their propagation by the GUM method to the output quantity, considering the mathematical models related to the adopted camera model.

1 Introduction

The increasing digitalization of objects of interest in different scientific and industrial domains is a notable trend in recent years, motivated by technological progress and the proliferation of optical, electronic, and computational resources. In this context, a significant transition occurred in the digitalization processes, from contact measurement of points in objects using coordinate measuring machines to non-contact measurement approaches based on scanning systems. This transition originated the following advantages: (i) a higher number of measurement points per unit of observation time; (ii) an increased ability in the visualization of large-scale objects with complex geometry; (iii) the non-contact measurement of fragile objects of high heritage historical value.

Infrared or laser scanning systems are currently used for the digitalization of interest objects, obtaining a high number of measurement points in a reduced amount of time, which can support the graphical representation of the digitalized object in the dimensional (spatial coordinates), radiometric (intensity of the received signal) and photometric (colour system components) contexts.

Three-dimensional digital reconstruction, supported in multiple images of the interest object, is an alternative approach to scanning systems owing to their operational complexity, in particular observation scenarios and high economic cost.

The origins of this optical approach can be found in the second half of the XIX century. The photogrammetry field of activity was supported by analogue images that were used in the determination of spatial coordinates of points in natural or built heritage. In the meanwhile, in the last quarter of the XX century, the technological evolution of computational resources enabled the application of previously developed mathematical and statistical models to the field of Computer Vision, this time using digital images.

This paper describes the application of a photogrammetric digital reconstruction approach in the structural condition assessment of sewers in an aggressive and complex observation environment, with operational restrictions on the use of scanning systems. The primary objective of this application is the generation of digital models for SI traceable dimensional measurement of interest elements with known accuracy, namely anomalies found in the visual inspection of sewers.

Structural investigation activities of sewer systems in urban areas are crucial for safeguarding public and occupational health and safety, environmental protection, and promoting a more sustainable society. Visual inspection plays a relevant role in assessing the condition and performance of vast and complex components of underground drainage systems. According to the standard EN 13508-1:2017 [1], the structural investigation aims to determine the integrity of the sewer system components, commonly achieved via visual inspection, supplemented by specialized techniques if needed.

Inspections allow the detection and characterization of anomalies, which can negatively affect the system's

* Corresponding author: lfmartins@lnec.pt

hydraulic, structural, operational and environmental performance. Direct visual inspection of large confined spaces by personnel walking through the sewer is doable when ensuring human safety. Otherwise, robots equipped with CCTV are used. Typical CCTV robots do not make direct measurements, only digital videos and images. During inspections by personnel, dimensional quantities are measured for each identified anomaly if within reach. The harsh environment inside a sewer makes the *in situ* dimensional measurement challenging.

In the following sections, the paper describes the photogrammetric digital reconstruction approach, namely, the applied experimental and computational procedures. Several examples of digital models applied related to large sewers in Lisbon (Portugal) are shown. The evaluation of measurement data resulting from the proposed digitalization approach is discussed.

2 Photogrammetric digital reconstruction

Photogrammetry is a dimensional measurement method of three-dimensional coordinates of points in an object of interest using bi-dimensional images of that object. It starts to be used in the second half of the XIX century in built heritage architectural records and mountain and glacier cartography. The development of computational algorithms, resources, and digital image acquisition devices at the end of the XX century extended its range of application to science and industry. For example, in the Civil Engineering context, it became an alternative solution for geodesic measurement, a time-consuming technique limited in the number of points and with restrictions regarding access and space required for instrumentation.

One of the most common techniques used in photogrammetry is the bundle adjustment, where stereoscopic images of the same object are not required, compared with other available techniques. It considers the perspective propagation of a beam of light from a certain point in the object, passing through a projection centre and up to the corresponding point in each image where the object point is visible.

Mathematically, the bundle adjustment aims to determine the three-dimensional coordinates of points in the object, intrinsic (focal distance, projection centre coordinates, and distortion coefficients) and extrinsic (position and orientation) parameters of the cameras used for image acquisition. This is achieved by the correspondence between points in the object and in the images, minimizing the re-projection error. The least squares method is used to solve the high number of non-linear collinearity equations, supported in optimization herein using the Levenberg-Marquardt algorithm. Therefore, the photogrammetric digital reconstruction based on the bundle adjustment is a high-dimension computational calculation process.

The recent evolution of parallel computing, supported by the dissemination of central and graphic processing units with multiple cores, allowed for overcoming memory and bandwidth restrictions of photogrammetric digital reconstruction calculation procedures, which were known to be extremely time-consuming and numerically unstable. In this context, it is important to point out the algorithms and applications developed by [2], characterized by a high-efficiency level and reduced processing time.

3 Experimental procedure

The experimental procedure includes the acquisition of multiple images in the observed sewer scenario, considering (i) the photographic scanning of the sewer interest region, assuring a high overlap rate in consecutive images and the visualization of reference objects (targets, for example), which can support the calculation of the scale coefficient of the digital model; (ii) the absence of movement in the interest object; (iii) the interest region must include heterogeneous elements and areas.

The proposed approach assumes a parallel geometrical relation between the image plane and the plane related to the recorded sewer anomaly or interest region, considering a uniform-scale orthographic model [3]. This defines a relation between an observed dimension L (expressed in millimetres, for instance) and the corresponding dimension in the digital model, p (expressed in a digital value), i.e.

$$L = K \cdot p, \quad (1)$$

where K is designated by scale coefficient (usually expressed in millimetres by digital value)

Dimensional measurements can be performed in the sewer digital model using a suitable computational application capable of providing digital values of points of interest and the parameterization of the scale coefficient, which is determined by

$$K = L_{ref} / p_{ref}, \quad (2)$$

where L_{ref} and p_{ref} the real (metric) and the digital (virtual) dimensions, respectively, of a visible reference object in the digital model in the same plane of the recorded sewer anomaly or interest region. In this context, reference objects in a sewer can be added targets and measurement instruments (crack width or graduated scales, metric tapes), the dimensions of the sewer's cross-section or construction elements (such as bricks, stones, aggregates, among others). The corresponding dimensional reference values must be determined using SI traceable calibrated measurement instruments.

In this work, reference targets (see Fig.1) were added to the observed scenarios for digital model generation. These were previously calibrated in a metrology laboratory, in a controlled environment, using an SI traceable optical measurement machine with known measurement accuracy, close to 10 µm. Since the targets were included in the sewer digital model, the scale coefficient was calculated based on the Euclidian distance between the same points, with known actual (metric) and digital spatial coordinates.

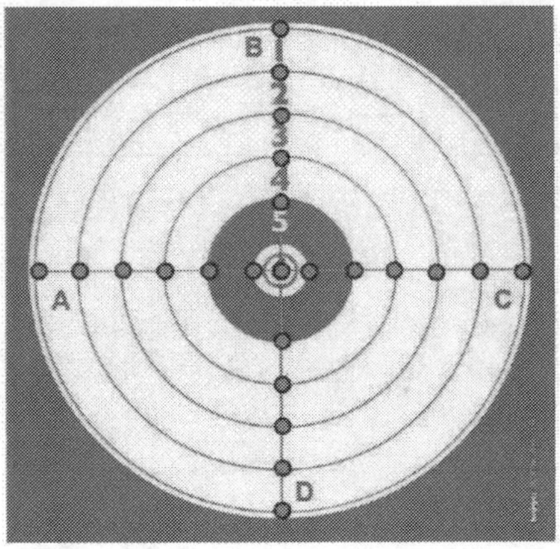

Fig. 1. Measured reference points in the applied target.

4 Computational procedure

The Visual SFM – A Visual Structure from Motion System application (version 0.5.26) was used in this study. It contains validated parallel processing algorithms proposed by [2]. In addition, the optional CMVS – Clustering Views for Multi-view Stereo algorithm [4] was also applied for the image decomposition in a set of clusters with a dimension suitable for parallel processing and independent for each cluster. This led to a reduced computation time without a significant loss of information when merging the resulting reconstructions.

In the Visual SFM application, the input data corresponds to the photos taken during the sewer observation from multiple views (camera positions and orientations). After loading the photos, pair-wise matching is carried out to calculate the missing match. The output data is a sparse cloud of points (with a low detail level) related only to the bundle adjustment parallel processing, and a dense cloud of points (with a high detail level) that results from the execution of the CMVS algorithm.

The obtained point clouds were loaded in the MeshLab application (version 2022.02) [5], aiming at the generation of a mesh of three-dimensional points and its edition, namely, removal of non-interest points and faces, mesh simplification, and surface and texture generation in the digital model. This application contains a tool dedicated to dimensional measurement, supported in the previously described orthographic model with uniform scaling, allowing the definition of the scale coefficient related to the observation scenario. The obtained digital model can be visualized with different magnifications and views suitable for the required measurement.

5 Examples

This section shows some examples of sewer digital models obtained using the previously described digital measurement approach.

The first example – shown in Figures 2 to 4 – is in a stone masonry sewer, built in the XVIII century, in Lisbon's historical downtown district (underground to Rua da Prata), with an inverted U-type cross-section with nominal dimensions of 2,15 m by 2,85 m.

Fig. 2. Stone masonry sewer underground Rua da Prata.

Fig. 3. Image of the digitalized region in the sewer.

Fig. 4. Sewer's digital model, showing the measurement of its cross-section dimensions.

In this case, the region digitalized through photogrammetric digital reconstruction corresponds to a connection to the main sewer. Due to the geometrical irregularity of the masonry stone elements, SI traceable reference targets were used, aiming at enhancing the scale coefficient measurement accuracy. In total, 32 overlapped photos were acquired (with a Nikon / D750 camera), with variable observation distances and camera orientations.

The second example is in a segment of the Alcântara large sewer (concrete arch type, with cross-section dimensions of 6,22 mm × 4 m) in Campolide, Lisbon (see Figure 5).

Fig. 5. Alcântara large sewer collector in the underground region of Campolide.

In this case, the selected observation for digitalization was a joint between sewer segments with visible signs of erosion. A reference target (shown in Figure 6) was added to the observed region, and a total of 35 overlapped photos were acquired and used as input data for the previously mentioned computational procedure.

Fig. 6. Image of the digitalized region in the sewer.

Figure 7 presents the obtained digital model, which can be used in the dimensional characterization of the sewer joint erosion. In this case, the approach can be applied for the consecutive generation of digital models in long-term monitoring of the observed anomaly based on SI traceable dimensional measurements.

An additional model – shown in Figure 8 – was also generated, aiming at the digitalization and measurement of the sewer's cross-section, based on the acquisition of 55 images with different observation distances and camera orientations.

Fig. 7. Digital model of a joint between sewer segments.

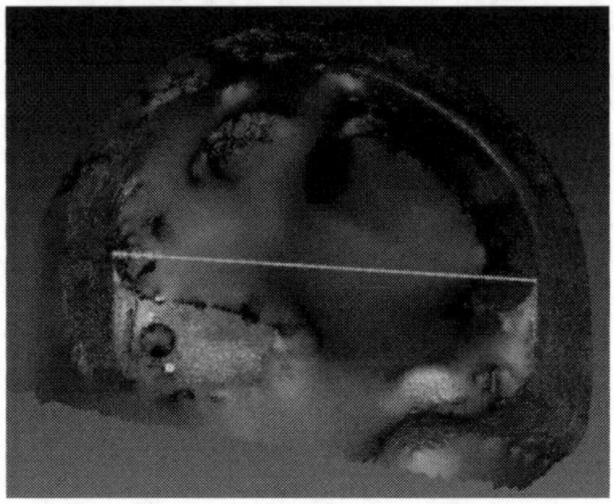

Fig. 8. Digital model of the sewer's cross-section.

The digital model presented in Figure 8 allowed the quantification of the section's width, although some regions were not digitally reconstructed due to the reduced illumination in the upstream region, and sewer flow (dynamic region of the observation scenario, that changes between multiple acquired images).

6 Evaluation of measurement data

In the proposed measurement approach, three input quantities are identified: the digital value and the reference dimension related to the calculation of the scale coefficient (intermediate quantity), and the digital value associated with the required dimensional measurement (output quantity).

The standard measurement uncertainty of the digital value gathers the contributions of two uncertainty components: the digital resolution and the operator's repeatability and reproducibility. The measurement tool embedded in MeshLab [5] provides a 0.1 digital resolution. Therefore, one can use a uniform probability distribution [6] with a semi-amplitude of 0.05 to calculate this uncertainty component, therefore equal to $0.05 / \sqrt{3} = 0,029$.

The operator's repeatability can be quantified by a dedicated experimental study where a repeatability condition is assured (same procedure, operator, measurement approach, operating conditions and location in the model) when performing replicate digital measurements on the same object. In the case of reproducibility, the measurement condition includes the effect of different locations in the model and operators (responsible for the spatial point selection in the model) in the obtained dispersion of digital values related to an object.

The standard measurement uncertainty of the reference dimension can have wide variability, depending on the use of calibrated targets and instruments or, as an alternative, cross-section and construction elements' dimensions. In the first option mentioned, a higher accuracy is expected since measurements are performed in a controlled environment (laboratory) and with transfer measurement standards. The second option, based on *in situ* measurements, is characterized by a lower accuracy due to the environmental factors inside the sewer and the spatial variability of the cross-section or construction element dimensions.

The application of the Law of Propagation of Uncertainty (LPU) [6] to expression (1) allows calculating the standard measurement uncertainty of the dimensional measurement performed in the digital models, $u(L)$, by

$$u(L) = \sqrt{[p^2 \cdot u^2(K) + K^2 \cdot u^2(p)]}, \quad (3)$$

where the measurement uncertainty of the scale coefficient, $u(K)$, is also obtained from the LPU, considering the expression (2), i.e.,

$$u(K) = \sqrt{[(1/p_{ref})^2 \cdot u^2(L_{ref}) + (-L_{ref}/p^2_{ref})^2 \cdot u^2(p_{ref})]}. \quad (4)$$

Expression (3) shows that not only the magnitude of the standard uncertainties of the input quantities (scale coefficient and of the digital value) is contributing to the dimensional uncertainty, as expected, but also their measurement estimates. Therefore, it is important to have a low magnitude scale coefficient, i.e., a high spatial resolution digital model, to achieve a lower dimensional uncertainty. According to expression (4), this can be reached with low standard uncertainties of the actual (metric) and digital reference values of a target (for example) and a high spatial resolution digital model (reduced estimates of actual and digital reference values).

From an experimental point of view, the spatial resolution of the digital model is related to the acquired photos. High spatial resolution digital images can be achieved by reducing the observation distance between the camera and the object, and by using an image sensor composed of pixels with lower size.

7 Conclusions

This paper described a digital measurement approach in the context of sewer visual inspection for structural condition assessment. This approach was applied and tested in large sewers in Lisbon, showing its suitability for the generation of digital models, from which measurements can be performed with SI traceability in the dimensional domain.

It was possible to confirm that the proposed approach has lower operational complexity when compared with the use of scanning systems. In addition, from an economic perspective, its application is also advantageous since it is based on the use of a single digital camera and open-source software (Visual SFM and MeshLab).

The experimental and computational procedures described in this paper are, therefore, available for use in the context of sewer visual inspections, being particularly useful for long-term structural monitoring of dimensional features and anomalies. Confidence in the performed dimensional measurements is assured by SI traceability, namely, when using reference targets calibrated before being added to the observation scenario.

The performed evaluation of measurement data, based on the GUM method, identified the main uncertainty components of the input quantities. It revealed the importance of studying the operator's repeatability and reproducibility since the approach is supported by the manual selection of points in the digital model, both in the scale coefficient intermediated stage and in the final dimensional measurement stage. The application of the LPU also showed the importance of the spatial resolution of the digital model for measurement accuracy. Acquisition of images with shorter observation distances and using image sensors with lower size pixels is recommended, whenever possible.

The authors acknowledge the Lisbon municipality (Sanitation department / Maintenance and Conservation division) for funding and supporting the research project Structured Evaluation of Large Sewers in the city of Lisbon – R8 Contributions for measurement quality enhancement.

References

1. EN 13508-1 – Investigation and assessment of drain and sewer systems outside building. Part 1: General requirement (European Committee for Standardization, 2012)
2. C. Wu, S. Agarwal, B. Curless, S. Seitz, Multicore bundle adjustment, in Proceedings of the Computer Vision and Pattern Recognition Conference, Colorado Springs, Colorado, USA, June 20-25 (2011)
3. R. Szeliski, Computer Vision. Algorithms and Applications (Springer, New York, 2011)
4. Y. Furukawa, B. Curless, S. Seitz, R. Szeliski, Towards Internet-scale multi-view stereo, in Proceedings of the IEEE Computer Society Conference on Computer Vision and Pattern Recognition, San Francisco, California, USA, June 13-18 (2010)
5. P. Cignoni, M. Corsini, G. Ranzuglia, MeshLab: an Open-Source 3D Mesh Processing System, in ERCIM News (2008)
6. Evaluation of measurement data – Guide to the expression of uncertainty in measurement (GUM), (Joint Committee for Guides in Metrology, 2008)

EPJ Web of Conferences **323**, 0100(21015) https://doi.org/(0.(05(/epjconf/10153130100(
22nd nIt enr Iai nr dMt Iei ai gylCi nget ss

Software in Metrology for the Digital Age: Addressing Compliance Challenges with MID, NAWID, and MDR

Martin Koval [1*], *Jiří* Tesař[1], *Martin* Staněk[2], and *Jaroslav* Foltýnek[3]

[1]CMI-Czech Metrology Institute, Okružní 31, 63800 Brno, Czech Republic
[2]FBMI nám. Sítná 3105, 272 01 Kladno 2, Czech Republic
[3]Slovak University of Technology in Bratislava, Vazovova 5, 81243 Slovak Republic

Abstract. In the digital era, software is integral to devices regulated by European directives like MID, NAWID, and MDR, ensuring accuracy, reliability, and safety. While metrology has been crucial, software now plays an equally significant role, enabling data processing, automation, and new functionalities. Emerging technologies like AI, IoT, or cloud computing introduce compliance challenges. This article analyzes and compares software requirements in MID, NAWID, and MDR, focusing on software lifecycle, regulatory gaps, and risk assessment.

1 Introduction

In the digital age, software has become an integral part of measuring devices. Directives such as the Measuring Instruments Directive (MID) 2014/32/EU [1], the Non-Automatic Weighing Instruments Directive (NAWID) 2014/31/EU [2] and the Medical Devices Regulation (MDR) 2017/745/EU [3] sets out requirements for placing a product on the market. The development of technologies such as artificial intelligence (AI), the Internet of Things (IoT), or cloud computing (CC) brings new opportunities but also challenges in the adjustment of software requirements. This evolution has an impact on data processing and storage, cybersecurity, and the overall integrity of measurement processes. The aim of this article is to analyse and compare the software requirements set out in the MID, NAWID and MDR, identify key differences and common features. Special attention will be paid to the software life cycle, risk management methods, and the possibilities of adapting regulations to modern technological trends.

2 The impact of software on measurement systems

The implementation of software in measuring systems can retrospectively be considered an extreme advance in the field of measurement when we realize that most of the measuring systems around us are equipped with software. This has brought about a fundamental step forward in data processing, storage and analysis. It gives measurement systems flexibility, the possibility of automated evaluation and integration with remote IT systems. Before software solutions, the accuracy, reliability and safety of measurement systems were ensured primarily by high-quality material processing and mechanical modifications. However, with the advent of digitalization, software solutions have been implemented in these systems, which have fundamentally expanded their functionality and efficiency. Software now enables automated correction of measurement processes and analyzes historical data for predictive purposes. Its main benefits include flexibility, higher accuracy and reliability thanks to the elimination of measurement deviations and automation that minimizes the need for manual manipulation. On the other hand, software in measurement systems also brings new challenges, such as cybersecurity, quality assurance and software trustworthiness.

3 Relationship between directives, standards and guides

In the regulatory environment of the European Union (EU), there is a hierarchy of legislative and technical documents that affect the placing of products on the market. European directives are legally binding documents that set out essential requirements for the safety, functionality and reliability of products. Compliance with the requirements of a given directive is essential for placing a product on the market within the EU. Manufacturers can demonstrate these requirements in various ways, one of the simplest being the use of standards. Standards can be divided into harmonised and non-harmonised. Harmonised standards are officially published in the Official Journal of the European Union (OJEU) [4] for each directive and compliance with them means that they meet certain requirements of the directive with a high degree of probability. This process is explained in detail by Regulation (EU) No 1025/2012 [5], which lays down

* Corresponding author: martin.koval@cmi.gov.cz

https://doi.org/(0.(05(/epjconf/10153130100(

the rules for the development and recognition of harmonized standards within the EU. Non-harmonized standards can be used to demonstrate compliance with the directive, but in that case it must be clearly documented how the specific standard reflects the requirements of the directive. It is also necessary to mention guidance documents, which can essentially also be used similarly to non-harmonized standards. Each of the directives (MID, NAWID, MDR) has harmonized standards however there is no harmonized standard specifically addressing software (status early 2025). NAWID has a harmonized standard EN 45501:2015[6], which contains some software requirements. MID has no harmonized standards for software in legal metrology. MDR also has no harmonized standards, but there are standards specifically aimed at software in medical devices, such as IEC 62304 [7], IEC 82304 [8] and IEC 81001-5-1 [9]. For each directive, there are guideline documents that provide detailed explanations on how to implement and understand the software requirements. Although the guides are not legally binding, they are an important source of recommendations.

Table 1. Overview of software in MID, NAWID, and MDR.

	MID	NAWID	MDR
Year of issue	2015	2014	2020
Number of requirements	3	0	17+
The word "software"	12	0	48
Harmonized standards	0	1	0
Non-harmonized standards	0	0	25+
Guides	7+	1	100+

4 Software requirements analysis

Directives set out the essential requirements that products must meet, but do not usually contain detailed technical specifications. It is therefore appropriate to link these requirements to relevant standards and guidance documents in a reasonable way. In the case of MID, it is possible to base it on WELMEC Guide 7.2 Software Guide [10]. Requirements are categorized based on common functions of software for measuring instruments, such as user and communication interface, software integrity, parameter protection, software protection and security, and data display trustworthiness. Furthermore, there are optional additional requirements such as data transfer, long-term data storage, software separation, software updates, or special requirements for operating systems in the case of more complex software. The following are requirements that are specific to measuring instruments under MID, such as data erasure prevention, fault recovery, back up, or requirements related to power failure. The checking of the fulfillment of these requirements is primarily based on technical documentation and performance of functional tests on the device that contains the software. The tests should be performed by a person who is not part of the software design. A total of 48 requirements are identified, with each requirement explained in detail. It explains what should be included in the submitted technical documentation, as well as instructions for the tester on what to check in the documentation and how to proceed with functional tests. Another interesting guidance document is OIML D31[11]. The number of requirements according to the final checklist is 31. In terms of the interpretation of the requirements, both documents are quite similar, with the difference that OIML D31 does not have requirements for specific measuring instruments. After reading both documents, the idea of fulfilling the requirements is clearer.

In the case of NAWID we can base ourselves on WELMEC Guide 7.5 Software in NAWIs [12]. The aim of this Guide is to bridge the requirements in EN 45501:2015 with WELMEC Guide 7.2, given that the standard has 20 requirements.

In the case of MDR, the software requirements are more specific than in MID. It is directly linked to risk, life cycle and also takes into account mobile computing platforms. An important standard is IEC 62304 Medical device software — Software life cycle processes. The standard briefly outlines four general requirements such as quality system, risk management, security, and legacy software. However, it primarily focuses on software design, leaving the identification of specific requirements to manufacturers within individual chapters of the standard. The IEC 82304 Health software standard Part 1: General requirements for product safety directly refers to the IEC 62304 standard but also includes more specific requirements such as interoperability and language support. Norme IEC 81001-5-1 Health software and health IT systems safety, effectiveness and security. As the name suggests, it is focused directly on security. The specific wording of the requirements is also left to the manufacturer, but there are specified areas that need to be addressed, such as testing, maintenance, or response to incidents reported from the real field. There are a number of guidance documents for MDR that are freely available, and sources such as MDCG [13], IMDR [14] or FDA[15] are certainly worth highlighting, where they are available for free.

Table 2. Overview of standards and guides related to MID, NAWID and MDR.

MID	
Standards	-
Guides	WELMEC Guide 7.2, OIML D31
NAWID	
Standards (harm.)	EN 45501:2015
Guides	
MDR	
Standards	IEC 62304, IEC 82304, IEC 81001-5-1
Guides	MDCG, IMDRF, FDA

5 Software lifecycle

Software lifecycle refers to every stage of software development, release and support. But only MDR works with software lifecycle and addresses all its stages, for MID and NAWID it is foreign term. This is shame because these two could easily benefit from this approach if it would be addressed properly.

It is important to realize what stages are in software lifecycle to correctly handle requirements of each stage. When it comes to medical device software, the most comprehensive and widely recognized standard for managing the software lifecycle is IEC 62304. This standard provides a structured framework for software development and maintenance, ensuring that all necessary safety and risk management processes are integrated throughout the software lifecycle.

Table 3. Software life cycle phases

Phase	Description
Planning	Defining project scope, objectives, regulatory requirements, and resources.
Development	Designing, implementing, testing, and integrating software components to meet defined requirements.
Maintenance	Managing software updates, bug fixes, performance improvements, and compliance adjustments.
Risk management	Identifying, analysing, and mitigating software-related risks.
Problem resolution	Detecting, documenting, and resolving software issues.
Decommissioning	Ensuring that the software is safely retired, data is properly handled.

6 Risk assessment

Risk assessment is mentioned in all three directives, but only MDR explicitly classifies medical devices into classes I, IIa, IIb, and III, where each classification reflects risk. Furthermore, MDR establishes additional requirements where risk is directly linked to software, ensuring that safety considerations are integrated throughout the software lifecycle. For MDR, the harmonized standard ISO 14971:2019 Medical devices — Application of risk management to medical devices [16] but the standard does not explicitly address software. However, a previous version of ISO 14971 is cross-referenced with IEC 62304. The idea is that manufacturers propose their own risk assessment, considering all relevant aspects, evaluating severity and probability, and proposing mitigation measures to reduce risks to an acceptable level.

Table 4. Example of a risk assessment for a medical device. (A-acceptable risk, N-unacceptable risk, Probability:1-Improbable, 5-Frequent, Severity:1-Negligible, 5-Criticial).

	Severity				
Probability	**1**	**2**	**3**	**4**	**5**
1	*A*	*A*	*A*	*A*	*N*
2	*A*	*A*	*A*	*N*	*N*
3	*A*	*A*	*N*	*N*	*N*
4	*A*	*A*	*N*	*N*	*N*

In contrast, for MID and NAWID, risk assessment follows guidance from WELMEC Guide 7.2, which categorizes risk into classes A–F, each with specific criteria determining when a particular risk class should be considered, based on level software protection, examination, and conformity.

Table 5. Definition of risk classes according to WELMEC Guide 7.2[10].

Risk Class	Software protection	Software Examination	Software Conformity
A	*LOW*	*LOW*	*LOW*
B	*MIDDLE*	*MIDDLE*	*LOW*
C	*MIDDLE*	*MIDDLE*	*MIDDLE*
D	*HIGH*	*MIDDLE*	*MIDDLE*
E	*HIGH*	*HIGH*	*MIDDLE*
F	*HIGH*	*HIGH*	*HIGH*

Another approach for MID/NAWID is outlined in WELMEC Guide 7.6, which introduces a quantitative risk assessment methodology. This methodology is based on a structured evaluation of assets, attack vectors, and attacker motivation, drawing upon principles from the ISO/IEC 27005:2011[17] standard, which is widely used for information security risk management.

7 Discussion

The analysis of directives from a software perspective has shown that not every directive has clearly defined software requirements. The most comprehensive approach is found in MDR, which is likely due to it being the most recent directive. Although there are ways to address software requirements in each directive, the approaches vary significantly. One key strength of MDR is that it leaves the definition of specific software requirements to manufacturers. This makes sense, as software is best understood by the manufacturer itself, and defining broad requirement categories rather than rigid specifications allows for greater flexibility. When it comes to risk assessment, the situation remains diverse. Since all three directives can apply to measurement systems, there could be a methodology that is applicable independently of the specific directive.

One major gap in MID and NAWID is missing requirements for the software lifecycle. Given the increasing reliance on software across all industries, this omission can be seen as a missing piece in these directives. MDR, on the other hand, fully incorporates the concept of a software lifecycle, providing a structured approach to software development, validation, and maintenance. Addressing this gap in MID and NAWID would be a significant improvement,

https://doi.org/(0.(05(/epjconf/10153130100(

helping manufacturers manage software updates, security patches, and long-term compliance more effectively. Looking ahead, one of the biggest challenges remains the creation of a harmonized standard for software in legal metrology. While MDR has at least software-related standards like IEC 62304. There is currently no harmonized standard specifically addressing software within MID and NAWID. Establishing such a standard would bring comprehensibility and consistency to software conformity in legal metrology. It is also essential to consider how directives are set to adopt the new technologies. As technology continuously evolves, applications such as Virtual Reality, AI tools, Cloud Computing, Arbitrary Devices, and IoT present new challenges. However, not all directives can integrate technologies into existing products.

Table 6. Adoption of new technologies from the perspective of directives. (* AI tools that continuously learn and adapt in real-time based on new data and interactions)

	MID	NAWID	MDR
Virtual Reality	+	+	+
AI tools*	-	-	-
Cloud Computing	-	-	+
Arbitrary device	-	+	+
IoT	+	+	+

8 Conclusion

The selection of MID, NAWID, and MDR for this analysis was intentional, as measurement systems play a crucial role in each of these directives. However, when a measurement system integrates software, the processes for market entry differ significantly across these directives. While MDR provides a more robust and structured framework, MID and NAWID lag behind in defining clear software-related requirements. One of the critical challenges across all three directives is the lack of harmonized standards for software. Despite this, numerous guidelines and non-harmonized standards exist that manufacturers can utilize. However, despite the availability of numerous approaches, their inconsistency leads to unnecessary complexity. Given that measurement systems are relatively stable, the lack of a unified framework results in regulatory fragmentation, making compliance more challenging than necessary.

It is important to recognize that measurement processes remain relatively stable, meaning that technological advancements, rather than fundamental measurement principles, will drive product attractiveness in the future. The most effective way to integrate new technologies into regulated measurement systems is to incorporate a structured software lifecycle and standardized risk management into directives where they are currently missing. Establishing such a more unified approach would enhance regulatory clarity, support technological innovation, and ensure consistent safety and compliance across all three directives.

The Acknowledgements
This work was partly funded by resources granted to the Czech Metrology Institute by the Ministry of Industry and Trade within the frame of internal research task IF2403601101 and UTR25E601102.

References

1. MID: European Parliament and Council, Directive 2014/32/EU on Measuring Instruments (MID), Official Journal of the European Union
2. NAWID: European Parliament and Council, Directive 2014/31/EU on Non-Automatic Weighing Instruments (NAWID), Official Journal of the European Union
3. MDR: European Parliament and Council, Regulation (EU) 2017/745 on Medical Devices (MDR), Official Journal of the European Union
4. Official Journal of the European Union (OJEU), available at: https://eur-lex.europa.eu/.
5. European Parliament & Council. (2012). Regulation (EU) No 1025/2012 on European Standardization. Official Journal of the European Union
6. CEN, EN 45501:2015 - Metrological aspects of non-automatic weighing instruments
7. IEC, IEC 62304:2006 + A1:2015- Medical device software – Software life cycle processes
8. IEC, IEC 82304-1:2016 Health software – Part 1 General requirements for product safety
9. IEC, IEC 81001-5-1:2021Health software and health IT systems safety, effectiveness and securityPart 5-1: Security — Activities in the product life cycle
10. WELMEC, WELMEC Guide 7.2 - Software Guide, 2023. https://www.welmec.org.
11. OIML, OIML D31 (2023) - General requirements for software-controlled measuring instruments, International Organization of Legal Metrology, https://www.oiml.org.
12. WELMEC, WELMEC Guide 7.5 - Software in NAWIs, 2020. https://www.welmec.org
13. MDCG, Medical Device Coordination Group Guidance Documents, https://ec.europa.eu/health/md_sector/new_regulations/guidance_en.
14. IMDRF, International Medical Device Regulators Forum Guidance Documents, http://www.imdrf.org.
15. FDAFDA, U.S. Food & Drug Administration - Medical Device Regulations, https://www.fda.gov.
16. ISO, ISO 14971:2019 - Medical devices — Application of risk management to medical devices
17. ISO/IEC, ISO/IEC 27005:2011 - Information security risk management

t pp s/dl o.gprj d(0g 0) (de: 3confd505) 1510100(

Quality infrastructure for sustainable hydrogen solutions in Namibia

Helga Hansen[1*], *Simasiku* Matali[2], *Moritz* Ackermann[1], *Fabian* Plag[1], *Olav* Werhahn[1], *Arne* Krietsch[1], *Arnas* Lucassen[1] and *Michael* Beyer[1]

[1]Physikalisch-Technische Bundesanstalt (PTB), 38116 Braunschweig, Germany
[2]Namibian Standards Institution (NSI), Department of Metrology, Windhoek, Namibia

Abstract. To ensure a sustainable and economically sound hydrogen supply, the ramp-up of hydrogen production in regions with large incident solar radiation is critically needed. Plans of the Republic of Namibia to set up a new infrastructure from scratch aiming at the export of ammonia as hydrogen carrier co-address questions with respect to the associated quality infrastructure (QI). Here, a regulatory framework is envisaged to define safety requirements and quality objectives for hydrogen generation, operating conditions of production facilities, and subsequent transportation. Standardization should secure access to the current level of technology and cover dynamic technological developments at the national and international level. New capacities will be required for services in metrology and accreditation, testing, certification, inspection and for monitoring the environmental impact. We present an overview of the essential components of a QI cooperation aimed at sustainable hydrogen production and export with project partner countries Namibia and Germany providing a case study. This article tackles technical requirements in the context of QI and showcases the cooperation between Namibia and Germany demonstrating how metrology supports both countries achieving their technical and economic goals.

1 Introduction

As part of the global transition to sustainable energy consumption, hydrogen will play a key role. Namibia is a country with high potential for renewable energy production. Currently, Namibia lacks the regulatory framework and quality infrastructure (QI), that shall go alongside the production of hydrogen and its derivatives. QI is also needed to ensure mutual accounting fairness. To address this gap, German and Namibian authorities are working together in a bilateral institutional partnership – a new instrument to share best practices of administration and to help establish efficient institutions.

1.1 Green Hydrogen Development

To be in line with the Paris Agreement and to "limit the temperature increase to 1.5°C above pre-industrial levels", the world needs to decarbonize its energy consumption. One promising field is the sustainable generation and use of hydrogen and its derivatives, such as ammonia and methanol. The ramp-up of this new technology opens up chances for industrialisation in countries with high solar irradiation and constant wind speeds like Namibia. Hydrogen has to be handled carefully, due to its explosive nature, molecular size, and related safety measures.

1.1.1 Namibian Hydrogen Strategy

Located on the western coast, in the south of the African continent, the Republic of Namibia offers ideal conditions for the use of renewable energy: About 300 sunny days and over 3,000 sun hours per year lead to solar irradiation values of 2,200 to 2,400 kWh/m². The southern coastline also offers constant wind speeds, which might yield around 2,800 MWh per installed MW of wind power. With *its Green Hydrogen and Derivatives Strategy*, the Namibian government sets the ambitious goal of producing "an estimated 140 mtpa of hydrogen equivalent in 2030 to 660 mtpa in 2050". This is estimated to be 5 to 8 percent of the worldwide green hydrogen production.[1]

Namibia's ambitions in establishing a green hydrogen industry were first laid out by Dr. Hage Geingob, the late President of Namibia, and his advisor James Mnyupe in 2019. Since then, the hydrogen strategy has become a part of the second *Harambe Prosperity Plan* and aims "to make a major contribution to solving the global climate crisis while also building broad-based prosperity for our citizens". It focuses on the production of four hydrogen-derivative products for export: ammonia, methanol, e-kerosene, and hot briquetted iron. In 2023, the Namibia Green Hydrogen Programme, led by James Mnyupe, was established by the Namibian government to implement the strategy.

Central to the Namibian Green Hydrogen Strategy is the question of sustainability, which shift the primary goal of merely energy production to implementing

* Corresponding author: helga.hansen@ptb.de

management controls that respond to climate change, government regulations, and customer demand for cleaner energy solutions. Production of green hydrogen in Namibia will therefore require a comprehensive and effective legal and regulatory framework that will help to manage sustainable production. This horizon therefore compels organizations to explore ways through which they can demonstrate environmental, social, and economic sustainability of their operations. This evolution highlights the growing importance for expanding its QI in response to the unique needs of this emerging industry

1.1.2 Hydrogen Strategies in Germany

In order to decarbonise its energy-intensive industry and the transport sector, the EU has set itself the goal of covering around 10 % of its energy needs by renewable hydrogen until 2050.[2] The *German Hydrogen Strategy* assumes an annual national need of up to 130 TWh of hydrogen by 2030, including hydrogen derivatives. With local electrolyser capacities aimed at 10 GW, the missing difference will have to be imported.[3]

1.2 Hyphen Pilot Project in Namibia

In 2021, the Namibian government announced Hyphen Hydrogen Energy as the successful bidder to develop its most ambitious green hydrogen and ammonia plant. The project proposal includes a combined hydrogen and power plant, water and hydrogen pipelines, electricity transmission and further processes at an industrial port site in the town Lüderitz on the south coast. The port will include facilities for water desalination, air separation and ammonia synthesis. The wind turbines, solar panels, as well as batteries and electrolysers will be installed in the nearby Tsau ǁKhaeb National Park in the Namib desert. Through pipelines, desalinated water will be supplied for electrolysis, and the green hydrogen routed back to the port. The targets are 7 GW renewable energy and 3 GW of electrolysis in 2030, and two million tonnes of green ammonia produced. Excess energy and potable water will go into the Namibian infrastructure.[4]

2 Institutional Partnership

To establish a safe and reliable green hydrogen infrastructure, as well as ensure accounting fairness, the concurrent establishment of quality infrastructure services and a regulatory framework for explosion protection is needed. To support the Namibian Ministries and Authorities in these tasks, an institutional partnership was agreed upon in 2023. Bilateral institutional partnerships are a tool of the German Federal Ministry for Economic Affairs and Climate Action (BMWK) to deliver advice in the setup of local authorities and support in adapting laws, guidelines and procedures as well as their implementation. To achieve this, training and further education of employees of partner institutions can also be provided.[5]

2.1 Partner institutions

On the Namibian side, two ministries are involved in the partnership: the Ministry for Industrialisation and Trade (MIT) and the Ministry of Mines and Energy (MME). Further institutions include the Namibian Standards Institution (NSI), an MIT agency, and the Energy Control Board (ECB), an MME agency. The NSI encompasses the Namibian National Metrology Institute as well as departments for Standards Development & Coordination, Testing & Inspection and Certification. The ECB is responsible for regulating the Namibian electricity supply industry with regard to efficiency and safety. Another partner is the University of Namibia (UNAM) with its Green Hydrogen Research Institute. The Namibian Green Hydrogen Programme is also involved in the partnership.

On the German side, the partnership is led by the German Federal Ministry for Economic Affairs and Climate Action (BMWK), which is also funding the partnership. Two of its subordinated agencies are taking part: The Federal Institute for Materials Research and Testing (BAM) and German National Metrology Institute (PTB), both of which are involved in hydrogen research and standardization. The fourth partner is the German Institute for Standardization (DIN), the national standards body in Germany. DIN has worked on the recently released German *Standardization Roadmap for Hydrogen Technologies* and is currently taking part in projects aimed at closing gaps in hydrogen standardization.[6]

2.2 Goals of this partnership

The aim of this institutional partnership is the development of quality infrastructure for the green hydrogen economy in Namibia. This includes the development of a regulatory framework to guarantee safety and quality during the production, distribution, transport, storage and utilisation of hydrogen, as well as its derivatives. Due to the explosiveness of hydrogen, special emphasis must be placed on proper explosion protection. Currently, no such regulation exists.

The second component concerns PTB and NSI. It includes an evaluation, which structural services should be provided by the metrology department of the NSI. Based on this, recommendations are developed for capacity building regarding physical equipment, as well as personnel training.

A further aspect of the Institutional Partnership is the advancement of national standardization efforts and participation in international standardization. This component is handled by DIN and NSI and includes the formation of a local Technical Committee (TC) on hydrogen technologies, mirroring the ISO/TC 197 of the International Organization for Standardization (ISO). Finally, UNAM and BAM are developing a system for welding capacity building. Both of these activities are outside the scope of this paper.

2.3 Prior developments

The institutional partnership builds on experiences gained during an earlier EU Twinning Project, intended to strengthen Namibia's participation in international trade agreements. It focused on improving standardization, accreditation and metrology related to fishery laboratories. Twinning project partners included MIT and NSI from Namibia and BMWK, PTB and DIN from Germany, as well as other institutions. During this project, the need for further advise on safety regulation was identified and consolidated into the proposal for an institutional partnership.

3 Hydrogen Metrology in Namibia

The overarching goal for the cooperation between the National Metrology Institutes is the establishment of new metrological services in Namibia, that help ensuring trust in the hydrogen industry.

3.1 Services for the hydrogen industry

During the different steps along the green hydrogen value chain, a variety of data will be measured and recorded – from wind speeds and solar irradiation, via purity and quantity of water and hydrogen, to temperature and calculations of efficiency. Together with the International Renewable Energy Agency (IRENA), PTB has developed *A Quality Infrastructure Roadmap for green hydrogen*, providing a comprehensive overview of all necessary steps in establishing required infrastructure services. It includes a checklist of over 30 metrological services, ultimately required in the green hydrogen sector.[7]

Currently, NSI has demonstrated calibration and measurement capabilities (CMCs) in mass and related quantities, as an associate member of the International Bureau of Weights and Measures (BIPM). It also offers accredited calibration services for the areas mass, dimension, temperature, and length/volume. Finally, NSI successfully undertakes comparisons in mass, dimension, and temperature to ensure credible and reliable metrology services to industries.[8]

3.2 Developing an action plan

To provide useful recommendations for addressing service gaps, a comprehensive overview of the planned hydrogen industry is needed. PTB is providing a desk study, detailing questions and factors to be considered in mapping out a strategy. One crucial aspect is the demand from stakeholders in industry, to avoid duplicated services as well as gaps in verification and calibration. Existing international cooperations with other National Metrology Institutes, e. g. in the framework of the CIPM MRA can be utilized or even expanded, especially for services that will rarely be used.[9] Further input is needed from the Namibian administration with respect to its priorities.

Based on the outcome of these discussions, recommendations for specific metrological services will be developed. To realise the services, the next step should be the development of an action plan, exploring funding possibilities and matching them with identified priorities. It is envisioned to include concrete recommendations for needed measurement equipment, as well as a recruitment and training plan for personnel.

4 Regulatory Framework for Explosion Protection

Regulations regarding explosion protection ensure that hydrogen is handled safely, and hydrogen plants are designed and used without harm. At the moment, no such regulations exist in Namibia. Recommendations will consider the specific needs of the country and allow for purposive, easy and fast implementation. A key focus must be the safety of workers – avoiding accidents, which otherwise might negatively affect the public acceptance of hydrogen infrastructures. Still, any regulations should also be oriented on the intended international trade and should not hinder for wide market access around the world. Monitoring and enforcing the compliance with regulatory requirements and standards will require governmental institutions – expanding existing bodies or establishing new ones.

4.1 Model legislation

First published by the United Nations Economic Commission for Europe (UNECE) in 2011, the document *A Common Regulatory Framework for Equipment Used in Environments with an Explosive Atmosphere* offers a comprehensive model for national regulation, aligned with internationally harmonized best practices. It references international standards and conformity assessment procedures developed by the International Electrotechnical Commission (IEC) and ISO. Relying on "a full life cycle approach", it covers selection, installation, maintenance, inspection, and repairs of equipment used in explosive atmospheres.[10]

The UNECE framework encompasses six Common Regulatory Arrangements (CRA). Similar to the European ATEX directives (from French "atmosphères explosibles" for "explosive atmospheres"), requirements for explosion protection are divided into two arrangements: Placing products on the market (like Directive 2014/34/EU) and safe use of the equipment and safety of service (like 1999/92/EC).[11, 12] To provide the presumption of conformity with this regulation, a reference list of ISO and IEC standards is given as the third arrangement.

Two further arrangements concern the recognition of conformity assessment bodies and market surveillance to ensure and monitor compliance with the requirements. Finally, a UNECE Steering Committee was proposed to update the regulation model, as well as an international system to distribute information about recently detected risks or faulty products. Both have not been instituted.

4.2 Fast and easy implementations

By using the international system of ISO and IEC standards the legislative system is relieved from detailing and constantly updating technical aspects of protection concepts. Large parts of the proposed list refer to standards developed in the IEC TC 31 Equipment for explosive atmospheres, where Namibia is already an affiliate member.

To further simplify the implementation of explosion protection principles, compliance with the IEC System for Certification to Standards Relating to Equipment for Use in Explosive Atmospheres (IECEx System) can be accepted as proof of conformity assessment, when installing equipment. Membership in the IECEx system is not mandatory but enables participation in its development.

4.3 Development of an institutional framework

Still, to monitor and enforce the compliance with regulatory requirements government bodies, institutions responsible for market surveillance and inspections are needed. Its tasks should include the fields of explosion protection, occupational safety and environmental protection, with inspections due before plant commissioning, after maintenance, repairs, and changes of the setup.

PTB is providing an overview of the needed aspects of explosion protection in regulatory frameworks with a desk study. After initial discussions and workshops on the topic, it has become clear, that more parties need to be involved in developing the needed regulations. Under the guidance of the MME the Namibian administration is thus setting up an extend working group with members from the Ministry of Justice, Ministry of Labour, Industrial Relations and Employment Creation and the Ministry of Works and Transport.

5 Discussion

The process of developing and implementing recommendations regarding explosion protection and metrology for a hydrogen infrastructure has been slower than initially expected. While some of the project partners have already worked together within the EU Twinning Project, the scope and processes in an institutional partnership are different. Additionally, new authorities and personnel have been brought in and needed onboarding.

The National Metrology Institute of Namibia, NSI, is dedicated to offering and extending its metrological services. Yet, due to the multitude of possible additions choosing the relevant services to be developed in a timely manner remains a challenge. Here, guidance from stakeholders and a clear vision of planned projects will be needed. Another key aspect is the current lack of funding for equipment. Establishing a long-term funding perspective has to be pursued, too.

While the general scope of recommendations for a regulatory framework in explosion protection was clear from the beginning, the intended circle of stakeholders proved to be too small. As laws and regulation in this field especially concern the health of workers, and not only encompass plants, but also e. g. transportation guidelines, more ministries and authorities need to be aligned with the project.

Some of the recommendations are expected to be easier implemented than others. Adopting the IECEx system for conformity assessment has already been done in other countries and provides a fast, safe and reliable solution. Also, the UNECE model legislation is supplemented by openly accessible guidelines and blue guides to aid national implementations. Establishing new administrative bodies or expanding existing ones to encompass new responsibilities is a challenge and further requires intensive training in the field of explosion protection. A fast decision and implementation will need a clear political vision.

Unforeseen delays to the partnership were also caused by the 2024 Presidential and National assembly election in Namibia. The year was also marked by the sudden passing of His Excellency the Namibian President Dr. Hage Geingob, who had spearheaded the green hydrogen initiative, in February 2022. Despite these challenging events, the Namibian Government has remained committed to the continued implementation of hydrogen strategies with the German Government.

References

1. Ministry of Mines and Energy, Namibia - Green Hydrogen and Derivatives Strategy (2022) Retrieved February 26, 2025, from https://gh2namibia.com/wp-content/uploads/2022/11/Namibia-GH2-Strategy-Rev2.pdf
2. European Commission, A hydrogen strategy for a climate-neutral Europe (2020) Retrieved February 26, 2025, from https://eur-lex.europa.eu/legal-content/EN/TXT/?uri=CELEX:52020DC0301
3. Bundesministerium für Wirtschaft und Klimaschutz, Fortschreibung der Nationalen Wasserstoffstrategie (2023) Retrieved February 26, 2025, from https://www.bmwk.de/Redaktion/DE/Wasserstoff/Downloads/Fortschreibung.html
4. Hyphen Hydrogen Energy, The Hyphen Project, Retrieved February 26, 2025, from https://hyphenafrica.com/the-hyphen-project/
5. Federal Ministry for Economic Affairs and Climate Action (BMWK), Institutional partnerships with the Federal Ministry for Economic Affairs and Energy (2021) Retrieved February 26, 2025, from https://www.bmwk.de/Redaktion/EN/Publikationen/Aussenwirtschaft/institutional-partnerships-with-the-federal-ministry-for-economic-affairs-and-energy-administrative-change.html
6. DIN, DKE, DVGW, NWB, VDA, Standardization Roadmap for Hydrogen Technologies (2024) Retrieved February 26, 2025 from

t pp s/dl o.gprj d(0g(0) (de: 3confd505) 1510100(

https://www.dke.de/en/areas-of-work/energy/standardization-roadmap-hydrogen-technologies

7. International Renewable Energy Agency, A Quality Infrastructure Roadmap for green hydrogen (2024)
Retrieved February 26, 2025, from https://www.irena.org/Publications/2024/Nov/A-Quality-Infrastructure-Roadmap-for-green-hydrogen
8. BIPM Key Comparison Database
Retrieved February 28, 2025, from https://www.bipm.org/kcdb/comparison/advanced-search?displayAdvancedResult=true&tab=2&keywords=&areaId=-1&subfieldId=-1&comparisonType=-1&organizationId=-1&_countries=1&countries=55&progressStatus=-1&startYear=&endYear=&validity=-1
9. A. Krietsch, O. Werhahn, CIPM MRA support for hydrogen metrology – A case study, Measurement **235**, 115041 (2024)
10. United Nations Economic Commission for Europe, A Common Regulatory Framework for Equipment Used in Environments with an Explosive Atmosphere (Second Edition), (2023)
Retrieved February 28, 2025, from https://unece.org/info/Trade/WP.6/pub/378872
11. Directive 2014/34/EU of the European Parliament and of the Council of 26 February 2014 on the harmonisation of the laws of the Member States relating to equipment and protective systems intended for use in potentially explosive atmospheres (recast), Retrieved February 27, 2025, from https://eur-lex.europa.eu/legal-content/EN/TXT/?uri=CELEX:52020DC0301
12. Directive 1999/92/EC of the European Parliament and of the Council of 16 December 1999 on minimum requirements for improving the safety and health protection of workers potentially at risk from explosive atmospheres (15th individual Directive within the meaning of Article 16(1) of Directive 89/391/EEC), Retrieved February 27, 2025, from https://eur-lex.europa.eu/legal-content/EN/TXT/?uri=CELEX:31999L0092

Digitalizing metrology: the quality infrastructure services portal of IPEM-SP

Robson Silva[1] and *Marcos* Oliveira Junior [2*]

[1]Instituto de Pesquisas Tecnológicas – IPT, Av. Prof. Almeida Prado, 532 - Butantã, São Paulo, Brazil
[2]Instituto de Pesos e Medidas do Estado de São Paulo – IPEM-SP, Rua Santa Cruz, 1922 - Vila Gumercindo - São Paulo, Brazil

Abstract. The digital transformation of Quality Infrastructure is one of the main challenges in the context of Industry 4.0. Not letting control be an obstacle to innovation is leading organizations to modernize and incorporate new practices and solutions. In Brazil, the Institute of Weights and Measures of the State of São Paulo (IPEM-SP) implemented a Quality Infrastructure innovation laboratory at the Technological Innovation Hub in the City of São José dos Campos. With the aim of bringing Quality Infrastructure closer to companies that promote innovation, enhancing products and services, IPEM-SP developed a Quality Infrastructure Services Portal (PSIQ) project, based on Artificial Intelligence, to provide initial assistance to those interested in learning about and using Quality Infrastructure tools. This Paper presents the PSIQ case study, a pilot project still under development.

1 Introduction

Quality Infrastructure (QI) is a powerful instrument of competitiveness in an increasingly complex market. One of the reasons for this situation is the role that innovation plays in the context of Industry 4.0. Anchored in information technology and connectivity, the 4th Industrial Revolution (4IR) is transforming society in various aspects, such as the way companies produce goods and services. The main impacts of the 4th Industrial Revolution are economic growth, company productivity and pressure on jobs, with the main factors for these impacts being the speed, scope and systemic impact of new technologies [1].

The ability to seize trade opportunities, compete in global markets and participate in the international value chain is often hampered by the difficulty of demonstrating compliance with quality requirements and trade rules. Organizing a QI system is one of the most positive and practical steps a developing nation can take on the path to becoming an economy based on prosperity, health and well-being [2].

Thus, one of the challenges of IQ is to digitally transform the system itself, which was structured in the context of the 3rd Industrial Revolution, with the control of the production line as its paradigm. With digital transformation, IQ systems are challenged to keep pace with the speed of new technologies. The potential to innovate is no longer an option, it's rather a necessity not only in production, but also in IQ, particularly in accessing markets [3]. The main IQ tools, such as conformity assessment, measurement traceability, and standards, to name a few, were designed and consolidated in an environment of predominance of mechanization, automation and increasing use of computing. One of the central issues of today is the transition from the control paradigm to the innovation paradigm. The challenge is how to promote innovation without control being an obstacle. It is not about abandoning control, but going beyond it, using it as a support for innovation itself.

One example is regulation, which can contribute to innovation, but can also be an obstacle to creativity and to the development and implementation of innovation solutions [4].

Brazil is a country of continental dimensions, with great distances to be covered, a large population and an irregularly distributed GDP, which requires regionalized public policies, especially regarding economic development.

Among the Brazilian states, São Paulo occupies a prominent position. It is the state with the largest industrial base, the largest consumer market and a significant agricultural population. With 45 million inhabitants, a GDP of around R$350 billion ($80 billion) and 250 thousand square meters [5], it is comparable to a European country.

One of the consequences for Brazilian QI is that a single national metrology organization is not capable of providing support for the needs of the entire country. One solution was to organize a networked system, in which state organizations connect to the federal level in a metrology and quality system [6]. One such organization is the Institute of Weights and Measures of the State of São Paulo (IPEM- SP) [7].

Created in 1967, IPEM-SP played a relevant role in the development of legal metrology in Brazil and in market surveillance. In Brazil, the National Institute of Metrology, Quality and Technology (INMETRO) has the prerogative of regulating legal metrology and assessing conformity in areas where there is no primary regulator, covering a large part of product safety [8]. INMETRO delegates to the states, through the state metrology institutes, with different names, the power of administrative policing and the provision of legal metrology services, such as verification of measuring instruments.

In response to a modernizing agenda for the state of São Paulo, IPEM-SP developed a strategic plan for the period 2023-2026 with an emphasis on innovation, with the aim of promoting its digital transformation and developing industrial metrology [9]. To become more efficient, IPEM developed actions to approach the

* Corresponding author: mhgojunior@ipem.sp.gov.br

productive sector, seeking to develop solutions for the main problems encountered by the industry.

Innovation is an important topic for Brazil, especially for São Paulo. According to the Brazilian Innovation and Development Index (IBID), the state leads all 7 pillars of innovation. Still, it seeks to increase its efficiency in converting inputs into results [10]. In 2025, the Secretariat of Partnerships and Investments (SPI-SP) will have a budget of 8.5 billion reais (1.5 billion dollars), an increase of 129% compared to the previous year [11].

Seeking to bring IQ closer to companies, IPEM-SP created the Quality Infrastructure Laboratory (LIQ) [12], in the São José dos Campos Technological Innovation Park (PIT) [13]. This is an innovation laboratory dedicated to IQ, with the scope of promoting projects in partnership with companies to generate innovative technologies and businesses in the state of São Paulo.

Fig. 1. Panoramic view of the Technological Innovation Park (PIT)

This article will present the experience of IPEM-SP, highlighting the first LIQ project, a service portal for companies based on the use of Artificial Intelligence (AI). The portal seeks to digitalize metrological processes and other IQ components, promoting accessibility, transparency and innovation. Markets based on digital platforms are increasingly prevalent, which requires companies and organizations in general to move faster [14].

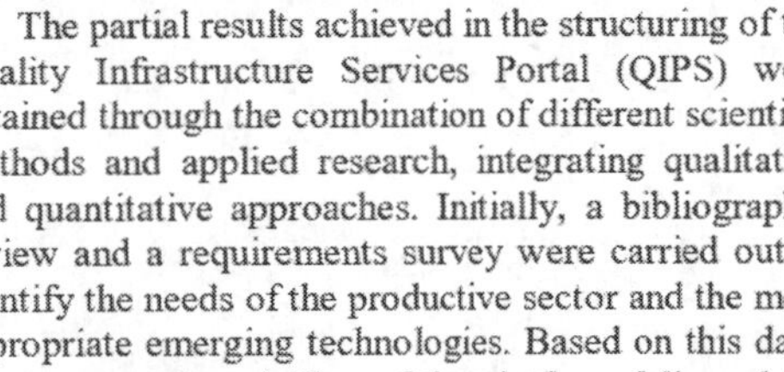

Fig. 2. Quality Infrastructure Services Portal (PSIQ)

The partial results achieved in the structuring of the Quality Infrastructure Services Portal (QIPS) were obtained through the combination of different scientific methods and applied research, integrating qualitative and quantitative approaches. Initially, a bibliographic review and a requirements survey were carried out to identify the needs of the productive sector and the most appropriate emerging technologies. Based on this data, the conceptual modelling of the platform followed the principles of Design Science Research (DSR), allowing the structuring of technological components, such as the Intelligent Virtual Assistant, Advanced Semantic Search, Big Data and Robotic Process Automation (RPA). The development and prototyping phase, corresponding to TRL 2 (Technological Formulation), used agile methodologies, enabling iterative adjustments and partial validations of the planned functionalities.

During the transition to TRL 3 (Experimental Validation), experimental methods were used, including usability testing, to ensure that the PSIQ components met the technical and regulatory requirements. The analysis of data collected during the tests was conducted using content analysis techniques, enabling evidence-based adjustments. Using this approach, it was possible to prove the efficiency of the virtual assistant in personalizing responses, the accuracy of the semantic search in retrieving technical information, and the optimization of automated processes via RPA. These results demonstrate that the integration of scientific methods with applied research has been essential to consolidate an efficient and interconnected digital ecosystem in the Quality Infrastructure, making PSIQ a reference model for the modernization of metrological and regulatory services.

2. IPEM-SP Innovation and Competitiveness Ecosystem

The state of São Paulo is Brazil's most important economic and industrial hub, home to a robust innovation ecosystem that drives the country's economic development. With a GDP larger than most countries, São Paulo has the largest industrial parks in the country and is a benchmark for sectors such as technology, healthcare, advanced manufacturing and agribusiness. This leadership role demands solid support for quality, trust and safety for products and services, making it essential to disseminate and strengthen IQ.

IQ is made up of 5 fundamental pillars – metrology, accreditation, standardization, conformity assessment and market surveillance – which guarantee competitiveness, safety and compliance for industrial production and the services provided, making it possible not only to drive innovation and efficiency, but also ensuring the integration of the state in the global value chain.

IPEM-SP, following its strategic planning, structured an innovation and technology center, published an innovation policy and transformed itself into an Institute of Science and Technology (ICT). ICTs, in the Brazilian legal system, aim to contribute to scientific and innovation production by promoting connections among government, academia and companies. This arrangement configures the triple helix of innovation, a concept presented in 1995 by Etzkowitz and Leydesdorff, who understood that economic development depends on this articulation [16]. Recently, the concept expanded to a quadruple helix by including society as another of its components, understanding that this component would be responsible for bringing innovation to the masses, civil society and the media [17]. Based on this concept, IPEM-SP sought strategic partnerships to form an innovation ecosystem focused on IQ. In January 2025, IPEM had already consolidated

https://doi.org/j 0.j 05j /ep3conf/(0(51(10100(

its ecosystem formed by recognized institutions, as shown in the figure below.

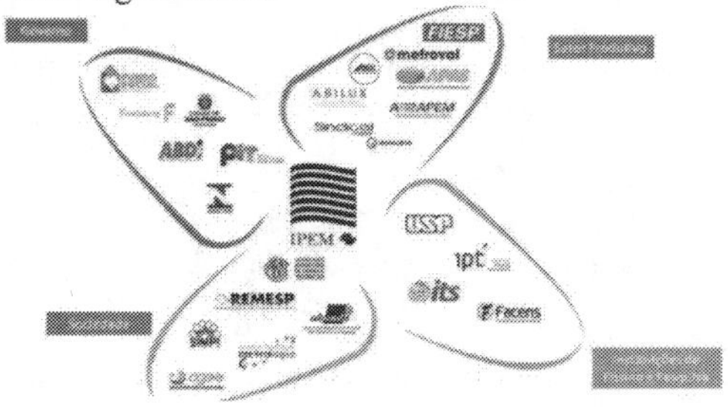

Fig. 3. IPEM-SP Innovation and Competitiveness Ecosystem

Another strategic action was to seek closer ties with the production sector. The main objective was to understand the challenges that companies face in the context of Industry 4.0. A pilot project was designed based on a previous experience of one of the authors of this article who, as President of INMETRO, led an initial experiment to create an IQ laboratory in the city of Foz do Iguaçu in 2021[18]. Despite its initial success, the laboratory did not consolidate. One of the factors was the distance from INMETRO and the lack of its own human resources to conduct the laboratory's activities, resorting at the time to a partnership with a local university. Seeking to correct the flaws found, IPEM-SP established a new laboratory, LIQ, in a city close to its technology center, using its own personnel, in a location with a concentration of companies focused on innovation.

This location was the city of São José dos Campos, located 100 km from São Paulo, with a strong technological vocation, being home to the Aeronautics Technology Center (CTA) and Embraer, a Brazilian aviation company. The city has an innovation park, the PIT, which has more than 300 associated companies, 135 of which are residents, as shown in the table below. LIQ began its operations in January 2024.

Total area of the PIT core	188 thousand m2
Special perimeter of the park	15.8 million m2
Related companies that are part of this universe	More than 300
Resident companies	135
Business Centers	4
Technological development centers	4
Business incubators	3
Local productive arrangements	2

Fig. 4. São José dos Campos Technological Innovation Park (PIT)

One of the first findings was that there is a huge pent-up demand for IQ. One of the factors is the lack of knowledge of IQ tools among companies themselves, especially companies focused on innovation. Every time LIQ introduced IQ to these companies, demand was generated, especially for information. The problem for LIQ became how to meet so many demands with limited human resources. The solution was to develop an IQ service portal, based on AI, to receive demands from companies, working on a funnel strategy to channel the most complex ones to the LIQ team.

Fig.5. IPEM-SP Quality Infrastructure Laboratory in São José dos Campos

3. Partial Results

The digital transformation of Quality Infrastructure (QI) has become a strategic factor for industrial development and global competitiveness. The Quality Infrastructure Services Portal (QISP) was designed to revolutionize access to metrology and conformity assessment services, promoting an efficient, integrated and accessible ecosystem. This advancement allows companies, regulatory bodies and society to use technical and regulatory information quickly, reliably and automatically, ensuring greater security and adherence to current standards.

The project is currently in the TRL 2 (Technological Formulation) phase, where the structural bases of the platform, its functionalities and technologies involved are defined. In the next six months, the transition to TRL 3 (Experimental Validation) will take place, in which the components and subsystems will be tested in controlled environments to ensure reliability, interoperability and operational efficiency. This validation will be essential to ensure that PSIQ accurately meets the needs of the production sector and the agencies responsible for regulating quality in Brazil.

One of the main differentiators of PSIQ is the implementation of an Intelligent Virtual Assistant, based on Artificial Intelligence (AI), which will provide personalized support to users. This technology will be able to interpret complex questions, suggest relevant standards and regulations, and offer specific guidance according to the user's profile. In this way, the aim is to eliminate barriers to accessing technical information and ensure that companies and professionals find quick and reliable answers on regulatory and metrological requirements.

The integration of Advanced Semantic Search will make access to information more intuitive and efficient. Unlike traditional search systems, this functionality will employ natural language processing to understand the user's intent and provide highly relevant and contextualized results. This will allow technical standards, ordinances and regulations to be located with greater precision, reducing ambiguities and optimizing the search for critical information for compliance and certification of products and processes.

The use of Big Data and Analytics will be essential to improve the management of Quality Infrastructure. By collecting and analyzing large volumes of data, PSIQ will be able to generate detailed insights into non-compliance patterns, regulatory trends, and opportunities for improvement in certification and metrology processes. This resource will provide a solid basis for evidence-based decision-making, benefiting both companies and regulatory bodies in building more effective policies and strategies.

Robotic Process Automation (RPA) will be one of the pillars of PSIQ's operational efficiency. By automating repetitive activities, such as document validation, certificate issuance and request processing, it will be possible to reduce response time, minimize errors and increase productivity. In addition, API integration will ensure that the platform can communicate with other institutional systems, promoting interoperability and connectivity between different components of the Quality Infrastructure.

The modernization promoted by PSIQ represents a significant advance for the Quality Infrastructure in Brazil, especially in a context where digitalization and connectivity are essential for sustainable development and global competitiveness. With the implementation of these technologies, IPEM-SP not only improves its internal processes, but also creates an innovative model for the digitalization of metrological and regulatory services, strengthening the productive sector and boosting the quality and safety of products in the national and international markets.

Furthermore, in its first year of operation, LIQ began a process of impacting the PIT ecosystem, highlighting the actions in the figure below.

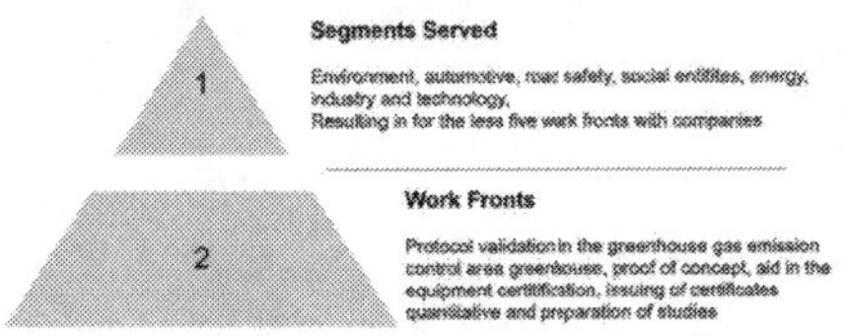

Fig. 6. LIQ Impact on the PIT Ecosystem

4. Conclusion

IPEM-SP has sought to put digital transformation concepts into practice at IQ, seeking to identify innovation projects to experiment with solutions that respond to the various challenges faced by the production sector. Industry 4.0 is having a strong impact on the market and IQ has challenges to overcome in all of its pillars. Examples include the development of remote calibration, smart standards, digital product passports, and others.

Understanding IQ as a system that provides services to the industry, with the aim of having reliable and safe products, in addition to contributing to competitiveness, the connection with companies is a critical factor for digitalization actions. Thus, the connection environment itself between institutions that directly or indirectly provide IQ services to companies must also occur in a virtual environment. With emerging digital technologies, these possibilities are greatly expanded.

LIQ and PSIQ are developments that aim to reduce this gap between IQ organizations and the productive sector, especially in Brazil, where the country's characteristics and dimensions often hinder integration and speed of solutions. With the validation of the portal, IPEM-SP will have a digital environment to meet various demands, especially in information, generating value for companies, particularly those dedicated to innovation.

This same principle can be applied to the same portal or to another one to be developed for different audiences, such as consumers, traders and governments. One of the recommendations in this article is that once the portal is validated, its scope should be expanded to other domains that can benefit from IQ.

The conclusion of this article is that organizations that work with IQ must seek innovative ways to modernize their services in order to be more efficient in the current context of 4IR, generating value for companies and trust for the market, thus being a factor in inducing Industry 4.0 itself.

References

Journal articles

1. Schwab, Klaus. The Fourth Industrial Revolution. Geneva: World Economic Forum, 2016.
2. UNIDO. Improving Trade, Changing Lives: The Impact of the Global Quality and Standards Programme. 2023.https://www.unido.org/news/improving-trade-changing-lives-impact-global-quality-and-standards-programme.
3. UNIDO. Guide for the Development of National Quality Policies. Vienna: UNIDO, 2016. https://www.unido.org/sites/default/files/2017-02/GUIDE_FOR_THE_DEVELOPMENT_OF_0.pdf.
4. Blind, Knut. "The Role of the Quality Infrastructure within Socio-Technical Transformations: A European Perspective." Technological Forecasting and Social Change 199 (February 1, 2024): 123019. https://doi.org/10.1016/j.techfore.2023.123019.
5. Brazilian Institute of Geography and Statistics (IBGE). n.d. São Paulo - Cities and States. Accessed March 1, 2025. https://www.ibge.gov.br/cidades-e-estados/sp.html.
6. National Institute of Metrology, Quality, and Technology (Inmetro). RBMLQ - Brazilian Network of Legal Metrology and Quality. Accessed March 1, 2025. http://www.inmetro.gov.br/fiscalizacao/rbmlq.asp.
7. Institute of Weights and Measures of the State of São Paulo (IPEM-SP). n.d. About IPEM-SP. Accessed March 1, 2025.

https://www.ipem.sp.gov.br/index.php/institucional/conheca-o-ipem-sp.

8. National Institute of Metrology, Quality, and Technology. "Official Inmetro Portal." Accessed March 1, 2025. https://www.gov.br/inmetro/pt-br.
9. Instituto de Pesos e Medidas do Estado de São Paulo (IPEM-SP). Strategic Plan. São Paulo: IPEM-SP, n.d. Accessed March 1, 2025. https://www.ipem.sp.gov.br/images/02ipem/conheca_o_ipem/planoestrategico.pdf
10. Instituto Nacional da Propriedade Industrial (INPI). Brazil Innovation and Development Index – IBID 2024. Rio de Janeiro: INPI, 2024. Accessed March 1, 2025. https://www.gov.br/inpi/pt-br/inpi-data/indice-brasil-de-inovacao-e-desenvolvimento-ibid/IBID_2024_PT.BRfinal.pdf.
11. Secretariat of Partnerships and Investments of the State of São Paulo. "SP Doubles Resources for Investment in Infrastructure Projects in 2025." Published on January 14, 2025. Accessed March 1, 2025. https://www.parceriaseminvestimentos.sp.gov.br/sp-mais-que-dobra-recursos-para-investimentos-em-projetos-de-infraestrutura-em-2025/.
12. Instituto de Pesos e Medidas do Estado de São Paulo (IPEM-SP). n.d. LIQ Services. Accessed March 1, 2025. https://www.ipem.sp.gov.br/index.php/cidadao/servicos/liq.
13. Brazil. Law No. 13,243, of January 11, 2016. Establishes legal frameworks for science, technology, and innovation. Official Gazette of the Federal Executive, Brasília, January 12, 2016. Accessed March 1, 2025. https://www.planalto.gov.br/ccivil_03/_ato2015-2018/2016/lei/L13243.htm.
14. Grau, Mateus, Leandro Franz, tadeu Vianna, Gabriela Scur, and Alexandre Massote. "Panorama Do Contexto Do Início Da Jornada Na Quarta Revolução Industrial." In Automação e Sociedade: Quarta Revolução Industrial, Um Olhar Para o Brasil. Brasport, 2018.
15. Brazil. Law No. 13,243, of January 11, 2016. Establishes legal frameworks for science, technology, and innovation. Official Gazette of the Federal Executive, Brasília, January 12, 2016. Accessed March 1, 2025. https://www.planalto.gov.br/ccivil_03/_ato2015-2018/2016/lei/L13243.htm.
16. Etzkowitz, Henry, and Loet Leydesdorff. "The Triple Helix -- University-Industry-Government Relations: A Laboratory for Knowledge Based Economic Development." SSRN Scholarly Paper. Rochester, NY: Social Science Research Network, January 1, 1995. https://papers.ssrn.com/abstract=2480085.
17. Aswal, D. K. "Quality Infrastructure of India and Its Importance for Inclusive National Growth." MAPAN 35, no. 2 (June 1, 2020): 139–50. https://doi.org/10.1007/s12647-020-00376-3.
18. Itaipu Technology Park. "Itaipu Technology Park to Establish Brazil's First Quality Infrastructure Laboratory Focused on Smart City Development." Published November 30, 2021. Accessed March 1, 2025. https://www.itaipuparquetec.org.br/parque-tecnologico-itaipu-brasil-tera-laboratorio-de-infraestrutura-da-qualidade-com-foco-no-desenvolvimento-de-cidades-inteligentes/

Establishment of Sustainability through Open Access to Research Infrastructure in a Calibration Laboratory for Extreme Electrical Metrology

Marija Cundeva-Blajer [1*]

[1]Ss. Cyril and Methodius University in Skopje, Faculty of Electrical Engineering and Information Technologies-Skopje, 18 Rugjer Boshkovic Str., 1000 Skopje, Republic of North Macedonia

Abstract. The laboratory sustainability aims at reducing environmental impacts of laboratory activities, like energy and water use, waste production, and greenhouse gas emissions, benefitting in cutting costs, improving laboratory reputation, supporting the UN SDGs of environmental protection, social justice, collaboration among laboratory staff and stakeholders. This can be achieved by inclusiveness and openness of the laboratory infrastructure towards different users, through defined procedure of "open access" to the laboratory research infrastructure. The sustainability measures implementation in the Laboratory for Electrical Measurements (LEM) at the Ss. Cyril and Methodius University in Skopje, is described. It is a calibration laboratory for instruments for electrical quantities, accredited according to EN ISO/IEC 17025:2017. The LEM sustainability maturity evaluation, through mapping and gap analysis is presented, enabling creation of strategic documents like the Quality and Sustainability Policy, Quality and Sustainability Manual and the Access Policy to the Research Infrastructure. Conflicting issues arise between openness and confidentiality, but these challenges are overcome. Two outputs are delivered by deploying risk-based thinking: 1) successful extension of the LEM accreditation scope in calibration of extreme electrical quantities, complying with EN ISO/IEC 17025:2017, including the point 4.2 (confidentiality requirements), and 2) strategic documents adoption, imposed by public funding conditions.

1 Introduction

The concept for laboratory sustainability aims to reduce the environmental footprint of laboratory activities, such as energy and water use, waste production, and greenhouse gas emissions, [1], improving the quality, safety, and efficiency of lab operations, but also the social and economic aspects of the laboratory practice, [2, 3]. This provides cutting costs, improved lab reputation and credibility, support of the global goals of environmental protection and social justice, promotion of innovation and collaboration culture among lab staff and stakeholders, [1]. However, a sustainable lab is expected to maintain efficient operations, and in the case of an accredited lab, to fulfill the quality assurance requirements of the international standard EN ISO/IEC 17025:2017, [4]. This can be achieved through creative activities, like inclusiveness and openness towards different users and stakeholders, by a defined procedure of "open access" to the laboratory Research Infrastructure (RI), [5]. One of the elements of the Horizon Europe, the EU's key funding programme for research and innovation, is the Open science policy, with mandatory open access to publications and open science principles applied throughout the programme, [6]. At international level, the General Conference of the United Nations Educational, Scientific and Cultural Organization (UNESCO), at its 41st session from 9 to 24 November 2021, has identified the needs and has provided the Recommendation on Open Science, [7]. To achieve the UNESCO recommendation on open science, several actions are foreseen, like enabling open access RIs (virtual or physical, including major scientific equipment or sets of instruments) needed to support open science and serve the needs of different communities. Open science infrastructures are often the result of community-building efforts, crucial for their long-term sustainability and therefore should be not-for-profit and guarantee permanent and unrestricted access to all public to the largest extent possible as addressed in [8]. The open approach contributes to some of the United Nations Sustainable Development Goals (UN SDGs): 1-No poverty, 4-Quality Education, 9-Industry, innovation and infrastructure, 10-Reduced inequalities and 17-Partnerships for the UN SDGs, [1], [5]. Here, the sustainability measures implementation in the Laboratory for Electrical Measurements (LEM) at the Ss. Cyril and Methodius University in Skopje (UKIM), by "open science" approach, will be provided. The LEM is a calibration laboratory for instruments for electrical quantities of extreme values, accredited according to the EN ISO/IEC 17025:2017. Due to accreditation, conflicting issues arise, like contradictions of openness and confidentiality. The developed methodology within

* Corresponding author: mcundeva@feit.ukim.edu.mk

the project "Development and Upgrade of Laboratory Resources for Research and Introduction of Novel Analytical Methods in Electrical Metrology", financed by the Ministry of Education and Science of Republic of North Macedonia, resolves these challenges.

2 Methodology and Tools for Establishment of Sustainability Measures through Open Access to Laboratory Research Infrastructure

Recently, the awareness on the lab environmental impact and the trend toward "sustainable laboratories" are rising, and diverse original methodologies for evaluation of the lab sustainability maturity are developed [9]. Some international initiatives, such as the MyGreenLab in the USA, [10] or the Sustainable European Laboratories network (SELs) in Europe, [11] are implemented. Several guidelines for introduction of laboratory practices contributing to the UN SDGs are published [12]. Another aspect of the laboratory sustainability, is the transformation from Industry 4.0 towards Industry 5.0, as re-humanization of the race towards automation, [13]. The laboratory sustainability directly contributes to the evolvement of the Metrology 5.0 and the laboratory of the future. Here a circular methodology for establishment of the laboratory sustainability measures is proposed as given in Figure 1.

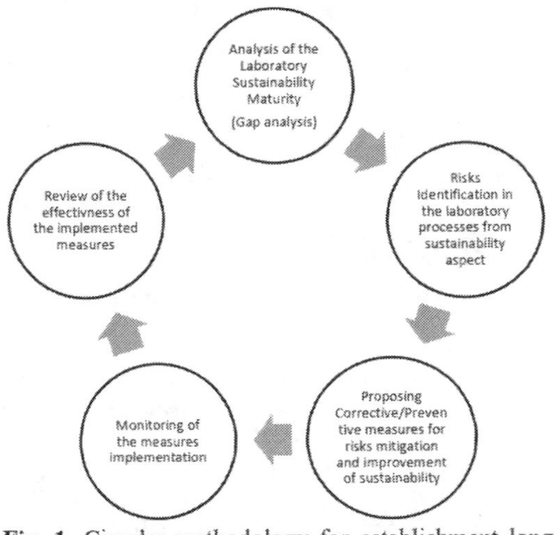

Fig. 1. Circular methodology for establishment long-term laboratory sustainability through gap analysis

The process of establishment long-term laboratory sustainability starts with analysis of the laboratory sustainability maturity, by mapping and gap analysis thoroughly presented in [1]. Based on the findings from the gap analysis in [1], one of the measures for achievement of fast and evident impact on the lab sustainability is the intervention the laboratory strategic documents, like the quality policy, the quality manual, as well as creation and adoption of access policy to the laboratory RI. This approach demonstrates potential for long-term determination of the laboratory to practice working processes oriented towards sustainability.

KnowSDGs (Knowledge base for the Sustainable Development Goals) is a web platform that provides tools and organises knowledge on policies, indicators, methods and data to support the evidence-based implementation and addressing of the SDGs, [14]. It maps policy documents with the SDGs and targets through specific keywords, [15, 16] as in Figure 2. The analysed documents in this on-line platform are processed using text mining and natural language processing techniques to identify relevant SDG targets within the text. The documents are uploaded in the SDG Mapper, and the tool is run to identify relevant SDGs in the text. Some SDGs are more prevalent than others along with their associated targets and indicators. The tool provides several visualisations showing how the SDGs are addressed in documents. The flowchart of the EU SDGs Mapper is given in Figure 3.

Fig 2. EU KnowSDGs - Knowledge base for the Sustainable Development Goals web platform [14]

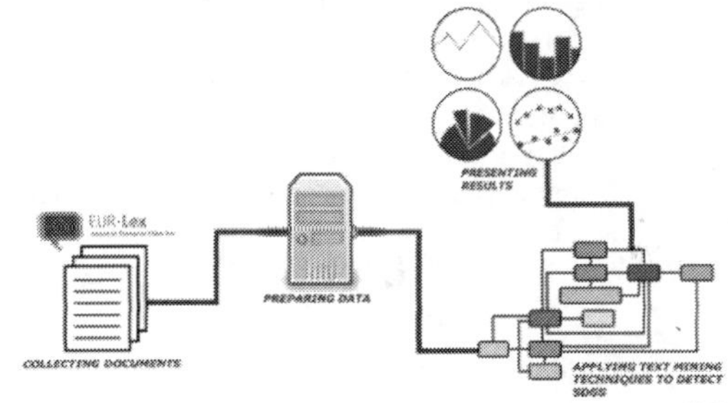

Fig. 3. EU KnowSDGs – SDGs Mapper flow-chart [14]

The circular methodology for introduction of the sustainability in the LEM starts by mapping of the already created and adopted strategic documents like the LEM Quality Policy and Quality Manual, in the EU KnowSDGs tool, with the results presented in [1]. These documents consider the specific operations of the electrical calibration laboratory, the requirements for confidentiality of the international standard EN ISO/IEC 17025:2017, and some general regulation like the EU GDPR, i.e. the harmonized national legislation. Based on the findings derived from the EU KnowSDGs on-line tool, these documents are thoroughly revised and submitted for a second check in the EU KnowSDGs tool, with significantly more positive results as in [1]. Another identified possibility for increasing the laboratory sustainability is the adoption of the Access Policy to the RI of the accredited LEM, which after the creation will be subjected to the assessment by the EU KnowSDGs on-line tool.

3 Challenges in Opening the Lab Research Infrastructures and Resolving Conflicting Issues in LEM

Some testing and calibration labs are an integral part of a more complex research facility, especially those metrology labs within public universities or research institutions opting for 'open access'. The labs, accredited according to ISO/IEC 17025:2017, have to fulfill the standard's requirements on confidentiality, i.e. clause 4.2. The confidentially requirement tangles the laboratory personnel, too. In general, the laboratory and its personnel are responsible for the information obtained or created during the performance of laboratory activities, and all information is considered proprietary information and shall be regarded as confidential, with exception to what is required by law. In the context of confidentiality in the laboratory practice, are also the requirements of the Regulation (EU) 2016/679 GDPR, [17], which have to be fulfilled by some labs. Balancing the requirements for 'confidentiality' and 'open access' introduces implementation challenges in the lab documentation and practice. In the paper, the example of the LEM, accredited calibration lab, and a RI within the UKIM Faculty of Electrical Engineering and Information Technologies (FEIT), public higher education and research institution, will be demonstrated through the process of development and implementation of the procedure for confidentiality and the Policy for Open Access to the Research Infrastructure of the Laboratory for Electrical Measurements. Independent faculty laboratories are established at UKIM-FEIT for practical implementation of the teaching-educational, scientific-research and application activities. LEM is one of them. The LEM is accredited since 2015, as a laboratory for the calibration of instruments for electrical quantities, electrical power and energy.

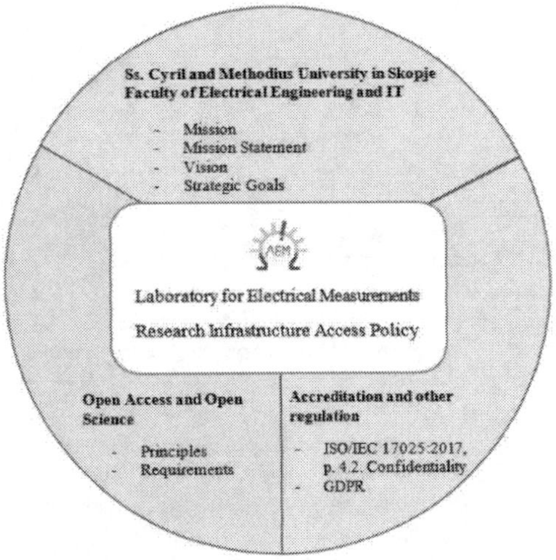

Fig. 4. LEM RI Access Policy-constraints

As a publicly funded RI, the LEM belongs to the category of smaller research infrastructures, [5], [18], with the objective of promoting cooperation between science, technology and industry, and providing a platform for the education of young scientists and engineers, with a strong motivation for development and adoption of a Research Infrastructure Access Policy in line with the Open Science approach. The RI Access Policy of LEM, as in Figure 4, has to comply with:

- the Mission and corresponding Mission Statement of the FEIT, the Vision of FEIT, as well as the strategic goals of FEIT publicly published in [19]
- the strategic agenda of the European Union for "open science", [6], and
- the accreditation requirements for confidentiality according to the ISO/IEC 17025:2017, p. 4.2., [4] and other applicable regulation, e.g. GDPR, [17].

Considering the contradictory requirements, the creation of the Access Policy to the LEM RI, is based on the already adopted university, faculty and LEM documents. The following terms and definitions are applied according to [5] and [18]:

Principles of open access – conditions under which a higher education institution creates access to its RI for use by different groups of users, inside and outside the organization.

Research infrastructure (infrastructure for conducting research) – physical structure (scientific institutes, laboratories, etc.), instruments, tools and other material, virtual resources and related services, necessary for conducting modern fundamental and applied scientific research.

Resources - RI, scientists and other researchers working with the infrastructure, personnel providing infrastructure services, infrastructure operation, maintenance and development, and infrastructure time.

Services – Open access services approved by the Dean of FEIT, based on the consent of the Head of LEM.

Recipient of open access services – a user (internal or external) who requested and received access to the RI.

User– a natural or legal person who orders services from the RI or requests access to this RI to perform research.

Working time of the RI – the total RI working time.

Experimental time – a period of time during which the RI can be used to perform scientific research and development work.

Technical time – the period of time during which the RI is technically maintained and users cannot use the RI to perform scientific research and development work, time reserved for maintenance and repairs.

Open access time – the period of time during which the RI is available to users either free of charge or for a fee.

Guaranteed time – the time period reserved for external users who made a real financial contribution to the development of the RI or participated in its support, which is regulated by a special agreement within the FEIT partner program.

Commercial time – the period of time during which the RI is available for payment.

The drafting of the LEM RI Access Policy, complies with the recommendation stipulated in [5] and [18], comprising the essential information and regulation on:

1. General provisions and definitions
2. Management of the LEM RI
3. Users of the LEM RI
4. Access to the LEM RI
5. Prices formation for LEM RI services

6. Income and use of funds received for providing RI services
7. Obligations related to confidentiality and protection of intellectual property
8. Resolution of disputes

The management of the LEM RI complies with the internal quality assurance documents and accreditation requirements. The services of the RI of LEM are used by the authorized members of LEM, and are provided to both internal and external users. Authorized members of LEM have access to the RI according to the decisions on appointment and authorization, and the Matrix of competence and responsibility of LEM. The users of the RI of LEM are classified as **internal users** - students of FEIT (of all three cycles of studies and students at the Lifelong Learning Centre), as well as employed scientific and research staff of FEIT, and **external users** – students or researchers (of all three cycles) at other faculties of UKIM, at other public or private universities/scientific institutions, employees in commercial research centres, researchers in government institutions, as well as members of the civil sector.

The procedure for granting access to laboratory resources by all types of users is described in the FEIT quality management system procedures and in Figure 5, [5]. For all users, the decision on access granting is based on risk-based thinking following the methodology for risk analysis prescribed in the LEM procedure, [20], including the risks related to the confidentiality requirements of ISO/IEC 17025. The LEM follows the methodology of Failure Mode and Effects Analysis (FMEA), [20]. The LEM RI is accessible to users according to the procedures defined by the time of access to the RI as in Figure 5. The working time of the LEM RI is divided into **experimental time** and **technical time**. Experimental time is divided into: free access time, guaranteed time and commercial time. Priority can be given to small and medium-sized enterprises (SMEs).

The prices of LEM's RI services are established according to the principle of reimbursing RI costs. The prices of the services for scientific researchers and development purposes are based on the principle of covering only material costs. The price of RI services is determined by the type of user, with an estimate of the duration of the operation of the equipment and human resources, consumables and other materials needed to perform work and other possible costs as given in Fig.5. For educational purposes within the accredited study programs of FEIT, the use of the RI of LEM is free and according to the number of hours of practical teaching within the subject programs. Access to LEM's RI for educational purposes is of the highest priority and is consistent with the FEIT lectures schedule. Access to the RI of LEM is enabled for students under the supervision of a subject teacher in charge of the realization of the specific course program or research, and in the presence of authorized member of LEM. Any material costs incurred for this purpose are covered from FEIT funds or from LEM's own funds, or from a dedicated educational or scientific research project. For educational purposes within the courses and training offered by FEIT through the FEIT Career Centre, prices are established according to the approved program and the number of hours of practical work within the course/training published on the FEIT website. Access to the LEM RI for lifelong learning purposes is a high priority and is consistent with the FEIT course/training schedule. Access to the RI of LEM is enabled for the students of the course/training under the supervision of teaching staff from FEIT in charge of the implementation of the specific training, and in the presence of an authorized member of LEM. Any material costs incurred for this purpose are covered by the income from the course/training and are an integral part of the price of the course/training. The prices of LEM's RI services are published publicly. Prices are revised taking into account changes in economic conditions, maintenance costs, administration and other costs related to RI activities. The income received from the provision of services through the RI of LEM is used for the sustainable development of the RI of LEM.

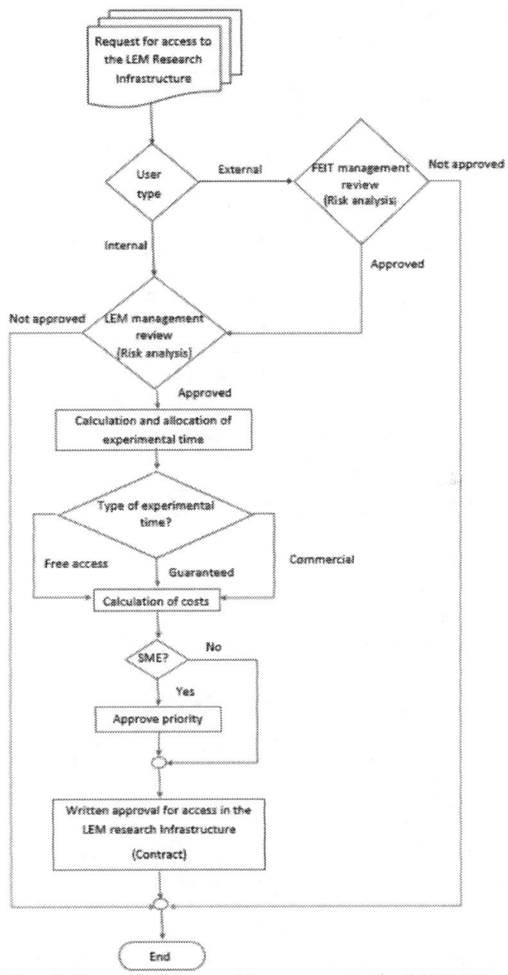

Fig. 5. Procedure for granting access to the LEM RI

The confidentiality of the results of any scientific research and/or experiment performed using the resources and/or services of the LEM RI must be insured. Exceptions may be specified by written agreement between FEIT and the external user. Pursuant to the Quality Policy and it is prescribed in the LEM RI Access Policy, that all members of LEM, including top management of FEIT, commit to confidentiality and protection of intellectual property arising from activities in the LEM RI. For this purpose, each of the participants in the processes of using the RI sign an appropriate Statement of Independence, Impartiality and Confidentiality. This complies with the item 4.2. of the LEM Quality Manual. Ownership and management of the intellectual property created in FEIT and confidentiality obligations are regulated by the legal regulations of R. N. Macedonia and the internal lab documents. In the case of research performed by external users, all intellectual property produced by the external user during the open access period shall be the intellectual property of the external users, unless otherwise specified in the mutual agreement between FEIT and the external user. In the case of research performed by external users as part of guaranteed or commercial access time, all intellectual property issues will be specified in the agreement or separate agreement signed for the specific access to LEM's RI. In the case of research conducted by internal users, a discussion may need to be held to make the results available Open Access, adhering to the principles of Open Science.

4 Evaluation of the LEM Access Policy Against the UN SDGs and Outcomes

The contribution to the laboratory sustainability by creating and adoption of the Research Infrastructure Access Policy of LEM is conducted by subjecting this strategic document for evaluation in the EU KnowSDGs on-line tool, [1]. In Figure 6 are the obtained results from the SDGs Mapper on the LEM Access Policy, indicating that the SDG 9-Industry, innovation and infrastructure is mostly addressed with 56 %, SDGs 1-No poverty and 4-Quality Education are represented with 20%, and SDG 17-Partnerships for the goals is present with 4%. In Figure 7 the particular SDG targets of the LEM Access Policy are displayed. After thorough drafting and inclusive discussion among the participants of LEM and other interested parties at FEIT, the Access Policy to the Research Infrastructure of the Laboratory for Electrical Measurements at UKIM-FEIT was officially adopted by the FEIT Management Board with Decision from 26.10.2023. In parallel regular assessment for re-accreditation and extension of the accreditation scope of LEM was conducted by the Institute of Accreditation of Republic of North Macedonia (IARNM) on 22.09.2023, during which the latest updated quality assurance documentation of LEM was assessed as well the drafted Access Policy to the Research Infrastructure of the Laboratory for Electrical Measurements was deeply analyzed by the accreditation assessment team. During the assessment it was confirmed that the Access Policy to the Research Infrastructure of the Laboratory for Electrical Measurements complies to the requirements of the ISO/IEC 17025:2017 as well the other documentation of the LEM quality assurance system, and in particular the requirement for confidentiality.

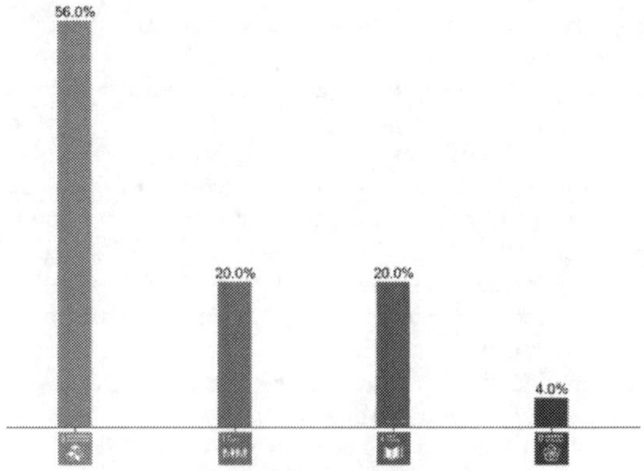

Fig. 6. UN SDGs tangled by the LEM Access Policy derived by the EU SDGs Mapper

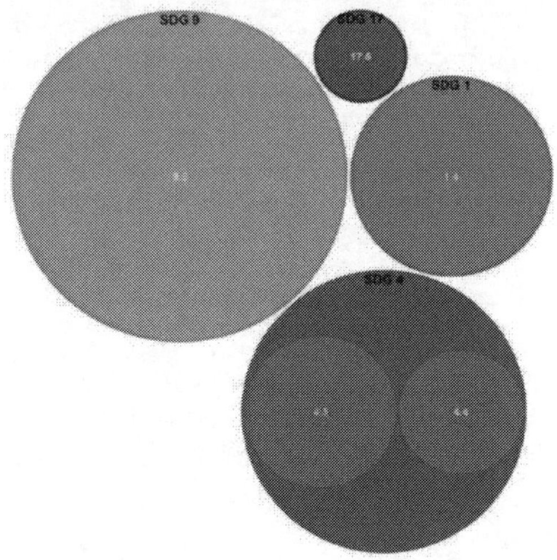

Fig. 7. SDGs targets addressed by the LEM Access Policy identified by the EU SDGs Mapper

The resolution of the contradictory issues has been successfully achieved in the procedures, documentation and best laboratory practice of LEM. This has led to realization of the main expected project outcomes, one of which is the adoption and implementation of strategic document 'Access Policy to the Research Infrastructure of the Laboratory for Electrical Measurements', imposed by the funding conditions of the public scientific grant. The evident benefits from the implemented approach are:

- defined transparent procedure for "open access" to the laboratory infrastructure,
- precisely defined users of the laboratory infrastructure,
- prescribed inclusiveness for entities from the academia, but also wider in the society, in particular users with insufficient access to cutting edge metrology facilities,
- most efficient usage of the laboratory infrastructure and fastest return of publicly invested funds,
- increased awareness on the "open access" approach contributing to the laboratory sustainability and the UN SDGs in general.

From the results obtained from the EU SDGs Mapper tool, the introduced strategic changes and the integrated approach to comply to the quality assurance requirements of the standard ISO/IEC 17025:2017 and the orientation towards the UN SDGs, contribute visibly to the fulfilment of the UN strategic development goals.

5 CONCLUSIONS

The paper presented the methodology for achieving long-term laboratory sustainability by the approach of open access to the RI in an accredited calibration laboratory. IT is gained by strategic intervention in the laboratory policy master documents defining the overall laboratory operations and practices. The effectiveness of the conducted procedure changes is evaluated by a verified EU software tool assessing the documentation against the UN SDGs. The implemented open access to a laboratory within a public university promotes the culture of inclusiveness and confirms contribution at micro-level to some of the SDGs like: 9-Industry, innovation and infrastructure, 1-No poverty, 4-Quality Education, 10-Reduced inequalities and 17-Partnerships for the goals (UN SDGs) the quality education.

The long-term performance and the efficiency of the undertaken systematic measures for sustainability, can be evaluated in a periodic time interval, synchronized to the period of regular laboratory management reviews, when most of the laboratory key performance indicators, including the sustainability indicators can be compared and chronologically benchmarked against posed targets. This is also in line with the proposed circular methodology for evaluating the effectiveness of the implemented measures for laboratory sustainability.

References

1. M. Cundeva-Blajer, M. Nakova, S. Cundeva, A contribution to sustainability – Towards green calibration laboratory for electrical instruments, Measurement: Sensors, 101619, (2024) ISSN 2665-9174, https://doi.org/10.1016/j.measen.2024.101619
2. G. Reid, H. Pain Sustainable laboratories-A community-wide movement toward sustainable laboratory practices, Royal Society of Chemistry, (2022), UK, https://www.rsc.org/globalassets/22-new-perspectives/sustainability/sustainable-labs/sustainable-laboratories-report.pdf [accessed 26.02.2025]
3. M. Srbinovska, M. Cundeva-Blajer, Optimization Methods for Energy Consumption Estimation in Wireless Sensor Networks, Journal on Sustainable Development of Energy, Water and Environment Systems, **Vol. 7, Iss. 2**, pp. 261-274, (2019)
4. ISO/IEC 17025, General requirements for the competence of testing and calibration laboratories, International Organization for Standardization, (2017)
5. M. Cundeva-Blajer, Research infrastructure open access approach – Implementation challenges and solutions for accredited calibration laboratories, Measurement: Sensors, 101613, (2024) ISSN 2665-9174, https://doi.org/10.1016/j.measen.2024.101613
6. Horizon Europe, Research and innovation funding programme until 2027, https://research-and-innovation.ec.europa.eu/funding/funding-opportunities/funding-programmes-and-open-calls/horizon-europe_en [accessed 26.02.2025]
7. UNESCO Recommendation on Open Science, United Nations Educational, Scientific and Cultural Organization, 7, place de Fontenoy, 75352 Paris 07 SP, France, (2021) https://unesdoc.unesco.org/ark:/48223/pf0000379949 [accessed 26.02.2025]
8. B. Fecher, G. G. Wagner, Open Access, Innovation and Research Infrastructure, MDPI Publications (2016), 4(2), 17, https://doi.org/10.3390/publications4020017
9. B.M Geronimo, G.G. Lenzi, Maturity Models for Testing and Calibration Laboratories: A Systematic Literature Review, Sustainability 2023, 15, 3480, https://doi.org/10.3390/su15043480
10. https://www.mygreenlab.org/ [accessed 26.02.2025]
11. https://sels-network.org/ [accessed 26.02.2025]
12. T. Freese, R . Kat, S.D. Lanooij, T.C. Böllersen, C.M. De Roo, N. Elzinga, et al. A guidebook for sustainability in laboratories, ChemRxiv. (2024) doi:10.26434/chemrxiv-2023-g3lmq-v3
13. K. Zupancic, T. Pavlek, J. Erjavec, Digital Transformation of the Laboratory - A Practical Guide to the Connected Lab, WILEY-VCH GmbH, (2021)
14. https://knowsdgs.jrc.ec.europa.eu [accessed 26.02.2025]
15. M. Trane, L. Marelli, A. Siragusa, R. Pollo, P. Lombardi, Progress by research to achieve the Sustainable Development Goals in the EU. A Systematic Literature Review, doi:10.3390/su15097055, JRC132860.
16. S. Borchardt, G. Barbero Vignola, D. Buscaglia, M. Maroni, L. Marelli,, Mapping EU Policies with the 2030 Agenda and SDGs, DOI: 10.2760/110687 (online), 10.2760/87754 (print), JRC130904
17. Regulation (EU) 2016/679 of the European Parliament and of the Council of 27 April 2016 on the protection of natural persons with regard to the processing of personal data and on the free movement of such data, and repealing Directive 95/46/EC (GDPR)
18. Regional Cooperation Council, Principals and Guidelines for creating a Policy for Open Access to Research Infrastructures, EU4TECH WB project (2017-2019), RCC Open Access Research Infrastructure in the Western Balkans Support Programme (2020)
19. Faculty of Electrical Engineering and Information Technologies at the Ss. Cyril and Methodius University in Skopje, Mission, Mission Statement, Vision and Strategic Goals, https://feit.ukim.edu.mk/en/about [accessed 26.02.2025]
20. S. Andonov, M. Cundeva-Blajer, FMEA for TCal: Risk Analysis in Compliance to EN ISO/IEC 17025:2017 Requirements, Proc. of 24th IMEKO TC4 International Symposium 22nd International Workshop on ADC and DAC Modelling and Testing IMEKO TC-4 2020 Palermo, Italy, September 14-16, (2020), pp. 222-227

Metrological characterisation of low-cost and wearable sensors for research on healthy buildings in a novel Living Laboratory

Francesca Rolle [1*], *Fabio* Favoino[2], *Giuseppina* Arcamone[2], *Anna* Pellegrino[2], *Ramona* Russo[1,2], *Paola* Iacomussi[1], *Chiara* Musacchio[1], Alberto Bottacin[1], *Stefano* Pavarelli[1], *Andrea* Prato[1], *Alessandro* Schiavi[1], and *Michela* Sega[1]

[1]INRiM, Istituto Nazionale di Ricerca Metrologica, 10135 Torino, Italy
[2]Department of Energy, Politecnico di Torino, 10129 Torino, Italy

Abstract. To achieve the EU targets in terms of ecological transition, and to assure people health, wellbeing and comfort in the indoor environment, research in the building sector plays a fundamental role. In the last decades the energy efficiency and indoor environmental quality (IEQ) of buildings have increased significantly, but a gap between the actual operational performances of sensors and the expected measurement results and still exists. The Italian project "MIRABLE - Measurement Infrastructure for Research on heAlthy and zero energy Buildings in novel Living lab Ecosystems", carried out in cooperation between the Italian National Metrology Institute, INRiM, and the Polytechnic University of Torino, aims to develop a methodology to reduce this gap by creating and validating a measurement infrastructure for monitoring the multi-domain indoor environmental conditions and the occupants' interaction in a full scale Living Laboratory (denominated "H-IEQ LL"). The final goal of the research is to support the realisation of healthy and smart buildings and to reduce energy use. Among the activities of the MIRABLE project, the development of methodologies for defining a ground-truth for low-grade and wearable sensors for IEQ measurements in ongoing. After a thorough analysis of the sensors available on the market, and of the best practices to monitor the occupants' comfort and interaction with buildings, a set of sensors were selected and metrologically characterised for the four domains on interest for the H-IEQ LL: thermal conditions, lighting conditions (spectral distribution included), acoustic conditions and indoor air quality. The monitoring of the response of the occupants to these variables, by means of low-cost sensors mounted on fixed monitoring stations in the LL and of wearable sensors, will allow to evaluate their feedbacks and interaction with the building systems in a dynamic mode. An overview of the results obtained from the metrological characterisation of IEQ sensors carried out at INRiM, and the preliminary calibration for some of the measured variables (e.g. temperature, sound pressure, CO_2 level, lighting), are presented in this work. The sensors will be installed in the LL, to create a sensor network for multi-domain monitoring of the physical environment and some wearable sensors will be used to monitor the occupant related quantities in a well-controlled environment. A methodology for the sensors *in situ* use, data collection and periodic calibration is also under definition.

1 Introduction

Office workers spend an average of 8.5 h in indoor environments [1]. Indoor environment conditions have a great influence on occupants' health, feeling and work productivity [2]. The World Health Organization (WHO) has demonstrated that approximately 30 % of employees experience a level of discomfort that results in a significant decrease in productivity [3].

In this context, Indoor Environmental Quality (IEQ) is a relative measure of comfort perception by people exposed to the indoor conditions [4]. The parameters for the design and assessment of the energy performance of buildings and IEQ cover indoor air quality, thermal environment, lighting and acoustics [5]. IEQ is evaluated using two strategies: Post Occupancy Evaluation (POE) and instrumental measurements [6]. The data collected by the instrument are treated as an objective assessment of the subjective evaluation made by the POE [6]. The interaction between IEQ parameters is characterized by significant variability in both space and time, due to the complex nature of these parameters [7]. Consequently, there is an increased focus on the utilization and development of instruments for measuring these parameters, which vary in type and quantity for each domain.

A number of recent studies have demonstrated the potential of low-cost instruments [8, 9, 10] and wearable devices [11, 12, 13] for monitoring IEQ, with the notable advantage of costing up to three orders of magnitude less than standard reference instruments [14]. Low-cost sensors used for measurements often have lower and more questionable data quality than the official monitoring stations conducted by EU Member States in accordance with European legislation and international standards methods at this stage of development [15]. However, low cost sensors are poorly characterized and the lack of standardized validation

* Corresponding author: f.rolle@inrim.it

methods for this systems is a significant obstacle to the market's orderly expansion [16]. Some of the most innovative research involves multi-sensors [17, 18], which attempt to integrate as many sensors as possible into a single instrument to capture environmental parameters that affect user comfort. It is clear that the variety and amount of these data make the development of such instruments a complex and necessarily multidisciplinary research process.

2 MIRABLE Project

Among the Research Projects of Relevant National Interest (PRIN) 2022 is the MIRABLE project - Measurement Infrastructure for Research on heAlthy and zero energy Buildings in novel Living lab Ecosystems", carried out in cooperation between the Italian National Metrology Institute, INRiM, and the Polytechnic University of Torino. The project aims to develop a measurement infrastructure for research on healthy and zero-energy buildings, focusing on the characterization of low-cost and wearable sensors within a Living Lab (LL) ecosystem. This project seeks to bridge the gap between expected and actual building performance by incorporating multi-domain studies of indoor environmental quality (IEQ) and occupant interaction.

The project will establish a methodology for monitoring various aspects of IEQ, including thermal comfort, acoustics, lighting and indoor air quality (IAQ) to understand their interactions and effects on occupants. This holistic approach contrasts with existing studies that often focus on single domains. The future monitor Living Lab (LL) will involve people in both monitoring and innovation, creating a real-life environment for research into IEQ and occupant behaviour, as well as advanced building technologies.

MIRABLE also emphasises the inclusion of the occupants as sensors. This involves the use of wearable sensors to both the environmental parameters that influence the occupant's comfort and some "human" parameters that provide immediate feedback on the human perception of the environment. A core objective is to define, calibrate, and test both static and wearable sensors to ensure reliable data. This includes developing metrological characterization protocols and ensuring traceability to national standards. This addresses the challenge of using low-cost sensors and wearable devices by developing a framework to define, calibrate and test them.

3 Low-Cost and Wearable Sensors for each domain

The European standard EN 15251:2007 [5] specifies indoor environmental parameters that have an impact on the energy performance of buildings, without directly considering occupant comfort and calibration method of instruments. The standard deals in detail with the thermal environment, acoustics, lighting and indoor air quality. The research therefore followed the same division of study areas, each of which is discussed in more detail in the following paragraphs.

3.1 Thermal domain

Air temperature is one of the environmental parameters contributing to the evaluation of the IEQ. However, sensors of different type, shown in Fig. 1, are included in the characterization protocol because an effective estimation of thermal comfort not only requires the knowledge of the environmental temperature, but also the study of correlations with the skin temperature of the occupant. Therefore, board mount thermometers will be characterized for the measurement of air temperature, whereas a wearable sensor and different infrared cameras will be test for the measurement of the occupant skin temperature.

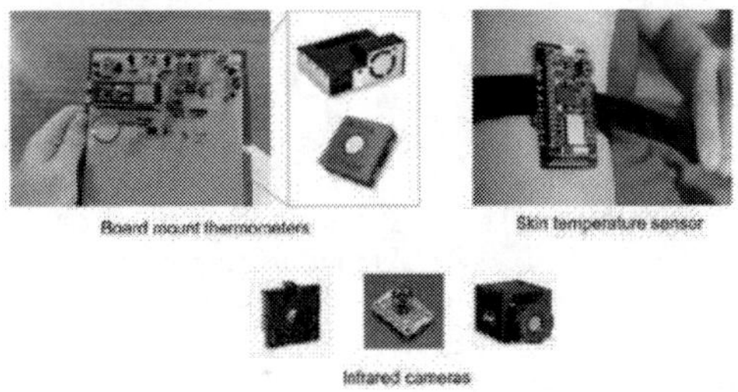

Fig. 1. Low-cost sensors under characterization for the thermal domain.

3.1.1 Board mount thermometers

Low-cost board mount thermometers can come in different design and working principles depending on the manufacturer. However, the accuracy of these sensors not only depends on the production quality or manufacturer calibration, but it can be mainly dependent on the position on the board, which should be optimized to reduce the influence of unwanted heat sources. Moreover, the coupling between the sensor and the medium of interest (air) should also be enhanced, as for example in Fig. 1 where a low-cost sensor is exposed to air by mounting it vertically.

Having in mind such design considerations, a batch of board mount thermometers will be characterized in a climatic chamber using reference Pt100 traceable to the ITS-90 (Fig. 2) to test their accuracy and production variability. During the characterization some sensors will be moved in different positions on the board prototype to check the influence of heat sources from other electronic components. After a year of full operation, it is planned to re-characterized the sensors to verify their stability and reliability over time.

The range of air temperature for the tests will be from 15 to 35 °C

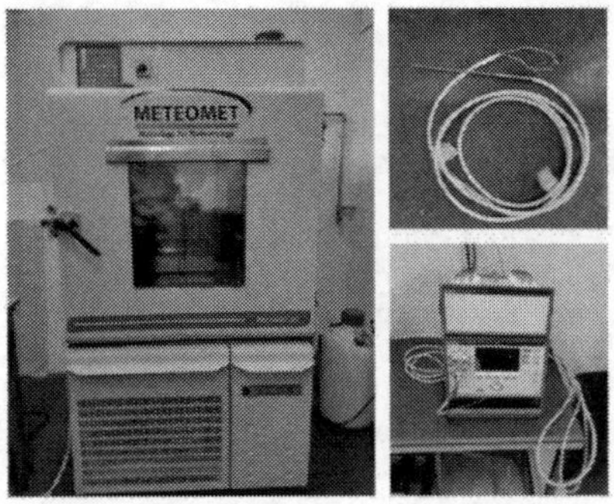

Fig. 2. INRiM laboratory setup: on the right the Kambic climatic chamber, whereas on the left the reference Pt100 and the Fluke DAQ temperature scanner.

3.1.2 Wearable skin thermometer and infrared cameras

The thermodynamic state of a wearable skin thermometer changes for two main causes: the heat conduction between the sensor and the skin and the convective heat transfer with the air. To characterize the behaviour of a wearable skin thermometer is therefore necessary the use of a controlled surface temperature source. The setup should be placed in a climatic chamber to increase the representativeness of the procedure and verify the influence of the environment on the sensor.

Based on the equipment available at INRiM laboratory, a surface temperature source will be obtained by circulating demineralized water of a thermostatic bath inside an aluminium box (Fig. 3). The developed system will be characterized by estimating the surface temperature using calibrated mini Pt100, and evaluating stability and uniformity of the surface. The wearable sensor will be placed on the surface for the characterization by comparison with the surface temperature estimated by the mini Pt100. This setup satisfies the accuracy required for the intended use, being also compatible with the use in a climatic chamber and allows to analyse the behaviour under different combinations of surface/skin and environmental temperatures.

Sensors will be tested in a range of temperature between 25 and 37 °C for ambient condition between 15 and 35 °C.

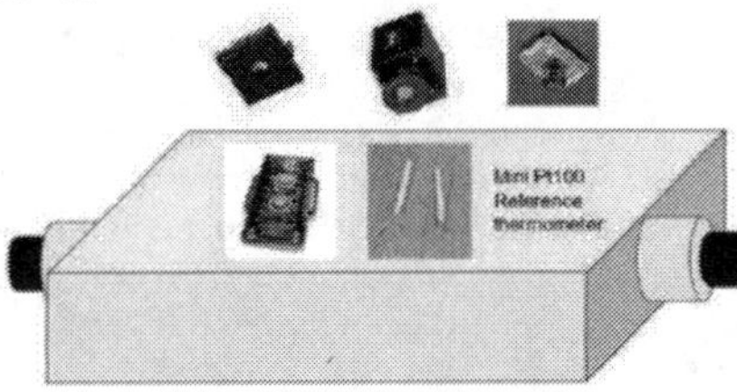

Fig. 3. Controlled surface temperature source for characterization of skin thermometers and tests of infrared cameras.

Exploiting the developed system, it is also possible to test low-cost infrared cameras. In principle, the characterization of these sensors requires high-grade equipment such as blackbody calibrators. However, having a stable surface temperature with an estimated homogeneity, it is possible to test the measurement repeatability of the cameras, the pixel-homogeneity, but also check their stability in the short and medium term.

3.2 Acoustic domain

The application of MEMS technology to acoustic sensors has led to the development of small and low-cost microphones with very high performance. MEMS microphones are fabricated on semiconductor production lines using silicon wafers and highly automated processes. Nevertheless, at present day, current standards do not provide adequate procedures for calibrating this kind of sensors, due to geometric limitations and other incompatibilities. The consequence is that reliability of data provided by MEMS microphone is not supported by uncertainty budget and traceability statement, being a relevant obstacle for safe and accurate implementations.

The characterization of the MEMS microphone (STM Model MP34DT05-DS) was carried out starting from the IEC 61094-5 standard [19], which provides a calibration method for comparison with standard laboratory microphones. This method consists of placing two microphones, the reference one and the one under test, at close distance (≤ 1 mm), facing the membranes of the two microphones in a sound pressure field. The detailed description can be found in [20]. By measuring the MEMS output voltage, the various acoustic parameters were obtained. Sensitivity, frequency response, stability, signal-to-noise ratio and distortion were measured in a semi-anechoic chamber. To measure the variation of sensitivity with temperature, the two microphones were placed in a small climate chamber, using a horn speaker as a source.

Fig. 4. The MEMS microphone and the reference microphone in a semi-anechoic chamber.

To evaluate the sensitivity and frequency response, pure tones from 20 Hz to 5 kHz with 1/3 octave step were generated for about 30 seconds, as shown in Fig 5.

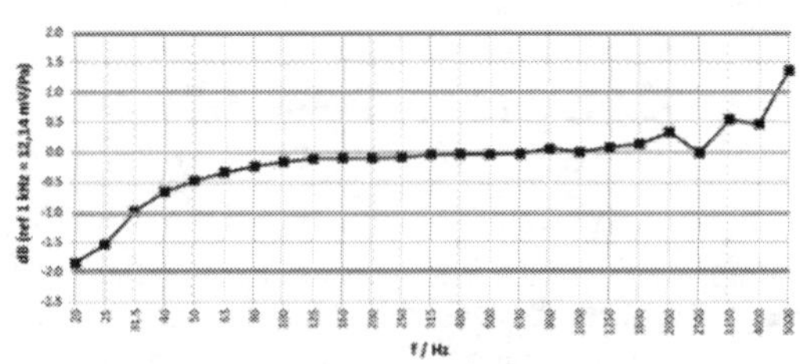

Fig. 5. Frequency response of the MEMS microphone

The measured sensitivity of the MEMS microphone is 12.14 mV/Pa (-38.32 dB, ref 1 V/Pa), at 1000 Hz. In

Fig. 5, the graph shows the frequency response of the MEMS microphone, normalized with respect to 1000 Hz and compared with the Sound Level Meter limits for Class 1 (green) and Class 2 (red).

The stability was measured using a pure tone at 1000 Hz for a period of 140 minutes. In particular, there is an increase of 0.1 dB in 813 seconds, an increase of 0.2 dB in 2030 seconds and an increase of 0.3 dB in 5095 seconds.

The measured internal noise of the reference microphone and the measurement chain was 17.5 dBA, while for the MEMS microphone 32.9 dBA were measured. In this case, A-weighting was used to eliminate the contribution of ambient noise due to low frequencies. This resulted in a S/N ratio of 61.1 dB (reference set to 94 dB).

For the measurement of distortion (THD), a 1000 Hz sinusoid was generated at 1 dB intervals starting from 110 dB up to 125 dB. Compared to the signal measured with the reference microphone whose distortion, below 140 dB, is completely negligible, a THD of 0.8% at 121 dB, 3.8% at 122 dB and 9.7% at 124 dB was obtained.

3.3 Lighting domain

The knowledge of individual light exposure plays a crucial role on studies on human health and wellbeing, especially since the discovery of photosensitive retinal ganglion cells (ipRGCs) having nonvisual effects on human release of various neurotransmitters and hormones (e.g. sleep / wake pattern) [21]. In addition, even the level and spectral distributions of light seem having effects on brain health [22] and eyesight defects (e.g. myopia) [23]. Low-cost, portable spectrometers capable of measuring the spectral power distributions of light sources and ad hoc wearable sensors are available on the market. They can capture spectral power density data in the visible and nearer ranges (near IR, blue light) and by using the tabulated ipRGCs spectral sensitivity functions stated in CIE S026:2018 report [24], calculate the relevant α-opic irradiances.

3.3.1 Preliminary tests

The first tests have been carried out on 14 LYS wearable sensor and one nano-Lambda miniaturized portable spectrometer. The tested quantities were illuminance, melanopic irradiance and Correlated Colour Temperature (CCT). Melanopic irradiance is crucial for understanding key impact of light on human well-being, monitoring IEQ and designing circadian friendly lighting. The sensors have been tested at different irradiance levels (from 3 lx up to 14 klx), CCT (3000 K, 4000 K, 6000 K) by exposing the sensors for short and long time to light (1 minute up to 3 hours). Further test will include PWM sensitivity and stress tests by cycling exposure to dark and light set-up. Preliminary results showed large discrepancies among the different LYS sensors and reference instruments (variable from 4% up to 30%, depending on the quantity of interest) and investigations are on the way because influences of LED flicker is supposed to explain discrepancies. Further tests will include PWM sensitivity and stress tests by cycling exposure to dark and light set-up.

3.4 Indoor Air Quality domain

Indoor Air Pollutant (IAP) is a generic acronym, including several categories of pollutants, including inorganic compounds (ICs) such as carbon monoxide (CO), carbon dioxide (CO_2), nitrogen oxides (NO_x) and ozone (O_3), among others [25].

The primary sources of CO, SO_2 and NO_2 in residential environments are the combustion process in gas stoves and woodstoves [25].

The main source of indoor CO_2 are combustion reactions during household activities and from human metabolism [25]. Metabolic CO_2 released by respiration has a major impact on the overall CO_2 concentration in office environments and transportation vehicles [25].

Various regulations and standards define acceptable CO_2 concentration levels for the design of ventilation systems in buildings. The European Standard EN 13779:2008 [26] sets the minimum indoor air guideline value (IAGV) for CO_2 at 800 ppm_v. In the United States, the Occupational Safety and Health Administration (OSHA) has established a Permissible Exposure Limit (PEL) for CO_2 at 5000 ppm_v averaged over an 8-hour workday [27].

3.4.1 Preliminary tests

The first activities carried out at INRiM in the IAQ framework within the MIRABLE project were focused on CO and CO_2, due to their importance as indoor air pollutants and their adverse health effects attributable to accumulation in indoor spaces. The first tests were carried out on a pair of low-cost CO sensor (model MQ-7, HANWEI ELECTRONICS CO., LTD., China).

The MQ-7 gas sensor is composed of a sensitive material, SnO_2, which exhibits reduced conductivity in clean air. The sensor detects CO in the presence of low temperatures (heated by 1.5 V), utilising method of cycle of high and low temperatures [28]. The sensor's conductivity increases in proportion to the gas concentration. It is necessary to utilise a simple electrocircuit to transform the change of conductivity into a corresponding output signal of gas concentration. In this instance, an Arduino board was employed, with specific programming.

In this study, two sensors of the same type were utilised. According to the technical datasheet [28], the initial stabilisation time required a minimum of 48 hours. The MQ-7_02 sensor had been activated in the days prior to the experimental trials for the purpose of conducting preventative analyses.

Figure 6 shows the short-term stability of the two sensors, MQ-7_01 and MQ-7_02, from the moment they were activated. It is evident that the MQ-7_01 sensor demonstrates greater stability than the MQ-7_02 sensor, which was previously warmed up before use. In addition, the MQ-7_02 sensor attained stability in a shorter time compared to the MQ-7_01 sensor. This occurrence can be attributed to the fact that the MQ-

7_02 sensor had previously been activated. The two data were then normalized, following the indications in the technical data sheet.

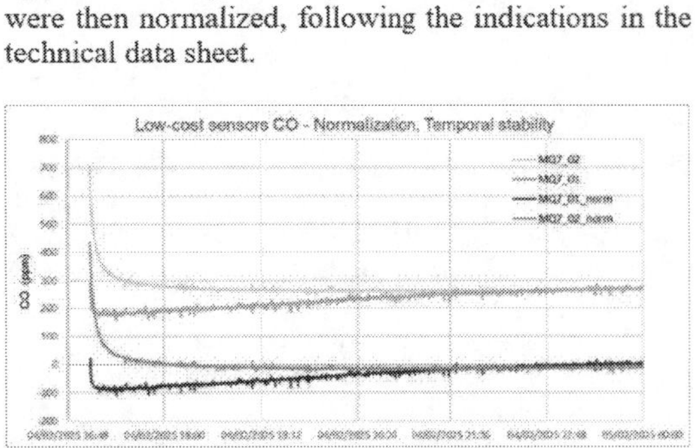

Fig. 6. Test on temporal stability of two CO low-cost sensors, namely MQ-7_01 and MQ-7_02.

Subsequently, the sensors were tested for their response time. The sensors were exposed to a source of smoke, containing CO, using a sheet of paper that was incinerated near the sensors. The response time of the sensors was investigated by repeatedly switching on and off the paper fire, and the results suggest that the sensors respond immediately, with a response time of few seconds.

3.4.2 Procedure for calibration of CO_2 and CO low-cost sensors

At INRiM, a procedure for the calibration of low-cost sensors (CO_2 and CO, but adaptable also to other analytes, e.g. nitrogen oxides) was developed. The system for the calibration of the sensors comprises an *ad hoc* climatic chamber (realised by Montepaone S.r.l., Italy), in which the sensors can be housed, with their corresponding Arduino microcontroller. The chamber can be evacuated and then filled with gas mixtures of CO_2 or CO at known composition, by using a system of mass-flow controllers (MFC) and a small dilution chamber. Certified reference gas mixtures are connected to one of the gas lines and diluted with a proper pure gas (either nitrogen 6.0 grade or synthetic air) to the final target concentration). The climatic chamber is then connected to a non-dispersive infrared analyser (NDIR, ABB model URAS 14, Switzerland), equipped with different measurement channels selective for CO_2 and CO, to allow the verification of the concentration of the mixtures filling the climatic chamber, and to compare the response of the low-cost sensors with a high-quality laboratory instrument.

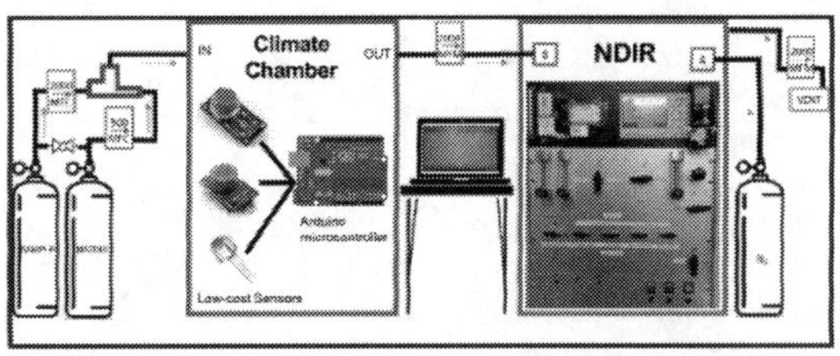

Fig. 7. Schematic representation of the INRiM set-up for the calibration of CO_2 and CO low-cost sensors.

In figure 7, the schematic representation of the system realised at INRiM for the characterisation and calibration of CO_2 and CO low-cost sensors is represented.

4 Conclusion

In summary, the aim of the project is to define, realise and demonstrate the effectiveness of a methodology for multi-domain research to be implemented in Living Labs, including the measurement of physical variables related to IAQ, thermal, lighting and acoustic environments, and the collection of non-physical data related to the occupant, their responses and interactions. The main outcome of the project will be the design and implementation of a working model for Living Labs dedicated to research on healthy and energy efficient buildings. In particular, a metrologically calibrated measurement infrastructure with high and/or low-grade sensors for monitoring the whole physical environment through static and dynamic measurements (wearable sensors for occupant related measurements) will be set-up. A very important part is the definition of measurement procedures and protocols for both environmental sensors and personal (wearable) sensors to ensure appropriate data sampling for each domain without compromising the realistic aspect of the environment.

Acknowledgment

The MIRABLE Project was funded by the Italian PIANO NAZIONALE DI RIPRESA E RESILIENZA (PNRR) - Missione 4 "Istruzione e Ricerca" - Componente C2 Investimento 1.1, "Fondo per il Programma Nazionale di Ricerca e Progetti di Rilevante Interesse Nazionale (PRIN)" Decreto Direttoriale n. 104 del 2 febbraio 2022. Progetto PRIN 2022 «MIRABLE – Measurement Infrastructure for Research on heAlthy and zero energy Buildings in novel Living lab Ecosystems» Codice di progetto: 2022ZNJHHY.

References

1. V. Surawattanasakul, W. Sirikul, R. Sapbamrer, K. Wangsan, J. Panumasvivat, P. Assavanopakun, S. Muangkaew, Respiratory Symptoms and Skin Sick Building Syndrome among Office Workers at University Hospital, Chiang Mai, Thailand: Associations with Indoor Air Quality, AIRMED Project, Int. J. Environ. Res. Public Health **19**, 17, 10850, (2022). https://doi.org/10.3390/ijerph191710850
2. J. Wu, J. Weng, B. Xia, Y. Zhao, Q. Song, he Synergistic Effect of PM2.5 and CO2 Concentrations on Occupant Satisfaction and Work Productivity in a Meeting Room, Int. J. Environ. Res. Public. Health. **18**, 4109 (2021). https://doi.org/10.3390/ijerph18084109
3. World Health Organization, World Health Organization eds: Indoor air quality: biological contaminants: report on a WHO meeting, Rautavaara, 29 August-2 September 1988. World Health Organization, Regional Office for Europe, Copenhagen, 67, (1990).

4. M. Piasecki, K. Kostyrko, S. Pykacz, Indoor environmental quality assessment: Part 1: Choice of the indoor environmental quality sub-component models, J. Build. Phys. **41**, 264 (2017). https://doi.org/10.1177/1744259117702882

5. EN 15251:2007 - UNI Ente Italiano di Normazione, (2017).

6. I. Mujan, A. S. Anđelković, V. Munćan, M. Kljajić, D. Ružić, Influence of indoor environmental quality on human health and productivity - A review, J. Clean. Prod. **217**, 646 (2019). https://doi.org/10.1016/j.jclepro.2019.01.307

7. T. Parkinson, A. Parkinson, R. de Dear, Continuous IEQ monitoring system: Context and development, Build. Environ. **149**, 15 (2019). https://doi.org/10.1016/j.buildenv.2018.12.010

8. G. Coulby, A. K. Clear, O. Jones, A. Godfrey, Low-cost, multimodal environmental monitoring based on the Internet of Things, Build. Environ. **203**, (2021). https://doi.org/10.1016/j.buildenv.2021.108014

9. M. Kim, H. Zhang, A. Tzempelikos, A. Gasparella, F. Cappelletti, New Low-Cost Sensing Network for Indoor Environmental Monitoring and Control in Buildings., 41st AIVC/ASHRAE IAQ- 9th TightVent - 7th venticool Conference - Athens, Greece - 4-6 May 2022, (2023).

10. M. Gola, A. Laghezza,Y. Yu, G. Settimo, S. Capolongo, How to promote health in indoor living and working spaces: quali-quantitative analysis to evaluate the indoor air quality through users' perception and low-cost sensors. Eur. J. Public Health. **34**, ckae144.491 (2024). https://doi.org/10.1093/eurpub/ckae144.491

11. B. Abboushi, S. Safranek, E. Rodriguez-Feo Bermudez, S. Pratoomratana, Y. Chen, M. Poplawski, R. Davis, A Review of the Use of Wearables in Indoor Environmental Quality Studies and an Evaluation of Data Accessibility from a Wearable Device., Front. Built Environ. **8**, (2022). https://doi.org/10.3389/fbuil.2022.787289

12. F. Salamone, S. Sibilio, M. Masullo, Integrated Approach for Human Wellbeing and Environmental Assessment Based on a Wearable IoT System: A Pilot Case Study in Singapore., Sensors. **24**, 6126 (2024). https://doi.org/10.3390/s24186126

13. M. Kong, J. An, D. Jung, T. Hong, Occupant-centered indoor environmental quality management: Physiological response measuring methods., Build. Environ. **243**, 110661 (2023). https://doi.org/10.1016/j.buildenv.2023.110661

14. L. Morawska, P. K. Thai, X. Liu, A. Asumadu-Sakyi, G. Ayoko, A. Bartonova, A. Bedini, F. Chai, B. Christensen, M. Dunbabin, J. Gao, G. S. W. Hagler, R. Jayaratne, P. Kumar, A. K. H. Lau, P. K. K. Louie, M. Mazaheri, Z. Ning, N. Motta, B. Mullins, M. M. Rahman, Z. Ristovski, M. Shafiei, D. Tjondronegoro, D. Westerdahl, R. Williams, Applications of low-cost sensing technologies for air quality monitoring and exposure assessment: How far have they gone? Environ. Int. **116**, 286 (2018). https://doi.org/10.1016/j.envint.2018.04.018

15. Measuring air pollution with low-cost sensors Thoughts on the quality of data measured by sensors, European Commission, JRC, (2017).

16. Pioneering next-generation air quality monitoring by metrological validationof low-cost particulate matter sensor, Euramet, Call 2023.

17. T. Parkinson, A. Parkinson, R. de Dear, Introducing the SAMBA indoor environmental quality monitoring system., 49th International Conference of the Architectural Science Association (2015).

18. A. Barbaro, P. Chiavassa, V. I. Fissore, A. Servetti, E. Raviola, G. Ramírez-Espinosa,E. Giusto, B. Montrucchio, A. Astolfi, F. Fiori, Data Acquisition, Processing, and Aggregation in a Low-Cost IoT System for Indoor Environmental Quality Monitoring. Appl. Sci. **14**, 4021 (2024). https://doi.org/10.3390/app14104021

19. IEC 61094-5:2001, Measurement microphones - Part 5: Methods for pressure calibration of working standard microphones by comparison. Available: https://webstore.iec.ch/en/publication/4489 (Accessed 20 Feb. 2025)

20. A. Prato, N. Montali, C. Guglielmone, A. Schiavi., Pressure calibration of a digital microelectromechanical system microphone by comparison, J. Acoust. Soc. Am. **144(4)**:EL297-EL303 (2018)

21. D. M. Dacey, H.W. Liao, B.B. Peterson, F.R. Robinson, V.C. Smith, J. Pokorny, K.W. Yau, P.D. Gamlin., Melanopsin-expressing ganglion cells in primate retina signal colour and irradiance and project to the LGN. Nature. **433**,749–754 (2025). doi: 10.1038/nature03387

22. K. A. Mazurek, L. Li, R.J. Klein, S. Rong, A. F. Mullan, D. T. Jones, E. K. St. Louis, G. A. Worrell, C. Y. Chen., Investigating the effects of indoor lighting on measures of brain health in older adults: protocol for a cross-over randomized controlled trial. BMC Geriatr 24, 816 (2024). https://doi.org/10.1186/s12877-023-04594-7

23. A. N. French, R.S. Ashby, I.G. Morgan, K.A. Rose, Time outdoors and the prevention of myopia. Exp. Eye Res. **114**, 58–68 (2013). doi: 10.1016/j.exer.2013.04.018

24. Commission International de l'Éclairage. CIE S 026/E:2018 System for Metrology of Optical Radiation for ipRGC-Influenced Responses to Light. Vienna: CIE, (2018).

25. L. R. López, P. Dessì, A. Cabrera-Codony, L. Rocha-Melongo, B. Kraakman, V. Naddeo, M. D. Balaguer, S. Puig, CO2 in indoor environments: From environmental and health risk to potential renewable carbon source, Sci. Total environ. **859** (2023). http://dx.doi.org/10.1016/j.scitotenv.2022.159088

26. UNI EN 13779:2008, Ventilation for non-residential buildings - Performance requirements for ventilation and room-conditioning systems. https://webstore.uni.com/en/uni-en-13779-2008

27. OSHA, Carbon Dioxide in Workplace atmospheres. Available: https://www.osha.gov/sites/default/files/methods/osha-id172.pdf (Accessed 24 Feb. 2025).

28. MQ-7 Semiconductor Sensor for Carbon Monoxide, Datasheet. Available: https://www.pololu.com/file/0j313/mq7.pdf (Accessed 24 Feb. 2025).

EPJ Web of Conferences **323**, 0100(25051)
22nd nIt enr Iai nr dMt Iei a gylCi nget ss
https://doi.org/(0.(01(/epjconf/50513530100(

Estimating the repeatability and reproducibility of an AI-embedded measuring device: application to road markings

Térence Bordet[1*], *Maxime* Redondin[1], *Stefan* Bornhofen[2], *Sébastien* Denaës[1] *Aymeric* Histace[2]

[1]CORE Center by COLAS, Data Science Digital Road Inspection and Material, 4 rue Jean Mermoz, F-78114, Magny-Les-Hameaux
[2] ETIS UMR 8051, Cergy Paris University, ENSEA, CNRS, F-95000, Cergy, France

Abstract. The road markings inspection using on-board cameras is gaining popularity, particularly for road inspection, despite most research focusing on autonomous vehicles. Traditional inspection methods rely on costly equipment like RetroTek-D, resulting in infrequent inspections. Recent advancements in artificial intelligence offer a more cost-effective solution, enabling the use of standard cameras with AI models for continuous road marking detection. While metrics such as F1-score evaluate AI performance, they do not ensure effectiveness on new sites or account for uncertainty in AI applications. Once deployed, AI systems may not adapt to new data, necessitating retraining for any updates. This paper proposes a method to estimate the repeatability and reproducibility of AI-based measurement devices, drawing inspiration from ISO 5725 standards, to enhance their reliability in road marking detection.

1 Introduction

A road marking material is a painting on the pavement with injected glass microbeads to ensure good nighttime visibility [1]. Beads reflect the light emitted by vehicle's headlights back to the driver. This phenomenon is called retroreflection and is measured by retroreflectometer such as RetroTek-D. The quantity of retroreflected light is expressed in mcd/m²/lx. This process checks if a given line respects a minimal service and current marking durability models are based on this method [2]. However, this operation is expensive and do not allow for more regular inspections than once a year.

Since the 90's [3], the main alternative has been an on-board camera inspection. This solution is less expensive but is not fully industrialized. Main obstacles are the need for a reliable algorithm that can detect lines and define a measure of their deterioration. The first is resolved since the 2010s, thanks to the development of driving aids partially based on the detection of road markings to define traffic lanes [4], [5]. The second is still an issue but two main solutions are proposed: to photograph a marking and given to assessors [6] or an AI [7] for them to evaluate the deterioration; to estimate the contrast between pavement and marking [8]. However, these solutions are still not industrialized and are dependent of environmental conditions.

Our final objective is to propose a full framework to ensure the proper use of marking inspection assisted by an on-board camera under the widest range of environmental conditions possible. The first step is to define the visibility geometry of the road, the type of deployable camera and the AI family useful for marking detection for road inspection purposes only. Following the current standards, the geometry defined is EN 1436, which establishes the markings visibility model for a driver. For the couple of cameras and AI, we need a method for detecting road markings.

This point is a widely researched field thanks to the development of autonomous vehicles. A good amount of traditional image processing approaches was and is still used to detect road markings [4], but in the last ten years, deep learning methods have revolutionized the field [5], to a point where road markings detection is today almost exclusively working with AI.

Measuring the robustness of an AI is not fully established. Main performance scores announced, such as the F1-score, are calculated from its test dataset. It is composed by chosen images supposedly representative of roads. Concretely, if an AI is trained on images taken in Sri Lanka [9], then is this AI still reliable on French roads? If not, is there an AI model capable of adapting to French roads based on a Sri Lanka dataset? Even assuming that the performance score is unbiased and certain, there is no way of knowing whether a randomly selected road will show this performance. Concretely, even if an AI shows a 90% probability of correctly detecting a line, this doesn't mean that 90% of lines on any given road will be detected. For a road maintenance company such as COLAS, it is important to have a procedure at the end of any inspection campaign to measure a valid performance score for this campaign.

To answer these questions, this paper introduces a combination of AI analysis approaches and metrological control of measurements. Our method uses the principles of the round-robin test to determine the repeatability and reproducibility of our AI-embedded measuring device. To use the round-robin test, we readapt important metrological elements to adapt them to our experiment, and we collect our own data on a specific road track, that will later be sampled using the Cochran sampling method and analyzed using an analyze of variance (ANOVA).

* Corresponding author: terence.bordet@colas.com

2 Related Work

2.1 Metrological standard and AI objectives

The method searches to respect ISO 5725-1:2023 [10].

Repeatability is the fidelity under repeatability conditions. Repeatability conditions are conditions where independent test results are obtained by the same method on identical test or measurement individuals on the same test or measurement facility, by the same operator, using the same equipment and over a short time interval.[10].

Reproducibility is the fidelity under reproducibility conditions. Reproducibility conditions are conditions where independent test results are obtained by the same method on identical test or measurement individuals on different test or measurement facilities with different operators and using different equipment.[10]

Although many types exist, AI models only categorize lines as continuous or discontinuous at best and can't specify the line type. Only continuous lines or discontinuous lines are considered as lines and should be detected by AI models.

2.2 Selected artificial intelligence models

An AI model efficiency is deeply tied to the dataset it is trained with. An appropriate dataset is required to build any AI-based application. A same model can behave differently depending on the dataset it was trained on. In this article, we define an AI as a couple of a model and a dataset.

YOLO is introduced in 2015 by Redmon *et al* [11]. It is an innovative single-staged object detection deep convolutional neural network (CNN). It became popular because of its high speed and detection accuracy, while being open source. YOLO divide the image into a grid of same sized cells. Each grid cell predicts several bounding boxes and a set of class probabilities, the latter regardless of the number of predicted boxes. The grid cell in which the center of an object fall is responsible for detecting that object. Doing detection and classification in one go, while reframing object detection as a regression problem enable YOLO to reach enough speed to be a real-time object detector. Today, YOLO is a collection of algorithms evolving and getting better at each iteration. Each iteration enhances the previous one, using lot of improvements like better backbone, better loss functions or better architectural design. Yolov8 can be used has a solid solution to detect road markings [5], [12] In this article, we use YOLOv8.

U-Net is introduced in 2015 by Ronneberger *et al* [13]. It is a two-sided, multi-layer fully CNN model aiming to segment biomedical images. The first side is the encoding part, known as contracting path. It is a succession of double-convolution and max pooling, used to extract features and contextual information while decreasing the spatial resolution. Each convolution results on this side will be used layer as skip connection. The second side is the decoding part, known as expansive path. It consists of a succession of double-convolution and up-convolution, reducing the number of features at each up-convolution. Skip connections are used to help the decoding part locate the features in the image. The final part of U-Net is a simple 1x1 convolution. The resulting output is a mask composed of a pixel-level classes annotation. In the biomedical field, it can be a mask locating cancerous tumors, as an example. U-Net as demonstrated such performance that it is used as a general segmentation algorithm, beyond the biomedical field. On the road, it has been used to segment road markings [5], [14]. In this article, we use U-Net to segment line-type road markings.

SCNN is introduced in 2017 by X. Pan *et al* [15]. It is a specifically designed CNN structure to more effectively learn spatial relationships of lane markings. Unlike traditional CNN, which are built using convolutional operations layer by layer, the SCNN propose a slice-by-slice convolutional method inside the feature map. The feature map is a 3D tensor of dimension C x H x W. Spatial operation separate this tensor into slices. There are four spatial operations: down, up, right, left. For example, the down spatial operation split the tensor into H slices, and each slice is sent into a convolution layer of C kernels, where the result is stored into the next slice. By doing these spatial operations, spatial coherence is reinforced and allow message to pass between pixels. SCNN demonstrate solid results in lane marking detection. In this article, we use it to detect line-type road markings.

Hough transform is introduced in 1962 by Hough, is a feature extraction method used to find simple shape in image, such as straight lines, circles or ellipses. While not being an AI model, the Hough transform is a very popular computer vision and image processing method, especially in the field of autonomous vehicle and road marking detection [4], [16]. Because line-type road markings are often straight or slightly incurved in most situations, a simple Hough transform may be enough to enable the accurate detection of road lanes detection. With good pre-processing techniques, the Hough transform can detect even the border of the road to more precisely detect lane even when there is no road marking, while still being way less computationally heavy than any AI alternative. In fact, a simple Hough transform can solve the lane detection problem in 90% of the highway cases [4], [17]. The remaining 10% are due to various issues like road illumination, shadows, rain, fog or glare for example [4]. In this article, we use a simple Hough transform to detect line-type road markings and observe how it behaves in various non-highway situations, compared to AI models.

2.3 Datasets

Training an AI model require a large amount of data, especially on the field of road marking detection due to the vast amount of different scenarios possible and the large number of different objects a driver or autonomous vehicle may encounter. Many road scene datasets have been created in the past, and for this experiment we chose three of them.

Mapillary [18] is a large dataset of 25,000 high-resolution street-level images dataset. It contains 100 instance categories and 124 semantic objects categories, covering different road instances across six continents. Images contains every possible condition, including different daytime, weather conditions, cameras and viewpoint. It is a very complete streetscape dataset. An example of an AI trained by Mapillary is [19].

Tusimple [20] is a dataset of 6,408 road images of US highways. It annotates lane-marking under various lighting conditions and different levels of occlusion. The resolution of Tusimple images is 1280x720. An example of an AI trained with Tusimple is [21].

CULane [22] is a dataset of 133,235 streetscape images located in Beijing and including various lightning and weather conditions. In addition, CULane reference eight lane scenarios: normal, crowded, night, no line, shadow, arrow, dazzle light, curve and crossroad. X.Pan is the reference example [15].

3 Method

Our goal is to determine a F1-score which corresponds more to the reality, while estimating the repeatability and the reproducibility of our AI-embedded measuring device, in our case, a camera. To achieve this, we create variation in our measuring system, in our measuring device and in our way of applying the method. Our strategy is to define different AI, different cameras and cameras resolution, different vehicles, different operators, choosing a single road circuit for the data acquisition and operate on it multiple times at different time of the day.

Then, when the data acquisition is complete and processed by our defined AI, we sample the processed frames to extract a fraction of frames representative of the global results. We use the Cochran sampling method [23] for creating the sample. Those results are then reviewed manually by our team.

Finally, with the newly reviewed results for every possible combination of AI, camera, operator and time of the day, we can compute the new more representative F1-score. With the newly computed F1-scores, we run an ANOVA method to extract all the information we want. We also use those newly computed F1-scores across our different groups to do a round-robin test, estimating the repeatability and reproducibility of our method. While not technically being an AI, it is the standard non-deep-learning method, and we use it to compare its behavior to real AI.

3.1 Road markings inspection strategy

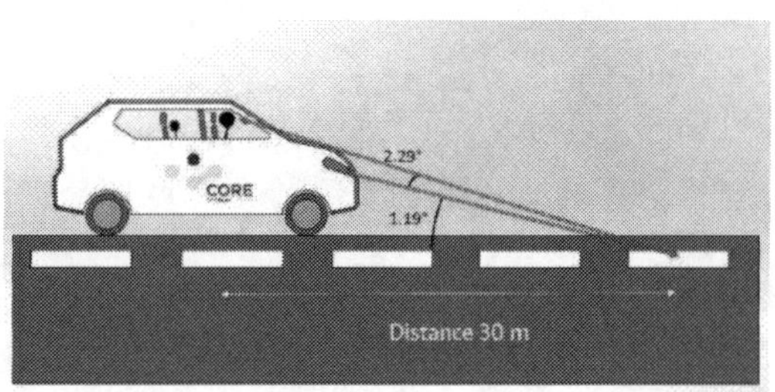

Figure 1 – EN 1436 standard

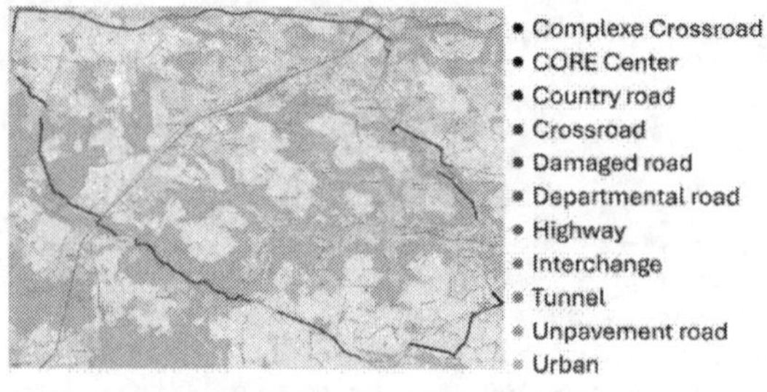

Figure 2 – Selected Road track for our study

An AI is defined as a couple between a model and a dataset. We define four AI: Yolov8 trained (by ourselves) with the Mapillary dataset; U-Net (by ourselves) trained with Tusimple; SCNN trained with CULane [24] ; a Hough Transform with no dataset [25].

We define a camera by its resolution: 1280x720 (720p), 1920x1080 (1080p) and 3840x2160 (4K). The objective is to check if the resolution could influence the performance of an AI. Cameras are mounted inside of the vehicle. The height and angle of the camera is inspired by the EN 1436 [26] geometry (Figure 1).

We chose three operators (drivers) and three vehicles. Before driving, operators remount the camera inside their vehicle. Each operator follows a road track, and their departure is spaced by a two-minute interval. Operators drives at different daytime of a same day: morning, noon and afternoon. We drove on dry day condition according to EN 1436. The road track covers standard French road scenarios: different markings material; road with no markings, different pavement, highway, urban (Figure 2)… We made a total of 9 videos of 100 minutes and 6000 images. Selected AIs processed each video and return the number of lines detected by image. It resulted in a total of 216,000 processed images to manually validate. This task is too much time-consuming and we need a smaller representative frame explained on the following section.

3.2 F1-score estimate and Cochran sampling

In our context, the F1-score (1) enables the quantity of correct detected lines (True Positives) against the quantity of false alarms (False Positives) and missed lines (False Negatives).

$$\mathbf{F1} = \frac{TP}{TP + \dfrac{FP + FN}{2}} \qquad (1)$$

Currently, the F1-score is determined on the test dataset to confirm the training process. Because this dataset may not be representative of given work site, the communicated F1-score may not be adapted. In our method, we estimate a F1-score for each video acquired.

Each video has the same or different operators, environment, measuring system, sample or time-lapse to estimate in second time the reproducibility and repeatability. However, we need to validate the predicted values on each processed image. To avoid this, the solution proposed here and summarized in Figure 3, is to perform a double Cochran sampling.

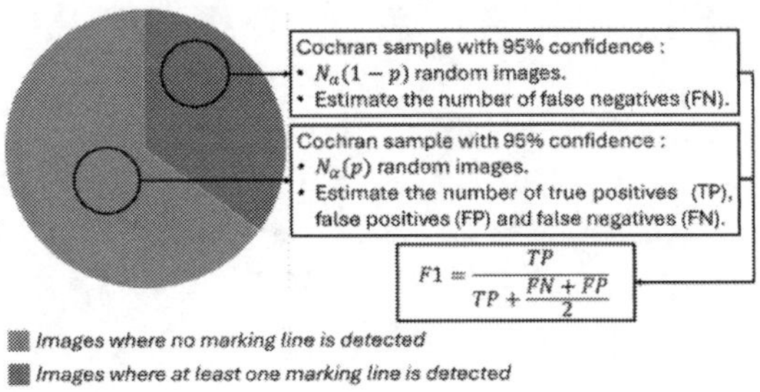

Figure 3 - Principle of Cochran sampling to control AI results

$$N_\alpha(p) = \frac{t_\alpha^2 \cdot p \cdot (1-p)}{(1-\alpha)^2} \qquad (2)$$

Introduced by Cochran [23] and adapted here to the detection of marking lines, the minimum size of a sample is set by equation (2) where α=0.95 is the desired confidence level, t_α=1.96 is the solution to F(x)=α with F is the cumulative density function of the centered-reduced normal distribution and p$\in$[0,1] is the empirical probability that at least one marking line is detected by the AI on an random image. The choice of a 95% confidence implies an acceptable risk of 5% to obtain a sampling not representative of the real AI performance. A sample size is between 0 and 384 images.

On a random image, one AI detects no line or at least one. To analyze those two classes of situation, two samples are produced. Sample $N_\alpha(p)$ represents images where AI has detected at least one line. The number of TP, FP are counted, number of FN is partially counted. Sample $N_\alpha(1-p)$ represents images where AI has detected no line. The number of FN is fully counted (Figure 3).

An F1-score is calculated for each AI and each video. According to the latest reviews, we require a minimum of 75% to accept an AI and validate an inspection campaign [27], [5]. Different F1-scores must be compared, and an ANOVA approach is introduced to estimate the difference according to the different camera and weather conditions.

3.3 ANOVA

Analysis of variance (ANOVA) is a statistical technique used to evaluate differences between the means of several groups. In our case, a group is either a specific AI, camera or daytime. The ANOVA is based on the comparison of variances: it examines the variability of the data within each group and the variability between groups. By breaking down the total variance observed into two main components, the between-group variance and the within-group variance, the ANOVA enables us to determine whether the differences observed in the means are not linked to chance, meaning the difference are significant and due to something. The results of an ANOVA are often presented as a p-value. A p-value below a predefined threshold (in our case 0.05) indicates that there are significant differences between the groups. If the ANOVA reveals significant differences, post hoc analyses can be performed to identify which groups are different from each other, like the Honestly Significant Difference (HSD) test, created by Tukey and aiming to know which pair of groups are different by calculating a critical value based on the range distribution studied, then used to compare the differences between the means of each pair. ANOVA also enable us to study interactions, defined as the existing differences between the groups of one factor and all the groups of another factor. If the difference is not the same, there is an interaction. In our case, our factors are the AIs, cameras and daytimes. In the next section, we study the significant differences and the interactions of our factors and groups.

4 Results

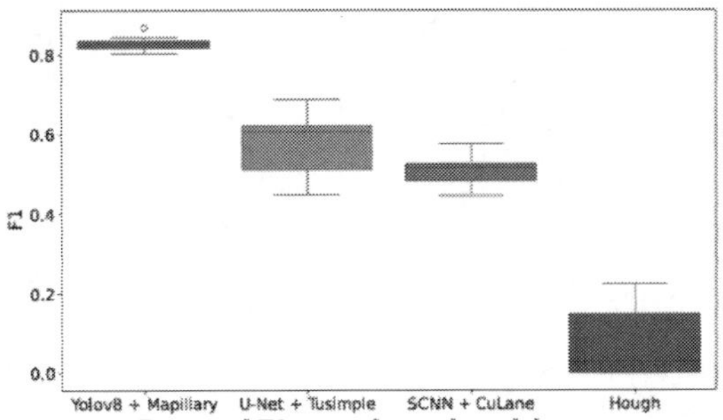

Figure 4 - Estimated F1-score for each model

Figure 4 shows F1-score per model, camera and daytime. Results are heterogeneous: Hough Transform shows an average of 8% with values being spread between 0% and 22% ; Yolov8 shows an average of 83% with values being spread between 80% and 87% ; U-Net is slightly superior to the SCNN, with respectively an average F1-score of 57% against 51% ; SCNN seems more constant and stable than U-Net, with an interquartile range (IQR) of 5% versus 13%. The IQR of Hough is 18%, and Yolov8 one is 3%. These raw results shows that Yolov8 is the most efficient.

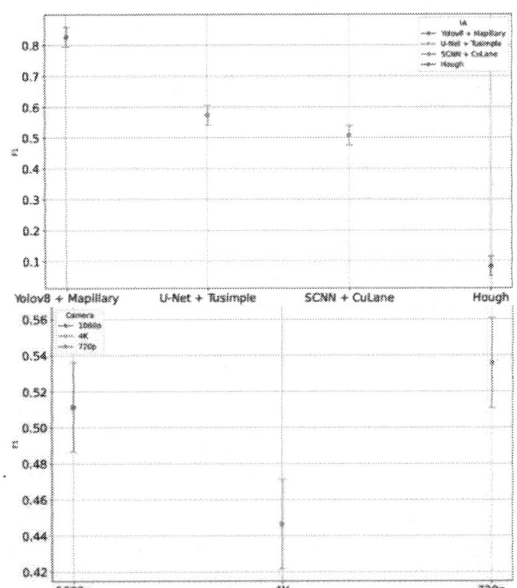

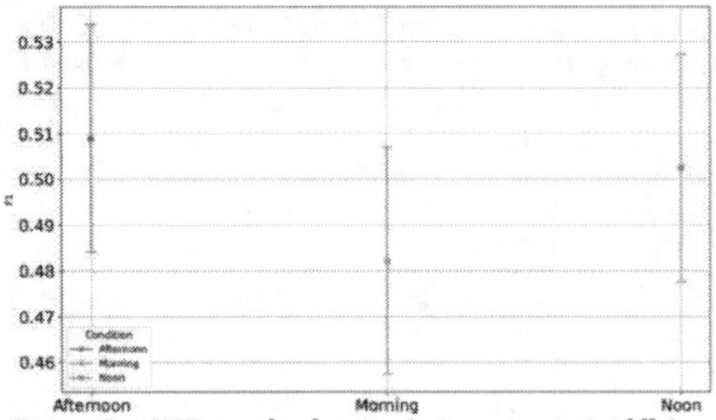

Figure 5 - HSD results for Ais (up), cameras (middle) and daytimes (down)

Figure 5 shows the HSD results between each group of a given factor. For AI, there is a significant difference between each AI. Especially between Yolov8+Mapillary and Hough. While the difference between the SCNN+CULane and UNet+Tusimple seems to be very small, it is still considered as significant. It means that the choice of an AI is fundamental for the methods, and they cannot be interchanged. For cameras, there is a significant difference between 720p and 4K, and 1080p and 4K. However, there is no significant difference between 720p and 1080p. Here, the 4K is the less performant camera resolution. In our case, because 720p and 1080p does not have significant difference, they can be interchanged. Finally, for daytimes, there is no significant difference between morning, noon, or afternoon. We can operate on the whole day without having an impact on our performances.

4.1 Interactions

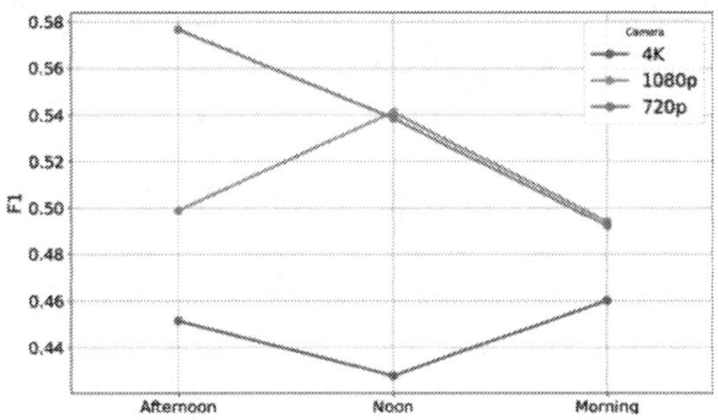

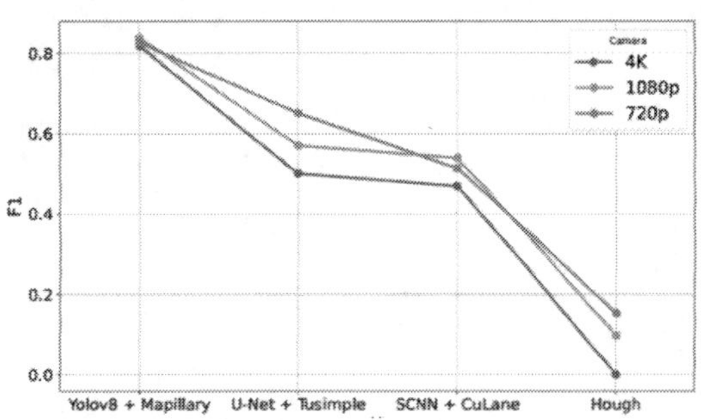

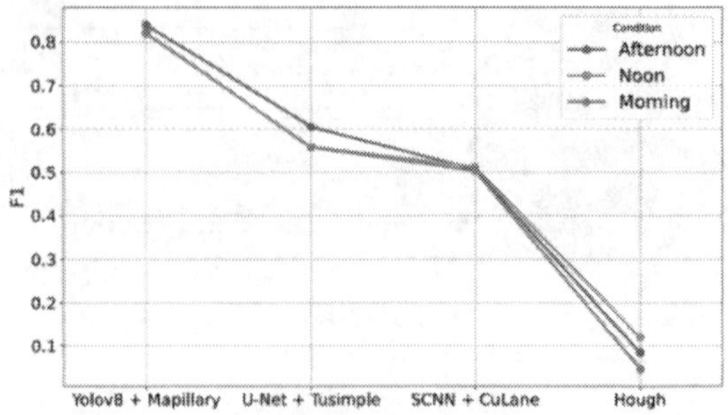

Figure 6 – Interactions results for Daytimes-Cameras (up), Ais-Cameras (middle) and Ais-Daytimes (down)

Figure 6 shows that there is no interaction between any of our factors. It means that no factor influences the others.

4.2 Repeatability and reproducibility

Table 1 - Round-robin test repeatability and reproducibility results

	Repeatability	Reproducibility
Variance	0.002	0.06
Standard deviation	0.05	0.25
Score 95%	**0.15**	**0.74**
Variation coefficient	9.26	46.23

Using the raw F1-score results we determined earlier on our road track, we can estimate the repeatability and reproducibility of our measuring method and AI-embedded measuring device (Table 1 - Round-robin test repeatability and reproducibility results). With 95% confidence, we can estimate our repeatability as 0.15 and our reproducibility at 0.74. It means that for a same measure on same conditions and a short time-lapse, two samples having a difference inferior to 15% are considered as the same sample. With varying factors, two samples having a difference inferior to 74% is considered as the same sample. These intervals are huge, but explainable (see Section 5).

5 Conclusion

This paper proposes a method to estimate the repeatability and reproducibility of an AI-embedded measuring device applied to road markings detection. The current way F1-score is determined, using a test dataset, is biased as the latter cannot be exhaustive. By using the principles of the round-robin test and adapting important metrological elements to adapt them to our experiment, we were able to compute a more accurate F1-score and estimate its representative repeatability and reproducibility. We used three AI models (Yolov8, UNet, SCNN) and one more classic image processing approach (Hough transform), and obtained average F1-score of 83% for Yolov8, 57% for UNet, 51% for the SCNN and 8% for the Hough transform. It is important to remind that our objective is to detect line markings and not lanes. SCNN and Hough are more suitable for detecting lanes, explaining those results compared to general literature. We then estimated the repeatability and reproducibility, scoring respectively 0.15 and 0.74. These results are huge, and it is explained by the fact that the different AIs (model+dataset) we used are too different from one another. The raw F1-score determined by our method was sufficient to separate these AIs. However, we demonstrated that it is possible to run round-robin tests for AI-embedded devices. We did obtain repeatability and reproducibility results.

Next step now is to use more similar AI models to Yolov8 to obtain coherent results of repeatability and reproducibility, because it performed extremely well in this paper. We also plan on taking this method on the next level to estimate the accuracy and the uncertainty of our AI-embedded measuring device.

References

[1] D. Babić, T. Burghardt, D. B.-I. J. for T. and, and undefined 2015, "Application and characteristics of waterborne road marking paint," *ijtte.comD Babić, TE Burghardt, D BabićInternational Journal for Traffic and Transport Engineering, 2015•ijtte.com*, vol. 5, no. 2, pp. 150–169, 2015, doi: 10.7708/ijtte.2015.5(2).06.

[2] R. Maxime, B. Laurent, D. D.-I. J. of, and undefined 2021, "Em approach for weibull analysis in a strongly censored data context-application to road markings," *ijpe-online.comR Maxime, B Laurent, D DimitriInternational Journal of Performability Engineering, 2021•ijpe-online.com*, Accessed: Feb. 26, 2025. [Online]. Available: https://www.ijpe-online.com/EN/Y2021/V17/I4/333

[3] P. Charbonnier, F. Diebolt, ... Y. G.-... of C. on, and undefined 1997, "Road markings recognition using image processing," *ieeexplore.ieee.orgP Charbonnier, F Diebolt, Y Guillard, F PeyretProceedings of Conference on Intelligent Transportation Systems, 1997•ieeexplore.ieee.org*, Accessed: Feb. 26, 2025. [Online]. Available: https://ieeexplore.ieee.org/abstract/document/660595/

[4] A. Bar Hillel *et al.*, "Recent progress in road and lane detection: a survey", doi: 10.1007/s00138-011-0404-2.

[5] Y. Zhang, Z. Lu, X. Zhang, ... J. X.-I. T. on, and undefined 2021, "Deep learning in lane marking detection: A survey," *ieeexplore.ieee.orgY Zhang, Z Lu, X Zhang, JH Xue, Q LiaoIEEE Transactions on Intelligent Transportation Systems, 2021•ieeexplore.ieee.org*, Accessed: Jun. 18, 2024. [Online]. Available: https://ieeexplore.ieee.org/abstract/document/9398517/

[6] Dumont Éric, "Évaluation du degré d'usure des marquages routiers par traitement d'images," Dec. 2001.

[7] J. Wu, W. Liu, Y. M.- Sensors, and undefined 2024, "Street View Image-Based Road Marking Inspection System Using Computer Vision and Deep Learning Techniques," *mdpi.comJ Wu, W Liu, Y MaruyamaSensors, 2024•mdpi.com*, Accessed: Feb. 19, 2025. [Online]. Available: https://www.mdpi.com/1424-8220/24/23/7724

[8] N. Hautière, R. Labayrade, and D. Aubert, "Real-time disparity contrast combination for onboard estimation of the visibility distance," *IEEE Transactions on Intelligent Transportation Systems*, vol. 7, no. 2, pp. 201–211, Jun. 2006, doi: 10.1109/TITS.2006.874682.

[9] O. Jayasinghe, ... S. H.-P. of the, and undefined 2022, "Ceymo: See more on roads-a novel benchmark dataset for road marking detection," *openaccess.thecvf.com*, Accessed: Aug. 02, 2024. [Online]. Available: http://openaccess.thecvf.com/content/WACV2022/html/Jayasinghe_CeyMo_See_More_on_Roads_-_A_Novel_Benchmark_Dataset_WACV_2022_paper.html

[10] "ISO 5725-1:2023 - Exactitude (justesse et fidélité) des résultats et méthodes de mesure — Partie 1: Principes généraux et définitions." Accessed: Feb. 20, 2025. [Online]. Available: https://www.iso.org/fr/standard/69418.html

[11] J. Redmon, S. Divvala, R. G.-... and pattern recognition, and undefined 2016, "You only look once: Unified, real-time object detection," *cv-foundation.org*, Accessed: Aug. 02, 2024. [Online]. Available: https://www.cv-foundation.org/openaccess/content_cvpr_2016/html/Redmon_You_Only_Look_CVPR_2016_paper.html

[12] C. Dewi, R. C. Chen, Y. C. Zhuang, X. Jiang, and H. Yu, "Recognizing Road Surface Traffic Signs Based on Yolo Models Considering Image Flips," *Big Data and Cognitive Computing 2023, Vol. 7, Page 54*, vol. 7, no. 1, p. 54, Mar. 2023, doi: 10.3390/BDCC7010054.

[13] O. Ronneberger, P. Fischer, and T. Brox, "U-net: Convolutional networks for biomedical image segmentation," *Lecture Notes in Computer Science (including subseries Lecture Notes in Artificial Intelligence and Lecture Notes in Bioinformatics)*, vol. 9351, pp. 234–241, 2015, doi: 10.1007/978-3-319-24574-4_28.

[14] M. Ghafoorian, C. Nugteren, N. Baka, O. Booij, and M. Hofmann, "EL-GAN: Embedding Loss Driven Generative Adversarial Networks for Lane Detection," 2018.

[15] X. Pan, J. Shi, P. Luo, X. Wang, X. T.-P. of the AAAI, and undefined 2018, "Spatial as deep: Spatial cnn for traffic scene understanding," *ojs.aaai.orgX Pan, J Shi, P Luo, X Wang, X TangProceedings of the AAAI conference on artificial intelligence, 2018•ojs.aaai.org*, Accessed: Jul. 30, 2024. [Online]. Available: https://ojs.aaai.org/index.php/AAAI/article/view/12301

[16] R. Mori, ... K. K.-S. 2004 A., and undefined 2004, "Hough-based robust lane boundary detection for the omni-directional camera," *ieeexplore.ieee.orgR Mori, K Kobayashi, K WatanabeSICE 2004 Annual Conference, 2004•ieeexplore.ieee.org*, Accessed: Jan. 23, 2025. [Online]. Available: https://ieeexplore.ieee.org/abstract/document/1491793/

[17] A. Borkar, M. Hayes, M. T. Smith, and S. Pankanti, "A layered approach to robust lane detection at night," *2009 IEEE Workshop on Computational Intelligence in Vehicles and Vehicular Systems, CIVVS 2009 - Proceedings*, pp. 51–57, 2009, doi: 10.1109/CIVVS.2009.4938723.

[18] "Mapillary Datasets." Accessed: Feb. 24, 2025. [Online]. Available: https://www.mapillary.com/datasets?locale=fr_FR

[19] Z. Yang, C. Zhao, H. Maeda, and Y. Sekimoto, "Development of a Large-Scale Roadside Facility Detection Model Based on the Mapillary Dataset," *Sensors 2022, Vol. 22, Page 9992*, vol. 22, no. 24, p. 9992, Dec. 2022, doi: 10.3390/S22249992.

[20] "TuSimple Dataset." Accessed: Feb. 24, 2025. [Online]. Available: https://paperswithcode.com/dataset/tusimple

[21] D. Neven Bert De Brabandere Stamatios Georgoulis Marc Proesmans Luc Van Gool ESAT-PSI and K. Leuven, "Towards End-to-End Lane Detection: an Instance Segmentation Approach".

[22] "CULane Dataset." Accessed: Feb. 24, 2025. [Online]. Available: https://xingangpan.github.io/projects/CULane.html

[23] R. R.-P. of the E. M. Society and undefined 1963, "w. G. Cochran, Sampling Techniques (John Wiley & Sons, 1963), ix+ 413 pp., 72s.," *cambridge.org*, doi: 10.1017/S0013091500025724.

[24] "GitHub - harryhan618/SCNN_Pytorch: Pytorch implementation of 'Spatial As Deep: Spatial CNN for Traffic Scene Understanding.'" Accessed: Feb. 24, 2025. [Online]. Available: https://github.com/harryhan618/SCNN_Pytorch

[25] "GitHub - chuanenlin/lane-detector: https://towardsdatascience.com/tutorial-build-a-lane-detector-679fd8953132." Accessed: Feb. 26, 2025. [Online]. Available: https://github.com/chuanenlin/lane-detector

[26] "Norme NF EN 1436." Accessed: Jan. 28, 2025. [Online]. Available: https://www.boutique.afnor.org/fr-fr/norme/nf-en-1436/produits-de-marquage-routier-performances-des-marquages-appliques-sur-la-ro/fa179243/81040

[27] D. Liang, Y. Guo, S. Zhang, ... T. M.-J. of C., and undefined 2020, "Lane detection: A survey with new results," *SpringerD Liang, YC Guo, SK Zhang, TJ Mu, X HuangJournal of Computer Science and Technology, 2020•Springer*, vol. 35, no. 3, pp. 493–505, May 2020, doi: 10.1007/s11390-020-0476-4.

Bayesian Analysis of Combustion Kinetic Models for Ammonia-Hydrogen Fuel Blends Using Artificial Neural Networks

Guanyu Wang[1*], *Fan* Wang[2], *Michael* Jones[3] and *Solmaz* Nadiri[1]

[1]Department of Physical Chemistry, Physikalisch-Technische Bundesanstalt, 38116 Braunschweig, Germany
[2]Faculty of Mathematics, Otto-von-Guericke-University Magdeburg, Universitätsplatz 2, 39106 Magdeburg, Germany
[3]Queen's University Kingston, 99 University Avenue, Kingston, Ontario, K7L 3N6, Canada

Abstract. Uncertainty quantification (UQ) plays a crucial role in predictive modeling in combustion chemistry, as it improves the accuracy of predictions and the reliability. To accurately predict ignition delay times and nitrogen oxides (NOx) emissions of ammonia (NH_3) and hydrogen (H_2) fuel blends, minimizing uncertainty in combustion kinetic models is critical. This study introduces a novel approach that integrates Bayesian analysis with Artificial Neural Networks (ANNs) to perform inverse UQ and update combustion kinetic models based on experimentally measured nitric oxide (NO) speciation time history. Traditional Markov Chain Monte Carlo (MCMC) methods are effective, but they are computationally intensive and require large datasets, which limit their practical applicability. ANNs are applied as surrogate models to replace traditional kinetic modeling, optimizing the combustion kinetic model of NH_3/H_2 fuel blends. By integrating Bayesian analysis with ANNs, the computational cost was significantly reduced compared to conventional MCMC methods, while maintaining high accuracy in uncertainty quantification and parameter optimization. This approach facilitates efficient exploration of parameter space and ensures reliable predictions, making it a valuable tool for complex combustion modeling.

1 Introduction

The transition to carbon neutrality requires the adoption of efficient, low-carbon alternative fuels. Ammonia (NH_3), recognized as a promising zero-carbon fuel, offers significant advantages such as ease of storage and transport. However, its application is limited by slow combustion rates and the production of nitrogen oxides (NOx) when burned alone. Blending ammonia with hydrogen (H_2) enhances combustion performance by reducing ignition delay times (IDTs) and NOx formation.

Accurate prediction of the combustion process through kinetic modeling is essential for improving the efficiency and reliability of energy systems. To improve these models, Inverse Uncertainty Quantification (UQ) is used to minimize uncertainty in predictions by refining model parameters based on experimental data. The concept of inverse UQ for kinetic models was introduced by Frenklach et al. [1], and methods like data collaboration and solution mapping techniques have been instrumental in refining models such as GRI-Mech 3.0 [2]. The Bayesian method is a probabilistic approach to tackle inverse UQ. By incorporating prior knowledge of system parameters and uncertainties, Bayesian analysis utilizes stochastic sampling to produce posterior distributions for model parameters and predictions. Wang and Sheen [3] explained that Bayesian methods provide probabilistic estimates of rate parameters, which improves predictive reliability by quantifying uncertainties and enabling more accurate extrapolation beyond the range of experimental data. A key technique in Bayesian analysis is Markov Chain Monte Carlo (MCMC), which iteratively generates correlated samples from posterior distributions. Although MCMC is widely employed, its computational demands make it challenging to apply to high-dimensional combustion models, often limiting its practical use to simpler combustion systems or smaller reaction sets.

Bayesian methods become increasingly challenging for complex systems, such as ammonia-hydrogen fuel blends. To improve computational efficiency, recent studies have integrated Artificial Neural Networks (ANNs) with MCMC, using ANNs as surrogate models to approximate combustion behavior. By capturing nonlinear relationships, ANNs enable faster and more scalable optimization, making Bayesian analysis feasible for high-dimensional systems. Wang et al. [4] introduced an ANN-assisted MCMC approach that improves the efficiency of Bayesian inverse UQ in combustion kinetics. They utilized ANNs as surrogate models, significantly reducing computational costs while maintaining accuracy in estimating the posterior distributions of kinetic parameters. This approach is particularly beneficial for complex combustion systems with restricted computational resources.

This study integrates Bayesian analysis with ANN-based surrogate models to perform inverse uncertainty quantification for ammonia-hydrogen fuel blend

* Corresponding author: guanyu.wang@ptb.de

combustion. By utilizing time-resolved NO concentration data [5], this approach optimizes pre-exponential factors (A-factors) in the Arrhenius equations, which are crucial for accurately predicting IDTs and NO emissions. By using surrogate models, we were able to reduce the computational effort compared to traditional MCMC methods, which makes Bayesian analysis more efficient and accessible for complex kinetic models. This approach provides a scalable framework that enhances the accuracy of combustion simulations, serving as a valuable tool for optimizing fuel blends and improving the sustainability of energy systems.

2 Methodology

Unlike the Frequentist approach, where parameters are assumed to be fixed but unknown, Bayesian methods treat parameters as probability distributions that can be updated with experimental data. In this work, the Bayesian approach is implemented to calibrate the simulation results from the knowledge of experiment data.

2.1 The Bayesian inference

Apart from the Frequentist approach, the true distribution of the is assumed unknown thus the parameters of the distribution are undetermined as well. The Bayesian Approach provides a way to inference the distribution as well as its parameters from the data sampled from the true distribution which is shown in the Equation (1),

$$p_{\text{post}}(\boldsymbol{\theta}|\boldsymbol{d}) = \frac{p_{\text{prior}}(\boldsymbol{\theta})p(\boldsymbol{\theta};\boldsymbol{d})}{\int p_{\text{prior}}(\boldsymbol{\theta})p(\boldsymbol{\theta};\boldsymbol{d})\,d\boldsymbol{\theta}} \tag{1}$$

where $p_{\text{post}}(\boldsymbol{\theta}|\boldsymbol{d})$ is the posterior distribution which is the inferred distribution of the parameters $\boldsymbol{\theta}$, and $\boldsymbol{d}$ is the given measurement data from the experiments. The Bayesian formula gives the possibility to calibrate inferred posterior distribution of the kinetic parameters according to the measurement of the experiments. The numerator of the right-hand side of the Equation (1) is multiplication between prior distribution of parameters $\boldsymbol{\theta}$ and likelihood function of collected experiment data $\boldsymbol{d}$. The prior distribution reflects the prior knowledge of $\boldsymbol{\theta}$ and the posterior influences the posterior significantly.

Meanwhile, the likelihood function models the uncertainty of the measurement. With the injection of measurement form experiment, the posterior is updated by leveraging the prior belief and likelihood of the measurements. While the integral term in the denominator, is known as the normalising or constant term, which is intractable. Therefore, we don ' t compute it explicitly. Hence the Equation (1) can be simplified as Equation (2) as follows

$$p_{\text{post}}(\boldsymbol{\theta}|\boldsymbol{d}) \propto p_{\text{prior}}(\boldsymbol{\theta})p(\boldsymbol{\theta};\boldsymbol{d}) \tag{2}$$

The prior distribution of $\boldsymbol{\theta}$ can be determined by the prior knowledge of $\boldsymbol{\theta}$, a common choice is uniform distribution or Gaussian distribution. We use uniform distribution as the parameters are uniformly sampled from the given sample domain. Besides the choice of prior, the choice of likelihood affects the quality of the posterior significantly as well. We use the multiplicative error model as suggested from [4]. And the likelihood is formulated as follows in Equation (3) and Equation (4):

$$p(\boldsymbol{x};\boldsymbol{d}) = \mathrm{C}\cdot\exp\left[-\frac{1}{2}\sum_{i=1}^{N}\left(\frac{\ln x_i - \ln d_i}{\sigma_i}\right)^2\right] \tag{3}$$

$$\mathrm{C} = \frac{1}{\prod_{i=1}^{N}\sqrt{2\pi\sigma_i^2}} \tag{4}$$

where N represents the total number of sample pairs of simulated results $\boldsymbol{x}$ and the collected experiment measurements $\boldsymbol{d}$. In which x_i and d_i are the sample pair for simulation and experiment respectively with identical parameter input. Variance σ_i^2 characterizes the uncertainty of the experimental measurement. Since the posterior distribution is not a known distribution, there is so analytic solution of it, it will be practically obtained by running MCMC simulation.

2.2 Markov Chain Monte Carlo

Bayesian inference is useful to infer the distribution of the parameters from the know information of the measurements, it combines prior knowledge with new data to compute a posterior distribution using Bayes' theorem. However, computing the posterior analytically is often infeasible in complex models. MCMC methods address this by providing a way to sample from the posterior distribution. MCMC uses a Markov chain to explore the sample space, generating samples that approximate the target distribution. This sampling approach makes MCMC an useful tool for solving high-dimensional problems in Bayesian analysis, particularly when direct integration is impossible. There are many ways to realize MCMC, and we used the Metropolis–Hastings (MH).

MH algorithm is a common method for MCMC for generating samples from a target distribution. It works by constructing a Markov chain with the desired distribution as its stationary distribution. At each step, a candidate sample is proposed from a proposal distribution, and then accepted or rejected based on a probability determined by the ratio of the target distribution to the proposal distribution. If accepted, the candidate becomes the new state; if otherwise, the chain stays at the current state. MH is flexible and can be applied to distributions with intractable normalizing constants.

2.3 Surrogate models

The ANN used in this work is a Multilayer Perceptron (MLP), employed as a surrogate model to approximate complex, high-dimensional non-linear simulations. It features GELU activation functions, AdamW optimizer for adaptive learning rates, and a batch size of 256 for efficient training. Regularization techniques, including dropout and batch normalization, are applied to prevent overfitting and ensure robust performance, making the model both computationally efficient and accurate in capturing complex relationships. Detailed settings are shown in Section. 4.2.

3 Kinetic modelling

The simulation of time-resolved NO concentration in the shock tube was conducted using an in-house Cantera code (version 3.0.0) [6] with a constant volume, 0-D homogeneous adiabatic, ideal gas reactor model. The kinetic model of ammonia hydrogen blend oxidation developed by Solmaz et al. [7] is employed for this study. The model contains 87 species and 460 reactions. To enhance the computational efficiency of the MCMC sampling process, the model was reduced to 50 reactions, focusing on the most influential reactions for NH_3/H_2 blend oxidation. This reduction significantly improved the efficiency of the optimization procedure while preserving the accuracy necessary for reliable predictions of ignition delay and emissions. The uncertainty factor (UF) for a reaction rate is defined as:

$$F = \frac{k_0}{k_{min}} = \frac{k_{max}}{k_0} \tag{5}$$

where k_0 is the nominal value of the rate coefficient, k_{max} and k_{min} represent the upper and lower bounds of the rate coefficient, respectively. Each rate coefficient $k_i$is assumed to follow a prior log-uniform distribution within the uncertainty range (k_{min} , k_{max}). The uncertainty factors for the rate coefficients were derived from literature compilations [8, 9]. A brute-force sensitivity analysis was performed for both IDT and the maximum NO concentration across all mixtures at three different temperatures: 1600 K, 1800 K, and 2000 K. In this approach, the rate coefficients of all reactions in the mechanism are individually doubled in each cycle, with the solver initialized to the reactor's starting conditions (T5, P5). The reactions identified as the top ten most sensitive for both IDT and NO maximum concentration are then compiled, resulting in a total of 29 reactions. These reactions were selected for further analysis in the MCMC study.

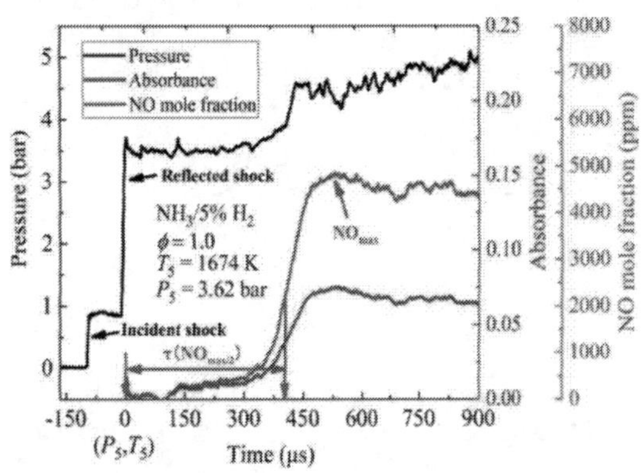

Figure 1. Measured pressure, absorbance, NO profile, and the definition of two characteristic parameters for the case of $NH_3/5\%H_2$ mixture [5].

The experimental data used in this work was obtained from Zhu et al. [5] [10] includes pure NH_3 and ammonia-hydrogen blends with hydrogen concentrations of up to 20%. Fig. 1 illustrates a typical measured NO time history for NH_3/H_2 blend in a shock tube. Two characteristic parameters were extracted from the NO time histories for more detailed quantitative analysis: NO_{max}, which represents the maximum NO mole fraction, and $\tau(NO_{max/2})$, the time from time zero (P_5, T_5) to the time corresponding to the position of half of the NO_{max}. These parameters capture the amplitude and phase of the NO profiles, respectively. And they represent the experimental data used in this work.

4 Results and discussion

4.1 Cantera-based MCMC

Sensitivity analyses (SAs) were performed to identify the most influential reactions in the kinetic model for both IDT and maximum NO mole fraction (NO_{max}). Fig. 2 illustrates an example of sensitivity analysis for IDT at a temperature of 2000 K and a pressure of 3.0 bar. Following the analysis, 29 key reactions were selected as the most important for both IDT and NO_{max}, based on their impact on the model predictions.

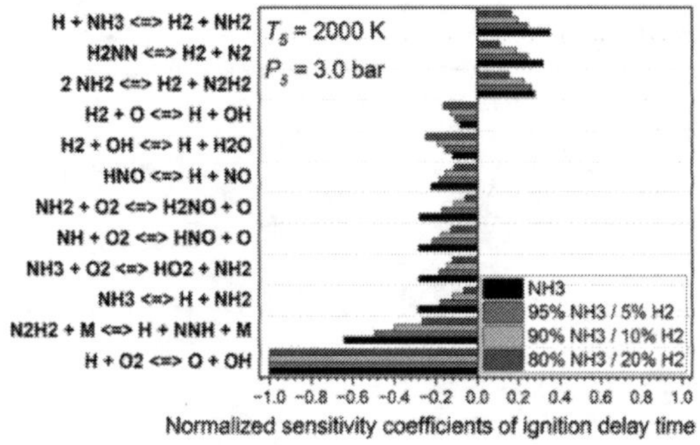

Figure 2. Sensitivity analysis of the IDT for all experimental conditions at $T_5 = 2000K$, $P_5 = 3$ bar

Following the sensitivity analysis results, the traditional MCMC method with the Metropolis-Hastings algorithm was used to sample reaction coefficients for the kinetic model, with the goal of minimizing discrepancies between model predictions and experimental data. This involved conducting a series of simulations to sample reaction rate coefficients (log A factors) and iteratively minimize the discrepancy between the model predicted values and experimental measurements. The MH algorithm proposed new values for the reaction rate coefficients, which were accepted or rejected based on the likelihood of improving the model fit to the experimental data.

The optimization process involved conducting 100,000 MCMC iterations, with convergence generally achieved after approximately 30,000 steps. In each iteration, the model was evaluated by computing the discrepancy between the simulated and experimental values, such as IDT and maximum NO mole fraction. These discrepancies were used to calculate the likelihood of each proposed set of reaction rate coefficients, guiding the MH algorithm to accept or reject the proposed solutions based on their relative likelihood. The mechanism that minimized the discrepancies was identified by evaluating the posterior distribution of the model parameters. This evaluation provided the most probable values for the reaction rate coefficients. As a result, the optimization process produced a refined set of log A factors, which significantly enhanced the model's predictions for both IDT and the maximum mole fraction of NO.

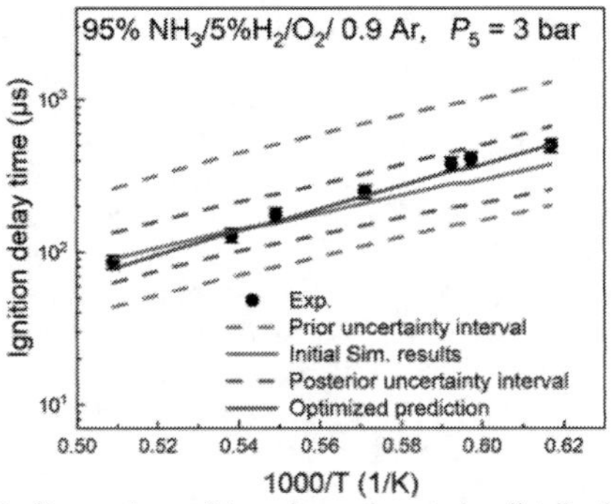

Figure 3. Comparison of the prior and posterior distributions of ignition delay time for 95% NH_3 / 5% H_2 fuel blends

Fig 3 shows the comparison of the prior and posterior distributions of IDT for 95% NH_3 / 5% H_2 fuel blends based on MCMC analysis. The measured data with an error bar ± 10%. The prior uncertainty interval was derived using Latin Hypercube Sampling for the rate coefficients within their uncertainty bounds, coupled with Cantera simulations. The posterior uncertainty interval was calculated from the output of the Cantera-based MCMC process. Notably, the posterior uncertainty interval is narrower than the prior, indicating a reduction in uncertainty. The optimized predictions (blue line) represent the best model generated during the MCMC process, and these predictions show a significantly improved match with the experimental data across the entire temperature range.

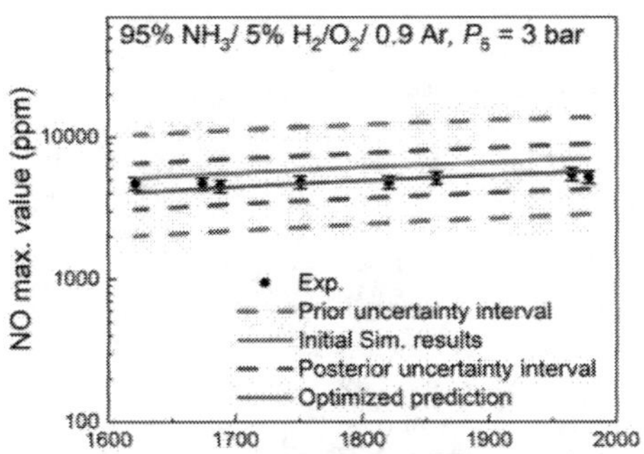

Figure 4. Comparison of the prior and posterior distributions of NO maximum value for 95% NH_3 / 5% H_2 fuel blends

Fig. 4 shows a comprehensive comparison of the prior and posterior distributions of the maximum NO mole fraction for 95% NH_3 / 5% H_2 fuel blends based on MCMC analysis. The method for deriving the prior and posterior uncertainty intervals was the same as for the IDT. The experimental data, shown with error bars representing a ± 10% uncertainty, is compared with the optimized predictions (blue line). The optimized mechanism shows significantly better results, with all the data points located within the uncertainty bounds.

Fig. 5 shows two examples of the NO time history for the 95% NH_3 / 5% H_2 fuel blends under different conditions. The left panel corresponds to $T = 1859$ K and $P = 3.26$ bar, while the right panel represents $T = 1621$ K and $P = 3.64$ bar. The NO peak value (NO_{max}) and the time to reach half of the NO peak ($\tau(NO_{max/2})$) are key parameters that capture the amplitude and phase of the NO profiles, respectively. NO_{max} and $\tau(NO_{max/2})$ were used in the MCMC process as discrepancy measures and for likelihood calculations. The predicted values for these parameters were optimized during the MCMC process by comparing the simulated data with experimental measurements. The optimized model (blue) provides a significantly improved match to the experimental data (black) for both NO peak and phase, compared with the original model (red).

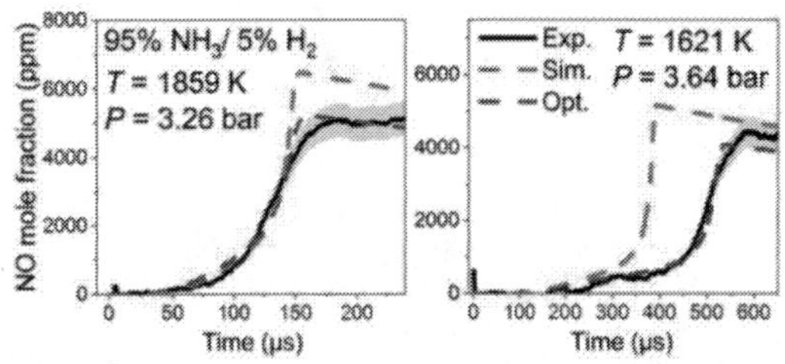

Figure 5. Comparison of measured NO mole fraction with original kinetic model and optimized model for 95% NH_3 / 5% H_2 fuel blends

4.2 ANN-based MCMC

4.2.1 ANN training result

The ANN framework is based on an MLP architecture implemented using the PyTorch framework. The ANN has 35 input features, which include gas compositions, temperature, pressure, and reaction rates, and two output targets: the log of the IDT and the peak NO value. The model architecture consists of 6 hidden layers with progressively fewer nodes. The training dataset, which consists of 310,000 data points, is generated from Cantera simulations. The dataset is split into 70% for training, 15% for validation, and 15% for testing. Data preprocessing involves scaling both the input features and target variables using StandardScaler to normalize the data and improve model convergence. The model is trained to minimize the mean relative error (MRE), and the learning rate is dynamically adjusted during training. The model's performance is evaluated using two metrics: R^2 and MRE. Predictions are compared against experimental data for NO emissions and IDT. Regularization techniques like dropout and batch normalization are applied to prevent overfitting and enhance generalization.

Fig.6 illustrates the training progress of the ANN model, with the MRE and R^2 values plotted against the number of epochs, based on the validation set. As shown, the MRE decreases significantly during the initial training epochs, dropping from approximately 0.02 to 0.006 within the first 50 epochs. The R^2 value increases steadily and reaches 0.999 towards the end of the training, indicating a near-perfect correlation between the predicted and actual values. These results demonstrate that the model effectively learned the underlying relationships in the data, providing highly accurate predictions with minimal uncertainty.

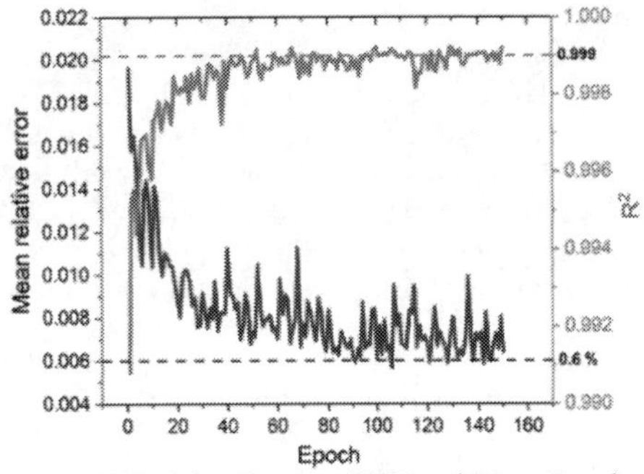

Figure 6. ANN Training Progress:MRE and R^2 vs. Epochs

4.2.2 Comparison of MCMC and ANN MCMC

This section compared the performance of traditional MCMC with the ANN-MCMC. Integrating ANNs with MCMC provides a robust framework for optimizing kinetic models and enhances optimization efficiency.

A time comparison between the ANN-MCMC approach with 100,000 steps and the traditional MCMC process is shown in Table 1. The results indicate that the ANN-MCMC approach significantly reduces overall computation time, with a total of 2203 seconds, compared to 170,905 seconds for the traditional Cantera-MCMC method. The key difference is observed in the model evaluation step, where Cantera-MCMC takes 170522 seconds, while the ANN-MCMC method requires only 326 seconds. However, the ANN training process adds 1504 seconds. The overall efficiency gain is considerable, as the combination of ANN and MCMC results in more than a 70-fold reduction in computation time. This demonstrates the effectiveness of the ANN-based optimization in accelerating the modeling process without sacrificing accuracy.

Table 1: Comparison of Computational Time: Cantera + MCMC vs. ANN + MCMC

	Cantera-MCMC	ANN-MCMC
Model evaluation	170522 s	326 s
Training of ANN	-	1504 s
MCMC process	331 s	324 s
Save the results	52 s	49 s
Total	170905 s	2203 s

To get a more detailed and accurate exploration of the parameter space, we expanded the number of steps to 1 million in the ANN-MCMC approach to further enhance the optimization process. Traditional 100,000 steps MCMC processes may fail to fully capture the complexity of non-linear systems, potentially missing important regions of the parameter space. Increasing the number of steps can achieve a much finer resolution in the posterior distributions, leading to a more reliable and accurate model. This extensive sampling ensures that the posterior distributions are well-converged and accurately reflect the joint distributions of the parameters, thereby improving the overall quality of the model's predictions.

Fig. 7 shows the prior and posterior distributions of the log A factors for two key reactions in the model. The prior distributions reflect the initial uncertainty in the reaction rate coefficients. These prior distributions capture a broad range of possible values before optimization. The posterior distributions (blue curves) are obtained from the ANN-MCMC optimization process with 1 million steps. The left plot corresponds to the reaction $H + O_2 \rightleftharpoons O + OH$, where the prior distribution of the log A factor is centred around 14.98. After the MCMC process, the posterior distribution shifts slightly to 15.045, showing a small increase in the rate constant. The right plot shows the reaction $NH_3 + H \rightleftharpoons NH_2 + H_2$. Similarly, the log A factor shifts from the prior center 5.81 to the posterior center 5.76 after the MCMC process, reflecting a slight decrease in the rate constant for this reaction. The figure shows that the posterior distributions are narrower than the priors, indicating a reduction in uncertainty after the optimization. The optimized predictions provide more precise values for the rate coefficients, leading to a more accurate model.

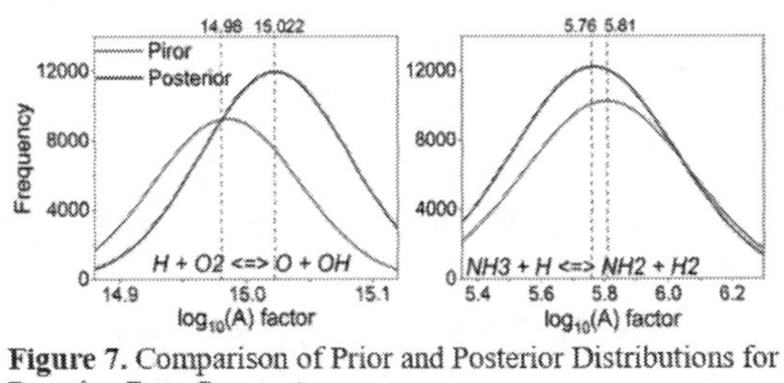

Figure 7. Comparison of Prior and Posterior Distributions for Reaction Rate Constants

Fig. 8 illustrates the joint distribution of the two reaction rate constants, $H + O_2 \rightleftharpoons O + OH$ and $NH_3 + H \rightleftharpoons NH_2 + H_2$, as shown in the contour plot. The plot shows the density of the log(A) factors, with darker shades indicating higher density and lighter shades representing lower density. The contours reveal the correlation between the two rate constants, illustrating regions of high probability where both rate constants are most likely to occur. The distribution indicates a strong relationship between the rate constants of the two reactions, with the densest regions concentrated around a specific set of values, indicating the most probable optimized rate constants. This joint distribution provides insights into the uncertainty and interactions between the rate constants, identifying the regions of parameter space with the greatest likelihood of accurate predictions.

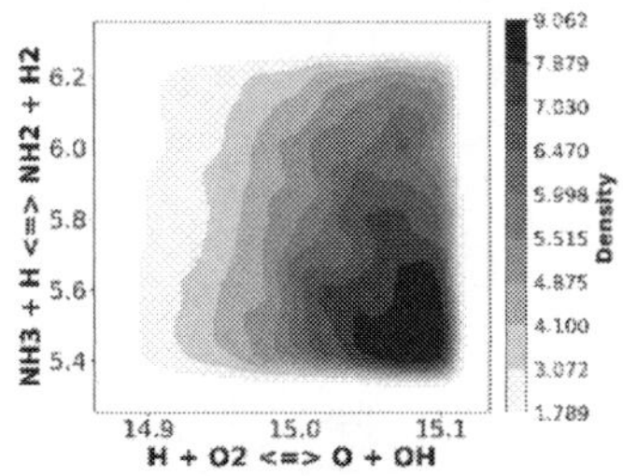

Figure 8. 2D Joint Distribution of Reactants and Products: $H + O_2 \rightleftharpoons O + OH$ and $NH_3 + H \rightleftharpoons NH_2 + H_2$

5 Conclusion

This study presents a practical approach for performing inverse uncertainty analysis on combustion kinetic models of ammonia-hydrogen fuel blends by combining Bayesian analysis with ANNs. The analysis focused on optimizing the pre-exponential factors (A-factors) in the Arrhenius equation, targeting 29 key critical parameters to accurately predict the combustion kinetics of NH_3/H_2 fuel blends.

By using ANNs as surrogate models, the computational cost was significantly reduced compared with traditional MCMC methods while still maintaining high accuracy in uncertainty quantification and parameter optimization. This approach provides an effective solution for dealing with high-dimensional systems. The narrower posterior distribution shows that the uncertainty has been reduced, leading to better alignment between the model's predictions and the experimental data. Additionally, the best-performing model is obtained during the MCMC process, ensuring that the optimized model provides reliable and accurate predictions for IDT and NO time history.

This work demonstrates how ANN-assisted Bayesian optimization can improve both the accuracy and efficiency of combustion modeling. By significantly reducing computational costs, this method is particularly useful for dealing with complex fuel blends or larger molecules that require more detailed kinetic models. The results presented here contribute to the broader goal of carbon neutrality, offering a robust tool for predictive modeling in fuel combustion research.

Guanyu Wang acknowledges the funding by the Deutsche Forschungsgemeinschaft (DFG, German Research Foundation) - 390881007, EXC 2163 Sustainable and Energy Efficient Aviation. Fan Wang acknowledges funding by the Deutsche Forschungsgemeinschaft (DFG, German Research Foundation) - 314838170, GRK 2297 MathCoRe.

References

1. M. Frenklach, H. Wang, and M.J. Rabinowitz, Optimization and analysis of large chemical kinetic mechanisms using the solution mapping method—combustion of methane. Prog. Energy Combust. Sci. **18**(1), 47-73 (1992) https://doi.org/10.1016/0360-1285(92)90032-V.
2. G.P. Smith, D.M. Golden, M. Frenklach, N.W. Moriarty, B. Eiteneer, M. Goldenberg, C.T. Bowman, R.K. Hanson, S. Song, W.C. Gardiner, V.V. Lissianski, and Z. Qin. Available from: http://www.me.berkeley.edu/gri-mech.
3. H. Wang and D.A. Sheen, Combustion kinetic model uncertainty quantification, propagation and minimization. Prog. Energy Combust. Sci. **47**, 1-31 (2015) https://doi.org/10.1016/j.pecs.2014.10.002.
4. J. Wang, Z. Zhou, K. Lin, C.K. Law, and B. Yang, Facilitating Bayesian analysis of combustion kinetic models with artificial neural network. Combust. Flame. **213**, 87-97 (2020) https://doi.org/10.1016/j.combustflame.2019.11.035.
5. D. Zhu, L. Ruwe, S. Schmitt, B. Shu, K. Kohse-Höinghaus, and A. Lucassen, Interactions in Ammonia and Hydrogen Oxidation Examined in a Flow Reactor and a Shock Tube. J. Phys. Chem. A. **127**(10), 2351-2366 (2023) https://doi.org/10.1021/acs.jpca.2c07784.
6. D. G. Goodwin, H. K. Moffat, I. Schoegl, R. L. Speth, and B. W. Weber, Cantera: An Object-oriented Software Toolkit for Chemical Kinetics, Thermodynamics, and Transport Processes. (Version 3.0.0)
7. S. Nadiri, B. Shu, C.F. Goldsmith, and R. Fernandes, Development of comprehensive kinetic models of ammonia/methanol ignition using Reaction Mechanism Generator (RMG). Combust. Flame. **251**, 112710 (2023) https://doi.org/10.1016/j.combustflame.2023.112710.
8. D.L. Baulch, C.J. Cobos, R.A. Cox, P. Frank, G. Hayman, T. Just, J.A. Kerr, T. Murrells, M.J. Pilling, J. Troe, R.W. Walker, and J. Warnatz, Evaluated Kinetic Data for Combustion Modeling. Supplement I. J. Phys. Chem. Ref. Data. **23**(6), 847-848 (1994) https://doi.org/10.1063/1.555953.
9. D. Baulch, C.T. Bowman, C.J. Cobos, R.A. Cox, T. Just, J. Kerr, M. Pilling, D. Stocker, J. Troe, and W. Tsang, Evaluated kinetic data for combustion modeling: supplement II. J. Phys. Chem. Ref. Data. **34**(3), 757-1397 (2005) https://doi.org/10.1063/1.1748524.
10. D. Zhu, Z. Qu, M. Li, S. Agarwal, R. Fernandes, and B. Shu, Investigation on the NO formation of ammonia oxidation in a shock tube applying tunable diode laser absorption spectroscopy. Combustion and Flame. **246**, 112389 (2022) https://doi.org/10.1016/j.combustflame.2022.112389.

Accurate Automation of Deadweight Force Standard Machine Based on Artificial Intelligent Model at NMCC-SASO-KSA

Hamad A. AlGhamdi*, Abdulelah A. Binown, Ahmed A. AlMatrawi

Saudi Standards, Metrology & Quality Org. – National Measurements & Calibration Center (SASO-NMCC)
Riyadh, Kingdom of Saudi Arabia
*h.gamdi@saso.gov.sa , a.binown@saso.gov.sa , a.matrawi@saso.gov.sa

Abstract

Accurate force measurements are critical in a various fields including metrology, material testing, and quality control. In this study, we propose an automated process for precise force measurements using Dead weight standard machines up to 1kN. This method leverages a combination of hardware and software components to achieve reliable results. The key steps in the automation process include the calibration Setup, which consists of a carefully calibrated force transducer used as a reference, which is selected based on its traceability to national standards. Automated Loading System (ALS) is the second item of the process, in which a motorized system places a known weights on the force transducer. The loading process was controlled to minimize disturbances and ensure accurate readings. The third step is Data Acquisition and Analysis, which includes a high-precision amplifier that collect force data during loading, process the acquired data, compensate for environmental factors (e.g., temperature and humidity) based on LabVIEW, and apply statistical analysis techniques to estimate the force values using python script based on classification machine learning. The full script is open source for all reader to apply in their different fields. The proposed automation process enhances measurement efficiency, reduces, cost, time, human errors, and ensures consistent results. This contributes to the advancement of force metrology and facilitates reliable force measurements in various applications.

Keywords:

LabVIEW, Python, Force, Machine, Digitization, Automation, Load cell, calibration.

1. Introduction

The National Metrology and Calibration Center (NMCC) at the Saudi Standards Metrology & Quality Organization (SASO), is committed to enhancing, advancing, and conserving the national standards of force, unit of Newton. The force laboratory also offers testing and calibration services to diverse sectors such as steel, concrete, military industrials, and scientific research, underscoring the pivotal role of the National Metrology Institute (NMI) in upholding a robust quality infrastructure. As defined by the Bureau International des Poids et Mesures (BIPM), metrology is the science of measurement, and it's vital for measurements of physical quantities like force to be conducted with a dependable stabilization system. This is of particular interest to researchers, scientists, equipment developers, and manufacturers who are invested in accurately measuring various substances. The NMI's metrology field primarily aims for high accuracy and precision in force lab from 200 N up to 5 MN [1,2,3,4].

The digital era has seen remarkable progress in big data, cloud computing, artificial intelligence (AI), and machine learning (ML). These technologies, including ML, deep learning, and neural networks, have been successfully integrated into metrology. The surge in computing and storage capabilities, coupled with increased data transfer speeds and the widespread availability of versatile sensors, has opened up new avenues for enhancing metrology tools, such as the Python programming language. Python is a versatile language used for machine learning, web development, desktop applications, and complex mathematical computations. Its simple syntax and ease of use make it an ideal choice. Python is particularly suited for ML, AI, descriptive and inferential statistics, and advanced mathematics, offering excellent results and accuracy with minimal resources and time. It boasts an extensive library system tailored for specific tasks; for advanced mathematics, libraries focusing on algebra, matrices, mathematics, visualization, exploratory data analysis (EDA), statistics, data pipelines, and data containers are utilized. One of our challenges is to digitalize the measurements of force and automate the process completely. In next sections we will introduce the three main steps in details.

2. Measurement system

The system of measurement consists of several connected equipment that works together in harmonized techniques as shown in the figure 1.

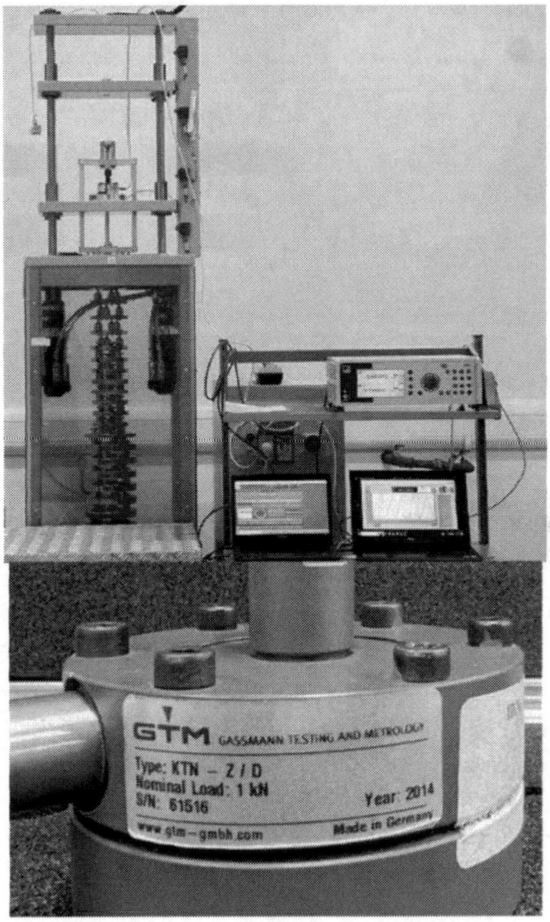

Figure 1. Force calibration Machine

2.1. Machine

Automated Loading System (ALS) is a motorized system places a known weights on the force transducer. The loading process was controlled to minimize disturbances and ensure accurate readings. Deadweight force machine code NMCC-MA-FO-003 has been used with several steps loading system [3].

Deadweight Force Standard Machines (DWMs) operate by using deadweights to measure force accurately. The weights are applied to a mechanical system to adjust the force. Weights are gradually added using precise motors, which automate the process of weight increment. The weights are either moved or adjusted by the motor to apply known amounts of force. Each weight represents a fixed value, such as 10 N or 50 N. The weights are added in successive steps to achieve the desired force. The calibration process with DWMs involves a series of precise steps to adjust and document the resulting force. During this process, 325 steps of commands (such as weight adjustments or motor modifications) are executed, while 81 precise readings are recorded, representing the measured force during calibration. Transducer calibration is carried out according to the ISO 376 standard, the transducer is connected to an indicator reading device, and then a known force (N) is applied using the DWMs. The resulting values are compared with reference values for accuracy. In order to convert the output signal from mV/V to Newton using a third-degree equation, it is essential to account for the relationship between the measured voltage (in mV/V) and the force (in Newton). A third-degree polynomial equation is commonly used when the relationship between voltage and force is nonlinear and requires precise correction to provide more accurate results, equation 1.

$$F = A\left(\frac{mV}{V}\right)^3 + B\left(\frac{mV}{V}\right)^2 + C\left(\frac{mV}{V}\right) + D \qquad 1$$

Where:

- F is the required force in Newtons (N).
- mV/V is the transducer output.
- A, B, C, D are constants determined through transducer calibration.

2.2. Measuring System

The measuring standard device used to acquire the reading data is DMP41 SN. 820669101. The DMP41 is a digital precision measuring amplifier known for its high accuracy and precision. It's often used in metrology specially in force measuring systems of strain gauge transducers, as well as transducers linked to weight, force, pressure, or torque. The Accuracy class is 0.0005 with resolution 6 digits and Long-term stability: ±5 ppm. DMP41 equipped with connectivity options: Ethernet, RS-232, USB.

3. Modeling and Algorithms

The automation model based on two main communicated programs, LabVIEW for automatic acquiring the data continuously from the DPM41 and store the collected pipeline of data to csv file and the second one is Python script that is coded with machine learning techniques based on classification and supported vectors.

3.1. LabVIEW

LabVIEW (Laboratory Virtual Instrument Engineering Workbench) is a graphical programming environment created, it's extensively utilized for applications involving testing, measurement, and control, enabling quick access to hardware and data insights. The program consists of two main parts, the front Pannel (figure 2) and block diagram (figure 3).

https://doi.org/10.1051/epjconf/202532306001

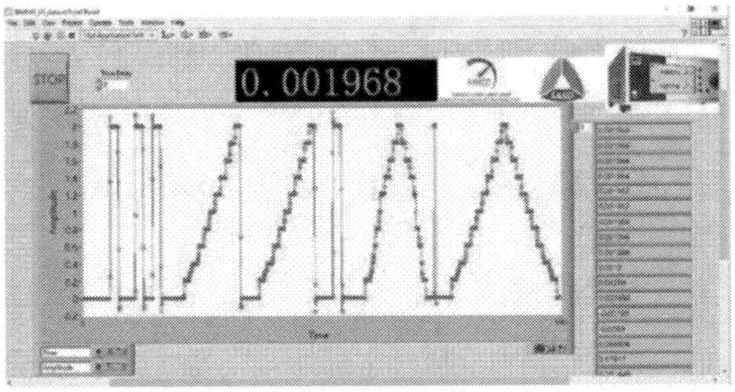

Figure 2. GUI Front Pannel

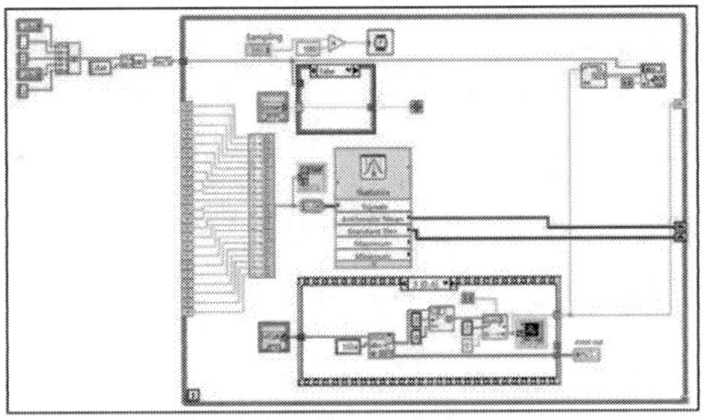

Figure 3. Block Diagram

The front panel consists of an indicator of live measurement, displaying chart for plotting the all acquired data and finally the last 50 consecutive readings with its mean, mode, median and standard deviation. The block diagram is the core of the program, it is start with LAN connection through VISA from DMP41 to the string reading (VISA-Read). The used code for this purpose is "MeAs?". The reading string handled with spitted technique again to separate the variable number into readable numeric. Finally, the numeric is acquired to csv file, connected to display and indicator in the front panel.

3.2. Python

Python is a versatile programming language known for its readability and simplicity. It is widely used for web development, data analysis, artificial intelligence, scientific computing, and more. Python is a popular choice for developing artificial intelligence (AI) applications due to its simplicity and the extensive libraries available for AI and machine learning [5-13]. We decided to use pythonic language in order to overcome the streamline pipeline of data that contains unwanted-polluted data (figure 4a) and scattered noise outliers (figure 4b). The challenge is how to extract only a specific step with its standard deviation and mean. This value is coming from a huge scattered data that reach in some cases to more than ten thousand of data.

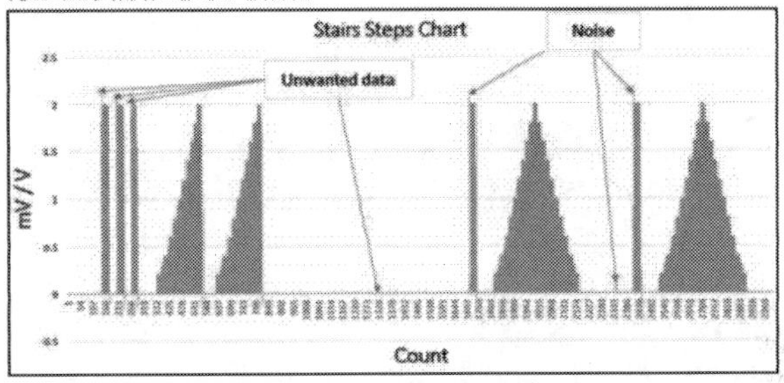

Figure 4.a Polluted data

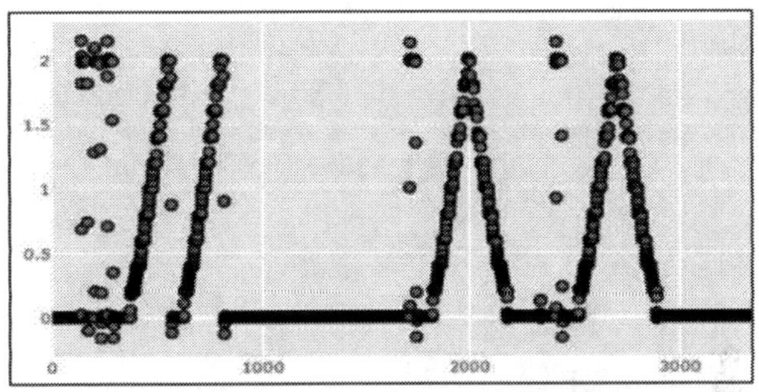

Figure 4.b Scattered data with outliers

The python script work under classification of data technique which is consider one of the strongest tools in machine learning. The full open script source in (Annex A),

4. Results

The calibration procedure begins with preloading the force-proving instrument three times to its maximum force in the direction in which the calibration forces will be applied. If the direction of loading is changed, the maximum force must also be applied three times in the new direction. Before applying the calibration forces, the force transducer is loaded to its maximum capacity three times, with each preload lasting between 30 to 60 seconds. After each preload, readings corresponding to no force are recorded after waiting at least 30 seconds for the force to be completely removed. A minimum of 3 minutes should pass between subsequent measurement series to allow stabilization.

In the calibration procedure, the zero signal is noted before starting. The calibration is performed by applying two series of calibration forces with increasing values, without disturbing the device. Then, at least two additional series of calibration forces with both increasing and decreasing values are applied at specific positions. These additional series are carried out after changing the angle or position of the force-proving instrument, typically at positions 0^0, 120^0, and 240^0, figure 5. The maximum force is applied each time the position changes. The time interval between successive loadings should be uniform, and no readings should be taken within 30 seconds after a force change to ensure accurate measurements, figure 5.

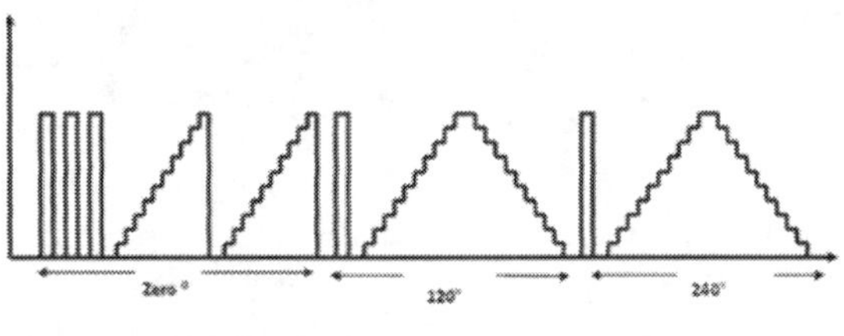

Figure 5.a Theoretical Scheme

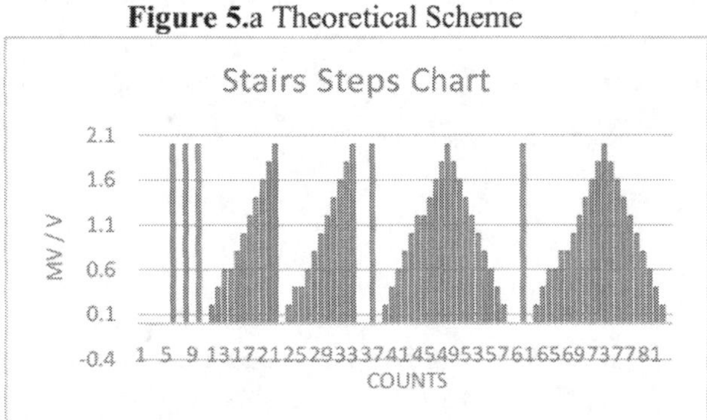

Figure 5.b clean data after classification

5. Conclusion

Machine learning model has been built in NMCC-SASO for accurate atomate the deadweights machine, the algorithm starts with acquire, handle, and stored the data as a phase one using LabVIEW. The second phase is coming with python code for selecting the proper data and extract only around 81 readings to link with the digital certificate in the soon future. The algorithm shows good performance for data ware during transition in the long series pipeline.

6. Reference

1. ISO 376:2011. "Metallic materials — Calibration of force-proving instruments used for the verification of uniaxial testing machines." International Organization for Standardization (ISO), 2011.
2. ASTM E4-16. "Standard Practices for Force Verification of Testing Machines." ASTM International, 2016. DOI: 10.1520/E0004-16
3. BIPM (Bureau International des Poids et Mesures). "International System of Units (SI)." International Bureau of Weights and Measures (BIPM), 9th edition, 2019. Available at: https://www.bipm.org/en/si
4. JCGM 100:2008 GUM. "Guide to the Expression of Uncertainty in Measurement." Joint Committee for Guides in Metrology, 2008. Available at: https://www.bipm.org/en/publications/guide
5. Jupyter Documentation (2024) retrieved from https://docs.jupyter.org/en/latest/
6. NumPy Documentation (2024) retrieved from https://numpy.org/news/
7. Pandas Documentation (2024) retrieved from https://pandas.pydata.org/docs/
8. Matplotlib Documentation (2024) retrieved from https://matplotlib.org/
9. Plotly Documentation (2024) retrieved from https://plotly.com/
10. SciPy Documentation (2024) retrieved from https://scipy.org/

11. Seaborn Documentation (2024) retrieved from https://seaborn.pydata.org/
12. statsmodels Documentation (2024) retrieved from https://www.statsmodels.org/stable/index.html
13. scikit-learn Documentation (2024) retrieved from https://scikit-learn.org/stable/

Annex-A Python Script

Import the required Liberaries

```
from dash import Dash, dcc, html, Input, Output
import plotly.graph_objects as go
import numpy as np
import pandas as pd
import matplotlib.pyplot as plt
import plotly.express as px
from plotly.subplots import make_subplots
import plotly.graph_objects as go
```

Read the stored data ¶

```
df = pd.read_excel(r't.xlsx')#, index_col='Date')
#df=df.dropna()
#df=df.drop(df.tail(1).index)
log = 0
```

```
app.layout = html.Div(
    [dcc.Graph(figure=fig, id='scatter-chart')]
)

@app.callback(
    Output('scatter-chart', 'figure'),
    Input('scatter-chart', 'relayoutData'),
    prevent_initial_call=True,
)
def update_title(relayout_data):
    try:
        x_min, x_max = relayout_data['xaxis.range[0]'],
        relayout_data['xaxis.range[1]']
        y_min, y_max = relayout_data['yaxis.range[0]'],
        relayout_data['yaxis.range[1]']
    except:
        avg = np.mean(y)
        min_val = np.min(y)
        max_val = np.max(y)
        y_pad = (max_val-min_val)/10
        std_val = np.std(y)
        n       = len(y)
        unc_val = std_val/np.sqrt(n)
        fig.update_layout(
            xaxis_range=[min(x), max(x)],
            yaxis_range=[min(y)-y_pad, max(y)+y_pad],
            title=f'Average: {avg:.0f},Std: {std_val:.0f}
            , n:{n}, unc: {unc_val:.0f}, Min: {min_val:.0f}
        , Max: {max_val:.0f}')
        return fig

    df_subset = df[df['x'].between(x_min,x_max)
    & df['y'].between(y_min,y_max)]
    avg     = df_subset['y'].mean()
    min_val = df_subset['y'].min()
    max_val = df_subset['y'].max()
    std_val = df_subset['y'].std()
    n       = len(df_subset['y'])
    unc_val = std_val/np.sqrt(n)
    #print(df_subset['y'].to_list())
    df_subset['y'].to_excel('out.xlsx',index=False, header=True)
    df_subset['y'].to_csv("out")
    fig.update_layout(
        xaxis_range=[x_min, x_max],
        yaxis_range=[y_min, y_max],
        title=f'Average: {avg:.0f},STD: {std_val:.0f}, n:{n}
        }, unc: {unc_val:.0f}, Min: {min_val:.0f}, Max: {max_val:.0f}',)
    return fig

if __name__ == '__main__':
    app.run_server(debug=True,port=8053)
```

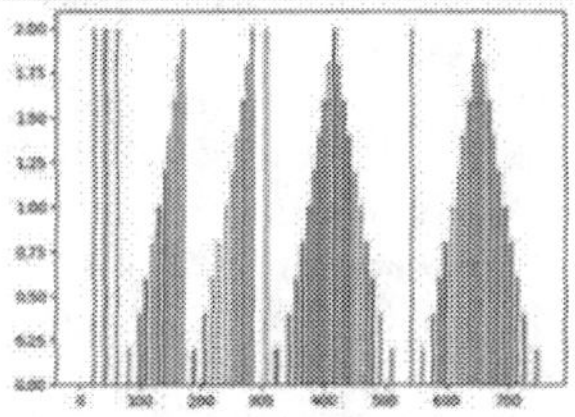

Criteria for filtering

```
#maximum = float(input('please enter Max level {}'))
#minimum = float(input('please enter Min level {}'))
criteria = float(input('Please enter the criteria {}'))
```

Please enter the criteria {} 0.0001

```
#df=pd.read_excel('t.xlsx')
#df = df[df.y<minimum]
#df = df[df.y>maximum]
```

```
data = df[df.columns[0]].to_list()
len(data)
```

6765

```
#d=[np.mean(i) for i,j in zip(data, data[1::]) if np.abs(i-j)<0.1]
#plt.scatter(y=data,x=np.linspace(0,len(data),len(data)))
```

```
[illegible]
```

```
tst=[]
for i in range (0, len(data)-1):
    if np.abs(data[i+1]-data[i])<criteria:
        tst.append(data[i])
    else:
        tst.append(0)

#plt.bar(np.linspace(0,len(tst),len(tst)),tst)
```

```
a = tst
split_value = 0

result = []
start = 0  # Initialize starting index for slicing

# Iterate through list to find
# indices of the split value
for i, value in enumerate(a):
    if value == split_value:

        # Add the sublist from start to the current index
        result.append(a[start:i])

        # Update start to next index after the split value
        start = i + 1

# Add the last sublist if there are remaining elements
if start < len(a):
    result.append(a[start:])
for i in range(0, len(result)):
    if result[i]==[]:
        result[i] = 0
    else: result[i] = np.mean(result[i])
result;
```

```
plt.bar(np.linspace(0,len(result),len(result)),result,width=4)
plt.show()
```

EPJ Web of Conferences **323**, 06001 (10125) Ht sp:/ odor. :g0ig02g:et jconf:101231306001
22nd nIt enr Iai nr dMt Iei a gylCi nget ss

Gauging error of pose acquired by vision systems in bin picking applications

Marek Franaszek*, *Prem* Rachakonda, and *Kamel S.* Saidi

National Institute of Standards and Technology, 100 Bureau Drive, Gaithersburg, MD 20899-8230, USA

Abstract. Picking a part from an unorganized pile of parts requires an accurate vision system integrated with a robotic arm. A proper metric for gauging pose error is therefore indispensable. Pose error is a combination of an error in the position vector and an error in the orientation matrix. Pose errors of a system under test (SUT) are calculated by comparing the poses obtained with the SUT with those obtained using a ground truth (GT) system whose measurements are registered to the SUT coordinate frame. Typically, the position error is calculated as the length of a vector connecting the SUT and the registered GT positions, and the orientation error is determined as the angle of relative rotation between the SUT and the registered GT orientation. However, many parts processed in industrial bin picking applications have axial symmetry and for such parts, the orientation cannot be determined uniquely. This causes the common metric for orientation error to be ambiguous and misleading. We show that a better and more reliable orientation metric can be calculated as the angle between the axes of symmetry for a part in the SUT and in the registered GT coordinate frame.

1 Introduction

Bin picking is a frequently deployed solution in manufacturing to automate tasks such as assembly or kitting. Its goal is to autonomously pick up a single part from an unorganized pile of parts and pass it to the next stage of the automated process. Successful completion of this goal requires a well calibrated robot integrated with the vision system, which must provide to the robot controller with the pose of each part. A part's pose (i.e., its position and orientation) needs to be accurately determined, to a degree related with a part's size, so that a gripper can approach and grab the part. Of the performance metrics that can be used to determine the suitability of a vision system for a particular application, pose error is a prominent one [1, 2].

However, pose error is usually not provided in the system's specification and there are few, non-trivial reasons for it. First, a six degree of freedom (6DoF) pose is rarely directly measured. Typically, raw data acquired either from 2D images or 3D point clouds are processed using various algorithms which output the 6DoF poses of parts [3, 4]. This means that the same data processed by different algorithms or different quality data input to the same algorithm may yield different results. Second, pose measuring systems provide their output in their own coordinate frames. Thus, the pose measured with the system under test (SUT) cannot be directly compared with that provided by a ground truth (GT) system. To calculate error in the SUT pose, the GT data must first be registered to the SUT frame and the registration error propagates into SUT pose error. Third, some objects may have axial symmetry and multiple equivalent orientations. Therefore, the standard way of gauging orientational misalignment as the angle of relative rotation between the SUT and the GT poses may be ambiguous and such objects are quite common in manufacturing applications.

In this paper, we specifically describe a novel method of gauging pose error of parts with axial symmetry that are randomly piled in a bin. We show that a better metric for such parts requires first fitting the computer-aided-design (CAD) model of the part to the SUT and GT point cloud data, and then reporting orientation error as the angle between the axes of symmetry of the two fitted CAD models. Attempts to derive pose errors directly from the 3D points acquired by the SUT and the GT sensors often yields ambiguous and incorrect results.

2 Previous work

For systems that determine pose from a set of markers, the influence of noise and bias in the marker locations on the derived pose was extensively studied [5, 6] and the standard for evaluating the performance of such systems was adopted [7]. For other systems, which do not rely on markers but derive pose from 3D point clouds, some bounds on pose variation may be obtained if the bounds of the noise affecting the 3D points are known [8], but such methods fail for objects with symmetry. The development of standards for 3D imaging system performance for use in automating the manufacturing process are an ongoing effort [9].

Symmetry of parts was specifically addressed in Maximum Symmetry-Aware Surface Distance (MSSD) used in benchmarking the 6D Object Estimation (BOP) challenge [10]. This metric has unit of length (e.g., mm)

* Corresponding author: marek@nist.gov

and requires prior determination of the symmetries that characterize a given part [11-13]. The MSSD metric is also used in a recently initiated perception challenge for bin picking [14].

3 Apparatus and test setup

In this work, two different systems were used to obtain the 3D data. The first one was a structured light camera mounted in a fixed position, the SUT. The second one was a laser line probe mounted on an Articulating Arm Coordinate Measuring Machine (AACMM), used as a GT system. The GT system acquires the data from various directions and automatically registers data. The SUT outputs data in the format of an organized 3D point cloud $\boldsymbol{s}_i$ of size $(N_{row}, N_{col}, 3)$, derived from the depth images of size (N_{row}, N_{col}), such as shown in **Fig. 1**. The GT system outputs an unorganized 3D point cloud $\boldsymbol{g}_j$. Both systems acquire the 3D point clouds in their respective coordinate frames.

Fig. 1. Example of a depth image acquired with the SUT.

Two different kinds of symmetric parts were used: M8 socket head cap screws and M12 hex nuts, both made from the same material. A bin was randomly filled with one kind of parts and scanned with both systems. This step was repeated for $K = 3$ different instances of random piles in the bin and for both kinds of parts.

4 Data processing

The data from the SUT were processed using the Segment Anything Model (SAM) algorithm [15]. SAM was applied to the depth images acquired by the SUT to automatically segment individual parts in the 2D Depth image of the bin. Once the resulting binary 2D masks of parts were obtained for each k-th instance of a pile in the bin ($k \leq K$), $M = 20$ masks were randomly selected, and their corresponding subsets of 3D points $\boldsymbol{S}_{m,k}$ were obtained, $m = 1, \ldots, M$ (see **Fig. 2**). This procedure was repeated for both the M8 screws and M12 nuts.

4.1 Registering GT to SUT frame

For each k-th instance of a pile of parts in a bin acquired by the SUT and the GT, the top part of a bin was manually segmented. The Iterative Closest Point (ICP) procedure was then used to get the rigid body transformation, $\boldsymbol{T}_k$, which can be used to register the GT frame to the SUT frame [16]. The outcome of this procedure is shown in **Fig. 3**. As the exit condition from ICP, the maximum number of iterations $I_{max} = 10$ was used.

Fig. 2. Example of segmentation masks generated automatically by SAM applied to 2D depth image (upper plot) and the corresponding 3D point cloud (lower graph). Segmented parts colored in blue.

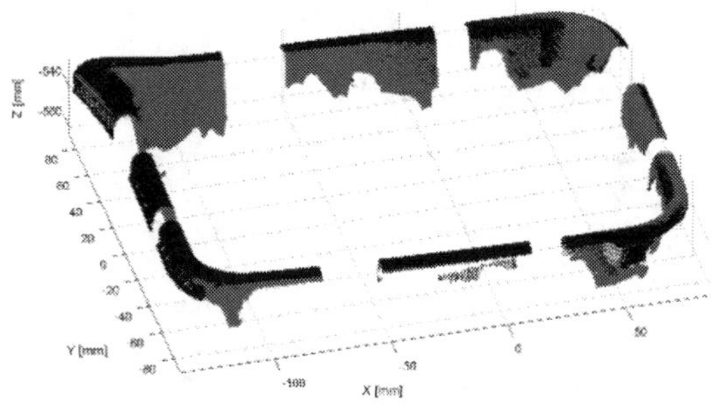

Fig. 3. Example of registering segmented bin from GT frame (black points) to SUT frame (blue points). For better visualization, portions of data are not displayed.

Once $\boldsymbol{T}_k$ was determined for each k-th instance of a pile, the GT data were transformed to the SUT coordinate frame. Then, for each selected earlier subset, $\boldsymbol{S}_{m,k}$ in the SUT data, the corresponding subset of 3D points, $\boldsymbol{G}_{m,k}$ from the transformed GT data was manually segmented.

4.2 Getting pose error without CAD fitting

For each k-th pile instance and each selected m-th part, the subset of 3D points, $\boldsymbol{G}_i$ was registered to $\boldsymbol{S}_i$ using ICP (to simplify notation, the part index i is used, $i = 1, \ldots, M \times K$). The outcome of this procedure is shown in **Fig. 4**. Initial pose for ICP was selected as in [17].

This step resulted in the individual transformations $\boldsymbol{T}_i = (\boldsymbol{R}_i, \boldsymbol{t}_i)$, where $\boldsymbol{R}_i$ is the rotation matrix and $\boldsymbol{t}_i$ is the translation vector. In this case, the position error p_i is expressed as the length of the translation as

$$p_i = \|\boldsymbol{t}_i\|, \tag{1}$$

and the angle β_i of rotation $\boldsymbol{R}_i$ is used as the orientation error, where

$$\beta_i(\boldsymbol{R}_i) = arcos((tr(\boldsymbol{R}_i) - 1)/2) \tag{2}$$

and $tr(\boldsymbol{R})$ is the trace of a matrix $\boldsymbol{R}$.

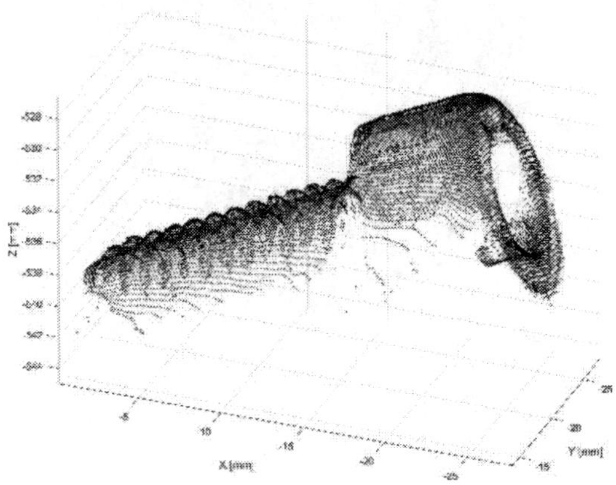

Fig. 4. Example of registering segmented 3D points $\boldsymbol{G}_i$ acquired by GT (black dots) to segmented $\boldsymbol{S}_i$ points (blue) acquired by SUT.

4.3 Calculating pose error using CAD fitting

Appropriate CAD models were also fitted to $\boldsymbol{S}_i$ and $\boldsymbol{G}_i$ using ICP for each i (i.e., each k-th pile instance and each selected m-th part), as shown in **Fig. 5**. This procedure yielded orientation matrices $\boldsymbol{\Omega}_{S,i}$ and $\boldsymbol{\Omega}_{G,i}$, and translation vectors $\boldsymbol{\tau}_{S,i}$ and $\boldsymbol{\tau}_{G,i}$. Based on these quantities, the orientation error $\omega_i(\boldsymbol{\Omega}_i)$, calculated as in (2), was determined as the angle of rotation of the relative rotation matrix $\boldsymbol{\Omega}_i$ as

$$\boldsymbol{\Omega}_i = \boldsymbol{\Omega}_{S,i}\,\boldsymbol{\Omega}_{G,i}^{-1} \tag{3}$$

where $\boldsymbol{\Omega}^{-1}$ is the inverse of matrix $\boldsymbol{\Omega}$. Position error e_i was then calculated as

$$e_i = \left\|\boldsymbol{\tau}_{S,i} - \boldsymbol{\tau}_{G,i}\right\|. \tag{4}$$

In addition, another orientation error α_i was calculated as the angle between the axes of symmetry $\boldsymbol{u}_{S,i}$ and $\boldsymbol{u}_{G,i}$ as

$$\alpha_i = arcos(\boldsymbol{u}_{S,i} \cdot \boldsymbol{u}_{G,i}) \tag{5}$$

where $\left\|\boldsymbol{u}_{S,i}\right\| = \left\|\boldsymbol{u}_{G,i}\right\| = 1$ and "·" is the dot product. Vector $\boldsymbol{u}_{S,i}$ was aligned with the axis of symmetry of a CAD model fitted to $\boldsymbol{S}_i$ and $\boldsymbol{u}_{G,i}$ was aligned with the axis of symmetry of a CAD model fitted to $\boldsymbol{G}_i$, as shown in **Fig. 6**.

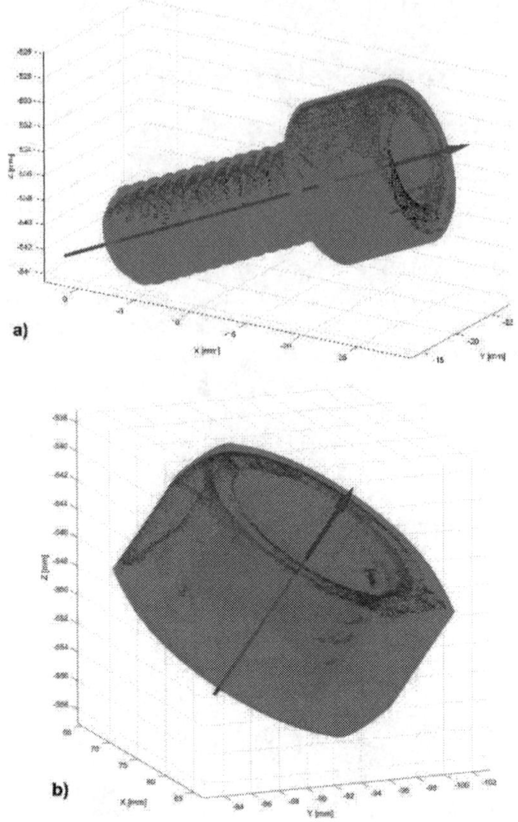

Fig. 5. Examples of CAD (in red) fitted to segmented 3D points (black dots) which belong to a): $\boldsymbol{S}_i$ acquired by SUT; b) $\boldsymbol{G}_i$ acquired by GT and transformed to SUT frame. Blue arrows represent axes of symmetry determined from CAD models.

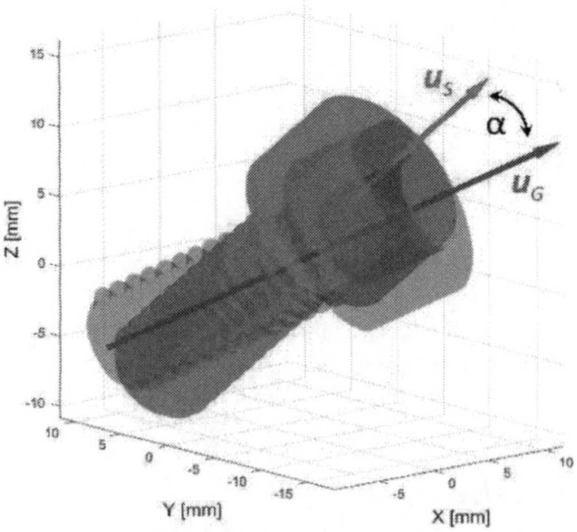

Fig. 6. Two CAD models fitted to $\boldsymbol{S}_i$ and the corresponding $\boldsymbol{G}_i$ subsets. Arrows represent the axes of symmetry, parallel to the unit vectors $\boldsymbol{u}_S$ and $\boldsymbol{u}_G$, the angle α is an acute angle between unit vectors.

5 Results

The outcome of the procedure described in Section 4.2. is presented in **Fig. 7** for a bin filled with M2 socket head cap screws. In this procedure, CAD models were not used and the pose error was calculated by registering the subset of 3D points $\boldsymbol{G}_i$ to $\boldsymbol{S}_i$ and by calculating the position error p_i from (1) and the orientation error β_i from (2). In addition, the residual ICP registration error e_{pc} is plotted in **Fig.** 7a and a distance Δ_i between two centroids $\overline{\boldsymbol{S}}_i$ and $\overline{\boldsymbol{G}}_i$ as

$$\Delta_i = \|\overline{\boldsymbol{S}}_i - \overline{\boldsymbol{G}}_i\| \ . \quad (6)$$

The corresponding results for a bin filled with M12 nuts are shown in **Fig. 8**.
The outcome of the procedure described in Section 4.3 is presented in **Fig. 9** for a bin filled with M8 screws. In this procedure, CAD models were fitted to each subset of 3D points $\boldsymbol{S}_i$ and $\boldsymbol{G}_i$, and the resulting two transformations $(\boldsymbol{\Omega}_{S,i}, \boldsymbol{\tau}_{S,i})$ and $(\boldsymbol{\Omega}_{G,i}, \boldsymbol{\tau}_{G,i})$ were used to characterize the error of the pose provided by the SUT. In **Fig. 9**a, the residual ICP error of fitting CAD to $\boldsymbol{G}_i$ is plotted. **Fig. 9**b shows distance e_i (calculated from (4)) between the positions of the fitted CAD models. In **Fig. 9**c, the rotation angle ω_i of a matrix of relative rotation $\boldsymbol{\Omega}_i$ determined from (3) is plotted. Finally, in **Fig. 9**d, the angle α_i (calculated from (5)) and illustrated in **Fig. 6**, is plotted.

The corresponding results for a bin filled with M12 nuts are shown in **Fig. 10**.

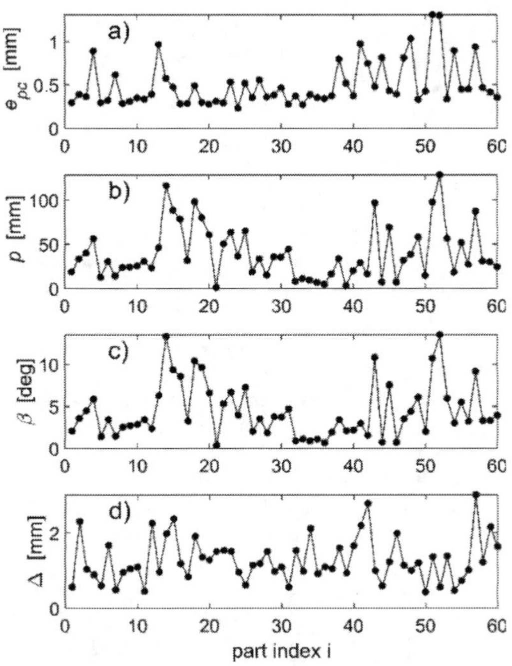

Fig. 7. Results for M8 screws: a) ICP error e_{pc} of registering point cloud $\boldsymbol{G}_i$ to $\boldsymbol{S}_i$; b) length p_i of the translation vector from ICP; c) rotation angle β_i from ICP; d) distance Δ_i between the centroids of $\boldsymbol{G}_i$ and $\boldsymbol{S}_i$.

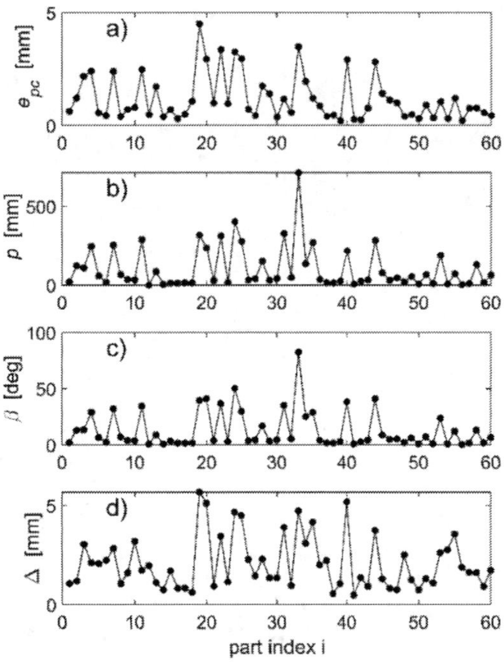

Fig. 8. Results for M12 nuts: a) ICP error e_{pc} of registering point cloud $\boldsymbol{G}_i$ to $\boldsymbol{S}_i$; b) length p_i of the translation vector from ICP; c) rotation angle β_i from ICP; d) distance Δ_i between the centroids of $\boldsymbol{G}_i$ and $\boldsymbol{S}_i$.

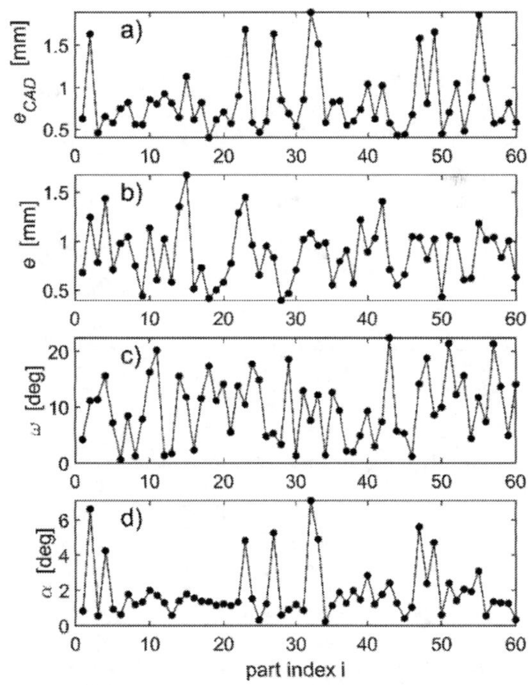

Fig. 9. Results for M8 screws: a) ICP error e_{CAD} of registering CAD to $\boldsymbol{G}_i$; b) distance e_i between the positions of CAD models fitted to $\boldsymbol{G}_i$ and $\boldsymbol{S}_i$; c) angle ω_i of relative rotation matrix $\boldsymbol{\Omega}_i$ in (3); d) angle α_i between axes of symmetry of CAD models fitted to $\boldsymbol{G}_i$ and $\boldsymbol{S}_i$.

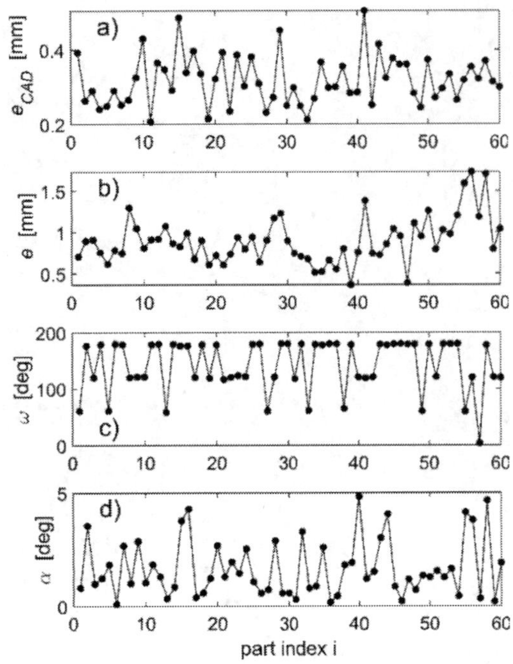

Fig. 10. Results for M12 nuts: a) ICP error e_{CAD} of registering CAD to $\boldsymbol{G}_i$; b) distance e_i between the positions of CAD models fitted to $\boldsymbol{G}_i$ and $\boldsymbol{S}_i$; c) angle ω_i of relative rotation matrix $\boldsymbol{\Omega}_i$ in (3); d) angle α_i between axes of symmetry of CAD models fitted to $\boldsymbol{G}_i$ and $\boldsymbol{S}_i$.

Table 1. Summary of mean errors

Mean Errors	Screws M8	Nuts M12
L_{min} [mm]	13.0	10.0
$\bar{e}_{pc}$ [mm]	0.50	1.11
$\bar{e}_{CAD}$ [mm]	0.83	0.32
$\bar{p}$ [mm]	39.43	96.69
$\bar{\Delta}$ [mm]	1.29	2.01
$\bar{e}$ [mm]	0.87	0.89
$\bar{\beta}$ [deg]	4.40	11.82
$\bar{\omega}$ [deg]	9.75	141.48
$\bar{\alpha}$ [deg]	1.88	1.65

6 Discussion

The ICP procedure was used in this study to register pairs of experimentally acquired, segmented subsets of points, such as shown in **Fig. 4**, or to fit CAD models to the experimental points, such as shown in **Fig. 5**. The rigid body transformations (rotations and translations) resulting from ICP were then used to evaluate different metrics, such as orientation errors β_i, α_i, ω_i and position errors p_i or e_i. Therefore, it is important to ensure that the poses obtained from the ICP procedure are correct, especially as the ICP process can be easily trapped in wrong local minima and can provide incorrect poses when an initial pose is not properly chosen.

All outcomes of ICP, such as displayed in **Fig. 4** and **Fig. 5**, were visually inspected, and the corresponding residual errors were checked. Examples of residual errors e_{pc} are plotted in **Fig. 7**a and **Fig. 8**a, and for e_{CAD} in **Fig. 9**a and **Fig. 10**a. Compared with the smallest size L_{min} of the bounding box containing the part, the registration was quite accurate as evidenced by small mean ICP errors $\bar{e}_{pc}$ and $\bar{e}_{CAD}$ in **Table 1**. Yet, the large values of some of the reported errors are in striking disagreement with visual evaluations and with the small values of the residual ICP errors.

Attempts to characterize pose error without fitting CAD models (as described in Section 4.2) yielded large orientation errors β_i displayed in **Fig. 7**c and **Fig. 8**c, see average errors $\bar{\beta}$ for screws and nuts in **Table 1**. The corresponding position errors p_i plotted in **Fig. 7**b and **Fig. 8**b seem to indicate a huge displacement between $\boldsymbol{S}_i$ and $\boldsymbol{G}_i$ 3D points (blue and black points in **Fig. 4**), which contradicts visual inspection and the displacements between centroids Δ_i plotted in **Fig. 7**d and **Fig. 8**d (compare also mean position errors $\bar{p}$ with mean displacements $\bar{\Delta}$ in **Table 1**).

It appears that incorrect displacement errors p_i, which are the length of the translation vectors $\boldsymbol{t}_i$ from ICP registration as in (1), are a consequence of ambiguous rotations $\boldsymbol{R}_i$ resulting from registering $\boldsymbol{G}_i$ to $\boldsymbol{S}_i$. In the ICP procedure, the translation vector $\boldsymbol{t}_i$ is obtained after the rotation matrix $\boldsymbol{R}_i$ is calculated as

$$\boldsymbol{t}_i = \bar{\boldsymbol{S}}_i - \boldsymbol{R}_i \bar{\boldsymbol{G}}_i \,, \tag{7}$$

where $\bar{\boldsymbol{S}}_i$ and $\bar{\boldsymbol{G}}_i$ are the corresponding centroids. If line-of-sight sensors are used to acquire 3D data (as is the case in many industrial bin picking applications) then the centroids $\bar{\boldsymbol{S}}_i$ and $\bar{\boldsymbol{G}}_i$ are not located on the part's axis of symmetry. Thus, the ambiguity of $\boldsymbol{R}_i$ in (7) must affect the vector $\boldsymbol{t}_i$ and this makes p_i an unsuitable metric for gauging position error (note the very strong correlation between p_i and β_i, displayed in **Fig. 7**b,c and **Fig. 8**b,c). Therefore, attempts to characterize the error of the pose based only on registration of the segmented 3D points $\boldsymbol{G}_i$ to $\boldsymbol{S}_i$ will be unsuccessful for parts with symmetry.

Deriving pose metrics from CAD models fitted to points $\boldsymbol{G}_i$ and $\boldsymbol{S}_i$, such as shown in **Fig. 5** and **Fig. 6**, is also challenging. While the position error e_i defined in (4) takes on reasonably small values in **Fig. 9**b and **Fig. 10**b (see mean errors $\bar{e}$ in **Table 1**), the orientation error ω_i, calculated from the matrix of relative rotation $\boldsymbol{\Omega}_i$ in (3) still has misleadingly large values ω_i plotted in **Fig. 9**c and **Fig. 10**c (see mean orientation errors $\bar{\omega}$ in **Table 1**).

It is worth noting that the ambiguity of the rotations $\boldsymbol{\Omega}_{S,i}$ and $\boldsymbol{\Omega}_{G,i}$ (from which $\boldsymbol{\Omega}_i$ is calculated) does not affect the translation vectors $\boldsymbol{\tau}_{S,i}$ and $\boldsymbol{\tau}_{G,i}$ (from which the position errors e_i are calculated) and, unlike position errors p_i which are flawed by large values, e_i provide appropriately small position errors. The root cause of the difference between p_i and e_i is that the centroids of the CAD models are located on the axes of symmetry and therefore, ambiguities in rotations $\mathbf{\Omega}_{S,i}$ and $\mathbf{\Omega}_{G,i}$ around those axes do not affect translation vectors $\boldsymbol{\tau}_{S,i}$ and $\boldsymbol{\tau}_{G,i}$.

It appears that the angle α_i between the axes of symmetry, as illustrated in **Fig. 6**, provides a more realistic estimate of the orientation error, as shown in **Fig. 9**d, **Fig. 10**d and characterized by mean angles $\bar{\alpha}$ in **Table 1**.

For parts used in this study (M8 socket head cap screws and M12 hex nuts), the mean angle $\bar{\alpha}$ was sufficient to describe rotational misalignment, but generally, rotations around the axes of symmetry may also contribute to the overall error. In such cases, the total error will have a contribution from rotating $\boldsymbol{u}_G$ vector to $\boldsymbol{u}_S$, as in **Fig. 6**, and then an additional angular component resulting from a rotation around $\boldsymbol{u}_S$.

Using CAD models fitted to SUT and GT data and the mean angle $\bar{\alpha}$ as an orientation error may be more practical than MSSD in bin picking applications. To execute a successful pick, planning a gripper's approach to a part requires knowledge of the full CAD surface, including sections of the surface occluded during data collection. Therefore, the angular error of the CAD orientation may be more useful than the distance provided by MSSD, which is calculated only from points covering a fraction of the part's surface within line-of-sight of the sensor.

7 Conclusions

For parts with axial symmetry, the commonly used orientation error (defined as the angle of relative rotation between CAD models fitted to SUT and GT data) provides estimates which are unreliable and inconsistent with visual inspection. The angle between two axes of symmetry corresponding to two fitted CAD models are more useful in gauging the orientation error for such parts. Position error defined as the distance between the positions of two fitted CAD models also provides a useful metric.

Use of CAD models is crucial as the errors derived from registering two subsets of 3D points acquired by the SUT and the GT provide a misleading metric, which is inconsistent with visual inspection of the two datasets.

References

[1] H. Alzarok, S. Fletcher, and A. P. Longstaff, "Survey of the current practices and challenges for vision systems in industrial robotic grasping and assembly applications," *Advances in Industrial Engineering,* vol. 9, no. 1, pp. 19-30, 2020.

[2] R.Bogue, "Bin picking: a review of recent developments," *Industrial Robot* vol. 50, no. 6, pp. 873-877, 2023.

[3] Z.He, W.Feng, X.Zhao, and Y.Lv, "6D Pose Estimation of Objects: Recent Technologies and Challenges - Review," *Applied Sciences,* vol. 11, 2021.

[4] G.Marullo, L.Tanzi, P.Piazzolla, and E.Vezzetti, "6D object position estimation from 2D images: a literature review," *Multimedia Tools and Applications,* vol. 82, pp. 24605 - 24643, 2023.

[5] J. M. Fitzpatrick and J. B. West, "The Distribution of Target Registration Error in Rigid-Body Point-Based Registration," *IEEE Trans. Medical Imaging,* vol. 20, no. 9, pp. 917-927, 2001.

[6] M. H. Moghari and P. Abolmaesumi, "Distribution of Target Registration Error for Anisotropic and Inhomogeneous Fiducial Localization Error," *IEEE Trans. Medical Imaging,* vol. 28, no. 6, pp. 799-813, 2009.

[7] *Standard Test Method for Evaluating the Performance of Systems that Measure Static, Six Degrees of Freedom (6DOF), Pose*, ASTM E2919-13, 2013.

[8] H. Yang, J. Shi, and L. Carlone, "Teaser: Fast and certifiable point cloud registration," *IEEE Trans. on Robotics,* vol. 37, no. 2, pp. 314-333, 2021.

[9] P.Rachakonda *et al.*, "Towards the development of standards and performance metrics for 3D imaging systems " in *SPIE Defense + Commercial Sensing 2024*, National Harbor, MD, US, 2024: SPIE.

[10] T.Hodan *et al.*, "BOP Challenge 2020 on 6D Object Localization," *arXiv:2009.07378v2 [cs.CV],*

[11] R. Bregier, F. Devernay, L. Leyrit, and J. L. Crowley, "Symmetry Aware Evaluation of 3D Object Detection and Pose Estimation in Scenes of Many Parts in Bulk," presented at the ICCV, 2017.

[12] H.Zhao *et al.*, "Learning Symmetry-Aware Geometry Correspondences for 6D Object Pose Estimation," in *ICCV*, Paris, France, 2023, pp. 14045 - 14054.

[13] W.Niu, X.Huang, H.Xiang, X.Wang, and S.Ji, "A symmetry-aware alignment method for photogrammetric 3D models," *ISPRS Journal of Photogrammetry and Remote Sensing,* vol. 204, 2023.

[14] OpenCV. (2025). *Perception Challenge for Bin-picking*. Available: https://bpc.opencv.org

[15] A. Kirillov *et al.*, "Segment Anything," *arXiv:2304.02643v1 [cs.CV],*

[16] P. J. Besl and N. D. McKay, "A method for registration of 3-D shapes," *IEEE Trans. Pattern Analysis and Machine Intelligence,* vol. 14, pp. 239-256, 1992.

[17] M.Franaszek, P.Rachakonda, and K.S.Saidi, "Improving Fitting CAD to 3D Point Cloud Acquired with Line-of-Sight Sensor," presented at the IEEE Int. Symposium on Robotic and Sensors Environment ROSE'23, Tokyo, 2023.

EPJ Web of Conferences **323**, 06001 (2025) https://doi.org/j 0.j 05j /ep3conf/202512106001
22nd nIt enr Iai nr dMt Iei ai gylCi nget ss

Automation and monitoring of lab- and industrial-scale food processing facilities for quality project management

Pierre Casaubieilh[1], Luidgi Résidant[1], Bertrand Heyd[1], Jérôme Bussière[1], Thomas Cattenoz[1], Matthieu Sénoville[1]*

[1]Université Paris-Saclay, INRAE, AgroParisTech, UMR SayFood, 91120 Palaiseau, France

* Corresponding author: pierre.casaubieilh@agroparistech.fr

Abstract. This paper presents the challenges and strategies for automation and monitoring in food processing at the pilot scale, within a teaching and research environment, the Technological Hall of the SayFood Laboratory. The objective is to ensure data accessibility, enhance quality management, and improve knowledge of unit transformation processes. Given the high heterogeneity of the equipments, various sensor technologies and data acquisition strategies are explored, along with software and hardware implementations tailored to support both research and industry needs. The integration of open-source solutions, Python-based tools, and web technologies is discussed, with a strong emphasis on the Industrial Internet of Things (IIoT) and interoperability.

1 Context

Processes in food and bioproduct engineering can cover serval domains from raw materials to the customers, and involves various contributors such as students, researchers, and industries. Their needs converge on accessing data and improving quality through monitoring physical parameters like temperature, pressure, humidity, mass, and energy consumption on multiple involved transformation processes like grinding, mixing, filtering and heating. In our facilities, laboratory- and industrial-scale equipments enable to support broad projects and research. In order to implement quality in our processes and project management, a plan has been set to investigate, define and develop solutions to monitor all equipments.

Processes equipments arrangements are with or without embedded control & monitoring software, electronics, and/or old instrumentations. Applications can be manually operated by users, controlled through commercial Human-Machine-Interface (IHM) or are in need for revamping to support new projects requirements. Some systems require data to be stored on the server for post processing; others mainly need to have the physical and process parameters to monitored in order to act manually on the changes.

Several softwares are commercially available (for example WinCC, PCVue, LabVIEW, EcoStruxure…) to develop Human Machine Interface for Supervisory Control and Data Acquisition (SCADA). Current laboratories and industries can limit their choice on some communication protocols (Serial, Modbus, Local Area Network), as software licences costs are dependent on the number variables and communication protocols to ease of data management.

Non of the solutions on market, or developed by other researchers suit our broad spectrum of food processing equipments.

A solution is then deployed to track and monitor equipments collecting, saving and arranging data for quality and metrology management.

2 Technological Platform & SayFood

SayFood is composed of 5 multidisciplinary teams dealing with raw-materials-to-consumers subjects. It has dedicated laboratories for chemistry, microbiology and sensory analysis, an experimental restaurant and a technological platform. In total, 200 equipments are then available for research, teaching & training and knowledge transfer.

The current paper concentrates on the Technological platform which is spread over 2720 m^2. It has 70 pilots with heterogeneous applications. It covers all aspects of food processing and transformation.

Over the manual, automatic or semi-automatic equipments being available in our facilities, case studies focus on three pilot-scale systems: the "*fluidised bed*", it required the installation of various sensors (air flow, humidity, temperatures, mass) and a signal acquisition strategy to help the user during the manual process; the "*tangential flow filtration*", a revamping and upgrading of its electronic is necessary; the "*plate heat exchanger*", pressure and temperature sensors were added to evaluate heat exchange parameters.

What's more, two solutions (IoT, commercial) are investigated for temperature monitoring in our cold chambers due to quality requirements.

A general objective is then to set-up and deploy a supervisory solution for all the equipments available at SayFood.

Ongoing efforts within the Technological Hall aim to improve automation and data accessibility. To support these initiatives, several key systems have been instrumented for monitoring and control, ensuring efficient data acquisition and process management.

3 Data-Acquisition and supervision strategy

The challenges in data acquisition for our pilot-scale equipments of the Technological Platform include equipment heterogeneity, data accessibility, and cost. A significant aspect is the heterogeneity of equipment landscape, as pilots often consist of devices employed in various food transformation processes and from different manufacturers, each utilising different communication protocol standards.

Processes equipments arrangements are with or without electronics and sensors. They may include or not embedded control and monitoring software, electronics, and/or legacy instrumentations.

Applications can be manually operated by users, controlled through commercial Interface-Home-Machine (IHM) or are in need for revamping to support new projects requirements. Some systems require data to stored on the server for post processing ; others mainly need to have the physical and process parameters to monitored in order to act manually on the changes. This diversity necessitates a versatile solution capable of interfacing with multiple protocols to ensure data acquisition and integration across all systems. Additionally, some manufactured systems are equipped with embedded sensors designed for only regulation purposes and their data are not readily accessible. This limitation drives us to develop custom solutions to access and record the necessary data.

Several commercial software solutions providing data acquisition and monitoring capabilities, such as WinCC, PCVue, LabVIEW, and EcoStruxure, are available as Human-Machine Interfaces (HMI) in Supervisory Control and Data Acquisition (SCADA) systems. Additionally, those commercialare often expensive for a research laboratory due to licensing fees, which are typically based on the number of variables monitored and the specific communication protocols used. This cost barrier makes it challenging to implement such solutions on a large scale and forces to limit laboratories and industries can limit their choice on some communication protocols (Serial, Modbus, Local Area Network), as software licences costs are depend to the number variables and communication protocols.

4 Pilots and current data

This section presents the actual data-acquisition methods and some data of the process pilots, in particular for the plate heat exchanger, the cold chambers, the fluidised bed and the tangential flow filtration. These reflect the diversity of equipments and uses that can be encountered at the Technological Platform.

4.1 Tangential Flow Filtration

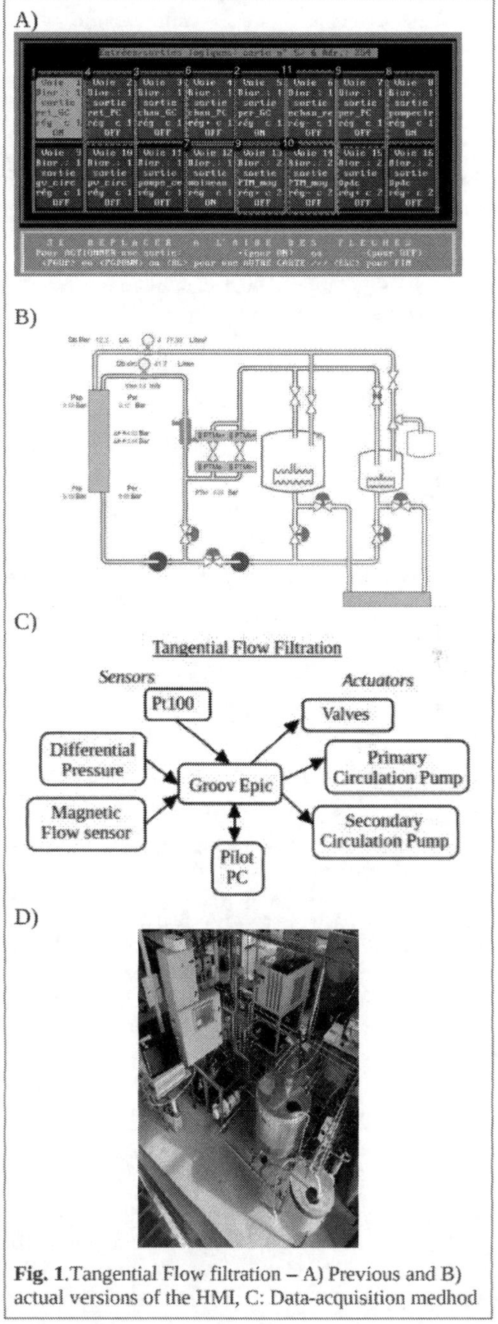

Fig. 1.Tangential Flow filtration – A) Previous and B) actual versions of the HMI, C: Data-acquisition medhod

The Labstak Tangential Flow Filtration (TFF) pilot, shown in (Fig. 1-D)), had an initial control and monitoring solution developed in our facilities with an human-machine-interface based-on MS-DOS (Fig. 1-A)). The control strategy has been revamped as Opto22 Groov Epic is incoporated with analog inputs and outputs and Pt100 modules. It has a web-based development tool and the HMI has the main parts being represented Fig. 1-B). This pilote is used for example in pre-filtration or to solution concentration applications. Without going to much in details in the experimental protocols, a first pump feeds to primary line, returning to the main tank. When the flow rate is stable, the second feed pump is turned ON to push the solution to the secondary line equiped with the filtration membrane. By applying a differential pressure across the filtration membrane, permeate and rententate are separated.

Doule jacket tanks are used with heating control either from the steam line at our infrastructure or using an independent heat regulation system.

The Groov Epic monitors the differential pressure, temperatures, magnetic flow (Optiflux 4300 (Krohne) + 800 series (Foxboro)) and controls a series valves (Gemü) and the pumps rotation speeds (Fig. 1-C)). It is also equipped with a P4Q-CV16 quick exhaust valve in case that critical pressure is reached. An example of results is presented on Fig. 2.

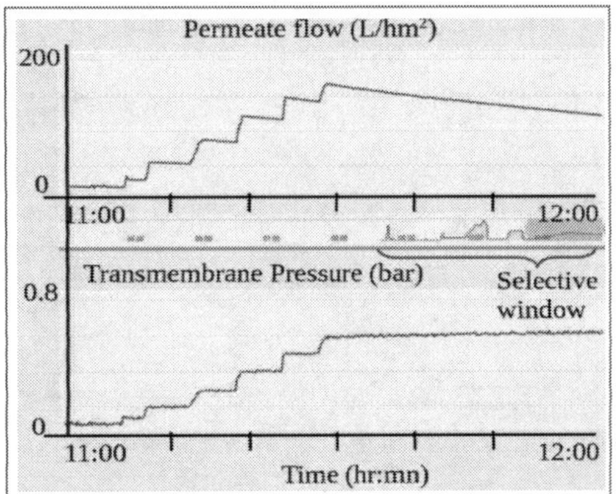

Fig. 2. Permeate flow and transmembrane Pressure

On the HMI, there is a section to visualise raw and calculated parameters as a function of time. As the pressure is increased across the filtration membrane, the formation of the "cake" is observed. With a selective window, it is possible to trace back the acquired data during the processes for verification or post data treatment.

4.2 Fluidised bed

The Glatt Fluidised bed is manually operated with electro- and pneumatic-control (Fig. 3-B)). It can be used for drying, agglomeration and particle coating.

A series of sensors are placed around the fluidised bed to monitor the process and to bring physical parameters information to the user. The environmental conditions (air flow, temperature) have to be reached to progress through the protocol. They can be adjusted according the materials characteristics (particle size, mass) being employed.

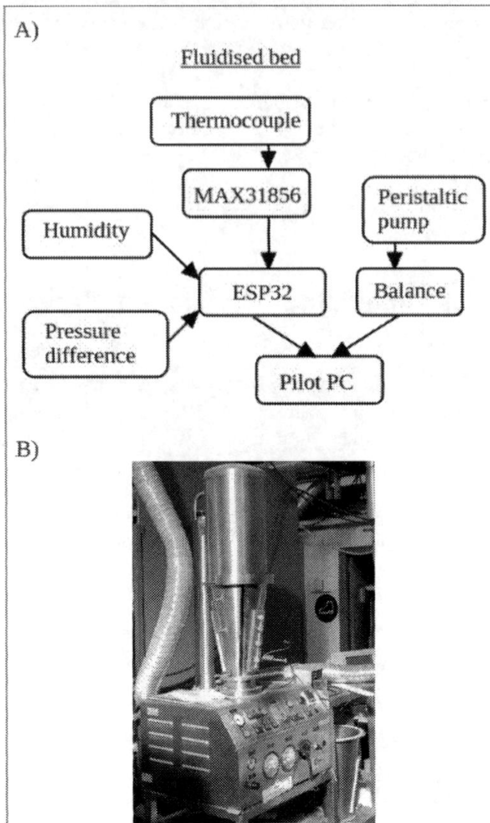

Fig. 3. Fluidised bed – A) Data-acquisition method, B) Fluidised bed pilot

A series of sensors are placed around the fluidised bed to monitor the process and to bring physical parameters information to the user. The steady environmental conditions (air flow, temperature) have to be reached to progress through the protocol. They can be adjusted according the materials characteristics (particle size, mass) being employed. The pilot is instrumented with two humidity transmitter (HF5A Rotronic) located at the air entrance and exit, three thermocouples and a differential pressure transmitter (FCX-AIV) for air flow measurement. A balance (Precisa LS6200D) is combined with a peristaltic pump (Petro Gas Berlin) to control the amount of liquid solution being sprayed through the nozzle at the top of the chamber. A desiccant dehumidifier (Munters M120) can be connected at the air entrance if a better control on the air humidity is required. An ESP32 board is prepared to acquire all data from the sensors (Fig. 3-A)). An HMI code is developed in Python to collect and display all data.

4.3 Spray Dryer

The Spray Dryer comes from GEA with built-in control based-on WinCC ((Fig. 4-B)). The user modifies the physical settings parameters (temperature, flow rate) of the process through the HMI of the Siemens Simatic TouchScreen. This communicates with an analog input and output PLC (S7-300) to control and monitor the equipments surrounding the pilot, such as Pt100 temperature measurement, peristaltic pump (Watson Marlow 530u), air flow measurement via differential pressure gauge and Rotronic Hygroflex (Fig. 4-A)).

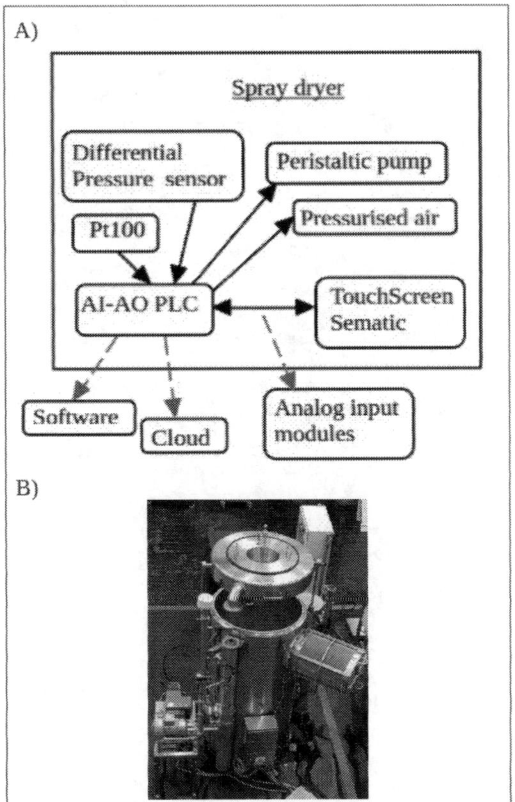

Fig. 4. Spray dryer – A) Control of the equipment, B) Spray dryer pilot

Simatic Cloud Connect Interface (CC712) and OPC Simatic NET Software are evaluated to get a remote access to all acquired data and to enhance the data transfer to the supervisory PC.

It is also investigated the possibility to employ Opto22 analog input modules (SNAP-PAC) or Groov Epic to interact with the transferred signals between the Simatic TouchScreen and the PLC, as expertise is already available in our facilities.

4.4 Plate Heat Exchanger

The Vicarb plate heat exchanger (PHE) is employed to calculate exchange coefficients between a cold and hot fluid lines (Fig. 5-B). This requires the combination of temperature and pressure and flow rate measurements and also having the characteristics of the PHE pilot [1, 2].

Four water pressure sensors from DFRobot (range: 0-1.6MPa; Accuracy: 0.5-1% Full Scale) and 4 Pt100 (connected to Adafruit Pt100 Amplifier: MAX31865) enable to monitor the temperatures and the pressures at the inputs and the outputs of the cold and hot water lines. Their signals are acquired with an ESP32. The water flows are adjusted with float flowmeters (Tubux M30, Mecon). A Raspberry Pi communicates with the ESP32 and makes a compact solution. Secure Shell (ssh) protocol is employed to get access through the local network (LAN) to remote user pc to transfer data, which are also saved on a back-up PC (Fig. 5-A)).

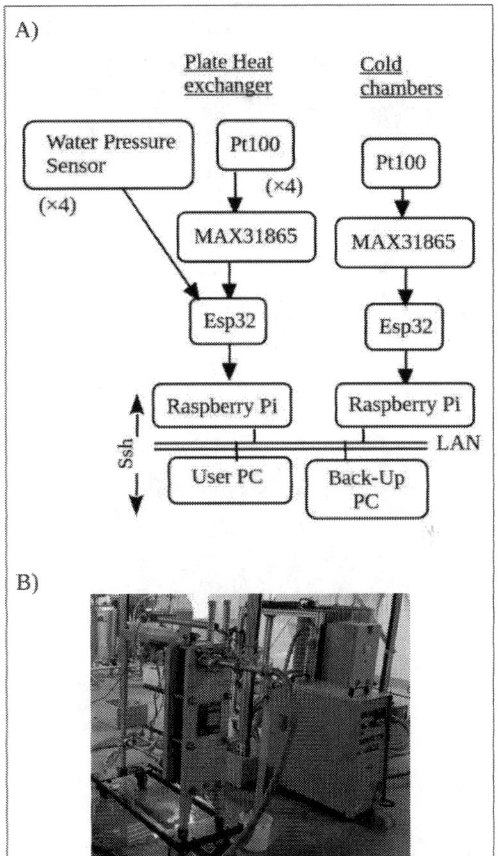

Fig. 5. Plate heat exchanger – A) Data-acquisition method, B) PHE pilot

4.5 Cold Chambers

Two methods have been set-up to collect the temperatures of the cold chambers (4 and -20° C) in separated locations (laboratories, Food grade area). Managing cold chambers temperatures is carried out automatically in our facilities and records not shared by the geostationary. For regulatory, management quality of our facilities and project collaborations, it is mandatory to have access to these data; this can help in identifying if preventive and curative maintenances are required.

On a similar approach to the PHE pilot, a Raspberry Pi collects data cold from chambers next to laboratories with Pt100 and is connected to the back-up PC (Fig. 5-A)). Fig. 6 shows the continuous monitoring of the cold chambers temperatures. Plots are updated every 2 mn. The peaks are due to a defrost process to avoid having ice-forming in the chambers.

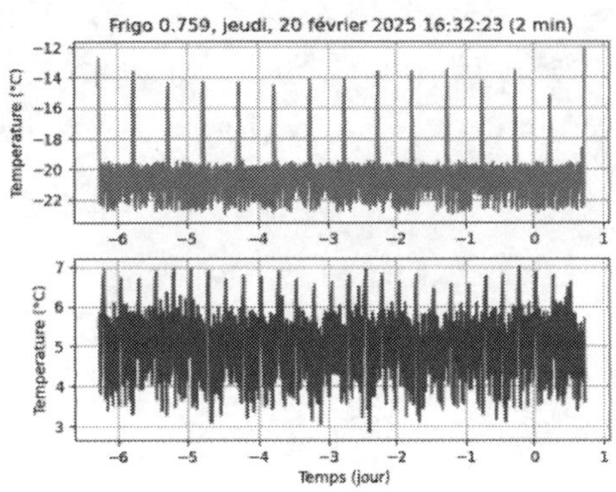

Fig. 6. Cold chambers temperatures monitoring displayed on the Back-up PC

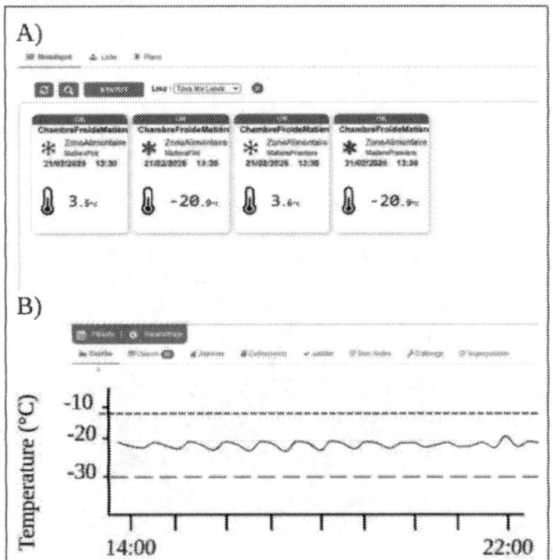

Fig. 7. Temperatures Monitoring of Cold Chambers for alimentary area ; __ __ : low-threhold and _._._._. : high-threshold for alarms

On the other hand, cold chambers are also located in the food grade area. Wireless FoxNet Temp recorder is employed to automatically send temperature measurements on cloud via RJ45 Ethernet connexion. The Thermotrack Webserve software, a remote temperature monitoring solution, a web enables to visualise the data (Fig. 7). It has automatic calibration documentation management to ease configurations. Fig. 7-A) is a real-time display of the actual temperatures. Alarms can be set if low and high thresholds are reached due to dysfunction and to take quick and necessary actions. Records are available for future investigations; an example is shown in Fig. 7-B), with the thresholds being set at at -30 and -12°C.

These two approches of temperature monitoring are incorporated in the supervisory solution.

5 Architecture deployment

The previous section shows the diversity of the pilots, the signals being acquired and the communication protocols considered (serial RS-232, Modbus, node-RED) of the available technical solutions.

Several data transfer protocols are possible for data transfer and deploying our solutions over the network. For IIoT solutions, just to site some, there are, for example, File Transfer Protocol (FTP), Hypertext Transfer Protocol (HTTP) and Secure Shell (SSH). Identifying which ones are suitable depends on parameters such as bandwidth requirements, latency requirements, range, energy efficiency, number of devices to be connected, compatibility with existing system to facilitate integration and operation.

The pilots PC's, based-on Windows or Linux operating system, are connected to the Virtual Local Area Network (VLAN) (Fig. 8).

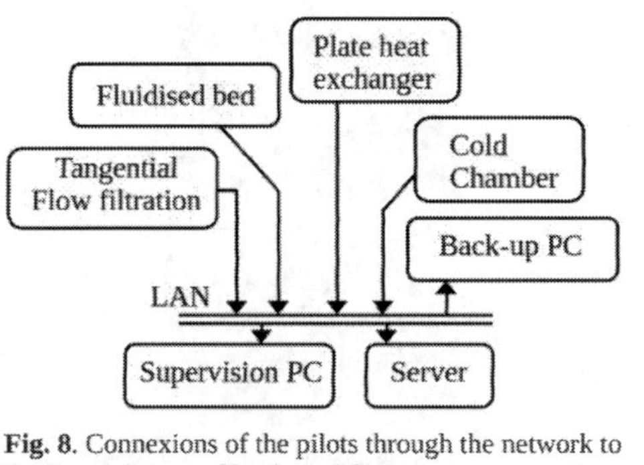

Fig. 8. Connexions of the pilots through the network to the Supervisory and back-up PC's

For our development, Message Queuing Telemetry Transport is chosen, being "Publish-Subscribe" protocol. It is reliable, easy to implement, suitable for IoT devices with limited bandwidth and power. The maximum size for each MQTT packet message that can be sent is 256MB. Also, due to its lightweight design, it can be incorporated in Raspberry Pi-based solutions.

An initial test was carried out generating and arranging random-data, with a time-stamp, and connecting several PC's with a Python code.

Following the development, MQTT data message from the pilots are continuously sent to the network. The HMI of the supervisory PC is designed to display the real-time data for the process occurring in the selected pilot. Attention is brought on getting and analysing the HMI requirements from researchers and trainers in pedagogic projects. The user has also the possibility to check the history. A copy of the data is directly sent to the server and the back-up PC. This facilitates managing and tracking pilot uses.

On the top of this, a generic web interface is developed for real-time data visualisation and metadata handling.

It used a webserver providing a Representational State Transfer in an Application Programming Interface (REST API) based-on FastAPI; it is a modern and high-performance web framework for creating APIs with Python and which has modules automating documentation. The user interface is developed in ReactJS, an open-source JavaScript library that builds user interfaces for web and mobile applications. The main advantage of ReactJS is that it is scalable, simple and fast.

The software development quality strategy uses version control (git), both automated and manual testing, continuous integration, environment consistency and isolation, an agile development methodology incorporating feedback from users and a comprehensive documentation. All components will have automated tests, both unit tests and integration tests, which are run automatically on code changes and/or on a scheduled basis using continuous integration tools.

The automation of data and metadata handling using the Dataverse APIs is also tested. The solution currently envisaged is a component on the user interface, with a specific metadata form and then use the Dataverse APIs to transfer the data to a long-term storage area.

6 Conclusion

The poster demonstrates that a Python-based open-source and web-based supervisory system can be deployed across a range of food and bioproduct processing equipment. The custom-built solution integrates multiple devices, IIoT and different protocols to provide a scalable and cost-effective alternative to commercial SCADA or HMI systems. Our developments fit for both educational and industrial applications.

The implementation is still in progress and future development will expend the number of supported pilots within our system. For convenience, current developments focus more on pilots that communicate via existing APIs, such as those coupled with an Opto22 Groov EPIC system.

The Groov Epic also offers the potential to be interfaced with Node-RED and MQTT for data transfer to and from database [3, 4]. C.-Y. Chen et al. demonstrated the combination of Raspberry Pi, Node-RED and MQTT in the development of a web-based plateform to control and monitor lighting and air conditioning in laboraory [5]. This shows that our considerations are promising.

Our approach is to gradually integrate additional protocols step-by-step, such as a Python client for Modbus TCP/IP or the MQTT protocol.

Regarding metadata entry, the required fields must be defined on a case-by-case basis, depending on the experiment. These specific metadata fields should align with ontologies developed by researchers, with also some aspects potentially being automated. Data formatting for compatibility with other databases, such as the PO2 database [6], will be proceed on the server side.

Similar processes are used in other domains (biotechnologies, chemistry, pharma, petrochemistry, cosmetics).

At SayFood, the instrumentation team has the potential to design, evaluate, test and implement strategies around food processing technologies and data management bringing expertises in electronics, automation, metrology, AI and quality.

Journal articles

1. A.P. Fraas, Heat Exchanger Design, New York: J. Wiley and Sons, 2nd edition, 1989
2. F.P. Incropera, D.P. De Witt, Fundamentals of Heat and Mass Transfer, 5th edition, 2002
3. Opto22, Case Study: netDNA Automates Water Management for Fracking & Water Transfer, (2019) https://documents.opto22.com/2319_Case_Study_NetDNA.pdf
4. Opto22, Getting Started with MQTT in Groov Products, (2022) https://documents.opto22.com/2350_Getting_Started_with_MQTT_in_groov_Products.pdf
5. C.-Y. Chen, S.-H. Wu, B.-W. Huang, C.-H. Huang, Cheng-Fu Yang, Web-based Internet of Things on environmental and lighting control and monitoring system using node-RED, MQTT and Modbus communications within embedded Linux platform. Internet of Things. 27, 101305 (2024) https://doi.org/10.1016/j.iot.2024.101305
6. M. Weber, P. Buche, L. Ibanescu, S. Dervaux, PO2/TransformON: A New Domain Ontology for Integrating Food, Feed, Bio-products and Waste in a Circular and Sustainable Approach, IFOW 2023 Integrated Food Ontology Workshop, 9th Joint Ontology Workshops (JOWO 2023), co-located with FOIS 2023, Sherbrooke, Canada, hal-04256248 (Jul 2023)

Status and future of metrology for dynamic measurement in Nordic and Baltic countries

Martti Heinonen [1*], *Jan* Johansson[2], *Jan C.* Petersen[3], *Aigar* Vaigu[4], and *Fredrik* Arrhén[2]

[1] VTT MIKES, Tekniikantie 1, 02150 Espoo, Finland
[2] RISE Research Institutes of Sweden, Brinellgatan 4,504 62 Borås, Sweden
[3] Danish Fundamental Metrology, Kogle Allé 5, 2970 Hørsholm, Denmark
[4] Metrosert, Teaduspargi 8, 12618 Tallinn, Estonia

Abstract. Methods and technologies for dynamic measurements have been developed and used for decades. To enable robust metrological traceability, uncertainty analysis methods for various applications have been derived and published by many scientists. In Europe, several research projects funded within European metrology research programmes (EMRP, EMPIR, Partnership on Metrology) have been focusing in dynamic measurements of mechanical, thermal and electrical quantities to provide new measurement and calibration methods. The European Metrology Network "Mathmet" drives the development of analytical methods related to dynamic measurement applications. The importance of dynamic measurement solutions has been boosted by digitalisation and rapid growth of computer power. Artificial intelligence combined with sensor fusion and sensor networks brings dynamism to wider measurement applications but may hide serious vulnerabilities to time dependent disturbances.At the moment most calibrations are performed under static conditions, i.e. the time dependency of the measurand is considered as a very small contribution to the overall calibration uncertainty. Calibrations at static conditions are often preferred due to practical reasons even if dynamic calibrations are available. In its recent strategy, the European Metrology Network "Smart North" has identified dynamic measurements as a field of regional competence and service development within Nordic and Baltic countries. This paper reviews most relevant research results and currently available calibration services in Europe. The study is focused on measurement needs related to machinery, combustion engines and electrical grids. Potential future needs for NMI level services in the region are analysed by considering specific needs of local industry, societal resilience and northern climate..

1 Introduction

In industry, measurement sensors are mostly used in non-static conditions but often they are calibrated in static conditions. There are many cases where dynamic characteristics of a sensor form a significant limiting factor for achievable measurement uncertainty. With proper calibration and analysis methods, the uncertainty could be significantly improved. The importance of dynamic measurement solutions has been boosted by digitalisation and rapid growth of computer power. Artificial intelligence combined with sensor fusion and sensor networks brings dynamism wider to measurement applications but may hide serious vulnerabilities to time dependent disturbances. In its recent strategy, the European Metrology Network "Smart North" has identified dynamic measurements as a field of regional competence and service development within Nordic and Baltic countries. Metrology related published research results and currently available calibration services are reviewed in this paper to provide a solid basis for strategic decisions in the region.

Eichstädt et al [1] define dynamic measurements as measurements involving at least one dynamic quantity whose value varies with time in such a way that this time dependence must be taken into account to characterize the quantity to the accuracy desired. The main challenges in establising robust metrological traceability for dynamic measurements are: evaluating the measurement uncertainty and calibrating the measurement system in such a way that the time dependency is appropriately taken into account [1 – 3]. Theoretical basis comprising definitions, concepts and analysis methods has been developed to dynamic measurements in general and applied to various fields [1, 4 – 10]. The state-of-the-art methods relevant to mechanical quantities and ultrasound is well described in [11]. When studying measurement challenges in more details, we need to look at different applications separately as the range of applications is very wide and the challenges vary with the application. To match with the needs specific to industry in Nordic and Baltic countries, we decided to focus on three applications fields: machinery, combustion engines and electrical grids. Needs in these application fields are discussed in Section 2. Research results on calibration methods and systems as well as calibration services provided by national metrology institutes are reviewed in Section 3. Using this information with industry landscape in Nordic and Baltic countries we analyse in Section 4

* Corresponding author: martti.heinonen@vtt.fi

future needs of dynamic metrology services in this region.

2 Dynamic measurements and application fields

2.1 Dynamic measurements and quantities

Dynamic measurement can be considered as the measurement of time-dependent quantities [12]. As an opposite approach, K.H. Ruhm states in [13] that a system is nondynamic if all quantities in the mathematical model of the measurement process except input and output signals depend only on their present values. However, the time dependency alone is not sufficient to consider a measurement dynamic: otherwise allmost all real-time measurements would fall into this category. It is decisive how the time dependency of the measurand is interlinked with the measurement system and the measurement result. When an instrument output reading show a significant time dependent deviation from the actual measurand values, the measurement should be treated as dynamic measurement. T. J. Esward et al. defines a dynamic measurements as "a measurement where the physical quantity being measured (the measurand) varies with time and where this variation may have a significant effect on the measurement result (the estimate of the measurand) and the associated uncertainty" [14]. To emphasize that the defining characteristics related to dynamic are not the absolute timescale nor physical application, A. Dienstfrey and P. D. Hale presented the definition as "one in which the measurand varies in time sufficiently fast relative to the response of the measurement system that corrections for finite-bandwidth effects are required to achieve the desired accuracy" [15]. S. Eichstädt et al. extends the definition to measurements involved with several quantities by defining a dynamic quantity as "any quantity whose value varies with time in such a way that this time dependence must be taken into account to characterize the quantity to the accuracy desired" and stating that "Measurements in which at least one of the involved quantities is dynamic are called dynamic measurements" [1].

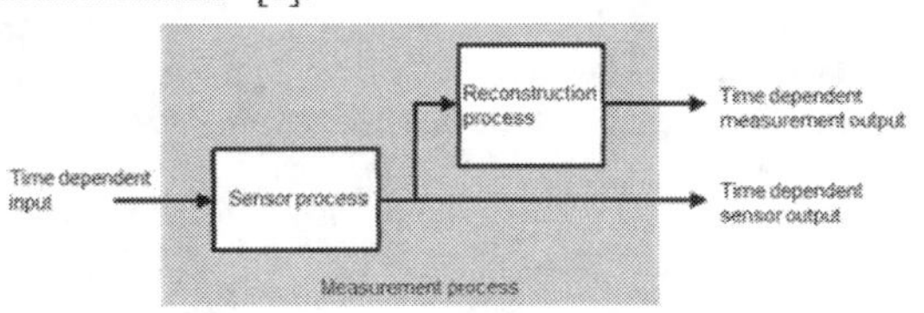

Fig. 1. Scheme of dynamic measurement process in instrument domain

Dynamic measurement process can be described with a block diagram in Fig. 1. In addition to a sensor process giving time-dependent sensor output, the process includes a reconstruction process (also called as estimation process) that generates measurement system output by applying an appropriate mathematical model. Signal processing methodologies are needed for analysing dynamic measurements [12, 16].

The reconstruction process is very sensitive to measurement noise, and the applied method causes systematic errors that cannot be omitted in the uncertainty analysis [12]. Mathematical theory for analysing dynamic measurement results and estimating their uncertainty has been studied in many scientific publications [1, 12 – 26]. A comprehensive overview is given in [11].

2.2 Applications within machinery, combustion engines and electrical grids

To ensure product quality and safety, fatigue tests and other mechanical tests are performed for materials, components and products within manufacturing processes. Dynamic force measurements record varying force acting on materials in tensile testers, compression testers, fatigue testers and viscoelasticity testers etc. [27, 28] Force and torque measurements are important in manufacturing engines and transmissions of ships, automobiles and aircrafts and for operating them in a safe and optimal way. In many cases, measurements are dynamic, which affects significantly the reliability of the recorded measurement data. Requirements for these dynamic measurements are becoming more stringent [28 - 31]. Dynamic torque measurements cover a wide range of applications such as the vibration of engines and motors and impact torque measurement by torque tools [32]. Reliable in-line torque measurement in the drive train of ships are needed for achieving the targets of reduced emissions in seafaring [33]. Regenerative braking in electric vehicles increases the need of dynamic torque measurements with proven quality. Forces acting on materials in press machines and rolling mills are real-time monitored with force transducers.

Another widely applied dynamic mechanical measurement is weighing: when manufacturing products in food, pharma and chemical industry and packaging them for transport and storage, dynamic weighing is commonly an integral part of the processes [34, 35].

According to the Intergovernmental Panel on Climate Change (IPCC), about 15 % of net global GHG emissions came from transport sector [36] in 2019. About 26 % of this is produced by ships and heavy freight vehicles [37]. Combustion engines are expected to continue as the main power source in this sector but the emissions will be reduced further by improving the engine efficiency, e.g. by improving the combustion system, gas exchange and thermal management [38]. More accurate dynamic pressure and temperature measurements are key to reduction of emissions by optimizing the combustion process in real time. Real time monitoring of cylinder pressure and temperature, fuel injection pressure and exhaust pressure and temperature enable optimizing the fuel injection and engine thermal management [39 - 42]. The measurement ranges of interest are from 1 MPa up to 30 MPa and up to 3000 °C [43, 44] with frequency up to a few tens of kHz [39].

Dynamic measurements are also relevant for engines used in light duty vehicles and cars which produce more than 50 % of GMG emissions in the transport sector [37]. However, electrification is expected to reduce the emissions in Nordic countries and the need for dynamic pressure and temperature calibration is not expected to increase significantly in the foreseeable future.

Dynamic measurements are crucial for the operation of electrical grids and for ensuring safety and durability of grid components. Measurement and analysis methods in line with principles presented in Section 2.1 are used in lightning impulse and partial discharge measurements, and the measurement quality is ensured by metrologically traceable calibrations. The methods have been implemented in the standard IEC 61083 [45]. Development needs have especially been identified in power measurements related charge-discharge efficiency of electric storage systems [46].

3 State of the art

3.1 Research on traceability of dynamic measurements

3.1.1 Force and torque

Metrological traceability and calibration of dynamic measurement systems in different applications have been studied in various research projects within European metrology research programmes in the last two decades. A traceability chain for metrological services in the field of force measurements was set up in the project ComTraForce [47]. This project delivered improved methods for static, continuous and dynamic force calibrations in a force range from 1 N to 1 MN at frequencies up to 1 kHz. A calibration setup and guidelines were developed for force calibration of testing machines under continuous and dynamic force. A guideline for dynamic calibration of material testing machine was published as DKD-R 9-4 [48]. NIST has developed a system for dynamic force calibrations using harmonic excitation and laser-interferometric acceleration measurement. An uncertainty less than 1.2 % (k = 2) was demonstrated for 2.2 kN and 1.3 kN force transducers [49]. Torque measurements in rotating systems like in wind turbines have been studied in the European research projects MNmTorque [50] and WindEFCY [51]. A development initiated at PTB in the project Dynamic has delivered a calibration system applying an oscillating torque load generating loads up to 20 N m in the frequency band 10 Hz to 400 Hz [52]. Also, a method for dynamic calibration of amplifiers used in conjunction with force and torque transducers was developed in the project Dynamic [53], and the work continued in the project ComTraForce [54]. NMIJ and KRISS have developed primary torque calibration systems applying the Kibble balance principle. NMIJ demonstrated an uncertainty of 0.3 % (k = 2) for a dynamic torque of 20 mN m to 40 mN m at frequencies up to 100 Hz [55]. KRISS expects to achieve an uncertainty level of 0.01 % in static torque calibrations up to 10 N·m. The system will be operating in dynamic calibration mode up to 100 Hz [56].

3.1.2 Pressure and temperature

To enable traceable dynamic pressure measurements, calibration systems applying three principles have been developed within the project DynPT: shock tube, fast opening valve and dropping weight [57]. Pressure and frequency ranges 0.1 – 400 MPa and 1 – 30 kHz, respectively, are covered with the developed setups. The development enabled SI-traceable dynamic pressure calibrations in the range from 5 MPa to 30 MPa, which is important for combustion engine applications. A relative uncertainty of 1 % (k = 2) was achieved with LNE/ENSAM's system combining shock tube and a fast-opening device in the pressure and frequency range up to 5 MPa and 100 Hz. At the frequency of 30 kHz, the uncertainty is about 7 % [58]. When generating the dynamic pressure up to 60 MPa with a drop-weight system developed by VTT MIKES an uncertainty of 1.7 % (k = 2) was achieved [59]. The uncertainty is recently reduced to 0.9 % in the range up to 500 MPa with a new design developed by VTT MIKES. The pulse width is 5 ms [60]. L. Combining a drop-weight test system with a high-speed camera and an accelerometer, Elkarous et al. have developed a dynamic calibration system for ballistic high-pressure sensors up to 350 MPa with a pulse width of 1 – 2 ms and achieved a calibration uncertainty of 2.4 % (k = 2) [61]. KRISS has developed a drop-weight secondary calibration system that generates 3 ms pressure pulses of 10 MPa to 200 MPa [62]. KRISS has also developed a primary dynamic pressure standard using a step pressure generator covering the range 1 MPa to 100 MPa with 1 ms rise time. The reported uncertainty at 70 MPa is 0.51 % (k=2) [63]. SPEKTRA has developed a primary dynamic pressure calibration system using a pistonphone exciter. The system generates sinusoidal pressure with frequencies up to 10 kHz and amplitudes up to 1 MPa (peak to peak). The estimated uncertainty is up to 2 % (k = 2) [64]. Zhang et al. generated a quasi-δ pressure pulse with a pulse width of 8 μs. The maximum static pressure level is 800 MPa and the amplitude 30 MPa. The amplitude-frequency error is estimated to 5 % [65].

A portable flame temperature standard was developed by NPL in the European project EMPRESS using the Rayleigh scattering thermometry technique. A relative standard uncertainty of 0.5 % was achieved [66]. The project DynPT resulted in three validated dynamic temperature calibration methods [57]: KTH achieved 3000 °C with a relative uncertainty of 2 % (k=2) using a shock tube setup. RISE developed a system based on a rapid shutter and high temperature blackbodies and estimated the uncertainty of calibration to be 2.2 °C and 4.5 °C at 500 °C and 2200 °C, respectively (k = 2). At NPL, a modified blackbody calibration setup provides traceability to the ITS-90 over a range of dynamic temperature from 800 °C to 2600 °C with a relative uncertainty of less than 1 %.

3.1.3 High voltage

To support testing ultra high voltage equipment, a calibration setup for gas insulated switchgear applications was developed in the European project UHV. This setup generates very fast transient over-voltages and provides robust metrological traceability. The calibration uncertainty ($k = 2$) is 1.1 % for 100 kV and 6 ns [67]. Several divider designs have been studied and compared for very fast transient measurements [68] and the dynamic effects of test impulse wave shapes were analysed for instrument transformer testing [69]. A Good Practice Guide for measuring ultra high voltage impulses was prepared within the project FutureEnergy. Among other topics, it describes a convolution and deconvolution method for estimate and reduce parameter errors in signal analysis [70]. The main developments achieved with the relevant European projects related to high voltage measurement procedures have been or are in implementation to relevant international IEC standards.

3.2 Measurement and calibration services

In November 2012, a BIPM Workshop on Challenges in Metrology for Dynamic Measurement concluded that developments are needed to clarify the terminology, enable appropriate uncertainty estimation and address specific urgent needs for dynamic measurement especially in the area of mechanical quantities [71]. As described in previous Sections 2.1 and 3.1, significant advancements have been achieved after the workshop. However, a search on CMCs published at the KCDB database by BIPM in January 2025 resulted no dynamic measurement related CMCs for mechanical or thermal quantities. Furthermore, dynamic calibration was only addressed under the theme Pressure in the service category lists of CIPM. In the high voltage area, published CMCs cover well the field of dynamic measurements. In Nordic countries, NMIs in Finland and Sweden cover well the high voltage needs of the region with their CMCs.

As described in Section 3.1, several European NMIs has developed expertise in the field of dynamic force, torque, pressure and temperature measurements within projects of the European metrology research programmes. Although this is has not yet resulted in new CMCs, the NMIs exploit the expertise in their customer service by providing test measurements, prototype instruments and consultancy (see e.g. [59, 72, 73]).

4 Analysis of the needs in Nordic and Baltic countries

Recent strategy documents of CCM and CCEM address the increasing importance of dynamic measurements. Establishing robust SI traceability to dynamic measurements is considered by CCM as one of the main topics for the next decade [74]. According to CCEM, the development of new technologies within e.g. electric vehicles, high frequency communications, renewable energy sources and quantum technology applications requires extending quality control of measurements from steady state to dynamic behaviour [75]. According to the strategic research agendas of the European metrology networks (EMN) Smart Electric Grids, Advance Manufacturing and Mathmet, metrology research in Europe should address the needs of reliable dynamic measurements including the development of relevant uncertainty estimation methods [76 - 78].

Within the stakeholder dialogue of the EMN Smart North, the reliability of dynamic measurements has especially been brought up with manufacturing of heavy duty engines, cars and trucks, measuring instruments and material testing. The needs of the evolving Nordic electric grid have been driving the strong contribution of the Finnish and Swedish national metrology institutes in the high voltage metrology. The electrification of vehicles has been creating needs both in mechanical and electrical measurements. Due to the recent geopolitical development, needs of defence sector have an increasing importance. Dynamic pressure measurements have an important role in testing ammunition.

According to our analysis, the first priority in the Nordic and Baltic countries should be given to the development of the dynamic pressure metrology and to the continuation of the relevant high voltage metrology. Also, dynamic force and torque measurements are of interest but it is not clear how the actual customer need will develop in the future. Overall, it is expected that the volume of dynamic calibrations will not increase rapidly within the next 5 years and they will be focused in specific application fields.

It is worth noticing that static and dynamic calibrations represent extremes from the time dependence point of view leaving an area in between whose importance is increasing. The development of uncertainty analysis methods and research on the optimal calibration approaches are needed to address increasing accuracy requirements and complexities in sensor network setups.

5 Summary

We reviewed published needs, research results and currently available NMI level calibration services related to dynamic calibrations. The review was focused in on measurement needs related to machinery, combustion engines and electrical grids because these were initially identified as the most important application fields in the Nordic and Baltic countries. Dynamic pressure calibrations and specific high voltage measurements were identified as the first priority topics of development in the area. It was also noted that the demand for NMI level dynamic metrology focuses on specific applications with limited growth potential.

References

1. S Eichstädt et al 2016 Metrologia 53 S125
2. T. J. Esward, C. Elster, J. P. Hessling, IMEKO 2009
3. A. Schäfer, S. Eichstädt, IMEKO TC3 2017
4. Andrew Dienstfrey and Paul D Hale 2014 Meas. Sci. Technol. 25 035001
5. K. H. Ruhm, Measurement 79 (2016) 276–284

6. S. Eichstädt, B. Arendacká, A. Link, C. Elster, EPJ Web of Conferences, 77, 0000 (2014)
7. S Eichstädt, K Ruhm, A Shestakov, Journal of Physics: Conf. Series 1065 (2018) 212018
8. Trevor Esward et al 2019 Metrologia 56 015002
9. O. Vasilevskyi et al, Proc. of SPIE Vol. 10808 108082E-1
10. I. Markovsky, Control Engineering Practice 43 (2015) 85–93
11. S. Eichstädt (ed.) Dynamic Measuring Systems: Fundamentals and application of time-dependent measurements, Berlin, Boston: De Gruyter Oldenbourg, 2024. https://doi.org/10.1515/9783110713107
12. S Eichstädt et al 2018 J. Phys.: Conf. Ser. 1065 212018
13. K.H. Ruhm, Measurement 79 (2016) 276–284
14. Esward T J, Elster C and Hessling P 2009 Analysis of dynamic measurements: new challenges require new solutions Proc. 19th IMEKO World Congress (Lisbon, Portugal, 6–11 Sept.) pp 2307–10
15. Andrew Dienstfrey and Paul D Hale 2014 Meas. Sci. Technol. 25 035001
16. Eichstädt S 2012 "Analysis of Dynamic Measurements - Evaluation of Dynamic Measurement Uncertainty", PhD Thesis, TU Berlin
17. Elster C and Link A 2008 "Uncertainty evaluation for dynamic measurements modelled by a linear time-invariant system", Metrologia, 45(4), 464-473
18. P. Hessling, "A novel method of dynamic correction in the time domain", Meas. Sci. Technol. 19, 075101 (10pp), 2008.
19. P. Hessling, "A novel method of estimating dynamic measurement errors", Meas. Sci. Technol. 17, pp. 2740-2750, 2006
20. J P Hessling 2011 Meas. Sci. Technol. 22 105105
21. Elster C, Eichstädt S, and Link A 2009 Uncertainty evaluation of dynamic measurements in line with the GUM Proc. 19th IMEKO World Congress (Lisbon, Portugal, 6–11 Sept.) pp 2311–14
22. O. Vasilevskyi et al, Proc. of SPIE Vol. 10808 108082E-1
23. Trevor Esward et al 2019 Metrologia 56 015002
24. S. Eichstädt, B. Arendacká, A. Link, C. Elster, EPJ Web of Conferences, 77, 0000 (2014)
25. S Eichstädt et al 2016 Meas. Sci. Technol. 27 125009
26. A. Link and C. Elster, "Uncertainty evaluation for IIR filtering using a state-space approach", Meas. Sci. Technol. 20, 055104 (5pp), 2009.
27. H. Dizdar, B. Aydemir, C. Vatan, Evaluation of the effect of dynamic verification on different types of force sensors, Joint IMEKO TC3, T5, TC16 and TC22 International Conference, 2022, DOI: 10.21014/tc3-2022.012
28. Mitra Djamal, Kazuhide Watanabe, Kyohei Irisa, Irfa Aji Prayogi, Akihiro Takita, Takao Yamaguchi and Yusaku Fujii, Metrol. Meas. Syst., Vol. XXI (2014), No. 1, pp. 59–66, DOI: 10.2478/mms-2014-0006
29. Nicholas Vlajic and Ako Chijioke 2016 Metrologia 53 S136, doi:10.1088/0026-1394/53/4/S136
30. Misaki Hamaji, Atsuhiro Nishino, Koji Ogushi, Measurement: Sensors 18 (2021) 100183
31. A. Tao Li, B. Xianglong Ma, Zhiqiang Qiao, Negative step dynamic torque calibration machine, Physics Conference Series, vol. 1740, no. 1, pp. 208-212, 2016
32. Misaki Hamaji et al 2022 Meas. Sci. Technol. 33 115901, doi.org/10.1088/1361-6501/ac8441
33. André Schäfer, Dynamic measurements as an emerging field in industrial metrology, PTB-Mitteilungen 125 (2015), No. 2, pp 62-67
34. Y. Yamakawa, T. Yamazaki, Simplified model of mass measurement system with consideration of variation of fulcrum position, Joint IMEKO TC3, T5, TC16 and TC22 International Conference, 2022,
35. André Schäfer, Sascha Eichstädt, Evaluation of dynamic measurement uncertainty for industrial applications, IMEKO 23rd TC3, 13th TC5 and 4th TC22 Int. Conf., 30 May to 1 June, 2017
36. IPCC, 2023: Sections. In: Climate Change 2023: Synthesis Report. Contribution of Working Groups I, II and III to the Sixth Assessment Report of the Intergovernmental Panel on Climate Change [Core Writing Team, H. Lee and J. Romero (eds.)]. IPCC, Geneva, Switzerland, pp. 35-115, doi: 10.59327/IPCC/AR6-9789291691647
37. IEA, Statista 2024
38. R D Reitz et al., IJER editorial: The future of the internal combustion engine, International J of Engine Research 2020, Vol. 21(1) 3–10, DOI: 10.1177/1468087419877990
39. Jan Hjelmgren, Dynamic measurement of pressure - a literature survey, SP Report 2002:34, 64p. ISBN 91-7848-925-3
40. Felix Leach, Gautam Kalghatgi, Richard Stone, Paul Miles, The scope for improving the efficiency and environmental impact of internal combustion engines, Transportation Engineering 1 (2020) 100005, DOI: 10.1016/j.treng.2020.100005
41. Dahham, R.Y.; Wei, H.; Pan, J. Improving thermal efficiency of internal combustion engines: recent progress and remaining challenges. Energies 2022, 15, 6222. doi: 10.3390/en15176222
42. Erick Garcia, Strategies for improving efficiency and emissions in heavy-duty diesel engines, PhD dissertation, The University of Michigan 2021
43. J Salminen et al 2020 Metrologia 57 045006, doi: 10.1088/1681-7575/ab8fb9

44. Alberto Sposito, Dave Lowe, Gavin Sutton, Int. J. Turbomach. Propuls. Power 2020, 5, 31; doi:10.3390/ijtpp5040031
45. IEC 61083
46. https://e-treny.eu/objectives/
47. Final Publishable Report, 18SIB08 ComTraForce, https://www.euramet.org/
48. DKD-R 9-4 Dynamische kalibrierung von werkstoffprufmaschinen, doi: 10.7795/550.20240606
49. Nicholas Vlajic and Ako Chijioke 2016 Metrologia 53 S136, doi:10.1088/0026-1394/53/4/S136
50. Final Publishable Report, 14IND14 MNmTorque, https://www.euramet.org/
51. Final Publishable Report, 19ENG08_WindEFCY, https://www.euramet.org/
52. Leonard Klaus, Michael Kobusch, Measurement: Sensors 18 (2021) 100149, doi: 10.1016/j.measen.2021.100149
53. Leonard Klaus et al 2015 Metrologia 52 72, doi:10.1088/0026-1394/52/1/72
54. L. Klaus, ACTA IMEKO, December 2020, Volume 9, Number 5, 200-204, ISSN: 221-870X
55. Misaki Hamaji et al 2022 Meas. Sci. Technol. 33 115901, doi: 10.1088/1361-6501/ac8441
56. MyeongHyeon Kim, IEEE Transactions on Instrumentation and Measurement, Vol. 70, 2021, 1005207
57. R. Högström et al., Development of measurement and calibration techniques for dynamic pressures and temperatures – results and achievements, Joint IMEKO TC3, T5, TC16 and TC22 International Conference, 2022, doi: DOI: 10.21014/tc16-2022.005
58. Christophe Sarraf 2021 Meas. Sci. Technol. 32 015013, doi: 10.1088/1361-6501/aba56a
59. J Salminen et al 2020 Metrologia 57 045006, doi: 10.1088/1681-7575/ab8fb9
60. Richard Högström et al., Measurement: Sensors, https://doi.org/10.1016/j.measen.2024.101686
61. Lamine Elkarous, Cyril Robbe, Marc Pirlot, Jean-Claude Golinval, Int. J. Metrol. Qual. Eng. 7, 201 (2016), doi: 10.1051/ijmqe/2016004
62. Rudi Anggoro Samodro; In-Mook Choi, Rev. Sci. Instrum. 90, 095111 (2019); doi: 10.1063/1.5108865
63. In-Mook Choi et al., Measurement: Sensors, https://doi.org/10.1016/j.measen.2024.101684
64. Thomas Platte, Measurement: Sensors 18 (2021) 100252, doi: 10.1016/j.measen.2021.100252
65. Yu Zhang, Jing Zu, Hong-Yan Zhang, Measurement 45 (2012) 1981–1988, doi: 10.1016/j.measurement.2012.04.024
66. Gavin Sutton, Alexander Fateev, Miguel A. Rodríguez-Conejo, Juan Meléndez, Guillermo Guarnizo, International Journal of Thermophysics (2019) 40:99, doi:10.1007/s10765-019-2557-6
67. Final Publishable Report, 15NRM02, www.euramet.org
68. A.-P. Elg, S. Passon, J Meisner and J. Hällström, "High voltage topologies for very fast transient measurements", 21st International Symposium on High Voltage Engineering (ISH 2019), 26-30 August 2019, Budapest, Hungary, https://doi.org/10.5281/zenodo.3244216
69. A.-P. Elg, "Quantifying a transient recorder for traceable measurements of very fast transients", Proceedings of Conference on Precision Electromagnetics Measurements (CPEM 2018), July, 8-13, 2018, Paris, France, https://doi.org/10.5281/zenodo.1473323
70. J. Hällström et al., Good Practice Guide on characterisation methods for UHV lightning impulse (LI) dividers, Deliverable Technical Report, 19ENG02 FutureEnergy, www.euramet.org
71. T. Usuda et al., Report on the BIPM workshop on challenges in metrology for dynamic measurement, Rapport BIPM-2013/01, www.bipm.org
72. www.ri.se/en/expertise-areas/test-demo/dynamic-pressure-testing
73. www.ume.tubitak.gov.tr/en/laboratuvarlarimiz/infrastructure-1
74. Strategy 2022-2032. Consultative Committee for Mass and Related Quantities (CCM), Version 1.8, 14 March 2022, www.bipm.org
75. Strategy 2020-2030 Consultative Committee for Electricity and Magnetism (CCEM), 18 May 2021, www.bipm.org
76. European Metrology Network Smart Electricity Grids - Strategic Research Agenda, Version 1.0 (04/2023), www.euramet.org
77. Strategic Research Agenda. European Metrology Network for Advanced Manufacturing, Version Live on JNP sharepoint, downloaded on 07.03.2024, www.euramet.org
78. European Metrology Network for Mathematics and Statistics - Strategic Research Agenda 2023 - 2033, Version 1.0 (07/2023), www.euramet.orgJ. Couturier, Y.H. Abou and E. Grolleau, Element of nuclear safety, (EDP Sciences, Les Ulis, 2019)

 https://doi.org/10.1051/epjconf/202532307001

Thermometry with embedded SI traceability for industrial applications

Jonathan Pearce [1*], *Henrik* Kjeldsen[2], *Jan* Nielsen[2], *Ingmar* Müller[3], *Christian* Krause[3], *Gavin* Sutton[1], *Alexander* Fateev[4], and *Aurik* Andreu[5]

[1]National Physical Laboratory, Hampton Road, Teddington, TW11 0LW, United Kingdom
[2]Teknologisk Institut, Kongsvang Alle 29, 8000 Aarhus, Denmark
[3]Physikalisch Technische Bundesanstalt, Abbestr. 2-12, 10587, Berlin, Germany
[4]Danmarks Tekniske Universitet, Søltofts Plads, Bygning 229, 2800 Kongens Lyngby, Denmark
[5]Advanced Forming Research Centre, 85 Inchinnan Dr, Inchinnan, Renfrew PA4 9LJ, United Kingdom

Abstract. Most industrial processes rely on temperature measurement, which directly influences product quality, energy efficiency, process optimization and emissions. The European Partnership on Metrology project "Thermometry with embedded SI traceability for industrial applications (ThermoSI)" is a 3-year research and development project (late 2024 – late 2027) which will overcome some specific process control challenges (calibration drift, surface thermometry, dynamic gas temperature variations) by implementing embedded traceable thermometry *in situ* through driftless practical primary thermometry and self-validation, hot gas temperature measurement, and new traceable surface temperature measurement methods. Measurement traceability will be either directly to the redefined SI kelvin, or indirectly via the International Temperature Scale of 1990 (ITS-90). The activities are grouped into four categories: 1) Develop techniques for traceable, quantitative thermal imaging from -100 °C to 500 °C; 2) Improve practical primary Johnson noise thermometry by developing sensing electronics and a robust probe for use up to 1200 °C; 3) Develop thermographic phosphor thermometry up to 1250 °C; 4) Develop artificial intelligence approaches to enable *in-situ* traceable thermometry. The approaches, and how they will be developed and trialled in collaboration with industrial stakeholders, are outlined.

1 Introduction

Advanced manufacturing, improved energy efficiency and measurement traceability in process optimization are key to the industrial strategy of many regions around the world [1-3]. Most industrial processes rely on temperature measurement, which directly influences product quality, energy efficiency, and emissions. All conventional temperature sensors exhibit calibration drift leading to inefficiencies. Inaccurate surface thermometry causes process control challenges in advanced manufacturing. Poor gas temperature measurement and control leads to sub-optimal noxious emissions, greenhouse gas emissions and reduced efficiency. This project will address and overcome specific process control challenges by implementing embedded traceable thermometry *in situ* through driftless practical primary thermometry and self-validation, hot gas dynamic temperature measurement, and new traceable surface temperature measurement methods. Traceability will be either directly to the redefined SI kelvin [4], or indirectly via the International Temperature Scale of 1990 (ITS-90) [5].

Reliable, traceable surface temperature measurement with thermal imaging is notoriously difficult. It requires knowledge of the surface emissivity and any reflected thermal radiation, including knowledge of the geometry of the scene. Contact probes are subject to heat flow effects which perturb the thermometer and the temperature being measured. There is a need for a completely new approach which can provide a reliable, non-perturbative measurement of the surface temperature in the field of view.

Long-term reliable temperature measurement and control is required to make autonomous production/Industry 4.0 a reality [2,3]. However, in the harsh measurement environments encountered in industry (e.g. high temperature), sensor materials degrade, leading to calibration drift. There is a need for practical 'primary' thermometers capable of measuring thermodynamic temperature directly, that do not drift, irrespective of any damage to the sensor.

Traditional techniques for surface temperature measurement such as thermal imaging are seriously compromised due to the aforementioned difficulties with emissivity of the surface and reflected and background thermal radiation. For welding, forming, forging and additive manufacturing, surface temperature measurement is not sufficiently accurate. Phosphor (also known as luminescence) thermometry offers a solution

* Corresponding author: jonathan.pearce@npl.co.uk

but robust coatings, new phosphor formulations and higher temperature operation (up to 1250 °C) are needed.

Self-validating thermometers which make use of an *in-situ* reference temperature are of growing interest for autonomous in-process recalibration but require manual intervention; automation requires recognition of characteristic features in temperature-time data which is beyond conventional software techniques, and artificial intelligence (AI) solutions are needed. Spectroscopic *in-situ* infrared gas temperature measurement for industrial hot gases (e.g. combustion and post-combustion) processes also relies on AI to retrieve the temperature, but this needs to be improved to reduce the temperature measurement uncertainty to ± 2 %.

All of these examples reflect the need to introduce traceability to the SI in process. The overall aim of the ThermoSI project is to enhance advanced manufacturing and process control by improving temperature measurement capability. The specific objectives of the project are:

1. To develop techniques for truly traceable, quantitative thermal imaging, by using at least 4 key engineering materials and selected thermographic phosphors with known temperature in the field of view of the thermal imager in the temperature range from -100 °C to 500 °C with an uncertainty of less than 5 °C. This will include characterisation (e.g. spectral, angular, and hemispherical emissivity) of the surface and of the phosphor itself and *in-situ* correction for camera non-uniformity.
2. To improve practical Johnson noise thermometry by bringing it up to a technology readiness level (TRL) of 6, with an uncertainty of less than 3 °C, and to provide truly driftless thermometry for harsh environments (e.g. nuclear power generation/decommissioning). In particular, to develop a robust probe assembly for measuring Johnson noise and demonstrate its performance in harsh environments (e.g. high temperatures up to 1200 °C, ionising radiation such as gamma rays and neutrons, and electromagnetic fields).
3. To develop robust thermographic phosphor techniques for surface temperature measurement with an uncertainty of less than 3 °C and up to temperatures of 1250 °C in collaboration with metals processing organisations and end-users (e.g. marine manufacturing) to progress towards the goal of zero carbon production (e.g. steel processing) and more generally improved energy efficiency of heavy industry.
4. To develop artificial intelligence (e.g. machine learning) approaches to enable traceable *in-situ* temperature measurement for industrial applications with an uncertainty of less than 2 % up to 1500 °C, demonstrated through at least three cases studies: 1) machine learning for autonomous operation of self-validating thermometers, 2) spectroscopic infrared thermometry for *in-situ* gas temperature and gas temperature profile measurements and 3) a reference surface temperature calibration insert for dry-block calibrators.

Significant progress in this collaborative research was made in the two EMPIR projects EMPRESS and EMPRESS 2 [6,7], particularly in developing working prototypes of several novel thermometers including a phosphor thermometer for surface temperature measurement, self-validating thermocouples, a portable standard flame and combustion temperature diagnostic techniques, and these, as well as the newer techniques, will be further developed to extend capabilities.

The focus of this project is to address specific process control challenges by demonstrating improved in-process temperature measurement traceable to the International Temperature Scale of 1990 (ITS-90) [5] or directly to the SI kelvin [4] during the life of the project.

Several European National Metrology Institutes are project partners including project coordinator DTI (Denmark), NPL (United Kingdom, providing technical leadership), CMI (Czech Republic), PTB (Germany), SMU (Slovakia), University of Ljubljana (Slovenia), VTT (Finland) and NSC-IM (Ukraine). Other university partners include the Danish Technical University (Denmark), Otto-von-Guericke University (Germany), and the University of Manchester (United Kingdom). Engagement is built into the project with the partnership of Beamex (Finland), Advanced Forming Research Centre at the University of Strathclyde, BAE Systems, CCPI Europe and Metrosol (United Kingdom). Each partner brings a specific area of expertise which will be employed as part of the collaborative activities. There is also a stakeholder community associated with the project, consisting of organisations interested in contributing to, or hearing about, the project activities, as well as workshops and other dissemination events.

2 The project

2.1 Thermal imaging

Thermal imaging is used to monitor surface temperature in a wide range of applications, including forming and forging, welding, annealing, spacecraft thermal vacuum testing, nuclear waste monitoring, and gas turbine manufacturing and operation. The difficulty of characterising the surface emissivity when performing quantitative thermal imaging results in measurement uncertainties which are often so large that the process quality/efficiency is significantly reduced.

There is a need for a completely new approach which can provide a reliable measurement of the local surface temperature without perturbing it. Thermographic phosphor spots can be adhered directly to the surface being measured and in the thermal imager field of view, allowing the surface emissivity to be determined and hence the true surface temperature to be determined, but this approach requires a) knowledge of the emissivity of the phosphor itself and b) knowledge of the inherent camera non-uniformity. Existing phosphor thermometry techniques are well established from ambient temperatures up to 750 °C, with prototype instruments able to approach 1000 °C. However, there is a growing need to measure below 0 °C, e.g. for the space sector, where traditional thermal imaging is particularly challenging due to the low signal levels and relatively high background thermal radiation, and above 1000 °C for manufacturing processes e.g. high reliability steel structures.

Due to the uncertain (often unknown) emissivity and reflected background thermal radiation, thermography can suffer from uncertainties in excess of ± 100 °C even at relatively modest surface temperatures. This project is overcoming these difficulties by employing thermographic phosphors in the form of a coated area in the field of view of the thermal imager. By using the phosphor (which is immune to the above confounding influences) to measure the surface temperature, the temperature indicated by the thermal imager can be calibrated by adjusting the emissivity setting, thus determining both the true surface temperature and emissivity simultaneously, dramatically reducing the measurement uncertainty to a target of around 5 K. To facilitate this, capabilities for measuring the emissivity of both the surface under investigation and the emissivity of the phosphor itself – which are both needed for the thermal imager correction – are being established, as well as the effect of perturbing environmental influences such as surrounding gas and humidity; these factors can limit the achievable uncertainty in the temperature measurement. These challenges are being addressed by several tasks:

- NPL is developing ITS-90 traceable calibration targets [8]. Emissivity measurements of the phosphors at PTB will enable a thermal model of the calibration targets to be developed, facilitating the connection between contact and non-contact thermometry.
- The emissivity of commonly used materials in industry under controlled environmental conditions such as pressure, relative humidity, and temperature are being measured by PTB. The reference emissivity data set will be made available to the public. This information will help industry to reduce the uncertainties and to extent the scope of application to non-contact thermometry.
- Large-area flat-plate reference blackbodies are being developed by VTT and Beamex. In conjunction with a digital twin of these devices, the temperature and heat flux distribution on the surface can be calculated. The blackbody sources will provide a compensated, high-resolution surface with a known, traceable thermal radiation temperature. This will be validated by comparison measurements by NPL and PTB.

2.2 Practical Johnson noise thermometry

Conventional thermometers are all prone to calibration drift which results in progressive loss of information about the process temperature and necessitates regular thermometer recalibration or replacement. Recent work by participants Metrosol and NPL [9], PTB [10], UL and CMI together with established routes to market will, for the first time, result in the world's first practical Johnson noise thermometers (JNTs) for industry with varying degrees of performance (and hence cost). All the JNTs exist as prototypes but the formidable technical challenges around electronics and probes fit for industry, as well as the unexplored traceability mechanisms, are common to all types of JNT. This is of great importance for applications where long-term monitoring and control is needed; examples include ionising radiation environments including nuclear waste storage and aerospace heat treatment. JNT is also needed for calibration laboratories.

JNT is very challenging because a) the noise voltage is minuscule [11] and needs to be extracted from other, much larger electrical noise and b) the requirement for sensing elements and probes are more demanding than for conventional thermometers. The route for traceability of the Johnson noise voltage measurement and resistance measurement to electrical standards, and a robust sensing element and probe assembly useable to 1200 °C need to be developed. Graphene is a promising candidate for the sensing element [12] but destructively oxidises at modest temperatures so the development and characterisation of a practical ceramic-encapsulated graphene sensing element is needed. JNT is one of the practical primary thermometry types recommended for further development by the BIPM Consultative Committee on Thermometry (CCT). It is in the CCT strategy (2021-2030+) as it implements the redefined kelvin by offering the possibility of thermometry free from calibration and drift. Joint development of the distinct JNT approaches is needed to provide a) diversity of design, metrological performance and cost, which translates into more options for customers; b) downward price pressure, and c) increased propagation to end users.

The redefinition of the kelvin in 2019 in terms of the Boltzmann constant opened the way for practical benefits through stimulating the development of practical primary thermometers which measure temperature directly, independent of any temperature scale. Primary thermometry therefore offers the possibility of a method that is free from calibration and is free from calibration *drift* in harsh environments. The type closest to commercialisation is the JNT. The temperature-dependent voltage arising from thermal motion of electrons can be measured, and thermodynamic temperature determined from first principles. Because all parameters associated with the thermometer which are degraded by harsh environments can be measured, a drift-free thermometer with continuous reference to the SI units based on fundamental constants can be implemented. Several JNTs exist in NMI laboratories, but they are essentially large physics experiments and are far from practical for industry. Four practical JNTs are currently being actively developed which are portable and practical to operate [9]. The key outstanding tasks are:

- The basic principle of the PTB dual-mode auto-calibrating resistance thermometer (DART) (which is called dual-mode because it is a joint JNT and resistance thermometer with the JNT used to calibrate the resistance thermometer *in situ*) and its electrical calibration have already been discussed in several publications [10]. However, the experiments presented were carried out with simplified prototypes which did not have the complete functionality of a practical noise thermometer. In this project a complete noise thermometer which makes traceable temperature measurements will be demonstrated.

- The JNT being developed by Metrosol and NPL (IJNT) is aimed at practical industrial use [11,13]. Currently it is a pure JNT, not dual mode. This thermometer has already had some testing at EMC facilities. Several factors limiting accuracy, calibration of the electronics, and improved stability for this thermometer need to be developed. Use in harsh environments such as high temperature, ionising radiation (gamma and neutron) and challenging electromagnetic environments (e.g. induction furnace) needs to be demonstrated.
- The JNT being developed at UL (ULNT) is also aimed at practical industrial use, using low-cost components such as a PC sound card. It operates over the temperature range from -196 °C to 300 °C. The uncertainty is approximately 0.5 °C. The device uses a relatively small 46 kHz bandwidth (i.e. audio frequency range); a key aim is to integrate this low-cost device with a practical probe suitable for industrial use and validate it.

This project is building on the existing JNTs by extending their temperature range (which is currently 0 °C to approximately 150 °C) up to 1200 °C, greatly increasing the range of applications in which they can be applied. A common theme for all four JNTs is the development of a robust sensor element and probe assembly. Conventional wire-wound resistive sensors and a completely novel sensor using graphene [14] will be developed. Boron nitride encapsulated graphene devices are robust against oxidation and can sustain high lattice temperatures up to about 1300 °C without degradation [15] and their resistance can be tuned to match the requirements of the measurement setup. This is being incorporated in a practical, robust probe assembly and tested in harsh environments.

Equally importantly, traceability of the Johnson noise voltage measurement and resistance measurement to electrical standards will be developed jointly by the project participants to ensure the accuracy and traceability of the JNT measurements. As the small signal in JNTs can easily be distorted by electromagnetic interference, testing in very high power electrical and induction furnaces will allow for unprecedented realistic testing of the suitability of the practical JNT in a very harsh environment. The participants will also assess the effect of high temperatures and ionising radiation environments. These three types of tests reflect the most likely stakeholder interest.

2.3 Phosphor thermometry to 1250 °C

Accurate and traceable non-contact temperature measurement of surfaces is challenging but is often the only option during high temperature dynamic processes. Traditional non-contact techniques such as thermal imaging are seriously compromised due to the unknown and changing emissivity of the surface being measured, background thermal radiation, and often rapidly changing temperatures. In industry such as marine, aerospace and space manufacturing, surface temperature measurement is not sufficiently accurate, and imaging capability is needed to obtain instantaneous temperature gradients. Phosphor thermometry offers a solution to these challenges and has been progressed substantially in EMPIR projects EMPRESS [6] and EMPRESS 2 [7]. However, although it can work at temperatures approaching 1000 °C, for consistent use it is currently limited to 750 °C for both single spot measurements and imaging. Robust coatings, new phosphor formulations and higher temperature operation for both imaging and single spot technologies are needed to extend the upper temperature to 1250 °C bringing many relevant applications in its purview e.g. steel processing and marine manufacturing.

Thermographic phosphor thermometry is being developed for operation at higher temperatures than previously attempted to validate surface temperature spot measurements to provide *in-situ* reference temperature 'spots' to facilitate qualitative thermal imaging. The maximum continuous temperature is currently 750 °C with intermittent use to 1000 °C; this project is elevating the maximum continuous temperature to a target of 1250 °C. This will be through development of enhanced instrumentation, robust coating formulations and application methods, and phosphor formulations that exhibit sufficient fluorescence at elevated temperatures. These will be demonstrated through in-process implementation in a range of manufacturing field trials. The techniques developed will be applied to practical devices for calibrating end-user thermometers, including contact surface temperature probes, ultimately for implementation as ISO 17025 [16] compliant services.

2.4 Artificial intelligence approaches for thermometry

New AI techniques are needed to address specific thermometry challenges:

- Self-validating thermometers which make use of an *in-situ* invariant temperature reference (which is based on the change of phase of materials) to overcome calibration drift [17] have been developed to the point where they are viable in industrial applications [18], and recent industry trials in aerospace heat treatment have proven their robustness and operational effectiveness. However, the feature which enables *in-situ* calibration, i.e. the 'change point', currently can only be identified manually by a human operator. Self-validating techniques based on change point detection (of the *in-situ* phase change materials) need to be automated before they can enter widespread use. Attempts to develop conventional algorithms for automating this process have failed. AI methods such as machine learning are needed to determine the change point and its uncertainty.

- The efficiency and effectiveness of noxious emission reduction of combustion processes (e.g. waste incineration for heat and electricity production) are strongly dependent on temperature. Gas temperature retrievals are mostly limited to atmosphere and planetary research, and industrial applications. In industrial applications local and effective gas temperature measurements are frequently made with the use of thermocouples (suction pyrometers) and hand-held pyrometers. The former is time consuming and prone to possible sensor contamination and blocking, while the latter can only give an overall picture of maximum gas and effective particle temperatures in distributed industrial systems such as boilers (power plants and waste incinerators) and large-scale high-temperature (glass, steel, gas-reforming) production. Non-uniform temperature profiles can reduce NO_x removal process efficiency (so-called SNCR or SCR processes) and lead to increased reagent (ammonia, urea) consumption and unnecessarily high NO_x/NH3 emissions. Infrared spectroscopic techniques are promising but the iterative algorithms needed to extract the temperature are far too slow to be used in real time.
- Reference surfaces for calibration of thermal imagers and phosphors are extremely difficult to implement in practice due to heat flow effects, which make it difficult to determine the areal surface temperature distribution, and the effect of placing items in physical contact with them.

AI is increasingly being used throughout society, and techniques are now available that can be adapted to solve some specific thermometry challenges in this project:

- Self-validating thermocouples are now mature. To enable their automation, an algorithm was recently developed, using training data from aerospace heat treatment trials [19], which uses machine learning to locate a single instance of a melting plateau and automate the corresponding *in-situ* recalibration. This algorithm showed promising results for data drawn from a single industrial furnace environment. However, the algorithm needs to locate multiple melting plateaus and perform well across a range of industrial scenarios. This will be achieved by enhancing the algorithm and performing testing under a wide range of operating conditions to make it robust to a wide range of industrial furnace environments.
- EMPIR project EMPRESS 2 pioneered the traceable measurement of temperature profiles along a path in combustion environments with a proof-of-concept demonstration in waste incineration [20]. Improved AI techniques to retrieve the temperature profile from the spectroscopic infrared measurements in these highly dynamic environments are being developed, to enable development of simplified equipment and compact, low-cost instrumentation. The temperature of the boiler/combustor walls is also needed in temperature profile retrievals, and the phosphor thermometry and emissivity measurements will be employed. These measurements cannot currently be performed in real-time; machine learning will enable faster processing to enable real-time thermometry.
- Reference surfaces which can be inserted in conventional dry-block calibrators are being developed. These make use of AI (a neural network) to interpolate between the temperatures indicated by a network of embedded sensors, in order to establish the areal temperature distribution at the surface. This will complement the thermal imaging and phosphor thermometry developments to enable the manufacture of a practical, low-cost surface thermometer calibration device.

3 Conclusion

A suite of current pan-European research activities aimed at improving SI traceable thermometry (and hence reliable process monitoring and control) suitable for harsh industrial environments has been described. These include:

1. Truly traceable, quantitative thermal imaging, by using at least 4 key engineering materials and selected thermographic phosphors with known temperature in the field of view of the thermal imager in the temperature range from -100 °C to 500 °C with an uncertainty of less than 5 °C.
2. To improve practical Johnson noise thermometry with a technology readiness level (TRL) of 6, and an uncertainty of less than 3 °C, and to provide truly driftless thermometry for harsh environments (e.g. nuclear power generation and decommissioning).
3. To develop robust thermographic phosphor techniques for surface temperature measurement with an uncertainty of less than 3 °C and up to temperatures of 1250 °C in collaboration with metals processing organisations and end-users.
4. To develop artificial intelligence (e.g. machine learning) approaches to enable traceable *in-situ* temperature measurement for industrial applications with an uncertainty of less than 2 % up to 1500 °C, demonstrated through at least three cases studies: 1) machine learning for autonomous operation of self-validating thermometers, 2) spectroscopic infrared thermometry for *in-situ* gas temperature and gas temperature profile measurements and 3) a reference surface temperature calibration insert for dry-block calibrators.

The project (23IND11 ThermoSI) has received funding from the European Partnership on Metrology, co-financed from the

European Union's Horizon Europe Research and Innovation Programme and by the Participating States.

References

1. E. Westkämper: Towards the Re-Industrialization of Europe - A Concept for Manufacturing for 2030, Springer-Verlag 2014
2. COM(2017) 479 final: Investing in a smart, innovative and sustainable Industry – A renewed EU Industrial Policy Strategy https://eur-lex.europa.eu/legal-content/en/TXT/?uri=CELEX%3A52017DC0479
3. COM(2014) 14 final: For a European industrial renaissance https://eur-lex.europa.eu/legal-content/EN/TXT/PDF/?uri=CELEX:52014DC0014&from=ET
4. Mise en pratique for the definition of the kelvin in the SI https://www.bipm.org/en/publications/mises-en-pratique
5. H. Preston-Thomas, The International Temperature Scale of 1990 (ITS-90), Metrologia 27 (1990) 3-10; erratum: Metrologia 27 (1990) 107 https://iopscience.iop.org/article/10.1088/0026-1394/27/1/002/pdf
6. J.V. Pearce, F. Edler, C.J. Elliott, L. Rosso, G. Sutton, A. Andreu, G. Machin, "EMPRESS: A European Project to Enhance Process Control Through Improved Temperature Measurement", Int. J. Thermophys. (2017) 38:118 https://doi.org/10.1007/s10765-017-2253-3
7. J.V. Pearce, A. Heyes, F. Edler, A. Fateev, G. Sutton, A. Andreu, G. Machin, Enhancing process efficiency through improved temperature measurement: the EMPRESS projects, proc. Tempmeko 2019, Journal of Physics: Conference Series 2554 012003 (2023) https://doi.org/10.1088/1742-6596/2554/1/012003
8. Sutton, G., Korniliou, S., Andreu, A. et al. Imaging Luminescence Thermometry to 750 °C for the Heat Treatment of Common Engineering Alloys and Comparison with Thermal Imaging. Int J Thermophys 43, 36 (2022). https://doi.org/10.1007/s10765-021-02963-1
9. http://www.johnson-noise-thermometer.com/
10. D. Drung, M. Kraus, C. Krause, Calibration of the dual-mode auto-calibrating resistance thermometer with few-parts-per-million uncertainty, Meas. Sci. Technol. 33(1) 015008 https://doi.org/10.1088/1361-6501/ac2c48
11. P. Bramley, D. Cruickshank, J.V. Pearce, The development of a practical, drift-free, Johnson noise thermometer for industrial applications, Int. J. Thermophys. 38, 25 (2017) https://doi.org/10.1007/s10765-016-2156-8
12. K.C. Fong & K.C. Schwab, Ultrasensitive and Wide-Bandwidth Thermal Measurements of Graphene at Low Temperatures. Phys. Rev. X 2, 031006 (2012) https://doi.org/10.1103/PhysRevX.2.031006
13. P. Bramley, D. Cruickshank, J. Aubrey, Developments towards an industrial Johnson noise thermometer, Meas. Sci. Technol. 31(5) 054003 (2020) https://doi.org/10.1088/1361-6501/ab58a6
14. Ferrari, A. C. et al. Science and technology roadmap for graphene, related two-dimensional crystals, and hybrid systems. Nanoscale 7, 4598–4810 (2015) https://doi.org/10.1039/c4nr01600a
15. F. Luo et al., Graphene Thermal Emitter with Enhanced Joule Heating and Localized Light Emission in Air, ACS Photonics 2019, 6, 8, 2117-2125 https://pubs.acs.org/doi/10.1021/acsphotonics.9b00667
16. ISO/IEC 17025:2017 General requirements for the competence of testing and calibration laboratories
17. D. Tucker, A. Andreu, C.J. Elliott, T. Ford, G. Machin, M. Neagu, J.V. Pearce, Industrial trials for integrated self-validating thermocouples up to 1329 °C, Meas. Sci. Tech. 29 105002 (2018) https://doi.org/10.1088/1361-6501/aad8a8
18. D. Tucker, J.V. Pearce, T. Ford, P. Cowley, P. Williams, P. Rau, *In-situ* traceability to the ITS-90 using integrated self-validating thermocouples – trials of the INSEVA thermocouple, AIP Conf. Proc. 3230, 090007 (2024) https://doi.org/10.1063/5.0235407
19. S. Bilson, A. Thompson, D. Tucker, J. Pearce, A machine learning approach to automation and uncertainty evaluation for self-validating thermocouples, AIP Conf. Proc. 3230, 090011 (2024) https://doi.org/10.1063/5.0235318
20. A. Fateev, From optimising waste incineration to internal combustion engines and defence applications, Johnson Matthey Technology Review 67(1) 25-35 (2023) https://doi.org/10.1595/205651323X16643556587827

EPJ Web of Conferences **323**, 07001 (10125
22nd nIt enr Iai nr dMt Iei ai gy|Ci nget ss

) llt sp:/ odor. :g0ig02g:et jconf:101231307001

Unscented Kalman Filtering for in-situ Bulk Identification of District Heating Meter Temperature Offsets and Service Pipe Insulation Level Detection

Peter F. Østergaard [1*], *Thomas S.* Daugbjerg[1], *Gertjan* Kok[2]

[1]Danish Technological Institute, Energy and Climate, Kongsvang Allé 29, 8000 Aarhus, Denmark
[2]VSL National Metrology Institute, Thijsseweg 11, 2629 JA Delft, Netherlands

Abstract. Unscented Kalman Filtering is applied to district heating meter data and GIS-data from a utility network to simultaneously identify temperature offsets in utility meters and service pipe insulation. Implementing estimation of the temperature in the main pipe allows for more accurate results, which also respect physical constraints. Unscented Transformations allow for easier implementation of the algorithm compared to existing solutions, as linearization is avoided. Correcting for potential offsets in the temperature measurement of the utility meter allows for a better estimation of the insulation level of the service pipe, improving the ability for the utilities to pinpoint their efforts in optimizing their renovation activities over several areas of interest.

1 Introduction

The European district heating network is distributed over more than 19,000 networks, with almost 200,000 km of distribution pipes. In 2022, it supplied a total of 608 TWh to more than 75 mio citizens. This corresponds to 13% of the total heating demand within the European Union. In some countries, like Denmark, more than two thirds of all residential buildings are heated by district heating [1].

The supply temperature in the district heating networks range from as high as 130 °C down to 60 °C or lower in certain 4th generation district heating networks [2]. As a district heating network has the goal of carbon neutrality, there is a movement towards even lower supply temperatures, as this allows for multiple, decentralized heating sources to be integrated into the network, such as accumulation tanks, heat pumps, surplus industrial heating, geothermal heating and similar sources. Many of these heating sources work best at temperatures below 60 °C [3], but to use such low temperatures in the district heating networks, it is a requirement that the insulation level is sufficiently good in all areas of the network. If not, the supply temperature will end up being so low at the consumer that domestic heating becomes troublesome, and the warm potable water ends up having a temperature which facilitates bacterial growth [4].

The European directive 2023/1791 [5] dictates that all utility meters must be remotely read by 2027.

While remotely read data from district heating utilities is often used by the utility to impose motivational tariffs [6,7] to the consumer, often by penalizing consumers who do not exploit the potential heat of the district heating water sufficiently and return water at a high temperature and reward the consumers who manage to return at a low temperature, it has also been used to calculate the insulation level of service pipes, allowing for more focused maintenance of the pipe network [8,9], monitoring installations [10,11], and leakage detection [12].

The meters, however, are mainly manufactured with a focus on measuring energy consumption by looking at temperature difference and volume flow. As such, the absolute temperature measured can deviate at levels defined by EN 1434-2022 [13].

Furthermore, when in service, a random sample of a given batch of utility meters from the same lot are spot-checked after 8 years to identify potential issues. If no issues are found during these checks of random meters, all meters in the batch are allowed to be in operation for an additional 8 years. During this time, no systematic monitoring of the potential drift of the sensors is conducted, potentially leading to false motivational tariffs to the consumers.

In this article, we propose a novel method, for identifying the utility meter temperature offset on top of the service pipe insulation level.

Added to the value found in previous works concerning insulation levels in service pipes, this method allows for a focused effort on changing faulty meters, thereby getting a better overview of the temperature in the network, allowing further reductions in supply temperatures without risking the public health, and for more fair motivational tariffs, as the temperatures used are corrected.

* Corresponding author: peo@teknologisk.dk

The method proposed in this article exploits Unscented Kalman filters [14] for identifying the state of the district heating network. Using an Unscented Kalman filter over e.g. an Extended Kalman filter [15,16] has benefits, as shown in Wan and Merwe [17] . These benefits include better state estimation and more accurate co-variance matrices, especially for highly non-linear state functions. Furthermore, it is easier to implement, as it does not require linearization of the equations.

2 Method

The method described in this article uses an Unscented Kalman filter as described in Wan and Merwe [17].

This method enables the continuous evaluation of the state of the system, which in the case of district heating is the insulation level of the service pipes and the offset of the utility meters.

Existing methods for evaluating the insulation level of the service pipes already exist in literature [8,9] , but these have some issues in their implementation and/or their assumptions.

The method described in Kongsgaard [9], uses an Extended Kalman Filter for evaluating the insulation level of the service pipe. As part of the evaluation, a constant temperature along the entire main pipe is assumed at each time step. This assumption is questionable as the flow through the main pipe consists of the sum of the sub flows going to the consumers at the various pipe branching points. As such, the flow in a main pipe going down a residential street decreases according to the consumption of the individual houses. If the last house on the street only has a small consumption, the flow at the end of the street will be low, and cooling in that part of the main pipe will be significant.

For the method described in Fester et al [8] a recursive algorithm is used to estimate the parameters in the network. This can lead to significant computational times, which is far from ideal, looking at the potential number of service pipes in European district heating networks.

2.1 Assumptions/requirements for running the algorithm

The method described here takes full advantage of the remotely read temperature and flow data from district heating utility meters. The method requires meter readings at a high frequency (hourly measurements or better). Furthermore, the data used for optimizing the parameters need to be obtained at time points, at which the hot water consumption is stable. As such, the best data arrives in the winter period during the night, when it is relatively safe to assume that any consumption is due to heating demands.

The algorithm works by estimating the temperature in the main pipe, based on the readings from the individual utility meters. The temperature profile in the main pipe is fitted using least squares fit to a physical model of the temperature profile along the pipe, given the insulation level and the partial flows in the different segments.

Using the fitted temperature in the main pipe, the temperature is backpropagated to the utility meter, giving an offset between the utility meter reading and the expected temperature from the model. This offset is used in the Kalman filter for optimizing the meter's temperature offset and the insulation level of the service pipe to best fit the system.

Since many district heating networks use shunts at the end of cul-de-sacs to avoid still-standing water and ensure warm water for the consumers at the end of the roads, the algorithm allows for the identification of a flow through such a shunt.

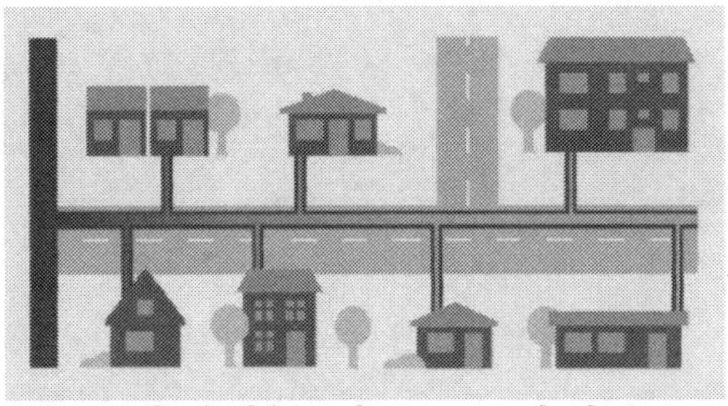

Figure 1: Sketch of district heating network. The main pipe, following the road, splits up into service pipes, each delivering district heating to individual houses. Insulation and flow levels at the different parts of the network determine the cooling of the water in each pipe segment.

2.2 Data quality requirements

2.3 Nomenclature

In the rest of the article, the following nomenclature is used:

T_{main}	Temperature at the main pipe
T_{supply}	Supply temperature at the utility meter
T_{ambient}	Ambient temperature
δT_{supply}	Offset of utility meter temperature measurement
P	Power loss through the pipe segment
Q	Flow
c_{H_2O}	Heat capacity of water
U	Thermal conductivity per length of pipe
L	Length of pipe segment

The energy loss in a pipe segment can, assuming steady state conditions, be found from two equations. The first way is to look at the temperature difference between the two ends of the pipe, and the second way is to look at the difference between the temperature of the water in the pipe and the ambient temperature:

$$P = (T_{\text{main}} - T_{\text{supply}}) \cdot Q \cdot c_{H_2O}$$

$$P = \left(\frac{T_{\text{main}} + T_{\text{supply}}}{2} - T_{\text{ambient}}\right) \cdot U \cdot L$$

Combining these two equations allows us to estimate T_{main} based on the measured temperature and flow at the consumer/utility meter and the ambient temperature. This gives

$$T_{\text{main}} = \frac{T_{\text{supply}} \cdot \left(c_{\text{H}_2\text{O}} \cdot Q + \frac{U \cdot L}{2}\right) - U \cdot L \cdot T_{\text{ambient}}}{c_{\text{H}_2\text{O}} \cdot Q - \frac{U \cdot L}{2}}$$

In this work, we assume that T_{ambient} equals the soil temperature, which is found through a meteorological source. The length of the service pipe is found through GIS-data, available from the utility network. To facilitate the analysis, T_{supply} is taken as the temperature indicated by the utility meter plus the meter offset, δT_{meter}, which we are interested in finding.

2.4 Unscented Kalman filtering for insulation level and offset estimation

Setting up the Unscented Kalman filter, three matrices/vectors need to be defined: The state vector, $\bar{x}$, containing the current expectation values for the temperature offsets and U-values, and the state covariance matrix, $\bar{\bar{R}}$, containing the covariance for the temperature offsets and U-values:

$$\bar{x} = \begin{bmatrix} \delta T_1 \\ U_1 \\ \delta T_2 \\ U_2 \\ \vdots \\ \delta T_n \\ U_n \end{bmatrix}$$

$$\bar{\bar{R}} = \begin{bmatrix} \sigma_{\delta T_1}^2 & \sigma_{U_1,\delta T_1} & \sigma_{\delta T_2,\delta T_1} & \cdots & \sigma_{U_n,\delta T_1} \\ \sigma_{\delta T_1,U_1} & \sigma_{U_1}^2 & \sigma_{\delta T_2,U_1} & \cdots & \sigma_{U_n,U_1} \\ \sigma_{\delta T_1,\delta T_2} & \sigma_{U_1,\delta T_2} & \sigma_{\delta T_2}^2 & \cdots & \sigma_{U_n,\delta T_2} \\ \vdots & \vdots & \vdots & \ddots & \vdots \\ \sigma_{\delta T_1,U_n} & \sigma_{U_1,U_n} & \sigma_{\delta T_2,U_n} & \cdots & \sigma_{U_n}^2 \end{bmatrix}$$

Finally, a matrix, containing the expected process uncertainty, $\bar{\bar{Q}}$, must be established. This matrix contains the expected noise in the system.

Initially we expect the temperature offset of the utility meters to be normally distributed: $\delta T = \mathcal{N}(0\,°\text{C}, 0.1\,°\text{C})$. The insulation of the service pipes is equally set to be normally distributed with $U = \mathcal{N}\left(0.10\,\frac{\text{W}}{\text{m}\cdot°\text{C}}, 0.01\,\frac{\text{W}}{\text{m}\cdot\text{K}}\right)$. Using the expected distributions of δT and U, both $\bar{x}$ and the diagonal elements of $\bar{\bar{R}}$ can be filled out.

Initially, all off-diagonal elements of $\bar{\bar{R}}$ are set to 0.

For the $\bar{\bar{Q}}$ matrix, the elements corresponding to process error for temperature are set to $\sigma_{\delta T,Q} = 0.01$ °C

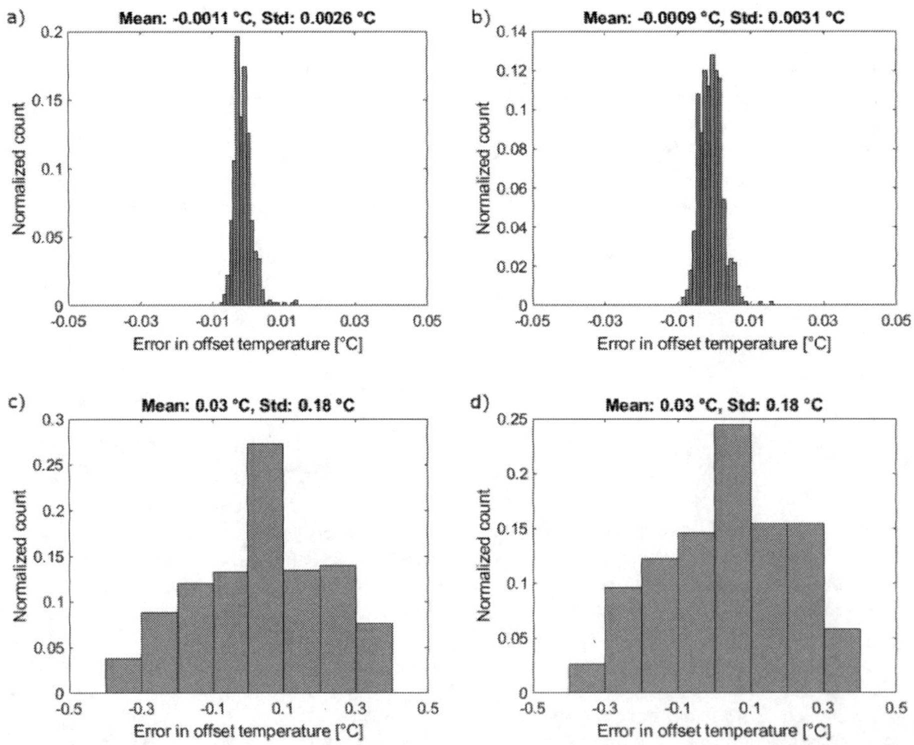

Figure 2: Deviations between utility errors and estimated errors found using the UKF. a) All data have high resolution and zero noise. Inlet temperature in main pipe is constant b) Data is rounded to same level as found in remotely read district heating meters. Inlet temperature to main pipe fluctuates. c) Individual, randomized service pipe insulation level and utility meter offset. d) Added uncertainty to location and length of service pipe.

and the process error for U to $\sigma_{U,Q} = 1 \times 10^{-5}\ \frac{\mathrm{W}}{\mathrm{m \cdot °C}}$. These values allow for the algorithm to converge towards stable solutions, without being too affected by noise in the measurements.

The diagonal elements of $\bar{\bar{Q}}$ are intentionally set lower than the diagonal elements of $\bar{\bar{R}}$ to obtain faster convergence.

3 Results

3.1 Synthetic data

To check the validity of the developed algorithm, the filter was run on 50 series of synthetic data [18]. Using synthetically generated data allows us to have a ground truth for the temperature offset and insulation level of the pipes.

The datasets are created in a way, which allows to add or remove noise for the different parameters. Using this feature, the Kalman Filter is first run on the synthetic data, where all information (meter readings, service pipe length, location of intersection between service pipe and main pipe) is known exactly, and the temperature at the beginning of the main pipe is constant. Using this data, the Kalman filter can identify the correct meter offsets with a standard deviation of 0.0026 °C.

In the second run, meter readings are rounded to a resolution of 0.01 °C and 0.01 m^3/h, identical to many actual utility meters. Furthermore, the temperature at the beginning of the main pipe is fluctuated. With this data, the Kalman filter can identify all the meter offsets with a standard deviation of 0.0031 °C.

For these two cases, the identification of the offset must be considered ideal, as it is better than the resolution of the meter.

In the third case, each consumer is given an individual consumption, as well as individual meter offsets and insulation level of the service pipe. Here, the algorithm can identify the offsets with a standard deviation of 0.18 °C.

The same standard deviation is found in case four, where uncertainty to the location and length of the service pipes is added to the data. Results from the four cases are shown in Figure 2.

In case four, it was noticed, much of the standard deviation originates from a general offset in the expected δT, leading to an offset in the expected temperature of the main pipe. By adding information on the temperature in the main pipe, the standard deviation of the error in δT can be reduced to 0.065 °C, as seen in Figure 3. In practice, this information can come from a reference thermometer. Using a reference thermometer would also introduce direct traceability to the SI-system.

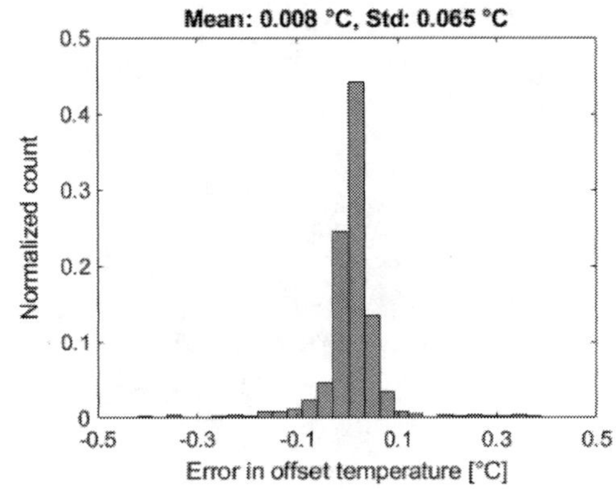

Figure 3: Deviation between error in temperature measurement and estimated error from the UKF.

3.2 Actual data

The Kalman filter has also been used on historical data from a Danish utility network. For this data, the actual offsets of the utility meters are unknown, and thus, the standard deviation on the error of δT cannot be analyzed as in section 3.1.

For the utility data, data from a single road is analyzed. The dataset has data for one year. To avoid issues with non-stationary consumption, the filter only uses data from midnight to 5 a.m. and only, when the meters show a flow rate higher than 0.04 m^3/h. This has the intended purpose of only analysing on the base load, used for heating.

Running the analysis shows, that for the road investigated, offsets are in the range [-0.4 °C; 0.4 °C] with uncertainties ($k = 1$) up to 0.08 °C. These δTs are within the expected range, as the ISO standard for energy meters allow δTs up to 0.5 °C.

Estimated errors in the temperature measurements of the meters from the test-area are seen in Figure 4.

For both synthetic and actual data, the insulation level of the service pipe is calculated simultaneously to the temperature offset. These results are similar to what has been found in previous studies [8,9] and will not be discussed here.

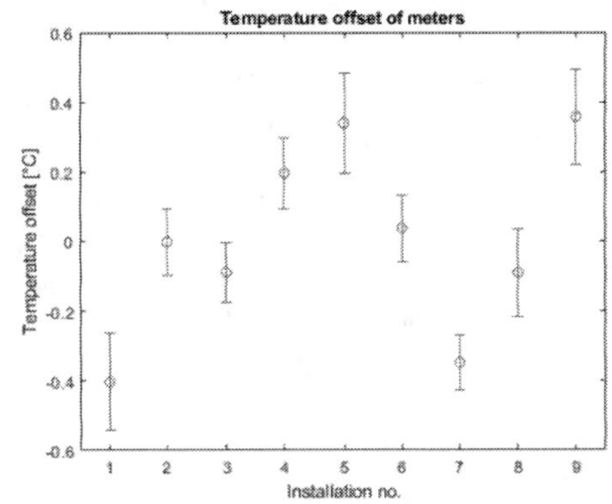

Figure 4: Estimated errors in temperature measurements on the test-area.

4 Potential pitfalls of Unscented Kalman Filtering for District Heating

In the above analysis of district heating data, both synthetic and actual data, the method appears to function

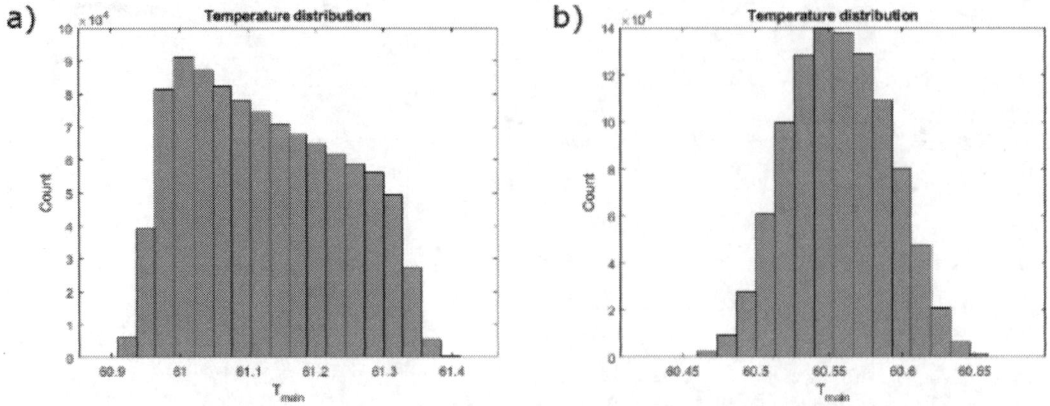

Figure 5 : Temperature probability distribution in the main pipe with a service pipe of 5 m. In both cases, the supply temperature is normally distributed N(60 °C, 0.02 °C). In a) the flow rate is uniformly distributed in the range [0.025 m3/h;0.035 m3/h], and in b), it is [0.055 m3/h;0.065 m3/h]

as expected. This is however not a guarantee that it will always work.

While unscented Kalman filtering does work significantly better on non-linear functions than regular Kalman filters and Extended Kalman filters, it still has some limitations when the transfer function is sufficiently non-linear. For district heating data this can be relevant when the flow in a pipe segment is low and the pipe segment is long. Here, the result of the transfer function can be shown to be skewed to a degree, as seen in Figure 5 a), which might cause issues. For such cases, it can be of interest to investigate other methods for parameter estimation, such as dual Unscented Kalman filters [19] or Particle Filters [20] (reference).

The temperature probability distribution in the main pipe, based on the temperature measurement at the utility meter can be seen in Figure 5 for a low flow ([0.025;0.035] m3/h) and a higher flow ([0.055;0.065] m3/h).

Another potential issue, which is generally true for all analyses of district heating data, is the frequency of the data gathering. Often, the flow rates in district heating networks are not stable or quazi-stable over the duration of one hour, as, e.g., taking a shower or cleaning dishes normally only takes a few minutes. Low duration events, if done at an unfortunate time, will lead to a meter reading showing a high flow, but low supply temperature (if the shower has just been started, and the warm water has not yet arrived at the house), or low flow and high temperature (if the shower has just ended, but the water at the utility meter is still warm).

5 Conclusion

We have found that it is possible to estimate critical parameters of a district heating network in the form of meter offsets, on top of the already characterized service pipe insulation levels using Unscented Kalman Filtering.

On synthetic data, the method can estimate the utility meter temperature offset for all meters on a road with a standard deviation on the error of less than 0.2 °C. If the temperature at the beginning of the road is known (e.g. by inserting a reference sensor here), the standard deviation of the utility meter temperature error is reduced to 0.065 °C, while also introducing direct traceability to the SI-system.

The method is used on real-world data, where offsets were estimated to be within the range [-0.4 °C – 0.4 °C], all within the tolerable limits as given by the relevant ISO-standard (Starndardization 2022).

The method described has potential issues with low flow rates, where the temperature probability density function in the main pipe becomes extremely non-Gaussian. These issues should be investigated, potentially using dual Unscented Kalman Filters or Particle Filters, capable of handling extremely non-linear transfer functions.

Bibliography

[1] "DHC Market Outlook 2024 Executive Summary". Euroheat & Power, 4. juni 2024. https://api.euroheat.org/uploads/Final_Market_Outlook_2024_0efcdb4b7e.pdf.

[2] Lund, Henrik, Sven Werner, Robin Wiltshire, Svend Svendsen, Jan Eric Thorsen, Frede Hvelplund, og Brian Vad Mathiesen. "4th Generation District Heating (4GDH)". *Energy* 68 (april 2014): 1–11. https://doi.org/10.1016/j.energy.2014.02.089.

[3] Bogdanov, Dmitrii, Rasul Satymov, og Christian Breyer. "Impact of Temperature Dependent Coefficient of Performance of Heat Pumps on Heating Systems in National and Regional Energy Systems Modelling". *Applied Energy* 371 (oktober 2024): 123647. https://doi.org/10.1016/j.apenergy.2024.123647.

[4] Toffanin, Riccardo, Vinicio Curti, og Maurizio C. Barbato. "Impact of Legionella Regulation on a 4th Generation District Heating Substation Energy Use and Cost: The Case of a Swiss Single-Family Household". *Energy* 228 (august 2021): 120473. https://doi.org/10.1016/j.energy.2021.120473.

[5] Directive (EU) 2023/1791 of the European Parliament and of the Council of 13 September 2023 on energy efficiency and amending Regulation (EU) 2023/955 (recast) (Text with EEA relevance), 231 OJ L § (2023). http://data.europa.eu/eli/dir/2023/1791/oj/eng.

[6] Lund, Henrik, Jan Eric Thorsen, Steen Schelle Jensen, og Flemming Pentz Madsen. "Fourth-Generation District Heating and Motivation Tariffs". *ASME Open Journal of Engineering* 1 (1. januar 2022): 011002. https://doi.org/10.1115/1.4053420.

[7] "HOT|COOL MAGAZINE SPECIAL COLLECTION 2/2022". Set 28. februar 2025. https://hotcool.dbdh.dk/view/390832837/14/?sharedOn=.

[8] Fester, Jakob, Peter Friis Østergaard, Fredrik Bentsen, og Brian Kongsgaard Nielsen. "A Data-Driven Method for Heat Loss Estimation from District Heating Service Pipes Using Heat Meter- and GIS Data". *Energy* 277 (august 2023): 127713. https://doi.org/10.1016/j.energy.2023.127713.

[9] Nielsen, Brian Kongsgaard, Fredrik Bentsen, Emil Andreasen Klahn, Jakob Fester, og Carsten Skovmose Kallesøe. "Supervision of Service Pipes in District Heating Networks". *SSRN Electronic Journal*, 2022. https://doi.org/10.2139/ssrn.4313579.

[10]Farouq, Shiraz, Stefan Byttner, Mohamed-Rafik Bouguelia, Natasa Nord, og Henrik Gadd. "Large-Scale Monitoring of Operationally Diverse District Heating Substations: A Reference-Group Based Approach". *Engineering Applications of Artificial Intelligence* 90 (april 2020): 103492. https://doi.org/10.1016/j.engappai.2020.103492.

[11]Theusch, Felix, Patrick Klein, Ralph Bergmann, Wolfgang Wilke, Wolfgang Bock, og Adrian Weber. "Fault Detection and Condition Monitoring in District Heating Using Smart Meter Data". *PHM Society European Conference* 6, nr. 1 (29. juni 2021): 11. https://doi.org/10.36001/phme.2021.v6i1.2786.

[12]Zhou, Shoujun, Zheng O'Neill, og Charles O'Neill. "A Review of Leakage Detection Methods for District Heating Networks". *Applied Thermal Engineering* 137 (juni 2018): 567–74. https://doi.org/10.1016/j.applthermaleng.2018.04.010.

[13]"EN 1434-2022 - Heat Meters". CEN.

[14]Julier, S.J., og J.K. Uhlmann. "Unscented Filtering and Nonlinear Estimation". *Proceedings of the IEEE* 92, nr. 3 (marts 2004): 401–22. https://doi.org/10.1109/JPROC.2003.823141.

[15]Ribeiro, Maria Isabel. *Kalman and Extended Kalman Filters: Concept, Derivation and Properties*. 1049-001 Lisboa, PORTUGAL: Instituto Superior Tecnico, u.å. https://www.researchgate.net/publication/2888846_Kalman_and_Extended_Kalman_Filters_Concept_Derivation_and_Properties.

[16]Lewis, Frank L. *Optimal estimation: with an introduction to stochastic control theory*. New York: Wiley, 1986.

[17]Wan, E.A., og R. Van Der Merwe. "The unscented Kalman filter for nonlinear estimation". I *Proceedings of the IEEE 2000 Adaptive Systems for Signal Processing, Communications, and Control Symposium (Cat. No.00EX373)*, 153–58. Lake Louise, Alta., Canada: IEEE, 2000. https://doi.org/10.1109/ASSPCC.2000.882463.

[18]Østergaard, Peter Friis. "Synthetic district heating meter data". Zenodo, 27. februar 2025. https://doi.org/10.5281/zenodo.14936551.

[19]Yu, Anxi, Ye Liu, Jubo Zhu, og Zhen Dong. "An Improved Dual Unscented Kalman Filter for State and Parameter Estimation". *Asian Journal of Control* 18, nr. 4 (juli 2016): 1427–40. https://doi.org/10.1002/asjc.1229 .

[20] Xu, Yabo, Ke Xu, Jianwei Wan, Zhengda Xiong, og Yuanyuan Li. "Research on Particle Filter Tracking Method Based on Kalman Filter". I *2018 2nd IEEE Advanced Information Management,Communicates,Electronic and Automation Control Conference (IMCEC)*, 1564–68. Xi'an: IEEE, 2018. https://doi.org/10.1109/IMCEC.2018.8469578 .

Frost/Dew Point Temperature and Relative Humidity Measurements: Primary and Secondary Calibration Methods

Andreia Furtado [1*], *Fitsum* Zenebe[1], *Özkan* Subas[1], *Michael* Schwinghammer[1], and *Praveen* Giri[1]

[1]Process Insights GmbH, Calibration Center, Max-Eyth-Str. 30, 70736 Fellbach, Germany

Abstract. Humidity measurements are crucial across various industries to ensure product quality, safety, and process efficiency. These measurements can be expressed as absolute quantities, such as frost/dew point, temperatures point, t_f/t_d, or as relative humidity, U, which relates to saturation at a given temperature. Chilled-mirror hygrometers are widely used in high-precision industrial and research applications due to their broad measurement range, stability, and accuracy. Ensuring metrological traceability requires rigorous calibration using traceable methods. The DAkkS-accredited Calibration Laboratory of Process Insights follows DKD-R 5-8 [1] guidelines and meets ISO 17025 [2] requirements, employing both primary and secondary calibration methods for t_f/t_d over the range [-90, 95] °C, and U over the range [1, 98] %rh. Primary calibration achieves the lowest uncertainties using in-house 1-pressure and 2-pressure humidity (U_{t_f/t_f}: 0.4 K - 45 mK and U_U: 0.10 - 0.39 %rh), while secondary calibration relies on stable CM hygrometers and commercial humidity generators (U_{t_f/t_f}: 0.54 K - 70 mK and U_U: 0.10 - 0.49 %rh). For relative humidity calibration, both t_f/t_d [1] and temperature [3] sensors require calibration. Humidity calculations follow established references, ensuring high accuracy [4, 7-8]. This work outlines the methodologies and challenges in maintaining traceability and accuracy in high accuracy humidity measurements at PI Cal.

1 Introduction

Humidity measurement plays a crucial role in various industrial and scientific applications, ensuring product quality, safety, and process efficiency. The characterization of humidity can be divided into absolute and relative quantities. Absolute humidity measurements provide direct information about the amount of water vapor contained in a gas and include parameters such as dew point temperature, t_d and frost point temperature, t_f [4]. On the other hand, relative humidity, U, expresses the relationship between the actual water vapor content and the saturation level at a given temperature [4]. The accurate determination of these parameters is essential across different fields, including climate monitoring, meteorology, pharmaceuticals, semiconductors, and industrial drying processes.

A variety of measurement techniques exist to determine humidity, each differing in complexity, measurement range, and associated uncertainty. Among these, chilled-mirror hygrometers stand out as one of the most reliable and accurate instruments [5], widely used in both industrial and research environments. Their popularity stems from their ability to provide direct, stable, and highly precise measurements over a broad humidity range. However, to maintain confidence in their measurements, metrological traceability is required, necessitating rigorous calibration using traceable methods.

The DAkkS-accredited Calibration Laboratory of Process Insights (PI Cal), GmbH ensures metrological traceability for humidity measurements through a combination of primary and secondary calibration methods. These calibration activities are conducted in compliance with DKD-R 5-8 [1] guidelines and meet the requirements established by ISO 17025 [2].

Frost and dew point temperature calibrations are performed over a range of -90 °C to 95 °C, utilizing both primary and secondary calibration methods. Primary calibration methods achieve the lowest measurement uncertainties by employing single or 1-pressure and 2-pressure humidity generators, which were originally developed by MBW Calibration AG when it functioned as the Swiss Designated Institute for Humidity [6]. These in-house developed generators produce a highly controlled humid gas stream, where the generated humidity is directly traceable to saturation temperature, t_s, and pressure, p_s. In contrast, secondary calibration methods rely on well-characterized chilled-mirror hygrometers with long-term stability, enabling comparative measurements against reference standards. Although secondary calibrations inherently have higher measurement uncertainties, they remain a reliable and widely used method for routine calibration of industrial humidity sensors.

In addition to frost and dew point temperature calibration, relative humidity calibration, in the range of 1 %rh and 98 %rh, is also part of the laboratory's

* Corresponding author: AFurtado@emea.process-insights.com

calibration measurement capabilities (CMC). In the case of chilled mirror hygrometers, this process requires calibration of both dew point/frost point temperature [1] and temperature sensors [3]. To ensure high accuracy across a broad temperature spectrum, humidity calculations follow well-established reference equations and internationally recognized data sources [4,7-8].

This paper aims to describe the operating principles and design of the PI Cal primary humidity generators used for frost/dew point temperature calibration. Additionally, the major uncertainty sources, as well, the acceptance criteria for calibration results, are also presented.

2 Calibration of frost/dew point temperature

2.1 Low range humidity generator (LRG)

2.1.1 Principle of operation

The low range humidity generator (LRG) is a 2-pressure generator based on the saturation of dry air, flowing over a plane surface of isothermal ice at a well-defined temperature, t_s and pressure, p_s.

2.1.2 Design

The LRS consists of 18 stacked electropolished stainless-steel trays, sealed with copper press seals, where ice is formed (Fig. 2). A preceding cooling coil serves as a heat exchanger for the incoming dry air (Fig. 2). Dry air sequentially flows through the trays, repeatedly passing over the ice surface to achieve thermodynamic equilibrium, ensuring full saturation with water at the bath's set temperature. The multiple flow diversions maximize contact with the ice, allowing the air to reach full saturation at the bath's set temperature. The generator operates at a slight overpressure relative to ambient pressure. The measured frost point temperature corresponds to the temperature at which the carrier gas is saturated, with minor corrections applied for pressure drops in the gas flow.

Saturator temperature control is managed via a thermoregulated bath using absolute ethanol as the refrigerant fluid. This setup results in an expanded uncertainty of approximately 2 mK due to instability and 3 mK due to inhomogeneity ($k = 2$).

A constant flow rate of 1 L/min is maintained as the gas mixture is accelerated to sonic velocity through a nozzle, ensuring a stable and controlled flow. Approximately 1.1 to 1.2 L of ultrapure water are required to fill the saturator.

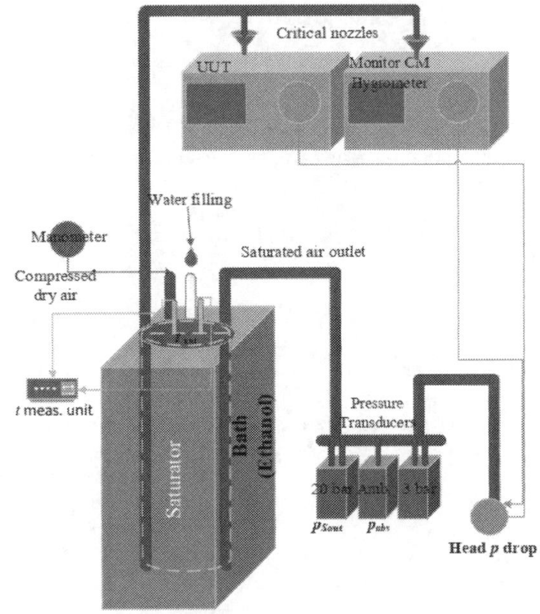

Fig. 1. Schematic diagram of the low range humidity generator (LRS) setup used for the primary calibration of frost/dew point temperature in the interval of [-90, -20] °C.

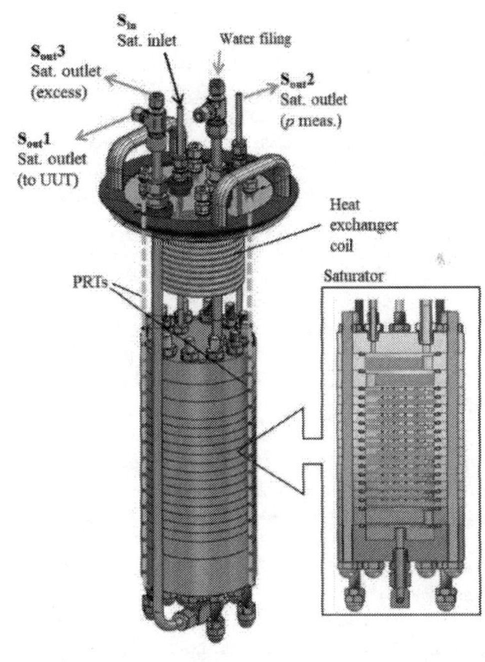

Fig. 2. Schematic diagram of the core of the low range humidity generator (LRS), consisting of a heat exchanger and a saturator. Legend: black arrow – dry air inlet; green arrows – humid air outlet; blue arrow – ultrapure water inlet.

2.2 High range humidity generator (HRG)

2.2.1 Principle of operation

The high-range humidity generator (HRG) operates in either single-pressure mode (1P) or two-pressure mode (2P), depending on the temperature range. In single-pressure mode, it covers dew point temperatures from 1 °C to 95 °C, while in two-pressure mode, it generates frost point temperatures from 0 °C down to - 20 °C.

In single-pressure mode, the dew point temperature corresponds to the temperature at which the carrier gas reaches full saturation. However, corrections must be applied for pressure drops occurring along the gas path to the point of use, including the unit under test and the reference chilled mirror hygrometer(s).

In two-pressure mode, the carrier gas is first saturated at an elevated pressure above ambient conditions. It is then expanded through a controlled expansion valve, leading to a reduction in pressure and temperature, thereby achieving the desired frost point temperature.

2.2.2 Design

The high-range generator (HRG) comprises three main components, all designed and manufactured by MBW [6]: a model G1HX humidity generator, which functions as a precision pre-saturator and pressure controller in two-pressure mode; the HRG main saturator with an integrated heat exchanger; and a motorized expansion valve assembly, connected to the outlet manifold and controlled by the G1HX, for regulating saturator pressure in two-pressure mode (Fig. 3).

Saturator temperature control is achieved using a thermoregulated bath with absolute distilled water as the refrigerant fluid. This configuration results in an expanded uncertainty of approximately 4 mK due to instability and 8 mK due to inhomogeneity ($k = 2$).

Dry air is first introduced into the G1HX pre-saturator, which operates in delta temperature mode at +5 °C relative to the desired frost/dew point temperature. The pre-conditioned humid air is then delivered via a heated stainless-steel hose to the saturator inlet. After achieving full saturation, the humid air exits the saturator through a heated stainless-steel hose, returning to the G1HX manifold before being directed to the unit under test (UUT) and the reference chilled mirror hygrometer. Heated stainless-steel hoses maintain a temperature approximately 30 °C above the frost/dew point temperature to prevent condensation.

The primary heat exchange and condensate formation occur within the heat exchanger coil, where condensation accumulates in the main saturator. As a result, only the final few mK of temperature drop take place inside the main saturator [6] (Fig. 4).

The HRG main saturator has a nominal internal volume of approximately 1 L. While the primary saturation surface is the internal wall of the cylindrical chamber, the equilibrium vapor pressure is primarily defined by the flat surface at the bottom of the bath, which is estimated to be a few mk lower than the wall temperature [6].

The generator operates as close as possible to atmospheric pressure, depending on the pressure resistance and internal flow restrictions of the unit under test. An individual flow rate of 1 L/min per unit under test is used for t_f/t_d below 0 °C, and 0.5 L/min per unit under test is used for t_f/t_d above 0 °C.

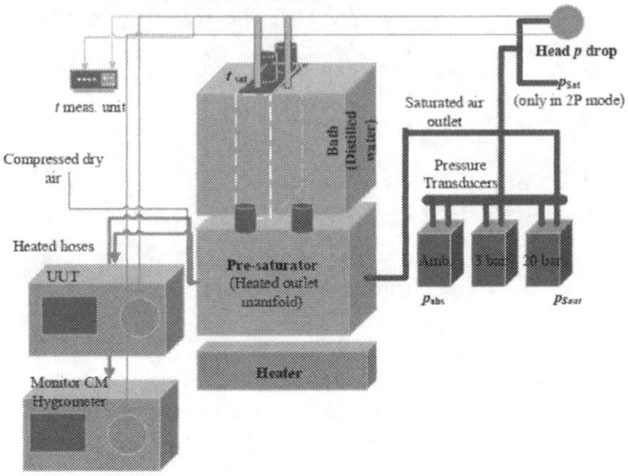

Fig. 3. Schematic diagram of the high range humidity generator setup used for the primary calibration of frost/dew point temperature in the interval of [-20, 95] °C.

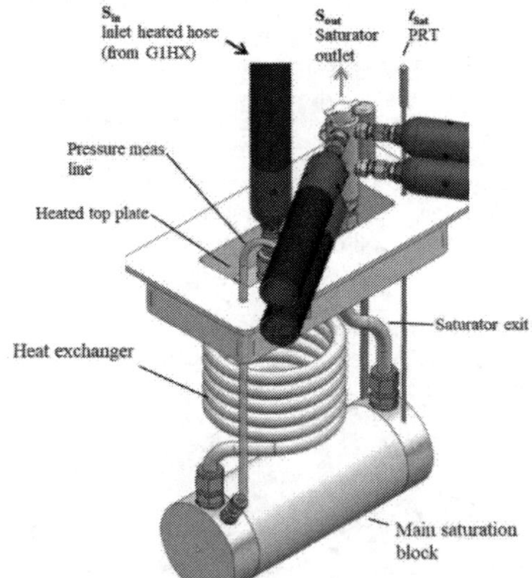

Fig. 4. Schematic diagram of the core of the high range humidity generator, consisting of a heat exchanger and a saturator.

2.3 Dry air

The air is compressed using an oil-free compressor, dried with a molecular sieve heat-regenerator dryer, and then fed through stainless-steel tubing to the saturator inlet. The fully saturated air exits via stainless-steel tubes to the unit under test and reference chilled-mirror hygrometers.

2.4 Temperature and pressure measurement in the saturators

Temperature measurement in the main saturator of each generator is performed using two platinum resistance thermometers (PRTs), calibrated at fixed points, with an expanded measurement uncertainty of 5.5 mK ($k = 2$). In the LRG, both PRTs are immersed in the bath fluid near the saturator exit (Fig. 2). In the HRG, one PRT is placed in the saturator block at the saturator exit, while the other is positioned in the bath fluid at the saturator exit side and serves as a verification sensor (Fig. 4). The PRT are used with resistance measuring units with an expanded measurement uncertainty of 1.2 mΩ ($k = 2$)

Pressure measurements are carried out using three digital pressure gauges in each generator. An absolute pressure transmitter, with an expanded measurement uncertainty of 0.29 hPa ($k = 2$), is used to measure ambient pressure. A 3 MPa differential pressure transmitter, with an expanded measurement uncertainty of 0.29 hPa ($k = 2$), is used to measure the pressure drop at the unit under test and the pressure drop in the LRS saturator. Another 20 MPa differential pressure transmitter, with an expanded measurement uncertainty of 0.79 hPa ($k = 2$), is used to measure the saturator pressure.

In the LRG, the saturator pressure measurement instrument is connected to a purged line with a large diameter. In the HRG, pressure measurement instruments are connected via two-way valves, allowing purging of the measurement lines during changes in saturator temperature and pressure to prevent condensation.

The above-mentioned expanded measurement uncertainties account for uncertainties from calibration, resolution, drift, and hysteresis. For temperature measurements, additional sources of uncertainty include nonlinearity, self-heating, and thermal coupling. For pressure measurements, interpolation, zero error, and height differences are also considered.

3 Calculation Formulas

Ideally, the humid gas exiting the generators (LRG and HRG), with a well-defined saturation temperature, t_{sat} and pressure, p_{sat}, is characterized by a water vapour mole fraction, x_w, given by the following equation [7]:

$$x_w = \frac{e_{i,w}(t_s)}{p_s} f_{i,w}(p_s, t_s) \quad (1)$$

where $e_{i,w}(t_s)$ represents the saturation vapour pressure in the pure phase, with respect to ice (i) in LRG or water (w) in HRG at the temperature t_s. The term p_s denotes the total pressure of the gas, while $f_{i,w}(p_s, t_s)$ is the enhancement factor, which accounts for the non-ideal behaviour of the gas.

The humidity of the gas at the outlet of the generators can also be expressed in terms of frost/dew point temperature, $t_{f,d}$. The quantity $t_{f,d}$ represents the temperature at which frost/dew forms when cooling a gas at constant pressure, corresponding to the temperature at which the gas is saturated in equilibrium with ice or water, respectively. In an ideal humidity generator, the saturation temperature, t_s and $t_{f,d}$ are identical.

The calculation of vapor pressure, $e_{i,w}$, from the frost/dew point temperature, $t_{f,d}$, and enhancement factor, $f_{i,w}(p_s, t_s)$, follows the ITS-90 formulations of Hardy [7] in the range -100 °C to 100 °C. For temperatures above 100 °C, vapor pressure calculations are performed in accordance with IAPWS [8], while humidity calculations above 100 °C (saturation vapor pressure via system pressure) follow VDI/VDE 3514 Part 1 [4], which describes the hypothetical saturation state.

The saturation temperature, t_s, is measured using platinum resistance thermometers (PRTs), as described in Equation (2):

$$t_s = t_{PRT}(R_{PRT}) \quad (2)$$

The saturator pressure, p_S, is determined based on the barometric pressure, p_{abs}, and the relative pressure measured at the saturator outlet. In the single-pressure (1P) mode, this outlet pressure is denoted as p_{Sout} (Eq. 3), while in two-pressure (2P) mode, it is referred to as p_{Sat} and is measured after the expansion valve (Eq. 4).

$$\text{In 1P mode}: p_S = p_{abs} + p_{Sout} \quad (3)$$

$$\text{In 2P mode}: p_S = p_{abs} + p_{Sat} \quad (4)$$

The pressure at the unit under test, p_{UUT}, is determined based on the operating range of the humidity generator. For high-range generator (HRG), where saturation occurs over water, p_{UUT} is given by:

$$p_{UUT} = p_{abs} + p_{Sout} \cdot \frac{p_{UUT}}{p_s} \quad (5)$$

For low-range generators (LRG), where saturation occurs over ice, the pressure at the unit under test is calculated by Eq. 6, where Δp_{UUT}, represents the pressure measured at the measuring head of the UUT.

$$p_{UUT} = p_{abs} + \Delta p_{UUT} \quad (6)$$

The water vapor partial pressure at the unit under test, e'_{UUT}, is then determined using the following equation:

$$e'_{UUT} = \frac{e_{i,w}(t_s) \cdot f_{i,w}(p_s, t_s)}{f_{i,w}(p_{UUT}, t_{f,d})} \cdot \frac{p_{UUT}}{p_s} \quad (7)$$

Since the vapor pressure equations used in this process cannot be solved analytically for the frost/dew point temperature, $t_{f,d}$, the value of $t_{f,d}$ is obtained iteratively using Eq. 8.

$$t_{f,d\,S} = t_{d,f}(e_{UUT}) \quad (8)$$

Finally, the relative humidity, $U_{i,w}$, is calculated as follows:

$$U_{i,w} = \frac{e_{i,w}(t_s) \cdot f_{i,w}(p_S, t_s)}{e_{i,w}(t_{air}) \cdot f_{i,w}(p_{UUT}, t_{air})} \cdot \frac{p_{UUT}}{p_S} \cdot 100\ \% \quad (9)$$

4 Acceptance Criteria

The acceptance criteria of the calibration results in primary and secondary calibration methods for frost/dew point temperature and relative humidity of a chilled-mirror hygrometer are presented in Table 1.

Table 1. Acceptance criteria of the calibration results in primary and comparison calibration methods for frost/dew point temperature and relative humidity of a chilled-mirror hygrometer. Note: in this context U_{CMC} refers to the accredited measurement uncertainty.

Acceptance criteria of calibration results
Primary method
· Difference from the monitor chilled-mirror hygrometer: t_f/t_d below -60 °C: ≤ 1/2 U_{CMC} t_f/t_d above -60 °C: ≤ 1/3 U_{CMC} · Standard deviation of primary ref. value: ≤ 20 % U_{CMC} · Standard deviation of the UUT: 25 % U_{CMC} · Repeatability of the UUT: t_f/t_d below -60 °C: ≤ 60 % U_{CMC} t_f/t_d above -60 °C: ≤ 40 % U_{CMC}
Comparison method
· Standard deviation of the reference chilled-mirror hygrometer: ≤ 20 % U_{CMC} · Standard deviation calibration of the UUT: ≤ 25 % U_{CMC} · Repeatability of the UUT: t_f/t_d below -60 °C: ≤ 50 % U_{CMC} t_f/t_d above -60 °C: ≤ 30 % U_{CMC} C

5 Measurement Uncertainty

The main contributions to the measurement uncertainty in primary and secondary calibration methods for frost/dew point temperature and relative humidity of a chilled-mirror hygrometer are presented in Tables 2 and 3, respectively. These uncertainty sources are categorized based on their impact on the reference value and the measured value obtained by the unit under test.

Table 2. Main contributions to the measurement uncertainty in primary calibration methods for frost/dew point temperature and relative humidity of a chilled-mirror hygrometer.

Primary method
Main contributions to the reference value
· Saturation efficiency and stability · Temperature inhomogeneity of the saturator · Determination of the saturation temperature, t_{Sat} · Determination of the saturation pressure, p_{Sat} · Gas pressure at the generator outlet, p_{Sout} · Correlation between pressure and temperature measurement · Contrib. due to the vapour pressure formulation [4,7-8] · For relative humidity calibrations: determination of the chamber/bath temperature and chamber/bath homogeneity and stability
Main contributions to the unit under test indication value
· Repeatability · Resolution · Pressure drop · Flow dependency

Table 3. Main contributions to the measurement uncertainty in comparison calibration method for frost/dew point temperature and relative humidity of a chilled-mirror hygrometer.

Comparison method
Main contributions to the reference value
· Reference value dew point temperature (reference chilled-mirror hygrometer, including; calibration, interpolation between calibration points, repeatability, temperature dependence of the electronics, drift) · Pressure drop · Flow dependency · For relative humidity calibrations: determination of the chamber/bath temperature and chamber/bath homogeneity and stability
Main contributions to the unit under test indication value
· Repeatability · Resolution · Pressure drop · Flow dependency

The calibration and measurement capabilities (CMC) of PI CAL related with chilled-mirror hygrometers are given in Table 4.

Table 4. Calibration and measurement capabilities of PI CAL in related with chilled-mirror hygrometers.

Frost/ dew point temperature	**Expanded Uncertainty (k=2)**
Primary method	
[-90, -80[°C	0.40 K ... 0.20 K(1)
[-80, -60[°C	0.20 K... 0.05 K(2)
[-60, -20[°C	0.050 K
[-20, 70[°C	0.030 K
[70, 90[°C	0.040 K
[90, 95] °C	0.045 K
Comparison method	
[-90, -75[°C	0.50 K... 0.20 K(3)
[-75, -60[°C	0.20 K... 0.07 K(4)
[-60, -20[°C	0.070 K
[-20, 60[°C	0.050 K
[60, 95] °C	0.070 K
Relative humidity	**Expanded Uncertainty (k=2)**
Primary method	
[1, 98 [%rh	0.10 ... 0.39 K
Comparison method	
[1, 98 [%rh	0.10 ... 0.49 K

Legend: (1) 0.2 K +$|t_f+ 80|$·0.02; (2) 0.05 K +$|t_f+ 60|$·0.0075; (3) 0.2 K +$|t_f+ 75|$·0.02; (4) 0.07 K +$|t_f+ 60|$·0.0087

6 Conclusion

This work presented a detailed description of the humidity generators used for primary calibration of frost/dew point temperature, along with the key contributors to measurement uncertainty and the acceptance criteria for calibration results. The uncertainty values for the comparison method and relative humidity calibration were also provided.

The Process Insights Calibration Laboratory has the capability to calibrate chilled-mirror hygrometers for frost/dew point temperature using both primary and secondary methods. Primary calibration covers the frost/dew point temperature range between -90 °C and 95 °C, with an expanded measurement uncertainty between 0.4 K and 45 mK, with a coverage factor $k = 2$, while secondary calibration yields to an expanded measurement uncertainty between 0.54 K and 70 mK, with a coverage factor $k = 2$.

Relative humidity calibrations can be performed within the range of 1 %rh and 98 %rh, with an expanded uncertainty between 0.10 %rh and 0.39 %rh for primary calibration and between 0.10 %rh and 0.49 %rh for secondary calibration, with a coverage factor $k = 2$.

These calibration capabilities ensure high accuracy traceability in humidity measurements, supporting industrial and research applications requiring rigorous calibration standards.

References

1. Guideline DKD-R 5-8, Edition 02/2019, Revision 0, Calibration of hygrometers for direct measurements of relative humidity, Physikalisch-Technische Bundesanstalt, Braunschweig and Berlin. https://doi.org/10.7795/550.20190214EN
2. DIN EN ISO/IEC 17025:2018, General requirements for the competence of testing and calibration laboratories (ISO/IEC 17025:2017), March 2018
3. Guideline DKD-R 5-1 Calibration of resistance thermometers, Edition 11/2023, Revision 0, Physikalisch-Technische Bundesanstalt, Braunschweig and Berlin. 10.7795/550.20231207
4. VDI/VDE 3514, Part 1: Measurement of gas humidity - Characteristics and symbols, Verein Deutscher Ingenieure e.V., 2016
5. VDI/VDE 3514, Pat 2: Measurement of humidity - Methods of measurement Verein Deutscher Ingenieure e.V., 2013
6. S. Wettstein & D. Mutter, Design and validation of the MBW standard humidity generators. *Int. J. Thermophys.*, 39(10), **116** (2018). https://doi.org/10.1007/s10765-018-2436-6
7. B. Hardy, ITS-90 formulations for vapor pressure, frostpoint temperature, dewpoint temperature, and enhancement factors in the range–100 to + 100 °C. in The Proceedings of the Third International Symposium on Humidity & Moisture, Teddington, London, England, April (1998), (pp. 1-8)
8. IAPWS, R7-97(2012): Release on the IAPWS Industrial Formulation 1997 for the Thermodynamic Properties of Water and Steam, International Association for the Properties of Water and Steam, 1997/2007
9. EA-4/02 M: Evaluation of the Uncertainty of Measurement in calibration, DAkkS, European Accreditation, 04/04/2022, Revision 3
10. BIPM, IEC, IFCC, ILAC, ISO, IUPAC, IUPAP, and OIML. Evaluation of measurement data - Guide to the expression of uncertainty in measurement. Joint Committee for Guides in Metrology, JCGM 100:2008. 10.59161/JCGM100-2008E.

Testing of Water Smart Meters Under Various Conditions

R. Ben-Mansour[1], A. Alsarkhi[1], A. Alshehri[1], E. Algazal[2], A. Alomar[2] and I. Alhemdda[2]*

[1]Mechanical Eng. Dep., KFUPM, Dhahran 31261, Saudi Arabia

[2]Legal Metrology Program "TAQYEES", SASO, Riyadh 11432. Saudi Arabia

Abstract. The accuracy Smart water meters are being widely used across developed and developing countries in order to avail accurate and updated billing for the consumers and provide more accurate data for the water companies to manage their water networks. The accuracy and reliability of these smart meters under different scenarios such as line pressures, existence of air bubbles in the water pipes, existence of sand particles and different water salinity and meter idle time; are extremely important for both consumers and suppliers. SASO and ME-KFUPM have worked together for the last two years to carry out rigorous tests according to recognized standards to investigate the accuracy of these meters under various conditions mentioned above. The results of these investigations have revealed interesting findings regarding the accuracy and reliability of both Ultrasound and electromagnetic smart meters across various pressure levels (0.5-2.5 bars), different flow rates (Q1 to Q3), and in measuring transient pressures and flow rates. Notably, when air bubbles were introduced into the flow stream, all meter types exhibited intriguing outcomes. These findings contribute to our understanding of the capabilities of these meter types in diverse scenarios.

1 Introduction

The accuracy and durability of smart water meters are crucial for effective water management, especially in environments where water quality is compromised by dissolved salts and suspended particles. Several studies have investigated the impact of water quality on water metering performance, highlighting issues such as sedimentation, scaling, and sensor degradation.

Research has shown that water containing high concentrations of salts and suspended particles can influence meter performance over time. Accumulation of sediments in mechanical and ultrasonic meters may lead to inaccuracies in flow measurement and increased maintenance needs (Arregui et al., 2018). Additionally, high salinity levels can contribute to corrosion of internal components, affecting long-term precision (Lee et al., 2020). Extended idle states in water meters can exacerbate measurement errors due to particle deposition and biofouling. Studies indicate that meters exposed to stagnant water for prolonged periods may experience drift in sensor calibration, leading to over- or under-reporting of consumption (van Zyl et al., 2017). The performance of smart meters, particularly those relying on ultrasonic or electromagnetic sensing, can deteriorate due to changes in internal flow dynamics after long idle phases (Ahmed et al., 2021). Modern smart meters incorporate self-cleaning mechanisms and advanced algorithms to compensate for environmental effects. However, their performance varies under different water conditions. Research comparing electromagnetic, ultrasonic, and mechanical meters suggests that non-contact technologies are more resilient to sedimentation but may still experience inaccuracies due to conductivity changes in high-salinity environments (Galeano et al., 2019).

In this work, we explore experimentally the effects of salt concentration, sand presence, non-operation (idle) duration, temperatures, pressures and flow rates on the accuracy of three commercial flow meters. The study emphasizes the importance of testing real scenarios on the accuracy of commercial flow meters before installation.

2 Methodology

A test loop was designed to simulate very closely the setup of water meters as they are installed in the field or as connected to consumers. Since the meters are tested one at a time, the actual distance between the meters is not important for the testing.
Figure 1 shows the setup of the system as it was installed in the laboratory. The main components of the loop include a 10-Hp pump which can deliver water flow with high pressures. The pump draws water from a one-cubic-meter reservoir (larger tank in Figure 1) and supplies to the main pipe loop through a PVC pipe network connected to the main Polyethylene black pipe of 100 mm diameter as typically used in water distribution systems. The water meters labelled as DN15, DN20 DN25, DN32, DN40 and DN50 of three supplier brands ('A', 'B', and 'C') were installed on the wall of the laboratory and were connected to the main pipe via polyethylene flexible pipes. The flowmeter labels indicate the pipe nominal diameter which translates to their flow rate capacity. The three commercial flowmeters were of different working principles; 'A' and 'B' utilized ultrasonic waves to measure the flow rates, while 'C' utilized electromagnetic waves to perform the same task. The installation of the water meters was performed as per the installation standards of the service provider. The meters' outlets were connected to the main Meter-Verification System (MVS). The outlets of all meters were connected to a manifold piping system (6 into 1) to minimize the contact with the metering tank (smaller tank in Figure 1). The metering tank was placed on a calibrated scale with an accuracy of 0.03%. This

* Corresponding author: e.ghazal@saso.gov.sa

accuracy has been verified with SASO-certified calibration weights.

Fig. 1. System Set-up as installed in the Fluid Mechanics Laboratory – KFUPM.

The error in measurement for all meters was computed as follows:

$$\text{Percentage Error} = \frac{M-\rho V}{M} \quad (1)$$

The experiment tested various factors that could affect flow meter accuracy. The density of water, which was measured with 1% accuracy, ranges from 998 kg/m³ at 20°C to 990 kg/m³ at 45°C. Adding salt between 2 and 12 g/kg leads to a density variation of ±1%, and the maximum error in mass measurement was determined to be ±1.3%.

For salt concentration effects, five different concentrations (180, 3000, 5670, 8738, and 27660 ppm) were tested. These concentrations, chosen for comparison between low and high extremes, were compared with the maximum salinity recorded by service provider's network (4200 ppm in the Eastern region). To test the effect of sand on flow meters, sand concentrations of 0.25%, 0.5%, and 1% were added to the water, as sand can be present in real systems after maintenance or pipe breaks.

Idle time effects were tested by leaving the flow meters non-operational for various durations, ranging from several hours to 8 months. These tests, conducted under a line pressure of 1.5 bars and medium flow rates, simulate idle periods seen in Saudi Arabia and situations where customers might not require water for extended periods. The effect of line pressure was also studied, with five different pressures (0, 0.5, 1, 1.5, and 2 bar) applied. Each pressure level was tested multiple times, and the cumulative errors for each flow meter were recorded.

The inclusion of air in the flow stream was tested by injecting controlled amounts of air upstream into the flow meters. The gas percentage in the mixture is critical, and the Gas Void Fraction (GVF) helps determine the flow regime. A GVF less than 3-5% results in a dispersed bubbly flow, and the flow pattern is primarily influenced by the flow rates, angle, fluid properties, and conduit diameter, rather than surface roughness.

$$GVF = \frac{\text{Flowrate of air}}{\text{Flowrate of air} + \text{Flowrate of water}} \quad (2)$$

Lastly, Temperature effects were tested from 20°C to 50°C, simulating varying environmental conditions. Flow rates were also examined at high, moderate, and low levels to assess meter performance. To test the different flowmeter operations under the different conditions, a pressure of 0.5 and 1.5 bar were chosen and the flow rate was ensured to be within Q_2 and Q_3 for each flowmeter according to the datasheets provided by the supplier. As per the datasheet, the acceptable cumulative error was reported to be ±6%. Any result outside of this range was deemed unacceptable.

3 Results and Discussion

3.1 Flowmeters operation with saline water

Figure 2 shows 'A' flowmeter errors at different salt concentrations. Most data fall within ±6% error, but all meters fail at the highest concentration. DN50 shows both positive and negative errors.

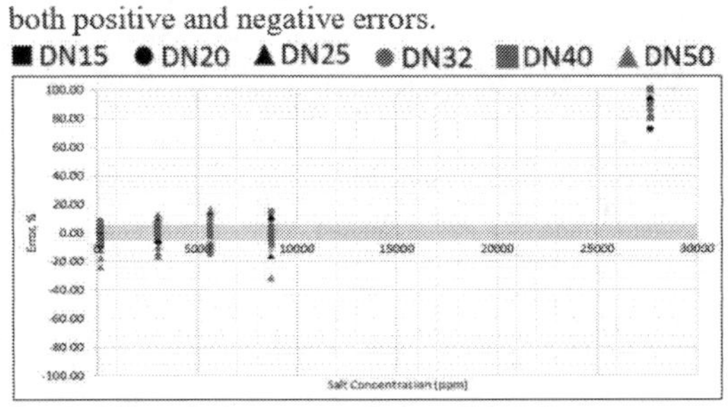

Fig. 2. Effect of salt concentration on all **'A' flowmeters**.

Figure 3 shows 'B' flowmeter errors. Most are within ±6% at low concentrations, but errors increase at moderate levels, and all fail at high concentrations. DN40 shows high errors at 3000 ppm, while DN20 and DN32 fail above 8738 ppm.

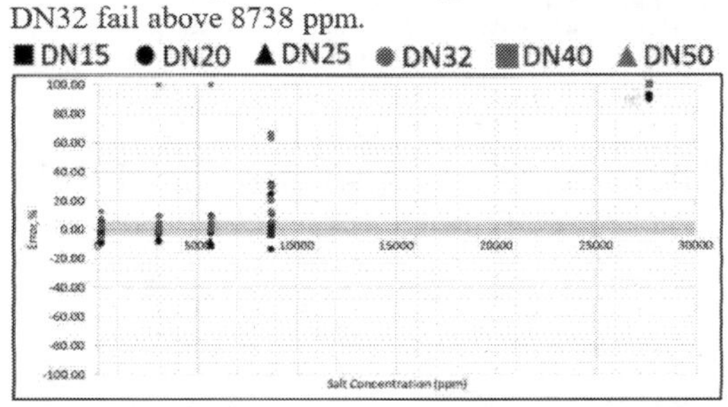

Fig. 3. Effect of salt concentration on all **'B' flowmeters**.

Figure 3 shows 'C' flowmeter errors. Most data fall within ±6%, but DN40 fails above 5670 ppm. All meters show errors at 5670 ppm but read accurately up to 27660 ppm.

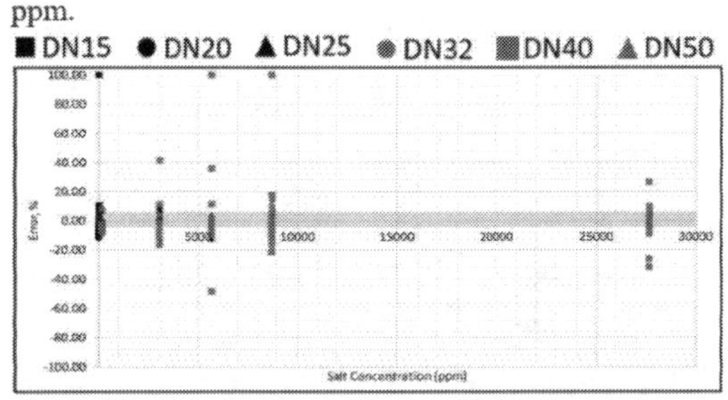

Fig. 4. Effect of salt concentration on all **'C' flowmeters**.

3.2 Flowmeters operation with water mixed with sand particles

Table 1 shows 'A' flowmeter errors. Most datapoints fall within the acceptable range, and all meters gave accurate readings at all sand concentrations.

Table 1: Average overall error at different sand concentrations for **'A' flowmeters**.

Sand conc. wt.%	Cumulative Error (%) of flowmeters DN-					
	15	20	25	32	40	50
0.25	-0.01	0.25	-0.01	0.25	-0.01	0.25
0.5	-0.01	0.5	-0.01	0.5	-0.01	0.5
1	0.00	1	0.00	1	0.00	1

Table 2 shows the error for different 'B' flowmeters, with cumulative errors of less than 1%, indicating acceptable accuracy.

Table 2: Average overall error at different sand concentrations for **'B' flowmeters**. NA indicates that no tests were done on the respective flowmeter.

Sand conc. wt.%	Cumulative Error (%) of flowmeters DN-					
	15	20	25	32	40	50
0.25	-0.02	0.00	-0.03	0.00	0.04	NA
0.5	-0.02	0.00	-0.01	0.01	0.03	NA
1	0.02	0.00	-0.02	0.02	0.90	NA

Table 3 shows the error for different 'C' flowmeters. Most data fall within the acceptable error, except for DN32, which performed poorly.

Table 3: Average overall error at different sand concentrations for **'C' flowmeters**. NA indicates that no tests were done on the respective flowmeter.

Sand conc. wt.%	Cumulative Error (%) of flowmeters DN-					
	15	20	25	32	40	50
0.25	0.01	0.03	-0.02	0.11	0.03	NA
0.5	-0.03	0.01	0.01	100	-0.02	NA
1	0.02	0.01	0.04	100	0.02	NA

Figure 5 shows DN40 has the highest fluctuations, with negative errors correcting positive ones. 'C' is the least reliable due to high fluctuations and DN32 failure.

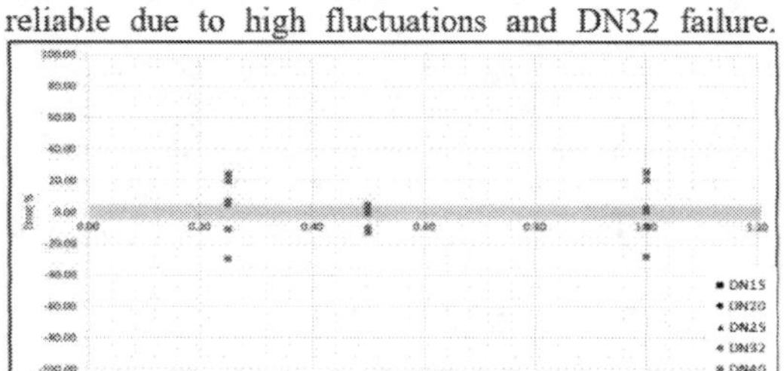

Fig. 5. Selected results showing the effect of sand concentration on **'C'-DN40 flowmeter**.

3.3 Flowmeters operation after different idle times

Figure 6.a shows cumulative errors for each flowmeter, and Figure 6.b shows steady-state error after 20 runs. All 'A' meters were acceptable, except DN50, which had consistent errors during idle times.

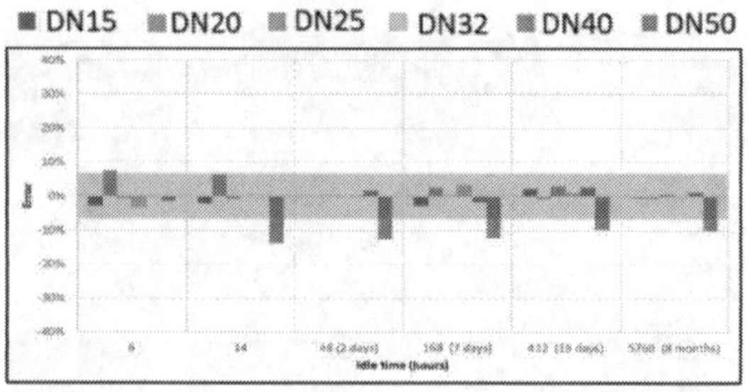

Fig. 6.a Error plot of all data collected under idle condition for **'A' flowmeters.**

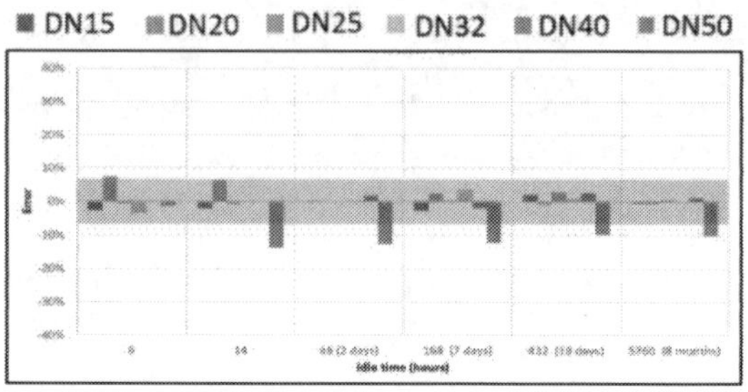

Fig. 6.b Error plot of last 4 data points collected under idle condition for **'A' flowmeters**.

Figure 7 shows the collected volume needed for accurate flow rate measurements, ranging up to 350 liters.

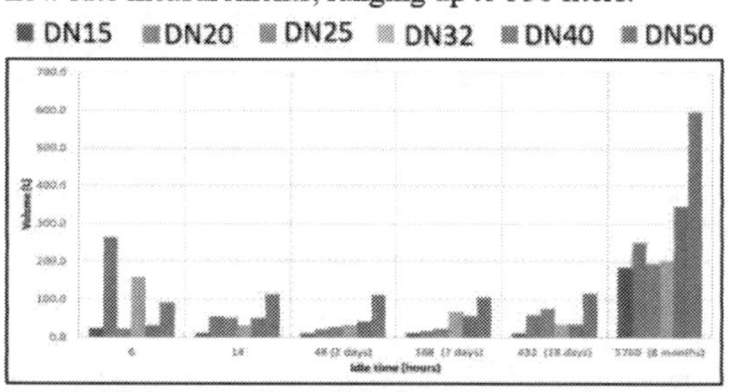

Fig. 7. Volume collected before final measurements were reported under idle condition for **'A' flowmeters**.

Figure 8 shows cumulative errors for 'B' flowmeters, and Figure 9 shows errors for the last 4 readings. DN15, 20, and 25 were acceptable, while DN32 and DN40 had errors at all idle times.

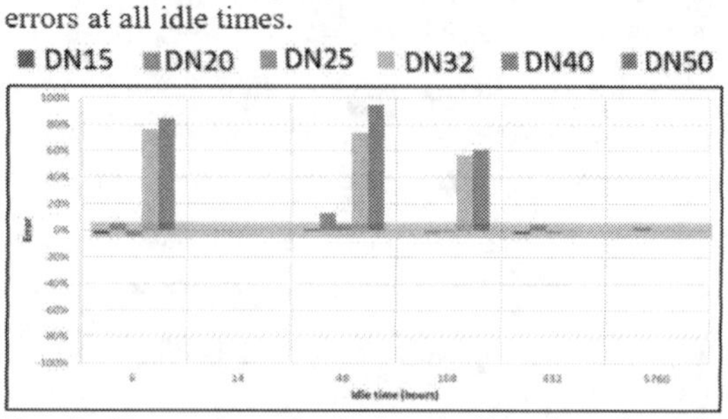

Fig. 8. Error plot of all data collected under idle condition for **'B' flowmeters.**

■ DN15 ■ DN20 ■ DN25 ■ DN32 ■ DN40 ■ DN50

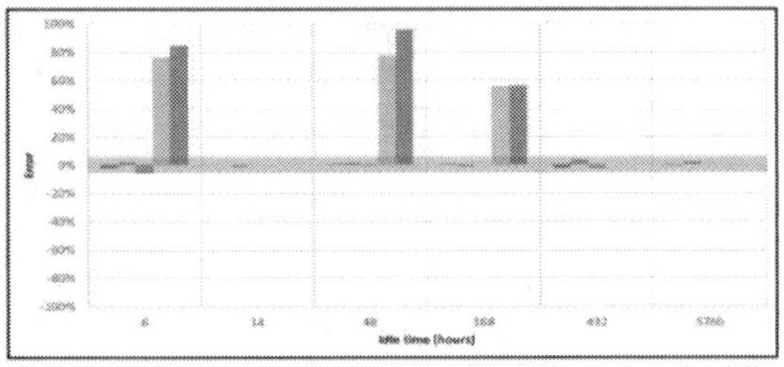

Fig. 9. Error plot of last 4 data points collected under idle condition for **'B' flowmeters**.

Figure 10 shows the collected volume needed for accurate flow rate measurements, ranging up to 80 liters.

■ DN15 ■ DN20 ■ DN25 ■ DN32 ■ DN40 ■ DN50

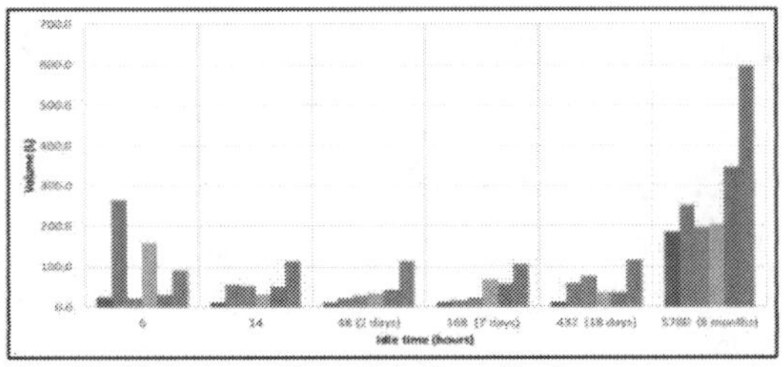

Fig. 10. Volume collected before final measurements were reported under idle condition for **'B' flowmeters**.

Figure 11 shows cumulative errors for 'C' flowmeters, and Figure 12 shows errors for the last 4 readings. Most flowmeters were acceptable, except DN40 at 7- and 18-day idle times, and DN32 at 7-day idle time after 300 liters.

■ DN15 ■ DN20 ■ DN25 ■ DN32 ■ DN40 ■ DN50

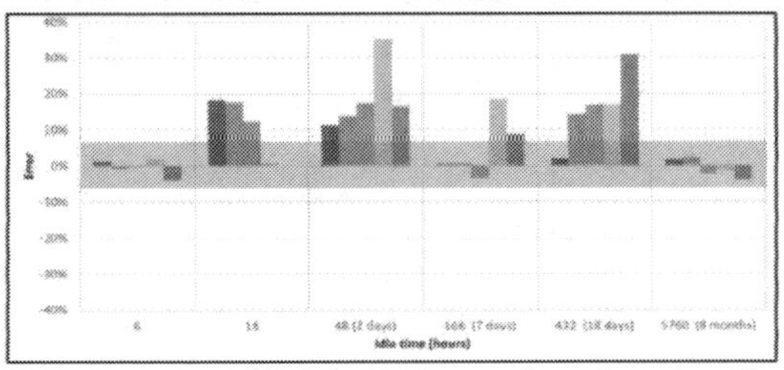

Fig. 11. Error plot of all data collected under idle condition for **'C' flowmeters.**

■ DN15 ■ DN20 ■ DN25 ■ DN32 ■ DN40 ■ DN50

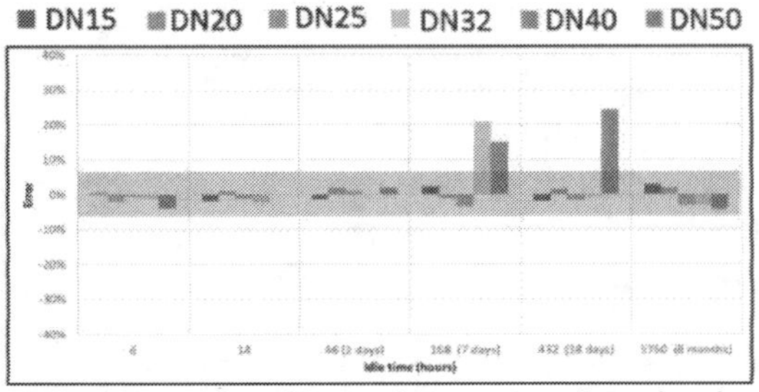

Fig. 12. Error plot of last 4 data points collected under idle condition for **'C' flowmeters**.

Figure 13 shows the collected volume required for final readings. The volume varies between flowmeters, with a maximum of around 212 liters.

■ DN15 ■ DN20 ■ DN25 ■ DN32 ■ DN40 ■ DN50

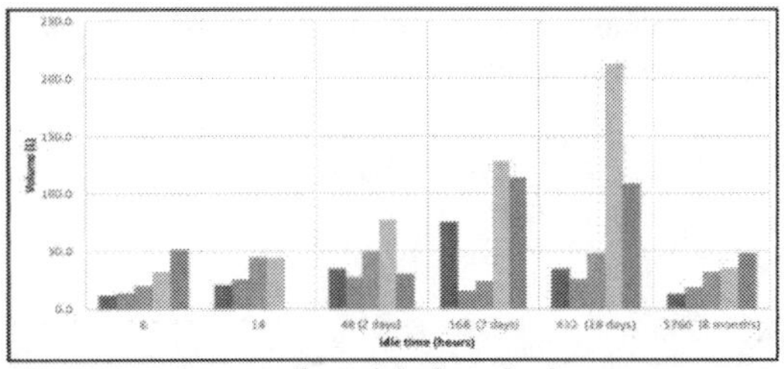

Fig. 13. Volume collected before final measurements were reported under idle condition for **'C' flowmeters**.

3.4 Flowmeters operation under different line pressures

Figure 14 shows the error at different line pressures for 'A' flowmeters. Most data points are within ±6%, with DN15 showing the highest average error.

■ DN15 ● DN20 ▲ DN25 ● DN32 ■ DN40 ▲ DN50

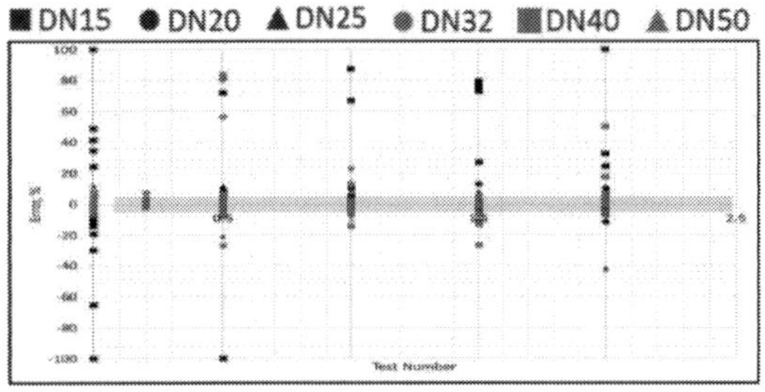

Fig. 14. Effect of pressure variation 0, 0.5, 1.5, 2 bar (gauge) on all **'A' flowmeters**.

Figures 15 and 16 show errors at various line pressures. Most points are within ±6%, with one 'B' flowmeter outperforming others. All flowmeters show excellent performance regardless of pressure.

■ DN15 ● DN20 ▲ DN25 ● DN32 ■ DN40 ▲ DN50

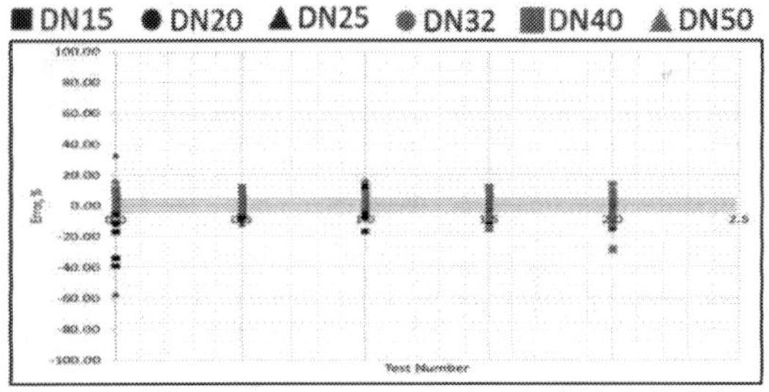

Fig. 15. Effect of pressure variation 0, 0.5, 1.5, 2 bar (gauge) on all **'B' flowmeters**.

■ DN15 ● DN20 ▲ DN25 ● DN32 ■ DN40 ▲ DN50

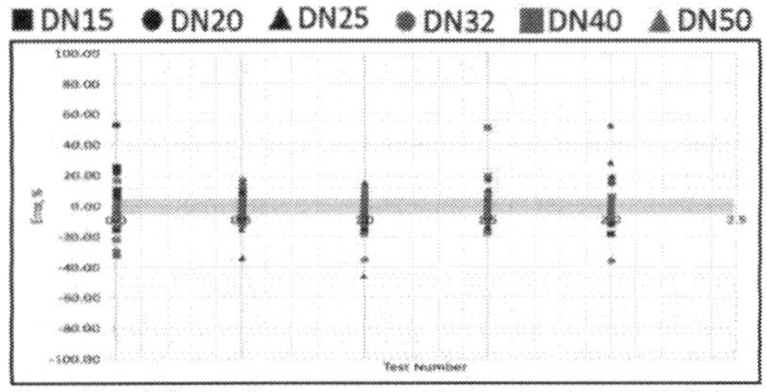

Fig. 16. Effect of pressure variation 0, 0.5, 1.5, 2 bar (gauge) on all **'C' flowmeters**.

3.5 Flowmeters operation under air bubble injection condition

Figure 17 shows GVF variation with percentage error for 'A' flowmeters. DN15 shows a +20% error at 4% GVF, DN20 a +80% error at 4.5% GVF, and DN25 a 45% error at 3.16% GVF. At GVF over 20%, the meters fail to record water.

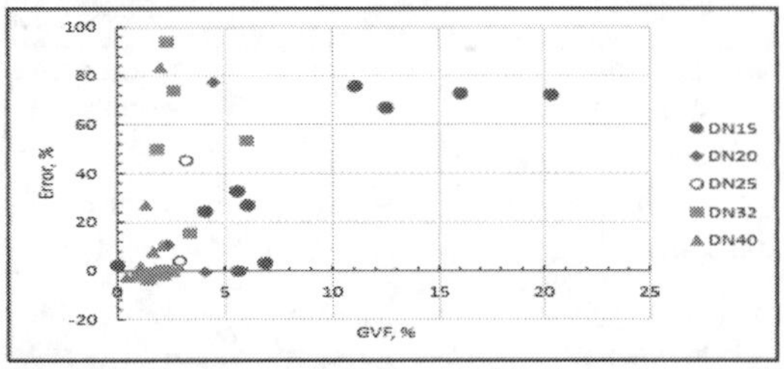

Fig. 17. Variation of GVF with % Error for all **'A' flowmeters**.

Figure 18 shows the GVF variation with error for 'B' flowmeters. They are sensitive to air bubbles, stopping at GVF values of 2-5%, with good accuracy for GVF <3%.

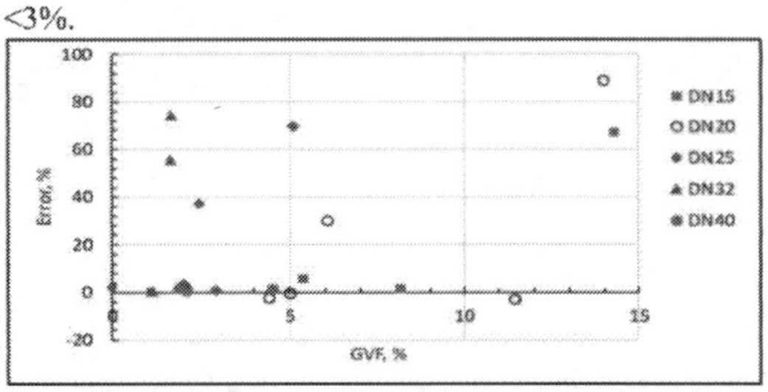

Fig. 18. Variation of GVF with % Error for all **'B' flowmeters**.

Figure 19 shows GVF variation with error for 'C' flowmeters. 'C' is less sensitive to air bubbles but often records more water than actual, with DN15 showing -21% error at 33% GVF and DN20 -22% at 23% GVF.

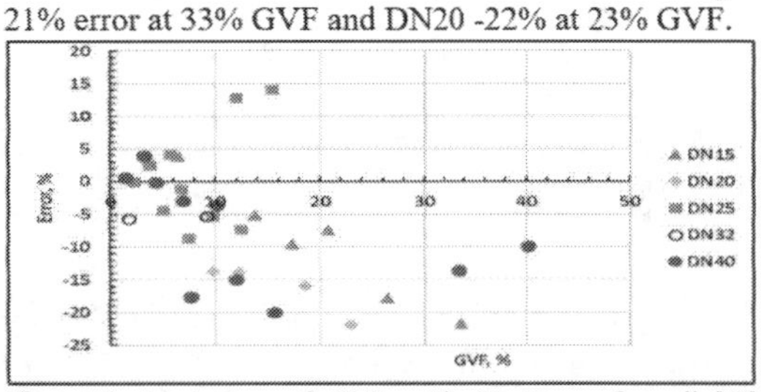

Fig. 19. Variation of GVF with % Error for all **'C' flowmeters**.

3.6 Flowmeters operation under different temperatures

A systematic analysis of temperature effects was not possible due to the lack of control mechanisms. However, natural temperature variations during testing provided sufficient data for evaluation. Temperature fluctuations, caused by viscous friction and heat transfer through convection and radiation, showed no clear correlation with measurement error.

'A' Meters: Tested between 20–37°C, with no significant impact on accuracy within the 5–50°C range (Figure 20).

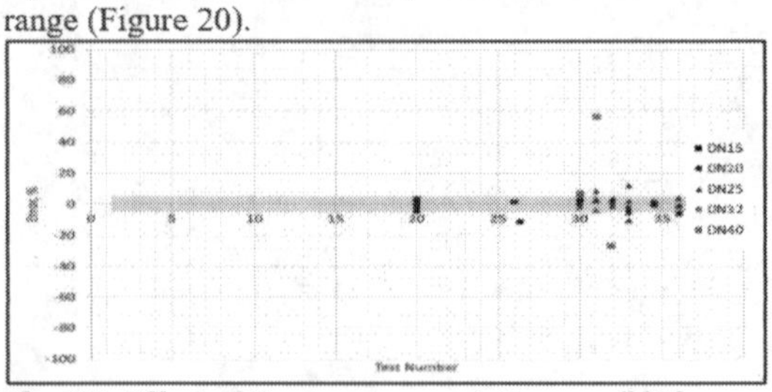

Fig. 20. Effect of Temperature variation on all **'A'** meters

'B' Meters: Tested between 27–55°C, showing no noticeable effect on error within the 70°C manufacturer limit (Figure 21).

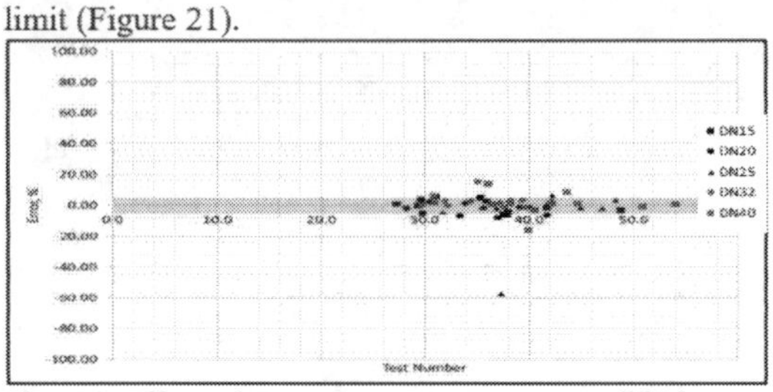

Fig. 21. Effect of Temperature variation on all **'B'** meters

'C' Meters: Tested between 31–46°C, confirming stable performance within the 50°C specification (Figure 22).

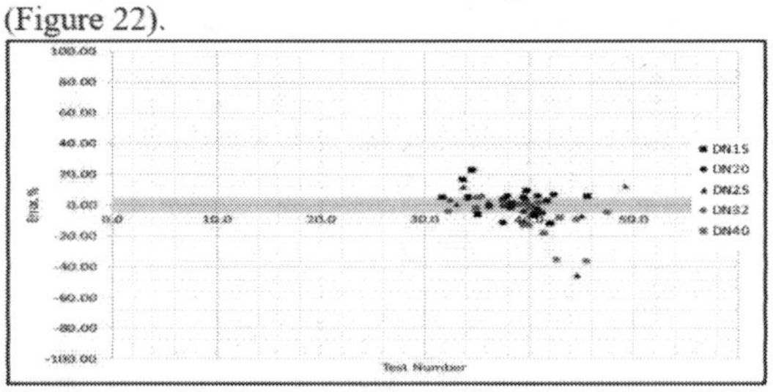

Fig. 22. Effect of Temperature variation on all **'C'** meters

Overall, temperature variations within manufacturer-specified limits do not significantly affect meter accuracy.

3.7 Flowmeters operation under different flowrates

The effect of high flow rates on the water meters was tested for three types: 'A', 'B', and 'C'. In most cases, the valve was fully open, with some instances at approximately 80% open. For all meters, most data points showed low errors (below ±2%), though a few data points for the DN15 and DN32 meters had larger errors. The DN50 meter's data was entirely faulty. Flow rate is influenced by pressure, with higher pressures leading to higher flow rates. The meters were operated below their maximum flow rates to ensure accuracy, with most errors for high flow rates staying below ±6%, except in a few cases.

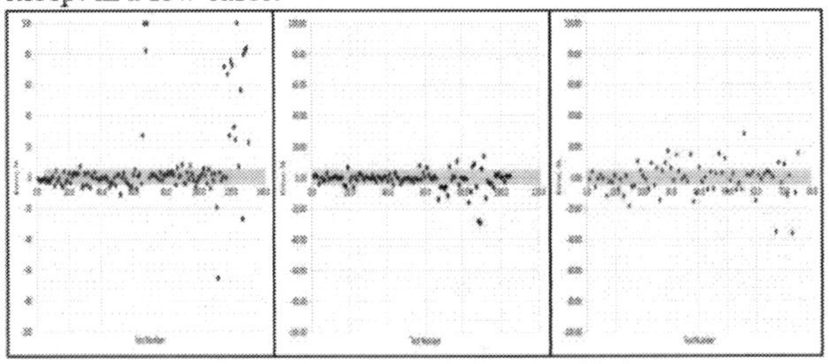

Fig. 23. Effect of high flow rate on 'A', 'B' and 'C' meters

For low flow rates, the testing produced the best results, with flow rates selected based on the minimum allowable ranges for each meter. The flow rates were controlled using a ball valve upstream of the meters, simulating typical service provider's installation conditions. A needle valve would offer even more precise flow control. Despite slight variations in the control valve, all 'A', 'B', and 'C' meters provided acceptable measurements, confirming their accuracy at low flow rates.

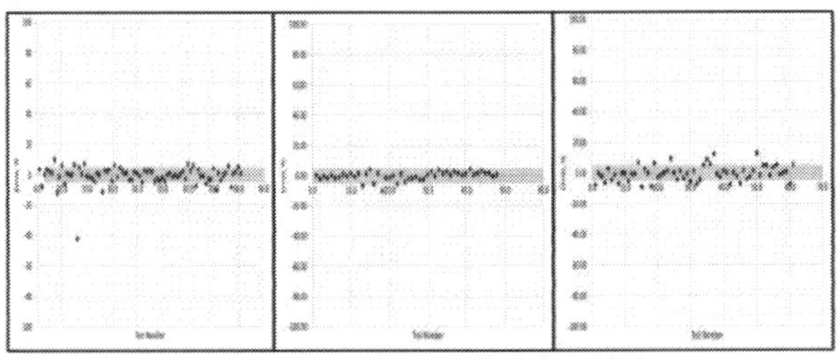

Fig. 24. Effect of low flow rate on 'A', 'B' and 'C' meters

4 Conclusion

Tests on 16 smart meters (11 ultrasonic, 5 electromagnetic) examined salt concentration, sand particles, and idle durations.

1. **Salt Concentration**: Ultrasonic meters worked up to 6000 ppm but failed at 27000 ppm. 'B' DN32 and DN40 had errors at 9000 ppm. Electromagnetic meters read accurately at 3000, 9000, and 27000 ppm but showed errors at 6000 ppm.
2. **Sand Particles**: Sand (0.25–1%) did not affect accuracy but caused damage to valves and pumps due to erosion.
3. **Idle Duration**: Durations from 6 hours to 8 months had little impact. Electromagnetic meters required more time and water to read correctly, while ultrasonic meters were less affected.
4. **Line Pressure**: 'B' flowmeters performed best across all pressures, while 'A' had the highest cumulative error.
5. **Air Injection**: All meters worked well with GVF below 3%. At higher GVF, 'A' and 'B' showed positive errors, while 'C' showed negative errors and was least affected.
6. **Temperature**: Temperature variations within the manufacturer-specified limits (20–55°C) did not significantly affect the accuracy of 'A', 'B', or 'C' meters, with no clear correlation between temperature fluctuations and measurement error observed during testing.
7. **Flow Rate:** At high flow rates, most meters maintained low errors (below ±2%), except for DN15 and DN32, which had occasional larger errors. The DN50 meter produced entirely faulty data. Most high-flow errors remained below ±6%. At low flow rates, all meters provided accurate readings, confirming their reliability under typical operating conditions.

- It is recommended to include idle duration and air injection tests in standard evaluations. Ultrasonic meters can meter salty water up to 6000 ppm, while electromagnetic meters can handle up to 27000 ppm.
- Standard evaluations should include idle duration and air injection tests.
- Flow rate variations should be considered in performance assessments. While meters generally maintained accuracy, high flow rates increased error margins, particularly for DN15, DN32, and DN50 meters. More precise flow control (e.g., using needle valves) could improve measurement accuracy in low-flow conditions.

References

1. Ahmed, N., Smith, R., & Brown, T. (2021). "Long-term performance of smart water meters under variable water quality conditions." *Water Resources Management, 35*(4), 987-1005.
2. Arregui, F., Cabrera, E., & Cobacho, R. (2018). "Influence of particulate matter on the accuracy of domestic water meters." *Water Science and Technology: Water Supply, 18*(2), 345-357.
3. Galeano, P., Martinez, L., & Ortega, J. (2019). "Comparative study of smart water meters: Performance under different environmental conditions." *Journal of Water Engineering, 25*(3), 215-230.
4. Lee, J., Kim, H., & Choi, S. (2020). "Corrosion and scaling effects on smart meter accuracy in high-salinity water environments." *Desalination and Water Treatment, 172*, 112-124.
5. van Zyl, J., Scheepers, H., & van der Merwe, B. (2017). "Effects of intermittent water supply on meter accuracy and reliability." *Urban Water Journal, 14*(5), 503-512.

A Wavelet-based Filtering Algorithm for Enhancing Signal Processing in Coriolis Flow Meters

David Wee Yang Khoo[1*], *Zhi Qun* Ng[2], and *Leong Keey* Seah[2]

[1]National Metrology Centre, Agency for Science and Technology Research, Singapore
[2]Nanyang Technological University, Singapore

Abstract. Applying signal processing method effectively for a Coriolis flow meter (CFM) requires robust filtering strategies. This is because in actual bunkering processes, various noise components can be generated resulting in unreliable mass flow rate measurements. This study introduces a wavelet transform-based filtering algorithm to denoise and extract relevant features from non-stationary signals. It can be observed that the db6 and sym6 wavelets, with SURE and FDR thresholding, achieve the highest SNR values and lowest RMSE. The sym6 wavelet & SURE threshold exhibited good noise reduction effect and were used for further analysis. It was also found that FFT with Zero Padding paired with Wavelet Denoising & Cross Correlation yielded a percentage error of < 1% when comparing with the original simulated signal.

1 Introduction

CFMs are widely used in the oil and gas industries, from upstream allocation to downstream bunkering and transmission pipeline custody transfer. Since 2017, the Maritime and Port Authority (MPA) has mandated the use of CFMs for ship-to-ship fuel oil custody transfers under Singapore Standard (SS) 648 (or ISO 22192) [1]. The CFM operates on the Coriolis force principle and comes in various designs, including straight-tube, S-shape, and V-shape [2]. In a U-shaped CFM, a driver excites the tube at its resonant frequency, causing fluid momentum and oscillatory motion to induce a Coriolis force, which results in a phase shift along the tube's length as shown in Figure 1.

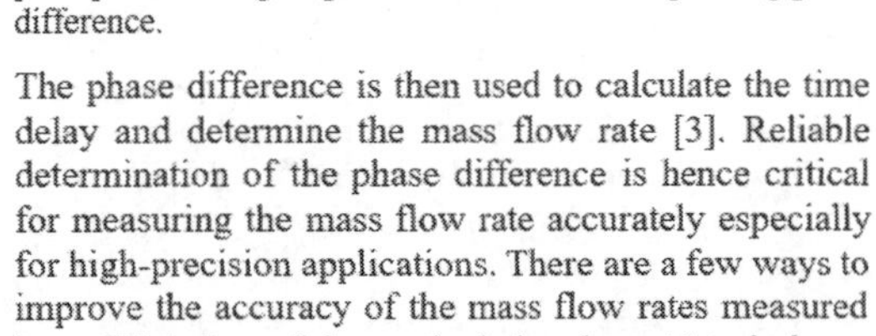

Figure 1: Schematic diagram of a U-shape CFM and the pickup sensors signal profiles with their corresponding phase difference.

The phase difference is then used to calculate the time delay and determine the mass flow rate [3]. Reliable determination of the phase difference is hence critical for measuring the mass flow rate accurately especially for high-precision applications. There are a few ways to improve the accuracy of the mass flow rates measured by a CFM. One of the methods involves AI techniques such as Long Short-Term Memory and Support Vector Machine that make use of sensor signals as sample characteristics to relate sensor signals to mass flow rate, but these algorithms can be time-intensive and difficult to interpret. Another method is to theoretically derive a solution and apply signal processing methods to develop an algorithm with high robustness and anti-interference capabilities. However, to apply the signal processing method effectively requires robust filtering strategies. This is because in actual bunkering processes, various noise components can be generated resulting in unreliable mass flow rate measurements. For annual bunker sales of 50 million tonnes, a small error of 0.1% may potentially cause a loss of approximately ~50,000 tonnes or US$25 million if a price $500/ton of bunker oil loaded in fuelling ships. External noise and vibrations are natural occurrences in the bunkering process and can affect CMF accuracy, making it challenging to extract reliable phase components [4]. Noise can come from sources like pumps, nearby equipment, or turbulence in the fluid, all of which can interfere with the vibrating tube of CMF and reduce measurement accuracy. As such, effective filtering techniques are required to remove the unwanted noise components while extracting reliable phase components information. Common filtering techniques include Moving Average, FIR/IIR Filters, Adaptive Notch Filters (ANF), Windowing Functions and Hilbert Transform [3-5].

Frequency-domain filtering like Window Functions often encounter spectral leakage where the truncation of signals and non-integer sampling rates distort the signals especially when using window functions with significant sidelobes. These sidelobes can lead to "ringing" effects which are unwanted oscillations or

* Corresponding author: david_khoo@nmc.a-star.edu.sg

ripples at the edges of the signals where the windows tapers off. In contrast, time-domain filtering is generally more effective at handling non-stationary signals and can mitigate some of the spectral leakage issues associated with frequency-domain filtering. However, its performance depends heavily on the noise characteristics and may also distort high frequency components. Therefore, selecting an appropriate filtering technique is imperative to accurately extract phase difference information in the presence of noise to ensure more reliable mass flow measurements.

To address this challenge, this work aims to develop a reliable filtering algorithm based on wavelet transform to suppress the noise interference generated during the bunkering process. Wavelet transforms were utilised to denoise the signals and extract relevant features, particularly in cases involving non-stationary signals or transient noise. This study analysed the impact of different wavelet functions and thresholding methods across various levels of decomposition on the filtering of simulated signals used in mass flow rate calculations. Cross-correlation was used to estimate the phase shift between the two sensor signals for the determination of mass flow rates.

2 Methodology Development

2.1 Numerical Signals and Boundary Conditions

A time-varying signal model, where the signal's frequency, amplitude, and phase change based on a random walk model [3] has been developed to represent CMF signals.

$$y_1(n) = A(n)\,sin[\omega(n) + \phi_1(n)] \cdot dt + e_1(n) \quad (1)$$
$$y_2(n) = A(n)\,sin[\omega(n) + \phi_2(n)] \cdot dt + e_2(n) \quad (2)$$
$$A(n) = A(n-1) + \delta_A \cdot \sigma_A \cdot e_A(n) \quad (3)$$
$$\omega(n) = \omega(n-1) + \delta_\omega \cdot \sigma_\omega \cdot e_\omega(n) \quad (4)$$
$$\phi(n) = \phi(n-1) + \delta_\phi \cdot \sigma_\phi \cdot e_\phi(n) \quad (5)$$

Where y_1 and y_2 are simulated sensor signals with amplitude A, angular frequency ω, phase lag ϕ and time step dt, $dt=1/f_s$. $e_1(n)$, $e_2(n)$, $e_A(n)$, $e_\omega(n)$, $e_\phi(n)$ are white noise following a Gaussian distribution and has no correlation with one another. δ_A,δ_ω and δ_ϕ are binary walk factors (0 – 1) with probabilities P_A, P_ω and P_ϕ [3]. Table 1 shows the boundary conditions of the parameter used for simulating the sensor signals. Figure 2 demonstrates the simulated signal and its corresponding frequency and phase difference profiles.

Table 1: Initialisations of signal parameters

Name	Initial Value
Amplitude	$A(0) = 5$mV
Frequency	$f = 105Hz$
Probabilities	$P_A = P_\omega = P_\phi = 0.5$
Sample frequency	$f_s = 2000Hz$
Step size	$\sigma_A = 10^{-4}$, $\sigma_\omega = 10^{-6}$, $\sigma_\phi = 10^{-4}$

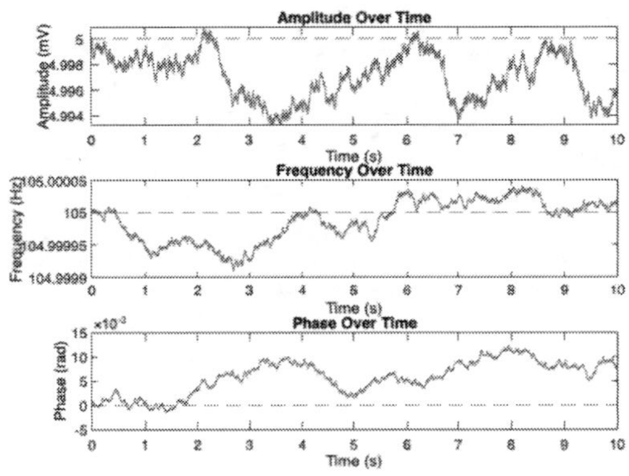

Figure 2: Simulated signal time domain plots

2.2 Wavelet Denoising

Noise reduction is a critical step in signal processing to improve the accuracy and reliability of measured data. Wavelet denoising leverages the ability of the Discrete Wavelet Transform (DWT) to separate a signal into frequency components at varying resolutions. This approach assumes that noise predominantly affects high-frequency components, while the key features of the signal are concentrated in the low-frequency components.

2.2.1 Wavelet Decomposition

The DWT decomposes a signal into wavelet coefficients, which represent the signal's approximation (low-frequency) and detail (high-frequency) components at multiple levels of resolution as illustrated in Figure 3.

The mathematical representation of the DWT is:

$$\alpha_{j,k} = \sum\nolimits_n x[n]\phi_{j,k}[n] \quad (6)$$

$$d_{j,k} = \sum\nolimits_n x[n]\psi_{j,k}[n] \quad (7)$$

Where, $\alpha_{j,k}$ represents the Approximation Coefficients and $d_{j,k}$ the Detail Coefficients. j is the level of decomposition, k is the position in time, $\phi_{j,k}[n]$ is the scaling function and $\psi_{j,k}[n]$ is the type of wavelet. The choice of wavelet function is critical, as it influences the effectiveness of the decomposition. Selecting an appropriate wavelet that aligns with the characteristics of the signal can significantly enhance the decomposition process, leading to a more precise separation between the signal and noise components. Factors such as symmetry, regularity, and support width determine a wavelet's suitability for a given signal [6]. In this study, wavelets such as Haar, Daubechies (db6), and Symlets (sym6) were evaluated for their performance in separating noise from signal components.

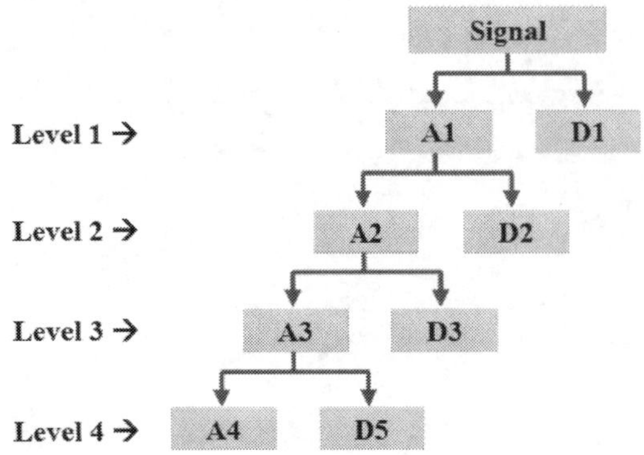

Figure 3: Wavelet Decomposition Tree

2.2.2 Thresholding Techniques

After decomposition, noise reduction is achieved by applying thresholding to the detail coefficients. By setting small coefficients—often attributed to noise—to zero or shrinking them toward zero, we can suppress noise while retaining the underlying signal structure. [6]. In this work, several thresholding techniques were assessed for wavelet denoising, such as the Universal threshold, SURE (Stein's Unbiased Risk Estimate), Minimax threshold, and False Discovery Rate (FDR). After thresholding, the signal is then reconstructed from the modified coefficients using the Inverse Discrete Wavelet Transform (IDWT). The reconstruction process also depends on both the selected wavelet function and the type of thresholding, ensuring that the key features of the actual signal are preserved with minimal distortion. This step combines the thresholder detail coefficients with the approximation coefficients to produce the denoised signal.

2.3 Phase Difference Extraction

Cross-correlation was used to determine the time delay by measuring signal similarity. By shifting one signal relative to the other and computing their pointwise product, the cross-correlation function identifies the time lag at which the signals align most closely. The cross-correlation between two time-domain signals $x(t)$ and $y(t)$ is defined as:

$$R_{xy}(\tau) = \int_{-\infty}^{\infty} x(t)y(t+\tau)dt \qquad (8)$$

Where τ represents the time lag. For discrete signals, the formula becomes:

$$R_{xy}[k] = \sum_{n=0}^{N-1} x[n]y[n+k] \qquad (9)$$

Where k is the discrete time lag (in samples) and N represents the length of the signal. To compute the cross-correlation for discrete signals, the process iterates over all possible lag values of k. Starting with $k = 0$, the two signals are aligned without any shift and their pointwise product is computed and summed. The iterative process continues for all positive and negative lag values, evaluating the similarity of the signals at each shift. At the highest R_{xy} value, the corresponding lag, k_{max} was extracted and calculate the phase shift (in degrees) $\Delta\,\theta = \frac{k_{max}}{fs} * 360 * f$.

3 Results and Discussion

Two performance indicators namely: Signal-to-Noise Ratio (SNR) and Root Mean Square Error (RMSE), were used to assess the precision and dependability of the wavelets. The SNR was selected as a performance metric because it measures the strength of the desired signal relative to the background noise. RMSE offers an interpretation of the units of the target variable. The SNR and RMSE formulations are as follows:

$$SNR = 10 \cdot \log\left(\frac{\sum_{n=1}^{N} f(n)^2}{\sum_{n=1}^{N}\left(f(n) - \hat{f}\right)}\right)^2 \qquad (10)$$

$$RMSE = \sqrt{\frac{1}{N}\sum_{n=1}^{N}\left(f(n) - \hat{f}(n)\right)^2} \qquad (11)$$

Where n is the number of test samples, $f(n)$ is the noise containing signal and $\hat{f}(n)$ is the signal after denoising. Figure 4 (a) illustrates the results of wavelet denoising using the haar wavelet with different types of thresholding. The blue signal represents the reconstructed signal after denoising, while the green signal represents the true signal. Ideally, if the blue signal closely matches the shape of the green signal, it will indicate high accuracy in the denoising process. A perfect match between the two signals would signify 100% accuracy in removing noise without distorting the underlying signal. Figures 4 (b) & (c) compare the performance of different wavelets and thresholding methods. It can be found that the db6 and sym6 wavelets, when used with SURE and FDR thresholding, achieve the highest SNR values. Additionally, these wavelets exhibit the lowest RMSE, indicating superior denoising performance compared to other combinations. The results are also consolidated and shown in Table 2.

The combination of the sym6 wavelet with SURE thresholding consistently produced the best denoising results for the sinusoidal signals in this study. While other thresholding methods, such as universal or minimax, tend to be more conservative and thus oversmoothed the signal, SURE adaptively selects a threshold that preserves essential signal features. At the same time, the sym6 wavelet which is designed to be nearly symmetric, exhibit approximately linear phase behaviour. This ensures that the reconstructed signal maintains its original phase alignment, preventing unwanted shifts. Moreover, sym6 has 6 vanishing moments, allowing it to efficiently represent polynomials of up to degree 5. Since sym6 can accurately model smooth, oscillatory behaviour like sinusoidal signals, it enhances the separation of signal-containing coefficients from noise-containing coefficients. This improved distinction allows for thresholding to be more effective. Making it easier to eliminate noise while preserving the signal components.

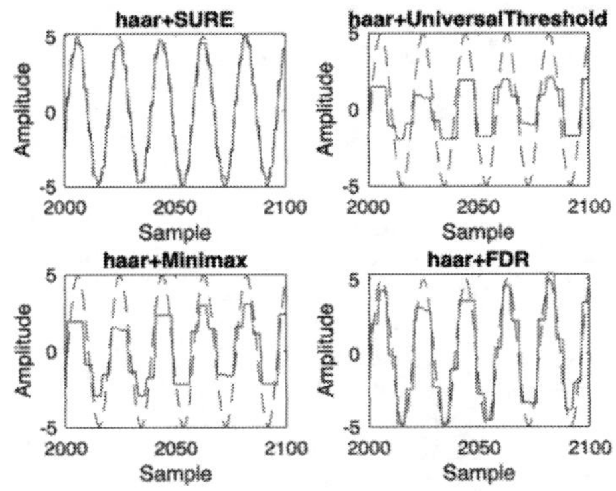

(a)

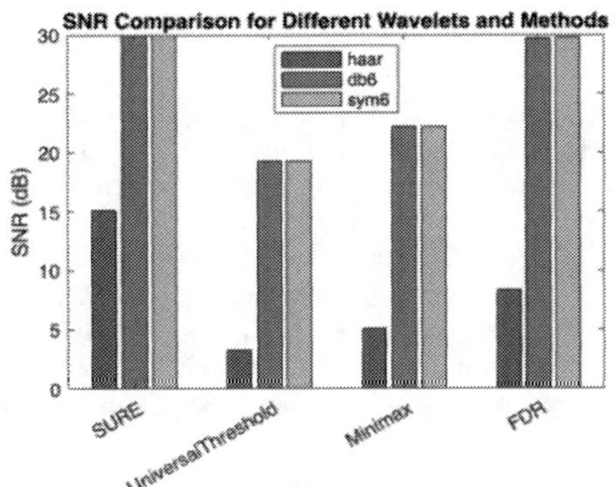

(b)

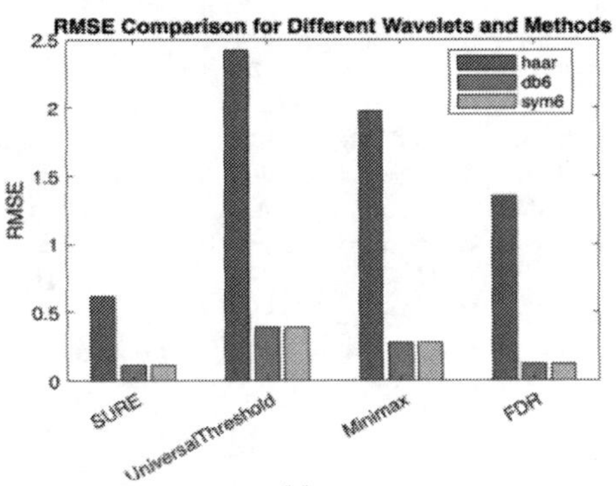

(c)

Figure 4: (a) Thresholding variations for haar wavelets, and the performance assessment for different wavelets and thresholding methods based on (b) SNR and (c) RMSE.

Table 2: Initialisations of signal parameters

Wavelet	Threshold Value	SNR	RMSE (mV)	Ranking
Sym 6	SURE	29.8624	0.1136	1
	Universal Threshold	18.9562	0.3987	4
	Minimax	21.8613	0.2854	3
	FDR	29.6268	0.1167	2

The combination of sym6 wavelet & SURE threshold exhibited good noise reduction effect and were used to obtain the phase difference using Cross Correlation. It was also found FFT with Zero Padding paired with Wavelet Denoising & Cross Correlation yielded a percentage error of < 1% when comparing with the pre-assigned boundary condition.

4 Conclusion and Future Work

The sym6 wavelet and SURE threshold effectively reduced noise and were used for further analysis. FFT with Zero Padding, combined with Wavelet Denoising and Cross Correlation resulted in a percentage error of < 1% compared to the pre-assigned sensor signal. A graphical user interface was created based on the designed numerical model and will be validated with experimental work for different mass flow conditions using the NMC liquid flow facility in the next stage of this research work.

References

1. SS 648 : 2019, Code of practice for bunker mass flow metering, Singapore Standards Council.
2. C. Tan, F. Dong, "Sensor instrumentation for flow measurement.", Encyclopedia of Sensors and Biosensors, vol. 3, pp. 536-554, 2023.
3. Y. Tu, H. Yang, H. Zhang, X. Liu "CMF signal processing method based on feedback corrected ANF and hilbert transformation." Measurement Science Review, vol. 14, 2014.
4. N. Chen, "Research on coriolis mass flowmeter filtering algorithm based on MALLAT algorithm." ICFTIC, pp. 861-865, 2023
5. M. Li, M. Henry, "Signal processing methods for coriolis mass flow metering in two-phase flow conditions." IEEE ICIT, pp. 690-695, 2016.
6. F. Xiao and Y. Zhang, "A comparative study on thresholding methods in wavelet-based image denoising." Procedia Engineering, vol. 15, pp. 3998–4003, 2011.

Acknowledgements

This research work was supported by the Agency for Science, Technology and Research (A*STAR) - Career Development Fund (CDF), <C233312022>.

Stability Study of Multicomponent Mixtures to Support Carbon Metrology

Florbela A. Dias [1*], *Cristina Palma* [1], and *Carlos J. Costa* [1]

[1]Instituto Português da Qualidade, Rua António Gião, 2, 2829-513 Caparica, Portugal

Abstract. The European project EPM SRT-v01 - MetCCUS (Metrology for Carbon Capture Utilization and Storage) is the first metrology project within the scope of CCUS (Carbon Capture Utilization and Storage), which, in the European ecological pact, European Commission's Green Deal, is listed as one of the priority areas to achieve a reduction in greenhouse gas emissions by 55 % by 2030 and carbon neutrality by 2050. This project, financed by EURAMET, aims to respond to the metrological challenges identified by the industry and aims to provide the primary standards, methods, good practice guides that will support the necessary measurements. This study successfully characterized four bicomponent mixtures: SO_2 in CO_2 matrix (two mixtures) and H_2S in CO_2 matrix (two mixtures) and four multicomponent mixtures SO_2+CO+O_2 in CO_2 (two mixtures) and H_2S+CO+CH_4+O_2 in CO_2 matrix (two mixtures) within a cylinder under a pressure of approximately 40 bar, and it entailed a stability study. The stability study was conducted over one year, employing statistical evaluation using the Normalized Error (E_n) function in accordance with the international standard ISO 13528:2022 for statistical methods.

1 Introduction

The European initiative EPM (European Partnership on Metrology) SRT-v01 - MetCCUS (Metrology for Carbon Capture Utilization and Storage) [1] represents the first metrology project dedicated to CCUS (Carbon Capture Utilization and Storage) in Europe. This initiative is a key element of the European Commission's Green Deal, an ambitious plan outlined in the European ecological pact. CCUS is identified as one of the priority areas for achieving the overarching goals of a 55 % reduction in greenhouse gas emissions by 2030 and achieving carbon neutrality by 2050. The project, funded by EURAMET, addresses significant metrological challenges faced by industry stakeholders. It aims to develop primary standards, methodologies and best practice guidelines to ensure precise and reliable measurements essential to support CCUS projects.

A critical aspect of this initiative lies in the preparation and use of primary gas mixtures, which plays a key role in environmental monitoring and decarbonization research. Reliable gas mixtures are essential for calibrating instruments that measure atmospheric pollutants and greenhouse gases, ensuring accuracy and consistency in data collection. Decarbonization itself refers to the process of significantly reducing carbon dioxide (CO_2) emissions resulting from human activities, with the goal of transitioning to a low-carbon or carbon-neutral economy. This transformation is a key strategy for mitigating climate change by directly reducing greenhouse gas concentrations in the atmosphere.

As part of the MetCCUS project, the Reference Gas Laboratory (LGR) at the Portuguese Institute for Quality (IPQ) is collaborating in the development of gas metrological capabilities. Specifically, the laboratory is preparing Certified Reference Materials (CRMs) to enable precise measurement of impurities in CO_2 with full metrological traceability [1, 2]. These materials are vital for validating analytical methods and calibrating the instruments used in carbon capture and storage processes.

To date, the LGR has prepared eight gas mixtures. These include four bicomponent mixtures (two consisting of SO_2 in a CO_2 matrix and two of H_2S in a CO_2 matrix) and four multicomponent mixtures (two containing SO_2, CO, and O_2 in a CO_2 matrix, and two with H_2S, CO, CH_4, and O_2 in a CO_2 matrix). These mixtures were successfully characterized to measure four pollutant gases and oxygen in a CO_2 matrix under high pressure, approximately 40 bar. The certification of these mixtures required an extensive stability study.

The stability of these mixtures was evaluated over one year using statistical methods. The Normalized Error (E_n) function, as specified by the ISO 13528 standard for statistical analysis, was employed to ensure accuracy and reliability in the results [3]. This rigorous approach underscores the project's commitment to providing industry and research sectors with robust and reliable metrological solutions.

* Corresponding author: florbelad@ipq.pt

2 Production of reference gas mixtures

The production of reference gas mixtures is done according to ISO 17034 [4] that specifies the requirements for the production of Certified Reference Materials (CRMs), ensuring high-quality and reliable standard gas mixtures. The process involves detailed documentation, and rigorous quality control to ensures high accuracy and traceability to the International System of Units (SI) [5, 6]. Producers must validate methods, assess uncertainties, and conduct stability studies to guarantee accuracy over time. Compliance with ISO 17034 ensures CRMs meet international standards for calibration, testing, and analytical measurements.

2.1 Preparation of gas mixtures

The preparation of gas mixtures following the ISO 6142-1 standard involves gravimetric methods, which are based on the precise weighing of components [7]. The process starts with the selection of a suitable gas cylinder, which must be thoroughly cleaned and evacuated to prevent contamination. The cylinder is then filled with the desired gas components, introduced sequentially, starting with the minor components (trace gases) and finishing with the balance gas, often nitrogen (N_2) or carbon dioxide (CO_2).

The mixture is prepared by gravimetric addition of each component. The mole fractions of the components in the final mixtures are calculated using the following equation [7]:

$$x_i = \frac{\sum_{A=1}^{P}\left(\frac{x_{i,A}\cdot m_A}{\sum_{i=1}^{n} x_{i,A}\cdot M_i}\right)}{\sum_{A=1}^{P}\left(\frac{m_A}{\sum_{i=1}^{n} x_{i,A}\cdot M_i}\right)} \quad (1)$$

Where: x_i is the mole fraction of the component i in the final mixture, i = 1,…., n; P is the total number of the parent gases; n is the total number of the components in the final mixture; m_A is the mass of parent gas A determined by weighing, A= 1,……, P; M_i is the molar mass of the component i; $x_{i,A}$ is the mole fraction of the component i.

Each gas is added using a high-precision mass comparator balance capable of measuring mass with a very low uncertainty. The mass of each component is calculated, considering the buoyancy effect of the surrounding air on the balance. Once all components are added, the total composition of the mixture is determined from the masses of the individual components and their respective molar masses.

After preparation, the mixture undergoes a homogenization process, which typically involves rotating the cylinder to ensure uniform distribution of gases within the cylinder. Finally, the prepared gas mixture is calibrated with others gas standards, by a suitable analytical method, to confirm its composition and validate the gravimetric calculations.

The traceable gas mixtures are widely used in calibration, environmental monitoring, and industrial applications.

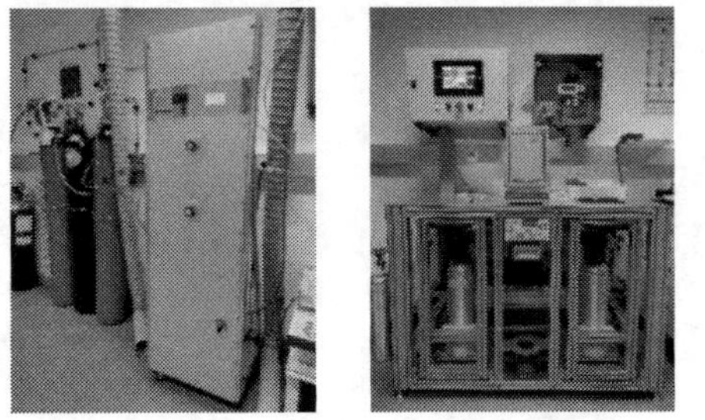

Fig. 1. Filling Station and the mass comparator balance.

2.2 Certification of gas mixtures

The ISO 6143 standard provides a systematic framework for the calibration of gas mixtures using a multi-point method [8]. This approach involves comparing the response of an analytical instrument to a set of calibration gas mixtures with known compositions, referred to as reference standards. The goal is to establish a reliable relationship between the instrument's response and the concentrations of the target components in the mixture being analysed.

Fig. 2. Certification of Gas Mixtures Facility.

The process begins by selecting reference gas mixtures that cover the range of concentrations expected in the sample. These reference standards must be traceable to SI and prepared with high accuracy, often using gravimetric methods according to ISO 6142-1 [7]. The instrument response to each reference mixture is recorded, typically using signals such as peak areas or voltages, depending on the type of analyser is used.

A mathematical model, such as a linear or polynomial regression, is then applied to describe the relationship between the instrument response and the concentration of the analyte. ISO 6143 [8] emphasizes the evaluation of uncertainties for both the reference mixtures and the instrument response, ensuring the calibration curve is accurate and reliable.

Finally, the established calibration curve is used to determine the composition of unknown gas mixtures by measuring their instrument response and interpolating within the range of the calibration standards. This process is essential for applications requiring high precision, such as environmental monitoring and industrial quality control.

3 Stability Study

The stability study of the eight bi-component and multi-component mixtures prepared was conducted over approximately one year. The analysed parameters included H_2S, CO, O_2, CH_4, and SO_2 in a CO_2 matrix. This research aimed to assess the chemical interactions and long-term stability of these gas combinations. Understanding their behaviour is crucial for industrial applications, storage, and transportation safety.

This study was conducted using Primary Reference Material (PRM) of several multicomponent mixtures (Table 1, Table 2, Table 3, Table 4, Table 5). All these reference gas mixtures were prepared in carbon dioxide matrix. The calibration curves were done using primary standards in nitrogen matrix. With these primary standards we can have traceability to the standards of these impurities in CO_2. In this case, the matrix will not influence the analysis because the analysers in question do not detect CO_2 just as they do not detect nitrogen. Each of them detects only the respective gas.

The purpose is to determine the shelf life of this type of mixtures, that is, the actual period during which a mixture can be considered stable concerning its original metrological specifications.

The study was conducted according to ISO 13528 standard [3], which provides various statistical evaluation methods that can be used in specific tests or measurements and for monitoring the ongoing performance of laboratories. In this context, it will be used to compare two concentrations: the concentration resulting from the initial certification and the concentration obtained in subsequent certifications according to the international standard ISO 6143 [8], over the lifetime of the standard.

In this study, we used the normalized error (*En*) statistical tool that is typically applied in comparison of measurement systems, calculated according to the following equation:

$$E_n = \frac{x_{cer1} - x_{cern}}{\sqrt{U_{cer1}{}^2 + U_{cern}{}^2}} \qquad (2)$$

Where x_{Cer1} is the concentration value from the first certification and x_{Cern} is the concentration value resulting from the nth certification. U_{Cer1} represents the uncertainty associated with x_{Cer1} while U_{Cern} is the expanded uncertainty associated with x_{Cern}. With this statistical tool, the results are considered satisfactory if $|E_n| \leq 1$ and unsatisfactory if $|E_n| > 1$.

4 Results

Four gas mixtures, Primary Reference Material (PRM), were carefully prepared for analysis, including two binary combinations of H_2S in a carbon dioxide matrix, designated as PRM108595, PRM108596 and two mixtures of SO_2 in CO_2, labelled as PRM408326 and PRM108593, were also carefully assembled. This study facilitated the comprehensive characterization of these four mixtures, each contained within individual cylinders maintained at an approximate pressure of 40 bar.

Furthermore, four multicomponent mixtures were prepared in a CO_2 matrix, PRM608395 and PRM308978 with the impurities SO_2, CO and O_2; and two, PRM202557 and PRM302530, with the impurities H_2S, CO, O_2, and CH_4. These mixtures were contained within four cylinders at an approximate pressure of 40 bar each. No stability study was conducted on the PRM308978 because this cylinder was sent for analysis to one of the participants of the MetCCUS project.

Table 1. Results of the stability study for the prepared binary mixtures of H_2S/CO_2

PRM108596	**H_2S/CO_2**		
Date	x µmol/mol	U µmol/mol	E_n
2023-09-11	9,64	0,47	-
2024-04-23	10,22	0,42	0,92
2024-11-08	10,02	0,34	0,66

PRM108595	**H_2S/CO_2**		
Date	x µmol/mol	U µmol/mol	E_n
2023-09-11	9,97	0,48	-
2024-04-23	9,87	0,35	-0,17
2024-11-08	9,61	0,29	-0,64

Table 2. Results of the stability study for the prepared binary mixtures of SO_2/CO_2

PRM408326	**SO_2/CO_2**		
Date	x µmol/mol	U µmol/mol	E_n
2023-09-04	19,52	0,51	-
2024-04-18	20,16	0,57	0,84
2024-11-18	19,9	1,1	0,31

PRM108593	**SO_2/CO_2**		
Date	x µmol/mol	U µmol/mol	E_n
2023-09-04	20,71	0,50	-
2024-04-18	20,71	0,58	0,00
2024-11-18	20,5	1,0	-0,19

Table 3. Results of the stability study for the prepared multicomponent mixture of SO_2+CO+O_2 / CO_2

PRM608395	SO_2+CO+O_2 / CO_2		
	SO_2		
Date	$x_{\mu mol/mol}$	$U_{\mu mol/mol}$	E_n
2024-04-18	14,24	0,77	-
2024-11-18	14,1	1,3	-0,09
	CO		
Date	$x_{\mu mol/mol}$	$U_{\mu mol/mol}$	E_n
2024-04-17	660,7	1,6	-
2024-11-22	653,5	1,6	-3,2
	O_2		
Date	$x_{cmol/mol}$	$U_{cmol/mol}$	E_n
2024-04-16	0,568	0,048	-
2025-01-23	0,572	0,017	0,08

Table 4. Results of the stability study for the prepared multicomponent mixture of H_2S +CO+O_2+CH_4 / CO_2

PRM202557	H_2S+CO+O_2+CH_4 / CO_2		
	H_2S		
Date	$x_{\mu mol/mol}$	$U_{\mu mol/mol}$	E_n
2023-09-20	9,83	0,48	-
2024-04-23	9,73	0,33	-0,17
2024-11-08	9,61	0,28	-0,40
	CO		
Date	$x_{\mu mol/mol}$	$U_{\mu mol/mol}$	E_n
2023-09-15	669,5	2,7	-
2024-04-17	662,3	1,6	-2,3
2024-11-22	654,4	1,6	-4,8
	O_2		
Date	$x_{cmol/mol}$	$U_{cmol/mol}$	E_n
2023-09-15	0,586	0,027	-
2024-04-16	0,582	0,048	-0,07
2025-01-23	0,586	0,017	0,00
	CH_4		
Date	$x_{cmol/mol}$	$U_{cmol/mol}$	E_n
2023-09-14	1,9685	0,0060	-
2024-04-17	1,9686	0,0061	0,01
2024-11-28	1,9706	0,0062	0,24

Table 5. Results of the stability study for the prepared multicomponent mixture of H_2S +CO+O_2+CH_4 / CO_2

PRM302530	H_2S+CO+O_2+CH_4 / CO_2		
	H_2S		
Date	$x_{\mu mol/mol}$	$U_{\mu mol/mol}$	E_n
2023-12-04	9,92	0,40	-
2024-04-23	9,60	0,36	-0,59
2024-11-08	9,16	0,33	-1,5
	CO		
Date	$x_{\mu mol/mol}$	$U_{\mu mol/mol}$	E_n
2023-12-14	677,0	1,8	-
2024-04-17	674,3	1,5	-1,1
2024-11-22	666,5	1,6	-4,3
	O_2		
Date	$x_{cmol/mol}$	$U_{cmol/mol}$	E_n
2023-12-18	0,602	0,051	-
2024-04-16	0,591	0,058	-0,14
2025-01-23	0,585	0,017	-0,32
	CH_4		
Date	$x_{cmol/mol}$	$U_{cmol/mol}$	E_n
2023-12-05	1,915	0,015	-
2024-04-17	1,9270	0,0059	0,74
2024-11-28	1,9284	0,0060	0,83

5 Summary

In conclusion, IPQ has demonstrated its ability to prepare and certify reference materials (CRM) for measuring impurities of H_2S, SO_2, CO, O_2 and CH_4 in CO_2, within the requested concentration with metrological traceability. The uncertainties obtained were as expected.

The stability study has confirmed that, except for CO, all components remain stable for about one year within the associated uncertainties. To further refine our understanding, a longer study will be conducted to determine the stability period of each type of mixture.

Looking ahead, this research may be extended to mixtures containing additional components. Additionally, to enhance the scope of the project, these mixtures will be analysed using alternative analytical methods to gather more data for further characterization of the mixtures.

References

1. MetCCUS Project https://metccus.eu/about-the-project/ (accessed 11 February 2025).
2. F. A. Dias, C. Palma, C. J. Costa, Preparation of Multicomponent Mixtures to Support Carbon Metrology, Measurement - Elsevier., **239**, 2025, 115453.
3. ISO 13528:2022 – Statistical methods for use in proficiency testing by interlaboratory comparisons.
4. ISO 17034:2016 – General requirements for the competence of reference material producers.
5. ISO/IEC 17025:2017 – General requirements for the competence of testing and calibration laboratories.
6. KCDB https://www.bipm.org/kcdb/ (accessed 11 February 2025).
7. ISO 6142-1:2015 – Gas analysis — Preparation of calibration gas mixtures — Part 1: Gravimetric method for Class I mixtures.
8. ISO 6143:2001 – Gas analysis — Comparison methods for determining and checking the composition of calibration gas mixtures.

EPJ Web of Conferences **323**, 09001 (10125)Ht sp:/ odor. :g0ig02g:et jconf:101231309001
22nd nIt enr Iai nr dMt Iei ai gylCi nget ss

Comparison of cavity ring-down spectroscopy and Fourier transform infrared spectroscopy for the isotopic composition determination of CRMs of CO_2 in air

Michela Sega [1]*, *Francesca* Durbiano[1], *Stefano* Pavarelli[1], *Francesca Romana* Pennecchi[1], and *Francesca* Rolle[1]

[1]INRiM – Istituto Nazionale di Ricerca Metrologica, Applied Metrology and Engineering Division, 10135 Strada delle Cacce 91, Torino, Italy

Abstract. Gaseous Certified Reference Materials (CRMs) characterised for the isotopic composition of carbon dioxide (CO_2) in air at ambient amount fraction are crucial for understanding the anthropogenic contribution to climate change. At INRiM, the Italian National Metrology Institute, the realization of gaseous mixtures, which are candidate CRMs of CO_2 in air at ambient level and known isotopic composition, is ongoing. Fourier transform infrared spectroscopy (FTIR) and cavity ring-down spectroscopy (CRDS) are used to verify the mixtures for their isotopic composition, in terms of δ^{13}C-CO_2 in the range from +1.3 ‰ VPDB to -42 ‰ VPDB. In this work, a comparison between the performances of the two analytical techniques FTIR and CRDS used at INRiM to assign the isotopic composition to the prepared candidate CRMs is presented.

1 Introduction

The past ten years, from 2015 to 2024, have been the warmest years in the 175-year observational record. World Meteorological Organization (WMO) and the international scientific community are actively considering several approaches to enable a prompt reporting on the exceedance of global temperature levels. One of these consists in estimating the warming that results from historical changes in key human drivers of the climate system such as greenhouse gases (GHGs) [1]. GHGs reached record observed levels in 2023 and real time data indicate that they continued to rise in 2024. Carbon dioxide (CO_2) is the most important anthropogenic GHG driving climate change. Its concentration has reached the current level of 420.0 ppm ± 0.2 ppm, which represents an increase of 51 % with respect to the concentration of the preindustrial era (around 278 ppm in 1750) [1]. The annual mean CO_2 value in the global surface atmosphere increased by 2.3 ppm from 2022 to 2023, thus marking the twelfth consecutive year with an increase greater than 2 ppm, which continues an already significant trend. The increase in atmospheric CO_2 is directly related to the amount of carbon emissions from fossil fuels, as it represents the net result of total carbon emissions surpassing total ocean and terrestrial biosphere carbon sinks. GHGs monitoring has to be carried out in a proper way, in order to obtain significant measurements and an objective quantification of emissions and removals, to support effective emissions reduction policies. These measurements must be precise and the instruments performing them well-calibrated, because the information about emissions resides in small gradients in space and time relative to a common global background. A fundamental aspect is also to track progress on climate action, sustaining these measurements over decades. [2]. Sound and affordable certified reference gas mixtures characterised for the isotopic composition of CO_2 in air at ambient amount fraction are requested to support the study of the anthropogenic contribution to climate change. Such mixtures, namely Certified Reference Materials (CRMs), are useful in the isotope measurement field, in particular for the spectroscopic techniques. On a broader scale, sound metrological references are fundamental to support the efforts ongoing in the metrological community to achieve the comparability of results and to assure accuracy and metrological traceability to the isotopic measurements of CO_2.

At INRiM, the Italian National Metrology Institute, the realization of CRMs of CO_2 in air at ambient level and known isotopic composition is ongoing starting from the activities carried out within the European Joint Research Projects (JRPs) 16ENV06 SIRS [3] and 19ENV05 STELLAR [4]. CRMs for the CO_2 amount fraction at atmospheric level in synthetic air are realised by the gravimetric method following the ISO standard 6142-1 [5], in high-pressure cylinders of aluminium alloy, achieving preparation uncertainties of 0.33 %. These mixtures are realised from parent mixtures at higher amount fraction, obtained from different pure CO_2 sources. Fourier transform infrared spectroscopy (FTIR) is used to verify the mixtures for their isotopic composition and assign their δ^{13}C-CO_2 value. More recently, a second analytical technique was chosen for

* Corresponding author: m.sega@inrim.it

the assignment of the $\delta^{13}C\text{-}CO_2$ values of the gravimetric mixtures, namely cavity ring-down spectroscopy (CRDS). The $\delta^{13}C\text{-}CO_2$ values of the mixtures span in the range from +1.3 ‰ to -42 ‰ VPDB.

In this work, a comparison between the performances of the two analytical instruments, a FTIR and a CRDS spectrometer, in assigning the isotopic composition to the prepared mixtures is presented, focusing on the more depleted $\delta^{13}C\text{-}CO_2$ values from -20 ‰ VPDB to -42 ‰ VPDB. An accurate instrument calibration is mandatory to obtain reliable results from the spectroscopic measurements of isotopic composition, and to carry out stability studies of the reference mixtures over time.

2 Materials and methods

A set of gas mixtures of CO_2 at atmospheric amount fraction in a matrix of synthetic air was gravimetrically prepared at INRiM starting from the following pure gases: CO_2 at +1.3 ‰ VPDB and -42 ‰ VPDB (99.998, SIAD, Italy), oxygen (99.9999, Air Liquide, Italy), argon (99.99999, LINDE, Germany), nitrogen (99.9999, Air Liquide, Italy). For the high precision weighing, the INRiM gravimetric facility is equipped with a mass comparator (PR 10003, Mettler Toledo, Switzerland), having a measurement range of [0.001–10010] g. The mixtures were prepared in cylinders of aluminum alloy (Luxfer, USA) with internal volume of 5 L, filled to a final pressure of 100 bar. After the preparation, the CO_2 amount fraction of each mixture was verified by means of a NDIR photometer (URAS 14, ABB, Switzerland), having a CO_2 measurement range of [0–1000] $\mu mol \cdot mol^{-1}$. Table 1 reports the characteristics of the mixtures, including the nominal $\delta^{13}C\text{-}CO_2$ value assigned on the basis of the information given by the CO_2 supplier.

Table 1. Characteristics of INRiM gas mixtures of CO_2 in synthetic air.

Mixture code	CO_2 amount fraction $\mu mol \cdot mol^{-1}$	$U(CO_2)$ $\mu mol \cdot mol^{-1}$ (k = 2)	Nominal $\delta^{13}C\text{-}CO_2$ ‰ VPDB
SIRS 010 (D580461)	390.04	0.40	-20
STELLAR 022 (15914)	404.72	0.40	-42
STELLAR 006 (12997)	409.46	0.40	-42

The mixtures were analysed by both FTIR and CRDS to verify their isotopic composition and assign the $\delta^{13}C\text{-}CO_2$ value. The two analytical techniques require different types of calibrations carried out by means of CO_2 in air reference gas mixtures with known CO_2 amount fraction and $\delta^{13}C\text{-}CO_2$ value. The approach used for FTIR consists of using reference gas standards having $\delta^{13}C\text{-}CO_2$ values similar to the mixture to be characterised and different CO_2 amount fractions bracketing the CO_2 nominal amount fraction of the mixture to be analysed. In CRDS, the reference standards have CO_2 amount fractions similar to the mixture to be characterised and different $\delta^{13}C\text{-}CO_2$ values bracketing the nominal $\delta^{13}C\text{-}CO_2$ value of the mixture to be analysed. In order to obtain the traceability to the VPDB scale [6], all the mixtures used in the present work were sampled in glass flasks and sent to the Max Planck Institute for Biogeochemistry (MPI-BGC) for the isotopic value assignment by isotope ratio mass spectrometry (IRMS).

2.1 FTIR analysis

A FTIR spectrometer (Nicolet iS50 Thermo Scientific, USA) equipped with a 2 m path length gas cell (Thermo Scientific, USA) and a MCT detector was used to analyse the CO_2 mixtures. A schematic picture of the measurement setup is reported in Figure 1.

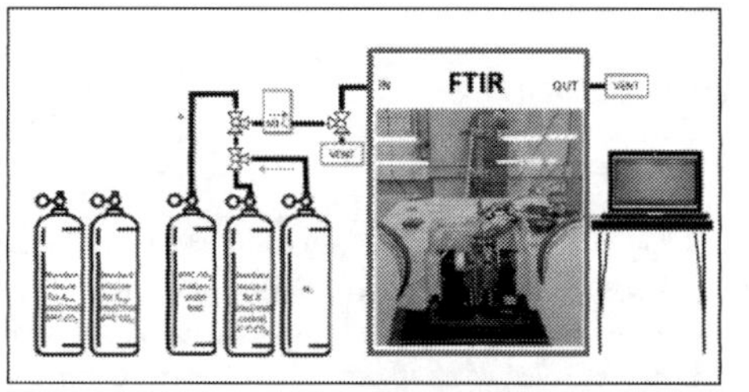

Fig. 1. Schematic of the FTIR measurement setup.

To calibrate the FTIR, two reference mixtures bracketing the CO_2 amount fraction values of the mixtures to be analysed were chosen and used as measurement standards. Moreover, an additional mixture was used as a control mixture to validate the calibration. For the acquisition and fitting of the FTIR spectra, the radiative transfer calculation code named MALT (Multiple Atmospheric Layer Transmission, University of Wollongong, Australia) was employed [7]. MALT uses the HITRAN database spectral lines to generate synthetic infrared spectra of gas phase mixtures. The software B-FOS developed at the Bureau International des Poids et Mesures (BIPM) has been used to interface MALT and the software of the FTIR (Thermo Fisher Scientific Omnic®).

The calibration approach, adapted from the BIPM procedure [8], is based on the use of two CO_2 standard mixtures of different amount fraction but similar isotopic values. The standards were analysed at the beginning and at the end of the analytical sequence in order to account for possible measurement drifts. The mixtures under investigation were analysed in between the two standards and in increasing CO_2 amount fraction value order. The analysis function was calculated according to the model equation (1), by using the

Calibration Curves Computing (CCC) software, developed at INRiM [9]:

$$y = a + bx \quad (1)$$

where:
y is the calculated value of $\delta^{13}C\text{-}CO_2$ (‰) in the mixture;
a is the intercept of the analysis curve;
b is the slope of the analysis curve;
x is the average of repeated FTIR spectra ($n = 6$).

2.2 CRDS analysis

A CRDS spectrometer (G2131*i*, Picarro, USA) was used to analyse the CO_2 mixtures. A schematic picture of the measurement setup is reported in Figure 2.

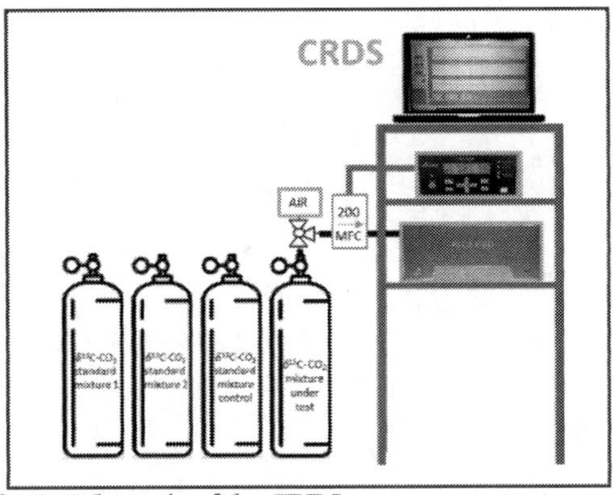

Fig. 2. Schematic of the CRDS measurement setup.

To calibrate the CRDS, two reference mixtures bracketing the $\delta^{13}C\text{-}CO_2$ values of the mixtures to be analysed were chosen and used as measurement standards. Moreover, an additional mixture was used as a control mixture to validate the CRDS calibration. The standard mixtures were analysed at the beginning and at the end of the analytical sequence in order to account for possible measurement drifts. The mixtures under investigation were analysed in between the two standards and in decreasing $\delta^{13}C\text{-}CO_2$ value order. The analysis function was calculated according to the model equation (1), where x is the average of repeated readings ($n = 100$) of the CRDS analyser. The final delta value was calculated as the average of three single measurement values x_i.

3 Results and discussion

Table 2 reports the $\delta^{13}C\text{-}CO_2$ values obtained for each mixture with the different techniques.

Table 2. $\delta^{13}C\text{-}CO_2$ values expressed in ‰ VPDB obtained by IRMS, FTIR and CRDS with the associated expanded uncertainty ($k = 2$).

Mixture code	IRMS ‰ VPDB	FTIR ‰ VPDB	CRDS ‰ VPDB
SIRS 010 (D580461)	-19.74 ± 0.04	-19.54 ± 0.60	-19.96 ± 0.35
STELLAR 022 (15914)	-41.94 ± 0.12	-41.87 ± 0.30	-42.24 ± 0.20
STELLAR 006 (12997)	-42.03 ± 0.04	-41.92 ± 0.30	-42.19 ± 0.16

The data presented in Table 2 for each mixture are compatible within the associated uncertainties. The spectroscopic measurements have uncertainty values greater than the IRMS, sometimes also by an order of magnitude. Such results are due to the intrinsic nature of the spectroscopic measurement principle.

The expanded uncertainty value associated with the IRMS data was evaluated by INRiM on the basis of the MPI-BGC measurement results, taking into account both the maximum uncertainty value for the single analysis and the standard deviation of the analyses carried out on the same mixture (different sample flasks). The FTIR uncertainty associated with the $\delta^{13}C\text{-}CO_2$ measurements takes into account several contributions, e.g. the stability of the FTIR, the HITRAN uncertainty for the CO_2 line parameters and the uncertainty of the regression algorithm, based on classical least squares (CLS), used by MALT. As for CRDS, the uncertainty takes into account the uncertainty of the standards, the instrument repeatability and the scattering among the three different measurement runs. Research activities are currently ongoing at INRiM to improve the measurement repeatability, in particular for CRDS, in order to obtain better estimation of the $\delta^{13}C\text{-}CO_2$ values and lower associated uncertainties.

In order to evaluate their stability in terms of $\delta^{13}C\text{-}CO_2$ values, additional CRDS measurements have been carried out on the mixtures which can be considered as candidate CRMs in accordance with the International Standard ISO 17034 [10]. Figure 3 reports the preliminary data.

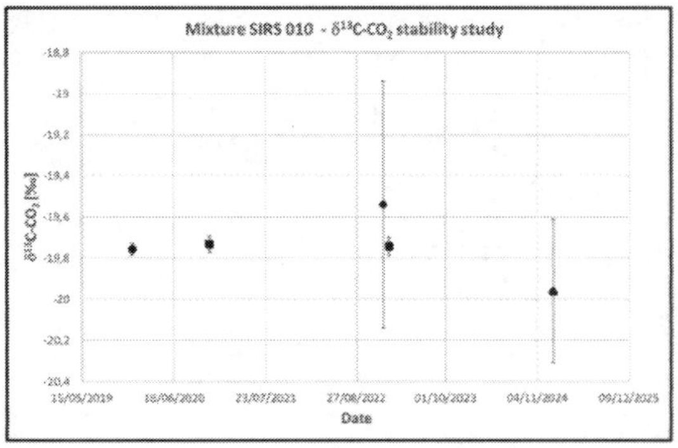

a)

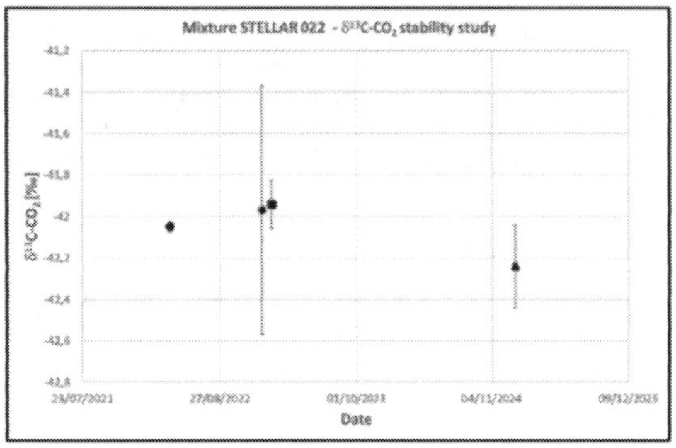

b)

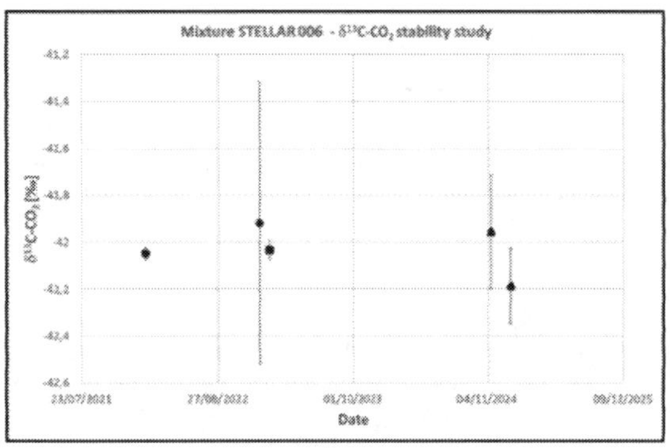

c)

Fig. 3. Stability studies of $\delta^{13}C$-CO_2 values: a) mixture SIRS 010; b) mixture STELLAR 022; c) mixture STELLAR 006. The error bars represent the expanded uncertainties (k = 2) associated with the analytical values. ●: gravimetric values; ♦: FTIR values; ■: IRMS values; ▲: CRDS values.

The stability study is essential to go towards the production of CRMs of CO_2 in air characterised for the isotopic values. Although different techniques show different uncertainty values, the data reported in Figure 3 are in agreement within their expanded uncertainties, thus confirming a good stability of the three mixtures, even for a 5-year period (Figure 3 a).

Part of this work has been funded by the Italian Ministry of University and Research (MUR) in the framework of the project "METRO-INN – National Infrastructure for the quality of measurements for sustainable innovation", under the Fund for the enhancing of public investments and national development (Law n. 160/2019).

4 Conclusions

The presented results show a good comparability of FTIR and CRDS for the assignment of $\delta^{13}C$-CO_2 values to the mixtures gravimetrically prepared at INRiM. In addition, they are promising in terms of the stability of the mixtures for $\delta^{13}C$-CO_2 values. Due to this premise, further activities are foreseen for extensive stability studies in the whole $\delta^{13}C$-CO_2 range in order to obtain the international recognition of Calibration and Measurement Capabilities for the production of CO_2 in synthetic air CRMs characterised for both CO_2 amount fraction and isotopic composition. Starting from the work carried out in the H2020 INFRAIA project "Metrology for Integrated Marine Management and Knowledge-Transfer Network – MINKE" [11], future developments are foreseen also in the application of isotopic measurements to the marine field, for the determination of the stable carbon isotopic content of seawater dissolved inorganic carbon ($DI^{13}C$).

References

1. World Meteorological Organization (WMO), State of the Climate 2024 - Update for COP29, WMO, 2024, https://library.wmo.int/idurl/4/69075
2. World Meteorological Organization (WMO), WMO Greenhouse Gas Bulletin No. 20 – 28 October 2024 The State of Greenhouse Gases in the Atmosphere Based on Global Observations through 2023, WMO, 2024 https://library.wmo.int/idurl/4/69057
3. https://www.euramet.org/research-innovation/search-research-projects/details/project/metrology-for-stable-isotope-reference-standards
4. https://empir.npl.co.uk/stellarproject/
5. International Standard ISO 6142-1:2015, Gas analysis — Preparation of calibration gas mixtures. Part 1: Gravimetric method for Class I mixtures, ISO, Geneva
6. H. Qi, H. Moossen, H.A.J. Meijer, et al, USGS44, a new high-purity calcium carbonate reference material for $\delta^{13}C$ measurements, Rapid. Commun. Mass Sp. **35**, e9006 (2021), https://doi.org/10.1002/rcm.9006
7. F. Rolle, M. Sega, Use of FTIR spectroscopy for the measurement of CO_2 carbon stable isotope ratios, in Proceedings of the 19th International Congress of Metrology, Paris, France, 24-26 September (2019), 05002, doi.org/10.1051/metrology/201905002
8. E. Flores, J. Viallon, P. Moussay, D. W. T Griffith, R. I. Wielgosz, Calibration Strategies for FT-IR and Other Isotope Ratio Infrared Spectrometer Instruments for Accurate $\delta^{13}C$ and $\delta^{18}O$ Measurements of CO_2 in Air, Anal. Chem., **89**, 3648 (2017).

https://doi.org/10.1021/acs.analchem.6b05063

9. CCC Software: https://www.inrim.it/en/services/software-and-databases/ccc-software
10. International Standard ISO 17034:2016, General requirements for the competence of reference material producers, ISO, Geneva
11. https://minke.eu/

EPJ Web of Conferences **323**, 09001 (2025) https://doi.org/j 0.j 05j /ep3conf/202512109001
22nd nIt enr Iai nr dMt Iei ai gylCi nget ss

On the autocorrelation of measurement results for gas volume and calorific value in fiscal metering in gas grids

Federica Gugole[1*], *Meng* Li[2], and *Adriaan M. H.* van der Veen[1]

[1]VSL, Data Science & Modelling Department, Thijsseweg 11, 2629 JA Delft, The Netherlands
[2]TU/e, Eindhoven University of Technology, Department of Mathematics and Computer Science, Eindhoven, The Netherlands

Abstract. The fiscal metering of natural gas is often performed using a flow meter and a gas chromatograph. The flow meter measures the volume flow rate of the gas and the gas chromatograph measures the composition, from which the calorific value is calculated. The energy is then calculated as the product of the volume and the calorific value. The uncertainty of the energy delivered (or received) is an important parameter for operating the gas grid. Currently, the energy values used to compute the total energy are considered mutually independent. However, the underlying processes affecting the gas flow through a pipe are continuous. We analysed the correlation between successive measurements due to temporal variations in the physical process by applying autoregressive moving average (ARMA) models to a set of measurement data taken at a metering station in the Dutch gas grid. The analysis showed that the volume time series can be modelled as an autoregressive model of order 1, while the time series of the calorific value can be described by an autoregressive model of order 2. These correlations lead to an increase of the instrumental measurement uncertainty associated to the total energy of about 50%.

1 Introduction

As part of the energy transition, required to achieve the net-zero greenhouse gas emissions targets for 2050, European gas grids are facing a diversification of the gas entering the grids. Renewable gases such as hydrogen, biogas and biomethane will replace fossil natural gas and the question arises whether the current infrastructure is still adequate. This infrastructure includes the instruments used at a metering station to determine the quantity (i.e., mass or volume) and the quality (i.e., the calorific value) of the gas, including data processing equipment used for calculating the total quantity or energy over a time interval. This equipment uses current modelling practices to calculate the uncertainty of the energy delivered (or received). Usually, the quantity of gas is measured by a flow meter, while a gas chromatograph determines the composition of the gas from which, e.g., the calorific value is calculated. Such measurements are important for financial transactions between buyer and seller, while the combined uncertainty of the measurements is an important parameter to ensure that suppliers can feed the grid and users can draw gas from the grid that is within legislative and contractual specifications.

Fiscal metering of energy gases is described in several standards and guidance documents, such as OIML-R140 [1], EN 1776 [2] and ISO 15112 [3]. The requirements for the measurement equipment to be calibrated and the measurement results to be metrologically traceable are common to all these documents, and so are the models described. The delivered energy is generally calculated as the sum of the energy increments over time, and in the evaluation of the measurement uncertainty, it is usually assumed that the quantities of interest (e.g., volume and calorific value at normal conditions) are mutually independent, and normally distributed. Whereas the latter assumption is usually unproblematic, it was shown that the former is unrealistic, see Van der Veen et al., 2025 [4].

Two sources of correlations between measurement results have been identified. The first cause of correlation is due to the use of the same instrumentation for all measurements, and the second is due to the continuous nature of the underlying physical processes. Whereas the latter effects can be small under steady-state conditions, their contribution can become substantial with a greater diversity of energy gases in gas grids and with larger fluctuations in supply and demand. In an era, where gas grids are facing a further diversification of the gas entering the grid and the fluctuations also increase, the uncertainty due to temporal effects is expected to become more relevant.

In this work, we show how time series models can be used to describe non-random features in gas grid data and quantify the correlation between subsequent measurements due to temporal effects. We then estimate the uncertainty both according to the current modelling practices and including the estimated temporal correlations. In section 2, we outline the methodology used for the analysis. We then present the results (section 3) and our conclusions.

* Corresponding author: fgugole@vsl.nl

2 Analysis

2.1 Time series

Data collected (and indexed) over time is called a time series. Just as with other series of data, there are different models that can be employed to describe and summarise the data. A basic time series model is the white Gaussian noise model, i.e., the data is assumed to be independent, identically and normally distributed. Many time series are however not centred around a specific mean, show trends, oscillating behaviour or other features. In gas grids, it is expected that measurement data will also contain such features due to, e.g., changes in supply and demand, blending with different gases or gas qualities or other events. Such phenomena give rise to the situation that the last measurement result depends on the previous one (and so on). Physically, one would expect that the current state at a metering point does not differ (too) much from a previous state, nor will it differ substantially from the next state. It takes time for the gas to respond to phenomena in the grid, and that will be reflected in the data.

If the current state depends on a previous state, then such dependencies affect the uncertainty about quantities evaluated using time series data. This kind of correlation is known as autocorrelation and it is different from, e.g., the correlations arising from the fact that the same instrumentation was used for the entire time series. Describing gas metering data using time series models aids at exploring the features in the time series and evaluating, among others, the autocorrelation between the measurement results in the time series.

An important concept in time series analysis is stationarity, which means that a time series has a constant mean and a covariance function that depends only on the time distance between the data points and not on the specific time at which the data have been collected [5, 6]. Using time series models, the mean and its associated uncertainty can be evaluated. Ignoring the specific features in the time series can lead to a wrong value for the uncertainty.

2.2 Data set

In this study, we analysed data that were collected at a metering station in the Dutch gas grid. The measurements were made with an ultrasonic flow meter, a gas chromatograph and temperature and pressure transmitters. The dataset covers a time window of two days with a time interval of 15 minutes between recorded measurement points.

The dataset consisted of the volume at normal conditions and the volumetric calorific value, also at normal conditions. Corrections for the actual pressure, temperature and calibration of the equipment had already been applied. The reported values for the volume represent the accumulated volume over the 15 minutes interval, while those reported for the calorific value are the average over the interval. The data are displayed in Figure 1.

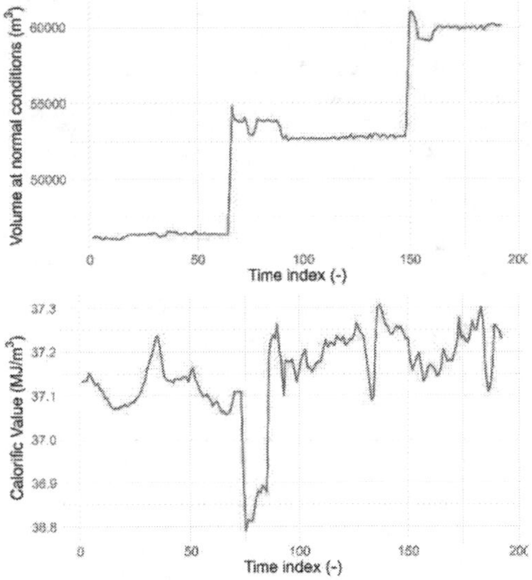

Fig. 1. The available measurement data at normal conditions (top: volume; bottom: calorific value) used in the analysis.

2.3 Time series model

We applied so-called autoregressive moving average (ARMA) models, a widely used class of time series models. ARMA models express the value observed at a particular epoch as a linear combination of a finite number of past values (AR part) plus an error defined as a linear combination of measurement errors affecting the current observation and a finite number of previous observations (MA part). The AR part describes the dependence of one datum with respect to its predecessors. The MA part instead, expresses the dependence of one datum with respect to the current and past instances of a non-identical to itself variable. The autocorrelation function (ACF) measures the correlation between observations at different distances apart. It is well suited to estimate the order of MA processes, since the ACF will be zero for distances larger than the order of the MA process. However, in case of AR processes the ACF alone gives little information. In that case it is helpful to look at the partial ACF (PACF). The idea of the PACF is to compute the correlation between two variables with the linear effect on a third variable removed. It is thus helpful to determine the order of AR processes. We invite the interested reader to check, e.g., Shumway and Stoffer, 2017 [5] for a more detailed explanation.

2.4 Automatic segmentation of the data

ARMA models can be used to describe series of observations provided that the series is (statistically) stationary. Many time series are not stationary. To get around the non-stationarity of the entire dataset, it is possible to look for stationary parts in the time series and locate those. To this end, we applied the binary segmentation method (Bai, 1997 [7]) to automatically detect stationary subsets of the available time series. The binary segmentation method is an approximate change point method that uses the mean of the series as criteria to determine the segmentation points. It is therefore well indicated to determine large changes in the time series, but it might not detect more subtle changes. As it can be seen in Figure 2, the binary segmentation method does a good job at detecting the biggest jumps first. It can then be applied recursively until the subseries satisfy the stationarity criteria, e.g., as tested by the augmented Dickey-Fuller test. This test tests the null-hypothesis that a unit root is present in the time series. If that is the case, the time series is non-stationary.

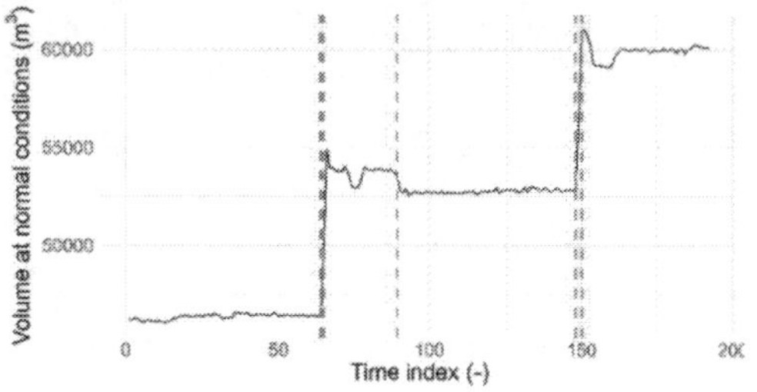

Fig. 2. Example of segmentation results using binary segmentation.

As a result of this analysis, we obtained three stationary subseries for the volume measurement data and two for the calorific value.

2.5 Fitting a time series model

Once stationary subseries of the volume and of the calorific value were identified, we computed the ACF and PACF to determine the order of the ARMA models to be used. The analysis revealed that the volume data are better described by an autoregressive (AR) process of order 1, meaning that the measurement result at time t is significantly correlated with the measurement result at time t-1. The calorific value time series turned out to be better modelled by an AR model of order 2 (see Figure 3), thus implying that the measurement result at time t is significantly correlated with the measurement results at time t-1 and t-2. Considering the resolution of the time series, t-2 corresponds to 30 min.

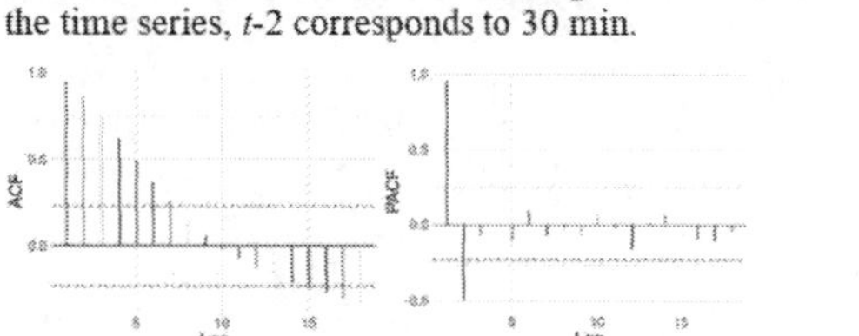

Fig. 3. ACF and PACF of one of the two stationary subseries of the calorific value time series.

The goodness–of–fit of the AR models has been evaluated by simulating 100 000 processes, where each simulation starts from the same initial value(s) (an AR(1) model requires one initial value, while an AR(2) model requires two starting points) as the series of the recorded measurement results and the following observations are simulated using the fitted AR models. The experimental data are within the 95 % confidence interval determined by the simulations (see Figure 4), thus the models are an adequate representation of the measurement data.

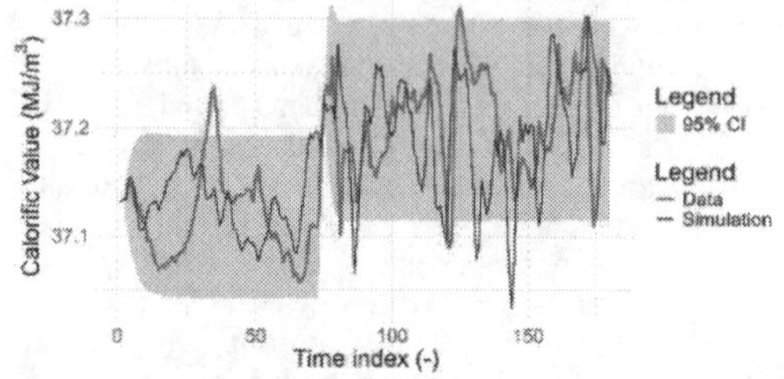

Fig. 4. Comparison between experimental data and simulated data.

2.6 Evaluation of uncertainty

The uncertainty is evaluated by applying the law of propagation of uncertainty with correlated input quantities [8]:

$$u_c^2(y) = \sum_{i=1}^{N}\left(\frac{\partial f}{\partial x_i}\right)^2 u^2(x_i) + 2\sum_{i=1}^{N-1}\sum_{j=i+1}^{N}\frac{\partial f}{\partial x_i}\frac{\partial f}{\partial x_j}u(x_i, x_j) \quad (1)$$

In the case of the total energy,

$$E_{tot} = \sum_{t=1}^{N} E_t = \sum_{t=1}^{N} V_t H_t \quad (2)$$

the double summation for the calculation of the covariance simplifies since the only correlation different from zero is between E_t and E_{t-1}, and between E_t and E_{t-2}. Furthermore, due to the stationarity of the time series, the correlation values are independent on the value of the index t. We note that the measured values have their own measurement models, describing predominantly the instrumental measurement uncertainty. Due to the fact that the entire time series is obtained from the same measurement equipment, there are correlations between the data due to the instrumentation. These come on top of the correlations identified in the time series analysis and are not considered in this work.

If only the instrumental measurement uncertainty had been considered, then the time series would have been modelled using a white noise model, so a model for independently and identically distributed data. When considering the serial correlation instead we consider the variance of the AR processes (AR(1) for the volume, AR(2) for the calorific value; see Chatfield, 1975 [6] for the formula of the variance of an AR process) and their corresponding correlations. Since the energy is given by the product of two random variables, we used the formula by Bohrnstedt and Goldberger, 1969 [9] to determine the covariance of the total energy, where we assumed that the volume and calorific value measurements are mutually independent. This formula considers all effects arising from the presence of covariances, this in contrast to the law of propagation of uncertainty from the Guide to the expression of Uncertainty in Measurement [8], which carries only the main contributors to the combined standard uncertainty of the output quantity.

3 Results

The effect of adding the serial correlation in the calculation of the uncertainty has been evaluated using two metrics, i.e.,

- the relative difference between the uncertainty of the total energy calculated including the serial correlation $u_{\mathrm{cor}}(E)$ and the uncertainty calculated under the assumption that the measurements are independent and identically distributed $u_{\mathrm{iid}}(E)$:

$$\Delta_{rel} = \frac{u_{\mathrm{cor}}(E) - u_{\mathrm{iid}}(E)}{u_{\mathrm{iid}}(E)} \cdot 100\% \qquad (3)$$

- the ratio between the calculated uncertainty under the two scenarios and the total energy (i.e., the relative uncertainty).

These metrics have been calculated over 100 000 simulated data obtained with the time series model fitted on the available measurement data. The results are displayed in Figure 5 and 6. The distributions of the uncertainty values calculated in the two scenarios are clearly separated with no overlap between their 95 % confidence intervals. The inclusion of the serial correlation leads to an increase of the measurement uncertainty by approximately 50 %, with the 95 % confidence interval covering the interval [38 %, 61 %]. Thus, when evaluating the measurement uncertainty without considering serial correlation, the uncertainty is severely underrated, which is expected to be the more relevant the more dynamic (and thus the less stationary) the gas flow is in the pipe.

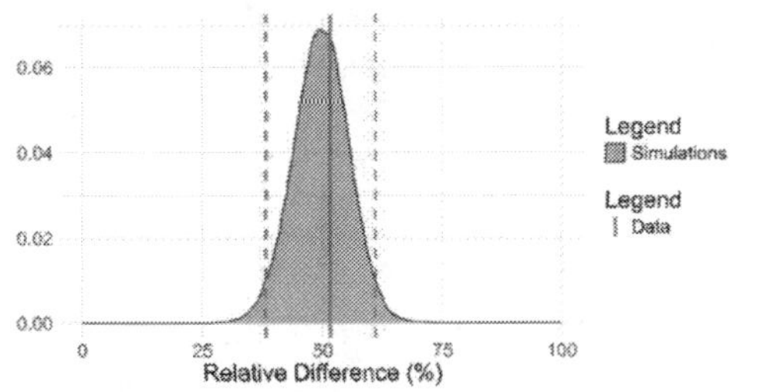

Fig. 5. Relative difference between the uncertainty values obtained including the correlation and the values obtained under IID assumption.

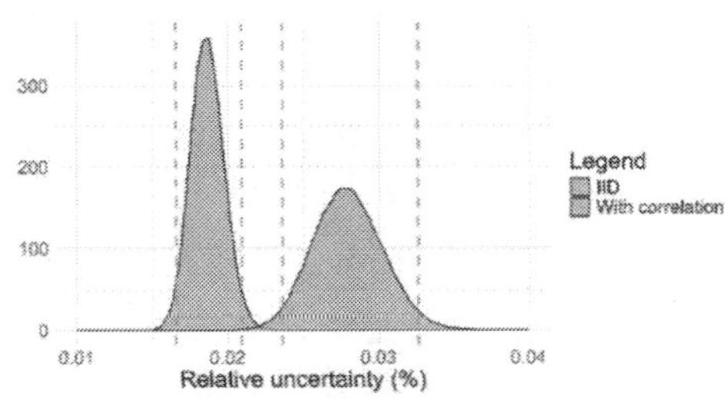

Fig. 6. The distributions of the values of the relative uncertainties associated to the total energy in the two considered scenarios.

4 Conclusions

With an increasing diversity of energy gasses entering the gas grid (e.g., hydrogen and biomethane), it is expected that the temporal effects due to the continuous process of the gas flowing through a pipe will substantially contribute to the uncertainty of the total energy. In this paper the time series of volume and calorific value measurement results from a metering station in the Dutch gas grid has been analysed to quantify the correlation between subsequent measuring results.

Since many time series models require stationary time series, a change point method called binary segmentation has been applied to automatically segment the given series of data into stationary subseries. Autoregressive models have then been applied to the resulting stationary subseries. In particular, it has been found that the volume measurement data could be described using an AR(1) process while the calorific value data are better modelled by an AR(2) process. The fitted AR process have then been validated by confirming that the experimental data are within the 95% confidence interval established by simulating a large number of data.

The simulated data have then been used to calculate the instrumental measurement uncertainty for the case with and without correlations. The results revealed an increase of typically 50 % in the uncertainty when including the temporal correlations. Considering the further diversification of the gas entering the gas grids in the foreseeable future, measurement data should not be treated as mutually independent when calculating the uncertainty to ensure safe and efficient operations of the gas grids. Further work is planned in the project 24GRD10 SmartGasNet to evaluate temporal correlations in case of non-stationary time series.

The authors would like to thank Robert Kruithof, Daniël Bos, Kjetil Folgerø and Astrid Marie Skålvik for helpful discussions during the preparation of this work.

The project 21GRD05 Met4H2 has received funding from the European Partnership on Metrology, co-financed from the European Union's Horizon Europe Research and Innovation Programme and by the Participating States.

The data used in this work have been shared with the authors by Gasunie for the purposes of the Met4H2 project.

Author contributions
Conceptualization: FG, ML, AvdV
Methodology: FG, ML
Software: FG, ML
Validation: FG
Formal analysis: FG, ML
Investigation: FG, ML
Resources: AvdV
Writing - Original draft: FG, AvdV, ML
Writing – Review & Editing:
Visualization: FG, ML
Supervision: AvdV
Project administration: AvdV
Funding acquisition: AvdV

References

1. International Organization for Legal Metrology, OIML R140 Measuring systems for gaseous fuel. (2007).
2. European Committee for Standardization, EN 1776 Gas infrastructure – Gas measuring systems – Functional requirements. (2015).
3. International Organization for Standardization, ISO 15112 – Energy determination. (2011).
4. A.M.H. van der Veen, K. Folgerø, F. Gugole, Measurement uncertainty in the totalisation of quantity and energy measurements in gas grids. (under review). https://doi.org/10.20944/preprints202412.0011.v1
5. R.H. Shumway and D.S. Stoffer, Time series analysis and its applications: with R examples, (EDP Springer International Publishing, 2017)
6. C. Chatfield, The analysis of time series: theory and practice (Chapman and Hall, 1975)
7. J. Bai, Estimating Multiple Breaks One at a Time, Economet. Theor., **13**(3), pp. 315–352, (1997). https://doi.org/10.1017/S0266466600005831.
8. BIPM, IEC, IFCC, ILAC, ISO, IUPAC, IUPAP, OIML, Evaluation of measurement data – Guide to the expression of uncertainty in measurement, JCGM 100:2008, GUM:1995 with minor corrections. (2008).
9. G.W. Bohrnstedt, A.S. Goldberger, On the exact covariance of products of random variables. J. Am. Stat. Assoc. **64**, pp. 1439–1442 (1969).

Low-concentration HCl gas mixtures in H_2: preparation and analysis

Corina Tabacaru [1], Daniel García-Nieto [1], Andrés Rojo [1], and Teresa E. Fernández [1]*

[1]Centro Español de Metrología, Reference Gas Laboratory, 28760 Tres Cantos, Madrid, Spain

Abstract. Measuring hydrogen chloride (HCl) impurities in hydrogen (H_2) produced by alkaline electrolysers is crucial in current "green" hydrogen systems. It aims to develop new gas standards and analytical methods, integrating both online and onsite monitoring and calibration at alkaline electrolyser facilities. These efforts are fundamental for setting industry-standard metrological practices that ensure reliable and consistent monitoring of hydrogen quality. Following strict standards such as ISO 14687:2019, which sets the quality requirements for hydrogen fuel and defines permissible contaminant levels like hydrogen chloride (HCl), highlights the importance of these initiatives. This study at Spanish Metrology Institute (CEM) aims to establish advanced capabilities for preparing and detecting hydrogen chloride (HCl) in hydrogen matrix mixtures at μmol/mol levels and below, as part of projects EPM 21GRD05 Met4H2 and the national Hydrogen Project-PRTR. To validate the in-house method, static gravimetric mixtures of HCl in hydrogen were prepared and analysed over a concentration range from 5 μmol/mol to 1 000 μmol/mol, revealing that while both gravimetric and analytical values align quite well at high concentrations, analytical measurements at lower levels report reduced HCl values-likely due to losses during successive dilutions.

1 Introduction

The transition to green hydrogen as a key energy source is growing rapidly, driven by its potential to decarbonize various sectors, including energy, transportation, and industry [1]. The EMP 21GRD05 Met4H2 project [2] addresses a critical need in the emerging hydrogen economy through one of the work packages, aims to address the challenges associated with hydrogen gas quality by developing methodologies and metrological frameworks that can be implemented at every stage of the hydrogen supply chain. The outcomes of this work will not only support the transition towards green hydrogen but will also facilitate the creation of a reliable infrastructure for hydrogen-based energy systems, strengthening trust in its role as a clean energy solution for the future.

As electrolysis becomes a key method for generating green hydrogen [3], the presence of impurities such as hydrogen chloride (HCl) in the produced hydrogen presents significant challenges [4]. Even trace amounts of HCl can negatively impact the purity and performance of hydrogen, potentially damaging infrastructure and limiting its use in sensitive applications. Therefore, ensuring the quality of hydrogen produced by electrolysis is essential, not only for optimizing process efficiency but also for ensuring the safety and reliability of hydrogen systems. In this aspect, ISO 14687:2019 [5] and UNE-EN 17124:2022 [6] provide essential guidelines for hydrogen fuel quality specifications and assurance.

As part of its involvement in the 21GRD05 Met4H2 project [2], the Reference Gas Laboratory of the National Metrology Institute of Spain (CEM) has carried out the preparation of primary reference gas mixtures (PRGM) of hydrogen chloride in hydrogen (HCl/H_2). These mixtures are prepared using the static gravimetric method, in accordance with ISO 6142:2015 [7], by carefully weighing the calculated mass of each component before introducing it into a gas cylinder. The PRGM will support the development and validation of a new analytical technique and provide traceable reference values for hydrogen quality testing laboratories.

2 Experimental

2.1 Preparation of standard gas mixtures

In the first place, as a preliminary step to preparation, an exhaustive study of cylinder passivation techniques was conducted, leading to the selection of ACULIFE® IV from Air Liquide wall treatment cylinders for the process (internal work carried out in CEM Reference Gas Laboratory within 21GRD05 Met4H2 EMP project) [2].

CEM has prior experience in preparing this type of mixture and has already set up an outdoor gas shed for

* Corresponding author: cntabacaru@cem.es

storing the pure gases, including H_2, N_2 and HCl. There, the pure HCl gas is connected to a control panel, where dry nitrogen is used as a purge gas. The HCl filling station is installed indoors, where nitrogen purging is performed before each filling to eliminate moisture traces. Additionally, modifications were made to the gas shed system to enable purging with dry nitrogen after replacing an empty HCl cylinder, ensuring precise and contamination-free gas preparation [8].

Standard gas mixtures are gravimetrically prepared at high pressure in 5 L aluminium alloy cylinders with appropriate passivation (ACULIFE® IV). To obtain low-concentration mixtures (µmol/mol), a multi-step dilution process is carried out, starting with pure hydrogen chloride (3.0 quality, Linde) and pure hydrogen (5.5 quality Praxair, 6.0 quality Linde). A detailed description of the filling process can be found in reference [8].

Before use, the cylinders were subjected to a vacuum of 10^{-2} mbar. Lower pressures are not reached to protect the internal treatment of the cylinders, as higher vacuum could potentially damage it.

2.2 Analysis of standard gas mixtures

The analytical measurements were performed with a ProCeas® analyser from AP2E/DURAG. It is an infrared spectrometer, based on optical feedback cavity enhanced absorption spectroscopy (OFCEAS) [9]. This custom-built instrument allows low level HCl and water (H_2O) analysis in various matrices (hydrogen, nitrogen, dry air and helium). It is equipped with two lasers: laser 1 for HCl concentrations below 10 µmol/mol and H_2O between 0 µmol/mol and 50 µmol/mol and laser 2 for HCl concentrations above 10 µmol/mol (up to 1 000 µmol/mol).

The measurement process begins by passing dry nitrogen through the OFCEAS analyser system for a minimum of 24 hours to reduce humidity as much as possible. Before starting the analysis, if the matrix of the mixture is another gas (H_2 in most cases), this gas is injected until the measurement stabilises. Furthermore, the pressure regulator is purged with the sample of interest (pressurising the dead volume and then depressurising it multiple times). After completing these steps, the cylinder is connected to the analyser system, and the gas sample is introduced with an outlet pressure of 1 bar with excess gas flow coming out of the vent (this is controlled with a rotameter).

3 Results and discussion

Previously, CEM gas laboratory was unable to analyse low-concentration mixtures, as the detection limit of the gas chromatography method used was approximately 900 µmol/mol [8]. This limitation has been overcome through the acquisition of the OFCEAS analyser mentioned above [10, 11].

For the purpose of testing the device three initial families of HCl/N_2 mixtures were prepared and analysed. Within the collaborative work of the project, one of the mixtures of 10 µmol/mol (HCl/N_2) was sent to the National Metrology Institute of the Netherlands (VSL). The measured HCl concentration reported by VSL was coherent with the analytical result obtained by CEM. Therefore, these mixtures served as a reference for assessing the system's response under controlled conditions.

Lately, several mixtures of HCl/H_2 were prepared and analysed over a wide concentration range as illustrated in Fig. 1.

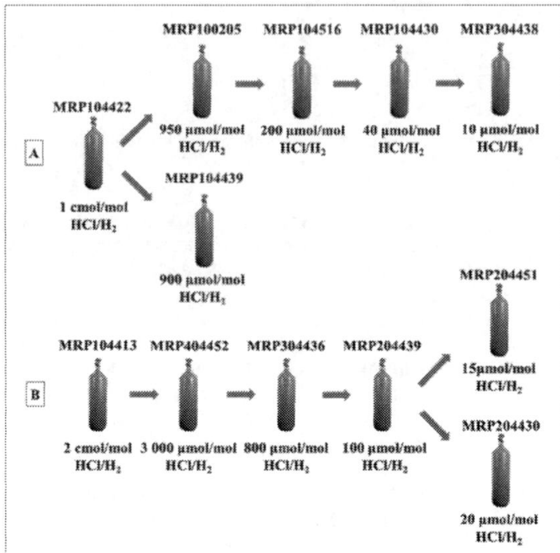

Fig. 1. Schematic representation of two sets of mixtures prepared through dilution steps, with the target HCl concentration indicated.

After preparation and analysis, the gravimetric and analytical values of HCl concentration in the mixtures were compared against each other. Although both values are similar for higher concentrations (e.g., around 900 µmol/mol), discrepancies were observed at lower levels (table 1). This is particularly notable in the low µmol/mol range, where the analytical results are below those expected according to gravimetry. There are several factors that could explain this discrepancy, most notably the loss of HCl during the successive dilutions required to prepare the low-concentration mixtures.

Table 1. Summary of the analysed samples.

Cylinder code	[HCl] (gravimetry) (µmol/mol)	[HCl] (OFCEAS) (µmol/mol)
MRP104439	920.91	919.78
MRP100205	919.11	919.56
MRP204430	20.17	13.90
MRP204451	16.08	9.23
MRP304438	9.71	4.03

Achieving a stable concentration value is a critical requirement for all these measurements. Due to the highly reactive nature of HCl, it was essential to use a short pipeline, and thoroughly purge the entire system, including the pressure regulators, prior to conducting measurements [12, 13].

A key challenge in OFCEAS analysis is the high gas consumption during measurement. The cylinders employed at CEM have a volume of 5 L, and despite preparing the standard gas mixtures at the maximum achievable pressure (close to 200 bar), this still constitutes a limiting factor. Fig. 2 and Fig. 3 present representative results of HCl determination carried out using the OFCEAS analyser.

Moreover, under these conditions, a minimum of 50 bar of the mixture is required to achieve stable measurements, which makes it challenging to undertake long-term stability studies of the mixtures, as initially planned.

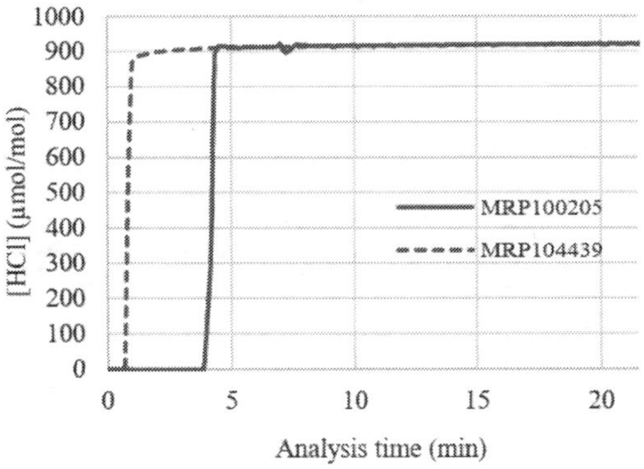

Fig. 2. OFCEAS measurement of two high-concentration mixtures.

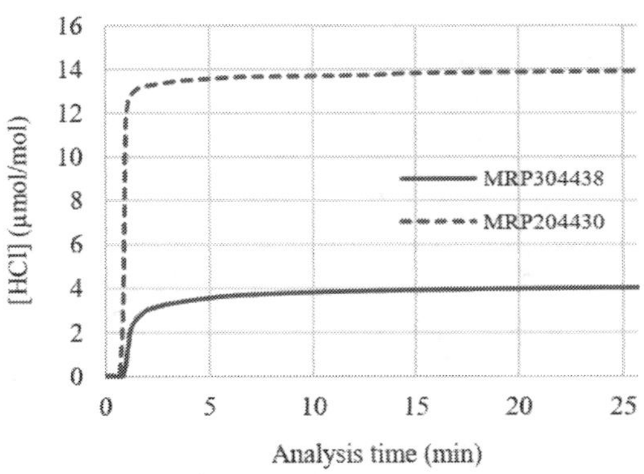

Fig. 3. OFCEAS analysis of two low-concentration mixtures.

4 Conclusion and further work

The CEM Reference Gas Laboratory has made significant progress in analytical techniques through the successful preparation and measurement of HCl/H_2 mixtures at the µmol/mol level. This achievement is especially significant as it represents an improvement over the previous analytical limit of 900 µmol/mol for HCl concentrations [8]. This current study builds upon that work, establishing a basis for the further development of the laboratory's hydrogen analysis methods, with a specific focus on detecting trace-level impurities such as HCl and H_2O in hydrogen. These impurities are critically important, as even small amounts can significantly affect the performance and quality of hydrogen, especially in applications such as fuel cell technology, hydrogen storage, and industrial processes.

A primary objective of this study is to address and optimize the preparation and analysis of low-concentration HCl mixtures (µmol/mol). We observed a discrepancy between the gravimetric values and analytical measurements, particularly at lower concentrations. This has been reported in previous works [13]. This discrepancy highlight the need for improvements in the preparation technique, especially during the final dilution steps, to ensure that the analytical results more accurately represent the true concentration of HCl in hydrogen mixtures. By optimizing the final dilution steps, we aim to reduce losses due to adsorption, enhance the reproducibility of results, and ensure that the analytical methods produce values more closely aligned with gravimetric concentrations. This refinement will not only improve the precision of HCl measurements but also strengthen the laboratory's capacity to detect trace-level impurities in hydrogen with greater accuracy and consistency.

Moreover, the improvement of the analysis process is crucial too. The use of treated sampling lines and pressure regulators with an appropriate coating such as SilcoNert® 2000 has demonstrated a reduction in HCl losses due to adsorption [12, 13]. It is also important to maintain minimal humidity both in the measurement system and in the mixtures [12, 13]. For the measurement system, this is already achieved by passing a continuous flow of dry nitrogen or hydrogen, as appropriate, before the analyses. For the mixtures, this could be improved by introducing a vacuum pump in the HCl filling station.

Moving forward, several key areas of focus will guide the next phase of this study. First, we will undertake a comprehensive validation of the existing analytical method to ensure its accuracy and precision across a broad spectrum of HCl concentrations. This validation process will involve refining the methodology to address potential limitations, particularly at trace concentrations.

Additionally, an ongoing stability study will be conducted to assess the long-term behavior and stability of HCl in H_2 mixtures at varying concentrations. This will ensure that prepared mixtures remain consistent over time, providing reliable analytical results.

We will also focus on improving the methodology for uncertainty evaluation. This will involve developing more robust procedures for quantifying uncertainties at different stages of the analytical process, thus improving the overall reliability and reproducibility of the results. Lastly, efforts will be made to expand the laboratory's capabilities to prepare and analyse HCl mixtures at the nanomol concentration level, enabling even greater sensitivity and precision in the detection of HCl impurities in hydrogen.

Through these efforts, this study aims to contribute significantly to advancing the laboratory's hydrogen analysis capabilities, ensuring more accurate and consistent impurity detection in hydrogen used for fuel and industrial applications.

This project 21GRD05 Met4H2 has received funding from the European Partnership on Metrology, co-financed from the

European Union's Horizon Europe Research and Innovation Programme and by the Participating States. Additionally, this work has been developed within the framework of the national Hydrogen Project, funded by MINTUR and the "European Union NextGenerationEU/PRTR". We sincerely thank Iris de Krom from VSL for her kindness and helpful contributions.

References

1. Q. Hassan, S. Algburi, A. Z. Sameen, H. M. Salman, M. Jaszczur, Green hydrogen: A pathway to a sustainable energy future. Int. J. Hydrogen Energy **50**, 310-333 (2024). https://doi.org/10.1016/j.ijhydene.2023.08.321

2. European Metrology project 21GRD05 Met4H2 Metrology for the hydrogen supply chain. https://met4h2.eu/

3. S. Dash, A. Singh K, J. S, V.H. Wilson D, E. D, S. K. Surapraraju, S. K. Natarajan, S. K. Natarajan, Advances in green hydrogen production through alkaline water electrolysis: A comprehensive review. Int. J. Hydrogen Energy **83**, 614-629 (2024). https://doi.org/10.1016/j.ijhydene.2024.08.157

4. Impact of impurities on water electrolysis: a review. H. Becker, J. Murawski, D. V. Shinde, I. E. L. Stephens, G. Hinds, G. Smith, 2023, Impact of impurities on water electrolysis: a review. Sustain. Energy Fuels **7**, 1565 (2023). https://doi.org/10.1039/d2se01517j

5. ISO 14687:2019 Hydrogen fuel quality - product specification. International Organization for Standardization (2019)

6. UNE-EN 17124:2022 Hydrogen fuel - Product specification and quality assurance for hydrogen refuelling points dispensing gaseous hydrogen - Proton exchange membrane (PEM) fuel cell applications for vehicles. Spanish Association for Standardisation (2022)

7. ISO 6142:2015 Gas analysis - Preparation of calibration gas mixtures - Part 1: Gravimetric method for Class I mixtures. International Organization for Standardization (2015)

8. A. Rojo, E. Santamaria, Preparation of hydrogen chloride in hydrogen standard gas mixtures for hydrogen purity requirements. International Congress of Metrology (2019) 20002. https://doi.org/10.1051/metrology/201920002

9. J. Morville, S. Kassi, M. Chenevier, D. Romanini, Fast, low-noise, mode-by-mode, cavity-enhanced absorption spectroscopy by diode-laser self-locking. Appl. Phys. B Lasers Opt. **80**, 1027 (2005). https://doi.org/10.1007/s00340-005-1828-z

10. K. Arrhenius, O. Büker, A. Fischer, S. Persijn, N. D Moore, Development and evaluation of a novel analyser for ISO14687 hydrogen purity analysis. Meas. Sci. Technol. **31**, 7 (2020). https://doi.org/10.1088/1361-6501/ab7cf3

11. C. Beurey, B. Gozlan, M. Carré, T. Bacquart, A. Morris, N. Moore, K. Arrhenius, H. Meuzelaar, S. Persijn, A. Rojo,A. Murugan, Review and Survey of Methods for Analysis of Impurities in Hydrogen for Fuel Cell Vehicles According to ISO 14687:2019. Front. Energy Res. **8**, 615149 (2021). https://doi.org/10.3389/fenrg.2020.615149

12. S. Persijn, E. Efremov, Sampling lines for HCl (VSL, Delft, The Netherlands). Output 1 - European Metrology project 17IND09 MetAMCII. https://empir.npl.co.uk/metamcii/wp-content/uploads/sites/43/2019/11/Sampling-lines-for-HCl-measurements.pdf

13. Deliverable D4 – Good practice guide on the handling and use of static HCl reference materials for end users, including a full uncertainty budget for providing the infrastructure to underpin the measurements of these priority AMCs (HCl, NH_3 and water vapour). European Metrology project 17IND09 MetAMCII. https://empir.npl.co.uk/metamcii/wp-content/uploads/sites/43/2021/09/D4-Good-practice-guide-on-the-handling-and-use-of-static-HCl-reference-materials.pdf

 https://doi.org/01.0150/epjconf/212532301110

Figures of merit of passive daytime radiative cooling materials

David Tichý [1*], *Lorenzo* Pattelli[2], *Chrysanthi* Efthymiou[3], *Margarita-Niki* Assimakopoulos[3], *Michal* Voldán[1]

[1]Czech Metrology Institute, Regional Branch Praha, Prague 102 00, Czech Republic
[2]Istituto Nazionale di Ricerca Metrologica (INRiM), Turin 101 35, Italy
[3]Department of Physics, National and Kapodistrian University of Athens, Athens 105 59, Greece

Abstract. Passive daytime radiative cooling (PDRC) materials represent an emerging technology that can provide sub-ambient cooling by dissipating heat as radiation through the long-wave infrared transparency window of the atmosphere. As such, they hold promise to alleviate our growing cooling needs and could find application in a broad range of areas. An increasing number of PDRC materials and applications is reported and tested each year. The fast-paced progress in this field also creates higher demand for reliable and universal methods for comparing the performance of novel materials and predicting their cooling abilities in different environments. However, clear figures of merit and standardised testing methods to evaluate real-world cooling performance are still lacking, so that the cooling performances of various novel PDRC materials presented in literature often cannot be compared. In this work, we review and discuss these issues from the specific viewpoint of the European Partnership on Metrology project PaRaMetriC, which aims at developing a metrological framework to classify and compare these materials.

1 Introduction

Reducing energy demands for cooling technologies has become one of the most relevant scientific challenges for sustainable development. Due to the imminent effects of global warming and growing urban areas, tripling of the cooling equipment installed capacity is expected before 2050 [1]. The prospect of the associated electricity consumption increase generates, among others, an urgent need for researching new cooling strategies and technologies. Passive radiative cooling (PRC) [2] process makes advantage of a spontaneous heat radiation towards a cold heatsink, which can potentially provide cooling of the material below the ambient temperature without the need of an external energy source. Key feature for utilizing PRC in cooling technologies is the ability of some materials to emit infrared radiation selectively in the wavelength range between 8 – 13 μm (long wave infrared atmospheric window, LWIR). Outer space can act as an infinite heat sink for thermal emitted radiation since the atmospheric gases don't have significant absorption bands in this range. An unobstructed access to a clear sky and high emissivity in the LWIR atmospheric window are therefore two main conditions for a successful PRC operation.

Thanks for this principle, reaching below-ambient temperatures by PRC during night is well documented since ancient times. On the other hand, passive daytime radiative cooling (PDRC) is far more challenging and was a subject of intensive research in the past decade. Achieving a net cooling effect under direct sunlight illumination [3] requires little to no absorptivity across the whole solar spectrum (0.3 – 2.5 μm). The well documented progress in both scientific understanding of PDRC phenomenon and development of its practical use (most prominently in cooling in the building sector [4]) brought many novel designs of PDRC materials [5], fabrication techniques and architectures of full-scale cooling systems [6-8]. However, there are still some shortcomings in the scientific coverage of the PDRC field, related to the adoption of inconsistent performance assessment methods and or the reporting of incomplete or incorrectly determined figures of merit, which makes it challenging to summarize the current state of the art [9]. Recognizing and overcoming these problems could help broadening the use of PDRC in real life and applying various scientific findings to address the current energy crisis. Overall, PDRC technology has the potential to reduce cooling energy demands and mitigate the urban heat island effect [10], significantly reducing cooling-related emissions of greenhouse gases while improving human comfort and air quality in urban environments. This study aims to identify the figures of merit for PDRC materials that can help define and expand the potential of this promising technology.

2 Coling performance assessment methods

Every year, more passive daytime radiative cooling materials and applications are reported and evaluated. Significant development in the field of PDRC in recent years creates an increased demand for accurate and universal methodologies for assessing the performance of innovative materials and forecasting their cooling

* Corresponding author: dtichy@cmi.gov.cz

capacities in varied situations. However, widely agreed methods have not been identified or validated yet. Bu *et al.* defines three main obstacles that result in inconsistencies in the measured data comparisons [9]: i) different measurement standards, ii) different experimental setups and iii) reporting different figures of merit for measured data. Figures of merit used in the majority of published studies are strongly dependent on both the experimental conditions and thermal properties of the materials, resulting in the current impossibility of comparing the performance of different materials directly against each other in a consistent way. In the following sections, frequently used figures of merit for PDRC materials will be described and various limitations associated with their use will be discussed.

2.1 Spectral properties

Considering the basics of PDRC, the spectral properties of the material are often used to characterise its suitability for these applications. The emissivity spectrum of the material has to be measured and its similarity with the ideal emitter models is then evaluated. Two options are most commonly used for designing PDRC materials: narrow-band emitter with high emissivity within 8 – 13 μm and broadband emitter with high emissivity within 4 – 25 μm. In both cases, the materials should have zero emissivity in the solar spectrum. Two main types of materials present specific advantages in different working conditions. Broadband emitters are able to radiate more heat outward, hence reaching potentially higher cooling powers, but only at a temperature above or slightly below the ambient. On the other hand, narrow-band emitters are suitable to realise larger sub-ambient temperature drops as their cooling power decreases more slowly with decreasing temperatures, and they are more radiatively insulated from atmospheric irradiance. Narrow-band emitters are therefore able to reach lower cooling temperature in absolute terms than broadband emitters [11]. However, broadband emitters can still be used for sub-ambient cooling, mostly in cold and dry areas with high atmospheric transmittance.

Some other ideal emissivity profiles have also been proposed, for instance featuring an additional drop between 9 and 10 μm to avoid radiative exchanges with the ozone absorption band in that wavelength range. However, such fine tailoring of the emissivity profile is difficult to achieve in actual samples [12].

Numeric analysis of different emissivity profiles and PDRC performance of the emitters can be also found in the work of Kecebas *et al.* [13]. According to their simulations, the ideal emissivity for reaching the lowest equilibrium temperature depends on the total heat load q acting on the surface coming from both radiative and non-radiative contributions. In the case of nearly insulated systems, values of q approach zero and lowest temperatures are reached when the emissivity is narrowed between 10 – 12 μm. However, with increasing q, the ideal emissivity broadens first to the usual narrow-band (8 – 13 μm) profile, and eventually to the broadband case.

Besides emissivity, solar reflectance is another parameter strongly correlated with PDRC performance. As suggested by Bu *et al.*, however, optical characterization and solar reflectivity measurements are often affected by common shortcomings in several recent studies on PDRC materials [9]. In ultraviolet-visible-near-infrared spectroscopy, standard reference samples are often measured prior to the actual PDRC material measurement, for calibration purposes. Unfortunately, most studies do not specify whether the reported reflectance values are absolute or relative to the reference standard. The reflectance of the standards is typically below 100 %, even within the specification of the manufacturers, which can lead to a significant reflectance overestimation if only relative values are reported. The approximation of the reflectivity of reference samples can lead to a critical underestimation of the overall solar absorption up to 25 %, introducing a systematic bias which affects the cooling performance prediction. It is therefore important to evaluate and include uncertainty estimation when presenting PDRC materials characterization.

Instead of reporting both infrared emissivity and solar reflectance values, spectral properties can be merged into one figure of merit. For example, Li *et al.* [14] proposed to use a simple metric called *RC*, which can be computed as:

$$RC = \varepsilon_{\text{sky}} - r\,(1 - R_{\text{solar}}), \qquad (1)$$

where ε_{sky} is the emissivity in the sky window, R_{solar} is a total reflectance in the solar spectrum, and r is the ratio of the solar irradiation power over the blackbody surface emissive power transmitted through the sky window. *RC* should be used to compare different PDRC materials at the same solar irradiation and weather conditions. The authors recommend using the "standard *RC*" by referring to a standard surface temperature of 300 K to calculate the emissivity, and using a standard r value of 10 (a typical peak solar irradiation of 1000 W m^{-2} and blackbody emissive power 100 W m^{-2}). The *RC* parameter has been used in various studies to compare different PDRC materials as it conveniently condenses the basic information about the emissivity and reflectance spectrum in one figure which does not depend on environmental conditions. However, the *RC* value cannot differentiate between broadband/narrow-band emitters, nor does it contemplate important aspects such as the angular dependence of the emissivity.

2.2 Cooling power

Cooling power P_{net} (W m^{-2}) is often reported as a result of a PDRC measurement or simulation. It can be calculated as an outcome of an energy balance of the PDRC surface (Eq. 2).

$$P_{\text{net}} = P_{\text{rad}} - P_{\text{atm}} - P_{\text{sun}} - P_{\text{nonrad}} \qquad (2)$$

Symbols on the right side of the equation represent thermal radiation power from the emitter, atmospheric and solar irradiations and contributions of the non-radiative heat transfer processes between the coating and ambient environment, respectively. The accuracy of P_{net} calculation however depends critically on the ability to correctly measure all contributing terms. When said contributions are approximated or neglected, the resulting P_{net} value might be misleading. Additionally, looking at Eq. 2, the final cooling power depends not only on the spectral properties of the material, but also on the experimental testing conditions and the other factors affecting PDRC performance. Therefore, when comparing various PDRC materials, it is not possible to rely solely on its cooling power as this quantity is largely dependent on the measurement conditions. Also, it should be noted that based on Eq. 2, an upper limit value for the cooling power attainable by an ideal PDRC material under ideal conditions (100% solar reflectance, perfect insulation from non-radiative heat gains) can in principle be estimated, which is typically reported at around 150 W m^{-2} [15].

For the experimental measurement of this quantity, Raman *et al.* [16] proposed a method to obtain P_{net} by heating a PDRC material using an external electric heating pad. Cooling power is then determined as the electric power dissipated by the heater when the temperature of the PDRC material equals the ambient temperature of the environment. To measure cooling power of a PDRC coating in real time, a feedback-controlled loop can be added to continuously tune the current flowing through the electric heater in such a way that the temperature of the coating under test matches that of the ambient air at all times. The measured value of the cooling power is correlated with the temperature fluctuations. This indicates that among other influences such as wind speed and solar irradiance, the accumulation of the heat in the measuring box or at the coating surface can also significantly affect the resulting cooling power, which is often reported as an average value from the whole cooling experiment.

This experimental approach to measure the cooling power of PDRC materials has some disadvantages. When reporting the experimental data, it is generally assumed that 100 % of the heat generated by the electric heater is transferred to the emitter and dissipated radiatively by it, i.e., assuming purely one-dimensional heat transfer from the heater to the cooled substrate. Any deviation from this condition can lead to significant cooling power overestimations and exaggerated cooling power claims. Possible solutions to this problem involve using more advanced heating systems with proper thermal guarding, as applied by Leroy *et al.* [17, 18].

Alternatively, the cooling power could be estimated using the controlled flux of a heat-transfer fluid kept in thermal contact with the backside of the emitter, as first exemplified in the work of Goldstein *et al.* [19]. An advantage of this method is that the inlet and outlet water temperatures can be measured with high accuracy, as well as the instantaneous flux. Moreover, the measured value would likely represent a conservative estimate, since any deviation from the ideal insulation of the system would result in an underestimation of the cooling power, rather than an overestimation.

2.3 Temperature reporting

The most basic characterization used during PDRC experimental tests is a direct temperature measurement. Several thermocouples are often used to monitor the temperature of the PDRC material surface or the substrates cooled down by it (T_s), to be compared with ambient temperature (T_{amb}). Most of the studies provide the results by showing just the lowest achieved temperature or more commonly a maximum temperature difference between T_s and T_{amb} (maximum temperature drop - MTD). The information about the temperature difference is beneficial for comparing various PDRC materials tested in similar working conditions or experiments with similar PDRC materials tested in various working conditions, but cannot be used for a more universal material comparison. Besides temperatures being strongly dependent on the experimental conditions, several shortcomings are also associated with the determination of T_{amb}, since its measurement depends critically on the placement of the thermocouple and its proper shielding from other external factors. Many of the exceptionally high temperature differences reported in the literature can probably be ascribed to significant overestimations of T_{amb}, obtained by measuring it under direct solar radiation, with insufficient shielding from other radiative and convective heat sources or by replacing T_{amb} with the "enclosure air temperature". When reporting the obtained temperature difference as an indicator of PDRC performance, it is therefore crucial to ensure accurate and consistent T_{amb} measurement [20]. This topic is also discussed in depth in a Viewpoint by Sui *et al.* [21], as well as other thermodynamic fundamentals of PDRC.

The term equilibrium temperature T_{eq} is also used for reporting in the literature. Most studies use this term referring to temperatures obtained under zero net cooling power conditions. Looking at Eq. 2, P_{net} and P_{rad} depend on the temperature of the material surface T_s, whereas P_{atm} depends on the ambient temperature T_{amb}. T_{eq} is therefore equal to T_s when cooling power $P_{net}(T_s) = 0$. Reaching the equilibrium condition can lead to T_{eq} being either lower or higher than T_{amb}. Ao *et al.* [22] considers the equilibrium temperature as a key parameter for PDRC performance, together with cooling power P_{net} at the ambient temperature T_{amb}. Working conditions of a PDRC material can be set either to reach the lowest equilibrium temperature T_{eq} or to obtain the highest cooling power P_{net} possible. As discussed before, spectral properties are the main parameter that can tune the performance of the PDRC material [23].

As a final remark, it should be noted that values of cooling power at T_{amb} and T_{eq} at $P_{net} = 0$ are typically presented as two alternative methods for the evaluation of the cooling performance of a PDRC material. However, their interpretation can be unified by considering them as two points on a single curve describing the dependence of the cooler temperature on the achieved cooling power. To obtain a more comprehensive characterisation of the cooler, more points of this curve should be reported [16], since the performance of PDRC materials can depend on the temperature of the emitter. Measuring more data points on the curve is on the other hand problematic due to the time needed for the temperature stabilisation of each value, which can lead to changes in external conditions and therefore to a distortion of the data, unless multiple copies of the same sample are tested simultaneously under different heating conditions

3 Conclusions

Summarizing of the current studies published on the topic of PDRC showed that the identification of universal figures of merit for PDRC materials remains as one of the major challenges in the field. Most of the studies suggest considering two basic indicators: maximum sub-ambient temperature drop and cooling power at ambient temperature, but a whole set of experimental conditions is needed to fully describe the PDRC performance of a given material. Some numerical methods have been suggested to approximately compare cooling materials using standard model atmospheres and other simplifications. However, for a more precise and effective comparison, the implementation of standard indoor or outdoor experimental test methods is needed in the scientific community, as well as the identification of a set of established PDRC materials with known properties [24], that should be tested in parallel with the other materials under study.

Acknowledgements

The project 21GRD03 PaRaMetriC received funding from the European Partnership on Metrology, co-financed by the European Union's Horizon Europe Research and Innovation Programme and from the Participating States.

References

1. Global Cooling Watch 2023. United Nations Environment Programme. (2023). https://doi.org/10.59117/20.500.11822/44243
2. X. Yin, R. Yang, G. Tan, S. Fan, Terrestrial radiative cooling: Using the cold universe as a renewable and sustainable energy source. Science **370**, 786 (2020). https://doi.org/10.1126/science.abb0971
3. M. Chen, D. Pang, X. Chen, H. Yan, Y. Yang, Passive daytime radiative cooling: Fundamentals, material designs, and applications. EcoMat **4**, 12153 (2022). https://doi.org/10.1002/eom2.12153
4. L. Chen, K. Zhang, M. Ma, S. Tang, F. Li, X. Niu, Sub-ambient radiative cooling and its application in buildings. Build. Simul. **13**, 1165 (2020). https://doi.org/10.1007/s12273-020-0646-x
5. X. Yu, J. Chan, C. Chen, Review of radiative cooling materials: Performance evaluation and design approaches. Nano Energy **88**, 106259 (2021). https://doi.org/10.1016/j.nanoen.2021.106259
6. D. Xu, S. Boncoeur, G. Tan, J. Xu, H. Qian, D. Zhao, Energy saving potential of a fresh air pre-cooling system using radiative sky cooling. Build. Simul. **15**, 167 (2022). https://doi.org/10.1007/s12273-021-0802-y
7. A. Aili, D. Zhao, J. Lu, Y. Zhai, X. Yin, G. Tan, R. Yang, A kW-scale, 24-hour continuously operational, radiative sky cooling system: Experimental demonstration and predictive modeling. Energy Convers. Manag. **186**, 586 (2019). https://doi.org/10.1016/j.enconman.2019.03.006
8. D. Zhao, A. Aili, X. Yin, G. Tan, R. Yang, Roof-integrated radiative air-cooling system to achieve cooler attic for building energy saving. Energy Build. **203**, 109453 (2019). https://doi.org/10.1016/j.enbuild.2019.109453
9. K. Bu, X. Huang, X. Li, H. Bao, Consistent Assessment of the Cooling Performance of Radiative Cooling Materials. Adv. Funct. Mater. **33**, 2307191 (2023). https://doi.org/10.1002/adfm.202307191
10. L. Carlosena, Á. Ruiz-Pardo, J. Feng, O. Irulegi, R.J. Hernández-Minguillón, M. Santamouris, On the energy potential of daytime radiative cooling for urban heat island mitigation. Sol. Energy **208**, 430 (2020). https://doi.org/10.1016/j.solener.2020.08.015
11. M. Zeyghami, D.Y. Goswami, E. Stefanakos, A review of clear sky radiative cooling developments and applications in renewable power systems and passive building cooling. Sol. Energy Mater. Sol. Cells **178**, 115 (2018). https://doi.org/10.1016/j.solmat.2018.01.015
12. C. Xu, X. Ao, B. Zhao, G. Pei, A novel selective emissivity spectrum for radiative sky cooling. Sol. Energy Mater. Sol. Cells **232**, 111380 (2021). https://doi.org/10.1016/j.solmat.2021.111380
13. M.A. Kecebas, P. Menguc, K. Sendur, Spectral Emissivity Profiles for Radiative Cooling. ACS App. Opt. Mat. **2**, 1010 (2024). https://doi.org/10.1021/acsaom.3c00092
14. X. Li, J. Peoples, Z. Huang, Z. Zhao, J. Qiu, X. Ruan, Full Daytime Sub-ambient Radiative Cooling in Commercial-like Paints with High Figure of Merit. Cell Rep. **1**, 100221 (2020). https://doi.org/10.1016/j.xcrp.2020.100221
15. E. Rephaeli, A. Raman, S. Fan, Ultrabroadband Photonic Structures To Achieve High-Performance Daytime Radiative Cooling. Nano Lett. **13**, 1457 (2013). https://doi.org/10.1021/nl4004283
16. A.P. Raman, M.A. Anoma, L. Zhu, E. Rephaeli, S. Fan, Passive radiative cooling below ambient air temperature under direct sunlight. Nat. **515**, 540 (2014). https://doi.org/10.1038/nature13883

17. A. Leroy, B. Bhatia, C.C. Kelsall, A. Castillejo-Cuberos, M. Di Capua H, L. Zhao, L. Zhang, A.M. Guzman, E.N. Wang, High-performance subambient radiative cooling enabled by optically selective and thermally insulating polyethylene aerogel. Sci. Adv. **5**, 9480 (2019). https://doi.org/10.1126/sciadv.aat9480
18. A. Leroy, B. Bhatia, J. Sircar, E.N. Wang, Thermal transport in solar-reflecting and infrared-transparent polyethylene aerogels. Int. J. Heat Mass Transf. **184**, 122307 (2022). https://doi.org/10.1016/j.ijheatmasstransfer.2021.122307
19. E.A. Goldstein, A.P. Raman, S. Fan, Sub-ambient non-evaporative fluid cooling with the sky. Nat. Energy **2**, 17143 (2017). https://doi.org/10.1038/nenergy.2017.143
20. L. Zhou, X. Yin, Q. Gan, Best practices for radiative cooling. Nat. Sustain **6**, 1030 (2023). https://doi.org/10.1038/s41893-023-01170-0
21. C. Sui, P.-C. Hsu, Standardizing the Thermodynamic Definition of Daytime Subambient Radiative Cooling. ACS Energy Lett. **9**, 2997 (2024). https://doi.org/10.1021/acsenergylett.4c00909
22. X. Ao, M. Hu, B. Zhao, N. Chen, G. Pei, C. Zou, Preliminary experimental study of a specular and a diffuse surface for daytime radiative cooling. Sol. Energy Mater. Sol. Cells **191**, 290 (2019). https://doi.org/10.1016/j.solmat.2018.11.032
23. Z. Huang, X. Ruan, Nanoparticle embedded double-layer coating for daytime radiative cooling. Int. J. Heat Mass Transf. **104**, 890 (2017). https://doi.org/10.1016/j.ijheatmasstransfer.2016.08.009
24. H. Xin, M. Jyotirmoy, R. Aaswath, Do-it-yourself radiative cooler as a radiative cooling standard and cooling component for device design. J. Photonics Energy **12**, 012112 (2021). https://doi.org/10.1117/1.JPE.12.012112

Metrological characterization of standards – plastic films, which are used for calibration of nano volume spectrophotometers

Veljko Zarubica [1*], *Edvard Kubičela*[1], *Boban Zarkov*[2] and *Milesa Srećković*[3]

[1]Laboratory for calibration and validation, Analysis d.o.o, Japanska 4 Belgrade, Serbia
[2] Bureau of measures and precious metals, Mike Alasa 14 Belgrade, Serbia
[3]Faculty of Electrical Engineering, Belgrade,Serbia

Abstract. UV-VIS spectrophotometers, including nano drop (volume) spectrophotometers, provide an answer to all challenges in scientific and industrial laboratories, whether for pharmaceutical, chemical or service laboratories, all the way to more complex applications such as quantification of DNA, RNA, and protein per second, using only 1-2 μL of the sample. Certified reference materials are used to check the measurement capabilities of nanodrop spectrophotometers and other analytical instruments. Since these are solutions, which by themselves are not practical in terms of handling, stability, availability, we were thinking of using materials for their calibration, which would have more suitable properties than the solutions. We decided to use plastic films, which are thin enough not to be a problem during manipulation and measurement, which are stable in terms of determining the regular absorbance, which are optically neutral in the wider spectrum of optical radiation, and which are temperature stable and do not change their metrological characteristics during prolonged exposure to light. The paper evaluates all these influential characteristics and presents the budget of measurement uncertainty of plastic films in the UV part of the optical radiation spectrum at wavelengths of 260 nm and 280 nm (Fig.6). The term "metrologically characterized materials" represent equivalent of the materials, with precisely define regular absorbance (e.g., absorption), as well as estimated influential parameters which may appear, thus contributing to the uncertainty of the measurement.

1 INTRODUCTION

Calibration of Nano volume spectrophotometers is usually performed with some of the standard reference solutions. It is foreseen by the manufacturer of these instruments, that the mentioned solutions are applied for one-time use. After using these solutions, any excess solution is thrown away, which is basically the negative side of these SRMs. Of course, the other negative side of this method of calibration is the high price of the SRM. Our wish was to try to find a solution, namely SRM, such that the price of SRM is acceptable and that there is a possibility of using these SRM for a longer period. In this way, we would be able to calibrate Nano volume spectrophotometers with a completely different type of standard reference materials - foils. Our goal was to characterize these foils metrologically and present them as CRMs, which will be able to be used for a long period of time, without losing, or in the best case, degrading, their metrological properties, especially in terms of long-term stability, accuracy of reproducing the standard values etc. Before the characterization itself, the mentioned standard reference materials-foils were defined in terms of their composition analysis. We used an IR spectrophotometer with Fourier transform (FT-IR) to analyse the composition of the mentioned foils in detail.

Fig. 1. Spectral analysis by FT-IR plastic foils

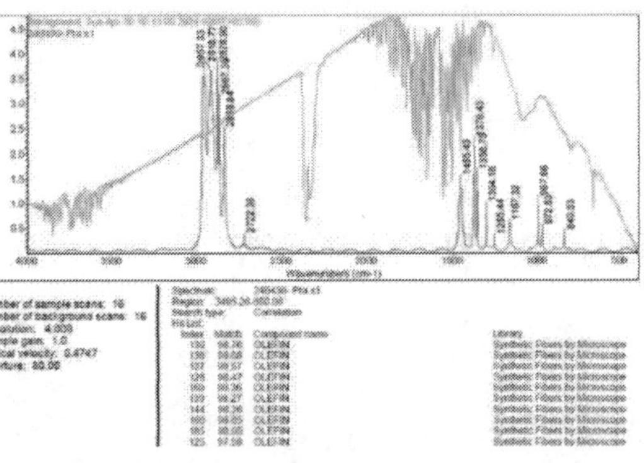

The results of the analysis are presented in Figure 1. It was important to determine the composition of the mentioned foils to see their hygroscopicity and resistance to UV radiation. It was found that they are olefins based on polypropylene, which represent materials with a poor hygroscopic characteristic and a very good characteristic of resistance to UV radiation, which is what we needed, because the key wavelengths for the application of these spectrophotometers were 260 nm and 280 nm. After analysing the foils, the metrological characterization of the foils was started:

* Corresponding author: veljko.zarubica@analysis.rs

repeatability, homogeneity, exposure of the foils to sunlight and temperature influence.

2 Measurement Equipment and Methods

The measuring equipment in Laboratory for calibration and validation, Analysis d.o.o includes: sets of standard reference materials as standards of spectral transmittivity coefficients (Figure 2. One standard set with tree different foils).

First task is measuring uncertainty of optical plastic foils for absorbtion coefficient: 0,1A, 0,2A and 0,3A. We usually split the operating range in three ranges. The measuring run means 10 measuring points and comparison with certificates. We usually apply Xenon flash lamp. Various spectrometer types demand different procedures. To determine the metrological characteristics of optical plastic foils, a primary spectrophotometric system was used in the UV/VIS part of the spectrum of optical radiation from 190 nm to 1100 nm. The source of optical radiation is a xenon flash lamp, with a single monochromator and a double split beam. A semiconductor cell was used as a detector. The influencing parameters that occur during the measurement of the spectral coefficient of absorbance, i.e. absorption, of optically neutral filters are as follows:

- homogeneity, exposure, temperature and atmospheric influences, long and short-term stability and the influence of dispersion.

In Laboratory Analysis d.o.o. a set of optically neutral foils type FOL1, FOL2 and FOL 3 of different values of spectral coefficient of absorption, were measured by placing a foil several micrometres thick on a plastic frame of appropriate dimensions of 25mm x 55mm.

2.1 Reproducibility determination of measurement of spectral coefficient absorption and wavelength setting

The determination of the repeatability of the measurement of the spectral coefficient of absorbance and the adjustment of the wavelength is carried out using filters of optical neutral foils in the UV and VIS areas of optical radiation.

Fig. 2. Absorption spectral characteristics foils type FOL

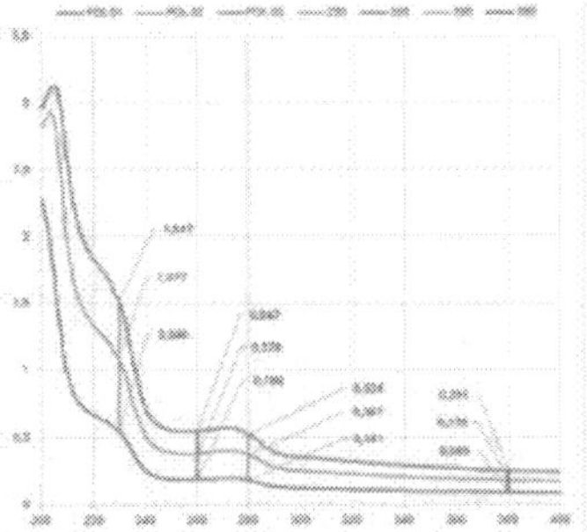

Reproducibility is performed in the UV part of the spectrum at wavelengths of 260 nm and 280 nm, while in the VIS part spectrum is performed at the beginning, middle and end of the VIS optical range. However, VIS optical range is not presented in this paper because the emphasis is in the UV part of the optical radiation. Which wavelengths we choose depends on the method used by spectrophotometer users. Since these are optically neutral foils, it is expected that at the mentioned wavelengths, the coefficient of spectral transparency is approximately the same value, nominally for foil (01) 0,20A, foil (02) 0,40A and foil (03) 0,60A. The spectral characteristics of our foils are shown in Fig 2.

Reproducibility is determined by repeating measurements after 24 and 48 hours, when talking about short-term stability, that is, measuring the foil over two years, when talking about long-term stability.

The paper was prepared during last two years, because the recalibration of plastic foils should be for one year, and in the worst case, 2 years.

The Fig. 3, 4 and 5 and table 1 show the absorption values of the filter foils obtained for monitoring over the course of one to two years.

Fig.3 FOL1

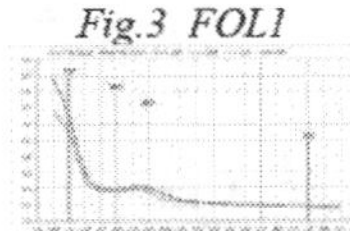

Fig.4 FOL2

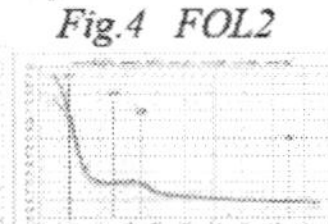

Fig.5 FOL3

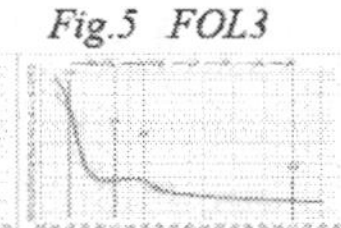

Table 1. Absorption values of the filter foils

Measuring the spectral coefficient of absorbance at a determined stability during a period of one year	FOL1		
	230 nm	260 nm	280 nm
Average value of spectral absorbance coefficient in 2022	0,5476	0,1833	0,1787
Average value of spectral absorbance coefficient in 2024	0,6505	0,1968	0,2052
Δ Absolute deviation	0,1029	0,0135	0,0264
Relative deviation of measurements (%)	18,79	7,39	14,79
Measuring the spectral coefficient of absorbance at a determined stability during a period of one year	FOL2		
	230 nm	260 nm	280 nm
Average value of spectral absorbance coefficient in 2022	1,0844	0,3848	0,3725
Average value of spectral absorbance coefficient in 2024	1,1980	0,4004	0,3934
Δ Absolute deviation	0,1136	0,0156	0,0209
Relative deviation of measurements (%)	10,47	4,05	5,60
Measuring the spectral coefficient of absorbance at a determined stability during a period of one year	FOL3		
	230 nm	260 nm	280 nm
Average value of spectral absorbance coefficient in 2022	1,5208	0,5489	0,5267
Average value of spectral absorbance coefficient in 2024	1,6415	0,5586	0,5594
Δ Absolute deviation	0,1208	0,0097	0,0326
Relative deviation of measurements (%)	7,94	1,77	6,19

Based on the results obtained over a period of 2 years, depending on which wavelength we are talking about, it can be seen that the relative deviation of the measured

absorbance values differs significantly between foils, and also the absorbance values for the same foil during a time period of 2 years.
Monitoring these foils for a period of less than a year gave much better results, showing that if these foils were to be used as a working standard, their calibration would have to be done for at least a year. We will show that in the further text of this paper. On Fig. 6 to 8 show the spectral characteristics of the absorption coefficient for three different filter foils, as well as the absorption values at precisely determined wavelength values monitored over the course of one year. Values are much better, which can be seen from Table 2. The RSD values, ie the standard deviations of the results in a period of one year, are significantly better.

Fig. 6. FOL 1 *Fig. 7. FOL 2* *Fig. 8. FOL 3*

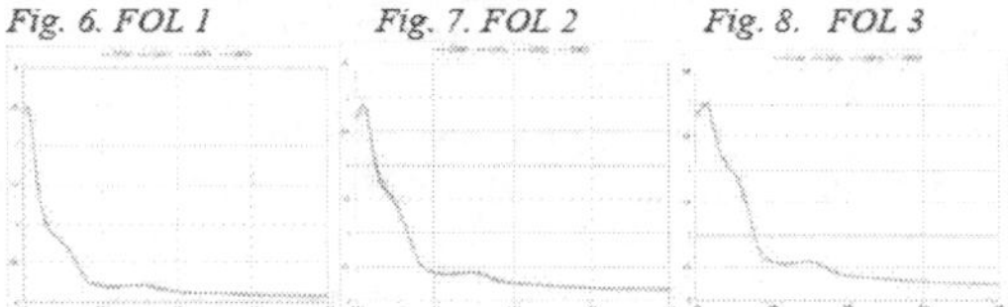

Table 2. Stability of coefficient absorbance during one year

Measuring the spectral coefficient of absorbance at a determined stability during a period of one year	FOL1		
	230 nm	260 nm	280 nm
240104	0,2275	0,5425	0,5323
240311	0,2244	0,5383	0,5275
240521	0,2204	0,5371	0,5226
240926	0,2277	0,5267	0,5194
241129	0,2233	0,5353	0,5137
Average τ	0,2247	0,0049	0,5231
u component of measurement uncertainty of stability	0,0070	0,0050	0,0059
u_{ave}	0,0104		
Measuring the spectral coefficient of absorbance at a determined stability during a period of one year	FOL2		
	230 nm	260 nm	280 nm
240104	0,0640	0,4018	0,4085
240311	0,0641	0,4017	0,4087
240521	0,0632	0,3990	0,4048
240926	0,0656	0,3999	0,3999
241129	0,0652	0,3924	0,3987
Average τ	0,0644	0,3989	0,4041
u component of measurement uncertainty of stability	0,0078	0,0050	0,0060
u_{ave}	0,0110		
Measuring the spectral coefficient of absorbance at a determined stability during a period of one year	FOL3		
	230 nm	260 nm	280 nm
240104	0,0215	0,2766	0,2745
240311	0,0229	0,2785	0,2782
240521	0,0230	0,2787	0,2784
240926	0,0223	0,2722	0,2710
241129	0,0228	0,2707	0,2709
Average τ	0,0225	0,2754	0,2746
u component of measurement uncertainty of stability	0,0142	0,0069	0,0069
u_{ave}	0,0173		

2.2 Determination of foil homogenity

The homogeneity test of optically neutral films is based on the method of determining the spectral absorbance of films at different positions, i.e. different points on the active surface of the film. Since these are relatively small dimensions of the active surfaces of the foils, the homogenity test is performed in small increments of a few mm to the left, right, up and down in relation to the central point of the foil, with a beam diameter of 1 to 2 mm. In this way, the best coverage of the active surface of the foil is achieved. The number of measuring points, of course, will depend on the size of the active surface, which in our case amounted to 5 measuring positions. The illumination of the measuring foil was achieved by the method shown in Figure 9. The integration sphere evenly illuminates the filter, where a part of the transmitted optical radiation passes through the telescope and reaches the photocell. The telescope is positioned to define the measuring field. In Figure 9. an optical diagram of the measurement method for checking the homogeneity of the filter is presented. The telescope consists of a collecting lens, an aperture mirror, a colorimetric lens and an eyepiece, which can be used to more easily define the measuring field on the filter. A collimator lens is needed to form a uniform light beam to illuminate the photocell evenly. An aperture and an aperture mirror are needed to define the measuring field. From the photocell, the signal is routed to a voltmeter via a transimpedance amplifier. The filter, which is located directly at the exit of the integration sphere, is located on a movable support with
a scale applied. The carrier can be driven manually along the x,y axis with the possibility of fine translation in steps of 1 mm. In this way, it is possible to test the homogeneity of the filter at different points. All measurements were performed in the Directorate of Measures and Precious Metals.

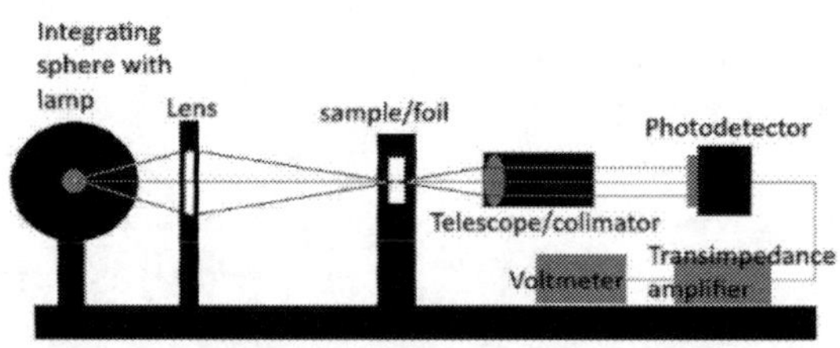

Fig. 9. Schematic representation of the method for verifying the homogeneity of filters of spectral coefficient of absorbance standards.

Table.3 Measurement uncertainty, resulting from inhomogenity of the three spectrophotometric filter fols

Measuring of the spectral coefficient absorbance on different position on the foil surface	FOL1	FOL2	FOL3
Mean valus of 5 different postions	**0,2270**	**0,6403**	**0,6306**
u – component of measurement uncertainty due to inhomogenity surface of foils	0,0000 6	0,0019	0,0025
U_{ave}	0,0032		

https://doi.org/01.0150/epjconf/(1(53(30111(

Based on the measured values of the spectral coefficient of absorbance at each point of the active surface for each film, the values of the measurement uncertainty of the measurement, which originate from the inhomogeneity of the filter, were obtained. Table 3 presents the calculated values of the measurement uncertainties for all three spectrophotometric optically neutral films separately, as well as the overall measurement uncertainty.

2.3 Determination of exposure of light radiation influence

The method of determining the influence parameter resulting from short-term exposure of spectrophotometric filters to optical radiation consisted in continuous exposure of all three spectrophotometric optically neutral foil filters to radiation in a period of 24 hours, with measurements of the spectral coefficient of absorbance performed before and after exposure. The measurements were performed on the primary spectrophotometric system at three different wavelengths of 230nm, 260nm and 280nm (Tables 4. and 5.). The reference conditions under which the measurements were carried out are as follows:

Table 4. Measuring the spectral coefficient of absorbance at a determined wavelength before light exposure	FOL1		
	230 nm	260 nm	280 nm
1	0,2275	0,6425	0,6323
2	0,2244	0,6383	0,6275
3	0,2204	0,6371	0,6226
Average value of spectral absorbance	0,2241	0,6393	0,6274
Relative deviation of measurement (%)	1,58	0,45	0,77

Table 5. Measuring the spectral coefficient of absorbance at a determined wavelength after light exposure	FOL1		
	230 nm	260 nm	280 nm
240104	0,2277	0,6425	0,4085
240311	0,2233	0,6383	0,4087
240521	0,2242	0,6371	0,4048
Average τ	0,2255	0,6393	0,4041
Relative deviation of measurement (%)	1,05	0,45	0,77
u component of measurement uncertainty of stability	0,0004	0,0028	0,0031
u_{ave}	0,0019		

u_{ave}- The mean value of the measurement uncertainty, which arises from the exposure of light for a given set of foils

2.4 Determination of temperature influence

The method of determining the temperature effects on spectrophotometric filters-films is performed using the primary spectrophotometric system and consists in measuring the spectral coefficient of absorbance of standard-spectrophotometric films at a room temperature of 20.5 °C and at a temperature of 7.5 °C at several different values of wavelengths of 230 nm, 260 nm and 280 nm.

The measurement was performed on a set of three foils FOL1, FOL2 and FOL3 with nominal values of spectral absorbance coefficient of (01) 0,20A, foil (02) 0,40A and foil (03) 0.60A.

The main problem of this method was to maintain the temperature within the given limits. The method consisted in determining the values of the spectral coefficient of absorbance at a temperature of 20.5°C before cooling the standard foils at a temperature of 7.5°C, and then comparing the values obtained. Why did they go for such a temperature interval? Primarily due to the possible impact of condensation formation or dew of the standard foil, which would lead to an error in reading the value of the spectral absorbance coefficient. It has been shown that the foils have quite satisfactory characteristics in terms of temperature influences. Very small deviations of measurement uncertainties at different temperatures were obtained, which are shown in Tables 6 and 7. The difference was only 0.00017 of the spectral absorbance coefficient.

Table 6. Measuring on 20,5 °C

Measuring results spectral coefficient absorbance on 20.5 °C	FOL 1	FOL 2	FOL 3
Mean value of series at 6 measuring	**0,2255**	**0,6288**	**0,6155**
Standard deviation	0,00004	0,00007	0,00003
RSD %	0,00016	0,00011	0,00005
Measurement uncertainty	0,00009	0,00006	0,00003
Uav	0,00011		

Table 7. Measuring on 7,5 °C

Measuring results spectral coefficient absorbance on 7,5 °C	FOL 1	FOL 2	FOL 3
Mean value of series at 6 measuring	**0,2222**	**0,6322**	**0,6161**
Standard deviation	0,00010	0,00011	0,00007
RSD %	0,00044	0,00017	0,00012
Measurement uncertainty	0,00025	0,00010	0,00007
Uav	0,00028		

2.5 The Influence of all components measuring uncertainty of the spectral absorbance of standard filter-foil (budget of measurement uncertainty)

Based on the measurements of all the influencing parameters due to the determination of the metrological characteristics of the standard filter films, we have obtained an overall assessment of the measurement uncertainty of the filter films themselves. The individual components of the measurement uncertainties are presented in Tables 8, 9 and 10, which also represents the budget measurement uncertainty of the spectral coefficient absorbance for each filter foil.

Tables 8, 9 and 10 show budget measurement uncertainty of the spectral absorbance coefficient for each filter foil

Table 8. The source of measurement uncertainty	FOL1	
	Contribution of standard uncertainty (Type A)	Contribution of standard uncertainty (Type B)
Component of measurement uncertainty of spectrophotometric system (dispersion of results, drift, stray light, resolution, fault radiation, setting wavelength...)		0,00104
Long stability of the results of measurement of spectral coefficient of absorbance after one year	0,0104	
Component of measurement uncertainty of homogeneity of filter structure	0,0006	
Component of measurement uncertainty of exposure of light radiation	0,0004	
Component of measurement uncertainty of temperature influence	0,0017	
Standard uncertainty by measurement of spectral absorbance coefficient	0,0106	0,00104
Combined uncertainty of the measurements of the absorbance coefficient with k=2	0,0213	

Table 9. The source of measurement uncertainty	FOL2	
	Contribution of standard uncertainty (Type A)	Contribution of standard uncertainty (Type B)
Component of measurement uncertainty of spectrophotometric system (dispersion of results, drift, stray light, resolution, fault radiation, setting wavelength...)		0,00104
Long stability of the results of measurement of spectral coefficient of absorbance after one year	0,0110	
Component of measurement uncertainty of homogeneity of filter structure	0,0019	
Component of measurement uncertainty of exposure of light radiation	0,0028	
Component of measurement uncertainty of temperature influence	0,0002	
Standard uncertainty by measurement of spectral absorbance coefficient	0,0115	0,00104
Combined uncertainty of the measurements of the absorbance coefficient with k=2	0,0231	

Table 10. The source of measurement uncertainty	FOL3	
	Contribution of standard uncertainty (Type A)	Contribution of standard uncertainty (Type B)
Component of measurement uncertainty of spectrophotometric system (dispersion of results, drift, stray light, resolution, fault radiation, setting wavelength...)		0,00104
Long stability of the results of measurement of spectral coefficient of absorbance after one year	0,0173	
Component of measurement uncertainty of homogeneity of filter structure	0,0025	
Component of measurement uncertainty of exposure of light radiation	0,0031	
Component of measurement uncertainty of temperature influence	0,0001	
Standard uncertainty by measurement of spectral absorbance coefficient	0,0177	0,00104
Combined uncertainty of the measurements of the absorbance coefficient with k=2	0,0356	

3 Conclusion

The purpose and intention of this paper was to expand the scope of work of accredited laboratories in the field of spectrophotometric measurements and to follow the modern tendency of nano measurements using instruments that provide this possibility - nano drop spectrophotometers. The idea was to implement standard filters, which would be a means of transferring values from higher hierarchical levels of spectrophotometric measurements to lower levels, i.e. to nano drop spectrophotometers, and thus carry out metrological traceability to the national standard. In addition to many materials, the choice fell on foils, which perfectly match the measurement geometry of nanodrop spectrophotometers and can be characterized relatively easily by metrology. This is how the process of metrological characterization of standard filter foils began, which, after the realization of this project, began to be a means of transmitting the values of the spectral coefficient of absorbance, i.e. absorption. In this way, we have realized a new type of spectrophotometric filters, which will be used for the calibration of nano drop spectrophotometers. At the same time, we have methodologically simplified the process of calibration of nanodrop spectrophotometers, and also reduced the cost of the calibration process. The filter film standards themselves have proven to be good standards in terms of metrological characteristics, both in the short and long term. The aim of this paper was primarily to create a new, cheaper and sufficiently reliable tool for the calibration of nano drop spectrophotometers. In order to achieve this, it was necessary to determine all relevant metrological parameters in terms of metrological characterization of the given standard-filter films, i.e. setting up methods for the characterization of filter films, measurement, analysis of the results obtained, as well as the estimation of the calculation of the measurement uncertainty of filter films. In this way, the story of realization of standard sets obtained from plastic foils is wrapped up.

4 References

1. F. J. J. Clarke, High-Accuracy Spectrophotometry at the National Physical Laboratory, Journal of Research

of the NBS-A. Physics and Chemistry, Vol. 76A, No.5, sptember-october 1972

2. International Vocabulary of Metrology, Fourth edition – Committee Draft (VIM4 CD), 11 January 2021 © JCGM 2021 – All rights reserved

3. K.D. Mielenz, K,L. Eckerle, R.P. Madden, J. Reader, New Reference Spectrophotometer, Applied Optics, p.p.1630, vol.12,No.7, July 1973

4. R. Mavrodineanu, J.R. Baldwin, NBS Special Publication 260-68, Standard Reference Materials, Metal-on-Quartz Filters As a Standard Reference Material For Spectrophotometry-SRM 2031, April 1980

5. Kenneth L. Eckerle, Jack J. Hsia, Victor R. Weidner, Absorbance MAP Service, NBS Special Publications 692, march 1985

6. W.H. Venable, Spectrophotometric Standards, Journal of Research of the National Bureau of Standards, vol. 76A, No. 5, sptember-october 1972

7. V. Zarubica, P. Vukadin, V. Škerović, The role of metrological provision in the use of absorption spectrophotometers for medical applications, International Conference: Quality and Reliability Management, Book 1. Belgrade, 26-27 June 2002

8. V. Zarubica, P. Vukadin, V. Škerović, Metrological protection of spectrophotometers, Tehnika-Journal of the Union of Engineers and Technicians of Yugoslavia, 2/2002

9. Organisation Internationale de Métrologie Légal, Bureau International de Métrologie Légal, Draft revision of International Document OIML D11, General Requirements for electronic measuring instruments, Technical committee OIML TC 5, 1994

10. F. Manoochehri, E. Ikonen, High-accuracy spectrometer for measurement of regular spectral absorbance, Applied Optics, Vol. 34, 1995.

11. T. C. Larson, S. S. Bruce, A. C. Parr, Spectroradiometric Detector Measurements, NIST Special Publication 250-41, February 1998

12. J. L. Gardner, Astigmatism cancellation in Spectroradiometry, Metrologia (volume 28), 1991.

13. J. Bastie, Les réalisations de l'INM dans les domaines de la radiométrie et de la photométrie, Bulletin du bureau national de métrologie, Vol. 25, No 96, avril 1994.

14. NIST Technical Note 1438, Optical Radiation Measurement with Selected Detectors and Matched Electronic Circuits Between 200 nm and 20 m, April 2001.

15. B. N. Taylor, C. E. Kuyatt, Guidelines for Evaluating and Expressing the Uncertainty of the NIST Measurement Results, NIST Techical Note 1297, 1994.

16. V. Zarubica, P. Vukadin, V. Škerović, Lj. Vulićević, M. Srećković, Calibration of absorption spectrophotometers in the UV/VIS region of the optical spectrum, Congress of Metrologists 2007, Zlatibor 2007, Serbia

17. V. Škerović, P. Vukadin, V. Zarubica and Lj. Zeković, Realization of a primary spectrophotometric system, Meas. Sci. Technol. 19 085103 (6pp), Print publication: Issue 8 (August 2008), Received 18 October 2007, in final form 8 May 2008, Published 10 July 2008

18. V. Škerović, V. Zarubica, B. Kasalica, S. Stojadinović, I. Belca, Metrological Assurance of Biodeviced – The New Method of Calibration of Biochemical Analizers, Analytical Letters, Certificate of Printing submitted on 10.09.2008., paper number 41180, Printing by the end of 2008.

 https://doi.org/01.0150/epjconf/212532300110

Low background facility for ionizing radiation at LNE LNHB: Design and traceability

J.M. Bordy *, O. Khattabi, C. Chardeur, K. Lahlal, J. Plangnard

Université Paris-Saclay, CEA, LIST, Laboratoire National Henri Becquerel (LNE-LNHB), F-91120, Palaiseau, France

Abstract. This paper presents the set up of a low background calibration facility aimed at calibrating environment survey meter. The facility is a lead box 100 cm x 100 cm x 125 cm with 2.5 cm thickness walls, the Caesium 137 source is located in a conical collimator including an internal cavity for the source. The ambient dose equivalent rate in the beam of this facility varies between 300 and 80 nSv/h. This quantity is traceable to the air kerma national references of LNE-LNHB. The standard uncertainty for the ambient dose equivalent rate is about 2% and the uncertainty of the calibration coefficient od a survey meter, depending meanly on the uncertainty if the background measure, is estimated between 5% and 10%.

1 Introduction.

The calibration coefficient of a survey meter is defined as the ratio between the reference value of the dosimetric quantity, in this case the ambient dose equivalent, and the corrected survey meter reading. Under conventional calibration conditions, the influence of background radiation on the value of the calibration coefficient and its associated uncertainty is negligible, since it is around 100 to 1000 times smaller than the reference value of the dosimetric quantity. This is no longer the case for low-rate calibrations, comparable to the level of radiation encountered in the environment. The uncertainty of the calibration coefficient increases drastically, reaching several tens of percents and the linearity of radiation meters at low ambient dose equivalent rates needs to be verified.

Radiative background consists mainly of two natural components (cosmic, telluric) and the possible influence of nearby or even distant nuclear facilities. In addition to underground or on boat calibration facilities, which largely eliminate natural components, ground-level calibration beams require shielding. The aim of this study is to set up a facility, similar to the National Metrological Institute of Japan one[1], for calibrating environmental dosimeters with very low ambient dose equivalent rates comparable to those encountered in the environment, i.e. a few tenth of nSv/h. In this publication, we present the design of the shielded facilty, and the study of the traceability of the measurements to the national references in terms of air kerma of the LNE-LNHB.

2 Design of the shielded facility.

Figure 1 shows the spectrum measured in air without a lead screen and without collimation using an ORTEC germanium detector model GMX 35P4-70-PLUS-1 cooled with liquid nitrogen. The origin of the peaks highlighted in orange is identified using the « Laraweb » website.[1]

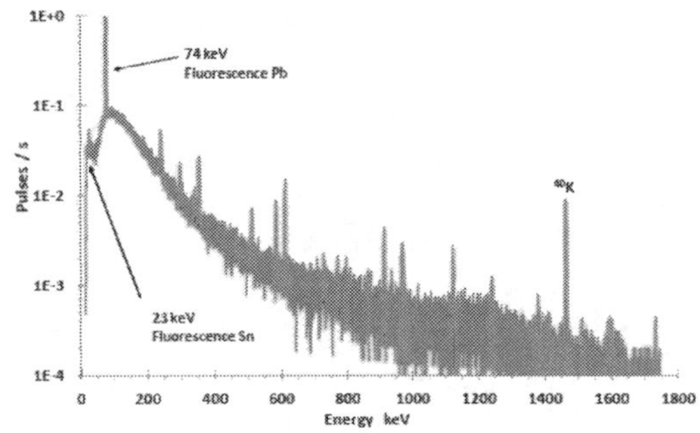

Fig. 1. Radiative background spectrum

The spectrum includes radionuclide's from the 4N (^{232}Th) and 4N+2 (^{238}U) natural decay families (^{224}Ra, ^{214}Pb, ^{228}Ac, ^{208}Tl, ^{214}Bi, ^{212}B, ^{226}Ra) and ^{40}K, plus a Kα lead fluorescence peak at 74 keV due to the measurement room environment, and a second fluorescence peak at 23 keV due to the presence of tin in the detector. The emission lines of these radionuclide's, identified on the spectrum, are used to choose the thickness of the walls through Monte Carlo modeling using the MCNP code [2]. The parallelepiped representing the enclosure is placed at the center of a sphere. Photons are emitted from the inner surface of this sphere, isotropically towards its center. The lead thickness is progressively increased by calculating the spectral fluence distribution for each thickness.

The analysis of the spectra reveals that the range of 25 to 30 mm of lead seems adequate. These results in terms

* Corresponding author: Jean-marc.bordy@cea.fr

[1] http://www.nucleide.org/Laraweb/index.php

of fluence are converted into ambient dose equivalent in order to quantify the influence of lead wall thickness in dosimetric terms. A 98.7% reduction in dose equivalent is observed across the entire background spectrum for a wall thickness of 25 mm. This performance is largely due to the drastic attenuation of low-energy photons (Table 1).

Table 1. Fraction of $H^*(10)$ remaining at the center of the enclosure for a 2.5 cm lead wall.

Energy	10-100 keV	0.1-0.5 MeV	0.1-1 MeV	1-2 MeV	Total
Remaining fraction of $H^*(10)$	0.1%	2.4%	9.2%	18.7%	1.3%

To reduce the influence of lead fluorescence radiation, a copper layer is added inside the facility. Optimi-zation between attenuation of 74 keV photons and production of photons scattered in the copper led to the choice of a thickness of 0.25 mm. It also makes possible to avoid the photons emitted by lead 210 contamination (X rays at 12.56 keV (22%) and 46.54 keV (4.3%)) and their decay products.

Source collimation is the key to defining the beam profile and the proportion of the scattered component of the radiation field in terms of dose equivalent. We chose a conical collimator with an internal cavity for the source. The sources are produced by LNE-LNHB there are made of a 3 mm diameter solid deposit on a plastic support surrounded by a plastic ring.

The variation of the total ambient dose equivalent and its component due to scattered photons was calculated along the axis of the beam in the enclosure as a function of its depth. The best compromise between the internal dimensions of the detectors to be calibrated, the total mass of the enclosure and this initial assessment of the dosimetric characteristics of the calibration conditions, led to external dimension of 100 cm x 100 cm x 125 cm.

Calibration of the transfert standard.

According to ISO 4037 [3] specifications, the scattered component of the radiation field must not exceed 5% in terms of air kerma, and for dose equivalent rates below 1 µSy/h a correction for radiative background must be implemented. We determined these corrections in an attempt to extend the calibration range below 1 µSv/h.

The spectral distribution of fluence between 100 and 1500 cm from a Cesium 137 source is calculated. The model takes into account the dimensions of the room and the design of our irradiator, in order to account for the scattered part of the radiation field at the point of measurement. The spectral distributions show a scattered component about two decades below the direct component represented by the radionuclide emission peak at 662 keV. Table 2 shows the ambient dose equivalent and air kerma rates from the Cesium 137 photon source. This calculation does not take into account the scattered component of the radiation field. The air kerma per photon emitted by the source is calculated for each spectrum (Table 3).

Table 2. Air kerma rates in the collimated beam of the multi-source irradiator on July 10, 2024 as a function of distance from the source.

Distance (m)	K_a Gy/h	Distance (m)	K_a Gy/h
1.00	5.02E-05	9.00	5.74E-07
2.00	1.25E-05	10.00	4.60E-07
3.00	5.48E-06	11.00	3.77E-07
4.00	3.05E-06	12.00	3.14E-07
5.00	1.93E-06	13.00	2.64E-07
6.00	1.33E-06	14.00	2.26E-07
7.00	9.67E-07	14.95	1.97E-07
8.00	7.34E-07	-	-

Table 3. air kerma per photon emitted by the source calculated by Monte Carlo and conversion coefficient from fluence to air kerma as a function of distance from source.

Distance (m)	K_a (pGy)	h* (pGy cm²)	Distance (m)	K_a (pGy)	h* (pGy cm²)
1	2.37E-05	2.83	9	2.76E-07	2.73
2	5.88E-06	2.83	10	2.24E-07	2.66
3	2.59E-06	2.83	11	1.86E-07	2.56
4	1.44E-06	2.83	12	1.58E-07	2.44
5	9.19E-07	2.82	13	1.38E-07	2.31
6	6.34E-07	2.81	14	1.23E-07	2.13
7	4.63E-07	2.80	14.95	1.16E-07	1.93
8	3.51E-07	2.77	-	-	-

The operating range of LNE-LNHB's reference beams under COFRAC IOS 17025 accreditation stops at 7m; to extend this range beyond this, in order to achieve lower kerma flow rates, we need to establish a correction that takes scattered radiation into account. The data in Tables 2 and 3 enable us to quantify this correction named $k_{spectrum,diff,Ka,D}$ as a function of the distance to the source, D. The air kerma at distance D is calculated according to the following equation.

$$k_{spectrum,diff,Ka,D} = K_{a,MC,D} \Big/ K_{a,MC,D=100cm}$$
$$= \int_E \phi_{E,D,MC}\, h_{E,K}\, dE \Big/ \int_E \phi_{E,D=100,MC}\, h_{E,K}\, dE$$

- $h_{E,K}$ is the conversion coefficient from fluence to air kerma of ICRU 57, expressed in pGv cm²,
- $K_{a,MC,D}$ is the air kerma at distance D obtained from the fluence calculated by Monte Carlo,
- $K_{a,MC,D=100cm}$ is the air kerma at 100 cm from the source calculated by Monte Carlo,
- $\phi_{E,D,MC}$ is the photon fluence at distance D calculated by Monte Carlo,
- $\phi_{E,D,MC}$ is the photon fluence at distance D calculated by Monte Carlo.

The calibration coefficient of the transfer standard, $N_{Ka,d,534}$, is measured according to the following equation.

$$N_{Ka,d,534} = \frac{\dfrac{K_{a,100cm}\ (100^2 / D^2) \exp(\mu_{att} \times \rho\ (100 - D))}{k_{spectre,diff,Ka,D}\ k_{profil\ 534,ref,D}}}{G_{brut,d,Cs/Co\ 534,D} - G_{BdF,d,Cs/Co\ 534,D}}$$

- $K_{a,100cm}$ is the air kerma at 1 m from the source traceable to the LNE-LNHB primary reference,

- μ_{att} is the average attenuation coefficient of the photon spectrum,
- $k_{spectre,diff,Ka,D}$ is the correction factor for scattered photon fluence and its influence on the conversion coefficient to air kerma at distance D,
- $G_{brut,d,Cs/Co\ 534,D}$ is the raw indication of the transfer dosimeter, d, during calibration measurement,
- $G_{BdF,d,Cs/Co\ 534,D}$ is the transfer dosimeter indication, d, during background measurement,
- $k_{profil534,ref,D}$ is the correction factor allowing to pass from the reference value of the dosimetric quantity defined at a point to the value averaged over the part of the beam profile occupied by the transfer standard, taking into account the dimensions of this standard and the profile of the calibration beams, this factor is taken equal to 1.

The standard uncertainties are the following:

- $u(K_{a,D})$ is equal to 0.41 %,
- $u(k_{spectre,Ka,D})$ is estimated from the uncertainty on the calculated spectral fluence distribution and that on the polynomial regression equations. The values of the fluence-to-air kerma conversion coefficient in ICRU 57 are conventionally considered to be without uncertainty. On average, the uncertainty on fluence in each energy channel is equal to 0.7%, but that on emission lines is between 0.03 and 0.05%. As the spectral fluence distributions are dominated at least 2 decades by the fluences of the Cesium 137 emission lines, however, in order not to underestimate the uncertainty, a standard uncertainty on the spectrum equal to 0.5% is applied. The maximum deviation between the polynomial regression equations and the data used to calculate them is in all cases less than 0.4%. Considering this deviation as the maximum width of a rectangular distribution, the uncertainty on the polynomial regression equations is estimated to $0.4/2\sqrt{3} = 0.115$ %. The relative standard uncertainty on this correction factor is estimated at 0.513%.
- The standard uncertainty on the calibration distance, measured with a laser pointer, is a maximum of 0.1%.

The uncertainty budget for the calibration coefficient (excluding measurement fluctuation) in terms of air kerma therefore gives a standard uncertainty, whatever the distance, equal to 0.652%.
The study of radiative background leads us to choose a number of measurements greater than or equal to 60, in order to achieve an uncertainty of better than 10% on the distribution of measurements and better than 1% on the distribution of mean values.
Figure 2 shows the variation of the transfer standard response as a function of photon energy. These results were obtained from ISO 4037 N series. It can be seen that this variation is close to that claimed by the supplier in terms of dose equivalent, to within about 10%. The angular sensitivity variation is good and in line with the manufacturer's data.

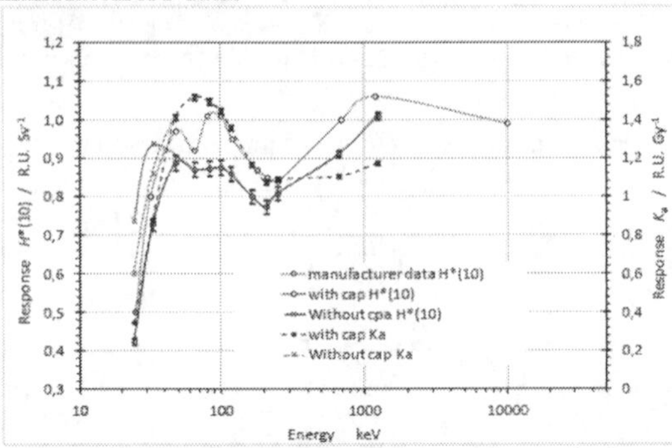

Fig. 2. $H^*(10)$ and K_a response of the transfer standard as a function of energy.

The transfer standard has been calibrated in terms of air kerma between 0.4 and 1 µGy/h. The calibration coefficient is equal to 0.897 µGy/h/ U.L. (U.L. = µSv/h), the standard deviation on these values is equal to 1.29%, we take this value for the uncertainty on the calibration coefficient of our transfer standard.

3 Establishment of the reference in terms of ambient dose equivalent in the shielded facility.

Prior to measuring the air kerma in the shielded facility using the transfer standard, the variation of the fluence spectrum along the axis of the beam and in the perpendicular plane is studied.
Figure 3 show the variation in ambient dose equivalent and the proportion of its scattered component as a function of distance from the source, with a 5% minimum between 60 and 80 cm. This range has been chosen as the calibration range in the shielded facility.
The value of the ambient dose equivalent, $H^*(10)_{BD}$, at the measurement point in the shielded enclosure beam is given by the following equation.

$$H^*(10)_{BD} = N_{Ka,d,534}\ G_{corr,d,BD}\ k_Q\ \overline{h^*}$$

- $N_{d,Cs/Co\ 534}$: Calibration coefficient of the transfer standard as determined in the previous section,
- $G_{corr,d,Cs/Co\ BD}$: Corrected indication of the transfer standard at the measurement point in the shielded facility,
- $\overline{h^*}$: Conversion factor from air kerma to ambient dose equivalent in the shielded facility,
- k_Q : Beam quality correction factor on the air kerma calibration coefficient of the transfer dosimeter.

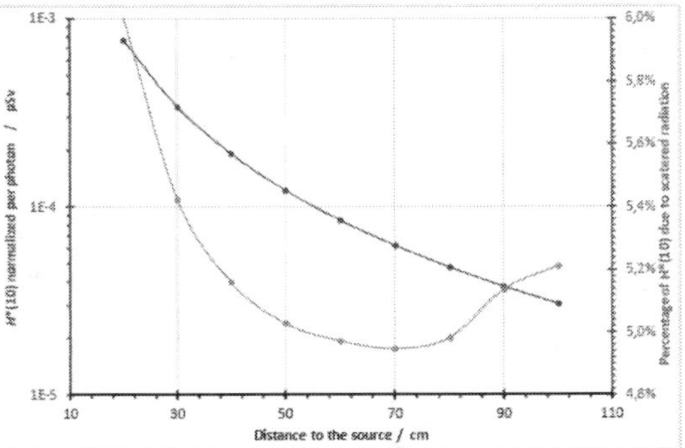

Fig. 3: Variation in ambient dose equivalent along the beam axis as a function of distance from the Cesium 137 source.

Te k_Q factor is the ratio of the calibration coefficients in the photon calibration beam (index "534") and in the shielded facility (index "BD").

$$k_Q = \frac{N_{d,Q,BD}}{N_{Ka,d,534}} = \frac{\left[\int_E \phi_{E,DB} h_{\phi K}\, dE \Big/ \int_E \phi_{E,DB} h_{\phi K}\, R_{E,d}\, dE\right]_{BD}}{\left[\int_E \phi_{E,534} h_{\phi K}\, dE \Big/ \int_E \phi_{E,534} h_{\phi K}\, R_{E,d}\, dE\right]_{534}}$$

- $h_{\phi K}$ is the conversion coefficient from fluence to kerma in air,
- $\phi_{E,DB}$ is the spectral fluence calculated in the low-flow chamber,
- $\phi_{E,534}$ is the spectral fluence calculated in the calibration facility,
- $R_{E,d}$ is the energy response of the transfer standard.

The standard uncertainty of this correction factor is calculated by taking into account the uncertainty of the calculated spectra, estimated as before (0.5%), and that of the energy-dependent response as measured, i.e. 1%. The average conversion coefficient from air kerma to ambient dose equivalent $\bar{h}^*$ is calculated from ICRU 57 data, its standard uncertainty calculated in a similar way to that on $k_{spectre,Ka,D}$ but in the absence of polynomial regression.
The closed-beam radiative background is evaluated using the cone-of-shadow technique, by applying a kM measurement correction factor to evaluate the component due to radiation transmission through the shutter from the calculated spectra. The uncertainty of this correction factor therefore takes into account the uncertainty of the spectra (0.5%) and that of the background measurements (1.0%), i.e. a total of 1.12%.

Table 4. Calculation of reference values in terms of ambient dose equivalent rate in the shielded enclosure as a function of distance from the source.

Distance cm	k_Q	$\bar{h}^*$ Sv/Gy	$N_{Ka,d,534}$ µGy/h R.U.	Raw measure R.U.	k_M
40	0.9358	1.223	0.897	322.04	0.053
50	0.9354	1.223		217.50	0.053
60	0.9352	1.223		158.17	0.052
70	0.9354	1.224		115.07	0.052
80	0.9357	1.224		95.81	0.052

Distance cm	Background R.U.	Corrected measure R.U.	$H^*(10)_{BD}$ nSv/h
40	33.91	303.40	311.5
50	28.03	199.52	204.7
60	26.04	139.13	142.8
70	20.96	99.09	101.7
80	21.87	77.85	80.0

Table 5. Uncertainty budget on the reference value of H*(10) in the shielded facility (an uncertainty of 0.4% on the calibration distance is added).

Distance cm	Standard deviation raw measure R.U.	Standard deviation background measure R.U.	Standard uncertainty on the corrected measure	
			R.U.	%
40	0.87	0.72	1.14	0.39%
50	0.54	1.26	1.37	0.63%
60	0.80	1.24	1.48	1.12%
70	0.70	0.91	1.14	1.22%
80	0.52	0.81	0.96	1.29%

Distance cm	$u(k_Q)$	$u(\bar{h}^*)$	$u(k_M)$	$u(N_{Ka,d,534})$	$u(H^*(10)_{BD})$
40	1.0%	0.50%	1.12%	1.29%	2.1%
50	1.0%	0.50%	1.12%	1.29%	2.2%
60	1.0%	0.50%	1.12%	1.29%	2.4%
70	1.0%	0.50%	1.12%	1.29%	2.4%
80	1.0%	0.50%	1.12%	1.29%	2.5%

4 Conclusions.

The expression for the calibration coefficient of a calibrated survey meter in the shielded facility beam is

$$N_{H*,d,BD} = \frac{H^*_{BD,D}\, k_{profile}}{G_{corr,d,BD,D}}$$

A profile correction is calculated according to the dimensions of the device to be calibrated. Its purpose is to correct the dose equivalent value obtained with the transfer standard, $H^*(10)_{DB}$. This correction factor is calculated from 2D mapping in the plane perpendicular to the source axis according to the following equation:

$$k_{profile} = \frac{\iint_{x\,y} H^*(10)_{x,y}\, dx\, dy}{H^*(10)_{DB}}$$

The value of this correction factor is a maximum of 4%, depending on the x and y dimensions of the survey meter, and the beam aperture radius is 24 cm at 70 cm from the source.

This study has enabled us to install and characterize Cesium 137 photon beams in a shielded facility for radiameter calibration against ambient dose equivalent rates comparable to those encountered in the environment. The reference value of the ambient dose equivalent in the low dose rate facility is traceable to the national references of the LNE-LNHB in terms of air kerma. The uncertainty on the calibration coefficient of a survey meter on this facility is estimated at between 5 and 10%; this uncertainty budget remains dominated by the uncertainty on the measurement of the radiative background.

References.

[1]Tadahiro Kurosawa & al, poster at AOCRP-4 ; 12 may 2014, Kuala Lumpur, Malaisia

[2] J. A. Kulesza, T. R. Adams, J. C. Armstrong, S. R. Bolding, F. B. Brown, J. S. Bull, T. P. Burke, A. R. Clark, R. A. Forster III, J. F. Giron, T. S. Grieve, C. J. Josey, R. L. Martz, G. W. McKinney, E. J. Pearson, M. E. Rising, C. J. Solomon Jr., S. Swaminarayan, T. J. Trahan, S. C. Wilson, A. J. Zukaitis. MCNP® Code Version 6.3.0 Theory & User Manual. Los Alamos National Laboratory Tech. Rep. LA-UR-22-30006, Rev. 1. Los Alamos, NM, USA. September 2022.

[3] ISO 4037 Series; Radiological protection — X and gamma reference radiation for calibrating dosemeters and doserate meters and for determining their response as a function of photon energy.

This study is made within the 21GRD02 **BIOSPHERE** (*Metrology for earth Biosphere: Cosmic rays, ultraviolet radiation and fragility of ozone shield*) research program. It has received funding from the European Partnership on Metrology, EPM, co-financed by the European Union's Horizon Europe Research and innovation Program and by Participating States. https://euramet-biosphere.eu/

EPJ Web of Conferences **323**, 0011(2(1(5)   https://doi.org/01.0150/epjconf/(1(53(30011(
22nd nIt enr Iai nr dMt Iei ai gylCi nget ss

What's obscure with previtamin D Action Spectrum – a challenge for AI

Irina Terenetskaya*

Institute of Physics, National Academy of Sciences of Ukraine, 03028 Kyiv, Ukraine

Abstract. The article discusses issues related to the significant difference between the Action Spectra of Vitamin D synthesis *in vivo* and *in vitro*. Experimental measurements of previtamin D photosynthesis *in vitro* under the quasy-monochromatic UV radiation at different wavelengths are presented, which indicate that nonlinear kinetics of previtamin D accumulation together with the wavelength effect on its side photoconversions, will lead to ambiguity in the Previtamin D Action Spectrum depending on the accepted erythema dose at which it was measured.

1 Introduction

As is known, solar ultraviolet (UV) radiation can cause both beneficial and adverse effects on health depending on the dose. The maximum admissible dose of UV radiation is associated with its erythemal biological activity and to date, the Erythema Action Spectrum adopted by CIE [1], Standard Erythema Dose (1 SED = 100 J/m2) [2] and the Global UV index [3], constitute the metrological basis for the use of AI for health protection.

The situation is less clear regarding the determination of the minimum required UV dose of sunlight required for natural synthesis of health-promoting vitamin D in human skin to balance the risks of vitamin D deficiency and skin cancer [4].

An important step towards this goal should be the construction of adequate Action Spectrum for calculating the vitamin D-synthesizing capacity of any UV radiation source and adequate assessment the so-called anti-rickets biologic dose of UV radiation in relation to the standard erythemal dose (SED) for various UV sources.

These are the issues that are discussed in this article.

2. Critical analysis of the Previtamin D Action Spectrum *in vivo*

The construction of the wavelength dependence for a given bioeffect, so called Action Spectrum, is one of the fundamental methods for analysis of an organism's responses to UV radiation [5]. By definition, the action spectrum (AS) of a specific biological effect of UV radiation is characterized by the spectral dependence of its magnitude, measured with monochromatic irradiation of different wavelengths with the same dose [5].

Hence, in theory, to determine the biologically effective irradiance E_{eff} (Wm^{-2}), the solar spectrum measured by a spectroradiometer is to be weighted (integrated over the wavelengths) according to the action spectrum of a specific biological effect [6]:

$$E_{eff} = \int E_{\lambda}(\lambda) * S_{\lambda}(\lambda) d\lambda \qquad (1)$$

Here $E_{\lambda}(\lambda)$ - solar spectral irradiance [$Wm^{-2}nm^{-1}$], $S_{\lambda}(\lambda)$ - action spectrum [relative units], λ - wavelength [nm].

The CIE erythema action spectrum [1] is widely used for estimation of the erythemal-active irradiance of sunlight and artificial UV sources.

An adequate assessment of the ability of sunlight to synthesize vitamin D also requires the Action Spectrum for vitamin D synthesis, especially in view of its widespread in the biosphere. It is known that vitamin D_2 is synthesized under sunlight from its precursor ergosterol (mainly in plants), and vitamin D_3 - from 7-dehydrocholesterol (7-DHC) in animals and humans. It is important that their synthesis occurs in the same way by two-stage monomolecular isomerization (Figure1).

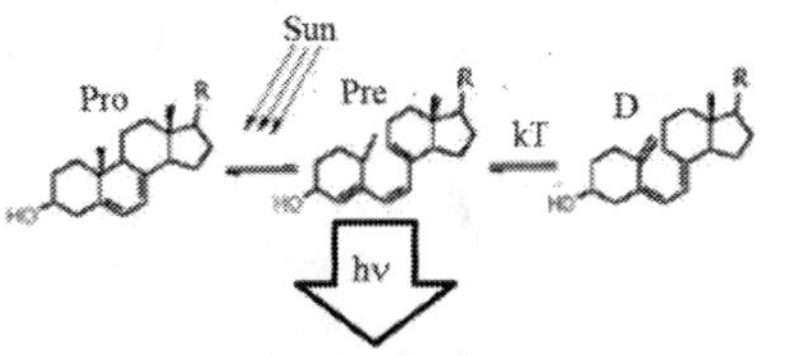

Fig.1 Simplified scheme of Vitamin D synthesis. Pro – Provitamin D, Pre – Previtamin D, D – Vitamin D. R = C_8H_{17} for vitamin D_3 series; R = C_9H_{17} for vitamin D_2 series.

At the first stage, absorption of UVB (280–315 nm) photons by provitamin D results in its conversion into previtamin D, which is then converted into vitamin D by heat. Thus, it is the amount of previtamin D accumulated during an UV exposure is a measure of the biologically effective anti-rickets dose of UV radiation.

In 2006, the CIE published an Action Spectrum for production of previtamin D_3 in human skin [7], based on the spectrum published by MacLaughlin et al. [8] with long-wavelength extrapolation up to 330 nm (Figure 2).

* Corresponding author: teren@iop.kiev.ua

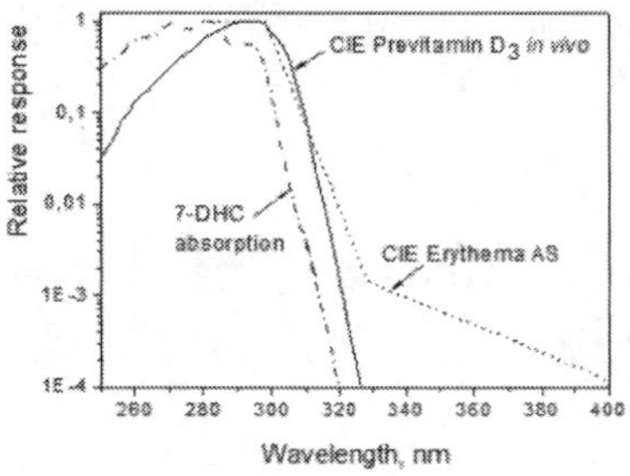

Fig. 2. The CIE Previtamin D Action Spectrum in human skin in comparison with absorption spectrum of provitamin D (extrapolated from 310 nm) and CIE erythema AS [1].

Several features in the graphs presented in Figure 2 are worthy of notice:

1. Difference in the wavelengths of maximum in the previtamin D AS (295 nm) and in the provitamin D absorption spectrum (282 nm),
2. Opposite relation of the two 'Vitamin D' spectra to the CIE erythema action spectrum around 310 nm,
3. Significant distinction between CIE erythema AS and both 'Vitamin D' curves in the UVA spectral range,
4. Starting from 305 nm and further towards longer wavelengths, the difference between the action spectrum of previtamin D and the absorption spectrum of provitamin D exceeds more than one order of magnitude (!), which contradicts the First Law of Photochemistry: '*Light must be absorbed for photochemistry to occur*'.

Moreover, the spectrum of previtamin D synthesis in human skin [8] does not correspond to the generally accepted methodology of measuring AS, since instead of measuring the spectral dependence of the amount of previtamin D synthesized under monochromatic irradiation of different wavelengths with the same dose, on the contrary, the dose required for the accumulation of no more than 5 percent of previtamin D was measured under irradiation at different wavelengths.

A simple mathematical analysis shows that with such a measurement, the AS should correspond to the absorption spectrum of the initial provitamin D (as was obtained for the AS *in vitro* [9]).

This discrepancy has been analyzed in detail [10], and the reason could be an incorrect concentration analysis that does not take into account the irreversible photoreactions of provitamin D, which play an important role during irradiation at the long-wavelength absorption edge of provitamin D [11].

In view of criticism [12,13], this AS of previtamin D synthesis in human skin has not yet been standardized by the CIE, but until a clear alternative becomes available, it is recommended [14] to use this existing CIE Action Spectrum to ensure spectral information on UV sources to enable comparison of results from different studies.

Another possible solution to this problem is discussed in this article, namely, measuring the amount of synthesized previtamin D *in vitro* in relation to the received erythema dose. The rationale for this approach is the linear correlation between *in vitro* previtamin D_3 synthesis and the increase in serum 25-hydroxyvitamin D_3 in humans after UV exposure [15].

3. Experimental technique

Experimental studies of the kinetics of previtamin D photosynthesis *in vitro* for radiometric characterization of the 'D-dosimeter' [16] were carried out within the framework of the BIODOS project at the Belgian Institute for Space Aeronomy (IASB) using a unique laboratory setup specially designed to characterize biological dosimeters of UV radiation. The laboratory facility has been described in detail [9], but only a small part of these measurements has been published until today [9,17].

3.1. UV source

Quasi-monochromatic UV radiation from the xenon arc lamp with a number of the narrow-band interference filters ($\Delta\lambda \sim 2.5$ nm) (Figure 3) was used to link physical and erythemal UV doses (Table 1) with concentrations of accumulated previtamin D.

Table 1. Characteristics of the UV irradiance with the narrow-band filters

Irradiation wavelength (nm)	Spectral irradiance (mW/m^2)	Erythema effective fluence rate (mW/m^2)	Irradiation time for 1 SED (min)
260	10.579	10.181	156
270	103.804	103.352	15
280	112.799	112.223	14
290	175.995	175.679	9
300	243.854	162.446	9.8
310	591.995	41.731	38

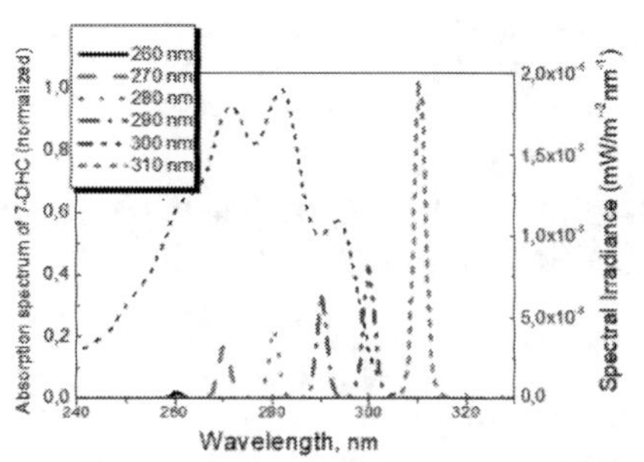

Fig. 3. Spectral characteristics of the narrow band filters in comparison with normalized 7-DHC absorption spectrum.

3.2. The measurements procedure

The ethanol solutions of 7-DHC (Sigma) ($C \sim 20$ µg/ml, $V = 2$ ml) were irradiated in standard quartz cuvettes (Helma) of 0.5 cm thickness located normally to the light beam. During the time when the cuvette with 7-DHC solution was exposed, the incident spectral irradiance was measured by the spectroradiometer SPEX 1672M. The absorption spectra of 7-DHC were recorded within 230 – 330 nm before and after several exposures using upgraded Beckman-34 spectrophotometer for further computer processing with specially developed original software for concentration analysis [18].

3.3. Spectrophotometric concentration analysis

As is known, when provitamin D is irradiated with UV light, a multicomponent mixture of photoisomers is formed due to the side photoconversions of previtamin D and the overlap of their absorption spectra (Figure 4).

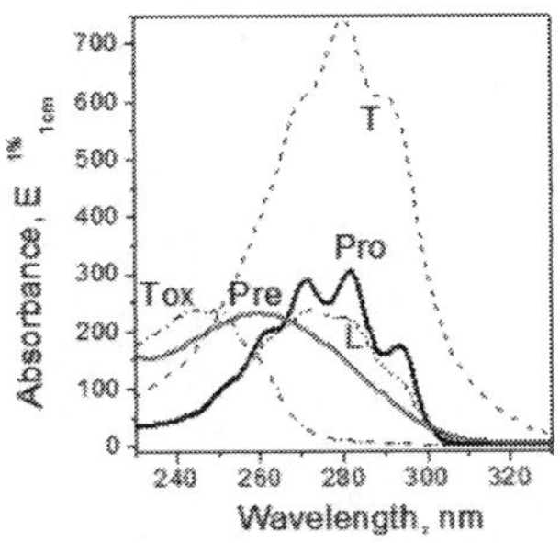

Fig. 4. UV absorption spectra of provitamin D and its photoisomers: T – Tachysterol, L – Lumisterol, Tox – Toxisterols. (The **Tox** spectrum was recorded after photolysis of 7-DHC in ethanol with excimer XeCl laser at 308 nm [19]) .

Concentration analysis of this multicomponent mixture is usually carried out using HPLC and the total concentration of the four main photoisomers is taken as 100%, i.e. irreversible photoconversions of previtamin D are not taken into account [8]. However, this neglect causes serious errors upon UV irradiation at the long-wavelength edge of provitamin D absorption band [20].

Therefore, in the described experiments, UV absorption spectroscopy was applied to monitor the course of the photoreaction, and the concentration composition of the photo-isomeric mixture was determined using an original spectrophotometric analysis [18, 21] developed with due consideration of its irreversible photodegradation.

Additionally, to verify the photoreaction model based on the system of rate equations [16, 20], the photoreaction kinetics was calculated at different wavelengths using the spectroradiometric data at the model input for comparison of the calculated and experimentally obtained kinetics.

4. Results and discussion

Due to the low intensity of UV radiation at 260 nm, only minor changes in the initial absorption spectrum of the 7-DHC solution occurred after almost three hours of exposure (Figure 5).

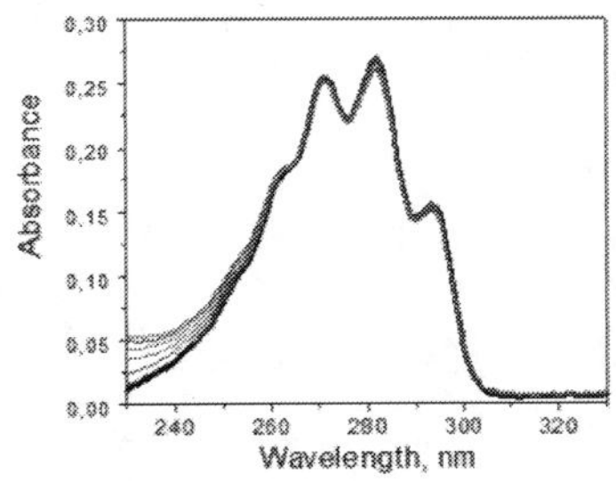

Fig. 5. Transformation of the 7-DHC initial spectrum upon UV irradiation at 260 nm recorded after 50, 80, 110, 140 and 170 min exposures.

The result of concentration analysis of previtamin D accumulation is presented in Figure 6.

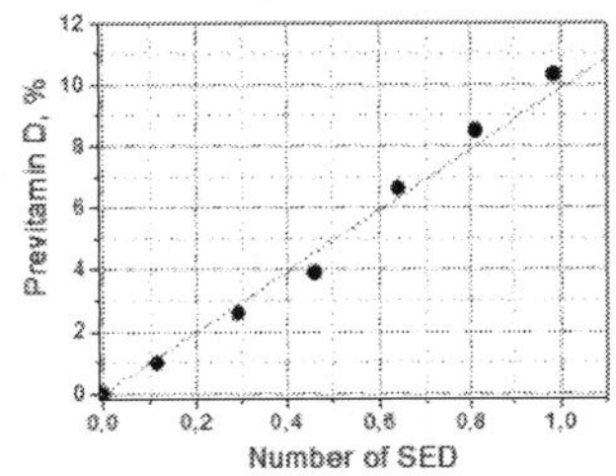

Fig. 6. Accumulation of previtamin D depending on the SED number: symbols – experiment, line – linear fit.

Note that Figures 4) and 5), indicating the sensitivity of the spectrophotometric analysis and the scatter of results, confirm previously published data on the dose of 0.5 SED required for the accumulation 5% of previtamin D [9].

Since the purpose of these experiments was not only calibration of the 'D-biodosimeter' [16], but also testing the adequacy of the photoreaction model, the exposure time was chosen to observe the full kinetics of previtamin D accumulation up to its maximum concentration, which could be indicated by the behavior of the optical density of the sample (its rise until the start of decline [22]), as is demonstrated in Figure 7.

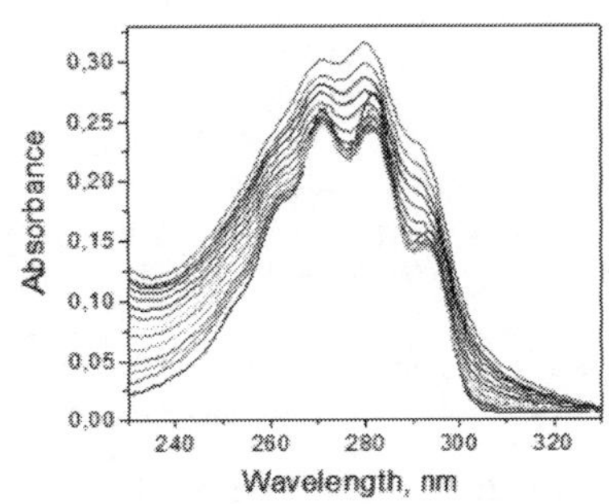

Fig. 7. Transformation of the 7-DHC initial spectrum upon UV irradiation at 280 nm with total exposure time 210 min; the exposures for individual spectra are visible from Figure 8.

The concentration kinetics obtained by computer processing of these spectra together with the results of model calculations are shown in Figure 8.

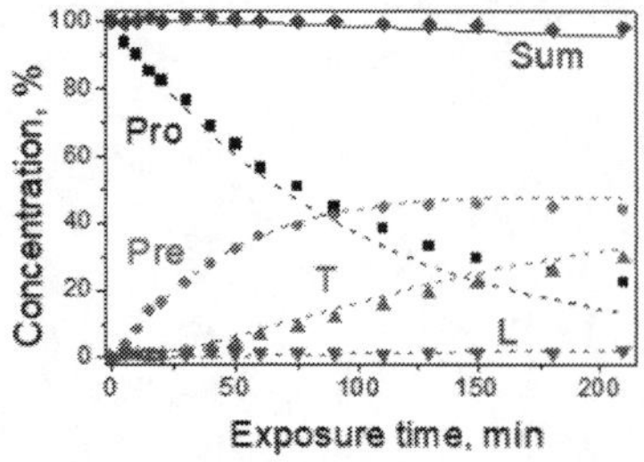

Fig. 8. Concentration kinetics: designations Pro, Pre, T and L as in Figs. 1) and 4); Sum – their summary concentration. Symbols – experiment, line – calculation.

It is important to note that in the longer wavelength region, where the efficiency of *cis-trans* isomerization is reduced, spectral transformation does not provide the possibility for fixation of Previtamin D maximum accumulation [22] (Figure 9).

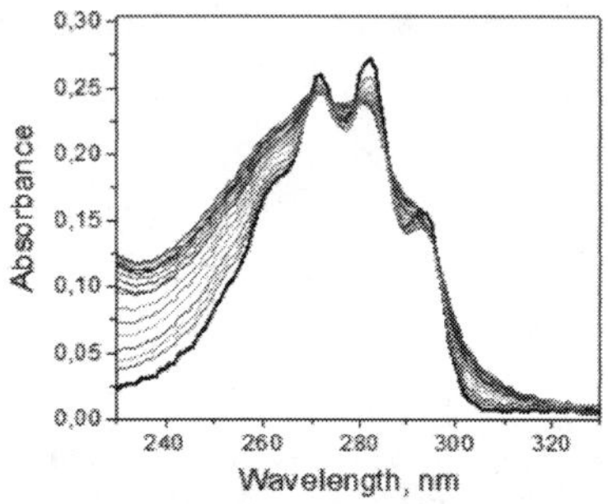

Fig. 9. Transformation of the 7-DHC initial spectrum upon UV irradiation at 300 nm with total exposure time 420 min.

This is demonstrated by Figure 10, where with a total irradiation time of 420 minutes, the maximum accumulation of previtamin D was not reached.

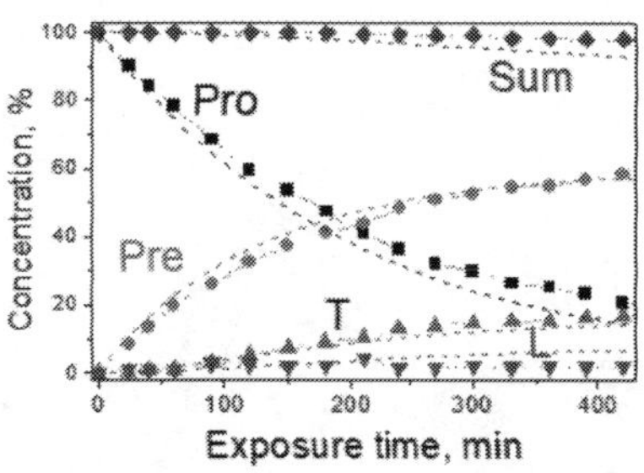

Fig. 10. Concentration kinetics: the notations are similar to Figure 8. Symbols – experiment, line – calculated kinetics.

Regarding the adequacy of the numerical modeling of the photoisomerization kinetics, from Figures 8 and 10 it can be concluded that there is rather good agreement (within 3%) with the experimentally measured kinetics at the initial stage of irradiation, but the match is slightly worse at the last stage.

The final results of the measurements of previtamin D accumulation in relation to the number of standard erythemal doses received during irradiation at all six wavelengths are shown in Figure 11.

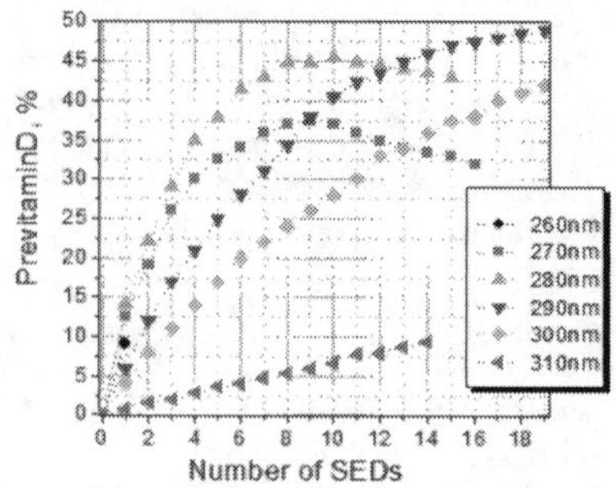

Fig.11. Previtamin D accumulation depending on the number of SED obtained

Analyzing the dependencies presented in Figure 11, one can come to an important conclusion about the absence of a monotonic increase in the concentration of accumulated previtamin D with an increase in the erythemal dose at all measured wavelengths. And when exposed to sunlight, the monotonous dependence is limited to a dose of no more than 8 SED, given that photons with a wavelength of less than 280 nm do not penetrate the earth's surface.

Based on the results shown in Figure 11, a dependence of previtamin D accumulation on the obtained SEDs number was constructed for different wavelengths (Figure 12) with the exception of $\lambda = 260$ nm, due to the lack of data for a dose exceeding 1 SED.

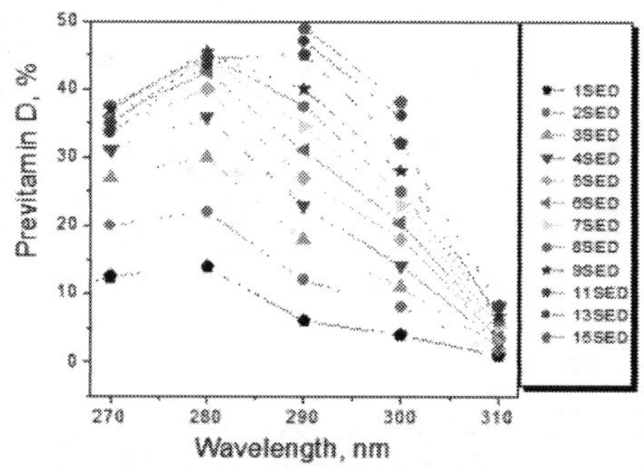

Fig.12. The wavelength dependence of previtamin D accumulated after irradiation with different SEDs.

The graphs in Figure 12 that are the basis for constructing the action spectrum of previtamin D synthesis, clearly demonstrate its ambiguity in relation to the maximum wavelength, i.e. its maximum is maintained at a wavelength of 280 nm only up to 10 SED, and with a larger number of SEDs it is gradually shifted to the longer wavelengths.

It is worth noting here that this result confirms the previously made conclusion, based on calculations of the photoreaction kinetics for different wavelengths [13,16], that the term 'spectral effectiveness' for the previtamin D photosynthesis can be considered in two aspects: either for the wavelength with the maximum rate of previtamin D formation, or for the wavelength with its maximum achievable concentration. A detailed examination of the ratio of the absorption spectra of provitamin D and previtamin D leads to the same conclusion [22].

5. Conclusions

The main result of these measurements is the revealed spectral dependence of previtamin D accumulation *in vitro* on the accepted UV dose at which it was measured that could suggest the ambiguity of its action spectrum.

To obtain an adequate action spectrum of previtamin D synthesis *in vivo*, further careful measurements using monochromatic UV irradiation are needed together with urgent development of non-invasive spectral-optical methods for measuring previtamin D formation in human skin.

In the meantime, in calculations of the vitamin D synthesis effective UV irradiance E_{eff} (W m^{-2}) it seems more appropriate to use the absorption spectrum of provitamin D (in relative units) as spectral weighting function $S_\lambda(\lambda)$ in formula (1) in accordance with the 1st Law of Photochemistry.

The simple procedure for determining the biologic dose of a UV source by integrating its effective irradiance E_{eff} over time [6], is unacceptable for an adequate assessment of the amount of synthesized previtamin D, that is, the anti-rickets UV dose should either be calculated using the photoreaction mathematical model, or measured with D-biodosimeter based on an *in vitro* model of vitamin D synthesis [23].

Acknowledgements

The author is grateful to Dr. Ann Webb for valuable discussions and to Dr. David Bolsee for assistance during experimental studies at the IASB (supported by the EC (Contract No. ENV4-CT95-0044).

References

1. A.F. McKinley, B.I. Diffey, A reference action spectrum for ultraviolet induced erythema in human skin. CIE Journal, **6**, 17 (1987)
2. B.L. Diffey, C.T. Jansen, F. Urbach, H.C. Wulf, D.H. Sliney, J-P. Cesarini, Standard Erythema Dose, a Review. CIE Journal, **125** (1997) ISBN 978 3 900734 81 7
3. World Health Organization, Global Solar UV Index. A Practical Guide. Geneva, Switzerland: WHO (2002)
4. R.L McKenzie, J.B. Liley, L.O. Bjorn, UV radiation: balancing risks and benefits. Photochemistry and Photobiology, **85**, 88 (2009)
5. T. Coohill, Historical Aspects of Ultraviolet Action Spectroscopy. Photochem. and Photobiol., **65**, 1235 (1997) https://doi.org/10.1111/j.1751-1097.1997
6. G. Horneck, Quantification of the biological effectiveness of environmental UV radiation. J. Photochem. Photobiol. B: Biology **31,** 43 (1995)
7. R. Bouillon, J. Eisman, M. Garabedian, M. Holick, J. Kleinschmidt, T. Suda, I. Terenetskaya, A. Webb, Action spectrum for the production of previtamin D_3 in human skin. CIE Journal, **174**, 1–12 (2006)
8. J.A. MacLaughlin, R.R. Anderson, M.F. Holick, Spectral character of sunlight modulates photosynthesis of previtamin D_3 and its photoisomers in human skin. Science, **216**, 1001 (1982)
9. D. Bolsee, A.R. Webb, D. Gillotay, D. Dorschel, P. Knuschke, A. Krins, I. Terenetskaya, Laboratory facilities and recommendations for the characterization of biological ultraviolet dosimeters. Applied Optics, **39**, 2813 (2000)
10. I. Terenetskaya, Mismatch between the *in vivo* and *in vitro* vitamin D synthesis action spectra: cause-and-effect relationship. CIE Division 6 meeting DR **6-41** (2014) DOI:10.13140/2.1.3158.8804
11. E. Abillon, R. Mermet-Bouvier, Effect of wavelength on production of previtamin D_2 . J. Pharm. Sci., **62**, 1688 (1973) https://doi.org/10.1002/jps.2600621023
12. M. Norval, L. Bjorn, F. de Gruijl, Is the action spectrum for the UV-induced production of previtamin D_3 in human skin correct? Photochem. Photobiol. Sci, **9**, 11 (2010) DOI: 10.1039/b9pp00012g
13. I. Terenetskaya, Inter-relation between the *in vivo* and *in vitro* action spectra of vitamin D synthesis, in Proc. of the 2nd CIE Symposium 'Lighting and Health', Ottawa, Canada, September 7-8, 182 (2006)
14. A. Webb, I. Terenetskaya, M. Holick, A van Dijk, R. McKenzie, R. Lucas, A. Young, P. Philipsen, F. de Gruijl, Previtamin D action spectrum: Challenging CIE towards a standard. Lighting Research and Technology, **55**, 487 (2023) DOI: 10.1177/14771535221122937
15. T. Orlova, J. Moan, Z. Lagunova, L. Aksnes, I. Terenetskaya, A. Juzeniene, Increase in serum 25-hydroxy-vitamin-D_3 in humans after sunbed exposures compared to previtamin D_3 synthesis *in vitro*. J. Photochem. Photobiol. B: Biology, **122**, 32 (2013)
16. O. Galkin, I. Terenetskaya, 'Vitamin D' biodosimeter: basic characteristics and potential applications. J. Photochem. Photobiol. B: Biology, **53**, 12 (1999)
17. I. Terenetskaya, Duality of solar UV-B radiation and relevant dosimetry: vitamin D synthesis versus skin erythema. SPIE Proceedings, **4896**, 144 (2003b)
18. I. Terenetskaya, K. Terenetsky, The method of bioactive ultraviolet radiation monitoring, Ukrainian Patent No. B4401247, Priority Date 08.04.94 (1994)
19. I. Terenetskaya, S. Gundorov, V. Kravchenko and E. Berik, Nanosecond laser photolysis of provitamin D, Sov. J. Quantum Electron., **18**, 1323 (1988) DOI 10.1070/QE1988v018n10ABEH012519
20. I. Terenetskaya, S. Gundorov, E. Berik, Characteristics of photolysis of provitamin D by long-wavelength radiation, Sov. J. Quantum Electron., 21, 472 (1991) DOI 10.1070/QE1991v021n04ABEH003843
21. I. Terenetskaya, Spectral monitoring of biologically active solar UVB radiation using an *in vitro* model of Vitamin D synthesis. Talanta, **53**, 195 (2000)
22. I. Terenetskaya, The wavelength effects in provitamin D photochemistry: a spectroscopist's view on the kinetics and maximum accumulation of

previtamin D, Trends in Photochemistry & Photobiology, **22**, 35 (2023)
23. I. Terenetskaya, Three operation modes of the Vitamin D Biodosimeter, Proc. of SPIE, **9887** (2016) DOI: 10.1117/12.2229756

Building a Radionuclide Metrology Algorithm Comparison Platform (NuCodeComP): Insights from Rapid Integration with Microsoft PowerApps

Eric Macedo [1,2*], *Liu* Haoran[3], *Zihao* Fan[3], *Marcus* Navarro[1], *José Guilherme* Peixoto[4], and *Romain* Coulon[2]

[1]Instituto Federal da Bahia, LabPROSAUD/IFBA, 41.745-715 Salvador, Bahia, Brazil
[2]Bureau International des Poids et Mesures, Pavillon de Breteuil, 92312 Sèvres Cedex, France
[3]National Institute of Metrology, 100029 Beijing, China
[4]Instituto de Radioproteção e Dosimetria (IRD/CNEN), Barra da Tijuca, 22780-160, Rio de Janeiro, Brazil

Abstract. An essential step in radionuclide activity measurement comparisons is the counting signal processing performed by laboratory-specific software. This has led to initiatives comparing software performance using a unique dataset from a list-mode data structure, as defined in IEC 63047:2021. A virtual Radionuclide Metrology Algorithm Comparison Platform was developed at BIPM to ensure a FAIR approach and facilitate broader laboratory participation. Beyond presenting the final product, this work highlights key insights from its development. The platform was designed to be reliable, adaptable, and future-proof, aligning with the D-SI framework to ensure machine-readable, structured, and interoperable data. A strategic decision was made to investigate Microsoft 365, leveraging its infrastructure to real-test software operations before investing in scalability. However, scalability limitations arise, requiring Azure solutions like SQL Server for big data applications. The drag-and-drop interface simplifies the platform's development in interface design while utilizing SharePoint tables for data structuring and access control. However, performance constraints exist, particularly with SharePoint's row-number limitation. Furthermore, non-M365 users face access barriers mitigated through basic M365 plans or per-app licensing. This case study serves as a model for digital metrology projects, balancing cost-effective IT solutions with scalability and accessibility challenges while ensuring alignment with SI Digital transformation.

1 Introduction

The digital transformation of metrology is changing how measurement data is generated, processed, and compared. In radionuclide metrology, interlaboratory comparisons have traditionally relied on the physical exchange of radioactive samples, posing logistical, regulatory, and reproducibility challenges [1]. Moreover, data analysis is a key aspect of any comparison—understanding how different laboratories process measurement data [2].

Unlike conventional approaches, where activity of radioactive samples using is estimated by primary measurement techniques, a code comparison framework focuses on the validation of downstream part of the measurement, the software, enable thanks to standardized structured list-mode data (IEC 63047:2021) generated by the measurement device [1–3].

Based on that demand, a project was started to develop a platform that manages that code comparison, a digital-first approach, leveraging structured list-mode data and FAIR (Findable, Accessible, Interoperable, Reusable) principles, offers a solution that aligns with the SI Digital Framework, as stated by the CIPM [4–6].

The Radionuclide Metrology Algorithm Comparison Platform (NuCodeComP) was developed at the BIPM to facilitate an interlaboratory assessment of data processing algorithms. The platform leverages BIPM's existing Microsoft 365 (M365) infrastructure to minimize deployment costs and ensure ease of access [7]. However, before committing to scalability investments, the platform was tested under real-use conditions, revealing both advantages and constraints.

The Consultative Committee for Ionizing Radiation (CCRI(II)), which oversees international comparisons of radionuclide activity measurements, recognizes the potential of software-based comparisons in complementing traditional methods [8].

This paper presents the insights gained during the platform's development and technical implementation, as well as lessons learned regarding the feasibility of adopting a digital-first approach in radionuclide metrology. By integrating FAIR principles and the D-SI framework, the platform may serve as a model for future digital comparison initiatives in metrology. However, challenges such as scalability, access management, compliance with the CIPM MRA, and long-term sustainability must be considered to ensure its adoption.

* Corresponding author: ematosmacedo@gmail.com

2 Radionuclide Activity Comparisons and Code Comparison

Interlaboratory comparisons are fundamental to ensuring measurement equivalence across National Metrology Institutes (NMIs), with the CCRI(II) coordinating their implementation in radionuclide metrology. The comparison process follows a structured flow (see Fig. 1) to maintain traceability to the International System of Units (SI) and adherence to the CIPM Mutual Recognition Arrangement (CIPM MRA) [8].

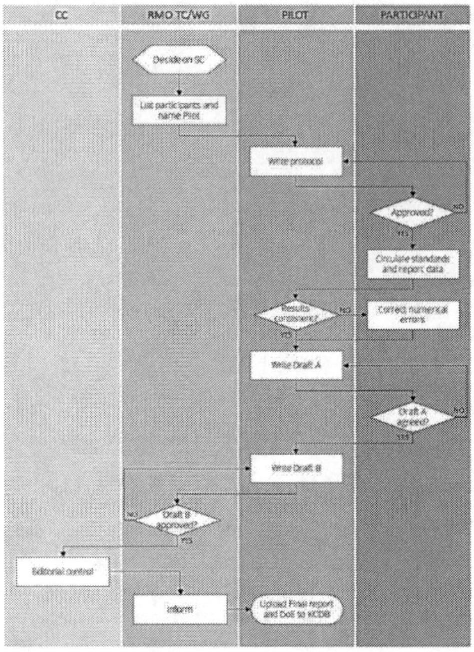

Fig. 1. Flowchart of CIPM and RMO key comparisons [8].

The comparison begins with the designation of a pilot laboratory, such as the BIPM or other NMI, responsible for defining the technical protocol. This document outlines the measurement methods, reporting formats, and uncertainty evaluation requirements governing the exercise. Participants receive a reference sample, such as an aqueous solution of technetium-99 (Tc-99), or sent a standard solution to the BIPM on-demand key comparison services (the SIR, SIRTI, and ESIR) [1].

Upon receipt of the test material, each participating laboratory conducts measurements according to its established methodologies. The results, including activity values and associated uncertainties, are submitted to the pilot laboratory for centralized analysis. The initial collation of data is compiled into Draft A, a preliminary report that presents individual laboratory results while maintaining confidentiality regarding deviations. At this stage, laboratories are permitted to review their own data for numerical or procedural inconsistencies, but no information is provided on the magnitude or direction of potential discrepancies, ensuring an unbiased reassessment [8].

Following participant feedback, the pilot laboratory refines the dataset, incorporating validated corrections and performing statistical analyses to establish the Key Comparison Reference Value (KCRV). The revised document, Draft B, undergoes further scrutiny by CCRI(II) (and/or KCWG(II)) before final approval. The degrees of equivalence, quantifying each participant's alignment with the KCRV, are determined and presented alongside the final results. Upon acceptance, the findings are published in the Key Comparison Database (KCDB), providing a globally accessible benchmark for radionuclide metrology.

While effective, this approach presents several challenges, such as regulatory constraints (international transport of radioactive sources), measurement variability (differences in laboratory setups, detector types, and measurement protocols), and focus on activity estimation, not data processing (traditional comparisons primarily assess measurement accuracy but do not systematically evaluate how different laboratories process list-mode data, which is a critical aspect of radionuclide metrology) [9,10].

2.1 The Code Comparison

In radionuclide metrology, while activity estimation typically follows data acquisition and analysis, specific investigations focus on the "data analysis" step, evaluating signal processing methodologies and their influencing parameters. A complementary to conventional comparisons is the code comparison approach, wherein laboratories analyze a common dataset rather than handling physical radioactive materials. This method establishes a controlled and reproducible framework for assessing the performance of signal processing algorithms and activity estimation techniques [2].

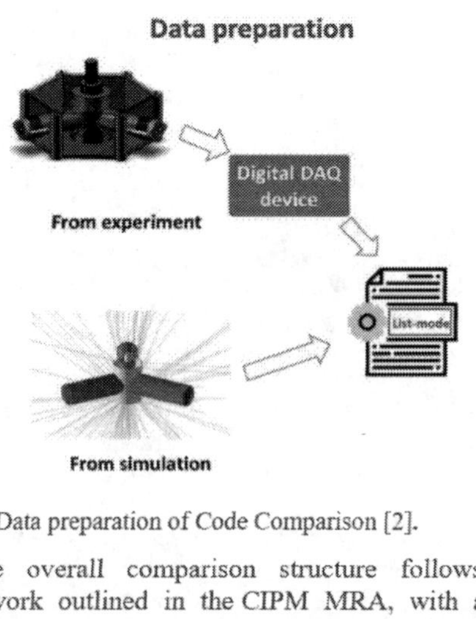

Fig. 2. Data preparation of Code Comparison [2].

The overall comparison structure follows the framework outlined in the CIPM MRA, with a key modification in the "Circulate standards and report data" phase. Instead of distributing radioactive sources, the pilot laboratory provides a list-mode dataset from either an experimentally validated measurement comparison, a prior algorithm comparison, or an

t pp s/dI o.gprj d01g01) 0de: 3conf615) (5(0011(

unvalidated dataset from a volunteer laboratory using a proper digitizer (see Fig. 2). Alternatively, the dataset may be generated through Monte Carlo simulations, allowing evaluation under various processing conditions [2,3,8,11].

Each participating laboratory processes the list-mode dataset using its proprietary software and submits the results accordingly (see Fig. 3). Subsequent steps remain unchanged, ensuring alignment with the standard comparison procedures while adapting the methodology to software-based evaluations.

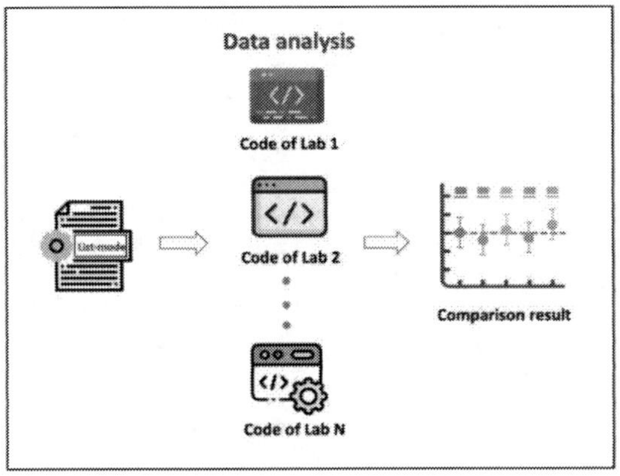

Fig. 3. Data analysis of Code Comparison [2].

3 Development of the Code Comparison Platform (NuCodeComP) for Radionuclide Metrology

3.1 Key Requirements and Design Principles

The NuCodeComP was developed at BIPM to provide a standardized environment for evaluating the performance of signal processing and activity estimation [2]. The objective was to create a FAIR-compliant system that supports structured, machine-readable, and interoperable data processing in line with the D-SI framework [5,12].

3.1.1 Design Requirements

The platform was designed based on the following principles:

• **Reliability and Data Integrity:** Ensuring a secure and auditable framework that maintains traceability of processed data back to the original list-mode dataset, in compliance with metrological standards [8].

• **Interoperability:** Compatibility with list-mode data formats, adhering to IEC 63047:2021 for radionuclide activity measurements [3].

• **Scalability and Future-Proofing**: Handle increasing data volumes and evolving metrological requirements, integrating cloud-based solutions.

3.1.2 Technology Stack

The M365 ecosystem was chosen for rapid deployment and cost efficiency, leveraging the BIPM inside it and using the following tools [7,13]:

• **PowerApps:** For building the user interface with drag-and-drop simplicity.

• **SharePoint**: Used as the primary database for structured storage of list-mode datasets and analysis results.

• **Power BI**: For data visualization and reporting, ensuring clear insights into software performance across laboratories.

• **Power Automate**: For future automation, such as sending e-mails automatically after each comparison step.

3.2 Insights from the Development Process

The development and implementation of the platform provided some insights that shaped its functionality and guided future improvements. A critical observation was the importance of real-world software testing at zero cost before investing in scalability. The initial prototype was developed within an already available M365 environment, leveraging PowerApps without additional expenses for infrastructure, database management, or hosting services. This approach allows the team to assess usability, identify performance bottlenecks, and evaluate access limitations using existing organizational resources.

Following initial validation, NuCodeComP can operate as the primary application for managing algorithm comparisons in radionuclide metrology, supporting this role within its current structure. The platform facilitates processing and validating final results while also tracking intermediate subset values throughout the comparison workflow [14]. This feature allows laboratories to evaluate specific processing steps, detect anomalies, and improve consistency before final reporting. These enhancements align with CIPM MRA guidelines, ensuring traceability in software-based radionuclide metrology comparisons [8].

The platform is accessed via a web browser using M365 accounts, with development simplified through PowerApps' drag-and-drop interface. Users familiar with Microsoft PowerPoint can adapt quickly to the PowerApps environment, enabling efficient development. SharePoint tables serve as the database, integrating pre-configured elements such as forms and galleries for structured data management.

Power BI is used for data visualization and structuring comparison results into interactive dashboards. Power Automate handles automated notifications and updates, supporting communication tasks such as comparison status alerts [13].

4 Implementation and Technical Considerations

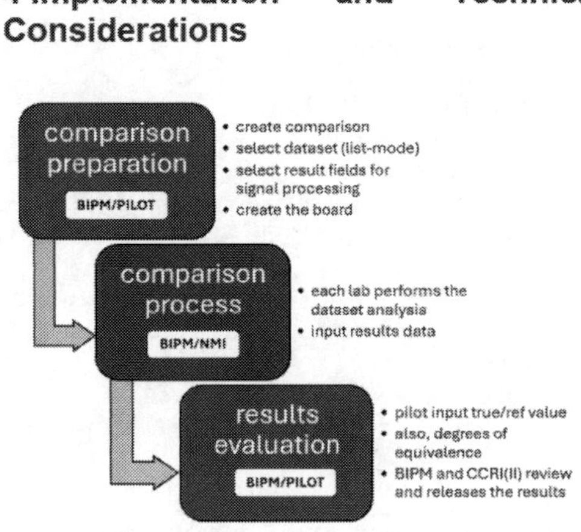

Fig. 4. Workflow Overview.

4.1 Platform Workflow and Data Processing

The NuCodeComP operates as a structured digital environment for interlaboratory evaluations, analyzing the results of those software-based activity estimations. The workflow (see Fig. 4) shows a general sequence of data submission, processing, and evaluation aligned with metrological standards and the D-SI Framework.

In the **Comparison Preparation** phase:

• In that phase, the Comparison Protocol was accepted by the comparison board members and the CCRI(II);

• BIPM or the Pilot Lab submits list-mode datasets following the protocol and IEC 63047:2021 specifications.

• Files are uploaded to SharePoint, where metadata (e.g., measurement conditions, equipment parameters) are registered.

• The necessary and optional fields for participants to input their results are configured.

• The comparison board is created and called to join in the comparison on the NuCodeComP.

In the **Comparison Process** phase:

• Participating laboratories download the dataset (including the list-mode data) and process it using their own software.

• Output files include processed activity results, uncertainty estimations, applied corrections, and rich metadata (parameters of digital measurement model) currently not considered in conventional comparisons.

• Processed results are re-uploaded to the platform.

In the **Results Evaluation** phase:

• Pilot Lab analyses and validates/corrects the pre-calculated evaluation parameters, such as true/reference value and the degrees of equivalence.

• A semi-automated validation script checks for format compliance and consistency with input parameters, reinforcing compliance with ISO/IEC 17025 [15].

• BIPM and CCRI(II) review and release the results.

For the visualization of comparison data:

• Power BI generates comparison charts.

• Users access a dashboard that highlights systematic deviations among laboratories according to access rules.

4.2 Scalability and Performance Limitations

Adopting an M365-based architecture provides a cost-effective and deployable solution for managing comparisons, but certain scalability constraints must be considered for long-term sustainability. A key limitation is SharePoint's data management, particularly the 20,000-row restriction per table for a fluid operation [16]. Based on projected data growth rates, NuCodeComP can operate within this limit for over 50 years. However, potential future expansions for additional applications should be evaluated before adopting M365 as the software platform.

Several scalability strategies are under consideration. One approach is migration to an SQL-based cloud storage solution, such as Azure SQL Server, which would enhance data handling efficiency and optimize query execution. While this transition involves additional costs, it ensures long-term scalability and faster data retrieval, supporting platform expansion. Alternatively, a hybrid model could be implemented, where metadata remains in SharePoint while large datasets are transferred to a cloud SQL database. This approach maintains SharePoint's cost efficiency while leveraging SQL for performance-intensive tasks, improving both accessibility and computational efficiency [17].

Another factor is user access and licensing limitations, particularly for non-M365 users. Currently, laboratories without M365 subscriptions face restricted access, limiting participation for institutions outside the Microsoft ecosystem. Possible solutions include institutional M365 subscriptions or per-app licensing plans (~$5–$6 per user/month). Additionally, Azure B2B authentication presents an alternative that allows external institutions to participate without requiring full M365 integration [18].

When scalability demands exceed expectations, migrating SharePoint data to an SQL-based system would be straightforward. Since data is already structured with defined types (e.g., CHAR, VARCHAR, FLOAT, INTEGER), transferring to cloud-based SQL storage would require minimal effort while maintaining data integrity and accessibility [19].

5 Impact on Digital Metrology and Future Developments

5.1 A Model for Other Metrology Applications

The NuCodeComP (see Fig. 5) applies a digital-first approach to radionuclide metrology comparisons, enhancing activity estimation algorithm evaluation by introducing a more detailed data processing analysis. This enables a comprehensive assessment of software performance and methodological
consistency throughout the measurement process.

This approach supports the digitalization of metrology, aligning with the D-SI framework to promote the use of structured, machine-readable, and interoperable datasets. The platform's architecture can also be adapted to other metrology fields that rely on digital signal processing, broadening its applicability beyond radionuclide metrology.

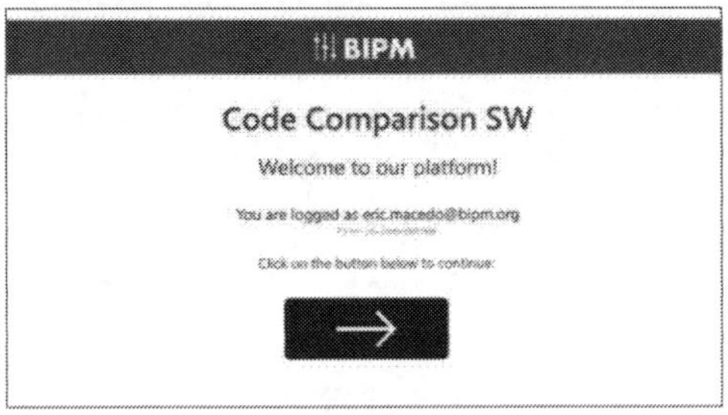

Fig. 5. NuCodeComP start page.

5.2 Future Improvements and Expansion

The NuCodeComP is advancing toward its first full version, with ongoing efforts to refine its functionalities and align with modern metrology frameworks. Current priorities include implementing Power BI dashboards for dynamic visualization and analysis of comparison results and integrating Power Automate into streamline communication workflows among participants. Additionally, the platform will be integrated with the D-SI framework, ensuring structured, interoperable, and machine-readable data principles through its reports. The platform's measurement data format will be interoperable with the recently developed machine-readable format for key comparisons in radionuclide metrology [20,21]. Expanding participant engagement will further validate usability, adaptability, and effectiveness in interlaboratory comparisons.

Beyond the initial deployment, future developments will aim to enhance automation, scalability, and real-time data processing capabilities. One possible envisioned expansion is the integration of measurement systems with the platform, enabling real-time data acquisition for quality control purposes.

The need for scaling computational and access management features will be assessed, identifying solutions for handling larger datasets and improving accessibility for laboratories outside the Microsoft 365 ecosystem.

Further iterations of the platform will incorporate advanced analytics and AI-driven automation to optimize data processing. Key enhancements include automated data quality checks and AI-driven detection of anomalies in submitted datasets.

In alignment with CIPM MRA, CCRI(II), and D-SI objectives, the long-term vision for NuCodeComP is to establish it as a reference model for software-based interlaboratory comparisons, extending its impact beyond radionuclide metrology [5,6,14]. This evolution will emphasize:

- FAIR Data Implementation, ensuring full compliance with Findable, Accessible, Interoperable, and Reusable principles [4].
- Interconnectivity with Global Metrology Networks, facilitating data exchange among BIPM, NMIs, and scientific repositories.

6 Conclusion

The Radionuclide Metrology Algorithm Comparison Platform (NuCodeComP) marks a significant step in the digital transformation of metrology, aligning with the CIPM Vision for Transforming the SI for a Digital World. The platform enables software-based comparisons and introduces a structured approach to interlaboratory comparisons, improving traceability, reproducibility, and efficiency.

Unlike traditional interlaboratory comparisons that focus solely on final activity estimations, NuCodeComP integrates intermediary processing steps, providing detailed insights into software performance and measurement methodologies. By structuring signal processing and activity estimation workflows, the platform ensures that each stage is documented, auditable, and reproducible, reinforcing the SI Digital Framework (D-SI).

The use of the Microsoft 365 ecosystem enabled rapid deployment without additional infrastructure costs, leveraging existing tools for data processing, access control, and interlaboratory collaboration. However, scalability and accessibility challenges—including SharePoint performance limitations and restricted access for non-M365 users—need future exploration of cloud-based SQL solutions and alternative authentication models to expand participation.

Despite these constraints, NuCodeComP's implementation has been effective, providing insights into software-based activity estimations and establishing a digital reference model for metrology. Future developments will focus on full D-SI framework integration, automated data validation, and AI-driven anomaly detection. Additionally, the platform will support machine-readable metrology reports, ensuring compliance with FAIR data principles and interoperability with global metrology networks, including BIPM and NMIs.

As metrology transitions to digital infrastructure, NuCodeComP demonstrates the feasibility of software-driven comparisons, contributing to cost-effective, scalable, and globally interoperable solutions for the future of measurement science.

References

1. Johansson L. Protocol for a CCRI(II) Key Comparison of 99Tc [Internet]. **v1.2** (2012) [cited 2025 Feb 9]. Available from: https://www.bipm.org/kcdb/comparison?id=1003
2. Liu H. Application of Müller EDT formulae to 4πβLS-γ coincidence counting at NIM. In: ICRM

RMT WG 2024[Internet] (2024) [cited 2025 Feb 9]. Available from: https://physics.nist.gov/ICRM/Application%20of%20Muller%20EDT%20formulae%20to%204pbLS-%CE%B3%20coincidence%20counting%20at%20NIM%20LIU.pdf
3. IEC. EN 63047. Nuclear instrumentation - Data format for list mode digital data acquisition used in radiation detection and measurement. EN IEC 63047 (2021).
4. GOFAIR. FAIR Principles [Internet] (n.d.) [cited 2025 Feb 5]. Available from: https://www.go-fair.org/fair-principles/
5. Lewis AJ, Yacoot A, Milton MJT, Lancaster AJ. A digital framework for realising the SI - A proposal for the metre. Metrologia **59**(4), (2022). DOI: 10.1088/1681-7575/ac7fce
6. CIPM-TG-DSI. CIPM Vision Transforming the International System of Units for a Digital World [Internet] (2023). Available from: https://www.go-fair.org/fair-principles/
7. Microsoft. Microsoft 365 for Enterprise [Internet] (2025) [cited 2025 Feb 9]. Available from: https://www.microsoft.com/en-us/microsoft-365/microsoft-365-enterprise
8. CIPM MRA. Measurement comparisons in the CIPM MRA - Guidelines for organizing, participating and reporting. CIPM MRA-G-11 [Internet] (2021) [cited 2025 Feb 9]. Available from: https://www.bipm.org/documents/20126/43742162/CIPM-MRA-G-11.pdf/9fe6fb9a-500c-9995-2911-342f8126226c?version=1.9&t=1630664744528&download=true
9. Ratel G, Michotte C. BIPM comparison BIPM.RI(II)-K1.Ba-133 of activity measurements of the radionuclide Ba-133 and links for the 1984 international comparison CCRI(II)-K2.Ba-133. Metrologia **40**(1A), 06011–06011 (2003). DOI: 10.1088/0026-1394/40/1A/06011
10. Michotte C, Nonis M. Experimental comparison of different dead-time correction techniques in single-channel counting experiments. Nucl Instrum Methods Phys Res A **608**, 163–8 (2009). DOI: 10.1016/j.nima.2009.06.010
11. Bouchard J. MTR2: a discriminator and dead-time module used in counting systems. Appl Radiat Isot [Internet] **52**, 441–6 (2000). Available from: www.elsevier.com/locate/apradiso
12. Hutzschenreuter D, Härtig F, Heeren W, Wiedenhöfer T, Forbes A, Brown C, Smith I, Rhodes S, Linkeová I, Sýkora J, Zelený V, Ačko B, Klobučar R, Nikander P, Elo T, Mustapää T, Kuosmanen P, Maennel O, Hovhannisyan K, Müller B, Heindorf L, Paciello V. Digital System of Units (2019). DOI: 10.5281/zenodo.3522631
13. Microsoft. Microsoft Power Platform [Internet] (2025) [cited 2025 Feb 9]. Available from: https://www.microsoft.com/en-us/power-platform/
14. CCRI(II). Guidelines for CCRI(II) key comparisons. Consultative Committee for Ionizing Radiation, Section II. Report No.: CCRI(II)/03-06 [Internet] (2003) [cited 2025 Feb 12]. Available from: https://www.bipm.org/documents/20126/48200031/working-document-ID-712/368f7f69-208a-7de4-1303-e2f8dc9b192b
15. ISO/IEC. 17025. General requirements for the competence of testing and calibration laboratories. International Organization for Standardization and International Electrotechnical Commission (2017).
16. Microsoft. SharePoint help & learning [Internet] (2025) [cited 2025 Feb 12]. Available from: https://support.microsoft.com/en-us/sharepoint
17. Microsoft. Azure SQL Database [Internet] (2025) [cited 2025 Feb 12]. Available from: https://azure.microsoft.com/en-us/products/azure-sql/database
18. Microsoft. Authentication and Conditional Access for External ID [Internet] (2024) [cited 2025 Feb 12]. Available from: https://docs.azure.cn/en-us/entra/external-id/authentication-conditional-access
19. Microsoft. Microsoft Power Fx overview [Internet] (2025) [cited 2025 Feb 9]. Available from: https://learn.microsoft.com/en-us/power-platform/power-fx/overview
20. Coulon R, Courte S, Judge S, Michotte C, Nonis M. Digitalization of the reporting of key comparisons for radionuclide metrology. Meas Sci Technol **33**, 024003 (2022). DOI: 10.1088/1361-6501/ac3fc4
21. Coulon R, Toro FG, Michotte C. Machine-readable data and metadata of international key comparisons in radionuclide metrology. Meas Sci Technol **34**, 074009 (2023). DOI: 10.1088/1361-6501/accd0b

EPJ Web of Conferences **323**, 00114 (2125) https://doi.org/01.0150/epjconf/212532300114
22nd nIt enr Iá nr dMt Iei á gylCi nget ss

Progress achieved in EURAMET project 21GRD09 MetroPOEM: Metrology for the harmonisation of measurements of environmental pollutants in Europe

Dirk Arnold[1†], *Rasmus* Andreasen[2], *Oktay* Cankur[3], *Lucille* Chambon[4], *Marcus* Christl[5], *José Antonio* Corcho Alvarado[6], *Betül Ari* Engin[3‡], *Arunas* Gudelis[7], *Karin* Hain[8], *Violeta* Hansen[9], *Steffen* Happel[10], *Mihail-Razvan* Ioan[11], *Johanna* Irrgeher[12], *Simon* Jerome[13], *Béatrice* Lalère[14], *Valérie* Lourenço[4], *Dmitriy* Malinovskiy[15], *Monika* Mazánová[16], *Jelena Krneta* Nikolić[17], *Johanna* Noireaux[14], *Habacuc* Perez-Tribouillier[5], *Daniel* Pröfrock[18], *Jixin* Qiao[19], *Ben* Russell[20], *Susanna* Salminen-Paatero[21], *Christian* Schöpke[22], *Sinikka* Virtanen[23], *Jochen* Vogl[24], *Clemens* Walther[25], *Stella* Winkler[26] and *Tea* Zuliani[27]

[1]Physikalisch-Technische Bundesanstalt, Germany
[2]Aarhus Universitet, Denmark
[3]Türkiye Bilimsel ve Teknolojik Araştırma Kurumu Ulusal Metroloji Enstitüsü, Türkiye
[4]Université Paris-Saclay, CEA, List, Laboratoire National Henri Becquerel, France
[5]Eidgenössische Technische Hochschule Zürich, Switzerland
[6]Labor Spiez, Switzerland
[7]Fizinių ir technologijos mokslų centras, Lithuania
[8]Universität Wien, Austria
[9]Göteborgs universitet, Sweden
[10]Triskem International, France
[11]Institutul Național de Cercetare Dezvoltare pentru Fizică și Inginerie Nucleară Horia Hulubei, Romania
[12]Montanuniversität Leoben, Austria
[13]Norges miljø- og biovitenskapelige universitet, Norway
[14]Laboratoire national de métrologie et d'essais, France
[15]National Measurement Laboratory, United Kingdom
[16]Český Metrologický Institut, Czech Republic
[17]Vinča Institut za Nuklearne Nauke, Serbia
[18]Helmholtz-Zentrum Hereon, Germany
[19]Danmarks Tekniske Universitet, Denmark
[20]National Physical Laboratory, United Kingdom
[21]Helsingin yliopisto, Finland
[22]Institutt for energiteknikk, Norway
[23]Säteilyturvakeskus, Finland
[24]Bundesanstalt für Materialforschung und -prüfung, Germany
[25]Leibniz Universität Hannover, Germany
[26]Helmholtz-Zentrum Dresden-Rossendorf, Germany
[27]Institut Jožef Stefan, Slovenia

Abstract. The European Green Deal's ambition for zero pollution requires development of highly sensitive techniques to detect ultra-low amounts of pollutants and determine their isotope ratios, where mass spectrometry is a key method. The project bridges the traceability gap between activity and mass measurements – particularly estimation of mass bias – and establishes new tools for pollutant tracing. SI-traceable reference materials and measurement procedures are being developed that significantly reduce measurement uncertainty and detection limits, to enable tracking pollution sources by commonly available mass spectrometers. This project supports strategies described by the European Metrology Network on pollution monitoring and the established EMN on radiation protection. Main areas of work are:

- Development of low-level radionuclide standards for ^{90}Sr and a series of actinides,
- Development of SI traceable high-precision analytical methods for isotope ratio determination of Li, B, Cr, Cd, Ni, Sb, Pb, and U in environmental matrices applicable to single and multi-collector ICP-MS systems.
- Generation of two reference materials – seawater and silica – spiked with radionuclides
- Production of certified seawater reference material for isotope ratio to validate analytical methods, support proficiency testing, and ensure quality control in future monitoring.
- Communication of project outcomes include peer reviewed papers, good practice guides, workshops, conference presentations and more.

† Lead Author, dirk.arnold@ptb.de
‡ Currently at LGC, UK

https://doi.org/01.0150/epjconf/212532300114

1 Introduction

The overall aim of the project is to bridge the gap between radiometric techniques and mass spectrometry for the characterisation and detection of polluting long lived radionuclides and stable elements and element tracers by comparing and linking both techniques, thus significantly improving measurement uncertainties and detection limits.
The specific objectives of the project are:

- To establish and compare the selectivity and detection limits of different types of mass spectrometers for selected radioactive pollutants using isotope reference materials and activity standards. This included assessing relative instrument performance with respect to current measurement challenges and establishing detection limits in relation to regulatory waste criteria levels or environmental regulations.
- To develop measurement methods for isotope ratios that are traceable to the SI by using multi-collector ICP-MS and apply these methods on more commonly available techniques (ICP-MS/MS, ICP-QMS) by providing suitable operating procedures focussing on selected stable polluting elements. This leads to producing recommendations for sample processing, treatment, uncertainty budgets and the quantification of the mass bias.
- To develop two radioactive reference materials with the sample matrix containing radioactive pollutants for use in an inter-laboratory comparison employing techniques used in the first objective, demonstrating the variations in parameters including detection limits, sample preparation requirements, sample introduction methods, total procedural time, and uncertainty budgets.
- To implement and validate the methods for isotope ratio measurements established in second objective by the development of one aqueous certified reference material (CRM) certified for the same stable polluting elements with lowest possible uncertainties using multi-collector instruments, in order to facilitate the calibration of single collector ICP-MS, instrument validation, as well as quality control.
- To facilitate the take up of the technology and measurement infrastructure developed in the project by the measurement supply chain, standards developing organisations and international organisations and end users.

These objectives are described in detail below.
Further information about the project can be accessed from the project website:
https://www.npl.co.uk/euramet/metropoem

2 Work Package 1: Establish and compare the selectivity and detection limits of different mass spectrometers

Mass spectrometry is increasingly being used in the measurement of medium and long-lived radionuclides (half-lives of approximately 20 years or longer). Approximately 25 radionuclides have up to now been measured using mass spectrometry techniques, including actinides, ^{90}Sr, ^{93}Zr, ^{99}Tc, ^{129}I and ^{135}Cs. The application areas for mass spectrometric measurement of radionuclides include contributing to safe and cost-effective decommissioning through accurate waste characterisation, nuclear forensics to determine the source of contamination, contributing to updated half-life measurements, and environmental radioactivity measurement. Mass spectrometry offers potential advantages over α- and β-particle counting techniques, including short measurement times of several minutes per sample, and the potential to measure several hundred samples each day depending on the instrument type and setup. Some instrument designs are also capable of online separation from interferences (for example through high resolution or collision/reaction cell capabilities), reducing reliance on relatively time-consuming offline chemical separation and further contributing to the high sample throughput.
The increasing application of mass spectrometry for radionuclide measurement needs to be supported with underpinning traceable standards and methods. The aim of WP1 is to develop a series of single and mixed standards of radionuclides relevant to mass spectrometry measurement. These standards are distributed to participating laboratories for measurement by a range of mass spectrometric techniques, as well as radiometric techniques through an inter-laboratory comparison exercise and report.

2.1 Determination of starting materials

Given the range of participating laboratories in the consortium, the first step was to send a survey to all laboratories to understand their measurement capabilities and what radionuclide and activity levels would make sense for the most valuable comparison exercise. It was decided at the start of the project to focus on actinides (^{237}Np, ^{234}U, ^{236}U, U_{nat}, ^{239}Pu, ^{240}Pu, ^{241}Am, $^{239/240}$Pu), ^{90}Sr and a mixed standard. Questions in the survey included the activity range measurable by each laboratory, the activity levels that would be of interest, interferences to be considered, the carrier the samples should be prepared in, and any national or international regulatory limits that should be considered when selecting the activity concentrations.
As expected, the survey results produced a range of activity levels. It was decided to focus on low-level measurements, which reflected the activity levels expected in environmental samples and the detection limits that needed to be achieved to comply with most regulatory limits. Some participating laboratories did not have the required licence to handle radioactive materials. However, by preparing standards at environmentally relevant levels, the samples could be considered as exempt for shipping purposes and safely sent.

2.2 Sample Preparation

All samples were prepared in dilute sub-boiled nitric acid, which can be directly measured by some mass spectrometry designs. A series of dilutions were performed from standardised single radionuclide standard solutions prepared at NPL and diluted in a dedicated source preparation facility containing calibrated five and six figure balances. For some radionuclides, these same starting standards were used for the preparation of the liquid and solid reference materials in WP3. The starting materials had previously been characterised for impurity levels but were remeasured by NPL with additional measurements being undertaken by CEA. The activity concentrations could be determined from the masses of material and carrier added, along with the characterisation of the standards by NPL with supporting measurements from CEA. Dilution checks were performed using Liquid Scintillation Counting for higher activity samples, and by Inductively Coupled Plasma Tandem Mass Spectrometry (ICP-MS/MS) for lower activity samples. A series of standards were also prepared for long-term homogeneity and stability measurements by ICP-MS/MS.

Materials were dispatched to eighteen participating laboratories. The aim was for all laboratories to receive the same starting activities for each radionuclide and mix of interest, even though not all laboratories were able to receive the same range of radionuclides due to measurement and/or sample handling restrictions. In some specific cases, higher activity starting materials were also requested. In the cases of laboratories receiving samples containing U and Pu isotopes, an export licence was required prior to dispatch, along with acknowledgement of safety and security considerations of handling the samples.

2.3 Sample Measurement and next steps

A range of mass spectrometric techniques are being used to measure the standards prepared, specifically quadrupole ICP-MS, tandem ICP-MS/MS, sector field ICP-MS, multi-collector ICP-MS, thermal ionisation MS, accelerator MS and decay counting techniques (α-spectrometry, liquid scintillation counting and γ-spectrometry). A template was prepared for submission of results from each laboratory. This included the activity levels (and where relevant isotopic ratio values) measured, the uncertainty budget, the measurement technique(s) used and details of any sample preparation. The details submitted through the template will form the basis of data analysis and the production of an interlaboratory comparison report. The report will provide a comprehensive overview of the advantages and limitations of different mass spectrometric techniques for measurement of the same starting materials. This will also support the development of a Good Practice Guide on the Measurement of radionuclides using mass spectrometry, that will be a valuable resource for current and potential future users of this technique.

3 Work Package 2: Advancing stable and long-lived radiogenic isotope ratio measurements of environmental pollutants

Determining isotope ratios in environmental pollutants has become a crucial tool in modern analytical chemistry, providing valuable insights into pollution sources, transformation processes, and environmental fate. Isotope ratio analysis enables researchers to trace the origins of contaminants, differentiate between natural and anthropogenic sources, and assess chemical pathways in various environmental matrices. Recent advancements in mass spectrometry techniques, single and multi-collector inductively coupled plasma mass spectrometry ((MC)-ICP-MS), have significantly improved the precision, sensitivity, and applicability of isotope analysis in environmental studies. Despite these advancements, several challenges remain in ensuring accurate and reproducible isotope ratio measurements. Matrix effects, instrumental mass bias, and sample preparation artifacts can introduce significant uncertainties, necessitating rigorous calibration strategies. A critical limitation in the field is the scarcity of SI-traceable certified reference materials (CRMs) for many non-traditional elements, which hinders method validation, interlaboratory comparability, and the establishment of standardized protocols. The lack of widely available CRMs also complicates the development of accurate mass bias correction models, which are essential for achieving high-precision isotope ratio determinations.

Work Package 2 of the MetroPOEM project is actively advancing the accurate and SI-traceable determination of isotope ratios for non-traditional elements using ICP-MS. New analytical methods are being developed to enable precise and traceable isotope ratio measurements of lithium (Li), boron (B), chromium (Cr), cadmium (Cd), nickel (Ni), antimony (Sb), lead (Pb), and uranium (U), ensuring robust metrological foundations. Analyte/matrix separation techniques are being optimized to improve the accuracy of isotope ratio measurements in complex environmental samples, effectively minimizing matrix-induced biases and interferences. At the same time, instrumental mass fractionation in ICP-MS is being evaluated and modelled by quantifying variations in instrumental isotope fractionation (IIF) across a wide mass range, from Li to U. This ongoing investigation, using multiple ICP-MS platforms and key elements, is enhancing the understanding of mass bias effects and improving the reliability of isotope ratio determinations. Collectively, these efforts are establishing high-precision, SI-traceable methodologies for environmental isotope analysis.

3.1 Development of SI traceable methods for determination of isotope ratios of Li, B, Cr, Cd,

Ni, Sb, Pb, U by MC-ICP-MS and single collector ICP-MS

Accurate determination of isotope ratios for elements such as Li, B, Cr, Cd, Ni, Sb, Pb, and U is essential in various scientific disciplines, including environmental monitoring, geochemistry, and nuclear forensics. Central to achieving this accuracy is the availability of well-characterized, SI-traceable certified reference materials (CRMs) for these elements. After an extensive search, the following isotopic CRMs were recorded; Li isotope measurements are commonly referenced against the LSVEC standard (NIST RM 8545), while boron isotope analyses utilize NIST SRM 951a as a primary reference material. Chromium isotope determinations often refer to NIST SRM 979, for Cd BAM-I012, for Pb the NIST SRM 981 and for U IRMM 184 are commonly used. However, the availability of CRMs for elements like B (NIST SRM 951a) and Ni (NIST SRM 3136) are not available anymore, while for Sb is non-existent, posing challenges for precise isotope ratio measurements. In the framework of the WP2 a re-characterisation of the reference material LSVEC for Li isotope ratio is underway by an interlaboratory comparison that aims to determine the absolute Li isotope ratio and to improve the measurement uncertainty of the reference material. A range of instrumental techniques are employed, including multi-collector ICP-MS (MC-ICP-MS), sector field ICP-MS, quadrupole ICP-MS, and ICP-MS/MS. The performance of these techniques was assessed and compared in terms of accuracy and precision.

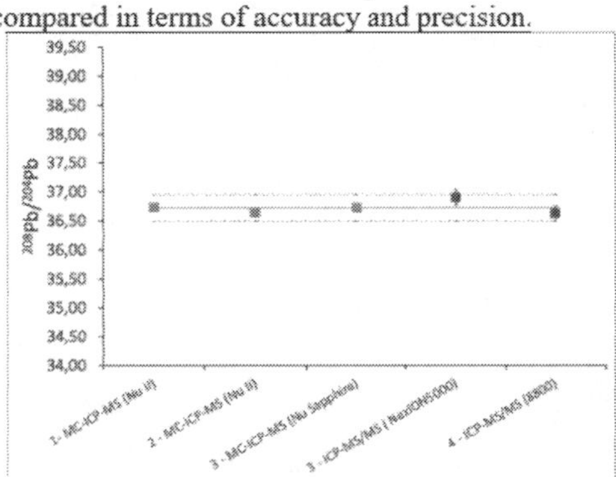

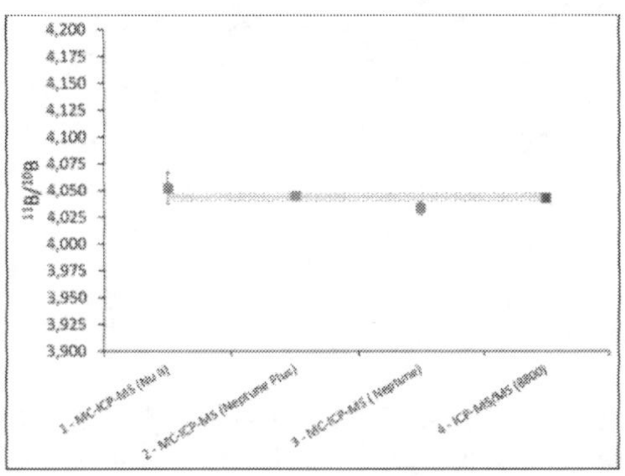

Figure 1: Comparison of isotope ratios for selected elements obtained with different mass spectrometers.

3.2 Development of analyte separation methods for high precision analysis

In order to obtain accurate and precise isotopic ratios in environmental samples, they need to be properly prepared. Several steps are usually applied before isotope ratio measurement. Depending on the type of the sample, there may be pre-treatment step needed. For solid samples, it consists of a digestion or extraction, while for liquids, usually a preconcentration is needed. Next is the separation step to isolate the element of interest from the sample matrix, and finally, the determination of the isotope ratios by measurement of the isotope responses and correction for instrumental isotopic fractionation. For the element isolation from the matrix different resins are being tested, as shown in Table 1.

Isotopic system	Resin
Li	AG 50W-X12
B	sublimation
	AG 50W-X8 and Amberlite IRA 743
	AG 50W-X8 and Microsublimation
Cr	BioRad AG 1-X8
Ni	Ni-Spec and others
	Chelex 100 chelating resin
Cd	BioRad AG 1-X8
	BioRad MP-1M
Pb	Sr spec
	DGA resin
	Pb Resin Triskem
	Anion exchange BioRad AG-1 X-8
U	Anion exchange BioRad AG-1 X-8

Table 1: Resins used for matrix removal.

3.3 Evaluating and modelling instrumental mass fractionation in ICP-based mass spectrometers

Instrumental isotope fractionation is a significant challenge in mass spectrometry, particularly in MC-ICP-MS. This phenomenon can lead to biased isotope ratio measurements, necessitating the development of correction methods. Traditionally, IIF has been corrected using empirical equations such as Power, Exponential and Russel law. However, a few studies show inaccuracy or significant deviations from true values when applying these conventional models. In the frame of WP2, current methods are being improved and new approaches developed based on inter-element normalisation and without a priori assumptions. One method that is being improved in the gravimetric isotope mixture approach, a primary method for the determination of SI-traceable isotope ratios. The latest variation of the approach introduces ion chromatography to determine the elemental mass fractions in the enriched isotope solutions. It significantly simplifies the classical isotope mixture approach. This new approach has been published [1] and it will be applied in the interlaboratory comparison on Li isotope ratios (CCQM-K182/P233) for testing the achievable uncertainty level and the comparability of laboratory results. Although the primary method is a strong asset, for routine use, the method has, unfortunately, some throwbacks like enriched isotopes are not available for many stable elements, and/or the required uncertainty level does not justify the costs and efforts of applying this method. Therefore, additional methods are required. For the isotopic systems where the gravimetric isotope mixture cannot be applied, and iRM are not available, modelling of the IIF is being tested. Another method that is being optimised is the regression method to correct for instrumental isotope fractionation. The method is based on simultaneous measurement of analyte, for which isotope ratios are to be determined, and internal standard with known isotope ratios. In this case, the IIF correction factor can be accurately determined for the internal standard from its measured and a priori known isotope ratios and then be extrapolated to the analyte. Altogether, the work done in WP2 will establish high-precision, SI-traceable methodologies for environmental isotope ratio analysis.

4 Work Package 3: Development of radioactive reference materials

The aim of WP3 was to produce two radioactive reference materials, a liquid and a solid, to mimic contaminated water and soil. The matrix of the liquid reference material was seawater and was the same as the reference material developed in WP4. Thus, the liquid RM was as close as possible to a real environmental sample, and the measurements included sample preparation steps, such as concentration and removal of interfering ions. Following a different approach, the solid material chosen was synthesised from scratch, in order to control the amount and activity concentration of radionuclides added and improve the homogeneity. A silica-type material was used, as it is readily synthesised via a *sol-gel* process and can be ground to yield a sand-like material. Those two reference materials will be used in an interlaboratory comparison, so that partners of WP3 can test their usual measurement methods.

4.1 Spiking procedure

The procedure used to obtain materials with well-controlled radionuclide levels is similar for both the solid and the liquid. First, starting materials, ie solutions of one radionuclide or several isotopes of the same element, were characterised at two different laboratories, at NPL and at CEA, using radiometric techniques and mass spectrometry. Specific uranium and plutonium isotopic compositions were selected, after discussion within the partners of WP3, shown in Table . Those solutions were first mixed and then used to spike seawater, or with silica liquid precursors.

Reference Material	Uranium	Plutonium
Liquid	Natural	^{240}Pu:^{239}Pu mass ratio ~ 0.1
Solid	Slightly enriched	^{240}Pu:^{239}Pu mass ratio < 0.1

Table 2: U and Pu isotopic compositions chosen for both RMs.

All the liquids used were weighed with high precision balances, so that the concentration of each radionuclide could be derived from the masses added. In addition, the characterisation of both final materials was performed by two metrology laboratories (CEA and NPL). These two approaches to characterise the property values of a reference material are described in the ISO 17034 standard [2], and their results can be compared.
The homogeneity and stability of the two reference materials were assessed at NPL and CEA, following the ISO 33405 standard [3] and this work is the subject of an article to be published.

4.1.1 Liquid RM

The seawater used as matrix was sampled from the German Exclusive Economic Zone (EEZ), as described in section 5.1, filtered, acidified and sterilised by γ-ray irradiation. The initial radioactive content in the sterilised and acidified seawater was assessed by several labs, before spiking. Forty litres of seawater were mixed with the radionuclide solutions and homogenised by stirring for two weeks. After homogenisation, the liquid RM was bottled into 80 samples and sent for characterisation, and to participants.

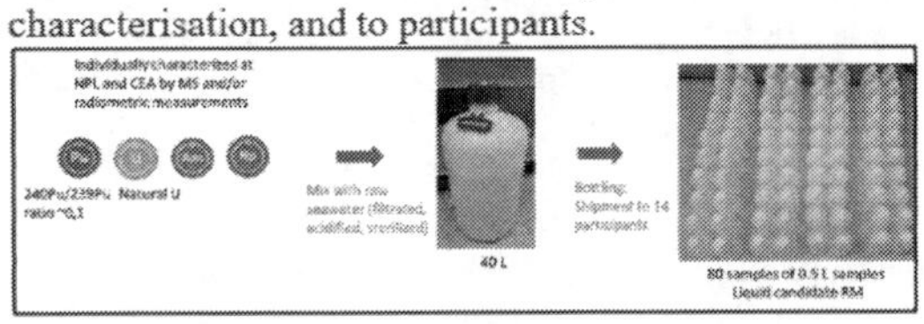

Figure 2: Schematics of the preparation procedure for the liquid RM samples.

4.1.2 Solid RM

The synthesis of the solid RM was adapted from Harms and Gilligan [4]. The radionuclide solutions (in nitric acid) were mixed with two silica precursors (tetraethyl orthosilicate and triethoxyoctylsilane), ethanol and nitric acid. The second silica precursor was used for its hydrophobic properties and generated a less hygroscopic material than pure silica one. After five days of stirring, the liquid reaction medium was transferred to trays, in order to facilitate the evaporation of ethanol. The complete solidification occurred 13 days after mixing, and the solid was dry after 22 days. It was then ground into a fine powder (particles smaller than 250 µm) with a jar miller and bottled into 82 samples.

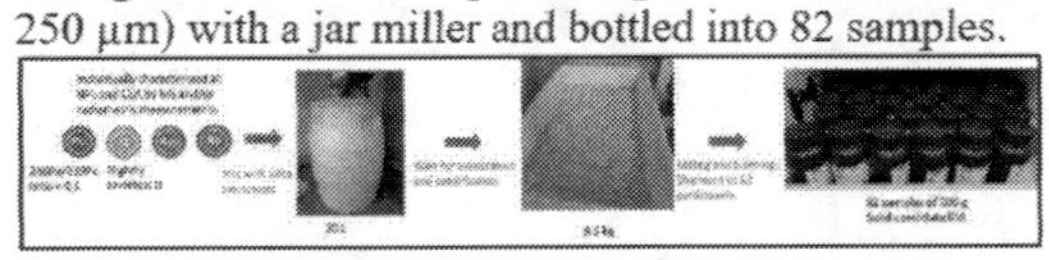

Figure 3: Schematics of the preparation procedure for the solid RM samples.

A batch of inactive solid was also synthesised using the same procedure, so that participants could test their dissolution procedure beforehand.

4.2 Organisation of an interlaboratory comparison

Both reference materials will be used in two interlaboratory comparisons. Participants will use radiometric and/or mass spectrometry measurements to determine the concentration of U, Pu, Am and Np, as well as the isotopic ratios of U and Pu, especially the ^{235}U:^{238}U mass ratio and the ^{240}Pu:^{239}Pu mass ratio. Around fifteen laboratories will take part in each comparison, including partners of WP3, and additional participants. The results are expected by the end of March 2025.

5 Work Package 4: Development of SI traceable certified reference material

The reference materials are crucial for metrological traceability of the measurement results in case of calibration of the measuring instruments as well as for providing objective evidence for the quality of measurement result by ensuring the validity of the methods used for the measurement. This work package of the project is dedicated to preparation and certification of one of the two reference materials in the MetroPOEM project for the isotope ratios of the target elements with stable isotopes. The studies in this WP is divided into tasks which are collection, processing, certification measurements which include stability, homogeneity and characterization measurements, and finally the value assignment. All the preparation steps are carried out following the requirements of ISO 17034 [2].

The target elements within the scope of the project are boron, lithium, chromium, nickel, cadmium, antimony, lead, uranium. The isotope ratio values of these elements are the most widely used ones in different areas for making decisions and scientific works. The method used for the certification measurements are mostly the ones developed in WP2 of this project and requires matrix separation before introduction into the plasma. The parameters aimed to be certified in the project for stable elements and their corresponding concentrations are given in table 3.

Element	Concentration /µg kg^{-1}	Measurand
B	5000 – 6000	$n(^{11}B)/n(^{10}B)$
Li	140 – 170	$n(^{6}Li)/n(^{7}Li)$
Cd	10 – 15	$n(^{114}Cd)/n(^{111}Cd)$ $n(^{113}Cd)/n(^{111}Cd)$
Cr	12 – 18	$n(^{53}Cr)/n(^{52}Cr)$
Ni	10 – 16	$n(^{60}Ni)/n(^{58}Ni)$
Pb	6 –8	$n(^{204}Pb)/n(^{206}Pb)$ $n(^{207}Pb)/n(^{206}Pb)$ $n(^{208}Pb)/n(^{206}Pb)$
Sb	5 – 10	$n(^{123}Sb)/n(^{121}Sb)$
U	3 – 5	$n(^{234}U)/n(^{238}U)$ $n(^{235}U)/n(^{238}U)$

Table 3. Concentration ranges of elements to be measured in the seawater candidate material and reporting measurands.

5.1 Sampling of the raw material

The sampling was conducted as part of the regular monitoring research cruise AT 020 (Start Bremerhaven, Germany, 2023-05-15, End Bremerhaven, Germany, 2023-05-26) with the RV ATAIR operated by the German BSH covering the entire German EEZ as shown on the map presented in figure 4. The sampling for candidate reference material was conducted at station UE67, which is located at the edge of the German EEZ.

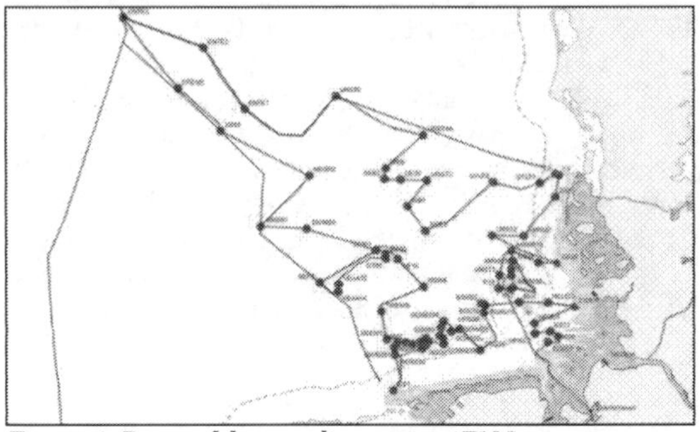

Figure 4: Route of the sampling cruise AT020

A total of 250 L of seawater for the reference material was into brand new 25 L carboys specified for food applications analysis. The carboys were cleaned by using a procedure where subsequent flushing with DI water, 1% acid solutions several times by keeping the inner surfaces of the carboys in contact with 1% HCl for 1 week and then rinsing with ultrapure water.

The water sample was collected by using the trace metal clean PVDF made clean seawater inlet system of the German research vessel ATAIR. The water was pumped into the ship from a depth of 5 m below sea level. The water was directly filtered using precleaned trace metal free filter cartridges (Pall AcroPak 1500 0.8/0.2 µm), into 25 L precleaned carboys. Before collecting the final sample each carboy was rinsed three times with ca. 1 L of seawater filtrate to precondition the surface of the carboy. In total two filter units were necessary to process the total volume ca. 250 L seawater. After filling the carboys they were closed and the outside was rinsed with MilliQ to remove any spilled seawater from the surface. The filtered raw material was acidified using 2 times sub-boiled HNO3 to stabilize the material. The carboys were sealed and individually packed in clean PE foil and stored at 4°C.

5.2 Processing and bottling of seawater reference material

The collected samples were transferred to Hereon laboratories where 50 mL aliquots from each carboy were taken under cleanroom conditions to allow a preliminary analysis of the trace metal content of individual samples. The purpose of the preliminary analysis conducted by using SeaFAST- ICP-MS/MS (Agilent 8900 QQQ) using a He/H_2 mixed gas mode [5]. The level of the parameters to be certified should be fit for purpose. In most circumstances, it is desired that the levels in the reference materials should be well above the method limit of detection values for providing results with uncertainties suitable for decision making either during the method development or in the calibration of the instruments. Since the levels for some of the target elements were found to be very low in original raw material, the material was spiked with NIST SRM 3100 series standards for Cd, Cr, Ni, Sb and Pb, where the elements were assumed to be at their natural isotopic composition. Then approximately 120 L of seawater was transferred into a 120 L HDPE tank and the material was homogenised for four hours. After filtration through 0.8/0.2 µm (Pall Corp, Supor® Membrane, AcroPackTM 1000, PN 12992), the material was filled into bottles manually. At the end, a total of 470 bottles each containing 250 mL of candidate reference material were obtained. All the steps in processing of the material, including spiking, homogenization and filling into bottles were carried out in ISO Class 6 Clean Chemistry Laboratory (CCL) at TÜBİTAK UME (Figure WP4-2). The whole batch of the reference material units were sent to the γ irradiation facility and irradiated with a total exposure of 25 kGy in order to ensure no biological activity afterwards.

Figure 5: Homogenisation and bottling in ISO Class 6 Clean Chemistry Laboratory at TÜBİTAK UME

5.3 Homogeneity and stability tests for seawater reference material

The reference material producer is responsible for the stability and the homogeneity of the material produced in the batch. According to ISO 17034, the producer should ensure the material stability and homogeneity and should provide objective evidence for them. The different approaches for homogeneity and stability tests and the statistical evaluation of the data produced form these test measurements are given in ISO 33405 [3]. In this project, although no instability is expected as the material is natural and stabilized by acidification, the tests were carried out to comply the requirements of standard ISO 17034 and to ensure the stability of spiked elements. Since the measurements require very sophisticated tools, requires large sample amount and specific sample preparation, and finally takes very long time, a combined approach for the assessments of homogeneity, short-term stability and long-term stability is used. The measurements were carried out by the participating partners who can measure the isotopic ratio values for target elements.

In the long-term stability (LTS) test, an isochronous design was applied for testing the stability of the material at 22 °C. The stability of samples was tested at 4 periods of time: 3, 6, 9 and 12 months. The temperature 4 °C served as reference temperature and taken as the 0th time point. Total number units to be used in long term stability testing were placed at test temperature and at the end of each period, 2 units of material were transferred to and kept at reference temperature. After the period of one year from the start of testing, all units had been transferred to the reference temperature. Since the measurements for each parameter takes long time and requires specific sample preparation steps, and thus to be carried out by different partners, separate sets of samples were reserved for each parameter and sent to the participating laboratories at the end of testing period.

The short-term stability (STS) is done for testing the stability of the material at the transportation conditions that the reference material is potentially subjected to during their transfer to the end users. In this project, a single test temperature, 45 °C with a single test duration, 3 weeks, is tested for short term stability of the material. Two bottles of the material are subjected to test temperature for the test period and then transferred to reference temperature to be measured isochronously with the LTS samples whose reference points would serve as well for STS samples. Since the measurements for each parameter for both long-term and short-term samples were to be carried out by the same project partner, the STS samples were sent to the measuring laboratories together with them. The stability measurements are still in progress at the time of the preparation of this manuscript. The reporting and the evaluation of the results are expected to be complete at the end of March 2025.

5.4 Characterization of seawater reference material

Characterisation is required where the certified value is to be assigned by the reference material producer. The assigned value can be either quantitative or qualitative. There are different approaches for the characterization of the reference materials. One of these approaches is the determination of the value to be assigned by an interlaboratory study between the competent laboratories where the consensus value between the participating laboratories is assigned as the certified value. In MetroPOEM project, this approach is selected for characterization. In addition to the project partners who agreed on getting involved during the preparations of the project, the other experienced laboratories in the field of isotopic measurements were also invited for the characterization measurements. A registration form was sent to the potential participating laboratories. They are asked to fill in the registration form by checking the parameters that they would like to participate in the measurements. The study protocol for the characterisation where the requirements for the measurements were explained was also sent to those laboratories. In total, there are 14 laboratories registered for the characterization study. Each laboratory received 2 units of samples unless they requested more samples for their measurements. The measurements are still in progress and results are expected to be reported by the end of March 2025.

6 Acknowledgement of funding

The project (21GRD09 MetroPOEM) has received funding from the European Partnership on Metrology, co-financed from the European Union's Horizon Europe Research and Innovation Programme and by the Participating States.

- Funder name: European Partnership on Metrology
- Funder ID: 10.13039/100019599
- Grant number: 21GRD09 MetroPOEM

References

1. L. Flierl, O. Rienitz, J. Vogl and A. Pramann, An advancement of the gravimetric isotope mixture method rendering the knowledge of the spike purity superfluous. Analytical and Bioanalytical Chemistry, **416(24)**,5325 (2024). https://doi.org/10.1007/s00216-024-05465-9
2. International Organisation for Standardisation, General requirements for the competence of reference materials producers. ISO 17034-2016, ISO, Geneva, Switzerland (2016)
3. International Organisation for Standardisation, Reference materials — Approaches for characterization and assessment of homogeneity and stability. ISO 33405:2024, ISO, Geneva, Switzerland (2024)
4. A. Harms and C. Gilligan, Development of synthetic environmental radioactivity reference materials. Applied Radiation and Isotopes, **70(9)**,1940 (2012). https://doi.org/10.1016/j.apradiso.2012.02.055
5. A. Ebeling, T. Zimmermann, O. Klein, J. Irrgeher and D. Pröfrock, Analysis of Seventeen Certified Water Reference Materials for Trace and Technology-Critical Elements. Geostandards and Geoanalytical Research, **46(2)**, 351 (2022). https://doi.org/10.1111/ggr.12422

Electric field probe calibration method by using a TEM cell for reference field generation

Seif Ben-Hassine[1*], *Jean-Marie* Lerat[1]

[1]Laboratoire National de métrologie et d'essais LNE, HF Metrology Department, 78197 Trappes, France

Abstract. The article presents a method to calibrate electric field probes using a transverse electromagnetic (TEM) cell as a reference. The TEM cell generates uniform and repeatable fields for accurate calibration. The process and setup are carefully detailed to ensure precise generation and measurement. We perform a full uncertainty analysis, considering factors like power delivery, septum-to-wall distance, impedance mismatch, and field inhomogeneity. The total uncertainty of the calibration is 10 % of the electric field amplitude, ensuring good accuracy. To validate the method, measurements are compared with data from an accredited laboratory over a frequency range of 9 kHz to 300 MHz. The results show excellent agreement, with errors within acceptable limits. This confirms the reliability and robustness of the method. The proposed approach provides a reliable solution for accurate electric field probe calibration.

1 Introduction

The accurate measurement of electric fields is critical in various domains, including electromagnetic compatibility (EMC) testing, environmental monitoring, and health and safety evaluations. The electric field probes are indispensable tools for these applications, but their performance heavily relies on proper calibration. Inaccurate probe calibration can lead to erroneous measurements, affecting the reliability of test results and assessments.

Several methods have been developed for the calibration of electric field probes, with on widely accepted approach involving the use of a transverse electromagnetic (TEM) cell. [1] first introduced the TEM cell as a reliable means of generating standard electromagnetic fields, later formalized in calibration methods described by [2, 3, 4]. These methods ensure a controlled electromagnetic environment, providing consistency in measurements and making the TEM cell an ideal tool for calibration purposes.

This article presents a comprehensive calibration method using a TEM cell as a reference source for electric fields. The method provides a controlled environment that enables precise calibration across a wide range of field strengths and frequencies, ensuring reliable probe performance.

The paper is structured as follows: Section 2 describes the calibration method, including the measurement setup, conditions, and uncertainty considerations. Section 3 focuses on the validation of the method through comparison with results from an accredited external laboratory. Finally, Section 4 concludes this work.

2 Calibration method

2.1 Measurement setup

The core of the calibration method involves using a TEM cell to generate the reference electric field. In this study, a Schwarzbeck TEMZ-type TEM cell is employed. The TEM cell consists of two parallel conductive ground planes separated by a central conductor, known as the septum. The septum is terminated at both ends with connectors, through which the RF signal is injected at one end generate the electromagnetic field inside the cell. Due to the design of the TEM cell, the electric field generated is vertical with respect to the septum plane.

Figure 1 presents the calibration setup for the electric field measurement. To measure the generated electric field, the setup includes an attenuator connected to the second connector of the TEM cell. The attenuated signal is then measured using a calibrated power probe of type R&S URV5-Z2 equipped with a millwattmeter. A 50-ohm matching load is connected to the probe to ensure proper impedance matching, which is critical for accurate measurements.

As noted by [5, 8], the TEM cell is effective in minimizing reflections and maintaining a uniform field distribution during calibration. The electric field strength inside the cell is adjusted by controlling the input power from the RF source, allowing for precise control over the field intensity.

* Corresponding author: seif.benhassine@lne.fr

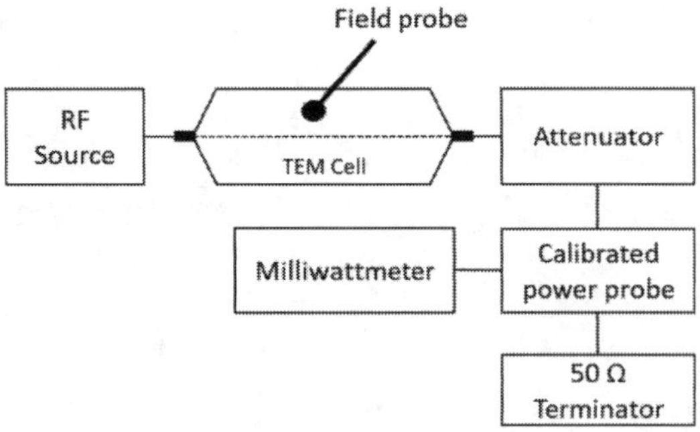

Fig. 1. Calibration setup of the reference electric field generation by using a TEM cell.

As shown in Figure 2, the probe to be calibrated is positioned at the 3D center of the cell, midway between the septum and the cell wall. The coordinates $P_c(x_0 = 0, y_0 = 0, z_0 = -100)$ designate this central position. In this study, we used a triaxial broadband isotropic electric field probe for measurements and validation. This setup ensures that the probe is exposed to a uniform and well-defined reference electric field.

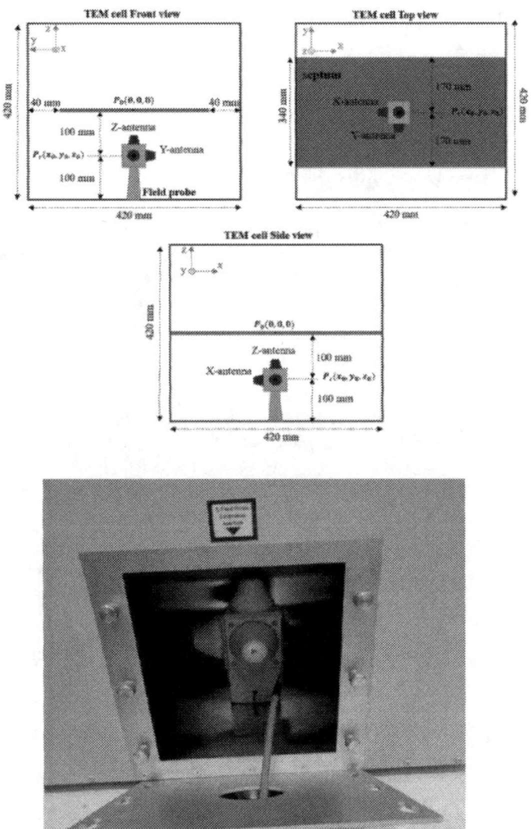

Fig. 2. Positioning of the field probe in the TEM cell.

2.2 Measurement conditions

The measurements are conducted within a controlled laboratory environment to ensure the accuracy and reliability of the calibration results. The laboratory is maintained at a stable temperature of 23±1.5 °C, which minimizes temperature-related fluctuations that could affect the performance of the electric field probes. In addition, the relative humidity in the laboratory is kept below 60 % to avoid moisture-related issues that could affect the measurements or the equipment. All ambient conditions, including temperature and humidity, are continuously monitored and recorded throughout the calibration process. This data is retained for reference and quality assurance, ensuring the any variations in environmental conditions are documented and can be taken into account during data analysis.

2.3 Uncertainty analysis for the measurement model

The electric field E_{TEM} generated within the TEM cell is modeled mathematically as follows:

$$E_{TEM} = \frac{\sqrt{P_{net}\mathrm{Re}(Z_0)}}{d} f(x,y,z) \qquad (1)$$

with:

- P_{net} is the net power delivered to the TEM cell.
- Z_0 is the characteristic impedance of the TEM cell.
- d is the distance between the septum and the lower wall of the cell.
- $f(x,y,z)$ is the inhomogeneity factor of the electric field along the x, y and z axes with reference to the central position $P_c(x_0, y_0, z_0)$. It is defined as:

$$f(x,y,z) = \frac{E_{TEM}(x,y,z)}{E_{TEM}(x_0,y_0,z_0)} = 1 + \varepsilon(x,y,z) \qquad (2)$$

where $\varepsilon(x,y,z)$ represents the uncertainty associated to the inhomogeneity factor along the x, y and z axes.
The uncertainty associated with the electric field is expressed as:

$$\frac{u^2(E_{TEM})}{E_{TEM}^2} = \frac{1}{4}\frac{u^2(P_{net})}{P_{net}^2} + \frac{1}{4}\frac{u^2(Z_0)}{\mathrm{Re}(Z_0)^2} + \frac{u^2(d)}{d^2} + \varepsilon(x,y,z) \qquad (3)$$

2.3.1 Input power measurement

The accurate measurement of the net power P_{net} delivered within the TEM cell is crucial for the uncertainty budget of the electric field calibration process. The mathematical model for P_{net} is expressed as:

$$P_{net} = \frac{C_p}{\left\|S_{21}^{cell}\right\|^2 \left\|S_{21}^{att}\right\|^2} \langle P_{mes} \rangle_n \qquad (4)$$

with:

- $\langle P_{mes} \rangle_n$ is the average of results from n measurements by the calibrated power probe.
- C_p is the calibration correction factor of the calibrated power probe.
- S_{21}^{cell} and S_{21}^{att} are the transmission coefficients of the TEM cell and attenuator, respectively.

The relative uncertainty associated with P_{net} is quantified by considering multiple sources of uncertainty. These components include the repeatability of power measurements, assessed through statistical analysis to evaluate measurement consistency. Additionally, the correction factor for the power probe is given from its calibration certificate. The potential drift of the probe over time is also taken into account. Furthermore, the uncertainties associated with the transmission coefficients of the TEM cell and the attenuator are included. These uncertainties are determined from measurements of the S-parameters using a calibrated vector network analyzer (VNA) in laboratory. Specifically, the uncertainty of the transmission coefficient of the TEM cell is estimated by considering the impact of the presence of a probe within the cell. The overall relative uncertainty can then be represented as:

$$\frac{u^2(P_{net})}{P_{net}^2}=\frac{u^2((P_{mes})_n)}{(P_{mes})_n^2}+\frac{u^2(C_p)}{C_p^2}+4\frac{u^2(S_{21}^{cell})}{\left|S_{21}^{cell}\right|^2}+4\frac{u^2(S_{21}^{att})}{\left|S_{21}^{att}\right|^2} \quad (5)$$

2.3.2 Error of cell septum distance

The uncertainty associated with the measurement of the distance d between the septum and the lower wall of the TEM cell influences the accuracy of electric field assessments. The distance is measured using either a laser rangefinder or a caliper. The measured distance can be expressed mathematically as follows:

$$d=(d_{mes})_n+C_q+C_j+d_{nom}\alpha\Delta T \quad (6)$$

with:

- $(d_{mes})_n$ is the average of n measurements taken with the laser rangefinder or caliper.
- C_q is the correction for quantization error during the measurement reading.
- C_j is the correction for measurement accuracy corresponding to the distance.
- d_{nom} is the nominal distance between the septum and the wall.
- α is the thermal expansion coefficient relevant to the TEM cell.
- ΔT is the temperature variation.

The correction for measurement accuracy C_j is neglected, along with the term involving the product of the nominal distance and the temperature variation ($d_{nom}\alpha\Delta T$). The relative uncertainty associated with the distance d is then expressed as:

$$\frac{u^2(d)}{d^2}=\frac{u^2((d_{mes})_n)}{d^2}+\frac{u^2(C_q)}{d^2}+\frac{(d_{norm}\alpha)^2}{d^2}u^2(\Delta T) \quad (7)$$

2.3.3 Inhomogeneity field factor

The evaluation of the inhomogeneity of the electric field is important for the calibration of the probe inside the TEM cell. This uncertainty component is assessed through CST simulations by evaluating the field within a distance of 20 mm from the central position $P_c(x_0, y_0, z_0)$, by varying the location along the longitudinal axis x, transverse axis y, and vertical axis z.

Figure 3 presents the variations of the electric field along the three axis for a frequency of 300 MHz. We observe that the field variations along the longitudinal axis x (the direction of propagation) are negligible. Therefore, the inhomogeneity depends primarily on the y and z components.

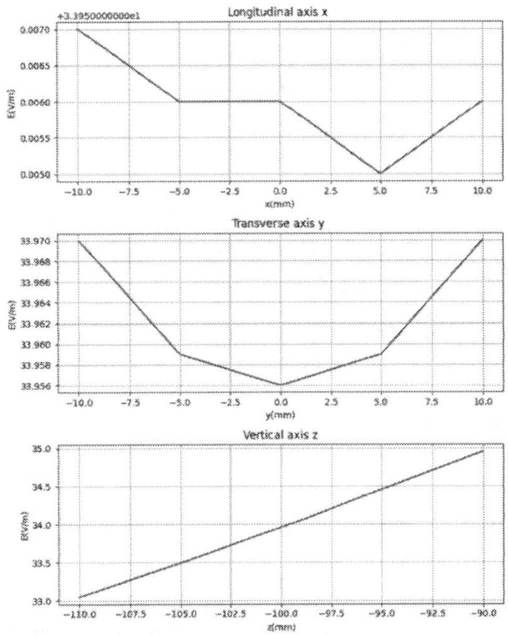

Fig. 3. Electric field distribution along the x, y, and z axes (CST simulation, f = 300 MHz), with respect to the central position $P_c(x_0, y_0, z_0)$.

The uncertainty component associated with the total inhomogeneity of the field is then given by:

$$\varepsilon^2(x,y,z)=u^2(y)+u^2(z) \quad (8)$$

The uncertainties associated with the field inhomogeneity along the transverse axis y and the vertical axis z, $u(y)$ and $u(z)$, are determined using a rectangular distribution, based on the maximum and minimum simulated values of the field.

2.3.4 Impedance mismatch error

The impedance mismatch of the TEM cell can lead to errors in the accurate determination of electric field values, impacting the reliability of the measurements. The estimation of the uncertainty related to the characteristic impedance Z_0 of the TEM cell is determined through measurements of its S-parameters. As shown in Figure 4, the TEM cell is modeled as a transmission line characterized by an impedance Z_0, with the load defined by an impedance Z_L and the source characterized by an impedance Z_s (typically set a 50 Ω) [6, 7].

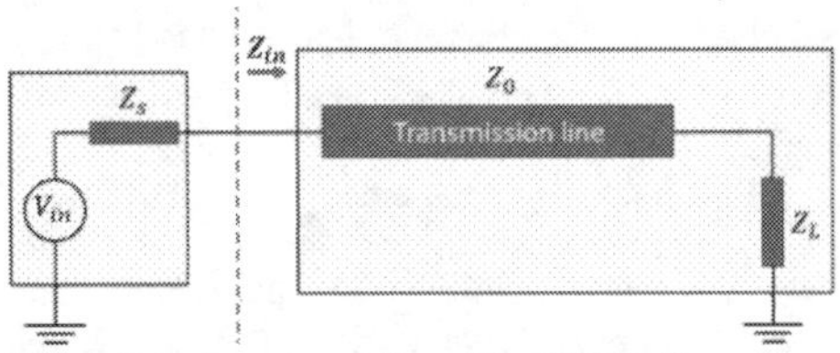

Fig. 4. Impedance modeling of the TEM cell.

The reflection coefficient of the cell S_{11} is defined based on the input impedance of the transmission line Z_{in} and the source impedance Z_s:

$$S_{11} = \frac{Z_{in} - Z_s}{Z_{in} + Z_s} \tag{9}$$

The input impedance Z_{in} is expressed as:

$$Z_{in} = Z_0 \frac{Z_L + Z_0 \tan\beta l}{Z_0 + Z_L \tan\beta l} \tag{10}$$

where β represents the phase constant of the transmission line, and *l* indicates the length of the transmission line segment. The input impedances for short-circuit and open-circuit conditions are expressed as follows:

$$Z_{in}^{cc} = \mathrm{j}\, Z_0 \tan\beta l = Z_s \frac{1 + S_{11}^{cc}}{1 - S_{11}^{cc}} \tag{11}$$

$$Z_{in}^{co} = Z_0 \frac{1}{\mathrm{j}\tan\beta l} = Z_s \frac{1 + S_{11}^{co}}{1 - S_{11}^{co}} \tag{12}$$

Here, S_{11}^{cc} and S_{11}^{co} are the reflection coefficients of the cell in short-circuit and open-circuit configurations, respectively. The characteristic impedance Z_0 of the TEM cell is derived from the measurements of its S_{11} parameter in both short-circuit and open-circuit conditions. It is defined by:

$$Z_0 = \sqrt{Z_{in}^{cc} Z_{in}^{co}} \tag{13}$$

The uncertainty associated with the mathematical model of the characteristic impedance Z_0 is expressed as:

$$\frac{u^2(Z_0)}{Z_0^2} = \frac{1}{4} u^2(S_{11}^{cc}) + \frac{1}{4} u^2(S_{11}^{co}) \tag{14}$$

The uncertainties $u(S_{11}^{cc})$ and $u(S_{11}^{co})$ are determined from S-parameter measurements using a calibrated VNA on the TEM cell in both short-circuit and open-circuit configurations.

2.3.5 Overall uncertainty budget

The evaluation of the overall uncertainty related to the calibration of the electric field E_{TEM} is based on the quadratic summation of individual uncertainty components, as detailed in the previous sections. Table 1 provides a summary of the uncertainty components and their respective contributions to the overall uncertainty budget, evaluated at the highest operational frequency of 300 MHz. The expanded overall uncertainty, with a coverage factor of 2, is standardized in this study to 10 % of the electric field amplitude.

Table 1. Uncertainty budget for TEM cell calibration at 300 MHz.

Component	Sensitivity coefficient	Uncertainty contribution (%)
Net power delivered to the TEM cell	0.50	0.10
Characteristic impedance of the TEM cell	0.50	1.13
Septum-to-wall distance measurement	1	0.46
Inhomogeneity factor (transverse axis)	1	0.04
Inhomogeneity factor (vertical axis)	1	4.85
Overall uncertainty (coverage factor = 1)	**4.90 %**	
Overall uncertainty (coverage factor = 2)	**9.80 %**	

3 Method validation

The validation of the method have been conducted by using a broadband isotropic electric field probe calibrated at the NPL (National Physical Laboratory), identified by the serial number s/n 101752. The measurements were carried out by comparing the correction factors for fields values from 1 V/m to 120 V/m across frequency points ranging from 9 kHz to 300 MHz, as shown in Table 2. The comparison have been performed separately along each antenna axis (X, Y, and Z).

Table 2. Parameters of the comparative study with NPL measurements.

Frequency MHz	Actual field strength V/m	Range V/m
0.009	10	30
0.01	10	30
0.015	10	30
0.02	10	30
0.03	10	30
0.05	10	30
0.07	10	30
0.09	10	30
0.1	10	30
0.2	10	30
0.5	10	30
1	10	30
10	10	30
30	10	30
100	1	10
100	3	10
100	8	10
100	10	10

100	10	10
100	20	30
100	30	30
100	30	100
100	50	100
100	100	100
100	100	300
100	150	300
100	200	300
180	10	30
300	10	30

The key indicator for this validation is the normalized error between the measurements from the laboratories. The external laboratory reports a maximum absolute uncertainty of 8 % for the correction factor within the measurement range applied in this comparative study.

Figure 8 presents the results of the normalized error between the two measurements on the three antenna axes.

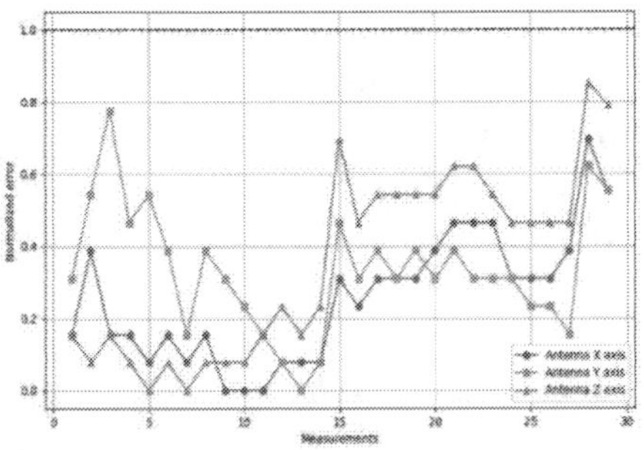

Fig. 5. Normalized error between measurements for the probe antenna along the X, Y, and Z.

We can observe that the error does not exceed 1 across the entire measurement range, which confirms the laboratory ability to meet the stated uncertainties in the 9 kHz to 300 MHz frequency range.

4 Conclusion

In this article, a comprehensive calibration method for electric field probes using a TEM cell as a controlled and reliable reference source has been presented. The calibration process is explained step by step, starting with the measurement setup. A Schwarzbeck TEM cell was used to generate uniform and reproducible reference electric fields. A detailed uncertainty analysis was performed, addressing all relevant sources of uncertainty, including the net power delivered to the cell, the septum-to-wall distance, field inhomogeneity, and impedance mismatch. The overall expanded uncertainty of the calibration was set at 10% of the electric field amplitude, which shows a high level of precision and control over the calibration process. To validate the method, measurements were compared with those from an accredited external laboratory across a wide frequency range (9 kHz to 300 MHz) for a triaxial isotropic probe. The evaluated correction factors showed excellent agreement between the two laboratories. The normalized errors remained within acceptable limits, confirming the robustness of the method and its ability to meet the required uncertainty specifications.

References

Journal articles

1. M. L. Crawford, "Generation of Standard EM Fields Using TEM Transmission Cells," *IEEE Transactions on Electromagnetic Compatibility*, vol. EMC-16, no. 4, pp. 189–195, Nov. 1974, doi: 10.1109/TEMC.1974.303364
2. J. P. Karst, C. Groh, and H. Garbe, "Calculable field generation using TEM cells applied to the calibration of a novel E-field probe," *IEEE Transactions on Electromagnetic Compatibility*, vol. 44, no. 1, pp. 59–71, Feb. 2002, doi: 10.1109/15.990711
3. S. Ishigami and M. Hirata, "A New Calibration Method for an Electric-field Probe using TEM Waveguides," in *2009 20th International Zurich Symposium on Electromagnetic Compatibility*, Jan. 2009, pp. 425–428. doi: 10.1109/EMCZUR.2009.4783481
4. X. Liu, M. Xie, D. B. Li, and J. Y. Li, "A Method to Calculate the Net Power Delivered into a TEM Cell Using a Directional Coupler in a Probe Calibration Application," *Applied Mechanics and Materials*, vol. 475–476, pp. 23–26, 2014, doi: 10.4028/www.scientific.net/AMM.475-476.23
5. M. Kanda, "Standard probes for electromagnetic field measurements," *IEEE Transactions on Antennas and Propagation*, vol. 41, no. 10, pp. 1349–1364, Oct. 1993, doi: 10.1109/8.247775
6. D. Nikolayev, Z. Kubík, P. Karban, and J. Skála, "Impedance analysis of transmission line cells for EMC applications using Agros2D," *Applied Mathematics and Computation*, vol. 289, pp. 381–387, Oct. 2016, doi: 10.1016/j.amc.2016.05.027

Books

7. D. M. Pozar, *Microwave Engineering: Theory and Techniques*. John Wiley & Sons, 2021
8. M. Kanda and R. D. Orr, "Generation of Standard Electromagnetic Fields in a TEM Cell," *NIST*, vol. 1319, Aug. 1988, Accessed: Nov. 25, 2024. [Online]. Available: https://www.nist.gov/publications/generation-standard-electromagnetic-fields-tem-cell

EPJ Web of Conferences **323**, 01((1 21(15)
https://doi.org/0(.0(50/epjconf/1(1531301((1
22nd nIt enr Iai nr dMt Iei ai gylCi nget ss

Traceability of the WBCO Standard Attenuator by Comparing With A Inductive Voltage Dividers

Houssemeddine KRRAOUI [1*], *Jean-Marie* LERAT[1]

[1]LNE Laboratoire National de Métrologie et d'Essais (LNE), Trappes, France

Abstract. A measurement system for the traceability of attenuation of a Waveguide Below Cut-Off attenuator standard (WBCO) is presented. This system consists of calibrating a lock-in amplifier at 10 kHz by frequency substitution using a WBCO at 30 MHz and a Inductive Voltage Dividers IVD as primary standards at 10 kHz. The new systems allows the establishement of a new traceability scheme at LNE, the French National Metrology Institue, The paper hereby describes the measurement method, and details the associated measurement model. Then a validation method is presented and the results are discussed.

1 Introduction

Attenuation is a key quantity in the field of high-frequency electrical metrology, as it affects many other key quantities in the high frequency domain, such as power, voltage, and reflection coefficients. It also has great importance in electronic system design due to its significant influence on system performance. The increasing demand for higher accuracy in measuring this electrical parameter has driven the development of precise measurement systems. In our laboratory, a Waveguide Below Cut-Off attenuator, (WBCO) serves as a primary standard at 30 MHz. The traceability to dimensional quantities makes it a very good attenuation standard, however, it suffers from several drawbacks due to its non-dissipative nature, as it reflects varying amounts of energy rather than absorbing it as the attenuation is varied, which leads to a limited range of achievable attenuation.

To correct the errors related to these physical phenomena and to establish the traceability of the WBCO to an even more accurate standard, we have devised a system to compare the voltage ratios obtained from the WBCO at 30 MHz standard and an inductive voltage divider (IVD) at 10 kHz using a serial mode substitution method [1]. The latter will also provide a more common attenuation standard, ensuring the mitigation of failure of any of both equipements. The voltage division obtained by the IVD can be realized with errors considerably less than 1 part per million of V, and such units find wide use as standards of voltage ratio in the discipline of electrical measurements.

Measurement uncertainty analysis of the broadband system has been conducted [3,4,5,6 and 7]. The expanded systematic measurement uncertainty (k=2) is estimated to be 0.002–0.02 dB for a 0–50 dB variable attenuator at 30 MHz. These systems have been used as the French national standard for microwave attenuation measurement.

2 Measurement method

The system below presents the measurement setup used for the calibration of the WBCO using an IVD.

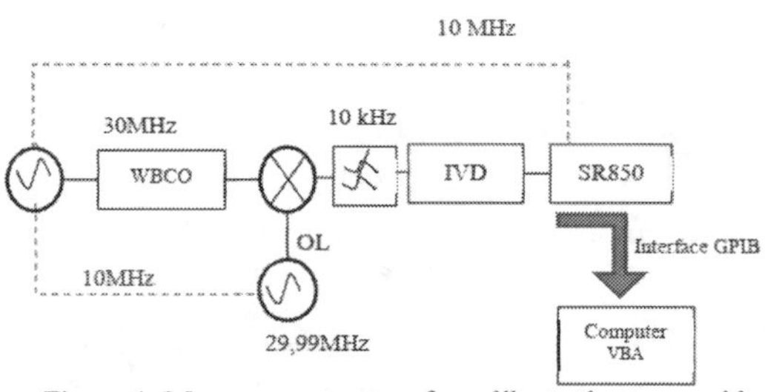

Figure 1: Measurement set up for calibrate the waveguide below cut-off attenuator using a reference inductive voltage divider

The RS850 lock-in amplifier is used to measure attenuation by monitoring voltage variation. The objective is to compare the WBCO attenuation with the reference attenuation obtained through voltage variation using the VDI.

The attenuation is calculated using the following formulas:

$$A_{dB}^{WBCO} = 20.\log_{10}\left(\frac{V_0}{V_1}\right) \tag{1}$$

and

$$A_{dB}^{IVD} = 20.\log_{10}\left(\frac{V_0}{V_1}\right) \tag{2}$$

where V_0 is the measured voltage at the reference position and V_1 is the voltage measured at the desired position of attenuation in dB.

2.1 Measurement Uncertainty Analysis

The uncertainties related to the different parameters are:

* Corresponding author: houssemeddine.krraoui@lne.fr

$$u^2(A) = \left(\frac{\partial A}{\partial V_0}\right)^2 . u^2(V_0) + \left(\frac{\partial A}{\partial V_1}\right)^2 . u^2(V_1) \qquad (3)$$

The attenuation A is in linear scale, is expressed by the following relation:

$$A = \frac{V_0}{V_1} \qquad (4)$$

The relative uncertainty is given by:

$$\frac{u^2(A)}{A^2} = \left(\frac{\partial A}{\partial V_0}\right)^2 . \frac{u^2(V_0)}{A^2} + \left(\frac{\partial A}{\partial V_1}\right)^2 . \frac{u^2(V_1)}{A^2} \qquad (5)$$

$$\frac{u^2(A)}{A^2} = 1. \frac{u^2(V_0)}{V_0^2} + 1. \frac{u^2(V_1)}{V_1^2} \qquad (6)$$

The uncertainty budget for this model is presented below:

a) DUT repeatability

The repeatability of the WBCO attenuation measurements A1 and the inductive voltage divider A2 are statistically estimated during the measurements.

The repeatability of the WBCO attenuation measurements varies between 0.001dB and 0.003 dB. And the repeatability of the DVI attenuation measurements varies between 0.001 dB and 0.009 dB.

b) Mixer's nonlinearity

The mixer's and receiver nonlinearities are also characterized using a step attenuator by varying the source power and the step attenuator by 5dB.
By calculating the deviation ($A-A_{ref}$):

1) We vary the generator power by AdB
2) Then we vary the step attenuator by Aref
3) The diviation is calculated as (A-Aref)

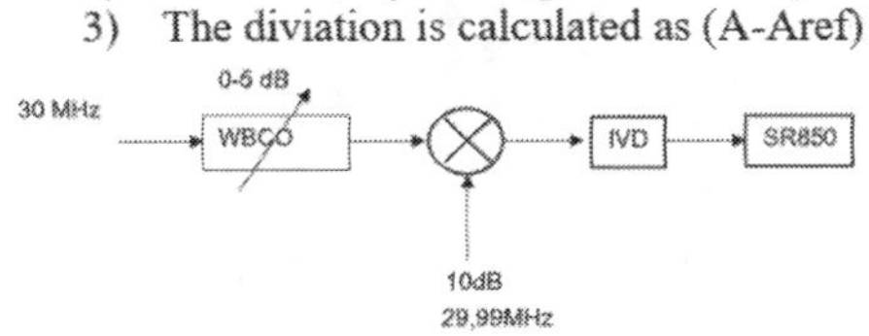

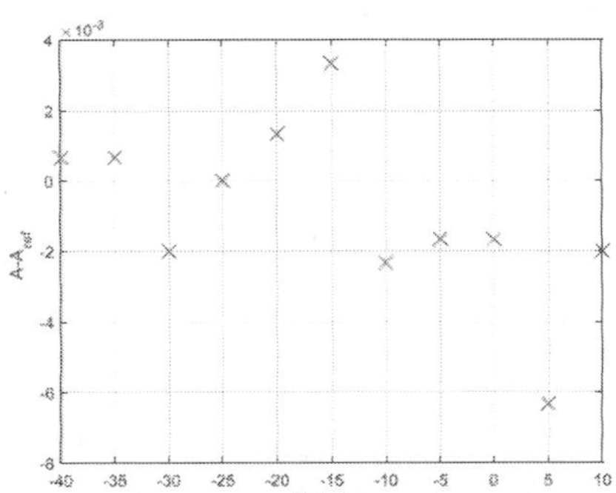

Figure 2: Non-Linearity of the system mixer and lock-in amplifier according to the power level

c) Mismatch uncertainty

The errors in the measurement of standard attenuation due to mismatch and the connector deficiencies have been analysed [1]
In the case of the step attenuator or variable attenuator, two setting values would be considered at each measurement frequency, one the initial value i.e 0 dB and the final value, the attenuation level to be measured.

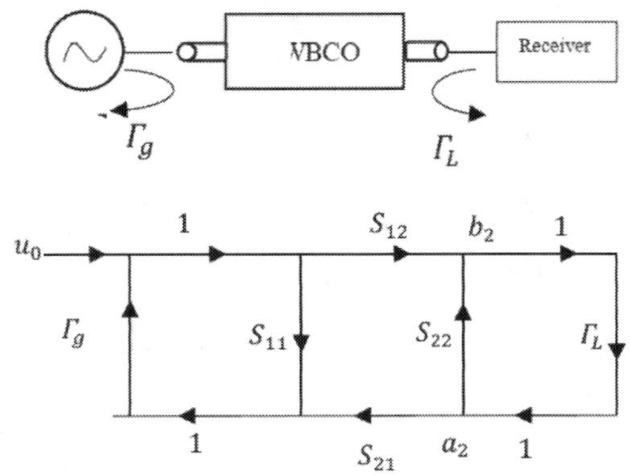

Figure 3: Modelling of the variable attenuator

So each attenuation value can be considered as one tow port attenuator is replaced by second two port attenuator, and mismatch for the step attenuator error (MSA) for incremental attenuation is given by [2]

$$MSA(dB) = 20\, log \left(\frac{(1-\Gamma_G S_{11})(1-\Gamma_L S_{22}) - \Gamma_G \Gamma_L S_{21} S_{12}}{(1-\Gamma_G S'_{11})(1-\Gamma_L S'_{22}) - \Gamma_G \Gamma_L S'_{21} S'_{12}}\right) \qquad (7)$$

Where :
Γ_G : effective source port match ;
Γ_L : effective load match ;
$S_{11}, S_{12}, S_{21}, S_{22}$: Scattering coefficientes of the attenuator (at the attenuation level) ;
$S'_{11}, S'_{12}, S'_{21}, S'_{22}$: Scattering coefficientes of the two port device at the initial state 0 dB.

The S-parameters of the variable attenuator were measured, and the MSA was calculated for different attenuation positions.

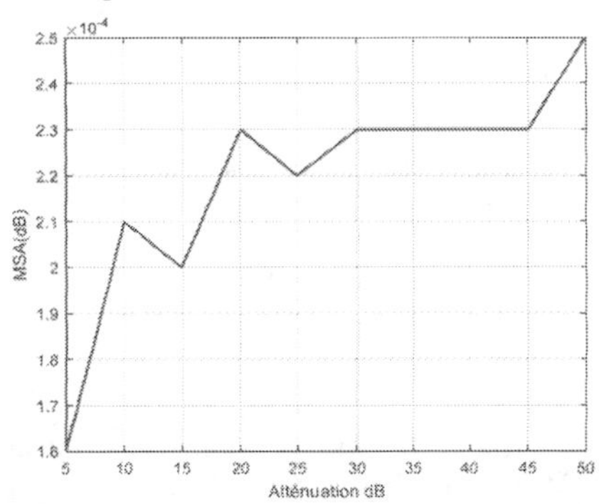

Figure 4: Variation of the MSA as a Function of Different Positions of attenuation

Figure 4 shows the variation of the measured MSA (dB) as a function of different positions of the attenuator.
To reduce the mismatch error, we have placed a fixed 10 dB attenuator pad.

d) Lock-in-detector fluctuation and noise

The noise of the lock-in amplifier was determined experimentally by calculating the standard deviation of the voltage variation as a function of time.

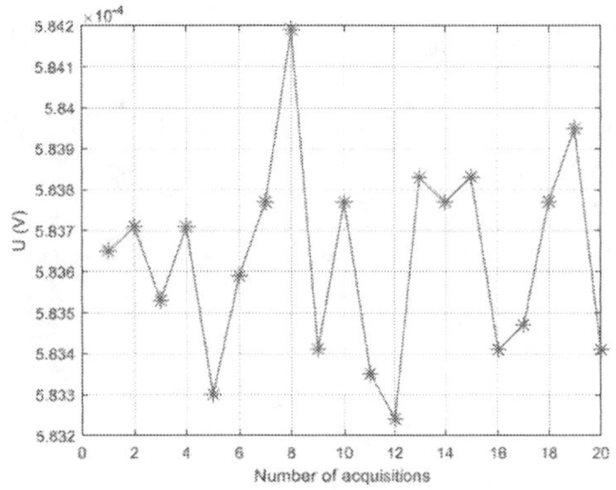

Figure 5: Measurement of the noise of the lock-in amplifier.

The error due to noise and fluctuation of the lock-in amplifier can be modeled using the following formula

$$e_n = 20\log_{10}\left(\frac{(D_2+\varepsilon)D_1}{(D_1-\varepsilon)D_2}\right) \quad (8)$$

Where:
D_1 and D_2: denotes the IVD ratio before and after the attenuation is changed, and ε represent the absolute error showen in the Figure 3.
To reduce this error, the data acquisition is automated for each measurement using a VBA program.
For each measurement, 30 acquisition were collected, and the average value was calculated to determine D_1 and D_2.
The noise is also present in the repeatability of the A1 and A2 measurements.

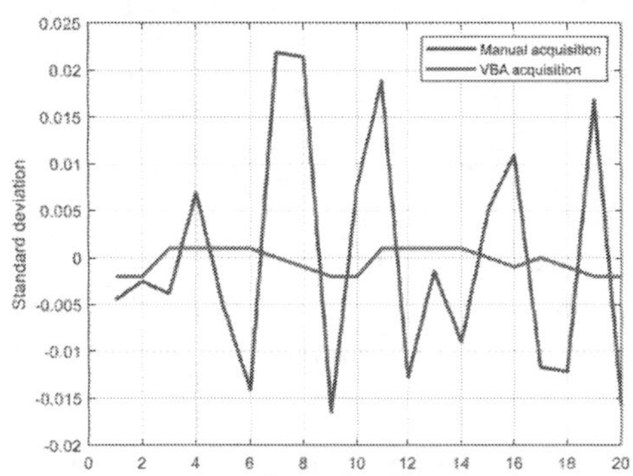

Figure 6: The effect of the automatic program and the number of acquisitions on the measurement results.

This figure illustrates the effect of noise, which is significant when the program uses a single acquisition. The standard deviation of the measurements becomes less than 0.005 dB when 30 automatic acquisitions are taken.

e) Leakage error

Receiver noise and leakage error are negligible for measurement of attenuation below 70 dB.

f) Uncertainty budget

Uncertainty Component		5dB	10dB	15dB	20dB
Repeatability IVD	/1	0.001	0.000	0.001	0.000
Repeatability WBCO	/1	0.001	0.001	0.001	0.001
IVD error	/2	1.01E-08	1.01E-08	1.01E-08	1.01E-08
Mismatch error	/√2	1.16E-04	1.49E-04	1.45E-04	1.65E-04
Receiver Noise	/2√3	5.19E-06	5.19E-06	5.19E-06	5.19E-06
U (k=2)		0.002	0.003	0.002	0.002

Uncertainty Component		25dB	30dB	35dB	40dB
Repeatability IVD	/1	0.001	0.002	0.001	0.001
Repeatability WBCO	/1	0.001	0.001	0.003	0.005
IVD error	/2	1.01E-08	1.01E-08	1.01E-08	1.01E-08
Mismatch error	/√2	1.56E-04	1.61E-04	1.63E-04	1.63E-04
Receiver Noise	/2√3	5.19E-06	5.19E-06	5.19E-06	5.19E-06
U (k=2)		0.003	0.005	0.007	0.010

Uncertainty Component		45dB	50dB
Repeatability IVD	/1	0.001	0.003
Repeatability WBCO	/1	0.005	0.009
IVD error	/2	1.01E-08	1.01E-08
Mismatch error	/√2	1.65E-04	1.78E-04
Receiver Noise	/2√3	5.19E-06	5.19E-06
U (k=2)		0.010	0.020

3 Validation

To validate our measurement system, we compare the measured values of two fixed attenuators, calibrated by an external laboratory and then measured by our system using a lock-in amplifier.

To evaluate the two results, we calculated the normalized deviation using the following formula:

$$E_n = \frac{|X_1 - X_2|}{\sqrt{U_1^2 + U_2^2}} \tag{9}$$

Table 1. Measurement results for the two attenuators using our measurement system.

Attenuator 50 dB	LNE results			
	Measured value		Calibration uncertainty.	
(1)	49,843	dB	0,020	dB
(2)	49,943	dB	0,020	dB

Table 2. External laboratory measurement.

Attenuator 50 dB	Reference results			
	Measured value		Calibration uncertainty.	
(1)	49,841	dB	0,023	dB
(2)	49,936	dB	0,023	dB

The normalized deviation for the measurements of attenuator 1 is equal to 0.05 and for the attenuator 2 equal to 0.24.
The normalized deviations for the two attenuators are less than 0.5, which demonstrates the reliability of our measurement and measurement system.

4 Conclusion

We have developed a precise microwave Attenuation measurement system for calibrating a national standard waveguide below cut-off (WBCO) at 30 MHz. This measurement standard is traceable to an inductive voltage divider (IVD) operating at 10 kHz. A detailed measurement uncertainty analysis has been developed to characterize the performance of the proposed method.
This system have been used as the French national standards for attenuation measurement at microwave and millimeter wave frequency.

The next work will concentrate on enhancing our measurement system to attain higher attenuation levels, reaching up to approximately 120 dB.

References

1. R. W. Beatty, Effects of connectors and adapters on accurate attenuation measurements at microwave frequencies, IEEE Trans. Instr. 13, 272-284 (Dec. 1964).
2. F.L. Warner, New expression for mismatch uncertainty when measuring microwave attenuation, IEE Proc. 127, 66–69 (1980)
3. I.A. Harris, F.L. Warner, Re-examination of mismatch uncertainty when measuring microwave power and attenuation, IEE Proc. 128, 35–41 (1981)
4. B.O. Weinschel, Standardization of precision coaxial connectors, Proc. IEEE 55, 923–931 (1967)
5. Warner, F. L., Herman, P., and Cummings, P.: 'Recent improvements to the UK National microwave attenuation standards', IEEE Transactions on Instrumentation and Measurement, 1983;LM-32:33–37
6. Warner, F. L., and Herman, P.: 'Very precise measurement of attenuation over a 90 dB range using a voltage ratio plus gauge block technique', IEE Colloquium Digest, 1989;53:17/1–17/7
7. Wollensack, Michael & Hoffmann, Johannes & Ruefenacht, Juerg & Zeier, Markus. (2012). VNA Tools II: S-parameter uncertainty calculation. 79th ARFTG Microwave Measurement Conference: Non-Linear Measurement Systems, ARFTG 2012. 1-5. 10.1109/ARFTG79.2012.6291183.

Nanoscale Calibration Standards for On-Wafer S-Parameters measurements up to 110 GHz

Daouda Seck [1,2*], *Djamel* Allal[1], *Florent* Marlec[2], *Clément* Lenoir[2], *Mohamed* Sebbache[2], and *Kamel* Haddadi[2*]

[1]LNE Laboratoire National de Métrologie et d'Essais, Trappes, France, France

[2]Univ. Lille, CNRS, Centrale Lille, Univ. Polytechnique Hauts-de-France, UMR 8520 - IEMN - Institut d'Electronique de Microélectronique et de Nanotechnologie - Lille, France

Abstract. We report the first experimental results on the design and fabrication of nanoscale on-wafer calibration standards operating up to 110 GHz. The propagation constant and effective permittivity of coplanar waveguide (CPW) transmission lines (TLs) are extracted from raw S-parameters using the Thru-Reflect-Line (TRL) method. Experimental data show deviations in extracted propagation characteristics when comparing nanostructures to microscale structures.

1 Introduction

The growing demand for miniaturization in on-wafer RF and microwave circuit design extends to the nanoscale. This scaling introduces challenges, particularly due to the high impedances that arise at such small dimensions. These high impedances create a mismatch with the vector network analyzer (VNA), which is typically designed and calibrated for a nominal impedance of 50 Ω [1], [2]. This mismatch negatively affects measurement sensitivity and accuracy. Moreover, commercially available calibration kits are not suited to the scale of these miniaturized components or nanodevices. Addressing these challenges requires equipping on-wafer probe stations with additional capabilities to enhance sensitivity [3], [4] and repeatability [4], [5].

It is also essential to miniaturize calibration standards to correct vector network analyzer (VNA) systematic errors at the nanoscale. The advancement of nanotechnology is largely driven by innovations in integrated circuit design which incorporate both miniaturized passive and active components. Passive components include transmission lines (TLs), which enable RF signal transmission across the circuit and support the design of impedance matching networks, couplers, dividers, and filters, among others. Planar TLs, such as microstrip lines and coplanar waveguides (CPW) [7], offer greater flexibility for component-mounting circuits. A key advantage of these structures is the ability to control losses through careful selection of conductor and substrate materials. High-frequency electrical performance of electronic devices is typically evaluated using a pre-calibrated VNA to measure their S-parameters, which represent the ratios of incident, reflected, and transmitted power waves. To obtain accurate S-parameters of the device under test (DUT), systematic errors inherent to the measurement system must be removed through calibration using traceable standards [8].

This article presents initial results on the design of a nanoscale calibration kit in GSG CPW topology, developed for on-wafer S-parameter measurements up to 110 GHz, based on a 50 Ω reference impedance [9].

2 Methodology

The measurement of S-parameters using a VNA rely on a concept that necessitates an error model or measurement model [10], depending on the DUT configuration, which can have one or two ports (as in this study). In the case of a two-port DUT, the measurement model accounts for systematic errors and the DUT itself, all represented as cascaded two-port networks.

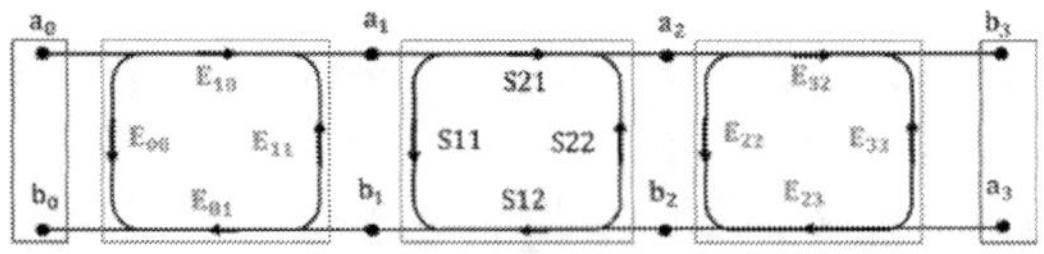

Fig. 1. Measurement error model.

The whole process is expressed by equation (1) where M represents the DUT data measured at the reference planes of the measurement system. X and Y represent the systematic errors on right and left sides. Finally, the term T_{DUT} denotes the true response in transfer matrix for the DUT.

$$M = X.T_{DUT}.Y \quad (1)$$

Knowledge of the transmission characteristics of a line, namely the characteristic impedance Z_c, the propagation constant γ and the effective relative permittivity ε_{reff} are required. Mark and Williams have demonstrated that

* Corresponding author: Daouda.Seck@lne.fr

impedance can be determined from measurements of the propagation constant and the linear capacitance of a transmission line [11], [12].
The Thru-Reflect-Line (TRL) calibration technique enables the determination of the propagation constant of a transmission line using the measured *S*-parameters of two calibration standards: a thru and a line. These standards are mathematically represented in a T-matrix format, which facilitates the extraction of the propagation characteristics of the transmission line.
The effective permittivity is directly related to the propagation constant through the following equation

$$\varepsilon_{reff} = -(\frac{c}{2\pi f}\gamma)^2 \quad (2)$$

where c is the speed of light in vacuum, f is the frequency, and γ is the TL phase constant.

3 Design and Fabrication

In our approach, we have designed CPW structures as calibration standards for on-wafer S-parameter measurements. These structures consist of two sections: a microscale section, optimized for contacting ground-signal-ground (GSG) probes with a pitch ranging from 50 µm to 100 µm and matched to a 50 Ω impedance, and a nanoscale section. To ensure impedance continuity between these regions, a tapered transition is implemented with an optimized geometric aspect ratio profile. The key contribution of this study lies in the miniaturized section, whose dimensions are scaled to match the calibration standards, enabling accurate high-frequency measurements at the nanoscale.

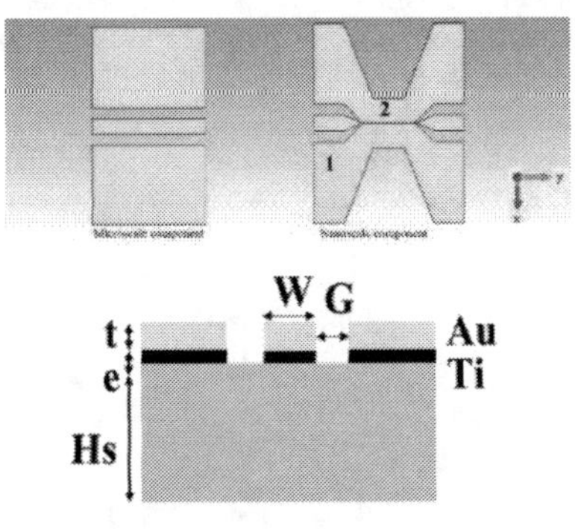

Fig. 2. View of the CPW structure designed in CST Studio.

The calibration structures were fabricated on a high-resistivity silicon substrate (ε_r=11.9). Gold was used as conductive material. A titanium adhesion layer was integrated, simultaneously as a resistive element with a sheet resistance of 48.9 Ω/□ for a deposited thickness in the range of 23–25 nm. The structural topology and dimensional parameters were optimized through full-wave 3D electromagnetic simulations in CST Studio, ensuring precise impedance control and minimal signal degradation. The detailed geometric specifications are provided in Table 1.

Table 1: Dimensional parameters.

dimension	W1	W2	G1	G2	Wg1	Wg2	t	Hs
µm	27	0.5	18.2	0.85	140	40	0.35	350

The calibration standards were fabricated using a three-step microfabrication process. First, alignment marks were patterned. Next, a Titanium layer was deposited to form the resistive elements. Finally, a 350 nm gold layer was deposited with an underlying titanium adhesion layer to enhance metal-substrate adhesion. The fabrication of these nanoscale structures presented significant technical challenges, using electron beam lithography (EBL) to achieve the required resolution. The process included an optimization of the EBL (to minimize proximity effects) and lift-off to ensure precise feature definition. This optimization was critical for achieving high-yield fabrication while operating at the resolution limits of the available microfabrication technology.
Two fabrication runs were conducted, with the first yielding a small number of defective devices, as illustrated in Fig. 3.

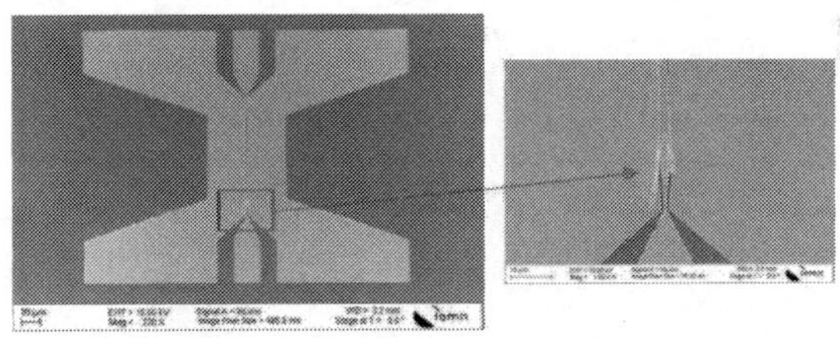

Fig. 3. Scanning electron microscope (SEM) view of a defective tapered TL (1st fabrication run).

After process optimization, the second run produced well-defined structures, as shown in Fig. 4.

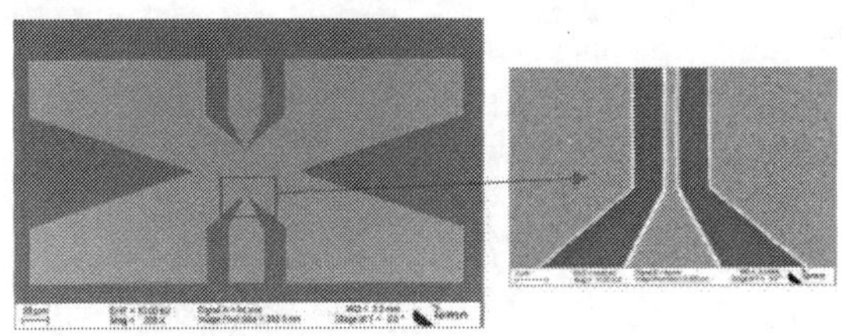

Fig. 4. Scanning electron microscope (SEM) view of a tapered TL (2nd fabrication run).

4 Measurement results

The Measurements campaign was performed from 250 MHz to 110 GHz using an on-wafer probe station and a Rohde & Schwarz ZVA67 VNA (Fig. 5). Initially, the LRRM calibration technique was applied using a commercial microscale calibration kit (ISS) to define the measurement reference planes at the GSG probe tips and verify the functionality of all fabricated standards (Fig. 6). The VNA output power was set to Pout = -15 dBm, with an IF bandwidth of 50 Hz.

t pp s/dl o.gprj d0(g0( ) 0de: 3confdl(1)21201((2

Fig. 5. On-wafer probe station.

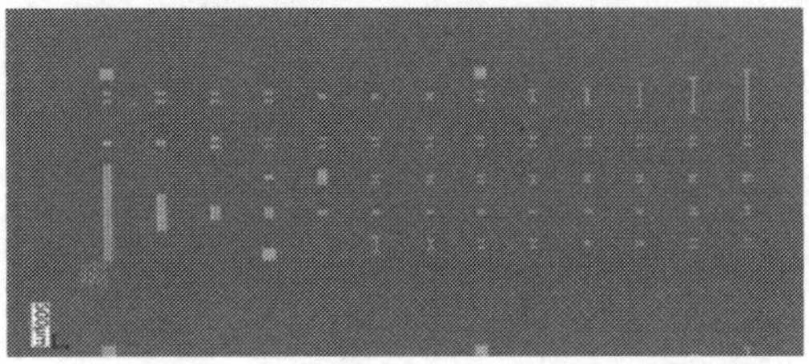

Fig. 6. HR silicon wafer with dedicated miniaturized CPW structures.

The TRL calibration technique was implemented using uncalibrated measurement data to establish the measurement reference planes at the input of the nanoscale DUTs. The calibration procedure employed a 200 μm line as the thru standard, a second line selected from a set ranging from 250 to 2250 μm as the line standard, and a pair of short circuits as the reflect standard. Given the high attenuation in the nanoscale structures, the TRL algorithm remained applicable with any combination of line standards.

The lateral miniaturization of CPW structures induces changes in their aspect ratio, leading to increased conductor losses, which in turn affect the effective permittivity, propagation constant, and characteristic impedance. To quantify these effects, a comparative analysis was performed between the extracted effective permittivity and propagation characteristics of the micro- and nanoscale structures. Fig. 7 presents the measured and simulated effective permittivity and propagation constants for micro- and nanoscale CPW structures over a frequency range up to 110 GHz.

As shown in Fig. 7, the real part of the effective permittivity for the microscale CPW line remains approximately 6.4 from 40 GHz to 110 GHz, which is consistent with the theoretical value for an ideal CPW line. In contrast, the nanoscale CPW line exhibits a higher and more frequency-dependent effective permittivity, varying from approximately 9.5 at 10 GHz to 7.5 at 110 GHz. The nanoscale TL also exhibits significantly higher losses, with an attenuation constant (α) reaching approximately 22 dB/mm (≈2.5 Np/mm) at 110 GHz, compared to only 2.2 dB/mm (≈0.25 Np/mm) for the microscale CPW TL. This increased attenuation is primarily attributed to higher conductor losses, which become more pronounced at smaller dimensions.

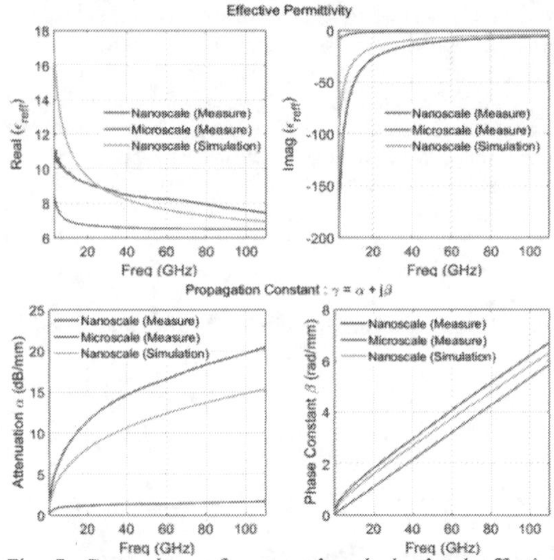

Fig. 7. Comparison of measured and simulated effective permittivity and propagation constants for micro- and nanoscale CPW structures. The top row presents the real (left) and imaginary (right) components of the effective permittivity ε_{reff}) as a function of frequency. The bottom row shows the attenuation constant (α, left) and phase constant (β, right) extracted from measurements and simulations.

Finally, a 300 μm CPW TL was measured as the DUT. In the TRL calibration, the measurement reference plane is defined at the center of the thru standard, with its two halves included in the error boxes. This calibration method effectively de-embeds all systematic contributions from the VNA, including cables and probes, to the defined reference plane.

Fig. 8 presents the measured transmission amplitude and phase of the transmission coefficient S_{21} of the DUT after applying both the ISS LRRM calibration and our TRL calibration, along with simulation results obtained using Keysight ADS. The ISS calibration results indicate higher attenuation, as it considers the entire structure between the probe tips, including contact resistances and parasitic effects. In contrast, the TRL calibration more accurately isolates the DUT response by referencing the calibration plane within the CPW nanoscale TL itself.

The observed deviation between the TRL-calibrated measurements and simulation results can be attributed to multiple factors. These include fabrication-related imperfections, such as scratches on CPW lines, which could locally alter the transmission characteristics, as well as a lower-than-expected conductivity of the deposited metal, leading to increased insertion loss.

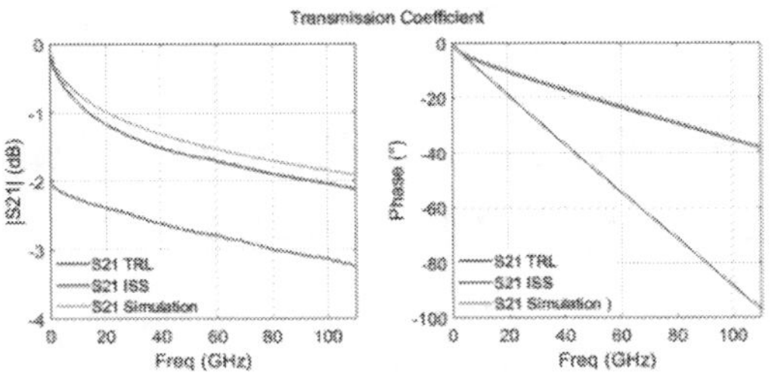

Fig. 8. Measured and simulated transmission coefficient S_{21} for the 300 µm CPW TL. The left plot shows the magnitude $|S_{21}|$ in dB, while the right plot presents the phase response (in degrees) as a function of frequency. The results compare the transmission coefficient obtained using the TRL calibration, ISS LRRM calibration, and Keysight ADS simulation.

5 Conclusion

We developed nanoscale S-parameter calibration standards for on-wafer characterization of nanodevices. The dimensional parameters of these standards were optimized through full-wave 3D electromagnetic simulations to ensure impedance control and calibration accuracy. Nano-fabrication posed significant challenges, initial measurement results demonstrated the feasibility of nanoscale on-wafer calibration, with TRL-calibrated data showing consistency with expected propagation characteristics. Further investigations are ongoing to assess factors influencing the performance of these nanostructures, with a comprehensive uncertainty analysis planned to quantify systematic and random measurement errors.

Acknowledgements

This project (BELC157) has received funding from the Réseau National de la Métrologie Française (RNMF) and from the Association Nationale de la Recherche et de la Technologie ANRT under grant 2022/0073. This work was partially supported by the French Renatech network.

References

1. H. Happy et al., "Measurement Techniques for RF Nanoelectronic Devices: New Equipment to Overcome the Problems of Impedance and Scale Mismatch," *in IEEE Microwave Magazine*, vol. 15, no. 1, pp. 30-39, Jan.-Feb. 2014.
2. K. Daffé, G et al., "On-Wafer Series-Through Broadband Measurement of Sub-fF55-nm MOS RF Voltage-Tunable Capacitors," *in IEEE Microwave and Wireless Components Letters*, vol. 28, no. 9, pp. 831-833, Sept. 2018.
3. R. Romano, F. Mubarak, M. Spirito and L. Galatro, "The HΓ-VNA, an Interferometric Approach for the Accurate Measurement of Extreme Impedances," *93rd ARFTG Microwave Measurement Conference (ARFTG)*, Boston, MA, USA, 2019, pp. 1-6.
4. K. Haddadi et al., "Multiport Vector Network Analyzer Configured in RF Interferometric Mode for Reference Impedance Renormalization," *IEEE MTT-S International Microwave Symposium (IMS)*, Boston, MA, USA, 2019, pp. 1276-1278.
5. C. Mokhtari et al., "Nanorobotics and Automatic On-Wafer Probe Station with Nanometer Positionning Accuracy," *2023 IEEE MTT-S International Conference on Numerical Electromagnetic and Multiphysics Modeling and Optimization (NEMO)*, Winnipeg, MB, Canada, 2023, pp. 22-24.
6. C. Mokthari et al., "Exploring Nanorobotics Integration with Microwave and Millimeter-Wave Techniques for Advanced On-wafer Measurement," *5th International Conference in Electronic Engineering, Information Technology & Education (EEITE)*, Chania, Greece, 2024, pp. 1-6.
7. R. N. Simons, "Coplanar waveguide circuits, components, and systems," *John Wiley & Sons*, 2004.
8. Andrej Rumiantsev, "Design of On-Wafer Calibration Standards," *On-Wafer Calibration Techniques Enabling Accurate Characterization of High-Performance Silicon Devices at the mm-Wave Range and Beyond. River Publishers*, 2022. 51-67.
9. D. Seck, D. Allal and K. Haddadi, "On-Wafer TRL Calibration Design for Microwave Nanoscale and High Impedance Measurement," *IEEE Symposium on Wireless Technology & Applications (ISWTA)*, Kuala Lumpur, Malaysia, 2024, pp. 260-263.
10. M. Zeier, D. Allal, and R. Judaschke. Guidelines on the evaluation of vector network analysers (VNA). *EURAMET Calibration Guide*, 2018, vol. 3, no 12, p. 507-521.
11. R. B. Marks and D. F. Williams, "Characteristic impedance determination using propagation constant measurement," *in IEEE Microwave and Guided Wave Letters*, vol. 1, no. 6, pp. 141-143, June 1991.
12. D. F. Williams and R. B. Marks, "Transmission line capacitance measurement," *in IEEE Microwave and Guided Wave Letters*, vol. 1, no. 9, pp. 243-245, Sept. 1991.

Enhancement of Reference Power Standard at SASO NMCC on AC power And revaluation of measurement uncertainty

Saleh Almojaewel[1*], Rashed Alrumie [1], Saad bin Qoud [1]
[1]NMCC-SASO- Saudi Arabia

Abstract

The accuracy and reliability of Power Standards for AC power measurements are significant subjects in current times and for the future. The rapid increase in smart electricity meters in Saudi Arabia necessitates the development of an NMCC (National Metrology and Calibration Center) reference power standard to meet legal metrology and industrial requirements. This study explores advancements in reference power standards, specifically focusing on the development of more precise and stable AC power measurement systems for high-current applications. The results demonstrate a significant reduction in the estimated uncertainty, leading to more accurate calibration of power meters. In a parallel case study, a calibration method is applied to a commercial power meter to measure AC power across high current values ranging from 10 A to 120 A using Refernce CT. The calibration method involves comparing the reference AC power system with the commercial power meter. The term 'DSWM' (Digital Sampling Watt Meter) refers to the reference AC power system, which utilizes sampling techniques to collect various data with a Unit under Calibration (UUC). Homemade software under the environment of LabVIEW software is used to controlling, optimizing, handling the data, statistically calculation and finally for exporting the well gathering data in the form in digitized certificates. The paper explains the components of the DSWM, the measurement results for AC power are presented, considering active and reactive power, which may impact various aspects such as voltage, current, and phase measurements. The evaluation of uncertainty was 40 µW/V.A for active power and 40 µvar/V.A for reactive power. Finally, the paper mentions future work in its concluding section.

Keywords: NMCC, UUC, CT, DSWM.

1. Introduction

since the demand of smart electricity meter used In residential and Industry In Saudi Arabia , Saudi Electric Company Install more than 10 million electric meters in different region of Saudi Arabia [1].however, Legal metrology in SASO required to satisfy all the requirements of OIML R 46 standard [2] which the accuracy test is one of the main test on any smart electricity meter. National metrology Institute is responsible to maintain the traceability of any of the measurement instuermnt . Power meter is the master device of electricity meter which can measure Ac power. Power and energy lab has ability to calibrate Ac power interments in National Metrology and calibration center "NMCC" .This paper aims to improve primary level system in the lab. The modular method used to calibrate the ac power source or meter called DSWM" Digital sampling watt Meter. DSWM Is sampling technic using sampling multimeters DMM 3458A. Operating principle of the standard is based on the use of two sampling voltmeters synchronized to the power source, fig. 1. Sinusoidal voltage and current signals or with steady-state harmonics are generated by the phantom power source and applied to the relevant input terminals of the
voltage and current measurement units. Regulated voltages are then applied to the voltmeters for sampling with the help of triggering synchronized to the power source[3,5].

2. Measurement Setup

The operational principle of the standard relies on the utilization of two sampling voltmeters that are synchronized with the power source, as illustrated in figure 1 below. The phantom power source generates sinusoidal voltage and current signals, or signals with steady-state harmonics, which are subsequently directed to the appropriate input terminals of the voltage and current measurement units. Regulated voltages are then supplied to the voltmeters for sampling, facilitated by triggering that is synchronized with the power source. [3].

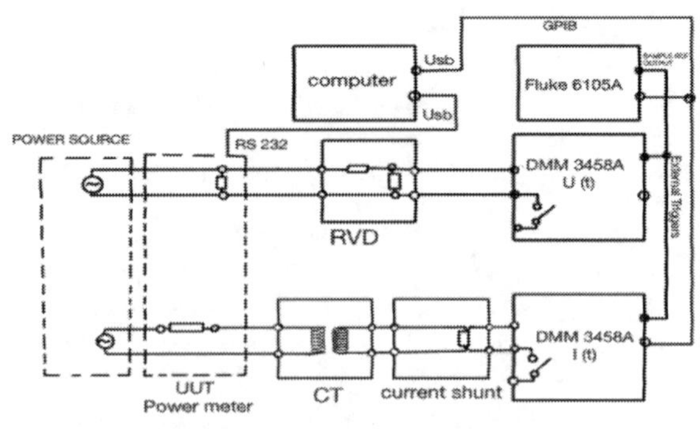

Fig.1 . the setup of AC power calibration

* Corresponding author: s.mojaewel@saso.gov.sa

© The Authors, published by EDP Sciences. This is an open access article distributed under the terms of the Creative Commons Attribution License 4.0 (https://creativecommons.org/licenses/by/4.0/)

The Components of modular measurement setups;

- Power source & phase locking :

The phantom power is the ac power system can deliver a sinusoidal voltage and current signal with different phase angle between them in period of cycle. It can generate active power and reactive power. The equation of ac power are [6]:

Active power

$$P = V * I * \cos(\varphi)$$

Reactive power

$$Q = V * I * \sin(\varphi)$$

Or other formal used based in power triangle :

$$(Q) = \sqrt{((S^2 - P^2))}$$

Where are

V. sinusoidal voltage signal

I. sinusoidal current signal

φ . The phase difference between voltage and current waveforms.

S .Apparent power which voltage multiply Current V.A.

6105A fluke used on this modular for phase locker that the external triggers of DMM connect to sample Ref OUTPUT of the fluke 6105A. The software controlled Phase-locking device.

- Voltage measurment unit:

Voltage measurment unit used a resisitive voltage divider which play the important role to cover input voltage from 30 V to 240V in 53 Hz and 60 Hz.the benfent of using resistive voltage divider to minmize the voltage input to 0.8V to get accurate measurermnet and achive the best uncertinty value.it is calibrated on Ratio & Phase displacmnet within less than 8 µV/V & µrad.

- Current measurment unit:

Current measurement unit is basically current shunt which cover current input from 62mA to 5A then convert the drop voltage as the output of the shunt. The output voltage is in the range of 1 V DCV to get the best accurate measurement and achieve the best uncertainty value.it is calibrated on Dc resistance value and AC-DC transfer value. For higher current value , the current transformer used to minimize the input current up (1A-4 kA) to reach 5A in secondary output of the current transformer.it is calibrated on CT ratio and Phase displacement.

- DMM & DSWM software :

DSWM is system using sampling technic which contents all unit list above and DMMs (keysight 3458A).Tow digital mulitmeters (DMMs) used to sample the voltage U(t) through a resistive voltage divider and current I(t) through current shunt with CT. .Both DMMs connect together in external trigger siginal with 6105A to provide a simultaneous voltage signals for Ac power calculation. In addition, all devices are connect through GBIP connection to computer for communications and controlling, enquiring data from DMMs. Mr.Rado Labuh cover many sampling technic using by 3458A .the sampling mode use in our Lab is DC voltage (DCV) same as Tubitak UME & RISE "Research Institutes of Sweden ". User define many parameters figure 2 such as :

- Communication part by using NI MAX from NI.
- DMMs , voltage and current set depends on the range .
- Accrue measurement by:
  A. Number of measurement :10 measurement
  B. Number of sample :Repeat counting measurements (128)
  C. Sampling period: time period per cycle (10)
  D. Frequency : what is the main frequency used in measurement .(60 Hz or 50 Hz)

after quering and collect data , the software will reprsent the voltage and current wave with copmaring the waves to calculate the phase angle between them. Base on the main scentifc equation on active and reactive power [6],the software can calculate the Ac power in high accurate mode.

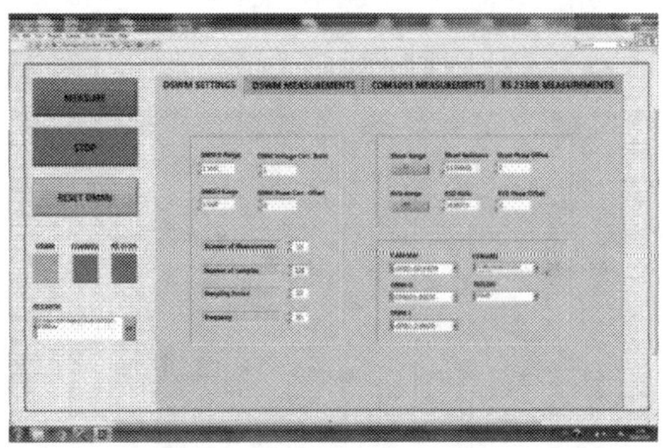

Fig.2 . configuration user and Front DSWM application

The values of data collection and calculation are represented in the software and store in Excel files immediately figure.3.

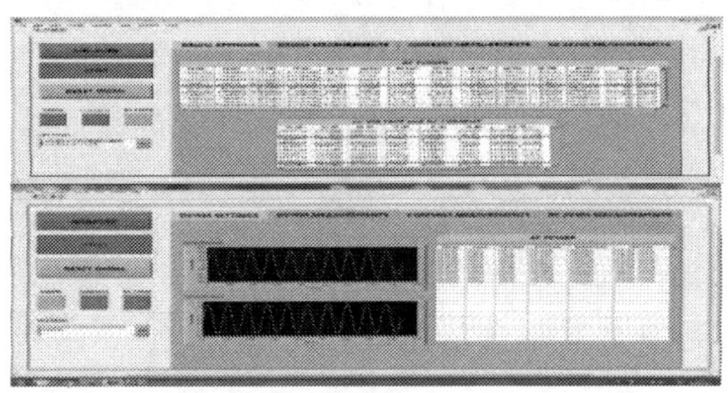

Fig.3 . Data present on DSWM system and UUT.

https://doi.org/04.0450/epjconf/14153130144(

3. Measurement Result

Base on inquiring data from various devices and apply it on many different equation to calculate the ac power, the experimental of calibration was implemented on one of the most commercial AC power meter RS 2330s that has accuracy 100 µW/V.A for active power and 100 µvar/V.A for reactive power. The equation used to compare the ac power (active, reactive, apparent power) used is:

$$Relative\ error = \frac{measured\ power\ value - nominal\ power\ value}{apparent\ power\ value} \times 10^{6}$$

Where are:

measured power value:Ac power measure indicate from UUT

measured power value=Ac power value indicate DSWM

apparent power value: Ac power indicate from DSWM

So far the table result give indicate value of the relative error compare with primary AC power standard.

- Active power result at 230 V 60 Hz

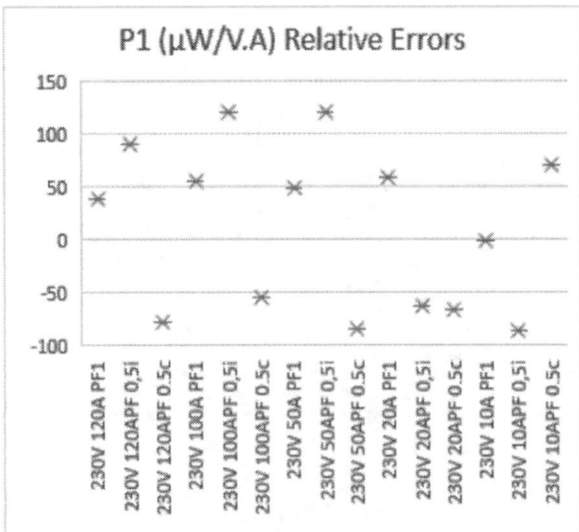

Fig 4: Active power in first phase at balanced system.

Fig 5: Active power in second phase at balanced system.

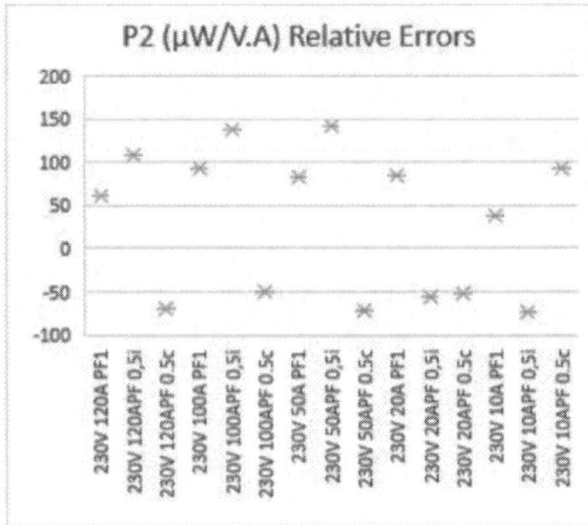

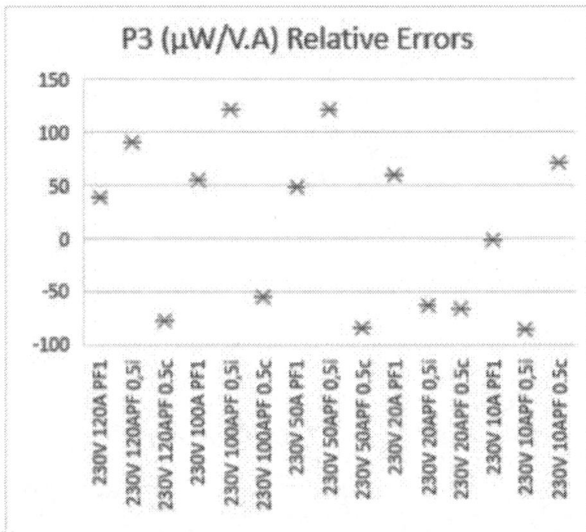

Fig 6: Active power in third phase at balanced system.

Fig 7: Total active power in three phase balanced system

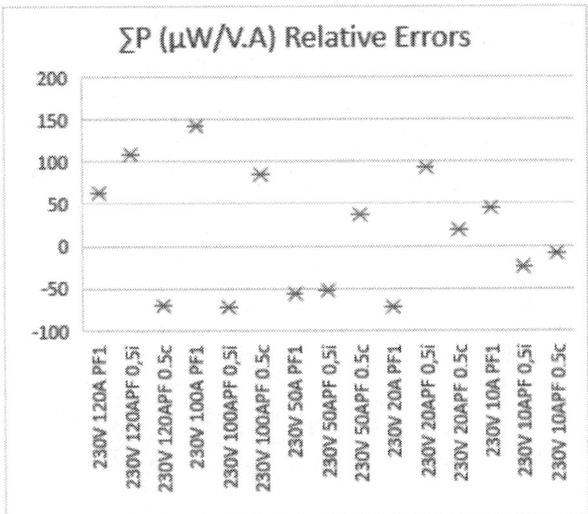

Where are

P1. Active power in first phase at balanced system.

P2. Active power in Second phase at balanced system.

P3. Active power in Third phase at balanced system.

∑P.Total active power in three phase balanced system.

- Reactive power result at 230 V 60 Hz

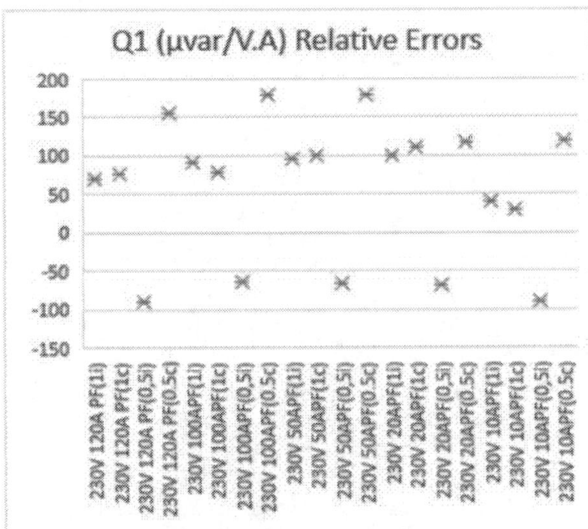

Fig 8: Reactive power in first phase at balanced system

Fig 9: Reactive power in second phase at balanced system

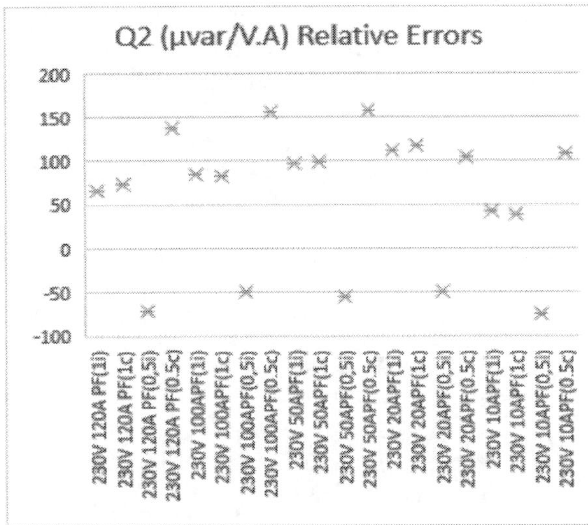

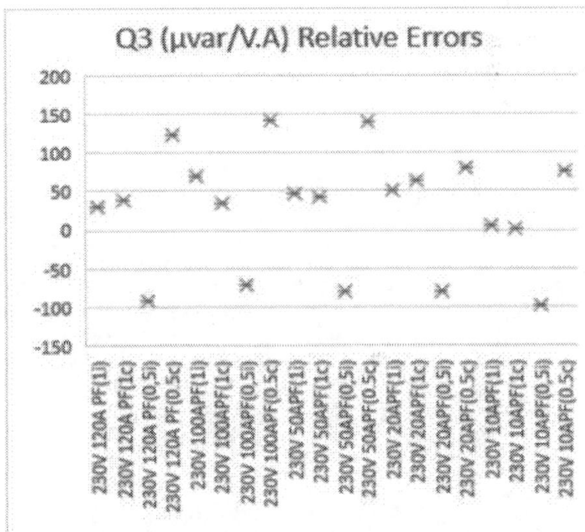

Fig 10: Reactive power in third phase at balanced system

Fig 11: Total Reactive power in three phase balanced system

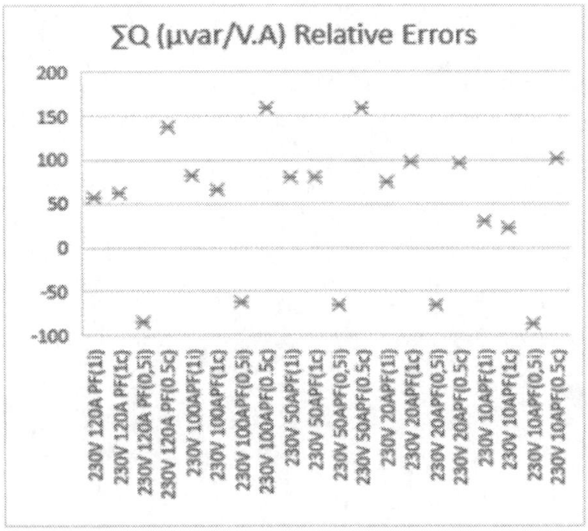

Where are

Q1. Reactive power in first phase at balanced system.

Q2. Reactive power in Second phase at balanced system.

Q3. Reactive power in Third phase at balanced system.

∑Q.Total Reactive power in three phase balanced system.

4. Uncertainty Evaluation

The following sample tables below shows a typical Uncertainty budget used by Power and energy lab (SASO-NMCC) in the calculation of its uncertainty values. After using CT in current measurement, the achieve uncertainty value is 40 W/V.A & 40 var/V.A for more than 10 A. And, uncertainty budgets of both sides for 53 Hz and 60 Hz measurements are given in Table below.

Summary calculation of measurement uncertainty[4].

Uncertainty evaluation for active power P in W/V.A and reactive power Q in var/V.A					
Main uncertainty components	Type method of evaluation	Standard uncertainty value u(xi)	Probability distribution	Sensitivity coefficient	Uncertainty Contribution (µW/V.A) or (µW/V.A)
Voltage meas. (U)/U	Here specify the type A or B of all sub uncertainty components	Here specify the value of all sub uncertainty components	Normal	cos(φ) for active power sin(φ) for reactive power cos(φ)	Root square sum of all sub uncertainty components value and Sensitivity coefficient (in V/V)
Current meas. u(I)/I			Normal		Root square sum of all sub uncertainty components value and Sensitivity coefficient (in A/A)
Phase shift meas. u(φ)			Normal	1	Root square sum of all sub uncertainty components value and Sensitivity coefficient (in rad)
Meas. setup	Type B		Rectangular	1	-
Std. uncertainty	Type A	Std.s/number of measurement	Normal	1	-
The standard uncertainty for active power P in W/VA is the root square sum of the standard uncertainty of the three independent components of the Main uncertainty components.					
Expanded uncertainty for active power P in W/VA or reactive power Q var/VA in is equal to standard uncertainty multiplied by 2 which gives 95.45% coverage factor					

Fig 12: Typical Uncertainty budget used by Power and energy lab

5. Future Work

Current and voltage measurement units will be re-evaluated for better measurement uncertainties to get lower uncertainty for low current value. Maintain the Ac power measurement traceability to the national standards inside Saudi Arabia. In addition, AC power quality is one major activity inside the lab, which it will be focused next stage too.

6. Conclusion

An AC power measurement standard has been established at SASO NMCC. Performance of the system was tested with a key comparison and achieve CMC in KCDB data base with in 60 µW/V.A [7]. The reported results were found in good agreement with the estimated measurement uncertainties. Further research work is planned for improvement in the measurement uncertainties and this paper aim to minimize the uncertainty values to 40 µW/V.A.

1. The Saudi Electricity Company (SEC) has completed the installation and replacement of over 10 million smart electricity meters, within its most important project towards digital transformation. https://saudienergyconsulting.com/10-million-smart-meters-set-to-transform-saudi-grid/
2. Technical requirement for effective electric energy meter : https://taqyees.sa/en/regulations
3. Establishment of Reference Power Standard at SASO NMCC and GULFMET Bilateral Comparison
4. GUIDE FOR SAMPLING POWER AND POWER QUALITY MEASUREMENTS
5. The book \Sampling with 3458A - Understanding, Programming, Sampling and Signal Processing", authored by Rado Lapuh [7] covers the entire sampling capabilities of the 3458A that can be used in various practical applications.
6. IEEE Standard Definitions for the Measurement of Electric Power Quantities Under Sinusoidal, Nonsinusoidal, Balanced, or Unbalanced Conditions IEEE Std 1459TM-2010
7. https://www.bipm.org/kcdb/cmc/search?domain=PHYSICS&areaId=2&keywords=&specificPart.branch=-1&specificPart.service=-1&specificPart.subService=-1&specificPart.individualService=-1& countries=1&countries=151&publicDateFrom=&publicDateTo=&unit=-1&minValue=&maxValue=&minUncertainty=&maxUncertainty=#comment-31920

EPJ Web of Conferences **323**, 01((2 5l(12)   https://doi.org/0(.0(20/epjconf/1(1231301((2
22nd nIt enr Ia nr dMt Iei a gylCi nget ss

NEW STRUCTURE FOR HIGH-SENSITIVITY COAXIAL THERMAL POWER SENSOR IN THE FREQUENCY RANGE FROM DC–50 GHz

Doudou BA[1*], and Jean-Marie Lerat[1]

[1]Laboratoire National de Métrologie et d'Essais, 29 avenue Roger Hennequin, 78197 Trappes, France

Abstract. This paper presents the design and development of a new thermal microwave power sensor for a frequency range spanning from DC to 50 GHz. The purpose of this new design is to propose a high-sensitivity thermoelectric power sensor suitable for microcalorimeter application that is a primary method of microwave power calibration. The core structure of the power sensor comprises a Grounded Coplanar Waveguide (GCPW) transmission line, two load resistors, a thermopile, and output pads for DC measurements. The optimized power sensor demonstrates promising simulation performance, with a return loss better than 20 dB across the frequency range and an efficiency exceeding 80%. At 50 GHz, the sensitivity of the power sensor reaches well over 0.240 mV/mW.

1 Introduction

In various domain of sciences and engineering such as telecommunication systems and wireless applications, power sensors are used for power monitoring, control antenna gain and so on. Indeed, the development of new telecommunication protocol and microwave applications in daily life induces an increased need for reliable and traceable power measurement while in the meantime the availability of the thermistor type of sensor is becoming more and more challenging for most of National Metrology Institutes (NMIs). Therefore, research and development of new type of power sensor in the millimetre wavelengths domain is growing faster [1].

There are essentially three conventional type of power sensor such as the diode, thermistors and thermoelectric that available in the market. The general principle and method for each type of sensor is based on the detection of power by using a termination loads. Regarding the requirement of compactness, high performance in a wide frequency range, the thermoelectric are the most widely used devices to fulfil all these requirements. Extensive research has been carry out on the development of thermoelectric type of power sensor. For instance, the thermoelectric power sensor developed by Dehe et al. [2] works in the frequency range between 1 – 20 GHz and presents some limitations regarding the sensitivity of the power sensor. Wang et al. [3] and Yi et al. [4], in their work propose solutions to optimize thermoelectric power sensor performance regarding the sensitivity. By optimizing the size of the thermopile, they achieve reasonable results in return loss and sensitivity over a frequency range of 1 – 20 GHz. Recently, similar results have been achieve by Zhang et al. [5] with thermoelectric power sensor developed in GaAs process for frequency range between 1 – 30 GHz.

The main goals of this research paper are to develop and optimize a new structure of thermoelectric power sensor that shows high performances regarding the return loss, better than 20 dB, high efficiency, with high sensitivity and working in a wide frequency range. To achieve the development of a power sensor with high performances, one need full analysing of the electromagnetic response as well as the thermal response of the power sensor. Therefore, the electromagnetic-thermal co-simulation concept [6] is applied for the design and optimisation of the power sensor. The electromagnetic performance of the power sensor is analysed by using the specification of the 2.4 mm end launch connector, which operate up to 50 GHz. To obtain high sensitivity, we conduct a detail studies on the power sensor thermal properties and response when we applied microwave power.

The remaining of this paper is structured as follow. In section 2 are described the power sensors, the different components, and the design principle as well. In section 3, we provide the power sensor performances optimisation regarding the return loss, efficiency and the sensitivity.

2 Specification, design and theory of the power sensor

The overview of the different components of the power sensor is given in Fig. 1. The elements of the power sensor are à GCPW transmission line, two loads resistors as termination, a thermopile and output pads

* Corresponding author: doudou.ba@lne.fr

for DC measurements. The power sensor is fed with microwave power by using a commercial 2.4 mm end launch connector type.

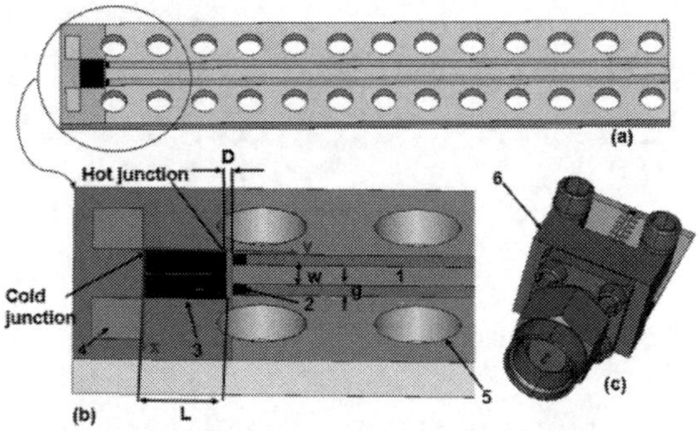

Fig. 1. (a) Internal structure of the power sensor. (b) Dimensions parameter of the power sensor. (c) 2.4 mm coaxial connector fixed to the power sensor. (1) GCPW li=transmission line, (2) load resistors, (3) thermopile, (4) output pads for Dc voltage, (5) via hole and (6) 2.4 mm coaxial connector.

The GCPW transmission line is conductor-backed coplanar waveguide (CPW). It consist of a central strip signal conductor with semi-infinite ground plane on either side, forming a ground-signal-ground structure that support quasi-TEM mode propagation. In the case of the GCPW line, an additional ground plane is located below the substrate, while a ground-signal-ground plane is deposited on top of the substrate. This additional ground plane is connected to the grounds of the upper plane by metallized vias holes [7] – [9]. The GCPW transmission line dimensions, including the width of the central strip (w) and the gap (g) between the central strip and the adjacent ground plane, were determined to achieve a characteristic impedance of 50 Ω, ensuring compatibility with the 2.4 mm end launch connector. The dimensions and positions of the vias as well as their number, were calculated and selected to prevent the appearance of a dominant rectangular waveguide mode with a cut-off frequency is given by the formula [7] below :

$$f_c = \frac{c}{2.\, d_{e.2e}.\sqrt{\varepsilon_r^{eff}}} \qquad (1)$$

Where c is the speed of the light, ε_r^{eff} is the effective relative dielectric constant of the substrate, $d_{e2e} = d_{c2c} - d_{via}$ is the edge-to-edge separation between two vias along the direction of the propagation, d_{c2c} is the center-to-center distance between 2 vias and d_{via} is the via diameter.

Considering the size of the power sensor, thirteen vias are placed across the direction of the propagation between the 2.4 mm end launch connector and the resistors as shown in Fig. 1. Therefore, $d_{e2e} = 0.775\ mm$ and accordingly to formula (1) above for the resonance frequency calculation is around $0.65 * f_c \cong 58\ GHz$. This is beyond the operating frequency of the power sensor designed.

For the computation, the central strip conductor, the ground planes on either side of the central strip and the additional ground at the bottom are made of thin film gold. Moreover, for the fabrication of the power sensor an additional layer of chromium is deposited on top of the substrate before thin film of gold. This additional layer is fully taken into account in the calculation and simulation.

The two parallel loads resistors are titanium sheet layer deposited at the end of the GCPW transmission line and between central strip and ground. The layer thickness is around 0.5 µm. The length (L) and the width (W) of the titanium sheet layer are optimised in order to match the 50 Ω impedance of the connectorised GCPW transmission line. Therefore the electrical resistance of each titanium sheet layer is:

$$R = \frac{R_S.\, L}{W} = 100\ \Omega \qquad (2)$$

The length of each titanium sheet layer is equal to the g parameter of the GCPW transmission line as shown in Fig. 1.

The couple alloy used or the thermopile is made of chrome/aluminium (Cr/Al) junctions with reasonable Seebeck coefficient. Regarding the fabrication process deposition of the Cr/Al couple alloy can be achieve by FEMTO ST (Franche-Comté Electronique Mécanique Thermique et Optiques-Sciences et Technologies) which is the manufacturing partner. The resulting output voltage (Vout) and the sensitivity (S) of the power sensor under microwave power are expressed, respectively as follow:

$$V_{out} = S_{Cr/Al} \sum_{i}^{N} \Delta T_i \qquad (3)$$

$$S = V_{out}/P_{in} \qquad (4)$$

Where $S_{Cr/Al}$ is the Seebeck coefficient of the Cr/Al alloy junctions, N is the number of thermocouples, ΔT_i correspond the temperature difference between the hot and cold junction of the thermocouples and P_{in} represent the input high frequency power.

The length of the thermopile, which refer to the distance between the hot and cold junction as shown in Fig. 1 ($L_{thermopile}$) is set at 500 µm. This value is largely sufficient for a stable ΔT_i [3]. It clearly has importance and impact on the power sensor performances, given the expression of equations (3) and (4), as the sensitivity increases when $L_{thermopile}$ is higher. However, one should consider the noise equivalent generated voltage that increase also [10] – [11], as shown by the expression of the thermal noise equivalent voltage that appears across every resistor device:

$$V_{noise} = \sqrt{4 * k_B * T_{ext} * R_e} \qquad (5)$$

Where k_B is the Boltzmann constant, T_{ext} is the external temperature and R_e is the electrical resistance of the thermopile which depends mainly to $L_{thermopile}$ parameter.

3 Power sensor electromagnetic and thermal response optimisation

3.1 Electromagnetic modelling

The modelling and the optimisation of the electromagnetic response (return loss, efficiency) of the power sensor were carried out using CST Studio Suite software. Since the GCPW transmission line is design to match 50 Ω of characteristic impedance, the power sensor matching characteristics regarding the return loss mainly depends on the positioning of the thermopile just beside the two load resistors. Therefore, we simulated the return loss performances of the power sensor with the distance between the thermopile and the two load resistors (D) in the range of 5 – 25 µm and the power sensor matching characteristic without the thermopile components is also calculated. All the power sensor components are considered as describe in section 1 and shows in Fig. 1. Fig. 2 shows the variation of the return loss across the frequency range from 1 to 50 GHz with D in range 5 – 25 µm. The results shows that the parameter D influenced the power sensor matching characteristics specifically when the frequency increase in the range 30 – 50 GHz. The return loss drop under 20 dB at 50 GHz when D = 5 µm. This degradation can be explained by the strong electromagnetic coupling effect between the thermopile and the two loads resistors when D is very small at high frequency.

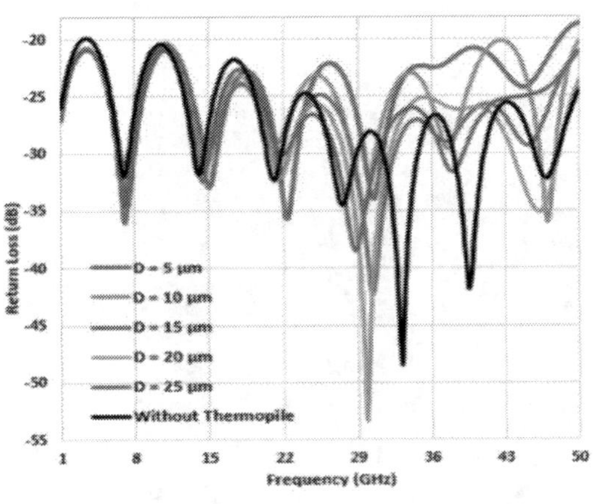

Fig. 2. Effect on changing the parameter D on the return loss of the power sensor

The power sensor effective efficiency η_{eff} as expressed in equation below correspond to the power sensor primary quantity.

$$\eta_{eff} = \frac{P_{absorbed\ by\ resistors}}{(1-\Gamma).P_{incident}} \qquad (6)$$

Where $P_{absorbed\ by\ resistors}$ is power absorbed by the resistors of the power sensor, $P_{incident}$ is power injected in the power sensor, $\Gamma = P_{reflected}/P_{incident}$ and $P_{reflected}$ is the amount of power reflected by the power sensor.

Fig. 3 shows the effective efficiency of the power sensor in the frequency range 1 – 50 GHz. As can be observed, $\eta_{effective}$ decreases when the frequency increases. When the distance D parameter in the range 15 – 20 µm, η_{eff} is higher than 80 % but it has a decreasing trend as D becomes smaller. The strong coupling effect between the thermopile and the two load resistors also affects η_{eff}, typically for D = 5 µm the effective efficiency drops below 80 % for frequency around 50 GHz.

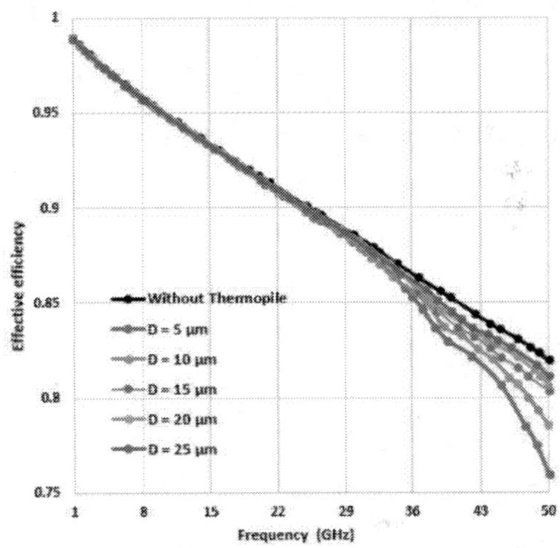

Fig. 3. Effect on changing parameter D on the effective efficiency of the power sensor

The results shows in Fig. 2 and Fig. 3 clearly highlighted the impact of the thermopile position regarding the power sensor electromagnetic response. To increase the power sensor sensitivity, one need to put the thermopile closer to the two load resistors for the temperature sensing without affecting the matching characteristics of the power sensor. Therefore, for the sensitivity analysis and calculation, the D parameter in the range of 10 – 25 µm is considered.

3.2 Thermal response and sensitivity analysis

The sensitivity calculation of a power sensor based on equation (4) depends on the thermopile sensing of the heat energy that is generated when microwave energy is absorbed and dissipated by the two load resistors. The power loss associated to the dissipated microwave power inside the power sensor depends on the electrical field distribution and the materials properties of the different components of the power sensor. The calculation and simulation of the thermal fields can be performed by using the power loss as heat source. Therefore, a multi-physics approach is implemented by running an electromagnetic and thermal co-simulation of the power sensor response when we applied power. To carry out this co-simulation, the CST Multiphysics Solver is used. Firstly, we calculated the electromagnetic fields distributions along the materials properties to evaluate the power loss as shown in Fig. 4. The results shows power loss are mainly distributed in the area where the two load resistors are located.

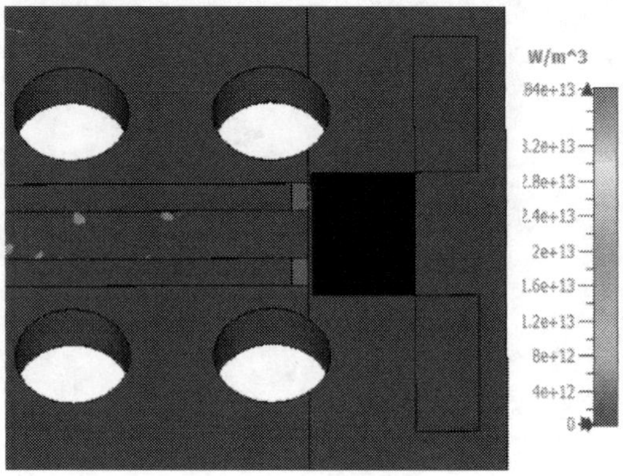

Fig. 4. Power loss density distribution of the power sensor at 50 GHz.

Table 1. Properties of materials involved in the design

Parameters	Value
Thermal conductivity (Ti)	11.3 W/(m.K)
Thermal conductivity (Au)	314 W/(m.K)
Thermal conductivity (Ni)	90.9 W/(m.K)
Thermal conductivity (Al)	90.9 W/(m.K)
Thermal conductivity (PTFE)	0.2 W/(m.K)
Thermal conductivity (Substrate)	1.5 W/(m.K)
Convection coefficient (Air)	5 W/(m.K)
Emissivity (Ti)	0.2
Emissivity (Au)	0.04
Emissivity (Substrate)	0.8
Seebeck Coefficient ($S_{Cr/Al}$)	22.5 µV/K
Ambient temperature	296.15 K
Convection coefficient (h)	5 W/(m^2.K)
Boltzman constant (k_B)	5.67* 10^{-8} W/(m^2.K^4)

The second step we performed the thermal field simulation by using the power loss results obtained in the first step as heat source. For the thermal setting, we used the parameter shown in Table 1. We consider two type of teat transfer that occurs in the power. The heat transfer by conduction between the two loads resistors, the substrate and the hot junction of the thermopile. The heat transfer by convection depends to the convective heat coefficient and the temperature difference between the surrounding air and the different components of the power sensors. Since the power sensor is design for microcalorimeter application with a maximum power level of 20 mW, we assumed the transfer type by radiation negligible and not considered for the computation and the calculation of the thermal response of the power sensor.

The temperature profile of the power sensor is shown in Fig. 5. Regarding the calculation, the parameter D is equal to 20 µm and with an applied microwave power of 10 mW through the power sensor at 50 GHz. As observed, the highest temperature value is located on the two load resistors and the nearby area. As we move away from the two load resistors layers, the temperature level decrease. This show the importance of the parameter D of the heat produce by the two load resistors.

As define in equation (4), the sensitivity of the power sensor depends on the output voltage define in equation (3). Therefore, we calculated the temperature difference between the hot and the cold junction across all the thermocouple in the thermopile as shown in Fig. 6. As expected, the temperature is maximum for hot junctions that are close to the two loads resistors. Overall, it shows a decreasing trend as we move away from the two loads resistors. It should be noted, at 50 GHz the maximum temperature difference for parameter D = 10 and D = 15 µm is very small, less than 0.1 K. This can be explain keeping in mind that the parameter η_{eff} is slightly better for D = 15 µm and as consequence the heat transfer by dissipation of the microwave power is more important.

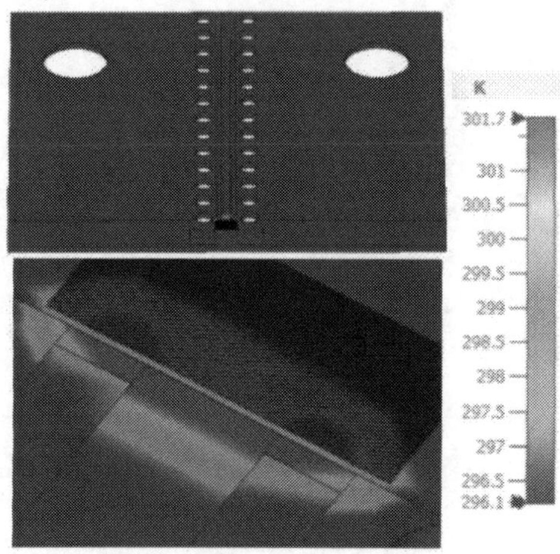

Fig. 5. (a) Thermal field distribution on the power sensor. (b) Temperature profile around the two load resistors.

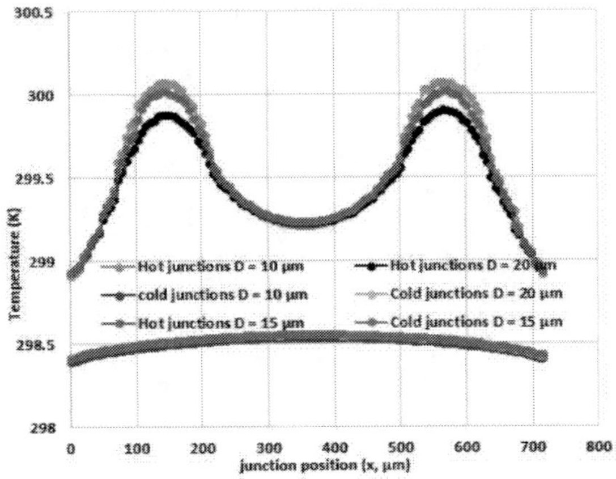

Fig. 6. Temperature distribution on the hot junctions and cold junctions of the thermopile at 50 GHz.

Fig. 7 shows the power sensor sensitivity with parameter D in the range 10 – 25 µm. The sensitivity is greater than 0.220 mV/mW across the entire frequency. At each frequency, it has a decreasing trend when parameter D increase. Regarding the performances, typically at 1 GHz, the sensitivity calculated in this paper is better when compare with similar power sensor reported in the literature.

This power sensor is design for the microcalorimeter applications with specific design goal such as reasonable return loss (up to 20 dB), efficiency higher than 80 % and high sensitivity as well. Therefore, when analysing the electromagnetic and thermal response, the power sensor with distance between the thermopile and the two load resistors of 15 µm is a reasonable compromise.

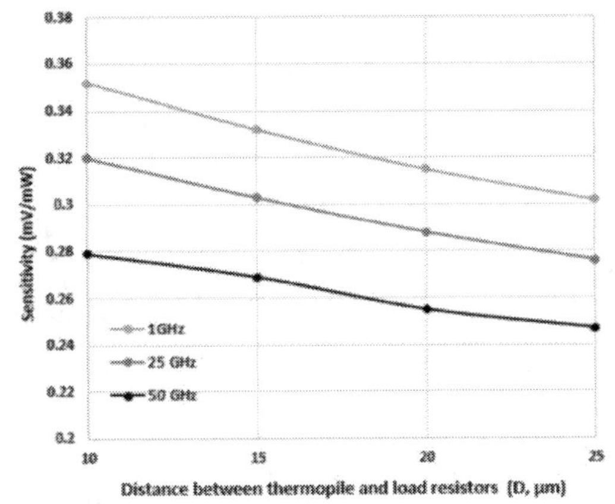

Fig. 7. Sensitivity of the power sensor vs distance between the thermopile and the two load resistors

4 Conclusion

We have reported a novel design concept of thermoelectric power for frequency range of DC – 50 GHz. The power sensor design combine a GCPW transmission line, titanium resistive load and chrome-aluminum thermopile. The optimise power sensor shows a return a loss better than 20 dB, and efficiency exceeding 80 % and high sensitivity across the entire frequency range. The sensitivity results, typically at 50 GHz, up to 0.247 mV/m was achieved which is suitable for microcalorimeter application since the applied microwave power does not exceed 20 mW.

References

1. A.S. Bush, Measurement of microwave power – A review of techniques used for measurement of high-frequency RF. IEEE Instrum. Meas. Mag. 2007, 38, 1473-1476.
2. A. Dehe, K. Fricke-Neuderth, V. Krozer, Thermoelectric power sensor for microwave applications by commercial CMOS fabrication. IEEE Electron Device Letters, 18(9), 450-452. 1997
3. D. B. Wang, X. P. Liao, T. Liu, Optimization of Indirectly-Heated Type Microwave Power Sensors Based on GaAs Micromachining. IEEE Sensors Journal, 12(5), 1349-1355. 2012
4. Z. Yi, X. Liao A 3D Model of the Thermoelectric Microwave Power Sensor by MEMS Technology. *Sensors* **2016**, *16*,921. https://doi.org/10.3390/s16060921
5. Z. Zhang, X. Liao, Zhang, Z., & Liao, X. Suspended Thermopile for Microwave Power Sensors Based on Bulk MEMS and GaAs MMIC Technology. IEEE Sensors Journal, 15(4). 2022
6. C. Mou, J. Chen, H. Peng, Electromagnetic-Thermal Co-Simulation of Planar Monopole Antenna Based on HIE-FDTD Method. MDPI-Electronics, 11(24), 4167. 2022
7. Z. Zhou, K.L. Melde, L. Development of a Broadband Coplanar Waveguide-to-Microstrip Transition with Vias. IEEE Transactions on advanced packaging, 31(4), 861-872, 2008
8. X. Hu, J. Tian, W. Tang, G. Zhang, Impact of Ground Via Placement and Size in Grounded Coplanar Waveguide Interconnects. IEEE International Workshop on Radio Frequency and Antenna Technologies, Shenzhen, China, 38-40. 2024
9. M. Grady, J.M. Kovitz, A. Iancovici, Y. Borenstein, Improved bandwidth using 3D Printed Quasi-Ideal Grounded Coplanar Waveguide Transmission Line. IEEE 22nd Annual Wireless and Microwave Technology Conference (WAMICON), Clearwater, FL, USA, 1-4. 2022.
10. O. Socher, O. Degani, Y. Nemirovskyl, Optimal consideration of CMOS compatible IR thermoelectric sensors. Sens. Act.A, vol. 71, no. 1 – 2, 107 – 115, Nov. 1998.
11. C.G. Mattsson, G. Thungstrom, K. Bertilssom, H-E Nilsson, H. Martin, Design of a Micromachined

Thermopile Infrared Sensor With a Self-Supported SiO_2/SU-8 Membrane. IEEE Sensors Journal, 8(12), 2044-2052. 2018.

12. F. Becher, Design of power sensor for measuring average power in the frequency band 110 GHz – 170 GHz, Ph.D. thesis, University of Paris-Saclay
13. S. Kodato, T. Wakabayashi, Q. Zhuang, S. Uchida, New Structure for DC-60 GHz thermal power sensor. IEEE MTT-S Int. Microw. Symp. Dig., Sanf Francisco CA, Jun. 1996, vol. 2, 871-874.

Establishment of AC-DC transfer standard at SASO-NMCC

Abdullah **Alrobaish**[1] *Ahmed* **Aljomaie**[1]

[1](NMCC, SASO, KSA) National Measurement and Calibration Center

Abstract. This paper documents the achievements of traceability and the technical evaluation of the newly established AC-DC Difference calibration service for AC voltage measurements at the NMCC, KSA. It gives details on the establishment and functioning of a new automatic calibrating system. This paper also includes instructions for the expanding uncertainty associated with the calibration system. Nevertheless, this study provides extensive review of heat converters and AC-DC difference measurements. The GULFMET.EM-S3 Supplementary Comparison data show the new system's capabilities, which cover the 2mV to 1000V @ 10Hz to 1MHz range. It also describes the new capabilities of AC-DC difference calibration services and the accomplishment of traceability for AC voltage measurements by the NMCC in Saudi Arabia. It explains the installation and functioning of auto-calibrating system. This paper also guides the construction of calibration systems and the related extended uncertainty. Although it is not very detailed, this document gives an idea of what heat converters and AC-DC difference measurements are all about—the results of the GULFMET.EM-S3 Supplementary Comparisons are used to show what the new system is capable of. These capabilities range from 10 Hz to 1 MHz and 2 mV to 1000 V.

Keywords. Automatic Calibration Systems, Thermal Converters, Thermal Transfer Standards, AC-DC Difference, and Uncertainty Calculations.

1. Introduction

The reference method to measure AC voltage and current is to compare the heating effect of the AC signal to the heating effect of a DC signal. This comparison generally uses thermal voltage and current converters (TVCs and TCCs), which are helpful in different level of uncertainties, from a few hertz to several hundred megahertz. These devices often consist of a thermoelement (TE) connected in series with a resistor for voltage measurements as a TVC or connected in parallel with a shunt resistor for current measurements as a TCC.

From tens to hundreds of thermocouples are connected along a heater structure, alternating the AC and DC signals with a thermoelement. When applying AC and both polarities of DC successively and observing the thermocouple output, the conventional concept of the AC-DC difference can be calculated as in formula (1)

$$\delta = \left(\frac{E_a - E_d}{E_d}\right)x10^6 \qquad (1)$$

When used with positive and negative polarities, the mean response from the DC value E_d equals the RMS AC amount E_a[1].

The majority of the present-day commercially available AC-DC thermal transfer standards are realized with the help of single-junction thermal converters (SJTC) [2–6] or solid-state transfer standards [7]. The SJTCs employ a single thermocouple to the heater wire; the output is 7mV to 12mV for full-scale input, and the output responds to the changes in the input signal in a manner proportional to the square of the input signal. These are applied in many commercial applications and are suitable for 10 Hz to 100 MHz frequencies. For all these devices, except range or shunt resistors and the measurement process, the best uncertainty is a few µV/V. The uncertainty rises at input levels below approximately half of the full scale and the frequency range limits. [8].

2. NMCC Thermal Transfer Standards Calibration Service

The characterizations of NMCC's thermal transfer standards across the different uncertainties are based on the following:

Among the standards for measuring AC are:

i. A set of multi-junction thermal converters (MJTC) in the range of 1V-1000V and an operating frequency range of 10Hz to 1MHz, as shown in Figures 1 and 2.

ii. Micro Potentiometers (MPOT) with outputs of 2 mV, 20 mV, 50 mV, 100 mV, and 200 mV and frequencies of 10 Hz, 100 Hz, 1 kHz, 10 kHz, 100 kHz, and 1 MHz as depicted in Figure3.

A build-up technique is calibrating the fundamental level thermal voltage converter (TVC) at half its nominal voltage (or at its lowest value applicable) and then calibrating the closest lower level TVC at half its nominal voltage (or at its lowest value applicable) using the calibrated converter [9]. A chain of converters up to 1000V can be calibrated in this way using a 3V basic-level thermal converter as showed in fig 4. In our case, PTB has calibrated the entry-level thermal converters that are used between 1 and 3 volts. These converters are compared and rechecked every two years. If the deviation of the results from the values indicated in the certificate is greater than the limits of uncertainty displayed in the certificate, the TVCs are adjusted in a similar way.

Fig. 1. Multi-junction Thermal Converters (MJTC)

Fig. 2. Thermal voltage replaced to MJTC

Fig. 3. Set of Micropotentiometer (MPOT)

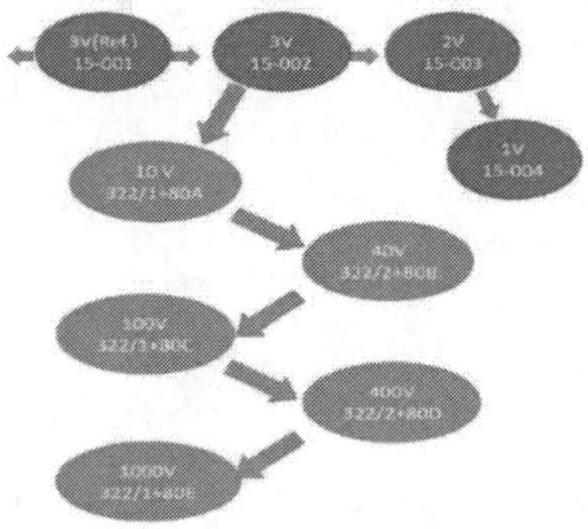

Fig. 4. Range-to-range build-up measurements

3. NMCC's Automated AC-DC Transfer Difference Calibration System

The NMCC has developed a state-of-the-art automated calibration system to facilitate the AC-DC transfer difference calibration process. This system involves a set of precision thermal converters incorporated in an extensive voltage and frequency range. The components comprising this system are:

Thermal Converters: NMCC reference standards include multijunction thermal voltage converters (MJTCs), micro potentiometers, and Fluke 792A. These converters play a significant role in voltage measurements where high accuracy is required. Conventionally, MPOT would represent the lower voltage ranges, and MJTCs would come in at higher voltages, where they would perform with relatively better accuracy and stability.

3.1 Measurement Devices

The system shall be equipped with high accurate nanovoltmeters for the measurements at the output of thermal converters that provide output electromotive forces (EMFs). These devices form the crucial link in establishing an AC-DC difference. In addition, the system shall use a multifunction calibrator to supply stable and precise sources for both AC and DC voltage. Fig 5 illustrate the circuit connection to perform the calibration

The system is designed in such a way that it works fully automatically; a computer with Labware software controls all operations. Consequently, automation allows continuous and exact measurements, decreases human error, and improves the efficiency of the calibration process. The software also allows real-time monitoring and data collection, allowing one to monitor performance and reliability.

3.2 Calibration Process

Each thermal converter is subjected to AC and DC voltages during calibration, and the response is recorded. The system accomplishes a brief AC-DC conversion by transferring a rapid switch that provides the necessary AC and DC alternation and a constant voltage supply to the converters. This makes it easier to measure the AC-DC difference with extremely high precision. To make the calibration information easily accessible to the user, every piece of information is written to the appropriate sections of the screen as fig 6 shows.

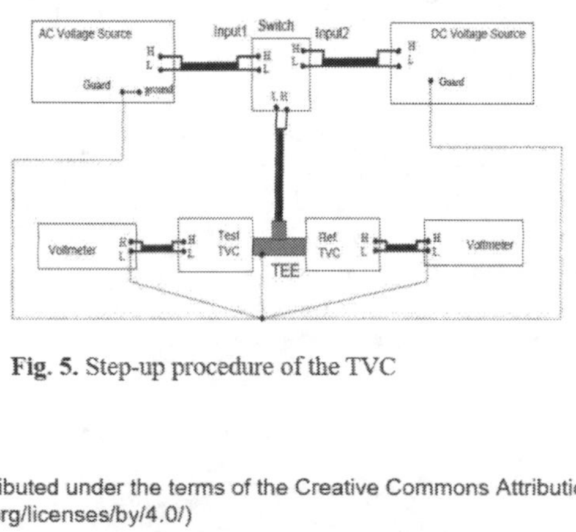

Fig. 5. Step-up procedure of the TVC

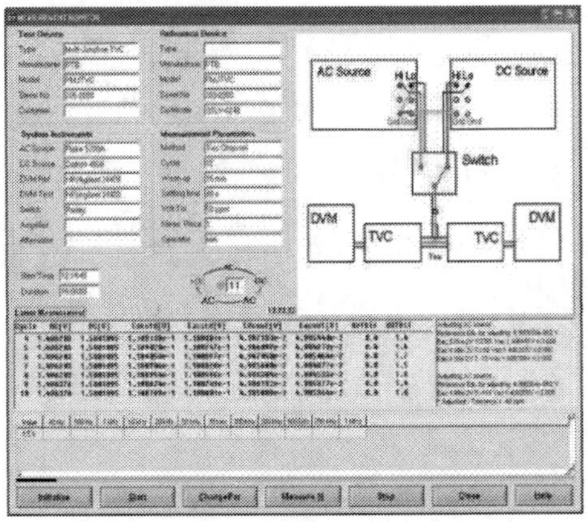

Fig. 6. A new automated calibration system in NMCC

Computers and systems running National Instruments software are in charge of the calibrating systems. During the calibration procedure, a graphics-based system control program called Labware is used as a virtual instrument, or VI, where data and conclusions are presented parallel to the measurements. Comparing this structure to previous language-based systems, it is a significant advance. When using the "virtual instrument" idea, the same screen serves as the system's input and output stages and is often shown for the duration of the calibration run.

As the calibration system is controlled and data is acquired through the IEEE-488 (GPIB) interface, an appropriate device is needed to connect the controller to the GPIB bus. The National Instruments NI-488.2 has successfully implemented the AC-DC calibration program. This application employs a system that toggles input voltage between ordinary and calibrated voltage converters. This calibrated DC source calculates an error of an AC source voltage. A sequence is performed where the first is a measurement of the DC input signal; the second is the switching to the AC signal and taking another measurement back to the DC input signal. Assistance is in recording drifts or signal changes with time to calibrate the voltage of AC accurately.

4. GULFMET.EM-S3 Comparison with Other Metrology Institutes

NMCC validated the performance of its AC-DC transfer standards by participating in the GULFMET.EM-S3 comparison. This comparison evaluated the accuracy and reliability of AC-DC difference measurements among other NMIs. Notable participants included UME (Turkey), NIS (Egypt), NIMSA (South Africa), and SASO-NMCC (Saudi Arabia). The results of this comparison are given in Tables 1 and 2.

Table 1. Results of the comparison of 10 mV @ 1 kHz

NMI	AC-DC Difference (µV/V)	Uncertainty (µV/V)
UME	7	32
NMCC	-3	28
NMIA	-15	49
NIS	-16	41

Table 2. Results of the comparison of 3V@100kHz

NMI	AC-DC Difference (µV/V)	Uncertainty (µV/V)
UME	16.4	5
NMCC	18	10
NMIA	17	10
NIS	19	22

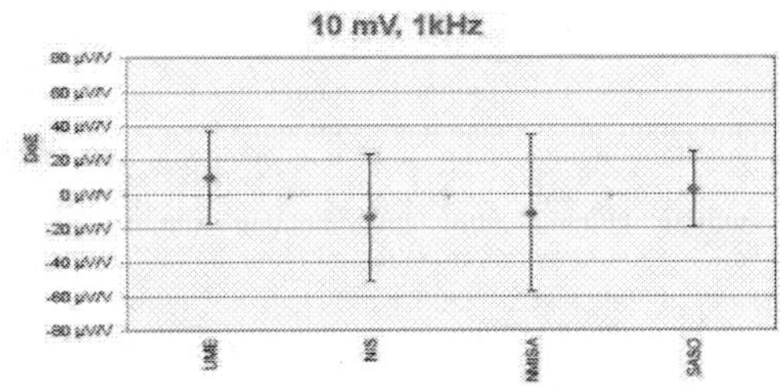

Fig. 7. Degree of Equivalences (DoE) @ 10 mV

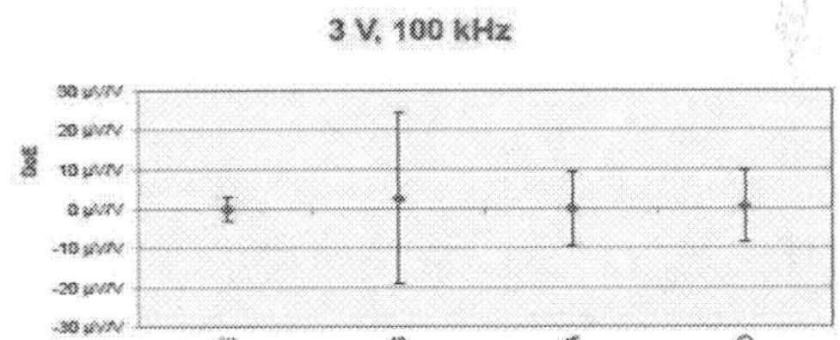

Fig. 8. Degree of Equivalences (DoE) @ 3V

The results showed good agreement among the participating institutes. All of the measurements were within the claimed uncertainties. Specifically, NMCC reported an AC-DC difference of -3 µV/V with an associated uncertainty of 28 µV/V at 10 mV which was the best uncertainty among all participant.

The agreement of these results proves NMCC's interoperability and precision of AC-DC transfer standards. This kind of comparison is critical to mutual recognition of calibration capabilities among NMIs, with a primary meaning only to support consistent and reliable measurements realized in different regions. Table 1 & 2 show some of the comparison results

5. Uncertainty Estimation

The uncertainties of NMCC's AC-DC Difference Calibration Service are evaluated according to M 3003, the Expression of Uncertainty and Confidence in Measurement, Edition 1, 1997 [10]. The standard uncertainty of the measurement is obtained by summing up the uncertainty components using root-sum-of-squares.

The Type A uncertainty is coming from statistical analysis of a series of measurement. All other uncertainty components are considered as type B uncertainty. These two types are combined using the RSS technique to obtain the combined standard uncertainty. The final or expanded uncertainty provided to the customer or for NMCC standards in a re-characterization is calculated by multiplying the combined standard uncertainty by a coverage factor (K) of 2. This allow a level of confidence of nearly 95 % [11].

The software will determine the uncertainty by including the standard deviations of a result with the Type B components evaluated for a particular type of thermal converter at the voltage and frequency. This will assist in evaluating some of the uncertainties to the measurements made by the automated system. Formula (2) and (3) represent the model function for calculating the delta for 1V to 100V and 100V to 1000V respectively [12]

Table. 3 represent the uncertainty contribution according to model function

$$\delta_x = \delta_{diff} + \delta_{ref} + \delta_{con} + \delta_{con} + \delta_{sys} + \delta_{level}. \quad (2)$$

- For the 100 V–1000 V voltage range

$$\delta_x = \delta_{diff} + \delta_{ref} + \delta_{con} + \delta_{sys} + \delta_{level} + \delta_{equip} \quad (3)$$

Where:

δ_x	The test transfer standard's AC-DC transfer difference
δ_{diff}	The difference between the reference transfer standard and the actual AC-DC transfer test
δ_{ref}	The AC-DC transfer Difference of the reference transfer standard
δ_{con}	Difference in AC-DC transfer from the connectors and connections
δ_{sys}	Difference in AC-DC transfer from the measurement system
δ_{level}	Difference in AC-DC transfer from the thermal converter's voltage dependence
δ_{equip}	Differences in AC-DC transfer from the use of various devices

Table 3. Components of Uncertainty

$u(\delta_{diff})$	The standard deviation repeatability and measurement uncertainty. The distribution is normal.
$u(\delta_{ref})$	Uncertainty of the reference AC-DC transfer standard with normal distribution and k=2.
$u(\delta_{con})$	The uncertainty caused by connections in the system. This uncertainty includes the inaccuracies brought on by using various TEEs and wires. It has a rectangular distribution.
$u(\delta_{sys})$	uncertainty resulting from the measurement system's estimation of the value of "n" which expresses the voltmeters' linearity inaccuracy. It has rectangular distributed.
$u(\delta_{level})$	uncertainty from the voltage dependence in the thermal converters' operating range. It has a rectangular
$u(\delta_{equip})$	uncertainty caused by several equipment. It has a rectangular distribution.

Tables 4 and 5 contains example of the uncertainty budgets for the AC-DC Difference calibration services at 10 mV/55 Hz and 3 V/1 kHz, respectively.

Table 4. The uncertainty budget of 10 mV @ 55 Hz.

Symbol	Distribution	Divisor	Contribution
$u(\delta_{diff})$	Normal	1	2.0 µV/V
$u(\delta_{ref})$	Normal	2	23 µV/V
$u(\delta_{con})$	Rectangular	√3	2.0 µV/V
$u(\delta_{sys})$	Rectangular	√3	4.0 µV/V
$u(\delta_{level})$	Rectangular	√3	8.0 µV/V
Total Variance			165 (µV/V)2
Standard Uncertainty			12.5 µV/V
Expanded Uncertainty (K=2)			25.8 µV/V
Declared Uncertainty*			27 µV/V

Table 5. Uncertainty Budget of 3V @ 1 kHz

Symbol	Distribution	Divisor	Contribution
$u(\delta_{diff})$	Normal	1	3.0 µV/V
$u(\delta_{ref})$	Normal	2	30 µV/V
$u(\delta_{con})$	Rectangular	√3	0.2 µV/V
$u(\delta_{sys})$	Rectangular	√3	5.0 µV/V
$u(\delta_{level})$	Rectangular	√3	1.0 µV/V
Total Variance			11.86 (µV/V)2
Standard Uncertainty			3.42 µV/V
Expanded Uncertainty (K=2)			6.83 µV/V

https://doi.org/01.0150/epjconf/61653630611(

Declared Uncertainty*	7.0 µV/V

Table 6. Extended Uncertainty Value Samples for Various Ranges and Frequencies

Voltage/Range	10 Hz	1 kHz	100 kHz	1 MHz
10mV /22mV	38	28	29	86
3V / 7V	11	7.0	10	28
1000V / 1000V	N/A	17	N/A	N/A

6. Conclusion

Due to the large number of tools and processes needed, a complete calibration system with high precision for AC voltage measurements and their applications is difficult to implement. The new automated calibration approach described in this study and technique recognizes this fact and the difficulty of accurately calibrating any heat transfer reference. This method makes it possible to calibrate the AC voltage with the help of high accurate nanovoltmeter and the AC-DC differences of the transfer standards. Significant high levels of automation provided by the new calibrating system result in great precision and confidence in NMCC and to be at the NMI capability level. This system deals with AC voltage measurements ranging from 2 mV to 1000 V at frequencies of 10 Hz to 1 MHz. the result of this system shows good agreement with the level of the NMIs. The system may achieve uncertainties in the wide range of voltage and frequency, from 6.0 µV/V to 86 µV/V. A chain of certified calibration certifications completed by accredited NMI with KCDB-published CMC has also helped NMCC, KSA to achieve AC voltage traceability.

References

[1] Mamdouh Halawa, A. Hassan, El-Sayed Shehab, El-Sayed Refai, "Integrated Calibration System for Accurate AC Current Measurements up to 100 kHz," *MAPAN, Journal Metrology Society of India*, July 2012.

[2] B. D. Inglis, "Standards for ac-dc transfer," *Metrologia*, 29, pp. 191-199, January 1992.

[3] F. C. Widdis, "Theory of Peltier- and Thomson-effect errors in thermal ac-dc transfer devices," *Proc. Inst. Elec. Eng.*, 109, pt. C (monograph 497 M) pp. 328-334, 1962.

[4] F. L. Hermach and E. S. Williams, "Thermal voltage converters for accurate voltage measurements to 30 megacycles per second," *Trans. AIEE (Comm. and Elec.)*, 79, pt. 1, pp. 200-206, July 1960.

[5] F. L. Hermach and E. S. Williams, "Thermal converters for audio-frequency voltage measurements of high accuracy," *IEEE Trans. Instrum. Meas.* IM-15, No. 4, pp. 260-268, December 1966.

[6] E. S. Williams, "Thermal current converters for accurate AC measurement," *IEEE Trans. Instrum. Meas.*, IM-25, No. 4, pp. 519-523, December 1976.

[7] E. S. Williams, "Thermal voltage converters and comparators for very accurate AC voltage measurements," *J. Res. Nat. Bur. Stand.*, 75C, pp. 145-154, July 1971.

[8] Thomas E. Lipe, "Operation and Reference Manual for the NIST AC-DC Calibration Systems and Software," *Natl. Inst. Stand. Technol.* NIST Special Publication 250-61, May 2004.

[9] Mamdouh Halawa and M. Rahal "A Step-Down Technique to Calibrate AC Current down to 10 µA Using a Precision 10 mA Current Shunt," *MAPAN, Journal Metrology Society of India*, Sept. 2012.

[10] M3003, The Expression of Uncertainty and Confidence in Measurement, Edition 1, December 1997, *UKAS*.

[11] EA-4/02, Expressions of the Uncertainty of Measurements in Calibration (previously EAL-R2), Apr. 1997.

[12] M. M. Halawa and Ahmed Hussein, "Improvement and Confirmation of a New Automatic System for AC-DC Calibration at NIS, Egypt" *Simposio de Metrologia, Mexico* Oct. 2006.

Towards a Traceable Calibration of Medium Voltage Transformers up to 150 kHz

Mohamed Agazar [1*], *Alf-Peter Elg*[2], *Angel Ramírez*[3], *Claudio Iodice*[4], *Domenico Giordano*[5], *Jari Hällström*[6], *Jorge Rovira*[3], *Mario Luiso*[4], *Palma Sara Letizia*[5], *Tatu Nieminen*[6]

[1]LNE, Laboratoire National de métrologie et d'Essais, 1 Rue Gaston Boissier, 75015 Paris, France
[2]RISE, Research Institute of Sweden, Box 857 SE-501 15 Borås, Sweden
[3]FFII, Fundación para el Fomento de la Innovación Industrial, LCOE, Getafe, 28906 Madrid
[4]Department of Engineering, Università degli Studi della Campania "Luigi Vanvitelli", Via Roma 29, 81031 Aversa, Italy
[5]*INRIM,* Istituto Nazionale di Ricerca Metrologica, 10135 Turin, Italy
[6]VTT Technical Research Centre of Finland Ltd, Finland

Abstract. The increasing integration of power electronics and renewable energy sources in modern electrical grids has introduced new challenges in medium voltage transformer calibration, particularly in the frequency range from 9 kHz to 150 kHz. Accurate and traceable calibration methods are essential to ensure reliable voltage measurement in electrical grids, where power quality and compliance with IEC 61869-1:2024 standards are critical. This study presents advancements in the development of traceable calibration techniques for medium voltage transformers operating within this frequency range. The approach includes the design of generators capable of simulating real world grid disturbances and the establishment of reference measurement systems at National Metrology Institutes. The study further explores generator configurations, such as parallel and series source arrangements, to extend calibration capabilities beyond existing limits. The proposed calibration methodology incorporates precision voltage dividers with high resolution, filtering and amplification techniques, and advanced data acquisition methods to achieve measurement uncertainties below 0.01% for fundamental components and between 0.2 % and 1 % for harmonic components. A key challenge is the ability to measure a fundamental voltage as high as 50 kV while superimposing harmonics with amplitudes as low as 5 V in the 9 kHz to 150 kHz range. These developments aim to enhance power system reliability, improve voltage measurement accuracy, and support the transition to more efficient and resilient electrical grids. The presented results lay the foundation for future calibration services.

1 Introduction

AC electrical power transmission and distribution systems have evolved significantly since the late 19th century to meet growing industrial and societal demands. Over the past two decades, however, substantial transformations have emerged, driven by advances in quantum and digital technologies. These advancements have facilitated the expansion of renewable energy sources, such as photovoltaic panels, wind turbines, fuel cells, and batteries, as well as energy storage solutions [1] [2]. Additionally, the increasing integration of power electronics in both conventional applications (e.g., lighting and power supplies) and emerging technologies (e.g., electric vehicles and decentralized energy production) has introduced significant disturbances within AC and DC networks, particularly in the frequency range up to 150 kHz [3].

Voltage transformers (VTs) play a critical role in power systems by converting voltage between their primary and secondary terminals while ensuring safe electrical isolation. These high precision devices are widely deployed in high (HV) and medium voltage (MV) networks, where accurate voltage measurement is essential for effective energy management. As smart grids continue to evolve, VTs must adapt to new power quality phenomena, making their characterization under realistic operating conditions increasingly necessary [4]. This characterization is crucial for managing their impact on grid performance, improving the reliability of energy systems, and ensuring compliance with updated power quality standards such as IEC 61869-1:2024 [5], which introduces new accuracy requirements for instrument transformers up to at least 150 kHz.

Despite these advancements, metrological challenges persist due to the absence of reference measurement systems, traceable calibration procedures, and validated experimental setups for precise voltage measurements in the 9 kHz–150 kHz range. While significant progress has been made for frequencies up to 9 kHz through the 19NRM05 IT4PQ project [6], further work is required for higher frequencies. To address this gap, a new project 22NRM06 ADMIT [7] has been launched with two primary objectives:

* Corresponding author: mohamed.agazar@lne.fr

The development of AC and DC voltage generators designed to simulate grid disturbances focuses on generating fundamental voltage components with amplitudes up to 36 kV for AC and 50 kV for DC. These generators will also superimpose frequency components in the 9 kHz to 150 kHz range, with amplitudes ranging from 5 V to 500 V.

Establishment of reference measurement systems at National Metrology Institutes (NMI) to provide traceability for voltage measuring instruments in the 9 kHz–150 kHz frequency range. This will enable the calibration of VTs with a 0.1% accuracy class. The target uncertainties are 0.01% for the fundamental component and between 0.2 % and 1 %, depending on the voltage level, for the 9 kHz–150 kHz components. For phase measurements, the target uncertainties are 0.01 crad for the fundamental component and between 0.2 crad and 1 crad for the 9 kHz–150 kHz components.

This paper presents the progress made toward achieving these two objectives, detailing the development of HV generators and the establishment of metrological infrastructures for precision voltage measurements in the targeted frequency range.

2 HV generators

To test VTs under real operating conditions, specifically, VTs that could be connected to the MV electrical grid and exposed to harmonics in the 9 kHz to 150 kHz range, it is crucial to develop generation techniques capable of producing disturbances that closely similar to those present on the grid. The facilities that generate voltage with controlled manner up to 150 kHz are very limited. Typically, the best NMI facilities do not go beyond 10 kHz. Similar results are noticeable on the market, where manufacturers of HV amplifiers propose systems that perform less than those at NMIs. Validated and stable generators remain an important tool, which is considered an essential part of the test circuit. Realistic AC and DC voltage with spectral content up to 150 kHz, must be identified for the characterisation of VTs . The project will make a major step by developing novel generation infrastructures allowing NMIs to offer new calibration services.

2.1 AC generator using two sources in parallel

This generator utilizes two grounded parallel generators to combine voltages through appropriate blocking elements and filters, as described in Figure 1. This technique has been commonly used in HV testing to superimpose impulses, such as lightning and switching impulses, onto AC or DC voltages, in accordance with IEC 60060-1 and IEC 60060-2 [8][9]. This technique has been successfully applied in the past for frequencies ranging from 4 kHz to 9 kHz [10], achieving a level of 1 kV in this frequency range, superimposed with 35 kV at 50 Hz. Based on these results, we have decided to further explore this approach to extend the frequency range up to 150 kHz.

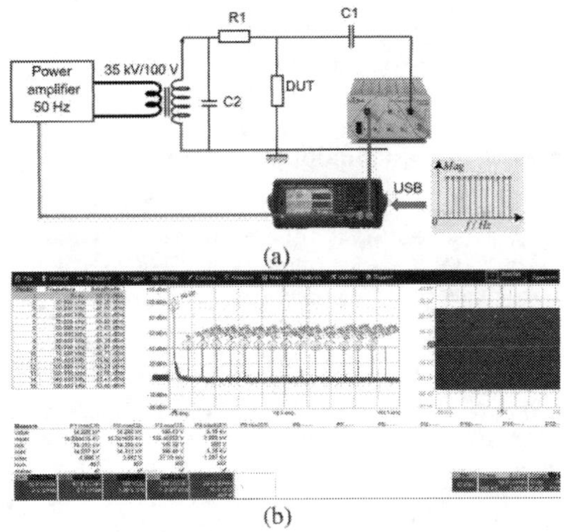

Fig. 1. The developed generator based on the use of two generators in parallel; a) design principle, b) example of the generation of 14 kV/50 Hz superimposed with multitoned harmonics from 10 kHz to 150 kHz with a step of 10 kHz.

The fundamental 50 Hz signal is generated by an voltage amplifier with a power rating of 6 kVA, capable of delivering voltages up to 120 V with a current of approximately 50 A. The output of this amplifier is stepped up from 100 V to 35 kV using a step up transformer with a power capacity of 5 kVA, which is necessary to supply the required energy to the components of the setup. The harmonic component is provided by an N4L LPA400 amplifier capable of delivering a voltage of 250 V rms with a maximum current of 50 mA. This amplifier can be replaced by a TREK PZD2000A amplifier, which can increase the voltage level to 500 V rms with a current of approximately 150 mA. Both amplifiers are controlled by an arbitrary voltage generator (AVG), which is itself controlled by software that allows for the desired frequency content. This can be a single harmonic or multiple harmonics simultaneously. Issues related to the phase of the signals are managed at the level of this AVG.

To ensure proper operation and protect each generator, two filters are included. A HV capacitor, C1, rated at 50 kV, is placed on the amplifier side. Together with the output impedance of the amplifier, it forms a high pass filter with a cut-off frequency in the range of several tens of kHz, ensuring that the 50 Hz component is sufficiently attenuated. Additionally, a resistor R1 and a capacitor C2 also rated at 50 kV, are used to protect the transformer from HF components. These elements form a low pass filter with a cut-off frequency in the range of tens of hertz, ensuring that HF components are significantly attenuated on the transformer side.

In Figure 1b, an example of the generation of 14 kV/50 Hz superimposed with multitoned harmonics from 10 kHz to 150 kHz with a step of 10 kHz. The FFT window lists frequency components with their respective amplitudes. The differences in harmonic levels are due to the frequency response of the HF amplifier, which is perfectly correctable. This generator operates correctly with voltage stability at 50 Hz better than 0.01% and better than 0.1% for harmonics up to 150 kHz.

2.2 AC generator using two sources in series

A variation of the generator discussed in the previous chapter consists of using both sources in series, Figure 2. A Step-Up Transformer (SUT) is fed by a Low-Frequency Amplifier (LFA) to generate the fundamental 50 Hz component at MV level. A High-Frequency Amplifier (HFA) is connected in series with the secondary winding of the transformer to generate harmonic components up to 150 kHz. The combination of LFA/SUT and HFA allows for the synthesis of a HV signal containing both the fundamental frequency (50 Hz) and HF harmonics. Two reference devices are used for measurement, one for fundamental tone (Low Frequency Reference Device, LFRD) and one for the HF tones (High Frequency Reference Device, HFRD).

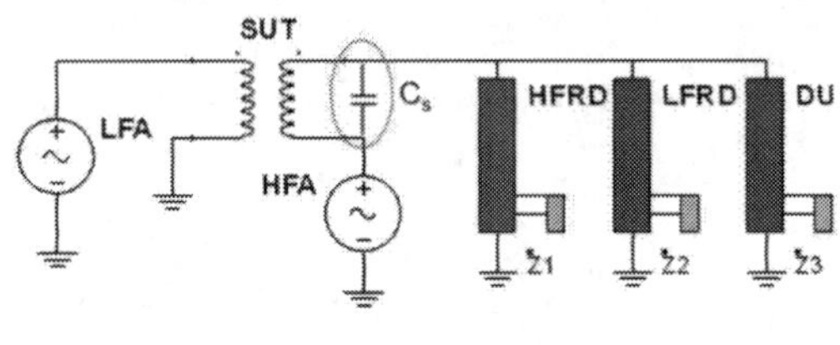

Fig. 2. The developed system based on the use of generators in series and its associated measuring systems

The arrangement of the generators is a critical consideration. If the HFA is positioned after the SUT at the HV point, it must be properly insulated to withstand the maximum voltage of the SUT. Achieving insulation for the HFA up to 35 kV requires powering all instrumentation with batteries, which presents significant challenges due to the intrinsic characteristics of the HFA. For this reason, we prefer the configuration shown in Figure 2, where the HFA is positioned before the SUT (low-voltage point), utilizing its natural insulation. In this setup, the HF current delivered by the HFA flows through the secondary winding of the SUT, which can lead to two potential issues. First, if the current flowing through the secondary winding exceeds its maximum allowable limit (typically a few tens of milliamperes at 35 kV), it may cause damage to the winding. Secondly, a significant amount of the generated high-frequency components willdrop in the secondary winding of the SUT. To mitigate this last effect, a capacitor Cs (typically in the nF range) is parallel-connected to the secondary windings of the SUT. However, this solution may significantly increase the power required for the LFA. The use of this capacitor, if correctly dimensioned, makes the portion of the HF current still flowing through the SUT negligible. Similarly, it is crucial to verify that the 50 Hz current flowing through the HFA via the ground return remains within its allowable limit.

2.3 AC generator using a step up transformer

This method consists of using a single voltage transformer to deliver both the 50 Hz frequency and harmonic frequencies up to 150 kHz, as shown in Figure 3. It is used to produce distorted voltages at MV using the simple circuit in figure compensating for the frequency behaviour of the generation setup components.

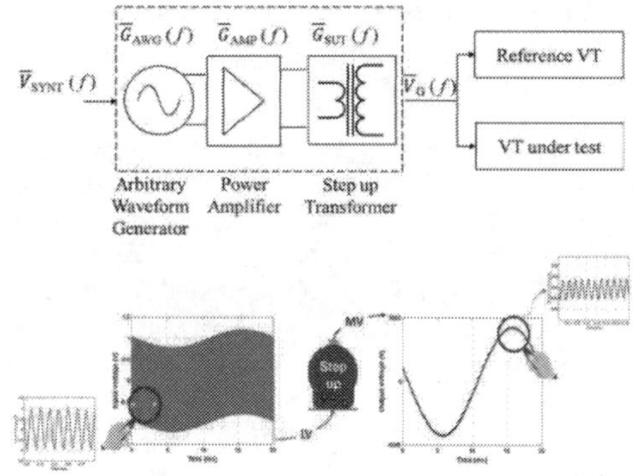

Fig. 3. Producing distorted voltages at MV using the simple circuit in figure compensating for the frequency behaviour of the generation setup components.

The arbitrary waveform generator produces a signal that includes the fundamental 50 Hz frequency along with its harmonics. It can be observed that the fundamental frequency has approximately the same amplitude as the harmonics. This signal is then amplified using a power amplifier to energize the step-up transformer, which boosts the voltage to meet the required test conditions while considering the frequency response of the transformer, which plays a crucial role in achieving the desired voltage levels accurately. Assuming that the transformer ratio at high frequencies is significantly lower than at the fundamental frequency, the fundamental component will be amplified more than the harmonics. As a result, the output of the transformer will deliver a high amplitude at fundamental frequency with harmonics at relatively lower levels. The compensating for the frequency behaviour of the generation setup components is performed. The amplified signal is then applied to the voltage transformer under test. A reference VT is used to compare the output and evaluate the performance of the transformer under test. Two key phenomena are considered in this setup. First, the frequency response of the transformer is sensitive to the load. To mitigate this effect, the frequency behaviour of the transformer must be characterized for each measurement campaign under the same conditions as its actual use. This characterization can be performed at low voltage using a frequency sweep method by using the same set up as that used in HV (figure 3). Second, the current flowing through the step-up transformer can increase significantly due to HF components, even if their amplitudes are limited. The rms current must be

https://doi.org/01.0150/epjconf/71753730711(

monitored to ensure it does not exceed its allowable limit due to the internal impedance of the transformer.

2.4 DC generator using two sources in series

The test system consists of two sources connected in series for DC generation, as illustrated in Figure 4. It comprises four key components: a HV direct current (HVDC) source, an arbitrary waveform generator (AWG) with a power amplifier, a HF voltage transformer (HFVT), and the DUT including the HV divider for measurement.

The HVDC source provides a stable 50 kV dc voltage with an adequate filtering mechanism to minimize harmonic distortion, ensuring that the primary voltage remains free from unwanted HF components that could interfere with the experiment. The arbitrary waveform generator, coupled with a power amplifier, generates the input signal containing harmonic frequencies up to 150 kHz. The power amplifier ensures that the signal meets the required test conditions, with a power requirement of approximately 1 kVA at 500V, a frequency range of 9 – 150 kHz, and an output voltage exceeding 50 V, allowing sufficient excitation of the HFVT.

The HFVT is a step-up HF transformer, designed to increase the applied voltage while maintaining a stable frequency response. Its key specifications include compliance with the same power and frequency as the power amplifier, a turn ratio of 10 to ensure effective voltage transformation up to 500 V, and insulation between primary and secondary windings up to 10 kV dc, preventing electrical breakdown under HV operation.

The DUT and the measurement system are used to measure the HV by comparison. The DUT is simulated using a capacitance of approximately 3.5 nF, ensuring that the system operates effectively for large capacitance values. The ground potential is set on the HVDC source side, with a sufficient blocking capacitor connected in parallel to the HVDC source to prevent HF currents from passing through. In this configuration, both the DUT and the reference measurement system can operate in a floating mode. Additionally, the voltage drop caused by the impedance of the secondary winding of the HF voltage transformer (HFVT) must be taken into account for accurate measurement.

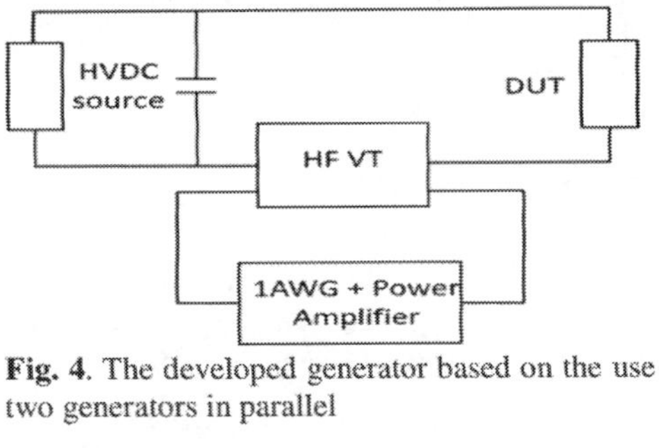

Fig. 4. The developed generator based on the use of two generators in parallel

The test results confirm the system's ability to superimpose a DC voltage with harmonic components across a frequency range of 9 kHz to 150 kHz, validating its suitability for HF applications. Additionally, the system successfully generates 500 V within the frequency range of ~75 kHz to 150 kHz, even under high-capacitance conditions, with the potential for higher voltage generation when capacitance is reduced. Furthermore, the system is capable of producing 1000 V within the 9 kHz to 75 kHz range, demonstrating its efficiency in voltage amplification at lower frequencies. These results highlight the system's effectiveness in handling both low- and HF voltage generation, with its performance influenced by capacitance and frequency-dependent characteristics.

3 Measuring systems

3.1 Specific challenges

The most commonly used method for measuring HVs exceeding 1000 V is the use of a high voltage divider. The HV is first divided using a HV divider, then transmitted via a coaxial cable to a digitizer capable of accurately measuring the transmitted voltage. The voltage divider, along with its digitizer, are essential components in ensuring the desired measurement uncertainty.

Regarding voltage dividers, two types are commonly used for measuring high DC or AC voltages at 50 Hz, superimposed with harmonics in the 9 kHz to 150 kHz frequency range. These are the RC mixed divider and the universal divider. The latter is similar to the RC divider but includes a small resistor in series with the capacitance, allowing fine-tuning of the frequency response at higher frequencies. Both dividers are highly effective for ensuring accurate HV measurements. Commercially available voltage dividers can achieve bandwidths extending up to several tens of MHz. Over the past three decades, NMIs have developed various dividers capable of measuring very HVs, with relatively wide bandwidths. However, these dividers are typically designed for DC, AC, or impulse voltage measurements and have never been specifically designed for applications where the fundamental frequency is superimposed with low amplitude of harmonics. The main challenge lies in measuring a 50 kVp (DC or AC/50 Hz) voltage superimposed with harmonics that can reach amplitudes as low as 5 V, corresponding to a dynamic range of 80 dB. Measuring such signal presents significant technical challenges due to the extreme dynamic range requirement. To achieve an accurate measurement of the 5 V harmonic up to 150 kHz with an uncertainty of 1%, a system sensitivity of at least 120 dB is required, which exceeds the capabilities of most conventional measurement systems. One of the primary challenges is the linearity and accuracy of voltage dividers, as even minor nonlinearity can introduce distortion or phase shifts in the measurement of HF harmonics. Furthermore, most analogue-to-digital converters (ADCs) have limited resolution when required to capture HF components up to 150 kHz. Typically, ADCs offer a dynamic range of around 100 dB, restricting their ability to accurately capture both the fundamental HV component and the low level harmonics simultaneously. Additionally, the ADC must meet several key requirements, including high bandwidth to minimize phase shift; High sampling frequency to correctly acquire the HF components and High dynamic range of at least 120 dB, which is extremely difficult to achieve with current technology. To overcome these technical constraints two solutions are proposed, the first one is to use a filtering and amplifying techniques. The second is to use a HV system with a very high sensitivity with a dynamic range of at least 120 dB.

3.2 HV system with enhanced supraharmonics sensitivity

A modular HV divider is designed to measure up to 60 kV DC, 42 kV AC_{rms}, and withstand 150 kV lightning impulse voltages. A schematic of the system is presented in Figure 5 and builds on the experience of an earlier design [11]. For future use in substations the divider to withstand 1.95 times the nominal phase voltage and if needed the HV modules can be stacked.

The voltage divider has two outputs, one for DC and AC fundamental components, and the other for harmonics measurement. The harmonics measurement branch incorporates a precision voltage divider, filtering, and amplification before data acquisition. Filtering is necessary to attenuate the fundamental component, while the amplifier enhances the signal for precise measurement using the data acquisition system.

The voltage divider, with a nominal scale factor (SF) of 15000, reduces the HV to measurable levels, lower than 2.0 V, 1.4 V, and 5.6 V for DC, AC, and impulse signals, respectively. It consists of HV/LV branches (720 MΩ/46 kΩ) and a capacitive branch for AC measurements from 0.5 Hz to 2.9 MHz (560 pF/6.9 µF) in series with damping resistors (120 Ω/0.01 Ω) which gives a bandwidth of 13 MHz (Figure 5).

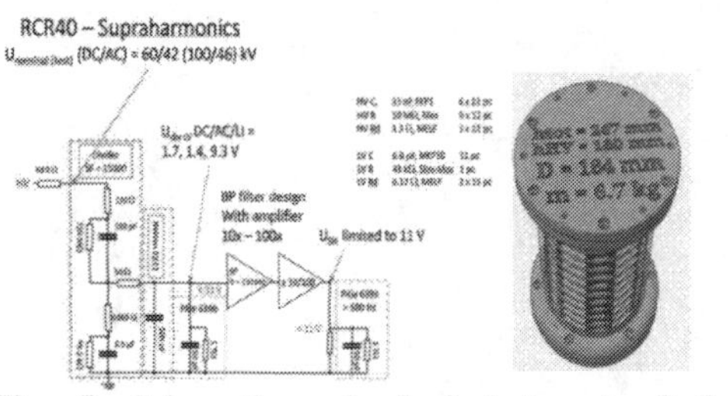

Fig. 5: Schematic and physical layout of the measurement system

For the divider, the components of both the LVand HV arms use the same type, value and batch of components to minimize the effects of voltage, frequency, and temperature variations. The raw output signal from the HV divider (DC – 13 MHz) is in parallel amplified in an active a band-pass filter (9–150 kHz) with selectable amplification factors of e.g., 10x - 100x to increase the sensitivity for supraharmonics signals. The raw and amplified signals are sampled simultaneously using a PXIe NI 6396 data acquisition board (8 differential simultaneously sampled channels, 18-bit resolution, ≤ 15 MS/s, 1 MHz bandwidth). The two channels per divider, one for DC to 150 kHz, and one for the filtered and amplified 9–150 kHz signal, gives an optimal dynamic range of about 120 dB. The measurement uncertainty is estimated to limit this to about 100 dB.

The physical construction of the divider is compact (165 mm diameter, 250 mm high, weighs 6.7 kg) and optimized for HF response and low signal distortion. The system ensures accurate HV measurements across a broad frequency range (DC–150 kHz), making it suitable for harmonic analysis and HV testing while addressing key challenges such as low noise, electromagnetic interference (EMI) immunity, and stable frequency response.

3.3 HV system with high sensitivity

The high sensitivity wideband system is based on a wideband divider [12] with 150 kV maximum peak input voltage. The divider can be used with or without an attenuator, and the total nominal scale factors are 200000 and 2000, respectively. The bandwidth extends from DC to 10 MHz. Voltages up to 500 V can be measured using the attenuator only. The divider and the schematic diagram showing the system component values is shown in Figure 6. All capacitors in the divider and in the attenuator are NP0 type surface mount components connected in series. Low TC type parallel resistors have been used. The wideband signal is then digitized using Applicos WFD20 data acquisition board [13] with 20-bit resolution, 2 MS/s maximum sampling rate, 2 MHz maximum bandwidth (-3 dB), and 108 dB spurious free dynamic range. The digitizer system has two simultaneously sampling channels. This allows calibration of both magnitude and phase errors of the measuring system connected in parallel with the reference divider. A waveform generator provides the sampling clock to the two digitizer boards. Sampling clock can either be tied with the source frequency or driven by software phase lock to ensure coherent sampling.

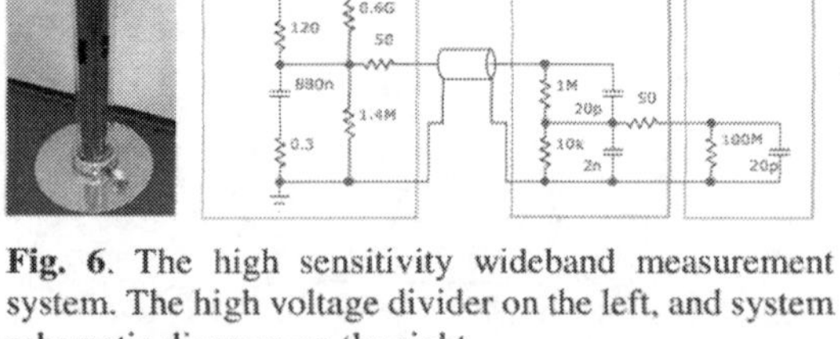

Fig. 6. The high sensitivity wideband measurement system. The high voltage divider on the left, and system schematic diagram on the right.

4 Conclusion

The traceable calibration of medium voltage transformers in the frequency range up to 150 kHz represents a crucial advancement in electrical metrology for modern power grids. This study demonstrated innovative approaches by developing both AC and DC generators capable of simulating realistic grid disturbances, effectively combining the fundamental voltage component with low-amplitude harmonics. By implementing reference measurement systems and high-sensitivity voltage dividers, the work achieved remarkably low measurement uncertainties (0.01% for the fundamental frequency and between 0.2% and 1% for harmonic components), even at voltage levels up to 50 kV. These advancements pave the way for enhanced characterization and calibration of transformers, thereby ensuring improved reliability in electrical systems and compliance with new standards such as IEC 61869-1:2024. Ultimately, the foundation laid by these developments supports the evolution toward smarter, more efficient, and resilient power grids that can better accommodate the growing integration of renewable energy sources and power electronic devices.

Funding

The project 22NRM06 ADMIT has received funding from the European Partnership on Metrology, co-financed by the European Union's Horizon Europe Research and Innovation Programme and by the Participating States.

References

1. S. Rönnberg, M. Bollen, Power quality issues in the electric power system of the future, The Electricity Journal, vol. **29**, Issue 10, 2016, pp. 49-61, https://doi.org/10.1016/j.tej.2016.11.006.
2. Jackson John Justo, Francis Mwasilu, Ju Lee, Jin-Woo Jung, AC-microgrids versus DC-microgrids with distributed energy resources: A review, Renewable and Sustainable Energy Reviews, vol. **24**, 2013, pp. 387-405, https://doi.org/10.1016/j.rser.2013.03.067
3. Agazar, M.; D'Avanzo, G.; Frigo, G.; Giordano, D.; Iodice, C.; Letizia, P.S.; Luiso, M.; Mariscotti, A.; Mingotti, A.; Munoz, F.; et al. Power Grids and Instrument Transformers up to 150 kHz: A Review of Literature and Standards. Sensors 2024, **24**, 4148. https://doi.org/10.3390/s24134148
4. L. Peretto, The role of measurements in the smart grid era, IEEE Instrumentation & Measurement Magazine, vol. **13**, no. 3, pp. 22-25, June 2010, doi: 10.1109/MIM.2010.5475163
5. IEC 61869-1; Instrument transformers - Part 1: General requirements. IEC: Geneva, Switzerland, 2024.
6. 19NRM05 IT4PQ project. Available online : https://www.it4pq.eu/
7. 22NRM06 ADMIT project. Available online : https://www.admit-project.eu/
8. IEC 60060-1; HV test techniques - Part 1: General definitions and test requirements. IEC: Geneva, Switzerland, 2010.
9. IEC 60060-2; High-voltage test techniques - Part 2: Measuring systems. IEC: Geneva, Switzerland, 2010.
10. M. Agazar, D. Istrate, P. Pradayrol, Evaluation of the Accuracy and Frequency Response of Medium-Voltage Instrument Transformers under the Combined Influence Factors of Temperature and Vibration. Energies 2023, **16**, 5012. https://doi.org/10.3390/en16135012
11. A.P Elg, T. Nieminen, J. Klüss, S. Passon, F. Gerdinand and J.Meisner, "A Modular Universal Divider for Calibration of UHVDC and Composite Waves up to 1400kV", Paper 645, ISH2023, Aug 2023, Glasgow. https://doi.org/10.5281/zenodo.8212695J.
12. J. Hällström, et al., Design of a modular wideband high voltage reference divider. Conference on Precision Electromagnetic Measurement (CPEM 2022), New Zealand. https://doi.org/10.5281/zenodo.8131452
13. WFD20 Applicos Card. Available online: https://www.salland.com/products/atx7006a/wfd20/

t pp s/dl o.gprj d0(g0()0de: 3confd5(5) 15101((0

Accuracy and reproducibility of ambient topographies at the nanoscale by AFM: several months of metrological monitoring

Ziad Gharibeh [1,2*], *Maxime* Leménager[2], *Hind* Bousbia[2], and *Rosine* Coq Germanicus[1]

[1]*Normandie Univ, Unicaen, Ensicaen, CNRS, Crismat UMR6508, 14000 Caen, France*
[2]*Murata Integrated Passive Solutions, 2 rue de la Girafe, 14000 Caen, France*

Abstract. With the high integration of microelectronic devices, nanoscale surface characterization is critical to process development. The widely used atomic force microscopy provides 2D characterization of the surface at the nanoscale. In this paper, a statistical study of the topographic mode PeakForce Tapping mode is performed. A silicon calibration sample with structures of 20 nm, is characterized, and from 28 days of measurements at the same location, data processing and analysis is proposed to determine the reproducibility of the height measured by AFM. From the section analysis, an uncertainty of 0.26 nm in air is determined. Statistical analysis is also used, and the mode is applied to characterize a dielectric material on the top of a highly integrated capacitor.

1 Introduction

With the high integration of microelectronic devices, the structural, electrical and mechanical properties of materials and system at the nanoscale is a key in the development. In recent years, Atomic Force Microscopy (AFM) has emerged as a key characterization technique[1], not only within research laboratories but also in industrial production lines, offering high spatial resolution and versatility[2]. Based on the interaction between the apex of a tip with the studied material, AFM allows to determine the topography by scanning the surface, measuring and controlling interaction forces at the nanoscale. The scanning direction has been a significant source of uncertainty from the comparison of three different AFM image processing software used to measure the step height of a monoatomic Silicon (111) crystal lattice[3]. Additionally, a comparison of SiO_2 nanoparticle size measurements using SEM and AFM revealed a higher level of uncertainty in SEM measurements, further demonstrating the accuracy and reliability of AFM for nanoscale metrology[4]. In this article, the intermittent Peak Force Tapping mode is studied in order to determine the reproducibility of the height AFM signal. For this, a microelectronic device consists of periodical step height of 20 nm structures was used. A metrological approach is investigated, Peak Force Tapping is used by two users and 28 days data are analysed. Furthermore, the method is applied on a high-integrated silicon capacitor sample for dielectric step height measurement.

1.1 A periodical Si/SiO_2 microelectronic sample

For the statistical and metrological study of nanoscale height determined by AFM, a commercial calibrated silicon sample is used. This sample ensures a reliable calibration in directions X and Y through the distinct size of the microelectronic structures, also a precise calibration in the Z direction through the fixed step height of 20 nm for all different geometries and shapes. The sample studied consists of a silicon chip, featuring fabricated silicon dioxide structures with different geometries like holes and pillars with circular, lines and square shapes. This silicon sample provides constant periodic arrays. All structures are fabricated on the same chip with a step height of 20 nm. Figure 1 represents a schematic view of the structure of the studied sample and a Scanning Electron Microscopy (SEM) top view.

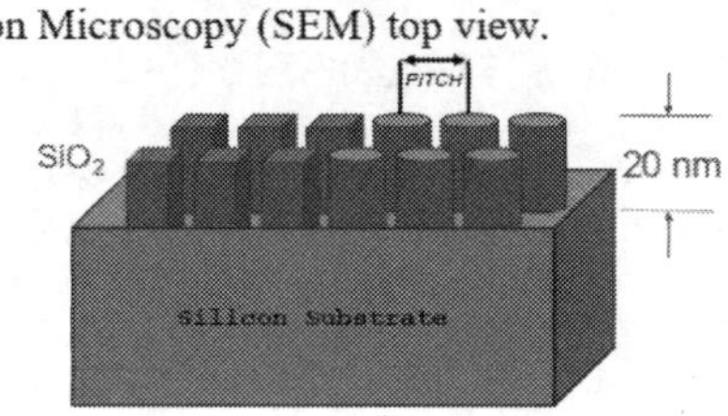

a)

* Corresponding author: ziad.gharibeh@murata.com

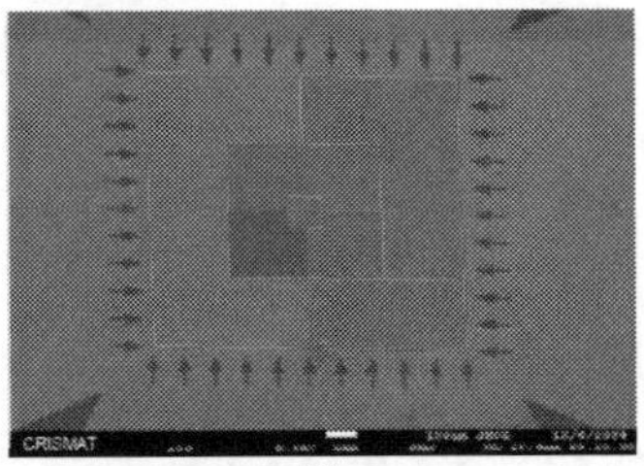

b)

Fig. 1. a) Schematic of the sample design showing circular and square pillars of SiO_2 having a 20 nm step height and b) SEM view of the calibration sample divided into three zones (colours are added to locate the region), in blue having a 10 µm pitch distance, zone 2 in green having a 5 µm pitch distance and zone 3 in red having only circular pillars with a 500 nm pitch distance.

SEM images, using a JEOL JSM 7200F were performed to get the contrast between the silicon substrate and the silicon dioxide structures as seen in Figure 2, Energy Dispersive X-ray (EDX) was also performed for silicon and oxygen. Elemental compositions maps are reported in the Figure 2, silicon and oxygen maps confirm silicon presence on all the scanned area and high oxygen concentration on the circular pillars, the higher concentration of oxygen on the circular pillars indicates the presence of silicon dioxide structures.

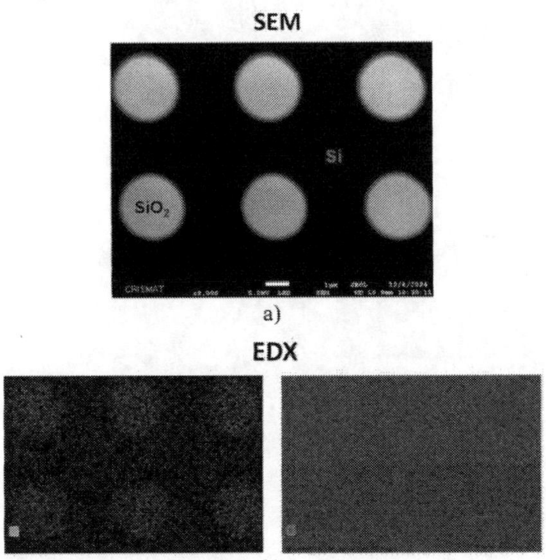

b)

Fig. 2. a) SEM image of the periodic array of circular pillars with a fixed 5 µm pitch distance, b) corresponding EDX (Energy Dispersive X-ray) silicon and oxygen maps.

1.2 Atomic Force Microscopy and used tip

A commercial Bruker dimension ICON AFM is used for all acquisitions presented in this paper. This AFM allows different topographic modes: in contact, no-contact, intermittent (also called Tapping) and PeakForce Tapping. The AFM is installed on an anti-vibration isolation table inside an acoustic isolation. Measurements were performed in ambient environments and a sensor of temperature and humidity was connected to monitor changes during scanning.

The tip used for all topographic measurements is a scan-asyst air tip. This tip is made of silicon nitride, consisting of a 100 µm V-shaped cantilever of 0.65 µm thickness having a reflective aluminum coating. This cantilever has alow spring constant of 0.4 N/m, a resonance frequency of 70 kHz paired with a very sharp triangular tip having a 2 nm radius. Figure 3 shows the SEM images performed on a new scan-asyst air tip. The apex of the tip can be observed.

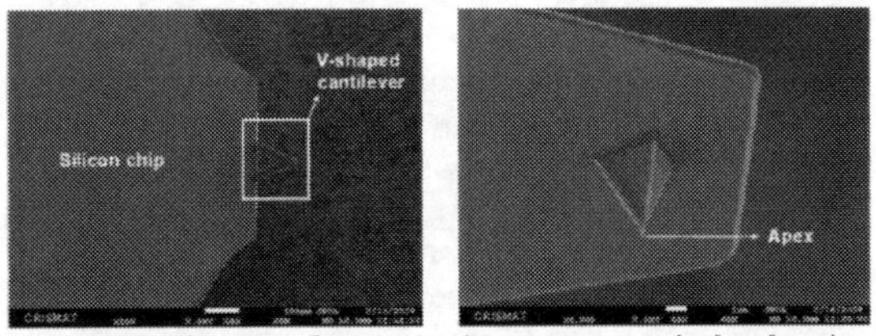

Fig. 3. SEM images of a new Bruker scan-asyst air tip, showing the V-shaped cantilever with its corresponding sharp tip attached to its end.

2 PeakForce tapping mode

First, the topographic mode PeakForce Tapping mode is used. This mode uses a sinusoidal wave having a 2 kHz frequency that induces the oscillation of the cantilever off its resonance frequency. A synchronization algorithm is set at about half of the period to extract the vertical maximum interaction force that is call PeakForce Tapping, this helps the reduction of the setpoint value with respect to the PeakForce value identified at each pixel [5]. The setpoint value is the maximum force applied by the tip onto the sample. Furthermore, another synchronization algorithm separates the tip sample interaction and non-interaction regions effectively so it can overcome the ringing signal fluctuation. The main advantage of this mode is its high scanning speed in parallel with accurate topography measurements with a minimum damage of the tip and the sample due to PeakForce control pixel by pixel. Figure 4 shows the schematic diagram of the PeakForce Tapping mode. Different stages are represented and the evolution of the force signal as a function of the time is reported.

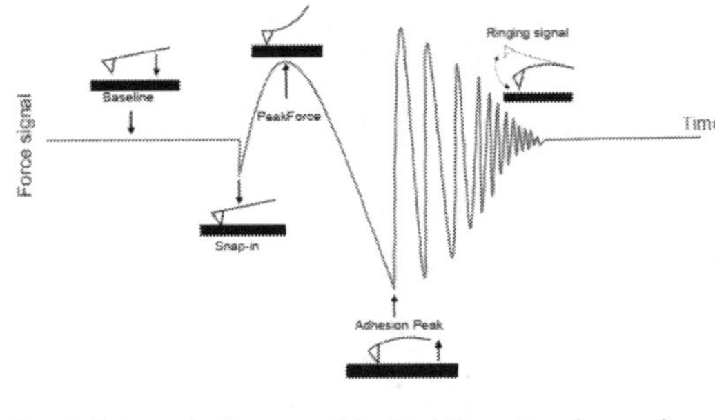

Fig. 4. Schematic diagram of the PeakForce Tapping mode.

The same scanning parameters were used for each repetitive scan performed in this paper. They are present in Table 1.

Table 1. The fixed scanning parameters with their corresponding values for each scan-asyst topographic measurement.

Scanning Parameter	Value
Scan Size	30 µm x 30 µm
Number Of Pixels	512 pixels x 512 pixels
Scan Rate	0.4 Hz
AC frequency	2 kHz

In order to characterize the used AFM tips, a sample called TGT1 consisting of a periodic array of peaks made of silicon is used. Topographic images are represented in Figure 5 (a). The PeakForce Tapping topographic measurement is performed on a single peak using a very slow scan rate of 0.1 Hz, a resolution of 512 × 512 pixels and a scan size of 1 µm x 1 µm for better accuracy. From this measurement, six section analyses are taken at the highest point of the acquisition while ensuring that each curve has the same maximum. This allows for the determination of the tip radius, which corresponds to the highest point across all six curves. The AFM 3D view of the used scan-asyst air tip, along with its corresponding section analyses, is shown in Figure 5 (c, b, and d) respectively. Based on the obtained graphs, the tip radius was found to be 2.7 nm, which is very close to that of a new tip, theoretically expected to have a radius of 2 nm. This result confirms that the PeakForce Tapping mode is a mode that minimizes the damage on the tip even after 6 scans.

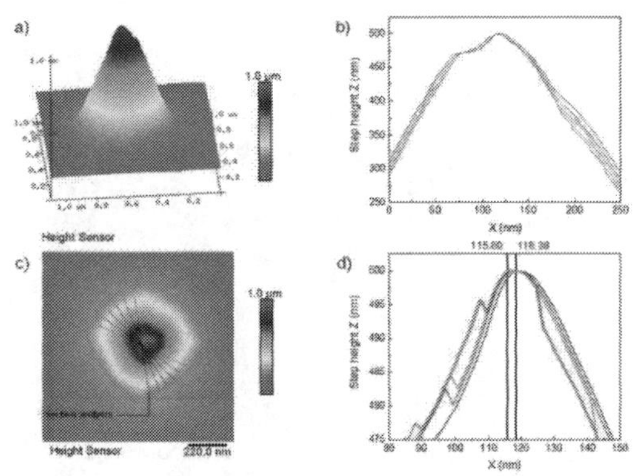

Fig. 5. a) 3D view of the AFM height sensor on the scan-asyst air tip, b) six section analysis on the highest point of the AFM acquisition on a single peak imaged, c) AFM 3D view of the height sensor acquisition of the used Bruker scan-asyst tip, and d) zoomed in view at the peak of graph b to extract the exact tip radius value.

3 AFM acquisition and image processing

After AFM measurements. NanoScope Analysis software is utilized for all image processing in this study. The calibration sample addresses sample tilt in the Z-direction, which can affect raw AFM data. To obtain accurate surface measurements, a flattening step is necessary to remove the sample tilt introduced when fixing the sample to the AFM holder. The flattening process can be complex and sensitive, potentially leading to inaccurate imaging results. In our case, 1st degree flattening is applied, which removes a linear tilt from the raw data. However, performing standard flattening on the whole AFM acquisition can produce misleading results for our samples that have structures with a 20 nm step height. A standard 1st degree flattening will take each line recorded on the acquisition and remove the tilt on each pixel, some lines will have the different shapes in our sample affecting the baseline level of our flattening leading to wrong results. To address this issue, a 1st degree flattening is implemented while excluding the silicon dioxide shapes from the calculation, in this case only the substrate is taken into consideration making the baseline at around 0 nm and leaving the real shapes of our SiO_2 structures. This approach ensures that only the baseline at around 0 nm is considered, preserving the true step height of our structures as seen in Figure 6 (b). The graph in Figure 6 (c) represents two cross section analysis, the red one corresponds to the raw data represented by the red line in (a) and the black line corresponds to the section analysis in (b) presented by the black line. This graph shows the importance of performing the right flattening step to obtain accurate AFM data without affecting the real step height of the SiO_2 structures.

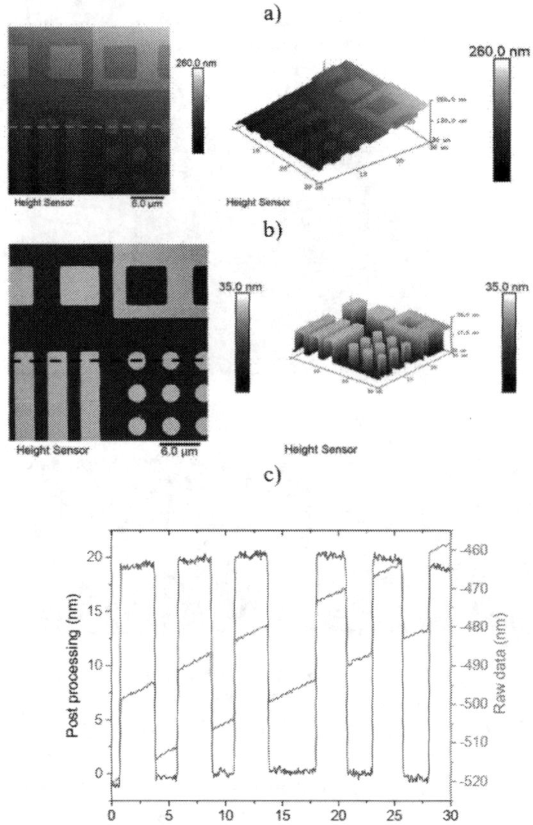

Fig. 6. a) The 2D map raw data AFM height sensor acquisition on the chosen zone of the sample with its corresponding 3D view b) flatten step with the excluded shapes, c) post flattening results on the height sensor acquisition with the 3D view and d) section analysis before and after the flattening process.

The designated area shown in Figure 6 is carefully selected for conducting all repetitive AFM measurements on the sample, motivated by two key factors. First, the area's distinct features allowed for easy optical detection, ensuring consistent positioning and enabling repeated measurements on the same structures across multiple sessions. Second, this region exhibited a variety of geometries, including square holes, square pillars, vertical lines, and circular pillars. This diversity within a single area provided a comprehensive representation of the sample's topographical features, facilitating a more thorough and efficient analysis of surface properties.

4 Section analysis on a single square pillar

For the metrological analysis, 28 measurements were recorded by two users. Figure 7 (a) represents the AFM acquisition of the calibrated sample with the use of six different tips of the same type. The total size of the acquisition is 30 µm x 30 µm. The height scale bar is 35 µm. From the AFM acquisitions, an area was selected for the metrological analysis. This area is the height of a square structure. An average section analysis having a size of 14 µm x 4 µm was taken in the red box represented in Figure 7 (a) for 28 different daily measurements. To be able to study the real step height variation of the square pillar present on this section analysis, the baseline should be at exactly 0 nm from its sides. To overcome this point, the mean value RMS from the baseline is subtracted from the image data scale to get a 0 nm baseline at the sides of the square pillar. After doing the same procedure for each of the 28 measurements, the plotted section analysis on the same graph is presented on Figure 7 (b), the focus will be on the variation of our step height on the pillar thus for x between 4 µm and 10 µm.

a)

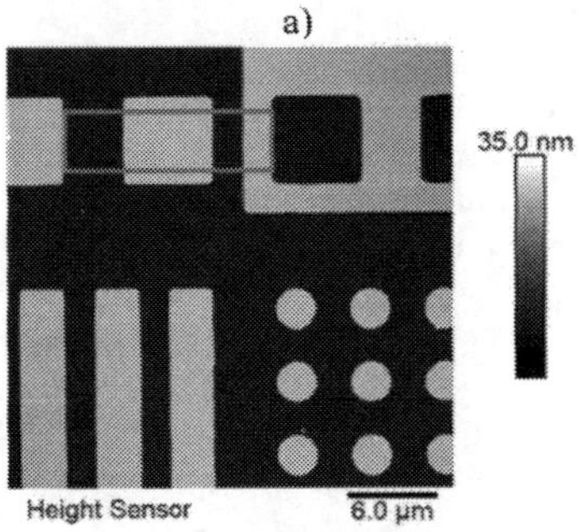

b)

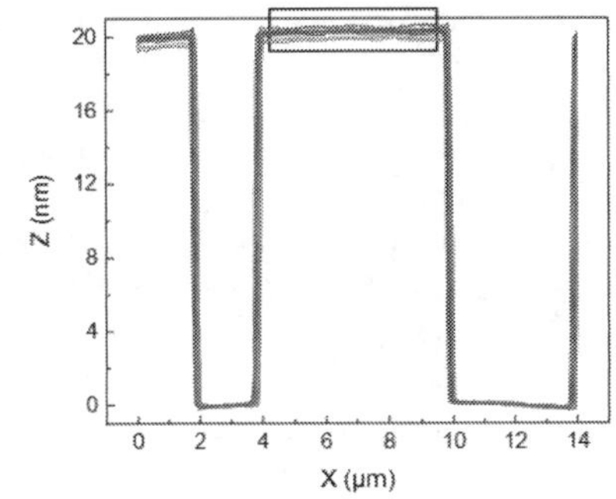

c)

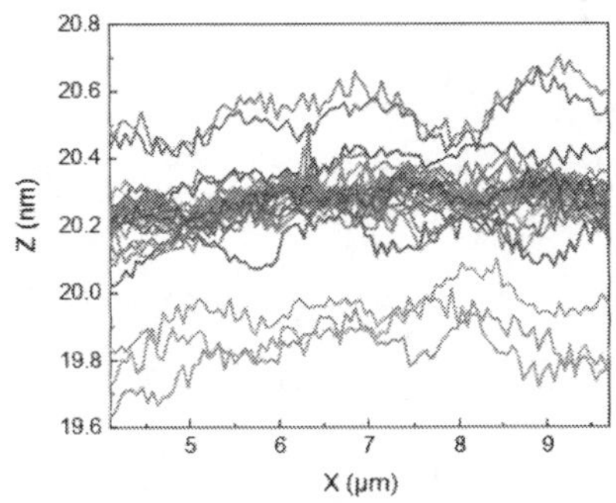

Fig. 7. a) AFM height sensor acquisition on the designated zone of the sample with a red box showing the place of the section analysis box, b) 28 curves for the same section analysis each one representing a day of measurement, c) zoomed in view on the square pillar for x between 4 µm and 10 µm.

For each curve recorded, the average value of the step height Z with its corresponding standard deviation was calculated and plotted with six different tips of the same type, each tip represented in a colour in Figure 8. The average step height value was found to be 20.260 nm with a standard deviation of 0.169 nm, thus the type A uncertainty (standard uncertainty of the mean) was of found to be 0.031 nm.

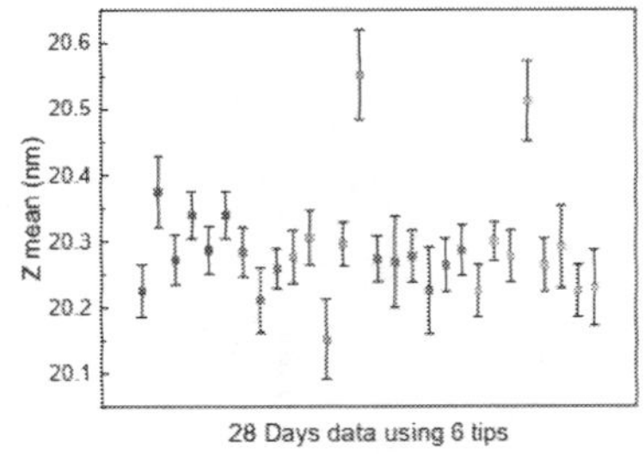

Fig. 8. Average value of the step height Z for each curve recorded on the square pillar, for 6 different tips used.

Moreover, the type B uncertainty is calculated by using the AFM uncertainties along the Z-axis given by the manufacturer Bruker. The uncertainty terms for the Z-axis taken into consideration are the Z noise, Z sensor performance, step height repeatability for a step of 20 nm and the roughness Rq. Table 2 shows the contribution of each term to finally add the type A uncertainty value and get the total uncertainty U with 95 % confidence. Finally, the step height is found to be 20.26 nm ± 0.26 nm.

Table 2. Uncertainty budget of the Bruker AFM dimension ICON for a step height of 20 nm.

TOTAL UNCERTAINTY U		
TERMS	**ESTIMATION**	**CONTRIBUTION**
Z Noise	0.035 nm	0.035 nm
Z Sensor performance	0.035 nm	0.035 nm
Step height repeatability (Z)	0.11 nm	0.11 nm
Roughness (Rq)	0.05 nm	0.05 nm
Type A uncertainty		0.031 nm
	Total U (95%)	**0.26 nm**

In addition, Figure 9 (a) shows a typical Gaussian distribution of the most found Gaussians distributions with its corresponding bins for the counts of the Z step height for 98 data points on each curve. Figure 9 (b) shows the histogram distribution of the step height Z for each curve analyzed on the chosen square pillar, each color on the histogram corresponds to a curve analyzed. We could clearly see on the histogram that the highest concentration of counts is for Z between 20.2 nm and 20.3 nm having a maximum of 1153 counts out of 2744 total data counts. For the curve distribution presented in Figure 9 (c), only 6 out of 28 curves that are not centered at the center of the Gaussian distribution at 20.26 nm.

a)

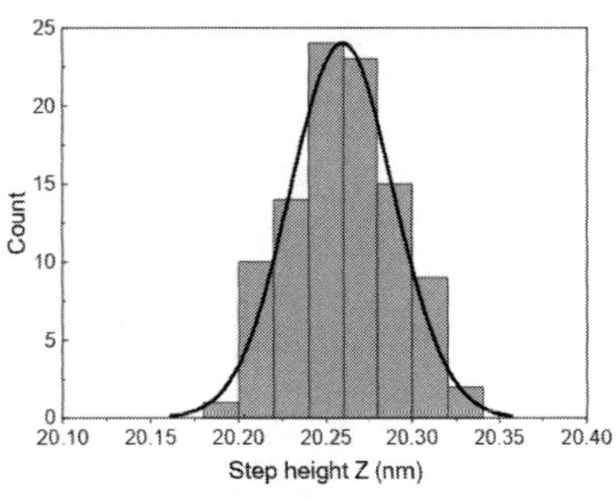

b)

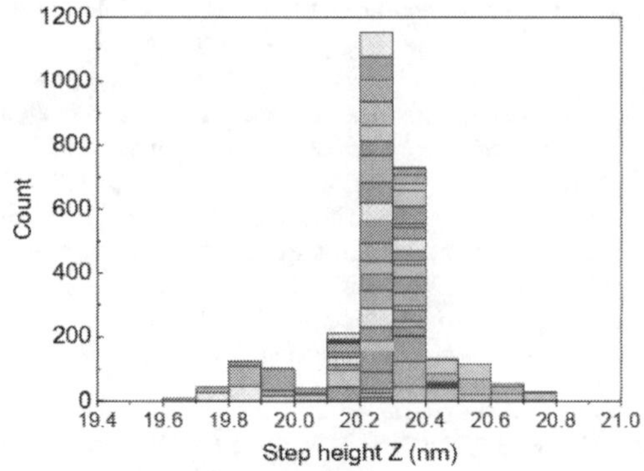

c)

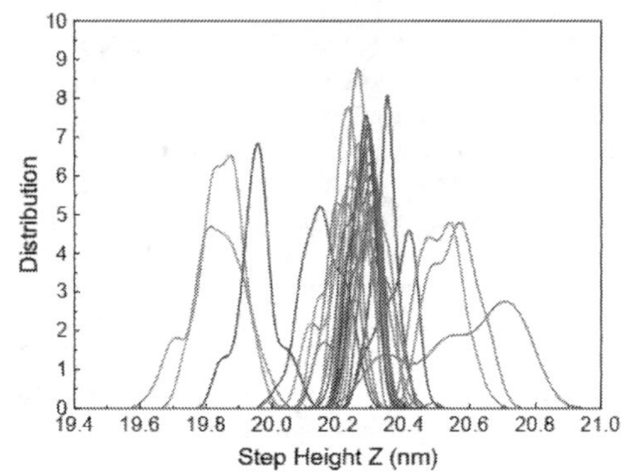

Fig. 9. a) Single curve distribution with its counts bins distribution, b) stacked histograms for all recorded curves and c) all recorded curves step height distribution.

5 Application

To illustrate the application of AFM for high integrated microelectronic device. Figure 10 shows two AFM topography measurements on the wafer surface using the PeakForce Tapping mode on a 3D Silicon capacitor manufactured by Murata Integrated Passive Solutions in Caen. Those capacitors are the second generation of its technology and consists of a metal-insulator-metal (MIM) configuration implemented within Si trenches to benefit from the third dimension of the silicon wafer to gain specific surface. Figure 10 (a) represents the top view of the 3D capacitor after the deposition of the top metal electrode. This electrode is made by depositing a highly doped polysilicon layer by Low Pressure Chemical Vapor Deposition (LPCVD). The size of this acquisition is 5 µm x 5 µm with a resolution of 512 x 512 pixels, the height scale bar is 650 nm. In order to reveal and measure the dielectric layer, a semi-automatic polishing step using polishing disks of 1 µm and 0.25 µm grain size is required. Figure 10 (b) shows the post polishing top of this capacitor. The scan size is 4 µm x 4 µm, the structure observed is the remaining Si 3D pillar after Bosch process, the dielectric layer and the trench filling with poly-Si. Most importantly, how the dielectric layer is polished differently from the top and bottom electrodes and have a step height Z of approximately 13 nm that is relatively close to the step height measured in this paper.

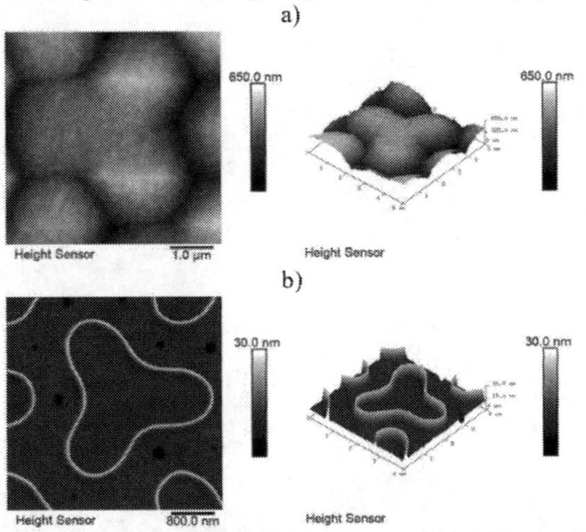

Fig. 10. a) Top view AFM topography acquisition (5 µm x 5 µm) on the 3D capacitor before polishing with its corresponding 3D view, b) top view AFM topography acquisition (4 µm x 4 µm) on the 3D capacitor after polishing with its corresponding 3D view.

This nano-metrological study on the step height measurement of the calibration sample and the studying of the reproducibility of our AFM topographic measurements using the PeakForce tapping mode will help to have accurate step height measurements on dielectric layer, characterized with the same mode and same conditions. Furthermore, this will help us perform very accurate topography mappings with a reproducible outcome with a low uncertainty budget, in parallel with very low damage on the tip and on the sample due to the PeakForce value adjustments pixel by pixel.

6 Conclusion

In this study, the reproducibility of AFM topographic measurements in PeakForce Tapping mode was evaluated using a calibration sample with 20 nm step height structures. The analysis revealed a step height measurement uncertainty of 0.26 nm, demonstrating the method's precision. This metrological approach contributes to accurate and reproducible step height measurements, particularly for dielectric thickness measurement on highly integrated capacitors having a MIM configurations. Additionally, the results confirm that repeated scans cause minimal tip damage due to the controlled PeakForce values, ensuring measurement reliability over time.

Acknowledgement: The authors would like to thank Mahima Chaudhary for her contribution to the SEM images of the sample and the AFM tip.

7 References

[1] A. Yacoot and L. Koenders, "Recent developments in dimensional nanometrology using AFMs," *Meas. Sci. Technol.*, vol. 22, no. 12, p. 122001, 2011.

[2] V. Constantoudis, G. Boulousis, K. Ellinas, and E. Gogolides, "Model-aided hybrid metrology for surface roughness measurement fusing AFM and SEM data," in *17th International Congress of Metrology*, B. Larquier, Ed., Paris, France: EDP Sciences, 2015, p. 14005. doi: 10.1051/metrology/20150014005.

[3] M. A. Lawn, Z. Bolton, L. Murphy, S. Gartner, Y. Oh, and V. A. Coleman, "Step height measurement of monoatomic silicon crystal lattice steps with a commercial atomic force microscope," *Meas. Sci. Technol.*, vol. 35, no. 10, p. 105018, Jul. 2024, doi: 10.1088/1361-6501/ad490d.

[4] A. Delvallée, N. Feltin, S. Ducourtieux, M. Trabelsi, and J.-. F. Hochepied, "Comparison of nanoparticle diameter measurements by Atomic Force Microscopy and Scanning Electron Microscopy," in *16th International Congress of Metrology*, J.-R. Filtz, B. Larquier, P. Claudel, and J.-O. Favreau, Eds., Paris, France: EDP Sciences, 2013, p. 06007. doi: 10.1051/metrology/201306007.

[5] K. Xu *et al.*, "Recent development of PeakForce Tapping mode atomic force microscopy and its applications on nanoscience," *Nanotechnol. Rev.*, vol. 7, no. 6, pp. 605–621, Dec. 2018, doi: 10.1515/ntrev-2018-0086.

Case Study of Genetic Algorithms in Metrology: Assessment of Inter-laboratory Comparisons

Romain Coulon [1*]

[1]Bureau International des Poids et Mesures, Pavillon de Breteuil, Sèvres, Cedex, F-92312, France

Abstract. This study reviews conventional consensus estimation methods, including mean-based, median-based, and pooling-based approaches, and evaluates their performance under challenging scenarios involving outliers and deviations from normality. While traditional methods such as the weighted mean and weighted median often fail to handle extreme values and non-Gaussian distributions, advanced techniques like the Monte Carlo Median (MCM) and Power Moderated Mean (PMM) offer improved robustness. The Genetic Algorithm (GA), a novel optimization-based approach, demonstrates exceptional resilience to outliers. To facilitate its application, the GA is made available through the Python package consensusGen, accessible via the Python Package Index and GitHub. This ensures that practitioners and researchers can easily implement the GA in their consensus estimation tasks, benefiting from its superior robustness and precision.

1 Introduction

In an inter-laboratory comparison, a set of measurements is represented by $X = (x_1, x_2, \dots, x_i, \dots, x_N)^{\mathrm{T}}$ with corresponding standard uncertainties $U = (u_1, u_2, \dots, u_i, \dots, u_N)^{\mathrm{T}}$. To determine a reference value μ that reflects the consensus of the dataset, a common approach involves aggregating the measurements using the Weighted Mean (WM), where the weights are defined as $w_i^{(\mathrm{WM})} = u_i^{-2}$. The reference value and its standard uncertainty are then calculated as follows:

$$\hat{\mu}^{(\mathrm{WM})} = \frac{\sum_{i=1}^{N} w_i^{(\mathrm{WM})} x_i}{\sum_{i=1}^{N} w_i^{(\mathrm{WM})}}, \quad (1)$$

$$u\left(\hat{\mu}^{(\mathrm{WM})}\right) = \left(\sum_{i=1}^{N} w_i^{(\mathrm{WM})}\right)^{-1/2}. \quad (2)$$

The standard Weighted Mean (WM) estimator is known to be sensitive to extreme values in a dataset, making it non-robust in such scenarios. A more robust consensus value can be derived by modifying the weight parameters to include a between-laboratory variance τ^2, often referred to as "dark uncertainty" [1]. In this approach, the weights are redefined as $w_i = 1/(u_i^2 + \tau^2)$. Estimation of τ^2 is typically achieved using optimization procedures, such as those based on the Birge ratio [2–6]. These procedures adjust τ to satisfy the following condition:

$$\frac{1}{N-1}\sum_{i=1}^{N} \frac{\left(x_i - \hat{\mu}^{(\mathrm{WM})}\right)^2}{u_i^2 + \tau^2} = 1. \quad (3)$$

The consensus value remains unchanged in this approach, but its uncertainty, $u\left(\hat{\mu}^{(\mathrm{WM}^*)}\right)$, is adjusted to ensure consistency with the dataset based on the Chi-squared test.

Another strategy, denoted as WM**, involves implementing a null hypothesis test to identify and reject potential outliers [7]. This approach is applied on the WM estimator when the Chi-squared test fails under the following condition:

$$P\left(\chi_{N-1}^2 > \sum_{i=1}^{N} \frac{\left(x_i - \hat{\mu}^{(\mathrm{WM})}\right)^2}{u_i^2}\right) < 0.05, \quad (4)$$

where χ_{N-1}^2 is the Chi-squared statistics with $N-1$ degrees of freedom.

To detect discrepant measurements, one of the following criteria can be used:

$$\left|x_i - \hat{\mu}^{(\mathrm{WM})}\right| > 2\sqrt{(1 - 2w_i)u^2(x_i) + u^2\left(\hat{\mu}^{(\mathrm{WM})}\right)}, \quad (5)$$

or

$$\left|x_i - \hat{\mu}^{(\mathrm{WM})}\right| > 2\sqrt{u^2(x_i) + u^2\left(\hat{\mu}_{-i}^{(\mathrm{WM})}\right)}, \quad (6)$$

where $u^2\left(\hat{\mu}_{-i}^{(\mathrm{WM})}\right)$ is the variance of the consensus value computed excluding measurement i from the dataset.

The WM** procedure ensures a minimum uncertainty value $u\left(\hat{\mu}^{(\mathrm{WM}^{**})}\right)$ by rejecting outliers. However, WM* is less precise but not destructive, as no measurements are excluded. A hybrid approach combining $WM*$ and $WM**$ is also sometimes employed and called the power-moderated mean (PMM) [8]. This approach is actively employed for key comparisons piloted by the section 2 of the Consultative Committee for Ionizing Radiation (CCRI) of the International Committee for Weights and Measures [9].

* Corresponding author: author@email.org

$\hat{\mu}^{(\mathrm{WM}^*)}$, $\hat{\mu}^{(\mathrm{WM}^{**})}$and $\hat{\mu}^{(\mathrm{PMM})}$ estimators rely on the Chi-squared statistic, which describes the distribution of the sum of squared standard normal random variables. As a result, they assume that the measurements follow a normal distribution, though real-world measurement statistics may deviate from this assumption [10,11].

As an alternative to mean-based estimators, the median offers inherent robustness against extreme values. To address the specific challenges of measurement dataset (X, U), the weighted median (WMD) has been proposed by J. W. Muller [12], incorporating weights $w_i^{(\mathrm{WMD})} = u_i^{-2}$. The weighted median is defined as:

$$\hat{\mu}^{(\mathrm{WMD})} = \underset{h}{\operatorname{argmin}} \left(\sum_{i=1}^{N} w_i^{(\mathrm{WMD})} |x_i - h| \right), \qquad (7)$$

and its associated uncertainty is calculated as:

$$u\left(\hat{\mu}^{(\mathrm{WMD})}\right) = \frac{1.9}{\sqrt{N-1}}$$

$$\underset{h}{\operatorname{argmin}} \left(\sum_{i=1}^{N} w_i^{(\mathrm{WMD})} \left| |x_i - \hat{\mu}^{(\mathrm{WMD})}| - h \right| \right). \qquad (8)$$

Another approach to estimating the median uses Monte Carlo sampling, treating the measurement as random variables drawn from a normal distribution, $X^{(r)} \sim \mathrm{NORMAL}(X, U^2)$. The Monte-Carlo median (MCM) is then computed as the mean of medians from each resampled dataset $X^{(r)} = \left(x_1^{(r)}, x_2^{(r)}, \dots, x_i^{(r)}, \dots, x_N^{(r)}\right)^{\mathrm{T}}$. The Monte Carlo median estimator [7] is given by:

$$\hat{\mu}^{(\mathrm{MCM})} = \frac{1}{M} \sum_{r=1}^{M} \mathrm{median}\left(X^{(r)}\right), \qquad (9)$$

and its variance is estimated as:

$$u^2\left(\hat{\mu}^{(\mathrm{MCM})}\right) = \frac{1}{M-1} \sum_{r=1}^{M} \left(\mathrm{median}\left(X^{(r)}\right) - \hat{\mu}^{(\mathrm{MCM})}\right)^2. \qquad (10)$$

This Monte Carlo sampling approach forms the foundation of the genetic algorithm originally introduced in [13] and described in the next section. By leveraging the bootstrapping technique, the genetic algorithm refines the estimation process, optimizing robustness and accuracy when determining consensus values.

2 Method

2.1 Preprocessing of the resampled measurement data

In this new approach, the resampled data $X^{(r)}$ are pooled into a single vector:

$$Y = \left(x_1^{(1)}, \dots, x_N^{(1)}, \dots, x_i^{(r)}, \dots, x_N^{(M)}\right)^{\mathrm{T}}$$

$$= \left(y_1, \dots, y_j, \dots, y_Z\right)^{\mathrm{T}}, \qquad (11)$$

where $Z = N \times M$. This technique, known as the *linear pooling procedure* (LP), was first formalized by M. Stone [14] and may trace its origins back to Pierre-Simon de Laplace [15]. LP serves as a foundation for generating the initial population in the genetic algorithm (GA). While LP considers only the resampled values $y_j = x_i^{(r)}$, the GA extends this approach by incorporating the provenance of each data point within the pooled dataset. This is achieved through a vector of labels $L = (\mathrm{A}, \mathrm{B}, \mathrm{C}, \dots)$, representing the N participants (e.g., "A", "B", "C"). These labels are stored in a $1 \times Z$ genome vector $G = \left(g_1, \dots, g_j, \dots, g_Z\right)^{\mathrm{T}}$, where the labels g_j for each y_j is given by $g_j = L_{j \bmod N+1}$.

Each individual in the dataset is therefore described by its value $y_j = x_i^{(r)}$ (its *phenotype*) and its corresponding label g_j (its *genome*). This pairing, formally represented as (y_j, g_j), creates a structured mapping for every data point $j \in \{1, .., Z\}$, where $Z = N \times M$. This structured representation enables the GA to evaluate consensus values while preserving information about the data's origin.

First, values in Y and G are sorted by ascending order of Y to produce $Y^{(0)}$ and $G^{(0)}$, where

$$y_j^{(0)} < y_{j+1}^{(0)}, \forall j \in \{1, .., Z-1\}. \qquad (12)$$

The sorted dataset $\left\{Y^{(0)}, G^{(0)}\right\}$ serves as the initial population for the genetic algorithm (GA).

A GA belongs to as a specific class of optimization algorithms inspired by evolution biology [16,17]. It iteratively applies evolutionary processes to a population of individuals, each characterized by their *phenotype* (e.g., $y_j^{(0)}$) and *genome* (e.g., $g_j^{(0)}$). At each generation t, a new population $t+1$ is created from the current one through selection mechanisms based on individual fitness.

The selection process follows Darwinian principles, often summarized as "survival of the fitness". The fitness of each individual is evaluated using a *fitness function*, which reflects how well the individual satisfies the problem's objectives. This function typically incorporates information from the genome and drives the evolution toward an optimal solution.

In this approach, the objective is to derive a consensual reference value from the pooled and bootstrapped data $Y^{(0)}$, using the corresponding genomes $G^{(0)}$. To achieve this, the genetic algorithm (GA) discourages inbreeding while promoting crossover within the population $\left\{Y^{(t)}, G^{(t)}\right\}$. Fitness function F_j is designed to penalize genetic similarity, fostering diversity between individuals in terms of their genomes.

2.2 Fitness Function Based on Cosine Similarity

For each individual $j = \{1, \dots, Z^t - 1\}$ at generation t, the fitness function F_j is given by:

$$F_j = 1 - \mathrm{cosine}\left(g_j^{(t)}, g_{j+1}^{(t)}\right), \qquad (13)$$

where $\mathrm{cosine}\left(g_j^{(t)}, g_{j+1}^{(t)}\right)$ measures the similarity of genomes between adjacent individuals based on frequency vectors $v(g)$. Each frequency vector $v(g) = \left(P_g(L_1), \dots, P_g(L_i), \dots, P_g(L_N)\right)^{\mathrm{T}}$ counts occurrences of each gene in L_i (participant label) in the genome g. The cosine similarity is defined as:

$$\text{cosine}\left(g_j^{(t)}, g_{j+1}^{(t)}\right) = \frac{v\left(g_j^{(t)}\right)^{\mathrm{T}} v\left(g_{j+1}^{(t)}\right)}{\sqrt{v\left(g_j^{(t)}\right)^{\mathrm{T}} v\left(g_j^{(t)}\right)} + \sqrt{v\left(g_{j+1}^{(t)}\right)^{\mathrm{T}} v\left(g_{j+1}^{(t)}\right)}}. \quad (14)$$

For example:

- If $g_j^{(t)}$ and $g_{j+1}^{(t)}$ are identical, $\text{cosine}\left(g_j^{(t)}, g_{j+1}^{(t)}\right) = 1$ (e.g., cosine(ABC, BCA) = 1), resulting in $F_j = 0$, and the individual has no chance of breading.
- If $g_j^{(t)}$ and $g_{j+1}^{(t)}$ have no genes in common, $\text{cosine}\left(g_j^{(t)}, g_{j+1}^{(t)}\right) = 0$ (e.g., cosine(ABC,EFG) = 0), resulting in $F_j = 1$, and the individual survives.
- For partial overlap (e.g., cosine(ABC, BGA) = 0.67), F_j falls between 0 and 1, with survival depending on whether F_j exceeds a user-defined threshold $S \in [0,1]$.

2.3 Breeding and Phenotype Update

If breeding is allowed ($F_j > S$), the new genome at generation $t + 1$ combines genes from the parents:

$$g_j^{(t+1)} = \text{CONCATENATE}\left(g_j^{(t)}, g_{j+1}^{(t)}\right). \quad (15)$$

The phenotype $y_{j+1}^{(t)}$ is generated as a random mixture of parental phenotypes:

$$y_j^{(t+1)} = a y_j^{(t)} + (1-a) y_{j+1}^{(t)}, \quad (16)$$

where $a \sim \text{uniform}(0,1)$.

2.4 Final Population and Reference Estimation

After W iterations, the GA yields a final population $(Y^{(W)}, G^{(W)})$. The consensus value $\hat{\mu}^{(\text{GA})}$ and its uncertainty $u\left(\hat{\mu}^{(\text{GA})}\right)$ are derived as:

$$\hat{\mu}^{(\text{GA})} = \frac{1}{Z^{(W)}} \sum_{j=1}^{Z^{(W)}} y_j^{(W)} \quad (17)$$

and

$$u^2\left(\hat{\mu}^{(\text{GA})}\right) = \frac{1}{N\left(Z^{(W)}-1\right)} \frac{Z^{(W)}}{Z^{(0)}} \sum_{j=1}^{Z^{(W)}} \left(y_j^{(W)} - \hat{\mu}^{(GA)}\right)^2. \quad (18)$$

The weight for each participant is proportional to the frequency of their original genome in $G^{(W)}$:

$$w_i = \frac{P_{G^{(W)}}(L_i)}{Z^{(W)}}, \forall i \in \{1, .., N\}, \quad (19)$$

with its standard uncertainty:

$$u(w_i) = \frac{\sqrt{P_{G^{(W)}}(L_i)}}{Z^{(W)}}. \quad (20)$$

The uncertainty of the deviation for each participant, $d_i^{(\text{GA})} = x_i - \hat{\mu}^{(\text{GA})}$, is given by:

$$u^2\left(d_i^{(\text{GA})}\right) = (1 - w_i) u_i^2 + u^2\left(\hat{\mu}^{(\text{GA})}\right) + \sum_{i=1}^{N} x_i^2 u^2(w_i). \quad (21)$$

Unlike conventional methods, the GA explicitly incorporates the uncertainty of participant weights, $u(w_i)$, providing a comprehensive evaluation of uncertainty associated with deviations from the reference. This robust framework ensures greater reliability in the consensus estimation while accounting for variability in individual contributions.

3 Results

To demonstrate the application of the Genetic Algorithm (GA), a dataset with seven measurements was analysed:

- Measurement values (X): $\{10.1, 11, 14, 10, 10.5, 9.8, 5.1\}$,
- Standard uncertainties (U): $\{1, 1, 1, 2, 1, 1.5, 3\}$,
- Participant labels (L): {A, B, C, D, E, F, G}.

In this dataset, point C (14) is moderately above the other values and precise, while point G (5.1) is significantly lower with higher uncertainty.

The GA was executed with the following parameters:

- Number of generations(W): 1,
- Resampled values (M): 1 000 000,
- Breeding threshold (S): 0.02.

The initial pooled dataset $Y^{(0)}$ from the linear pooling (LP) reflects the distribution of the resampled measurements and is represented by the blue distribution in Fig. 1. This distribution includes equal contributions from all participants.

After applying one generation of the GA ($Y^{(1)}$) with selection and breeding, the resultant distribution is displayed as the orange distribution in Fig. 1. The GA procedure reshapes the distribution toward a monomodal distribution inherently centred around its main mode.

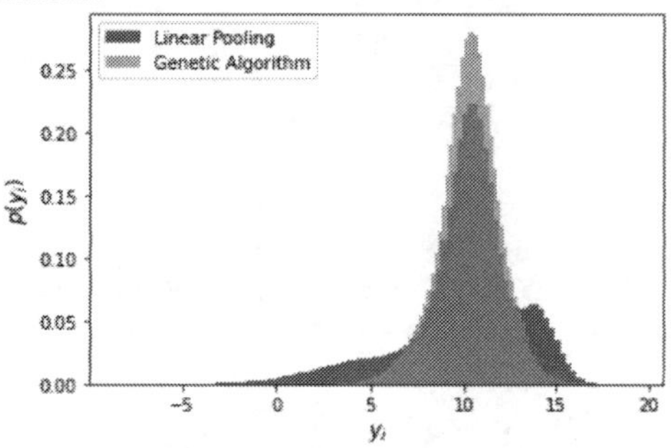

Fig. 1. Distribution of the values $\boldsymbol{Y}^{(0)}$ and $\boldsymbol{Y}^{(1)}$.

The GA-based approach demonstrates robustness against the influence of extreme points, particularly for outliers like C (14) and G (5.1) (see Fig. 2). This robustness is evident when analyzing the weights assigned to each participant in the final generation (here $W = 1$), as shown in Fig. 3.

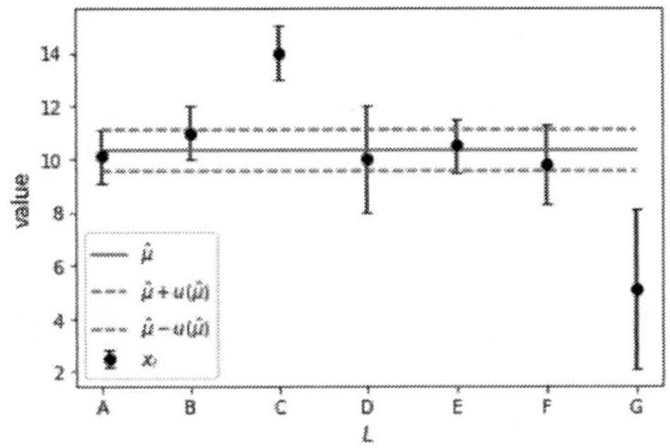

Fig. 2. The measurements and reference value in red line with standard uncertainties in dash lines.

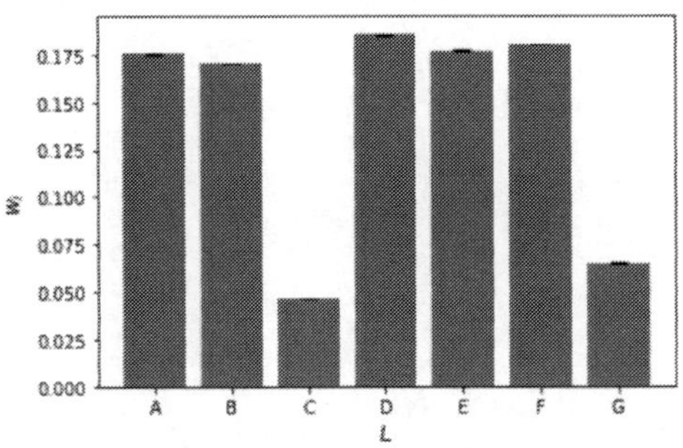

Fig. 3. Weights assigned to each measurement in the estimation of the reference value.

The GA selection process significantly reduces the population size Z with each generation, reflecting the algorithm's filtering strength. Fig. 5 illustrates this reduction for the given example, where the initial population size decreases to 62.3 % after the first generation, and only 9 % of the original population remains by the seventh generation. The threshold S allows for control over the "killing rate" between generations. A higher S value leads to stricter selection and faster population reduction, while a lower S retains more data. Whatever the tuning of S, the first selection step results in a substantial improvement of the precision and shifts the reference value toward a better consensus compared to the linear pooling (LP) method. Beyond the first step, additional selection rounds yield minimal improvement in consensus quality while significantly degrading precision due to excessive loss of data (see Fig. 4). In this example, no notable gains are observed in the reference value after the first generation, indicating that further iterations are unnecessary. Based on these observations, one or two generations of the GA is recommended for most applications. For fine-tuning, adjusting the threshold S can control the tradeoff between consensus quality and data retention.

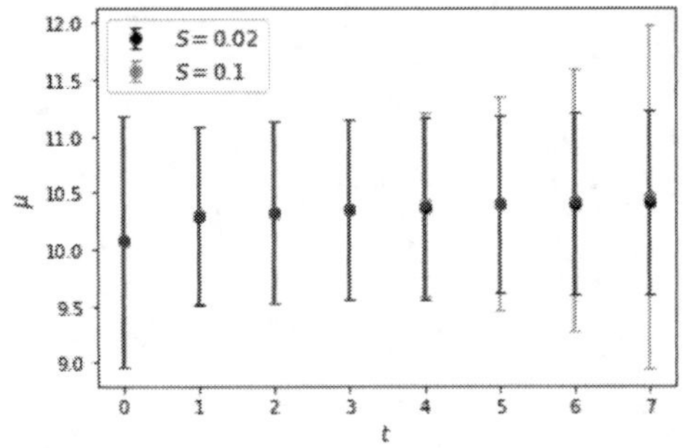

Fig. 4. Estimated reference value as a function of the evolution step.

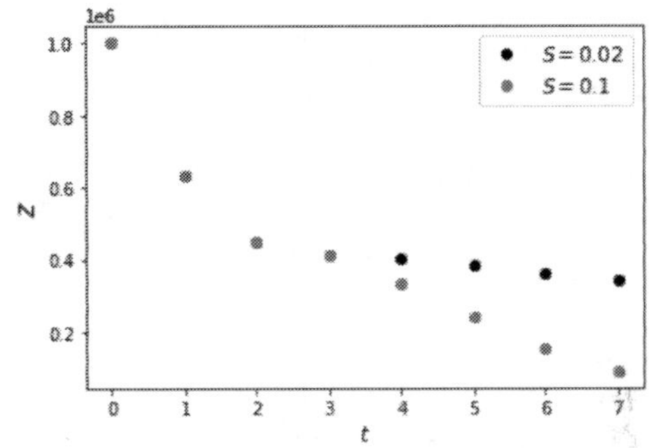

Fig. 5. Population size as a function of the evolution step.

It is important to note that this statistical approach serves as an assessment tool and does not replace the necessary scientific discussions on extreme values, which are overseen by an international committee responsible for comparison exercises.

4 Conclusion

Among all consensus estimators, the Genetic Algorithm (GA) emerged as the new reliable and versatile estimator with exceptional robustness against outliers. For practical applications, the GA is readily available as the Python package **consensusGen**. It can be accessed on the Python Package Index at https://pypi.org/project/consensusGen/ and its development repository on GitHub at https://github.com/RomainCoulon/consensusGen. This accessibility ensures that researchers and practitioners can seamlessly integrate the GA into their workflows, leveraging its robust performance for consensus estimation tasks.

References

1. M. Thompson and S. L. R. Ellison, Accreditation and Quality Assurance **16**, 483 (2011)
2. O. Bodnar and C. Elster, Metrologia **51**, 516 (2014)
3. R. DerSimonian and N. Laird, Control Clin Trials **7**, 177 (1986)
4. R. C. Paule and J. Mandel, J Res Natl Bur Stand (1934) **94**, 197 (1989)

5. A. A. Veroniki, D. Jackson, W. Viechtbauer, R. Bender, J. Bowden, G. Knapp, O. Kuss, J. P. Higgins, D. Langan, and G. Salanti, Res Synth Methods 7, 55 (2016)
6. R. T. Birge, Physical Review **40**, 207 (1932)
7. M. G. Cox, Metrologia **39**, 589 (2002)
8. S. Pommé and J. Keightley, Metrologia **52**, S200 (2015)
9. R. Coulon, C. Michotte, S. Courte, M. Nonis, T. Ziemek, J. Marganiec-Gałązka, E. Lech, P. Saganowski, M. Czudek, and A. Listkowska, Metrologia **60**, 06001 (2023)
10. D. C. Bailey, R Soc Open Sci **4**, 160600 (2017)
11. R. Coulon, C. Michotte, and V. Gressier, in *MathMet Conference* (2022)
12. J. W. Muller, *Rapport BIPM-2000/6, Weighted Medians* (Sèvres, 2000)
13. R. M. Coulon and S. Judge, Metrologia (2021)
14. M. Stone, The Annals of Mathematical Statistics **32**, 1339 (1961)
15. M. Bacharach, J Am Stat Assoc **74**, 837 (1979)
16. D. B. Fogel, IEEE Trans Neural Netw **5**, 3 (1994)
17. D. E. Goldberg, *Genetic Algorithms in Search, Optimization and Machine Learning* (Addison-Wesley Longman Publishing Co., Inc.75 Arlington Street, Suite 300 Boston, MAUnited States, 1989)

EPJ Web of Conferences **323**, 0144(2(4(5)
22nd nIt enr Iai nr dMt Iei a gylCi nget ss

https://doi.org/04.0450/epjconf/(4(53(30144(

Risk-aware decisions: taking into account admissible risk and measurement uncertainty in setting the acceptance limits

Alessandro Ferrero [1], *Harsha Vardhana* Jetti[2], *Sina* Ronaghi[1*], and *Simona* Salicone[1]

[1]Dipartimento di Elettronica, Informazione e Bioingegneria (DEIB), Politecnico di Milano, Italy
[2]Department of Engineering, University of Perugia, Italy

Abstract. Document JCGM 106:2012, encompassed in the ISO-IEC Guide 98-4, provides guidelines for comparing a measurement result with a tolerance interval, considering that, according to the Guide to the Expression of Uncertainty in Measurement (GUM), a measurement result is not a single value but rather a distribution of values. Therefore, the comparison does not always lead to a fully certain decision. In fact, when the distribution crosses the tolerance limits, there is a risk of making an incorrect decision. JCGM 106:2012 offers general recommendations about setting acceptance or rejection limits, without providing details on how to compute them under practical situations. This paper addresses most practical situations, considering cases of normal and non-normal distributions and cases where the distribution of values that can be reasonably be attributed to the measurand are obtained through Monte Carlo simulations. Additionally, it allows for considering any desired level of decision risk, which can be set based on the specific situation or application.

1 Introduction

Measurement results are generally used as input elements in decision-making processes, which are crucial for conformity assessment. This task is critical in many fields, ranging from industrial applications [1], where product features must meet given specifications, to environmental protection, healthcare, legal, and forensic domains [2], where decisions typically involve verifying that the amount of a substance (such as a pollutant or drug) or the error of an instrument does not exceed a specified maximum admissible limit.

Ensuring compliance requires that the measurand value lies within a range of admissible values. If the measurand is measured with negligible uncertainty, this can be easily assessed by directly comparing two numerical values: the measured value and the tolerance limits of the admissible range. In such cases, the decision appears to be made with no risk of error.

However, when measurement uncertainty is not negligible - as is often the case in practice - the Guide to the Expression of Uncertainty in Measurement (GUM) [3] states that a (coverage) interval should be provided around the measurement result. This interval encompasses a large fraction of the distribution of values that can be reasonably attributed to the measured quantity. Consequently, the decision-making process involves comparing an interval, with a given coverage probability, against the tolerance limits, which introduces a risk of false decisions (false acceptance or false rejection).

This issue is addressed in document JCGM 106:2012 [4], encompassed in the ISO-IEC Std. Guide 98-4 [5], which specifically deals with the problem of determining whether a measured quantity falls within a given tolerance interval - defined as the permissible range of values for a property. The tolerance interval can be either two-sided or one-sided. The document defines acceptance limits, stating that, given a certain measurement uncertainty, the measurand is considered conforming if the measured value falls within these limits and non-conforming if it falls outside them. It also explores different decision rules and methods for evaluating the risk of incorrect assessments based on measurement uncertainty.

It can be readily observed that the risk of a false decision, given a tolerance limit and an acceptance limit, depends on the probability distribution associated with the set of values that can be attributed to the measurand, and not just on the expanded uncertainty. Moreover, in many cases, particularly in industrial applications as well as in environmental protection, healthcare, and forensics, it is more practical to define a maximum admissible risk [6-9]. This allows for the proper adjustment of acceptance limits based on the estimated measurement uncertainty, ensuring that the risk of exceeding the tolerance limits remains below the desired maximum admissible risk.

This paper presents a method that, given:

- the distribution of values that can be attributed to the measurand (whether assumed, estimated, or obtained via Monte Carlo simulation),
- the tolerance limits,
- and the desired maximum admissible risk,

* Corresponding author: sina.ronaghi@polimi.it

determines the corresponding acceptance limits. The defined method has been also included into a general-purpose tool developed in Python, making it freely available to the Readers across multiple platforms.

2 Background: the problem

When a measured value x_m (without considering its uncertainty) is compared with a given threshold, it is immediate to take a decision, as shown in Fig. 1 [10]. On the other hand, the decision-making procedure becomes quite cumbersome when an uncertainty interval is associated to the measured value x_m [10], as shown in Figs. 2-3, in particular in the case of Fig. 3, where the uncertainty interval crosses the threshold.

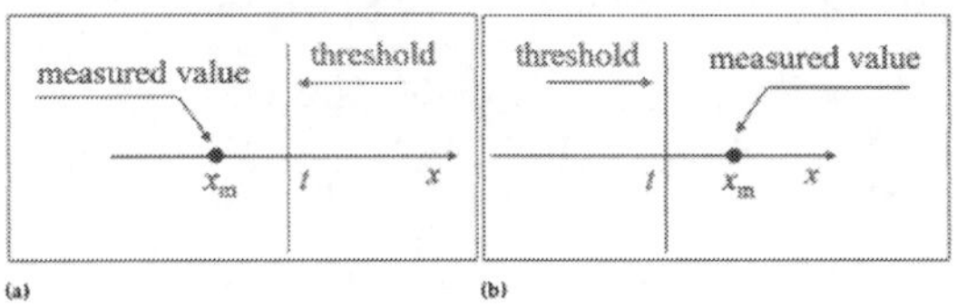

Fig. 1. Comparison of a single measured value with a threshold, when the measured value x_m is lower (a) and greater (b) than threshold t.

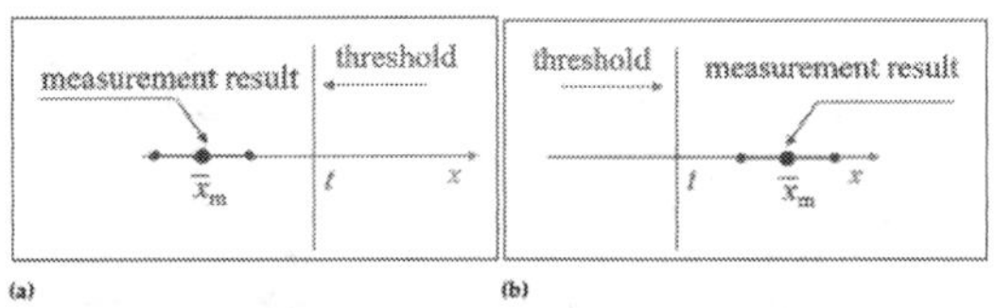

Fig. 2. Comparison of an uncertainty interval with a threshold t, when the uncertainty interval is completely below (a) or above (b) the threshold.

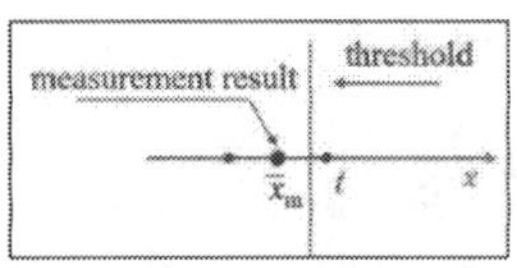

Fig. 3. Comparison of an uncertainty interval with a threshold t, when the threshold falls within the interval.

However, it is important to underline that in all the above situations there is a risk of taking a wrong decision.

In the case of Fig.1, where the decision is simply taken by considering whether $x_m < t$ or $x_m > t$, the risk can reach 50% when $x_m = t$, [10]. In fact, the decision is simply taken by considering the measured value x_m and its position with respect to t, but it is known that, because of uncertainty contributions, a probability distribution is always associated to x_m [3]. Therefore, supposing this distribution is symmetric, half distribution will be above t and half distribution will be below t, when $x_m = t$, thus giving a probability of 50% of a wrong decision.

In the case of Fig. 2, where the uncertainty interval is considered, a risk of a wrong decision could be still present, since the width of the interval is strictly related to the probability distribution and the considered coverage factor [3]. In Fig. 3 the risk of a wrong decision is even more evident.

To consider this problem in decision making procedures and in conformity assessment, document JCGM 106:2012 [4], encompassed in the ISO-IEC Std. Guide 98-4 [5], proposes a more precautionary approach, as described in Fig. 4 and reported in [10].

In short, when acceptance or rejection decisions need to be made based on measured values, the threshold is increased or decreased in order to widen or narrow the interval, in the direction of making a more precautionary decision.

As an example, in Fig. 4, the measured value must be lower than an upper threshold T_U (up) and therefore the resulting decision will be considered positive (accepted) only if the measured value satisfies $x_m < A_U$, where $A_U < T_U$ and the width w of the guard band is determined as a multiple of the expanded uncertainty associated to x_m; or it must be included between a lower and an upper threshold T_L and T_U (down), and therefore the decision will be positive (accepted) only if the measured value satisfies $A_L < x_m < A_U$.

This approach represents an improvement with respect to the case that does not consider measurement uncertainty but does not yet provide step-by-step guidance on how to evaluate w in practical cases. This paper aims to provide an answer to this problem.

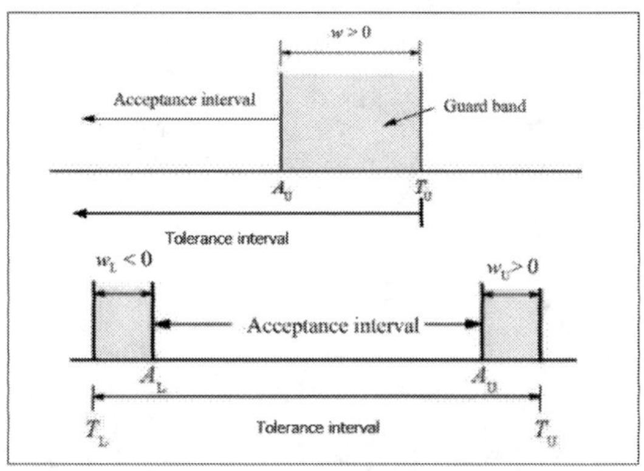

Fig. 4. Decision rule based on guarded acceptance. Up: a one-sided tolerance interval upper limited by T_U. Down: two-sided tolerance interval between lower and upper limits T_L and T_U.

3 Decision rule based on the maximum admissible risk

The GUM [3] states that a probability distribution is always associated to a measurement result. Furthermore, documents JCGM 106:2012 [4] and ISO-IEC Std. Guide 98-4 [5] state that such distribution is always obtained from two components: the one available before performing the measurement (called *prior* information) and the additional information supplied by the measurement, combined through the well-known Bayes' theorem.

In practical applications, information about the measurement result is provided either in terms of a known probability distribution function (PDF) or as a set of measurements belonging to an unknown PDF. In this section, it is shown how to evaluate values A_U and A_L, according to the available information of the measurement result and to the maximum admissible risk (*MAR*), that is, the maximum risk that can be accepted in the specific application domain. In particular, Sec. 3.1 covers the case where the PDF of the measurement result is known, while Sec. 3.2 covers the case where the shape of the PDF is not known, and multiple measurements are available.

3.1 Known PDF

The width of the guard bands must be determined in relation to both the probability density function (PDF) of the measurement result and the Maximum Allowable Risk (*MAR*). In this section, several common PDFs are examined to formulate relationships for A_U and A_L (which represent the upper and lower acceptance limits in the context of guarded acceptance), as well as for R_U and R_L (which denote the upper and lower rejection limits in the context of guarded rejection). It is also important to note that, these relationships are expressed as a function of *MAR*.

The reported equations (the readers are addressed to [10] for the details) are evaluated starting from the following simple considerations.

Given PDF $p(x)$ associated to the measurement result, the cumulative distribution function (CDF)

$$F_X(x) = \int_{-\infty}^{x} p(t)dt \quad (1)$$

represents the probability that variable X is lower than x; similarly, $1 - F_X(x)$ represents the probability that variable X is greater than x. Therefore, if the tolerance limits T_U or T_L shall not be exceeded and the *MAR* is given, the following inequalities shall be satisfied:

$$\begin{cases} F_X(T_U) \geq 1 - MAR & \text{when } x < T_U \text{ is required} \\ F_X(T_L) \leq MAR & \text{when } x > T_L \text{ is required} \end{cases} \quad (2)$$

The acceptance or rejection limits are hence evaluated by considering the specific measured value (which is also the mode of the considered PDF) for which, in equation (2), the equalities hold.

3.1.1 Normal PDF

Let's suppose $p(x)$ is normal, with standard deviation σ. Then, it follows [10, 11]:

$$A_U = T_U - \sqrt{2}\sigma \cdot \text{erfinv}(1 - 2 \cdot MAR) \quad (3)$$
$$A_L = T_L + \sqrt{2}\sigma \cdot \text{erfinv}(1 - 2 \cdot MAR) \quad (4)$$
$$R_U = T_U + \sqrt{2}\sigma \cdot \text{erfinv}(1 - 2 \cdot MAR) \quad (5)$$
$$R_L = T_L - \sqrt{2}\sigma \cdot \text{erfinv}(1 - 2 \cdot MAR) \quad (6)$$

where erfinv is the *inverse error function*.

Figs. 5 and 6 show an example where a resistor with nominal resistance R_n = 100 Ω is considered and its conformity to a ±2% tolerance must be assessed. It is assumed that a normal PDF is associated with the measured value, with a standard deviation σ = 0.5 Ω; the tolerance limits are: $T_U = 102$ Ω, $T_L = 98$ Ω, and the *MAR* is set to 0.05.

The application of equations (3)-(6) provides the following values for the acceptance and rejection limits: $A_U = 101.18$ Ω; $A_L = 98.82$ Ω; $R_U = 102.82$ Ω; $R_L = 97.18$ Ω. In Fig. 5, the pink line shows a normal PDF with the given standard deviation and centred exactly on A_U and the pink area shows the probability that this PDF exceeds the tolerance limit T_U. This area is exactly equal to the set *MAR*. Similarly, the green line shows a normal PDF with the given standard deviation and centred exactly on A_L and the green area shows the probability that this PDF exceeds the tolerance limit T_L. This area is exactly equal to the set *MAR*. Similar considerations can be done for Fig. 6, where the PDFs are centred on the rejection limits R_L and R_U.

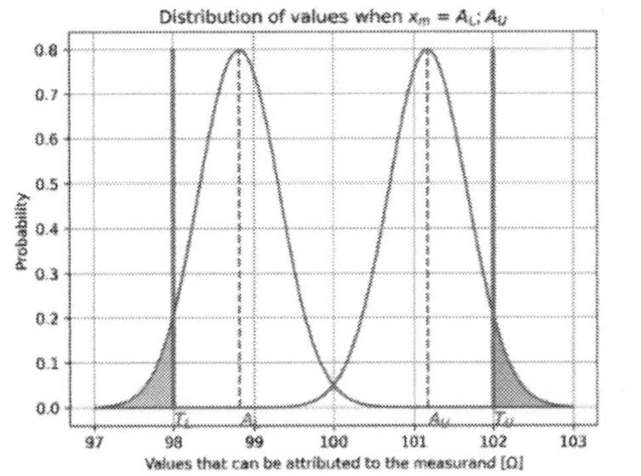

Fig. 5. Example of evaluation of A_U and A_L (guarded acceptance) with a normal distribution.

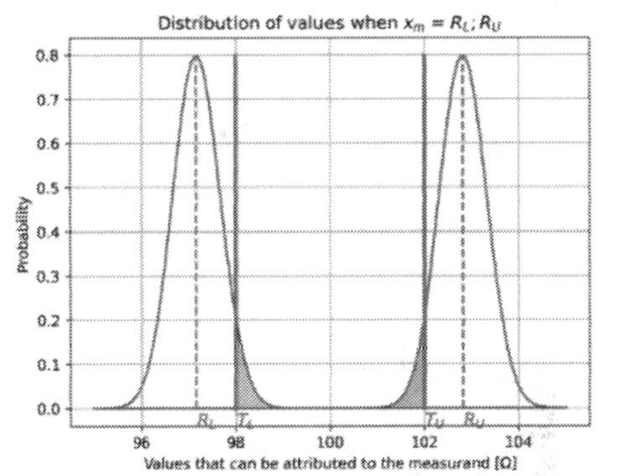

Fig. 6. Example of evaluation of R_U and R_L (guarded rejection) with a normal distribution.

3.1.2 Uniform PDF

Let's suppose $p(x)$ is uniform, with support $2a$. Then, it follows [10, 11]:

$$A_U = T_U - a \cdot (1 - 2 \cdot MAR) \quad (7)$$
$$A_L = T_L + a \cdot (1 - 2 \cdot MAR) \quad (8)$$
$$R_U = T_U + a \cdot (1 - 2 \cdot MAR) \quad (9)$$
$$R_L = T_L - a \cdot (1 - 2 \cdot MAR) \quad (10)$$

Figs. 7 and 8 show the results obtained considering the same example as in section 3.1.1, where it is now assumed that the considered PDF is uniform with a = 1 Ω, the tolerance limits are still $T_U = 102$ Ω, $T_L = 98$ Ω, and the *MAR* is set again to 0.05. Equations (7)-(10) leads to the following values for the acceptance and rejection limits: $A_U = 101.10$ Ω, $A_L = 98.90$ Ω; $R_U = 102.90$ Ω; $R_L = 97.10$ Ω. Similar considerations as those reported for Figs. 5 and 6 apply to these figures too.

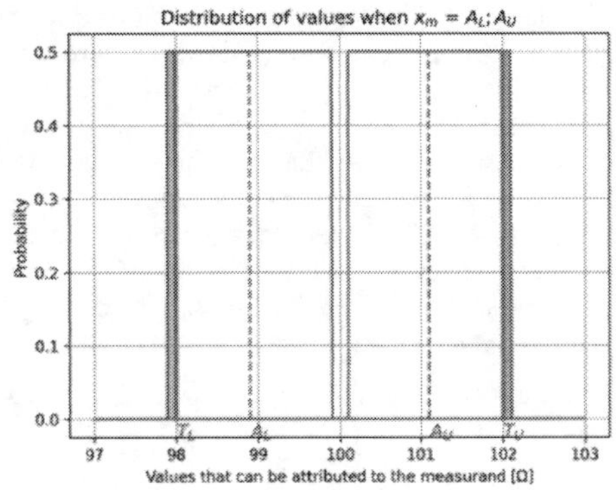

Fig. 7. Example of evaluation of A_U and A_L (guarded acceptance) with a uniform distribution.

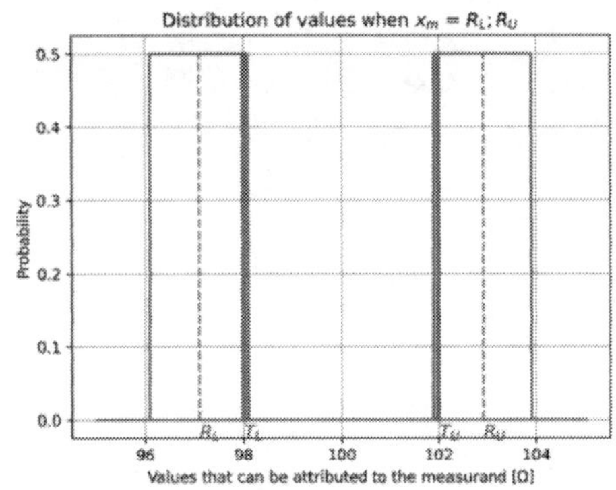

Fig. 8. Example of evaluation of R_U and R_L (guarded rejection) with a uniform distribution.

3.1.3 Triangular PDF

Let's suppose $p(x)$ is triangular, with support $2a$. Then, it follows [10, 11]:

$$A_U = T_U - a \cdot \left(1 - \sqrt{2 \cdot MAR}\right) \quad (11)$$

$$A_L = T_L + a \cdot \left(1 - \sqrt{2 \cdot MAR}\right) \quad (12)$$

$$R_U = T_U + a \cdot \left(1 - \sqrt{2 \cdot MAR}\right) \quad (13)$$

$$R_L = T_L - a \cdot \left(1 - \sqrt{2 \cdot MAR}\right) \quad (14)$$

Figs. 9 and 10 show the results obtained considering the same example as in section 3.1.1, where it is now assumed that the considered PDF is triangular with $a = 1\ \Omega$, $T_U = 102\ \Omega$, $T_L = 98\ \Omega$, and the MAR is set to 0.05 again. Equations (11)-(14) lead to the following values for the acceptance and rejection limits: $A_U = 101.32\ \Omega$; $A_L = 98.68\ \Omega$; $R_U = 102.68\ \Omega$; $R_L = 97.32\ \Omega$. Similar considerations as those reported for Figs. 5 and 6 apply to these figures too.

3.1.4 Trapezoidal PDF

Let's suppose $p(x)$ is trapezoidal, with major base $2a$ and ratio of the minor base to the major base β. Then, it follows [10, 11]:

$$A_U = T_U - a \cdot \left(1 - \sqrt{2 \cdot MAR \cdot (1 - \beta^2)}\right) \quad (15)$$

$$A_L = T_L + a \cdot \left(1 - \sqrt{2 \cdot MAR \cdot (1 - \beta^2)}\right) \quad (16)$$

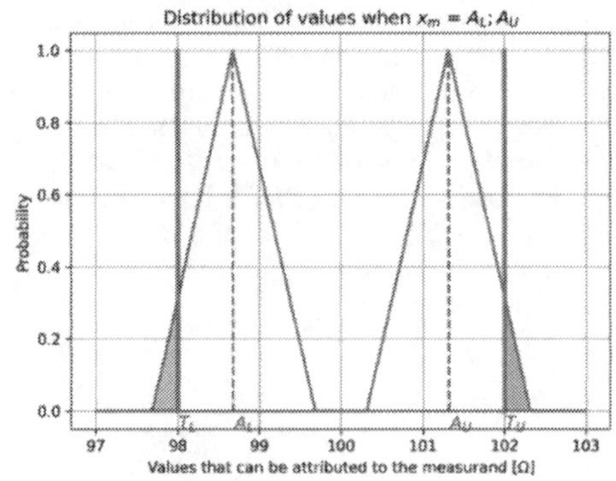

Fig. 9. Example of evaluation of A_U and A_L (guarded acceptance) with a triangular distribution.

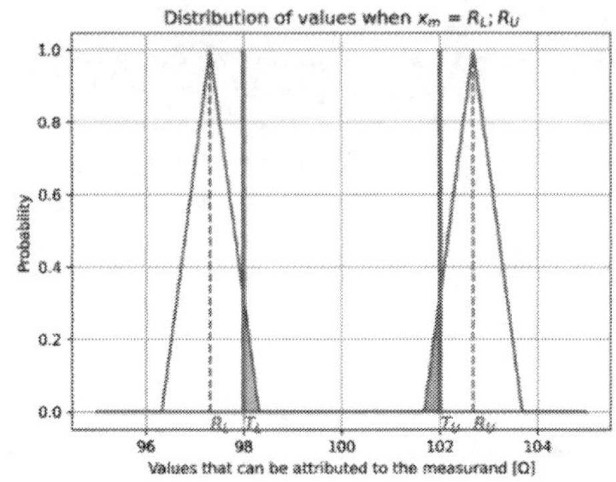

Fig. 10. Example of evaluation of R_U and R_L (guarded rejection) with a triangular distribution.

$$R_U = T_U + a \cdot \left(1 - \sqrt{2 \cdot MAR \cdot (1 - \beta^2)}\right) \quad (17)$$

$$R_L = T_L - a \cdot \left(1 - \sqrt{2 \cdot MAR \cdot (1 - \beta^2)}\right) \quad (18)$$

Figs. 11 and 12 show the results obtained considering the same example as in section 3.1.1, where it is now assumed that the considered PDF is trapezoidal with $a = 1\ \Omega$, $\beta = 0.75$, $T_U = 102\ \Omega$, $T_L = 98\ \Omega$, and the MAR is set to 0.05 again. Equations (15)-(18) lead to the following values for the acceptance and rejection limits: $A_U = 101.21\Omega; A_L = 98.79\ \Omega; R_U = 102.79\ \Omega$; $R_L = 97.21\ \Omega$. Similar considerations as those reported for Figs. 5 and 6 apply to these figures too.

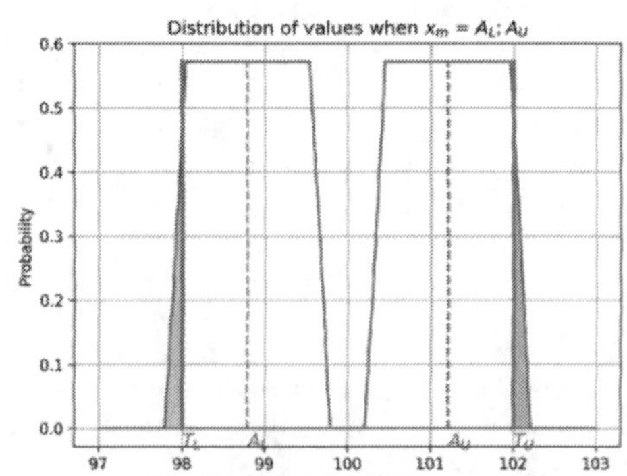

Fig. 11. Example of evaluation of A_U and A_L (guarded acceptance) with a trapezoidal distribution.

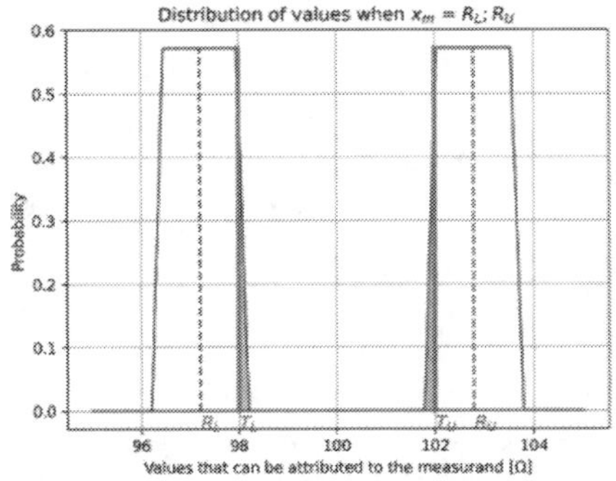

Fig. 12. Example of evaluation of R_U and R_L (guarded rejection) with a trapezoidal distribution.

3.2 Unknown PDF

In the previous section, mathematical relationships have been presented that related tolerance limits, measurement uncertainty, acceptance/rejection limits and risk of exceeding the tolerance limits, under the assumption of specific PDFs. These relationships improve the guidelines in [4, 5]. The presented relationships in (3)-(18) are significantly useful in practice, since they represent most of the practical situations for measurement results and their associated uncertainties.

However, since other scenarios cannot be excluded a priori, a generalized approach has also been developed to ensure the broad application of the proposed decision-making procedure [11].

When the mathematical equation of the PDF is not known, it is not possible to have a mathematical equation of the CDF and find closed-form formulas for the acceptance and rejection limits. Under this situation, by applying a Monte Carlo simulation (as also recommended by [12]), or by experimentally repeating the measurement procedure, if possible, N values are obtained for the measurand, and their PDF can be approximated by the histogram of the relative frequencies. This histogram is initially supposed to have a mean value exactly in either T_U or T_L. Its associated CDF can be hence numerically evaluated as:

$$F_X(x) = \sum_{-\infty}^{x} h(x) \quad (19)$$

where, for each class of the histogram, $h(x)$ represents the relative frequency of the class.

Then, according to $F_X(x)$, the value x_{MAR} can be numerically found. In particular, in case of guarded acceptance, x_{MAR} has to satisfy to:

$$x_{MAR} | F_X(x_{MAR}) = 1 - MAR \quad (20)$$

when $x < T_U$ is considered; and to:

$$x_{MAR} | F_X(x_{MAR}) = MAR \quad (21)$$

when $x > T_L$ is considered [11].

On the other hand, in case of guarded rejection, x_{MAR} has to satisfy to:

$$x_{MAR} | F_X(x_{MAR}) = MAR \quad (22)$$

when $x < T_U$ is considered; and to:

$$x_{MAR} | F_X(x_{MAR}) = 1 - MAR \quad (23)$$

when $x > T_L$ is considered [11].

The evaluation of x_{MAR} on the CDF allows us to shift the CDF on the left or right, so that the risk of exceeding the threshold becomes exactly MAR [11]. The following equations for the acceptance and rejection limits are found as [11]:

$$A_U = R_U = 2 \cdot T_U - x_{MAR} \quad (24)$$

$$A_L = R_L = 2 \cdot T_L - x_{MAR} \quad (25)$$

Let us again consider the previous example where $T_U = 102\ \Omega$, $T_L = 98\ \Omega$ and the MAR is set to 0.05. Figs. 13 shows the histogram associated to the measurement values with a mean value equal to T_U. The associated CDF is evaluated as in (19), while x_{MAR} is evaluated as in (20) or (22), when, respectively, guarded acceptance or guarded rejection are considered. The acceptance and rejection limits are then evaluated as in (24). Although the formula is the same, it will provide two different values for A_U and R_U, since equations (20) and (22) provide a different x_{MAR} value. In particular, in the considered example, it will be: $A_U = 101.15\ \Omega$ and $R_U = 102.83\ \Omega$.

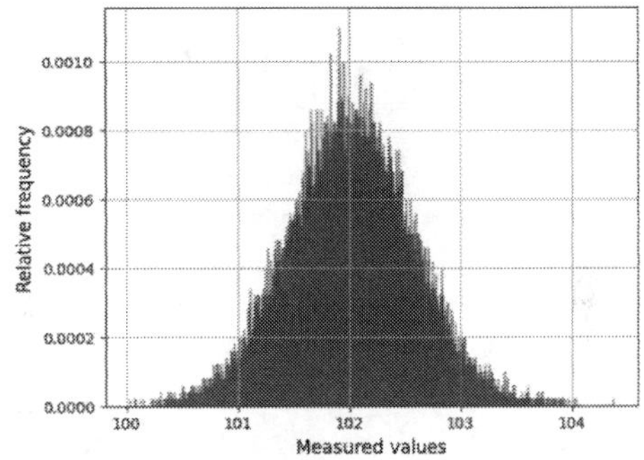

Fig. 13. Histogram of the relative frequencies associated to the measured values, centred on T_U.

This is shown in the left side of Figs. 14 and 15, where the pink lines represent the CDFs of the shifted, with respect to the original (in Fig. 13), histogram to the left and right respectively, in order to be centred on A_U and R_U respectively. In fact, according to equations (20) and (22), the shifted histograms have a probability of exceeding the threshold exactly equal to the set MAR, as shown by the pink lines in the figures.

Similar considerations can be done when the lower threshold T_L is considered. In this case, the initial CDF (19) is evaluated according to a histogram similar to the one shown in Fig. 13, but centred on T_L. In this case, x_{MAR} is evaluated as in (21) or (23), when, respectively, guarded acceptance or guarded rejection are considered, while the acceptance and rejection limits are evaluated as in (25). In the considered example: $A_L = 98.80\ \Omega$ and $R_L = 97.18\ \Omega$ are obtained, as shown in Figs. 14 and 15, as well as the shifted CDFs (green lines).

4 Phyton tool

A Jupyter Notebook, implemented in Python, has been developed to compute the acceptance and rejection limits given the MAR, the PDF of the values that can be reasonably attributed to the measurand, and the tolerance limits. This notebook, which is available open-source and can be accessed in [13], allows one to reproduce the presented results using the same parameters, as well as different ones.

Furthermore, in cases where the distribution of measurements at the tolerance limits are unknown and the results cannot be obtained in a closed-form solution, a Monte-Carlo simulation has been performed by generating two random sets from a normal distribution, each consisting of 5000 values. These sets are centred at 98 Ω and 102 Ω, respectively. The generated distributions are included in the repository and can be used as T_U and T_L to determine the acceptance limits (A_U, A_L), as well as the rejection limits (R_U and R_L) from (24) and (25).

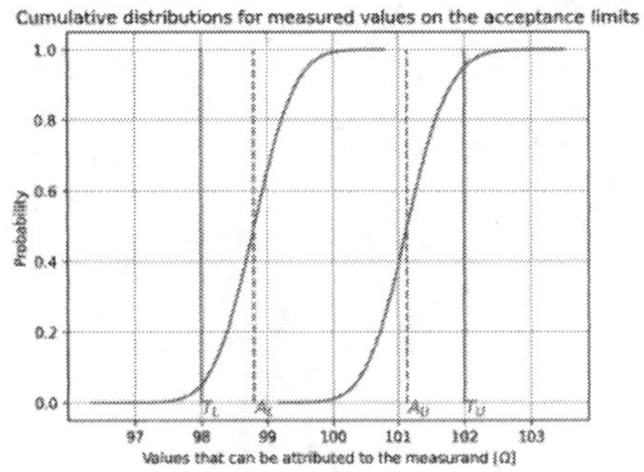

Fig. 14. Example of application of the general method when guarded acceptance is considered.

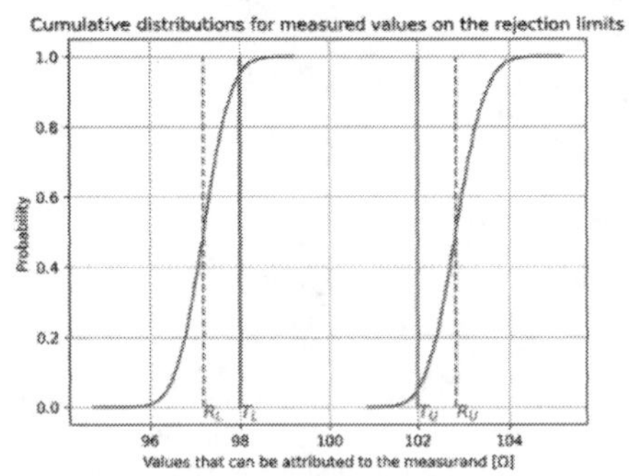

Fig. 15. Example of application of the general method when guarded rejection is considered.

5 Conclusions

The work aims to fill a gap in the JCGM 106:2012 standard regarding methods for considering measurement uncertainty in conformity assessments. The standard provides only general guidelines and does not specify a universally applicable methodology to link acceptance (or rejection) limits, uncertainty, and the risk of false decisions. The article analyses the most common probability distributions used to characterize the distribution of values reasonably attributable to the measurand and provides practical guidance for calculating one of the above parameters as a function of the other two.

In summary, this paper introduced a decision-making framework that enhances the practicality of the recommendations in JCGM 106:2012 by considering measurement uncertainty and the maximum allowable risk in real-world scenarios. The study derived equations for known unimodal probability distributions, as well as for cases where the distribution of values reasonably attributed to the measurand is obtained through Monte Carlo simulation. To ensure applicability and reproducibility, the authors also developed an open-source Python script, available in a public GitHub repository, which readers can utilize and build upon.

References

[1] A. Ferrero, V. Scotti. Uncertainty and Conscious Decisions". In: Forensic Metrology: An Introduction to the Fundamentals of Metrology for Judges, Lawyers and Forensic Scientists. Cham: Springer International Publishing, 2022, pp. 115–124. ISBN: 978-3-031-14619-0. DOI: 10.1007/978-3-031-14619-0_8. URL: https://doi.org/10.1007/978-3-031-14619-0_8.

[2] J. M. Pou, L. Leblond. Smart Metrology: From the metrology of instrumentation to the metrology of decisions. Ed. by Array. 2017. DOI: 10.1051/metrology/201701007. URL: https://doi.org/10.1051/metrology/201701007

[3] JCGM 100:2008. Evaluation of Measurement Data – Guide to the Expression of Uncertainty in Measurement, (GUM 1995 with minor corrections). Joint Committee for Guides in Metrology. 2008.

[4] JCGM 106:2012. Evaluation of measurement data – The role of measurement uncertainty in conformity assessment. Joint Committee for Guides in Metrology. 2012.

[5] ISO/IEC Guide 98-4:2012. Uncertainty of measurement. Part 4: Role of measurement uncertainty in conformity assessment. 2012.

[6] L. R. Pendrill. Using measurement uncertainty in decision-making and conformity assessment. Metrologia 51.4 (2014), pp. 206–218. DOI: 10.1088/0026-1394/51/4/S206. URL: https://iopscience.iop.org/article/10.1088/0026-1394/51/4/S206

[7] A. Allard, N. Fischer, I. Smith, P. Harris, L. Pendrill. Risk calculations for conformity assessment in practice. Ed. by Array. 2019. DOI: 10.1051/metrology/ 201916001. URL: https://doi.org/10.1051/metrology/201916001

[8] Puydarrieux, S. et al. Role of measurement uncertainty in conformity assessment. Ed. by Array. 2019. DOI: 10.1051/ metrology/201916003. URL: https://doi.org/10.1051/metrology/201916003

[9] E. Cruz de Oliveira, F. R. Lourenço. Risk of false conformity assessment applied to automotive fuel analysis: A multiparameter approach. Chemosphere 263 (2021), p. 128265. ISSN: 0045-6535. DOI: https://doi.org/10.1016/j. chemosphere.2020.128265. URL: https://www.sciencedirect.com/science/article/pii/S0045653520324607

[10] A. Ferrero, H. V. Jetti, S. Ronaghi, S. Salicone. A method to consider a maximum admissible risk in decision-making procedures based on measurement results. Acta IMEKO, vol.12, n. 2, 2023. DOI: https://doi.org/10.21014/actaimeko.v12i2.1518

[11] A. Ferrero, H. V. Jetti, S. Ronaghi, S. Salicone. A general Monte-Carlo approach to consider a maximum admissible risk in decision-making procedures based on measurement results. Acta IMEKO, vol.12, n. 4, 2023. DOI: https://doi.org/10.21014/actaimeko.v12i4.1602

[12] JCGM 101:2008. Evaluation of measurement data – Supplement 1 to the Guide to the expression of uncertainty in measurement – Propagation of distributions using a Monte Carlo method. Joint Committee for Guides in Metrology. 2008.

[13] Python scripts to find suitable acceptance limits according to ISO-IEC Guide 98-4. https://github.com/alessandro-ferrero/Acceptance-limits

AUTHOR INDEX